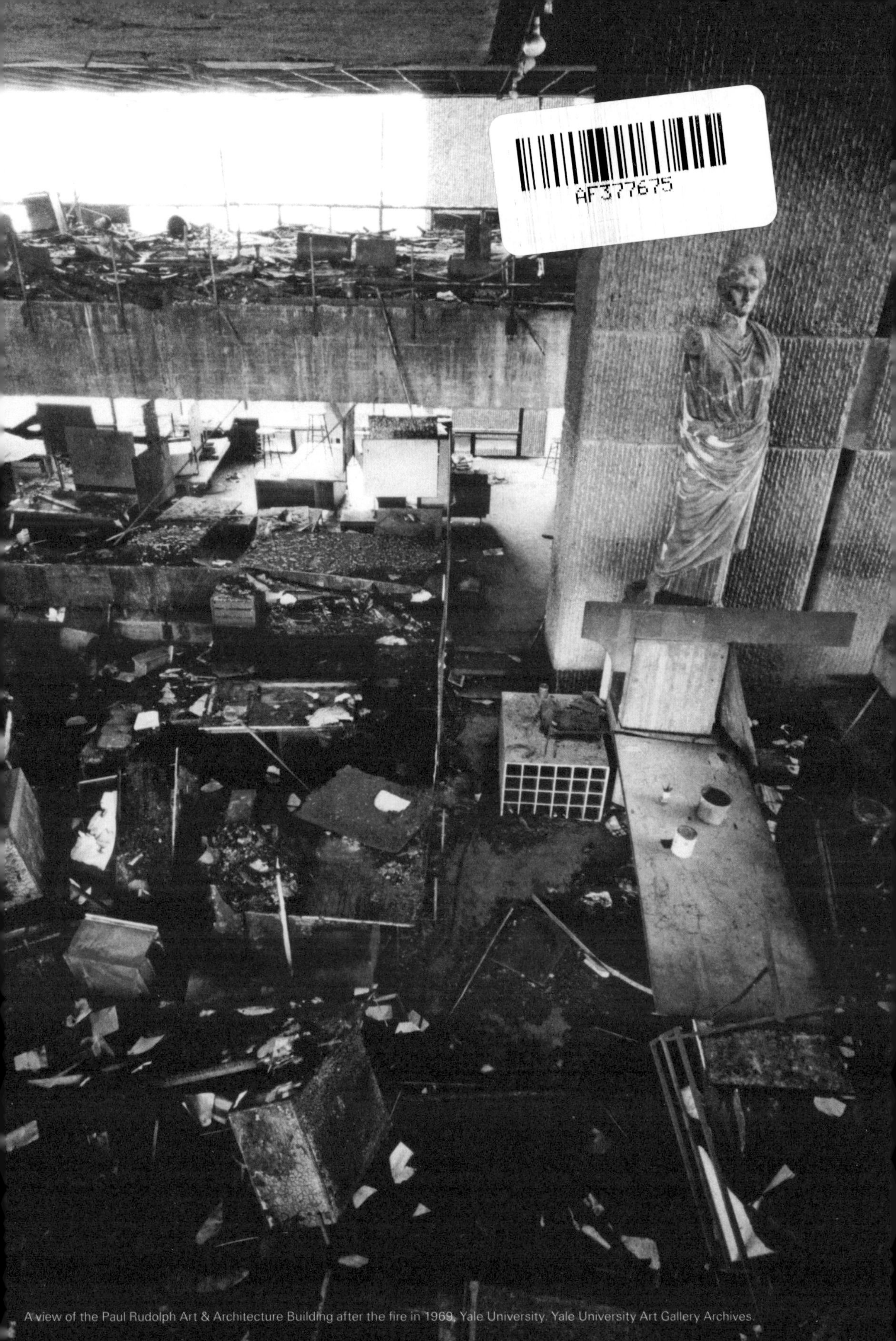

A view of the Paul Rudolph Art & Architecture Building after the fire in 1969, Yale University. Yale University Art Gallery Archives.

HISTORY OF ART AND SCHOOL

Marta Kuzma
with Angela Y. Davis and Linda Nochlin
edited by Angie Keefer

Yale School of Art, New Haven
Verlag der Buchhandlung
Walther und Franz König, Köln

Published by Yale School of Art
1156 Chapel Street, New Haven, CT 06511

Verlag der Buchhandlung Walther und Franz König
Ehrenstraße 4, D-50672 Köln

Bibliographic information published by the Deutsche
Nationalbibliothek The Deutsche Nationalbibliothek lists
this publication in the Deutsche Nationalbibliografie;
detailed bibliographic data are available on the Internet
at dnb.d-nb.de.

ISBN 978-3-7533-0005-4

Library of Congress Control Number: 2021915361

Printed and bound in the Netherlands

Distribution:
Europe
Buchhandlung Walther König
Ehrenstraße 4,
D – 50672 Köln
Tel: +49 (0) 221 / 20 59 6 53
verlag@buchhandlung-walther-koenig.de

UK & Ireland
Cornerhouse Publications Ltd. – HOME
2 Tony Wilson Place
UK – Manchester M15 4FN
Tel: +44 (0) 161 212 3466
publications@cornerhouse.org

Outside Europe
D.A.P. / Distributed Art Publishers, Inc.
75 Broad Street, Suite 630
USA – New York, NY 10004
Tel: +1 (0) 212 627 1999
orders@dapinc.com

CONTENTS

women faculty are not a luxury was produced by Anne Ghory-Goodman (BA 1971;
MFA 1973), a member of the first class of women undergraduates at Yale
College. According to Ghory-Goodman, she made the piece, which was distributed as a leaflet, when the School of Art was reviewing the appointment of
Inge Druckrey as an adjunct rather than a full-time, tenure-track faculty member.
Ghory-Goodman recounts that by 1971 she "had been radicalized by the
inequities and indignities women students encountered. In the spring of 1969,
the Art School had gone up in flames and art majors were bussed to studios
on the periphery of campus. In the spring of 1970, May Day and the Bobby Seale
trial shut down the school; in the spring of 1971, academics ground to a halt
when students supported the Workers' Strike. This document was a product of
those times. In 1971, there had been women in the School of Art for 102 years,
yet no women had had a full-time faculty appointment. That record continued
through my time in the graduate program in Graphic Design. The information
in *women faculty are not a luxury* describes the status of women faculty in the
School of Art during my time there as an undergraduate and graduate student.
It was an untenable record. These flyers were distributed to people exiting
a meeting of University advisors, most likely the University Council Committee
on Art and Architecture and/or the Art School Steering Committee or the Yale
Corporation. A footnote to this document is Alvin Eisenman's response to it.
He was the founder and longtime chair of the Graphic Design Department and
was incensed that Polly Lada-Mocarski was referred to as a 'token woman.'
Polly taught a bookbinding elective. Alvin believed that her worth as a teacher
was being denigrated while, in fact, it was meant to highlight the fact that
she wasn't given a more robust appointment."

Anne Ghory-Goodman in conversation with Angela Chen
July 23, 2021

women faculty are not a luxury

<u>University Directives on the Status of Women:</u>

The Greene Report, May 1971
    'We therefore recommend that the University temporarily set aside a
    number of tenure faculty positions for the specific purpose of rec-
    ruiting senior women academicians until such time as a more favorable
    balance of representation has been achieved.

Charles Taylor, The Provost's Office, Sept. 9, 1971
    First: the University's difficult budgetary problem does not reduce its
    obligation to make every effort to attract qualified members of under-
    represented groups (women) to the Yale faculty as openings occur.
    Second: All communications seeking candidates for any faculty or
    professional positions which may become open must include the explicit
    statement that the University seeks qualified candidates who are women...
    Third: At the time appointments or promotions to faculty positions are
    proposed, deans and chairmen will be expected to explain in writing the
    efforts which have been made to recruit women...

Charles Taylor, The Provost's Office, Dec. 15, 1971
    Since qualified women or members of minority groups may be insufficiently
    known to schools and departments, the committee points out that invit-
    ations to participate in colloquia or as lecturers or visitors may
    often be helpful in making appropriate judgements. Where department
    budgets or lecture funds may not be adequate or available, application for
    honoraria or other special assistance may be made to the office of the
    Provost in particular cases.

<u>The Realities of Female Participation on Yale Art School Faculty:</u>

1970-71
    2 visiting faculty in sculpture hired, both male, no women considered.
    1 assistant to director of studies in sculpture hired, male, no women
    considered.
    1 director of sculpture hired, male, no women considered.
    7 members of the University Council Committee on Art and Architecture,
    all male.
    5 Faculty Emeriti, all male.
    10 Faculty in Painting and Printmaking, all male.
    3 Faculty in Sculpture, all male.
    15 Faculty in Graphic Design, 13 male and 2 token women (visiting instructor

The Realities of Female Participation on Yale Art School Faculty (cont.)

    4 Faculty in Filmmaking, all male.
    8 Research Associates in art, all male.
    All classes of the Art School have included women, from its beginning.
    Therefore there is no dearth of qualified women in the applicant pool.

1971-72
    As of March 1, 1972 neither of the women listed as visiting lecturers
    in Graphic Design has taught.
    Both visiting lecturers in photography for this academic year are male
    though a rostrum of eminent women photographers available has been
    compiled by the department.
    8 women will receive MFA degrees from the art school this June and will
    be prime candidates for the position being vacated by Jack Lembeck.

<u>Current Response to These Facts</u>: A discussion of the University Council
Committee on Art and Architecture with the Art School Steering Committee

Louis Finklestein:
    My wife is an artist and I know that art department faculties in
    particular discriminate against women.

Ivan Chermayeff:
    We all agree (that there should be more women on the faculty) and
    you have my sympathy, so why should we discuss this?

Diane Krieger:
    Because I've been saying this (that there should be more women in the
    Art School) for two years and we've gotten only sympathy and no action.

William Bailey:
    (The reason there are no women on the faculty is that) There have been
    no positions open.

    <u>Note</u>: 4 positions in sculpture filled last year.

Anne Goodman:
    A male faculty is self-perpetuating.

PREFACE

The impetus for this book emerged from a conversation with Barbara Chase-Riboud (MFA 1960)—the first known Black woman graduate of the Yale School of Art MFA program—that took place in her apartment in Paris in the summer of 2019. I recall Chase-Riboud's account of independently steering herself through a graduate education: that no one bothered to mentor her, and that no one bothered with her much at all, until, finally, they did, when her eligibility for a degree was called into question at the end of her studies because she hadn't received permission to produce her final project. At the time of that trip and my visit with her, I had been reading a concise and forceful book by Isabelle Stengers and Vinciane Despret called *Women Who Make a Fuss*. In their introductory chapter, "We Who Are at the University," the authors' description of the often fleeting nature of generational memory would stay with me throughout my tenure as dean at the Yale School of Art:

> We are among those women who entered the university certainly knowing that not everyone (male or female) would be allowed entrance, but without really thinking about the fact that, as girls, we posed a particular question. One quickly forgets the history, once a right is acquired and one is living in the general conditions permitting one to benefit from that right. If we wanted it, if we were "good" enough, and if we were lucky, we could even have an academic career. … In short the question of the democratization of access to the university could surely be posed, and was, moreover, but it didn't concern us specifically, "as women."[1]

That first conversation with Chase-Riboud was followed the very next day by one with Sheila Hicks (BFA 1957; MFA 1959), during which Hicks also spoke to me about her experiences at Yale, and led to numerous other conversations, interviews, correspondence, and archival research, all of which gradually accumulated into a new and unfamiliar story of the Yale School of Art, one that had until recently been relegated to the margins. This process was

1   Isabelle Stengers and Vinciane Despret, *Women Who Make a Fuss: The Unfaithful Daughters of Virginia Woolf* (Minneapolis: Univocal Publishing, 2014).

spurred along by an invitation from the Yale University Art Gallery
to contribute a chapter on fifty years of the School's history,
from 1969 to 2019, for a catalogue that would accompany an
exhibition commemorating the 150th anniversary of women at
Yale University. I quickly discovered that a sufficiently detailed and
nuanced account could not be contained within the constraints
of a single, short chapter. And so, while simultaneously serving as
the first woman dean in the history of the School of Art, I found
myself committed to an ambitious research program that soon
evolved into an oral history project and archival excavation, which,
after more than two years of digging, investigating, and collecting,
has ultimately resulted in a book that seeks to provide a more
accessible and lasting record of that "particular question" alluded
to by Stengers and Despret.

One well-known version of the School's modern history and
pedagogical legacy is anchored in the foundational teachings of
Josef Albers, who joined the Yale School of Art faculty in 1950,
importing the pedagogical model that he had helped to develop
at the Bauhaus in the 1920s and 1930s. Albers was an active
member of the School's faculty until 1958, his official retirement,
after which he became Professor Emeritus. The years following
Albers' tenure at Yale were marked by educators of significant—
although lesser—renown, some of whom also attained international
recognition. What remains unknown to many, however, is that
women faculty members, in particular, who greatly contributed to
shaping the School of Art into a leading institution during the post-
Albers decades, were most often engaged under conditions of
employment that would be deemed precarious by any standard.
They faced unique obstacles to promotion under a School led by
a governing group of senior male faculty members that continued
to exclude women for several decades following the passage of
important antidiscriminatory legislation in the early 1970s that
effectively increased gender equity in faculty composition and the
governance of educational institutions nationally. By presenting
testimony from some of the women involved in the School
over the past five decades, this publication attempts to recover
from the margins a version of the School's history that, while
necessarily specific to the Yale School of Art, may resonate with
the experiences of faculty and graduates from other MFA programs
bracketed by the same historical, social, political, and intellectual
movements pertaining to women's liberation and civil rights.

The story is told not only through first-person accounts, but through a plethora of images, including photographs, memos, ephemera, and news articles. The latter include documentation of events and works mentioned in the text, as well as more tenuously—or associatively—linked visual materials, presented here with the intent to elevate and preserve sources that may serve other, future histories yet to be written, and to acknowledge that any effort to distill a fifty-year period of an institution as intricate as a school of art into a singular narrative will only succeed in broaching the vast complex of stories that comprise a full history.

This revised account of the Yale School of Art's history is accompanied by two key texts to mark the beginning and the end of the historical period in question—Linda Nochlin's canonical essay, "Why Have There Been No Great Women Artists?" first published in 1971, and the transcript of an original lecture by Angela Y. Davis delivered at the School in fall of 2020 when she was a Hayden Distinguished Speaker. Nochlin's essay postulated that systemic social, cultural, and political barriers prevented the career development of women artists. It was a concerted attempt to address what she described as "one of the perennial questions used to challenge women's demand for true, rather than token, equality by examining the whole erroneous intellectual substructure upon which the question 'Why have there been no great women artists?' is based."[2] Nochlin's approach resounds in many of the testimonies collected here. Davis, speaking to current students at the School about philosophical aesthetics, as well as her own experiences working with collective resistance movements that have included artists, reminded her audience that, "We use the category 'woman,' but there's no such thing as an abstract woman, and there's no such thing as an abstract Black person … Race is always gendered and classed, and class is always raced and gendered," but that "art can yield a kind of knowledge that is not categorical."[3]

Importantly, this book has been a collective endeavor, made possible by the generous participation of more than thirty interview subjects, and by the estimable effort of a devoted team. Our editor, Angie Keefer (BA 1999), worked side by side with me to help shape a narrative and a book that would be balanced while remaining courageous. Associate Editor Edi Dai (MFA 2019), whose research into the history of women at the Yale School of Art began as an extension of her artistic practice during her

2   Linda Nochlin, "Why Have There Been No Great Women Artists?" ARTnews (January 1971).

3   Angela Y. Davis, "Diving into the Wreck: Rethinking Critical Practice," lecture (ART 949), October 27, 2020, Yale School of Art, New Haven, transcript.

first year of MFA study, shone the headlights that allowed us to steer across what had been unilluminated terrain. Without Dai's dedication and acumen for sustained record recovery, it would have been impossible to assemble this story. Angela Chen (MFA 2020), our photo editor, lent her expertise to the collection of materials and rights for publication. Willis Kingery (MFA 2019), publications coordinator, contributed several interviews with recent graduates of the Department of Graphic Design and fastidiously managed the project, ensuring the book made it onto press and into the hands of readers. Beth Lovell (MFA 1991), Assistant to the Dean at the School of Art, provided invaluable help with research and coordination. Finally, Irma Boom, who has served as Critic at the School for nearly three decades, honored the project by giving form to this story with the design of the book itself.

Recognizing that a landmark anniversary provides an important opportunity to revise and enrich existing legacies, to fill in oral histories not previously told, and to bring to light materials not already known or cited, this book depicts the Yale School of Art since around 1969 from the perspective of an author whose understanding of that period has been informed by avidly listening to a number of exemplary women associated with the School during this time, either as students, faculty, or both. It aims to acknowledge and reflect a constellation of individuals, events, and experiences that have been historically peripheralized, while admitting that too many individuals will still be overlooked, and many more stories are as yet unfolding. This volume is only a first attempt to convey a complicated, multidimensional, and extensive history that asks to be retold many more times, at length, and through counterpositions, keeping in mind that while a 150-year anniversary calls for commemoration and celebration, the task cannot be merely laudatory nor perfunctory. Above all, the account to follow demonstrates that since 1969, the gender binary that once dominated the School has gradually shifted toward gender nonconformity, profoundly influencing its pedagogical perspective.

Marta Kuzma   New Haven, Connecticut
                     June 30, 2021

A LEGACY
REVISITED

Marta Kuzma

The history of the Yale School of Art has been entangled with questions of inclusivity from its very beginning. The Yale School of the Fine Arts, as it was then called, officially opened on October 15, 1869, supported by a generous donation from Caroline Mary Leffingwell Street and her husband, Augustus Russell Street, an 1812 Yale graduate, with the stipulation that admission be open to both male and female students. It was a radical proposal at the time, since women weren't admitted into University art programs in the United States. Although Augustus Street died prior to the completion of the building, Caroline Street proceeded to select John Ferguson Weir as the first Director and to endow two professorships—the William Leffingwell Professorship of Painting and Design and the Street Professorship of Drawing. The School's inauguration occurred two months before the territory of Wyoming (which was not yet a state) became the first to adopt as law a woman's right to vote and hold public office. Despite Street's mandate for coeducation, media coverage around the School's opening exhibition belied the presence of women. As reported by the *New York Times*: "We have never had a school of high art where young men could receive an artistic training that would fit them for the actual work of their profession, and we congratulate the authorities of Yale College on having so far succeeded …"[4] A curious omission, considering that the "young men" in the first class of only three or four students included two women, Alice and Susan Silliman (who were the daughters of Yale Professor of Chemistry Benjamin Silliman, Jr.).[5] It would be some eighty years before the School would graduate the first known African American woman, and another decade to graduate the first known African American woman from the MFA program, Barbara Chase-Riboud. An additional sixty years would pass before she would be widely recognized for that fact,

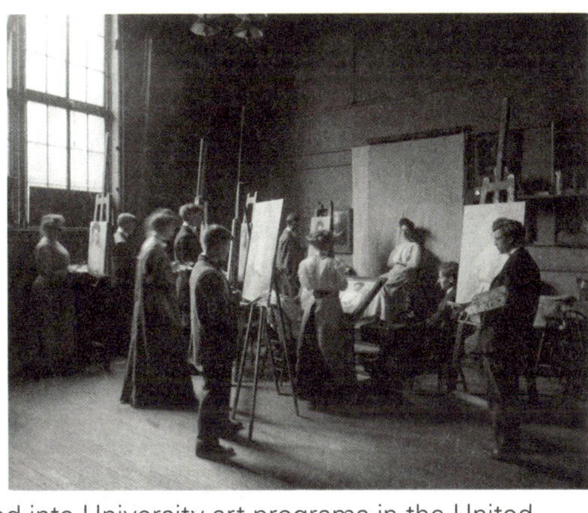

Co-educational studio painting class at the Yale School of Fine Arts, ca. 1900–20. Photographs documenting the School of Fine Arts, Yale University (RU 890). Manuscripts and Archives, Yale University Library.

in August 2019. This delay was due in part to the fact that no one had asked the question, much like the *New York Times* of 150 years earlier, in its omission of women.

Chase-Riboud, who enrolled at Yale in 1958, was commissioned to realize a fountain located in a shopping mall in Wheaton, Maryland [see p. 18], that same year. She pursued its fabrication at a local factory and went on to install the work (where it remained through the 1970s). The School's thesis

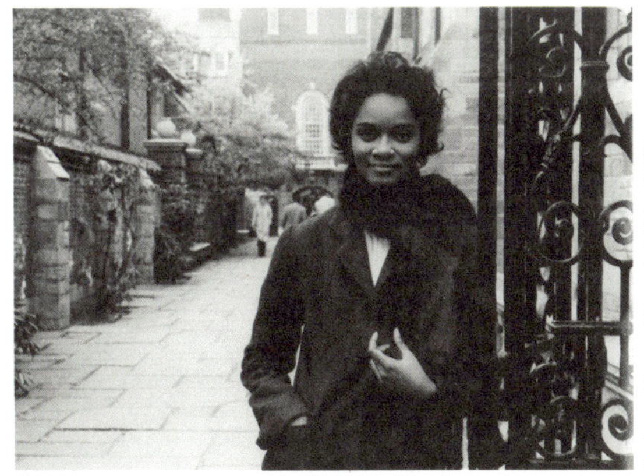

Barbara Chase-Riboud at Yale, 1960. Photo by Mei Lou Klein.

4   "The Exhibiton at Yale College," *New York Times*, July 22, 1867.

5   It is unclear whether the first class was three or four students.

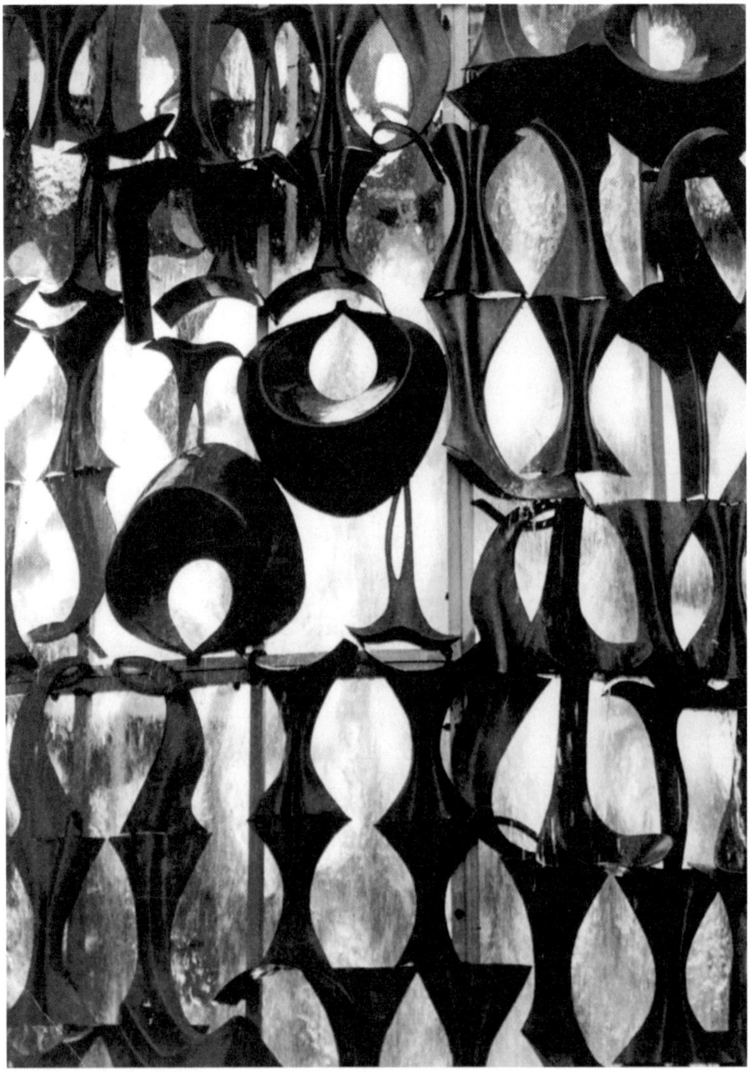

Barbara Chase-Riboud, <u>Wheaton Plaza Fountain</u>, 1960 (detail).
Courtesy Barbara Chase-Riboud.

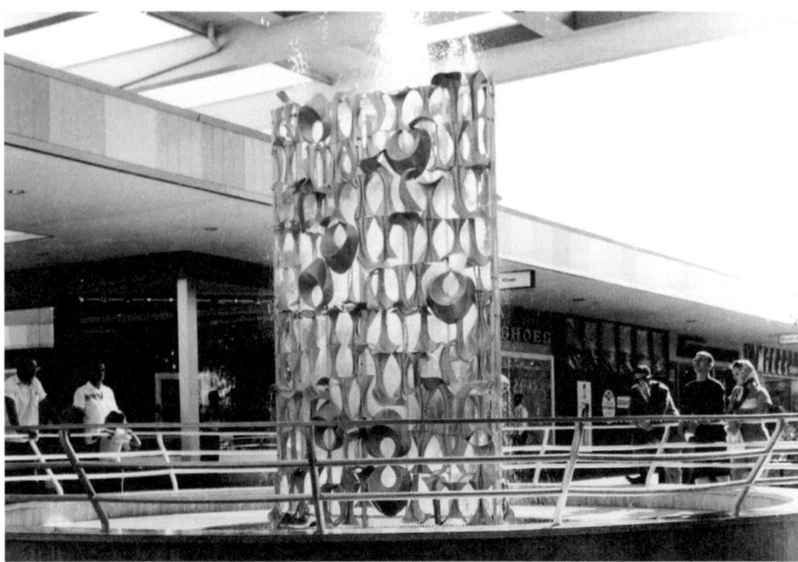

Barbara Chase-Riboud, <u>Wheaton Plaza Fountain</u>, 1960. Courtesy Barbara Chase-Riboud.

review committee, however, rejected the commission (hence, denying her the credentials to graduate) as Chase-Riboud's final project, claiming that it had not been properly supervised. Chase-Riboud explains, "It is true that I didn't ask anybody if I could do the commission. I mean, I didn't ask the administration, I didn't ask the Dean. I didn't ask any professors. I just did it. I had no designated supervisor." When the visiting critics learned that Chase-Riboud would not graduate, they collectively threatened to withhold everyone's degree in protest. "It was the most silent revolution I've ever heard about, I didn't even realize it took place," Chase-Riboud notes. She was subsequently offered the right to graduate on the condition that a new thesis project be submitted, a requirement she fulfilled three weeks later in the form of a bound book of etchings based on Arthur Rimbaud's *A Season in Hell*.[6]

In order to provide context for the School of Art's history from 1969 onwards, one must refer back to the 1950s and early 1960s, since the curriculum changes of those years and the central role of Josef Albers significantly impacted the School in the decades to follow. Charles Sawyer, Dean of the School of the Fine Arts (1947–57), recruited Albers from Black Mountain College in North Carolina, in 1950, appointing him as Chair of the Department of Design, entirely replacing, at least in name, the existing Departments of Painting and Sculpture, and dramatically revising the previous curriculum of the School, which had been modeled on the French Beaux Arts tradition of classical training that upheld ancient Roman and Greek forms as the pinnacle of artistic achievement. Sawyer conceived of Albers' appointment as an effort to "secure a common foundation with the architectural curriculum."[7] Sawyer also appointed Alvin Eisenman at this time in response to a student petition to include graphic design classes.[8] Albers, who had been part of a visiting committee formed two years earlier by the President of the University to study the School, was hired to establish an experimental program that would explore the relationship of painting and sculpture to design and architecture at a time when rationalism in city planning was being heavily criticized. Sawyer and Albers had both arrived in the wake of the federally sponsored Housing Act of 1949, which brought Yale University into active institutional partnership with the city of New Haven in a program of government-administered social welfare extending to the built environment, referred to as "urban renewal."[9] Albers' pedagogy, initially developed in the 1920s at the Bauhaus, where he taught after first

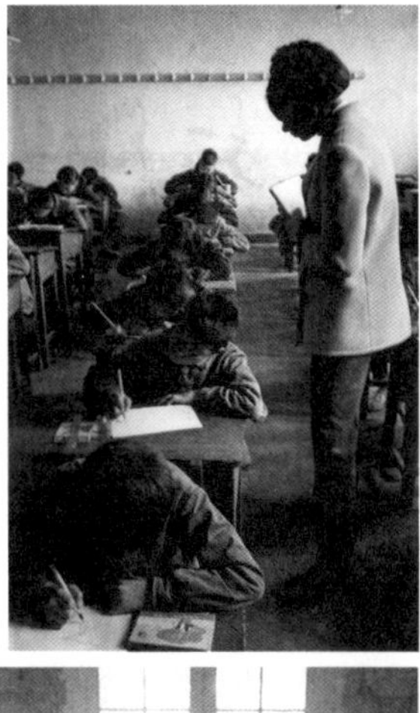

Barbara Chase-Riboud visiting a primary school during a drawing lesson in China, 1965. © Barbara Chase-Riboud.

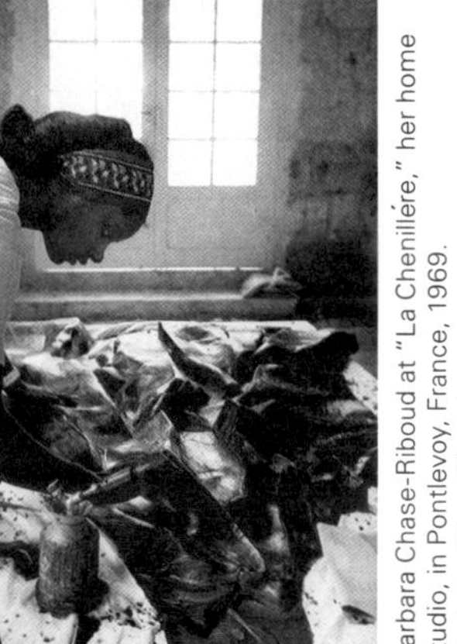

Barbara Chase-Riboud at "La Chenillére," her home studio, in Pontlevoy, France, 1969. Photo by Marc Riboud.

Barbara Chase-Riboud at the exhibition Barbara Chase-Riboud: Four Monuments to Malcolm X at Bertha Schaefer Gallery, 1970.

6   Barbara Chase-Riboud, conversation with the author, June 10, 2019.

7   "In the revision of the curriculum a special effort would be made to secure a common foundation with the architectural curriculum and also to provide for an orderly transition from the liberal arts or general education which will be the usual requirement for admission." Charles H. Sawyer, letter to Josef Albers, June 16, 1950. School of Art and Architecture, Yale University, Records (RU 189). Manuscripts and Archives, Yale University Library.

8   Jerry L. Thompson and Alvin Eisenman. "Teaching the Practice of Photography at Yale: A Conversation with Alvin Eisenman, February 2006." *Yale University Art Gallery Bulletin*, 2006, 124–31. www.jstor.org/stable/40514665.

9   Brian Goldstein, "Planning's End? Urban Renewal in New Haven, the Yale School of Art and Architecture, and the Fall of the New Deal Spatial Order," *Journal of Urban History*, 2011: 401.

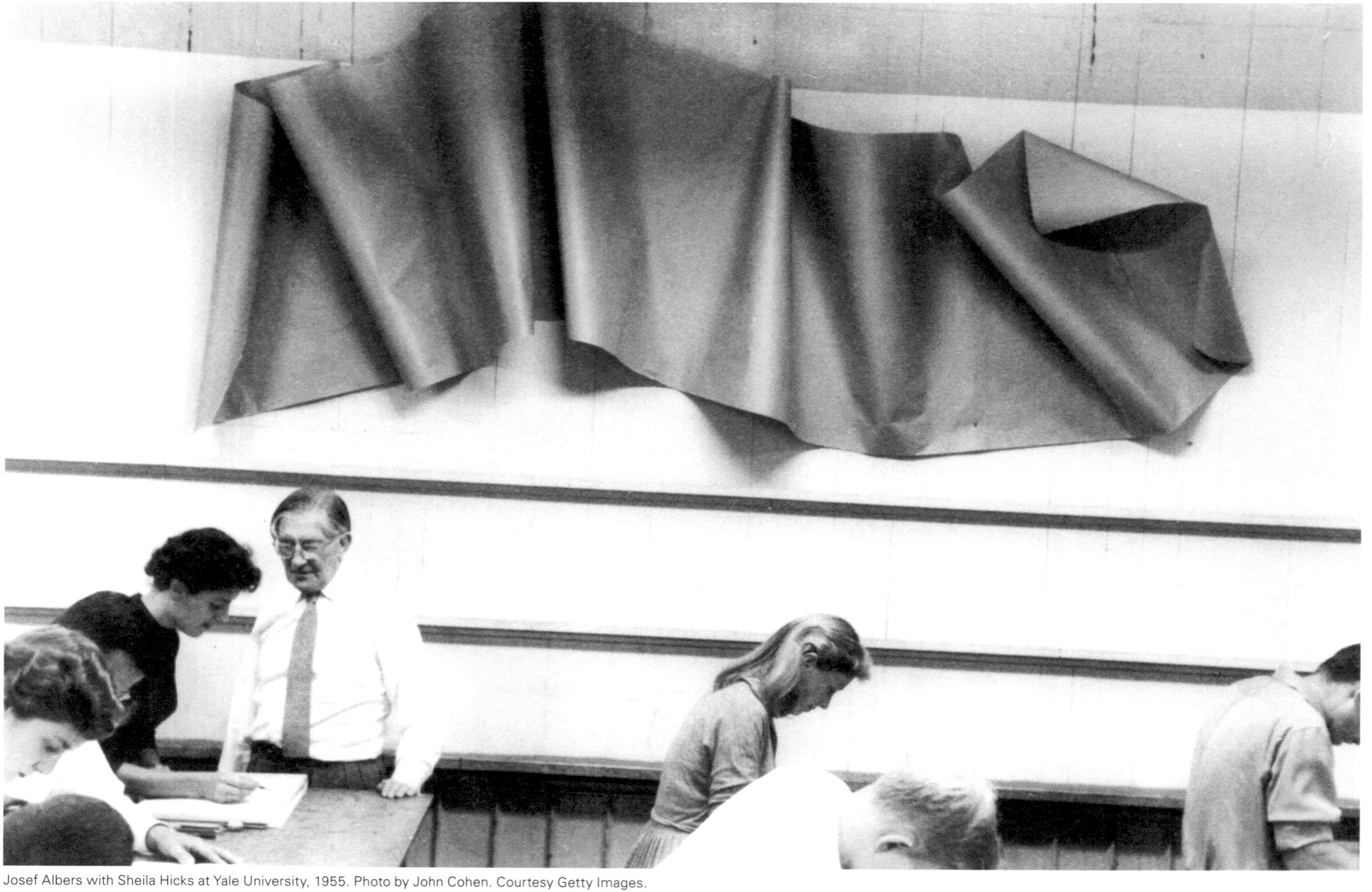

Josef Albers with Sheila Hicks at Yale University, 1955. Photo by John Cohen. Courtesy Getty Images.

attending as a student, was premised on the acquisition of technical skill through direct observation and revolved around a study of color as a unifying thread weaving through all disciplines. Although Albers' legacy is historically irrefutable, his tenure ended polemically with the criticism that his approach was overly formalist and denied social aspects of the lived environment. In a 1955 letter from Dean Sawyer to President Griswold, Sawyer refers to a "City Planning Section" that, like Albers' "Graphic Arts program in design," was "adopted in 1950 on a five-year experimental basis as a means of determining the University's program in this field." He continues, "The coordination with architecture that was presumed, never really took effect and our Council Committee has been critical of the narrowness of the program which has stressed primarily the physical and visual aspects of planning."[10] By the end of the 1950s, graduate students at the School had begun to challenge what they viewed as an "authoritarian mode of urban design," seeking instead a "greater engagement with the people whom architects and planners served."[11] The School established a Department of City Planning in 1960.

Albers submitted his final annual report as Chairman of the Department of Art in 1958 (before becoming Professor Emeritus of Art), writing of the faculty that "they have developed as excellent and truly successful teachers, admired and liked by their students. They realized that a subsequent specialized study depends on a thorough training in observation and articulation instead of a directionless and aimless laissez-faire of so-called self-expression."[12] By 1969, the Bauhaus approach he instilled at the School had been exhausted amid broader social and political struggles affecting universities throughout the U.S. and internationally. At the Yale School of Art and Architecture, as it was then called, this shift was led predominantly by graphic design, architecture, and city planning students who demanded greater community engagement, increased racial diversity within their respective fields, influence in university planning, and increased involvement in university governance.[13]

Upon Albers' departure as Chairman of the Art Department in 1958, Jack Tworkov was appointed to that role, and he reasserted the School's commitment to painting and object-making, pursuing a curriculum overseen by an expanded list of visiting faculty comprised of acclaimed painters from the New York art world, rather than from academia. The Art Department's full-time faculty also drew from artists who remained based in New York City, rather than ones who would relocate to New Haven, cementing the School's satellite relationship

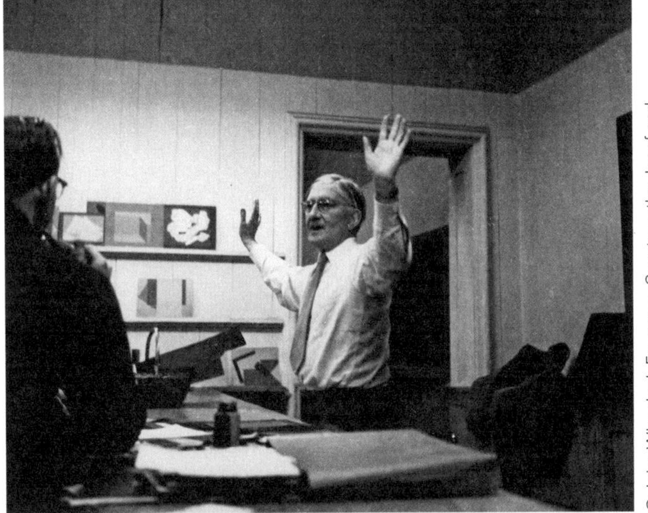

© John Wheelock Freeman. Courtesy the Josef and Anni Albers Foundation.

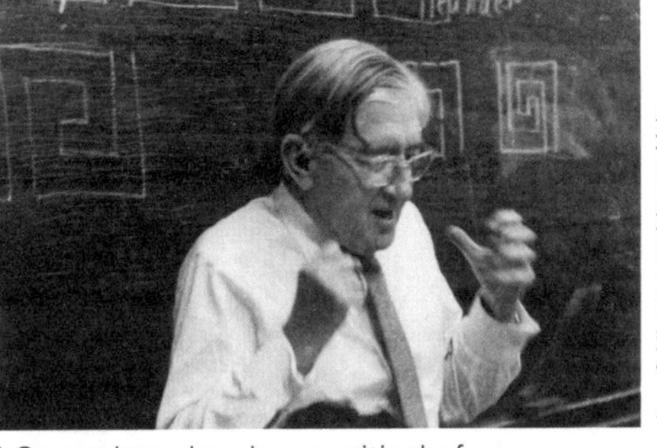

Josef Albers teaching at Yale University, 1955–56. Photo by John Cohen. Courtesy the Josef and Anni Albers Foundation. © John Cohen.

10   Charles Sawyer to A. Whitney Griswold, April 18, 1955, Records of A. Whitney Groswold, President 1950–63, RY-22, box 25, Yale University Manuscripts and Archives. Quoted in Robert A. M. Stern and Jimmy Stamp, *Pedagogy and Place: 100 Years of Architecture Education at Yale* (New Haven: Yale University Press, 2016), 153.

11   Goldstein 2011, 402.

12   "Josef Albers, Eighth Annual Report, 1957–58." Yale University Art Gallery Archives. June 27, 1958.

13   Goldstein 2011.

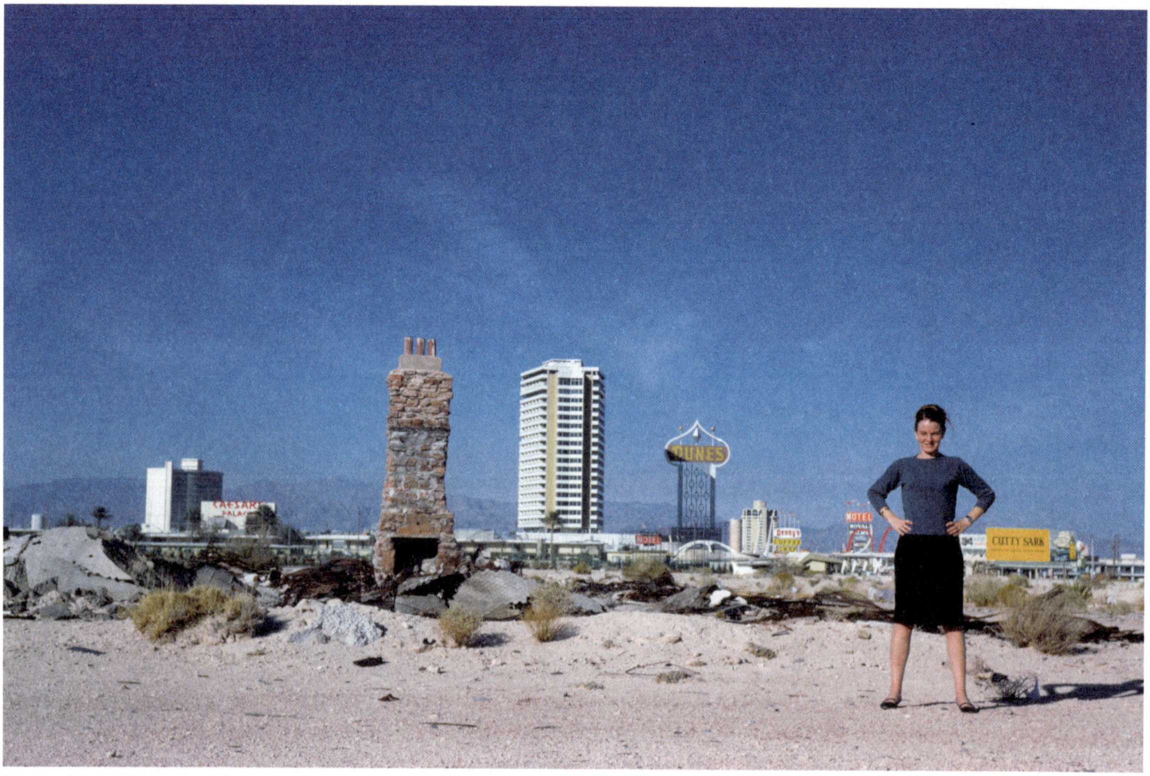

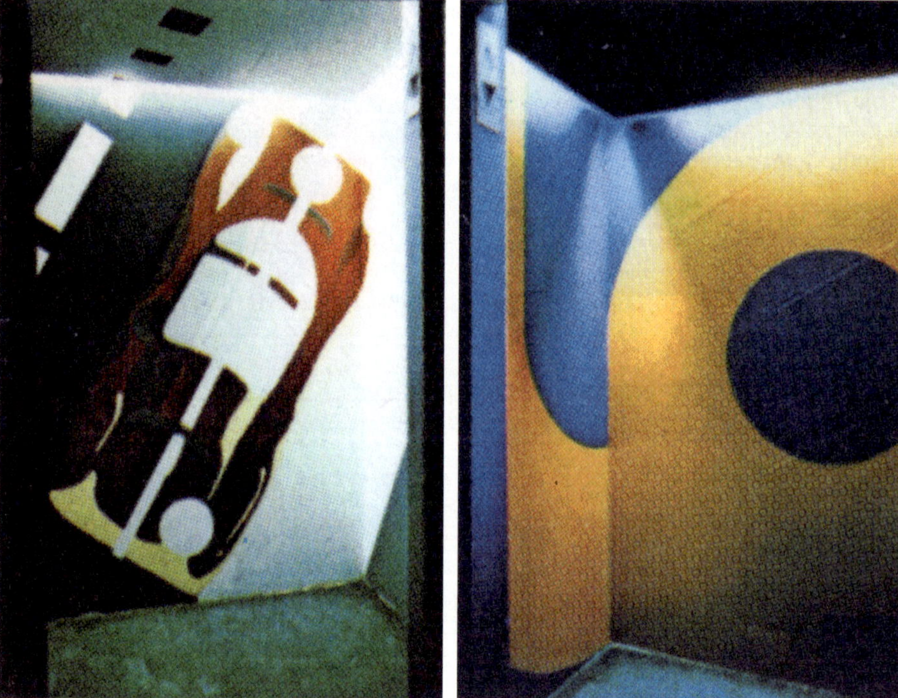

The Las Vegas Strip as seen from the desert, with Denise Scott Brown, Learning from Las Vegas Studio, 1966.
Photo by Robert Venturi. Courtesy Denise Scott Brown.

Barbara Stauffacher Solomon's elevator design problem given to Yale architecture students,
New Haven, Connecticut, 1968. Photo by and courtesy James Righter.

to New York.[14] Throughout the 1960s, the culture of the School of Art and Architecture was split among students committed to career development within the elite New York art world and students in the Departments of Design, Architecture, and City Planning, who were calling for greater political and social engagement on the part of the School with the city of New Haven.[15]

The year 1969 was characterized by ongoing student activism at Yale University following a variety of national and political events, including the occupation of Columbia University in New York; the protests at Chicago's Democratic Convention; the Black Freedom movement; the Vietnam War; and emerging freedom of sexual choice. It was also the year that African American studies was established at Yale, the Afro-America Cultural Center (later Afro-American Cultural Center) opened, and the first Asian American and Chicanx student groups were founded on campus. The Yale School of Art and Architecture was not isolated from student engagement with these issues. It was a space of dissonance within the University, where artists, designers, architects, and city planners converged under the same roof with a heightened sense of political urgency and desire for direct political action, challenging University policies with respect to education and broader civil rights. A year earlier, the 1968 research studio led by Robert Venturi, Denise Scott Brown, and Steven Izenour had taken an excursion to California and Las Vegas, which resulted in a seminal document regarding the aesthetics of "the Strip," which would revise a canonical understanding of how communication dominates space as an element in architecture and landscape. That same year, Barbara Stauffacher Solomon led a project in which students applied two dimensional supergraphics to the School of Art and Architecture elevators in what was heralded as a protest against the establishment.[16] And in 1969, Barbara Chase-Riboud produced her *Malcolm X* stelae as a memorial to the human rights activist who had been assassinated four years earlier. "Most activism sacrifices the aesthetic for the message," Chase-Riboud said recently. "For me, the message is the message. We had to deal with something that should have been dealt with in 1865."[17]

Experimental filmmaker Abigail Child (BFA 1970; MFA 1970) recalls the Living Theatre—the oldest experimental theater group in the nation, founded in 1947—taking to the streets after a performance of *Paradise Now* in 1968; she also remembers attending screenings held by the Yale Law School, which also hosted lectures, including one by the psychologist and writer Timothy Leary in November 1969 titled "The Politics of Joy," organized by the Yale Political Union.[18] Child later worked professionally with another former student Nick Doob (BA 1969; MFA 1973), who had participated in May 1st Media, a film collective that included classmates in the Architecture and City Planning programs. The group documented student activism on campus and worked with members of the New Haven chapter of the Black Panther Party in support of the city's breakfast program for children, among other initiatives.[19] Students from the School had occupied Dean Howard Sayre Weaver's office in the fall of 1968 to demand that Yale address two critical issues: the University's inadequate commitment to the School and the staffing of the School with mediocre faculty. These demands were followed by protests calling for uniform procedures to allocate financial aid on the basis of need in all schools, and to increase aid overall at the art school. In May 1969, nearly one hundred students from Art, Architecture, Music, and Drama marched on Woodbridge Hall after University President Kingman Brewster maintained there were no available funds for the professional art schools. The protest continued for a second day with what students referred to as "guerilla theater" and a mock funeral in which a coffin was unloaded onto Beinecke Plaza.[20]

14   Irving Sandler, "The School of Art at Yale: 1950–1970: The Collective Reminiscences of Twenty Distinguished Alumni." *Art Journal* 42, no. 1 (1982): 17. www.jstor.org/stable/7776486

15   Goldstein 2011.

16   Eve Blau, "This Work Is Going Somewhere: Pedagogy and Politics at Yale in the Late 1960s." *Log* 38 (2016): 131–49. www.jstor.org/stable/26323794.

17   Barbara Chase-Riboud, conversation with author, June 10, 2019.

18   Abigail Child, telephone conversation with the author, February 1, 2020; see Charles C. Meeker, "Leary Praises Youth Hits Old Moral Values," *Yale Daily News*, November 18, 1969.

19   Nick Doob, telephone conversation with the author, February 5, 2020.

20   Tom Warren, "A and A Protesters Hold Mock Burial," *Yale Daily News*, May 5, 1969.

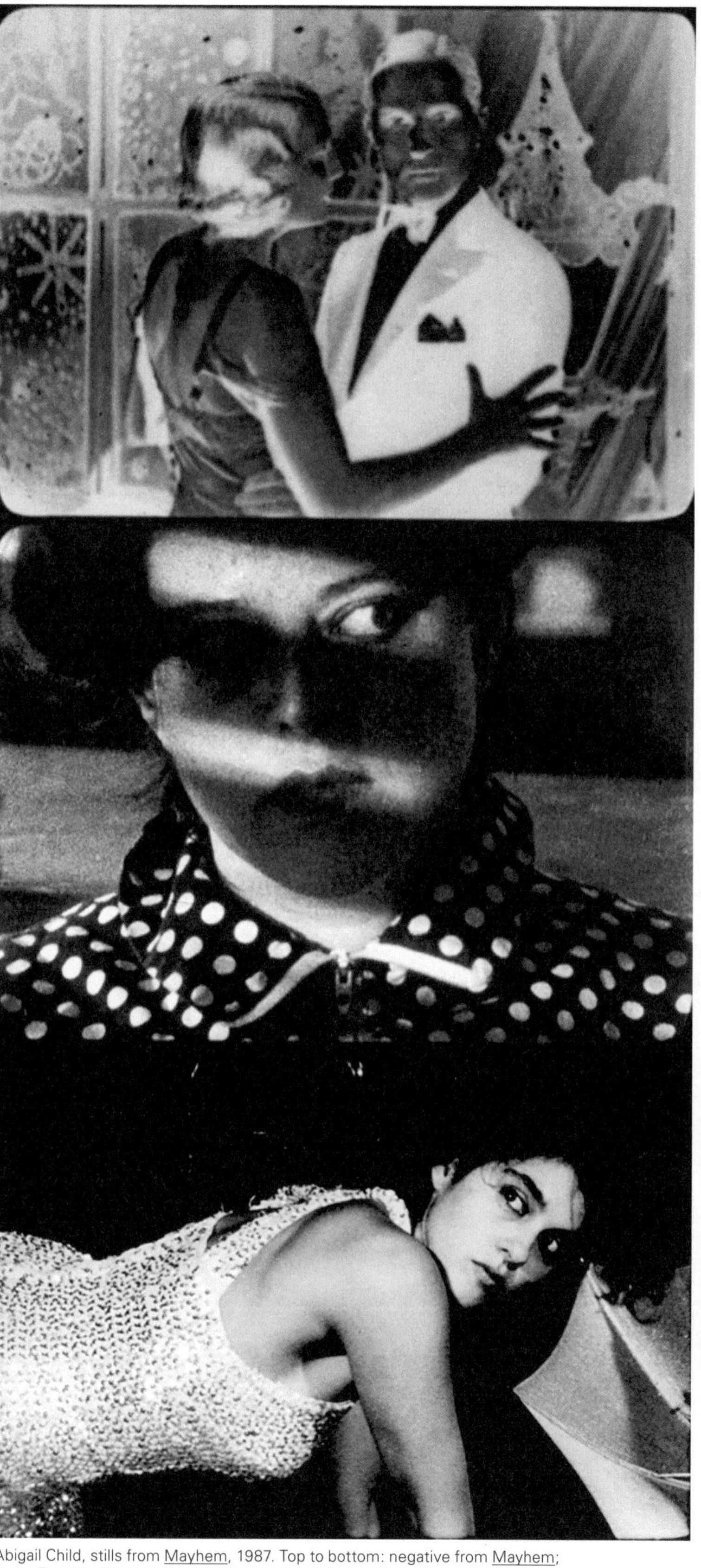

Abigail Child, stills from <u>Mayhem</u>, 1987. Top to bottom: negative from <u>Mayhem</u>; Diane Torr; Ela Troyano. Courtesy Abigail Child.

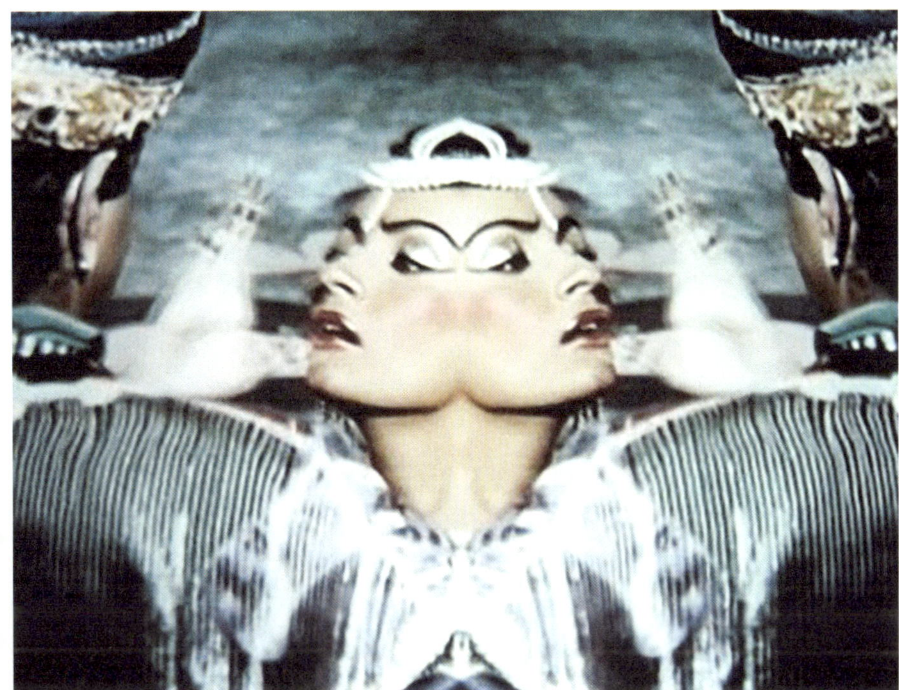

Abigail Child, still from <u>Mirror World</u>, 2006. Courtesy Abigail Child.

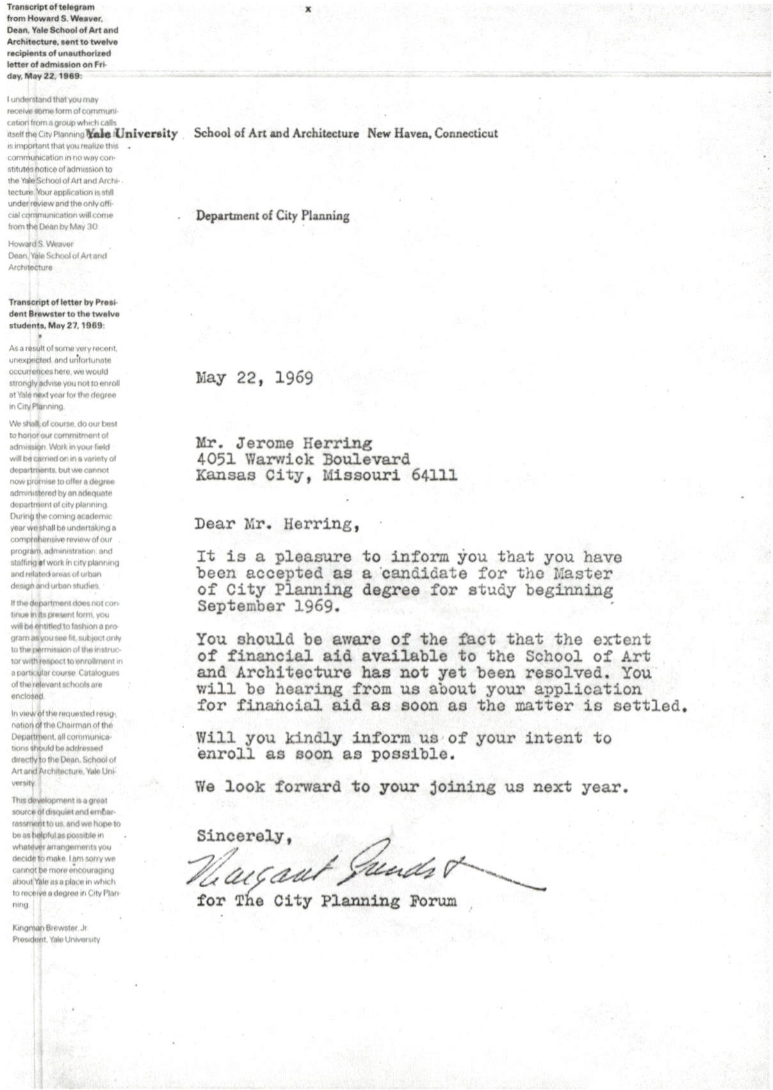

Yale University   School of Art and Architecture   New Haven, Connecticut

Department of City Planning

May 22, 1969

Mr. Jerome Herring
4051 Warwick Boulevard
Kansas City, Missouri 64111

Dear Mr. Herring,

It is a pleasure to inform you that you have been accepted as a candidate for the Master of City Planning degree for study beginning September 1969.

You should be aware of the fact that the extent of financial aid available to the School of Art and Architecture has not yet been resolved. You will be hearing from us about your application for financial aid as soon as the matter is settled.

Will you kindly inform us of your intent to enroll as soon as possible.

We look forward to your joining us next year.

Sincerely,

for The City Planning Forum

Copy of unauthorized acceptance letter written by the City Planning Forum, signed by Margaret Grundstein, 1968, and reproduced in Perspecta 29: Into the Fire, 1998. Courtesy Margaret Grundstein and Perspecta.

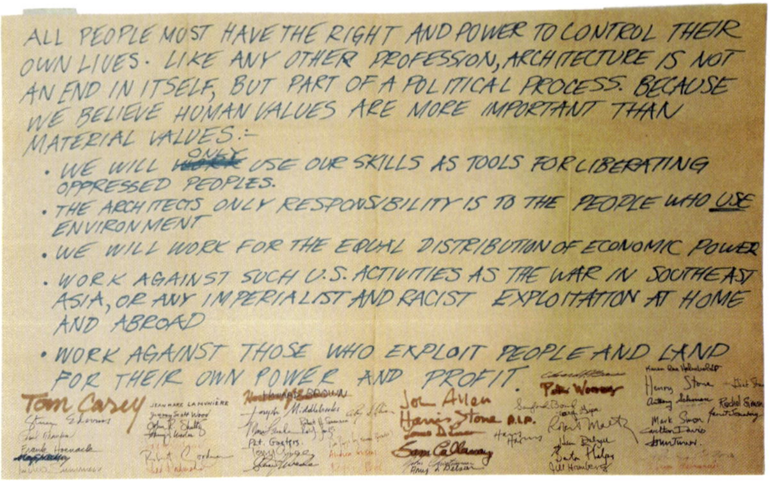

Statement adopted by students critiquing the American Institute of Architects Conference, 1968. School of Architecture, Yale University (RU 906). Manuscripts and Archives, Yale University Library.

21 Amy Vita Kesselman, "Women's Liberation and the Left in New Haven, Connecticut 1968–1972," *Radical History Review* 81 (2001): 17, 26. muse.jhu.edu/article/30187.

22 Ibid, 17.

23 Ibid.

24 Ibid.

25 Ibid, 22.

26 Ibid.

27 Ibid.

28 Ibid, 24.

29 Ibid, 24–25.

30 Thomas Kent, "Women Seek Liberation," *Yale Daily News*, March 6, 1970.

With the admittance of the first women undergraduates into Yale College and the rise of the women's movement nationally, the American Independent Movement (AIM) was formed in New Haven by a group of "antiwar activists at Yale that had run a candidate for Congress in 1966 on an anti-Vietnam War platform" and who "continued to see themselves as part of a broader movement for social and economic revolution," even as women's liberation became their focus, as Amy Vita Kesselman writes in "Women's Liberation and the Left in New Haven, Connecticut 1968–1972."[21]

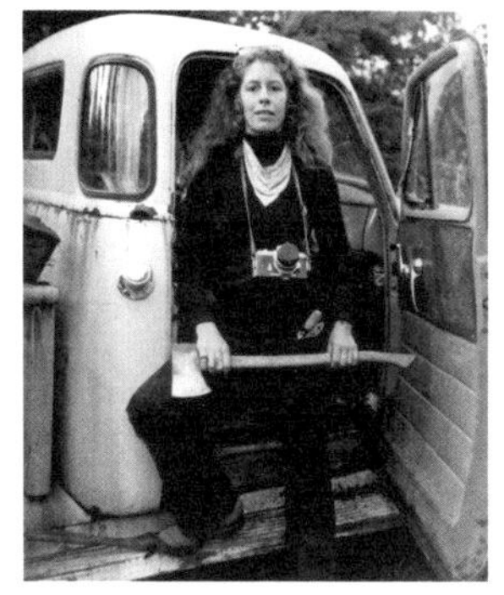

Margaret Grundstein at a commune at Flora's Creek, Oregon, ca. 1973. Courtesy Margaret Grundstein.

Kesselman continues, "By 1968, AIM had grown into a lively, multi-faceted group that was organizing New Haven residents around local workplace, antidevelopment issues, as well as against the war."[22] The organization also created several "alternative institutions," including "a children's school, a coffeehouse, and a printing press."[23] AIM was comprised largely of white members, although "they worked closely with an African American community organization called the Hill Parents Association." Kesselman describes a July 1969 cover of the AIM Newsletter as featuring, "an illustration of a barbed-wire-wielding capitalist flanked by six figures who represented various oppressed groups; all of the figures were male."[24] The image includes the slogan, it's a system that keeps us apart.[25] The organization began to engage in what the New York group Redstockings coined as "consciousness raising," with members "examining their own experience for insights into women's position in society."[26] The women ran "a weekly radio show (including a serial soap opera entitled *The Liberation of Lydia)*, women-and-our-bodies courses, a speaker's bureau, a women's liberation rock band, and forums and conferences in the community and at area colleges."[27] Women activists also "used their organizing skills in a wide variety of projects in the early 1970s to change laws and challenge existing sexist practices," including "a campaign to assist the organizing efforts of clerical and technical workers at Yale; a child care alliance that staged a 'child-in' at a Yale board meeting; a campaign against Mory's (the men-only bar [that Yale faculty and administrators attended]);

a 'camp-in' on the town green to protest the cuts in the grants to welfare recipients; a class action suit challenging Connecticut's abortion law; and an 'offensive defense squad' that challenged sexual harassment on the street."[28] An article appearing in the *Yale Daily News* in March 1970, titled "Women Seek Liberation," read, "A lot of young ladies have been acting very unladylike in the past few months. Eighteen from the Yale community swept into Mory's all-male lunch hour several weeks ago and demanded to be served … 200 of them refused to admit men to meetings they held at the Law School last weekend. And a few emblazoned 'Up from Under—Women Unite' in red paint on Beinecke Library and Woodbridge Hall two days ago."[29]

Just one month after the student protests and mock funeral on Beinecke Plaza, the Paul Rudolph-designed Art and Architecture Building, which housed the School of Art and Architecture, caught fire in June 1969, and was extensively damaged. The fire, suspected

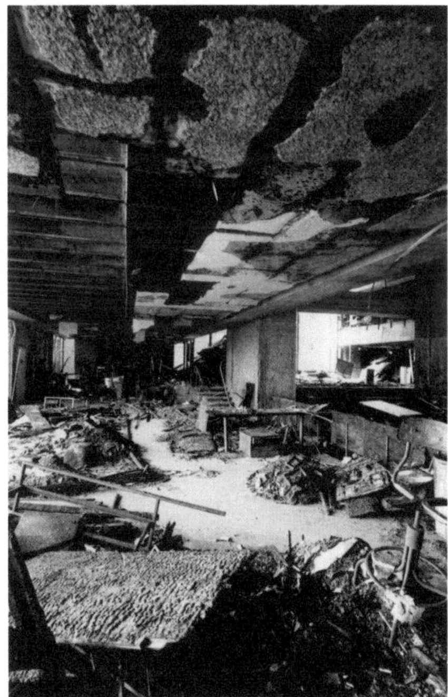

A view of the Paul Rudolph-designed Art & Architecture Building after the fire in 1969, Yale University. Yale University Art Gallery Archives.

BLACK AND BLUE:

"Yale is the wrong place for a black radical."

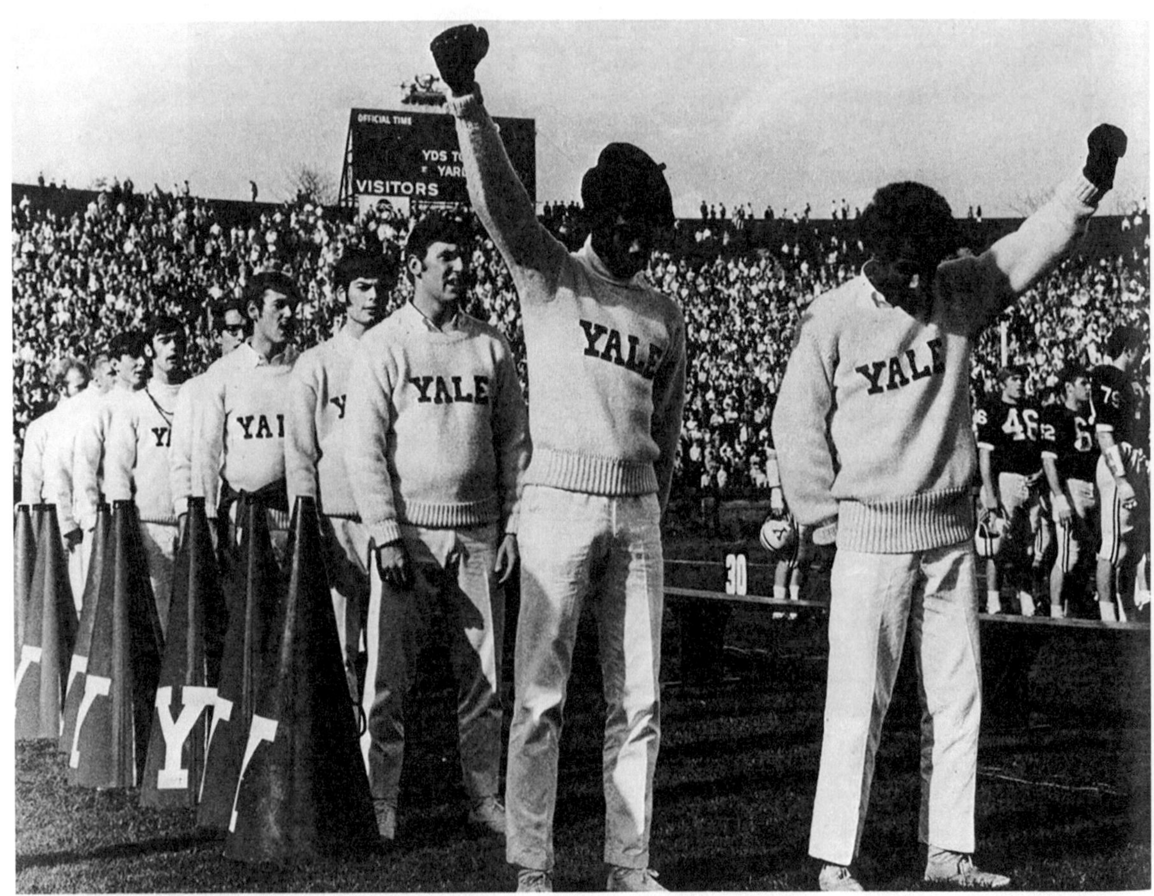

54

Theodore A. Burrell's "Black and Blue: 'Yale is the wrong place for a black radical,'" <u>Yale Banner</u>, 1969. Manuscripts and Archives, Yale University Library.

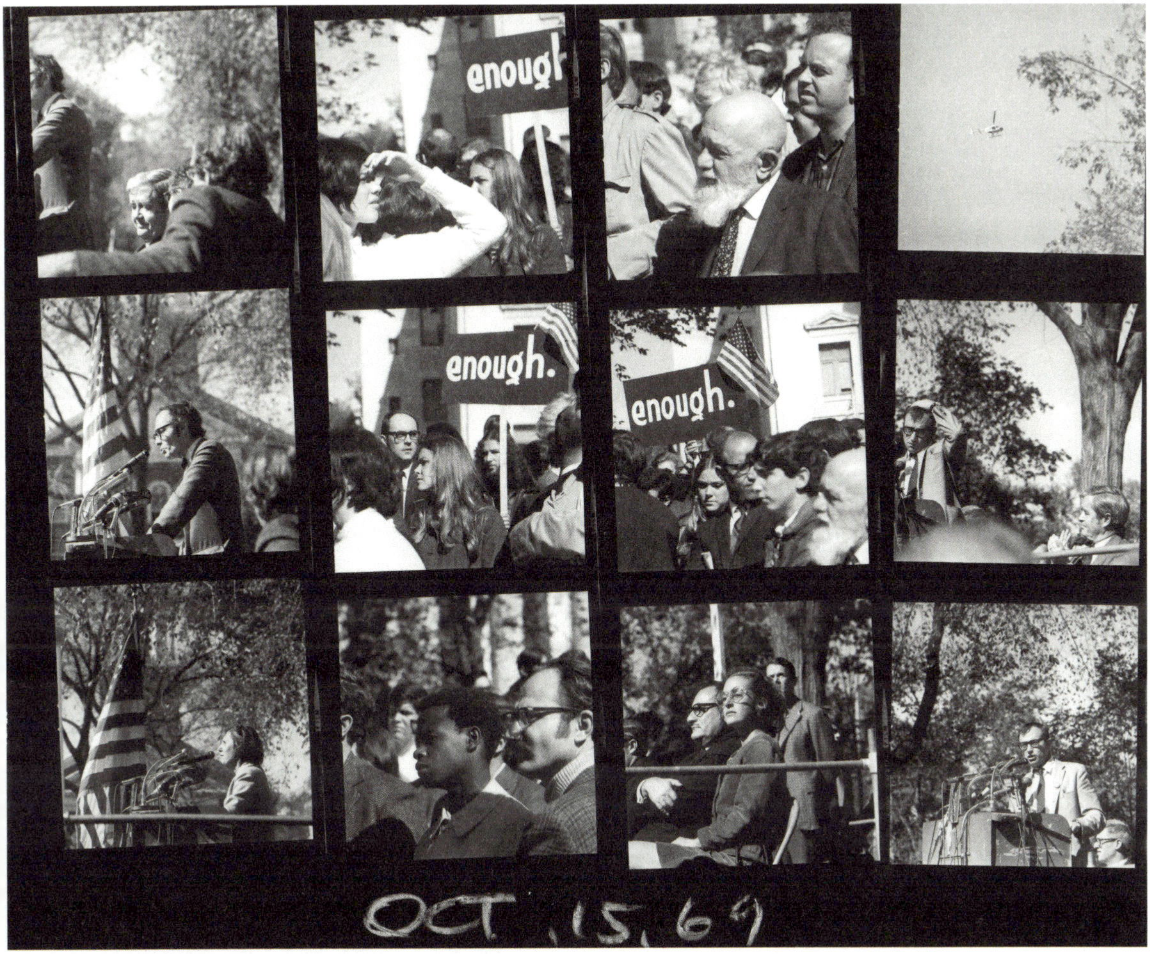

Images of speakers and attendees at the Vietnam Moratorium rally held on the New Haven Green, 1969. Yale Events and Activities Photographs (RU 690). Manuscripts and Archives, Yale University Library.

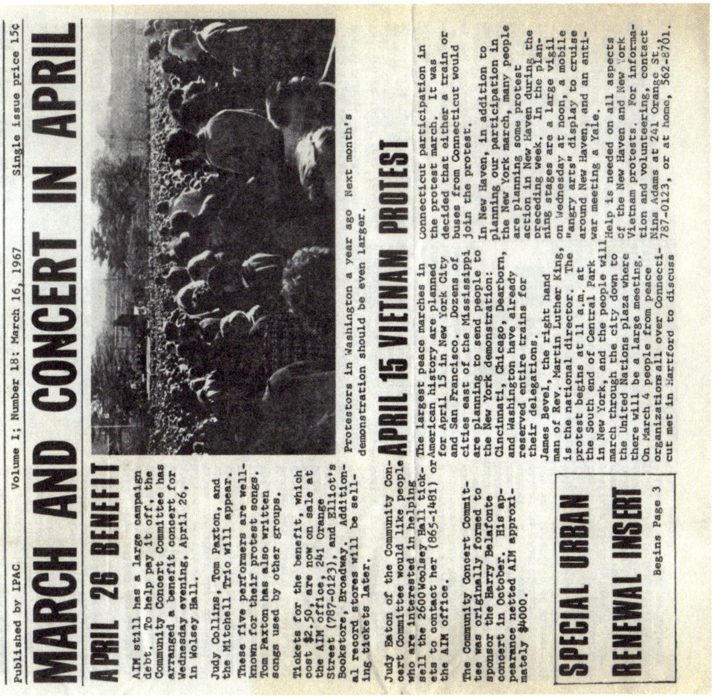

AIM

THE BULLETIN OF THE AMERICAN INDEPENDENT MOVEMENT

Published by IPAC   Volume I; Number 18; March 16, 1967   Single issue price 15¢

MARCH AND CONCERT IN APRIL

APRIL 26 BENEFIT

AIM still has a large campaign debt. To help pay it off, the Community Concert Committee has arranged a benefit concert for Wednesday evening, April 26, in Woolsey Hall.

Judy Collins, Tom Paxton, and the Mitchell Trio will appear. These five performers are well-known for their protest songs. Tom Paxton has also written songs used by other groups.

Tickets for the benefit, which cost $2.50, are now on sale at the AIM office, 241 Orange Street (787-0123), and Elliot's Bookstore, Broadway. Additional record stores will be selling tickets later.

Judy Eaton of the Community Concert Committee would like people who are interested in helping sell the 2600 Woolsey Hall tickets to contact her (865-1481) or the AIM office.

The Community Concert Committee was originally formed to sponsor the Harry Belafonte concert in October. His appearance netted AIM approximately $4000.

SPECIAL URBAN RENEWAL INSERT

Begins Page 3

Protestors in Washington a year ago   Next month's demonstration should be even larger.

APRIL 15 VIETNAM PROTEST

The largest peace marches in American history are planned for April 15 in New York City and San Francisco. Dozens of cities east of the Mississippi are planning to send people to the New York demonstration: Cincinnati, Chicago, Dearborn, and Washington have already reserved entire trains for their delegations.

James Bevel, the right hand man of Rev. Martin Luther King, is the national director. The protest begins at 11 a.m. at the South end of Central Park in New York, and the people will march through the city down to the United Nations plaza where there will be a large meeting. On March 4, people from peace organizations all over Connecticut met in Hartford to discuss Connecticut participation in the protest march. It was decided that either a train or buses from Connecticut would join the protest.

In New Haven, in addition to planning our participation in the New York march, many people are planning some protest action in New Haven during the preceding week. In the planning stages are a large vigil on Wednesday at noon, a mobile "angry arts" display, to cruise around New Haven, and an anti-war meeting at a Yale.

Help is needed on all aspects of the New Haven and New York Vietnam protests. For information and volunteering, contact Nina Adams at 241 Orange St., 787-0123, or at home, 562-8701.

Cover of AIM: The Bulletin of the American Independent Movement, vol. 1, no. 18, March 16, 1967. William Sloane Coffin, Jr. Papers (MS 1665). Manuscripts and Archives, Yale University Library.

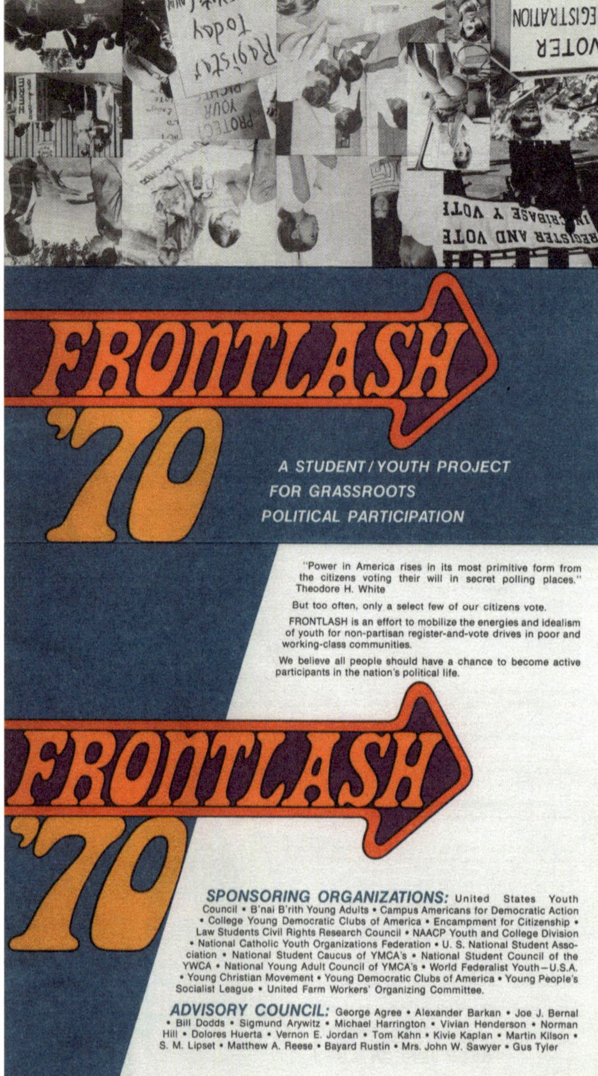

Advertising brochure for Frontlash 70, a student/youth project for grassroots political participation, 1970. Dwight Macdonald Papers (MS 730). Manuscripts and Archives, Yale University Library.

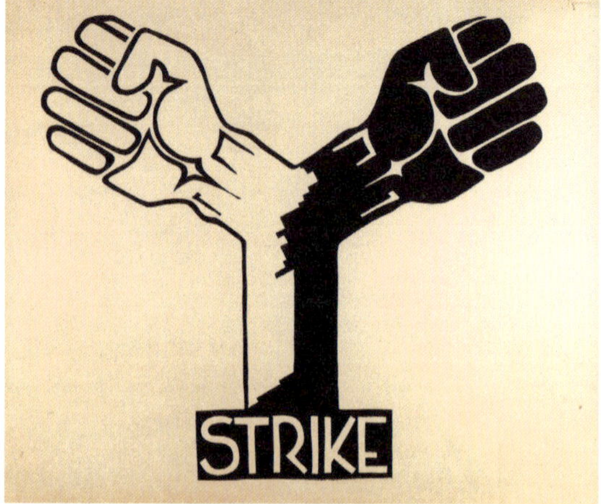

Yale "Strike" poster, ca. May 1970. May Day Rally and Yale Collection (RU 86). Manuscripts and Archives, Yale University Liabrary.

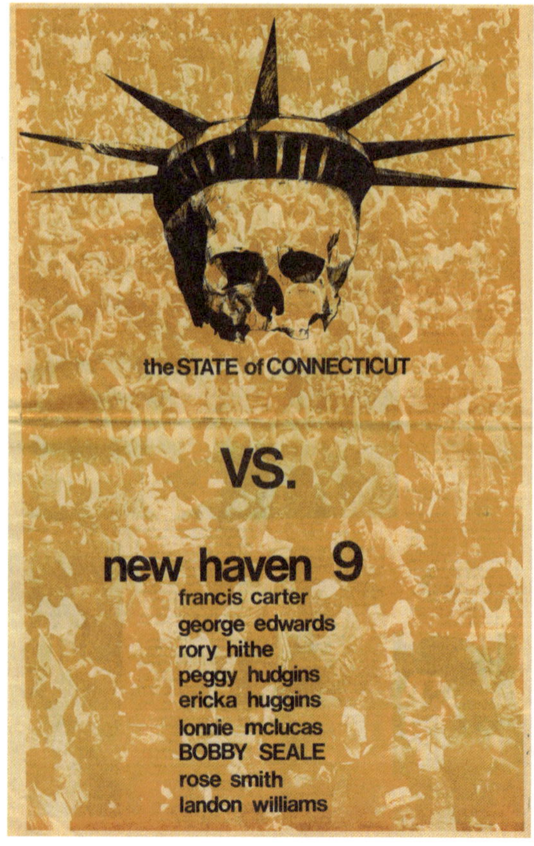

Front page of the State of Connecticut vs. New Haven 9 newspaper, ca. April 1970. Office of the President, Yale University, Records Concerning the May Day Rally (RU 16). Manuscripts and Archives, Yale University Library.

to be an act of arson by disgruntled students, put pressure on the administration to deliver a set of resolutions that would answer students' growing frustrations with leadership. In a faculty meeting demanded by students in the fall of that year, Weaver proposed the adoption of a revised organizational structure that would include a Director of Studies for each of the three programs (Painting, Sculpture, and Graphic Design); these directors would serve as an executive committee of the faculty. According to Weaver's memo from September 15, 1969, they would "conduct programs of study on a regular basis … be regularly available to students, and [would] meet as various questions arise and then report back to the entirety of the faculty for further action on these matters."[30] One of the meeting attendees feared that this plan might reinstate previous power structures, though Weaver attempted to reassure them that the Directors of Studies would "act on matters pertaining to specific areas of study on a regular basis and would not make independent decisions on such matters as promotions, appointments, etc."[31] He referred to the postfire semester as a moment for reappraisal and put forth a vision to include undergraduate studies in the School's future. Three months after the meeting, in January 1970, Weaver submitted a written report to President Brewster titled "Studies in Visual Arts in the University," in which he noted:

> The principal characteristics of advanced or graduate studies in the visual arts are independent exploration, a colleague relationship between student and student and student and teacher, and relief from external pressures. This freedom allows him to challenge himself with entirely new modes of exploration and standards discovered in the community of artists and in the general university community. … It happens that the Yale M.F.A. degree is incidentally a reasonably effective meal ticket. There is irony in this because nothing in the program is remotely related to teacher training, nothing is provided for the student to equip him or her to teach, and no credits are accumulated towards any sort of "certification" anywhere. The fact is that studies in visual art are deficient nearly everywhere, and Yale has set the highest standard for relating investigation in visual arts to general education. Yale graduates came to be in demand because they are regarded as most *liberated* from the constraints and the myopia characteristic of many art schools. The key to this liberation is the emphasis on investigation as opposed to the indoctrination of style.[32]

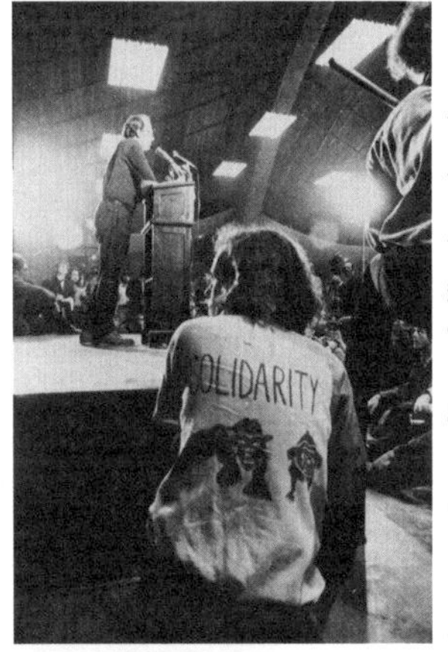

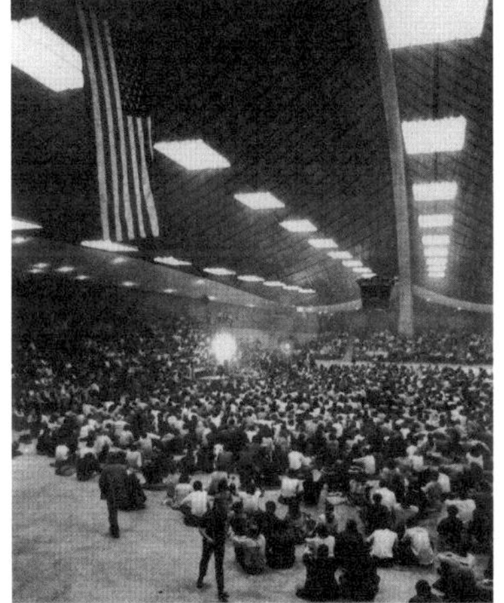

Reverend William Sloane Coffin, the university chaplain and prominent anti-war leader, speaking at Ingalls Rink, April 21, 1970. Photo by Stephen West. Courtesy Stephen West, Yale Class of 1970.

A 4,500-strong crowd, mostly students, listens to speeches about striking in solidarity with the Black Panthers, Ingalls Rink, New Haven, Connecticut, April 21, 1970. Photo by Stephen West. Courtesy Stephen West, Yale Class of 1970.

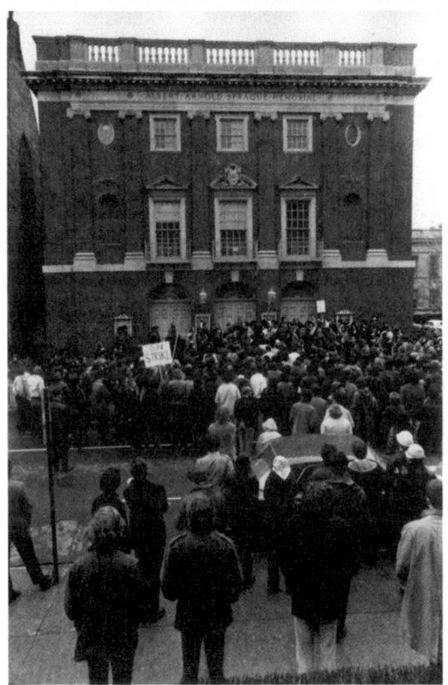

A crowd of 900 demonstrators at Sprague Hall, where a meeting of the Yale College faculty debated and passed, overwhelmingly, a set of demands formulated by a committee of Black faculty members, April 23, 1970. Photo by Stephen West. Courtesy Stephen West, Yale Class of 1970.

rec'd Apr. 16, 1970

M O R A T O R I U M

Last night in WLH there was a meeting of 600 Yale
students and faculty. The meeting voted to begin, immediately,
a three-day moratorium on classes. The only purpose for
attending classes during this period will be to raise issues
relevant to the defense of the Black Panther Party. If no
discussion is permitted, alternative classes will be held
to discuss these issues. The meeting also voted to demand
$500,000 from the Yale Corporation for the Panther defense
fund.

It was then decided to hold meetings in the individual
colleges. At thesemeetings, strong support was expressed
for the moratorium.

The moratorium begins today. It will focus on the
Panther trials and on Yale's relation to the trials and
to the New Haven community in general.

A communications center has been established on the
second floor of Dwight Hall. Phone 436-1480 anytime.

The campus continued to rally in advance of the May 1970 trial in New Haven of Black Panther Party co-founder and chairman Bobby Seale [see p. 34], who, along with eight other members of the Black Panther leadership, had been indicted for the murder in Middlefield, Connecticut, of Black Panther member Alex Rackley. On April 23, nearly 750 demonstrators marched from Beinecke Plaza to President Brewster's home on Hillhouse Avenue with a list of demands regarding not only Yale's response to the charges against the "New Haven Nine" [see p. 30 bottom right] but also University real-estate expansion, wages, retirement plans, childcare, and more.[33] The following day, on April 24, the Art and Architecture School and the Drama School adopted resolutions declaring active solidarity with the aims, means, and goals of the demonstrators. On May 1–3, 1970, which came to be known as May Day Weekend, a large public rally took place on the New Haven Green [see pp. 40–41], with University faculty and students joining members of the New Haven community in support of the Black Panther Party. The Art and Architecture administration, attempting to quell student discontent within the School, began setting out structural changes that would eventually result, in 1972, in the formation of two separate schools—the School of Art and the School of Architecture—each with its own unique faculties and dean.

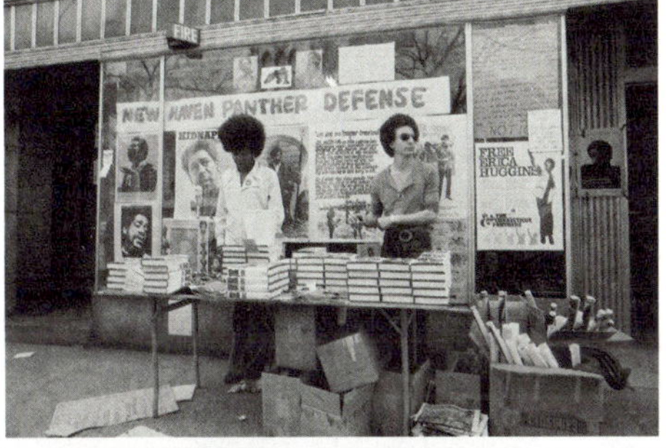

Black Panther Party member at Woolsey Hall rally, April 13, 1970. Photo by John T. Hill. Photographs Used in the Publication of the Yale Alumni Magazine (RU 694). Manuscripts and Archives, Yale University Library. © John T. Hill.

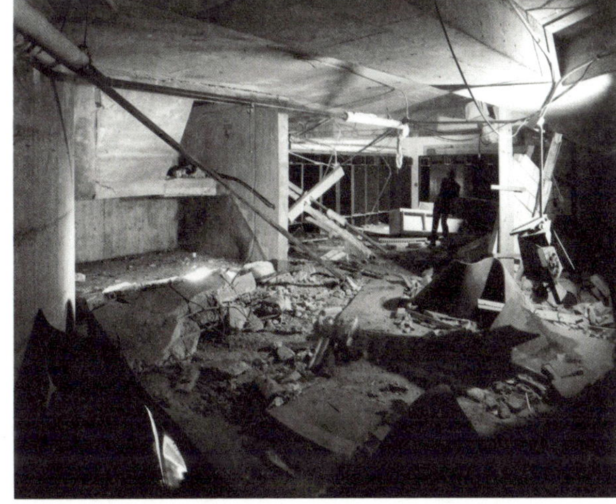

In front of the Black Panther Party organization office, New Haven, May 1 or 2, 1970. Photo by David Fenton. Courtesy Getty Images.

David S. Ingalls Rink, May Day bomb damage, 1970. Photographs of David S. Ingalls Rink, Yale University (RU 629). Manuscripts and Archives, Yale University Library.

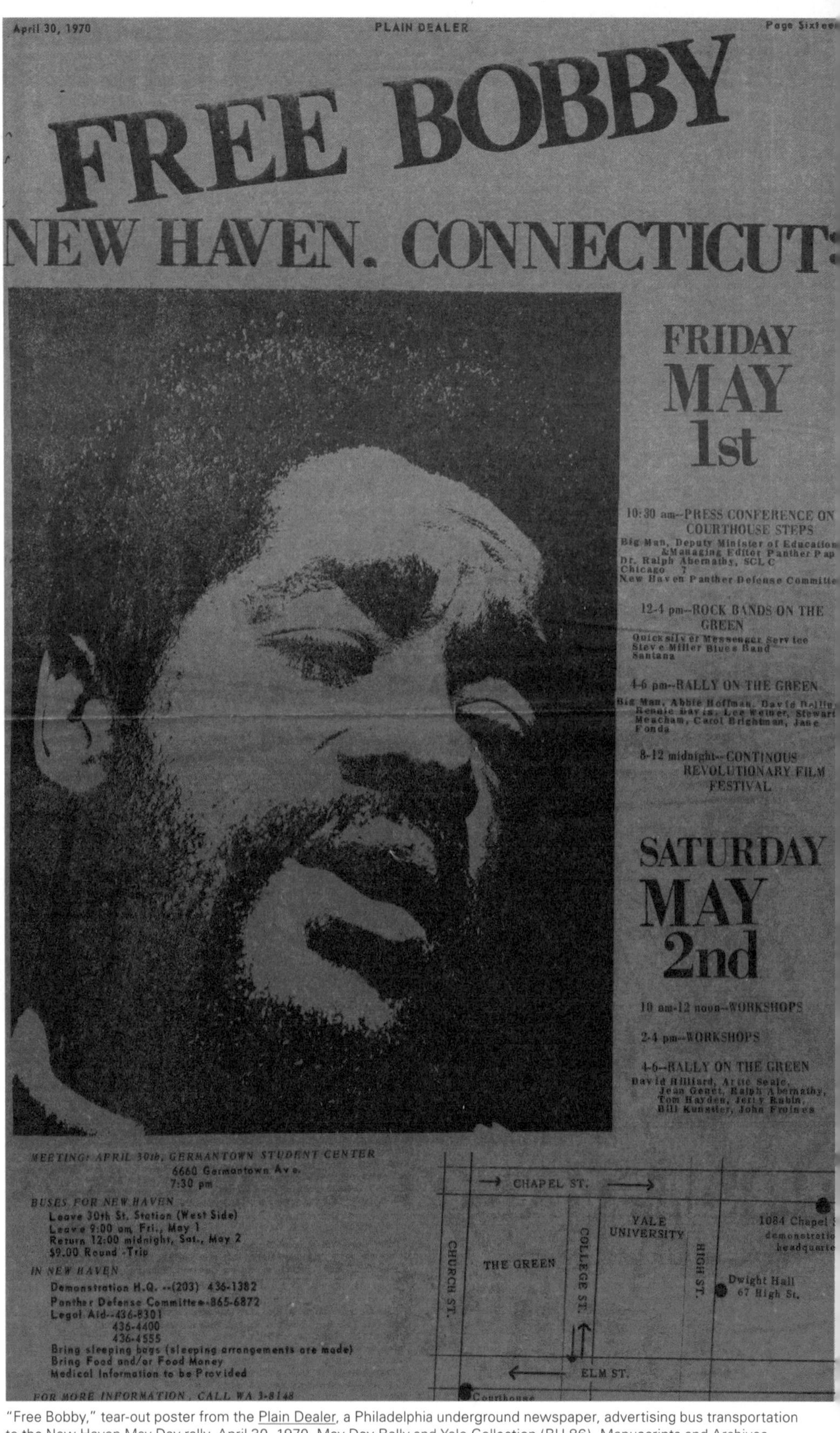

"Free Bobby," tear-out poster from the <u>Plain Dealer</u>, a Philadelphia underground newspaper, advertising bus transportation to the New Haven May Day rally, April 30, 1970. May Day Rally and Yale Collection (RU 86). Manuscripts and Archives, Yale University Library.

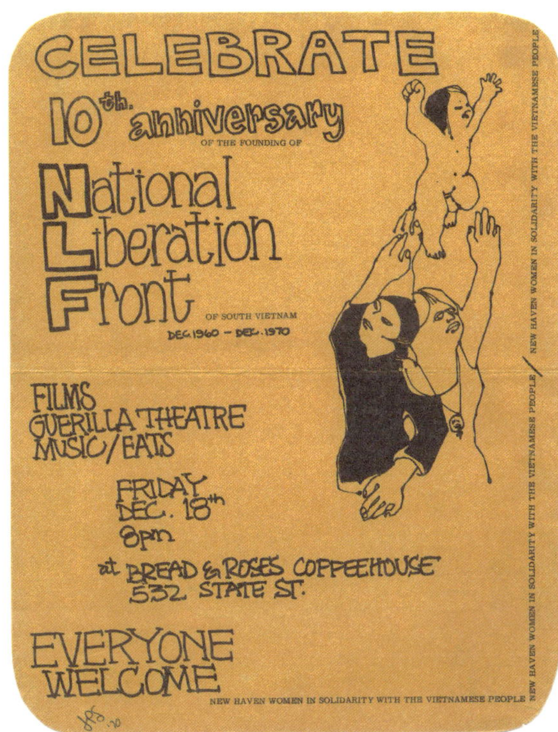

Poster for an event celebrating the tenth anniversary of the founding of the National Liberation Front, hosted by the New Haven Women in Solidarity with the Vietnamese People, December 18, 1970. May Day Rally and Yale Collection (RU 86). Manuscripts and Archives, Yale University Library.

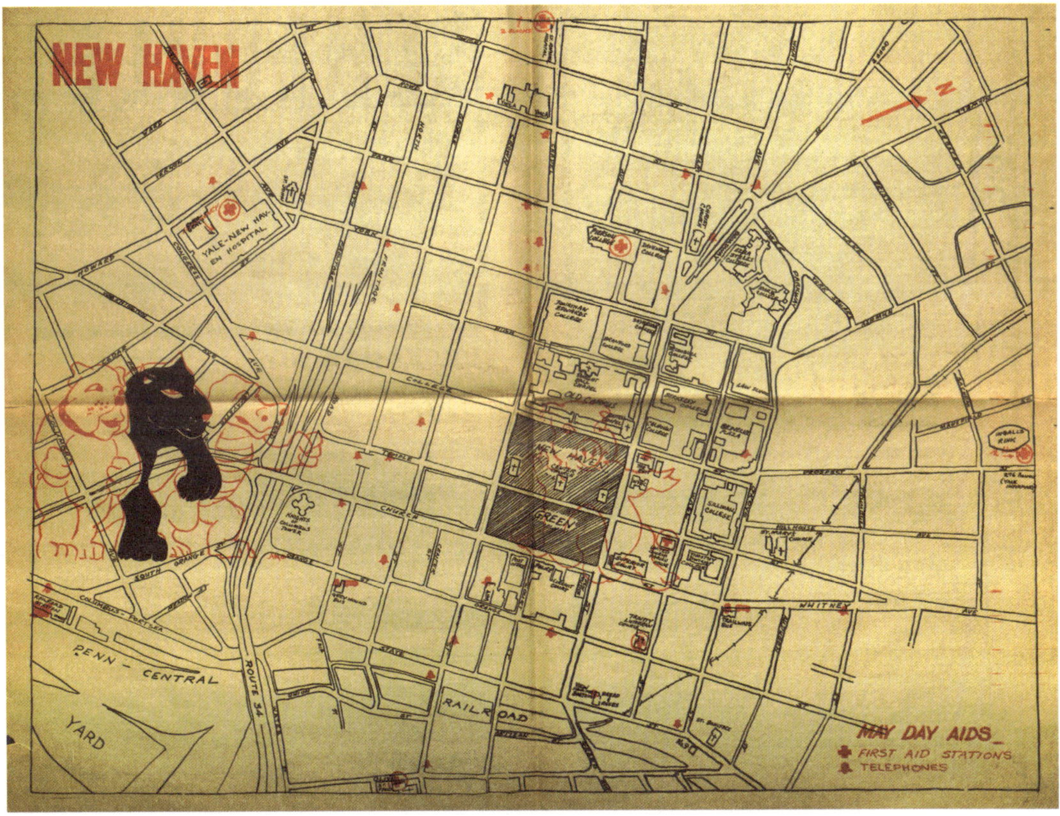

Fold-out map insert from the May Day New Haven information newspaper showing locations of first aid stations and telephones. Office of the President, Yale University, Records Concerning the May Day Rally (RU 16). Manuscripts and Archives, Yale University Library.

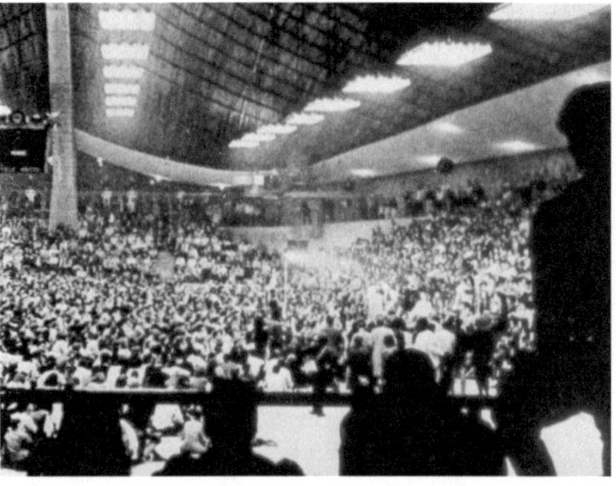

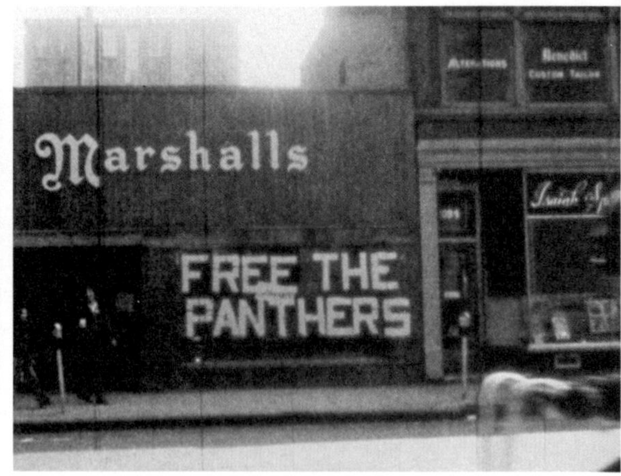

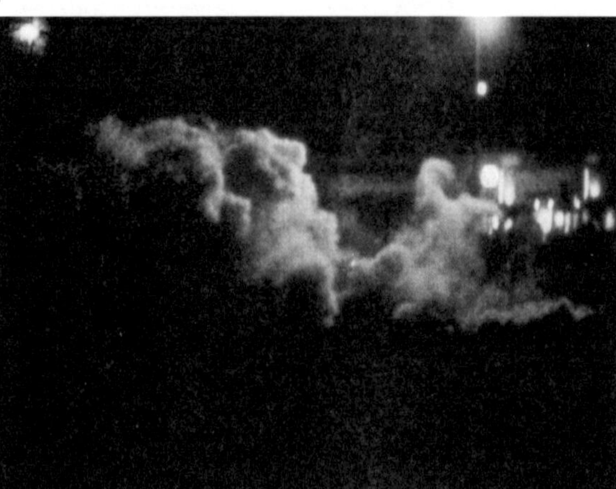

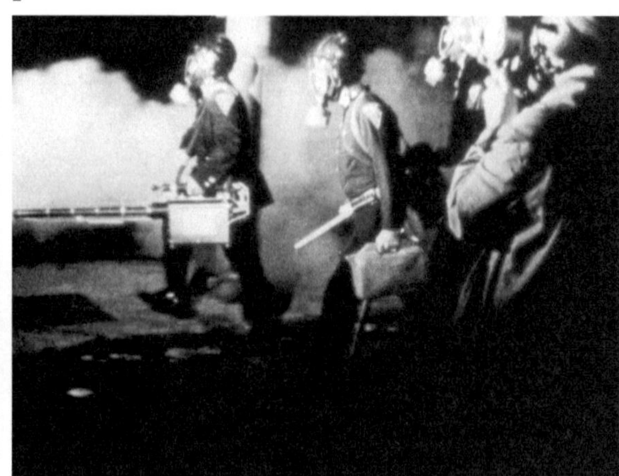

1   May 1st Media, still from <u>Mayday</u>, 1970. Ingalls Rink, New Haven, April 29, 1970.

2   May 1st Media, still from <u>Mayday</u>, 1970. "FREE THE PANTHERS" on the front façade of Marshalls on Chapel Street, New Haven.

3   May 1st Media, still from <u>Mayday</u>, 1970. Cloud of tear gas dispersing on the New Haven Green after a rally in support of the Black Panthers, May 2, 1970.

4   May 1st Media, still from <u>Mayday</u>, 1970. Nighttime view of police releasing smoke after the Black Panther support rally, New Haven, May 2, 1970.

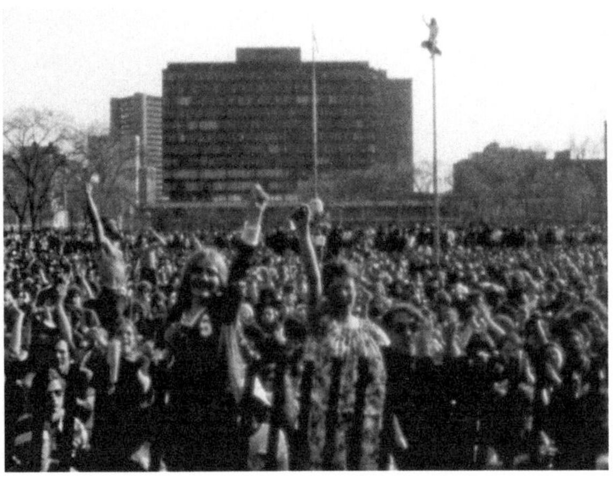

5

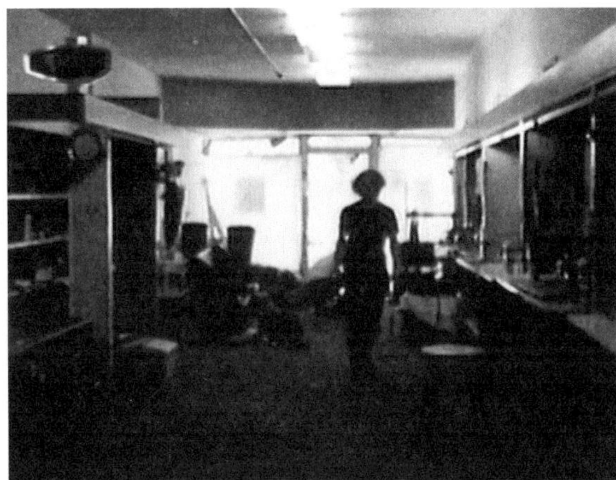

6

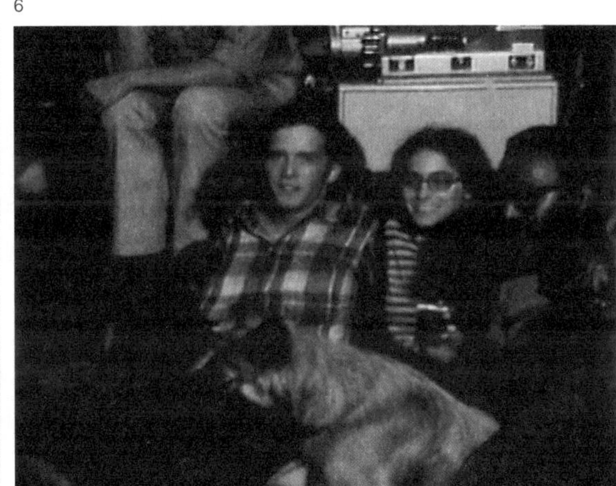

7

8

5   May 1st Media, still from <u>Mayday</u>, 1970. Large crowd at the Black Panther support rally during a speech by Kenneth Mills on the New Haven Green, May 1970.

6   May 1st Media, still from <u>Mayday Home Movie</u>, 1970. Interior of Aldon Parlor, New Haven.

7   May 1st Media, still from <u>Mayday Home Movie</u>, 1970. Josh Morton, Alberto Lau, Lorry Newhouse, and Nick Doob at Aldon Parlor, New Haven.

8   May 1st Media, still from <u>Mayday Home Movie</u>, 1970. Nick Doob, Trudi Miller, and other members of the May 1st Media collective at Aldon Parlor, New Haven.

Courtesy the filmmakers: Nick Doob, Josh Morton, and Alberto Lau and Managing Archivist Brian Meacham at the Yale Film Archive.

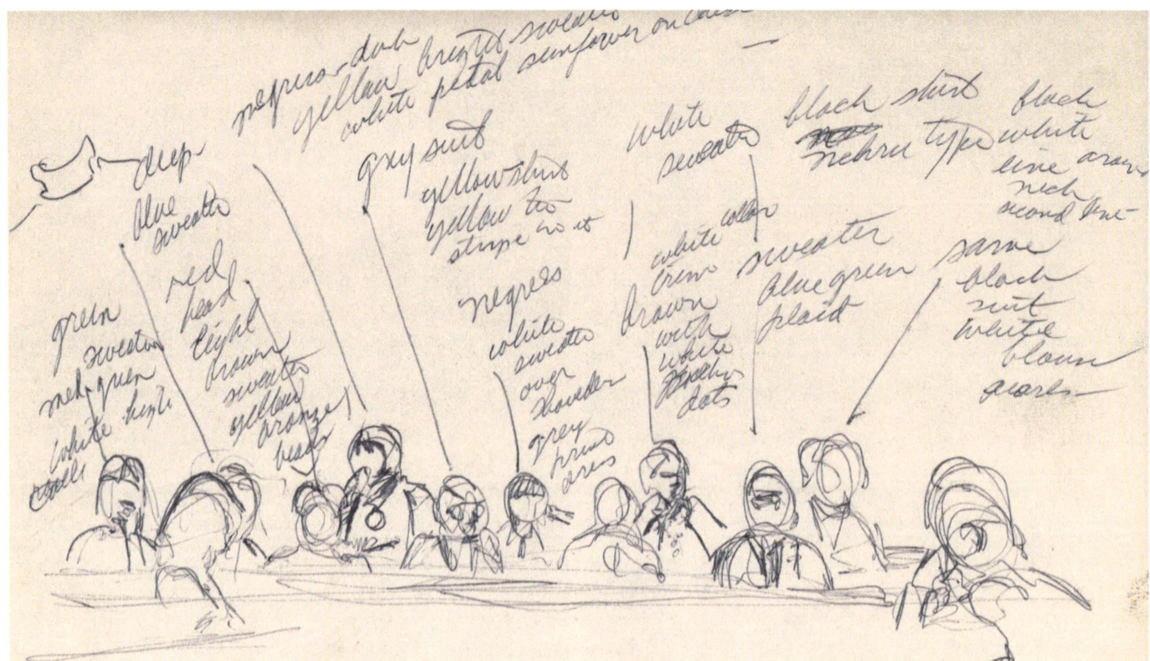

Robert Templeton, sketch from a sketchbook that includes notes about the trial and forty-one preliminary sketches of the participants and courtroom, 1971. Robert Templeton Drawings and Sketches Related to the trial of Bobby Seale and Ericka Huggins, New Haven, Connecticut. Yale Collection of American Literature, Beinecke Rare Book and Manuscript Library. © Robert Templeton Estate.

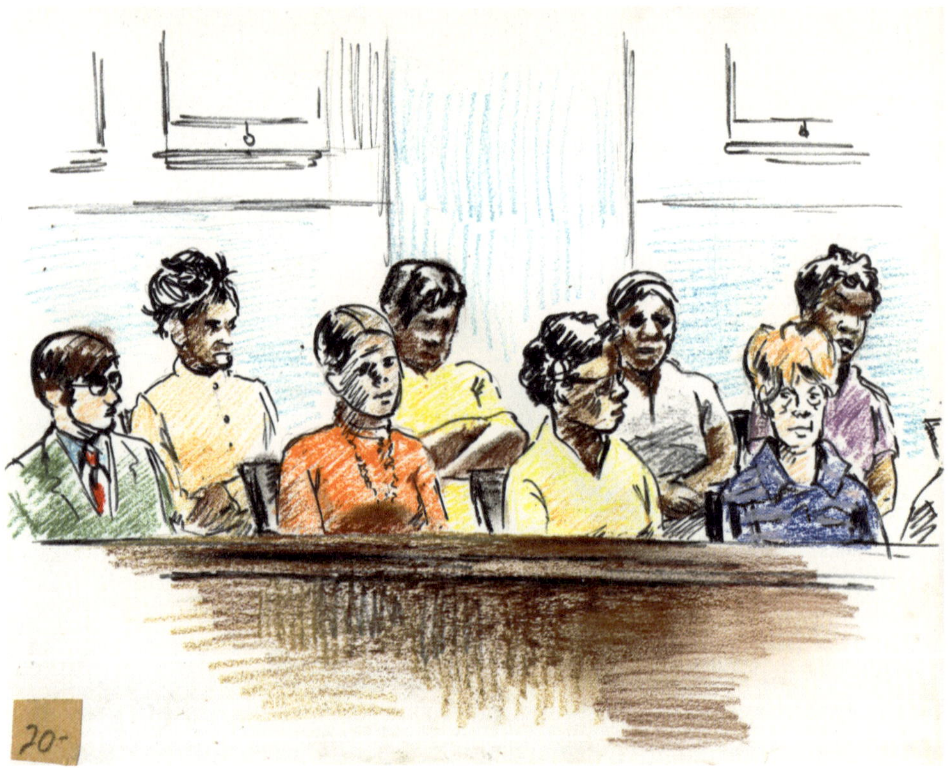

Robert Templeton, drawing of jurors at the Bobby Seale trial, 1971. Robert Templeton Drawings and Sketches Related to the trial of Bobby Seale and Ericka Huggins, New Haven, Connecticut. Yale Collection of American Literature, Beinecke Rare Book and Manuscript Library. © Robert Templeton Estate.

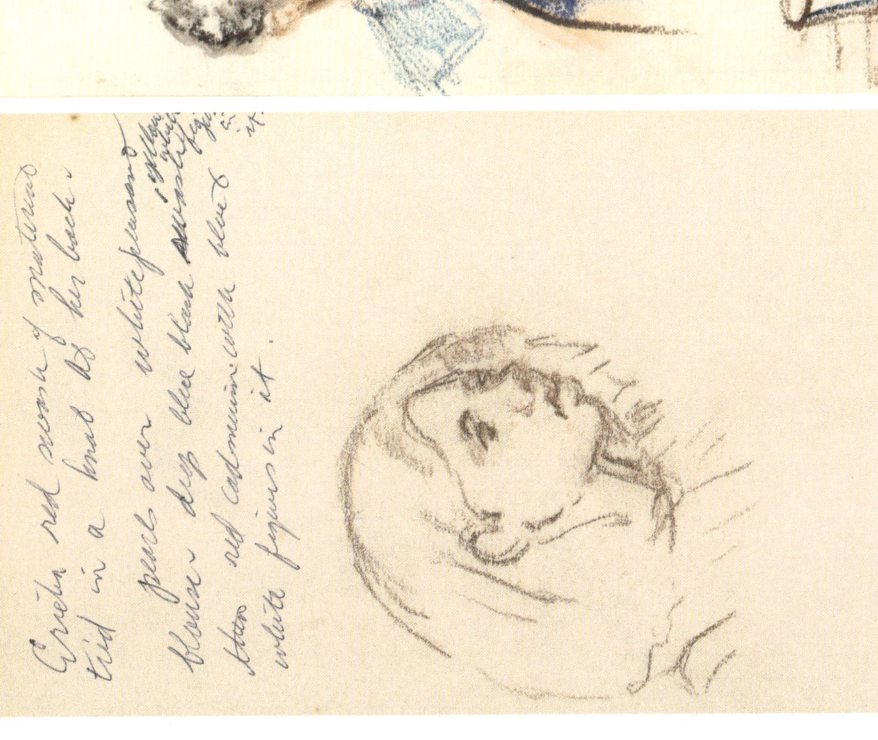

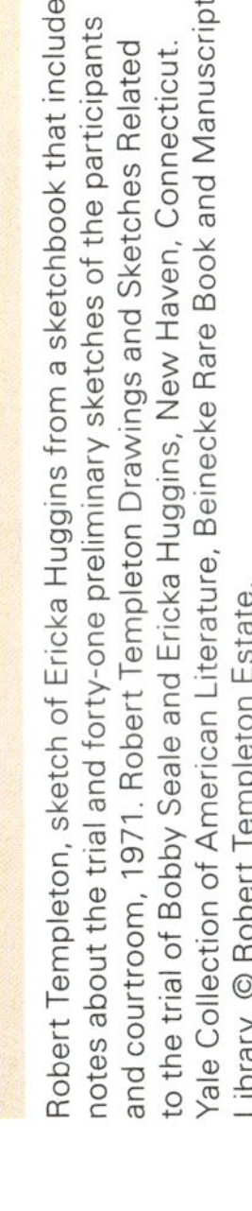

Robert Templeton, drawing for CBS Evening News of Bobby G. Seale with Arnold Markle, State's Attorney for the Judicial District of New Haven, in the background, 1971. Robert Templeton Drawings and Sketches Related to the trial of Bobby Seale and Ericka Huggins, New Haven, Connecticut. Yale Collection of American Literature, Beinecke Rare Book and Manuscript Library. © Robert Templeton Estate.

Robert Templeton, sketch of Ericka Huggins from a sketchbook that includes notes about the trial and forty-one preliminary sketches of the participants and courtroom, 1971. Robert Templeton Drawings and Sketches Related to the trial of Bobby Seale and Ericka Huggins, New Haven, Connecticut. Yale Collection of American Literature, Beinecke Rare Book and Manuscript Library. © Robert Templeton Estate.

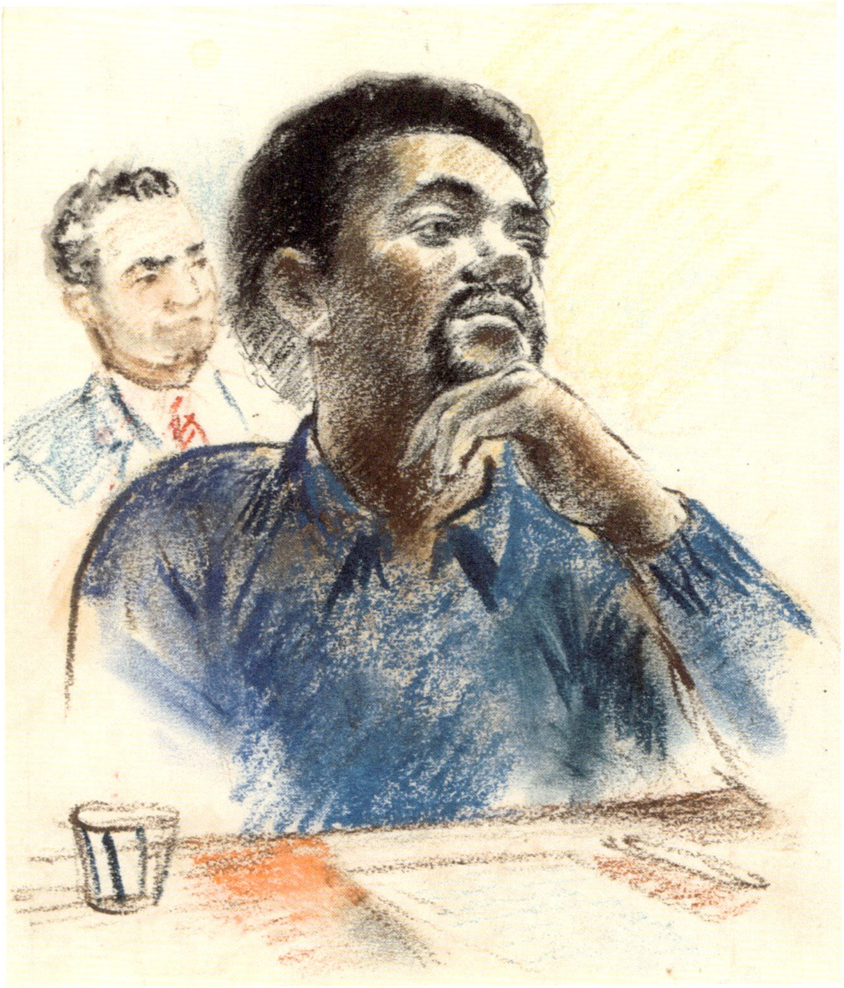

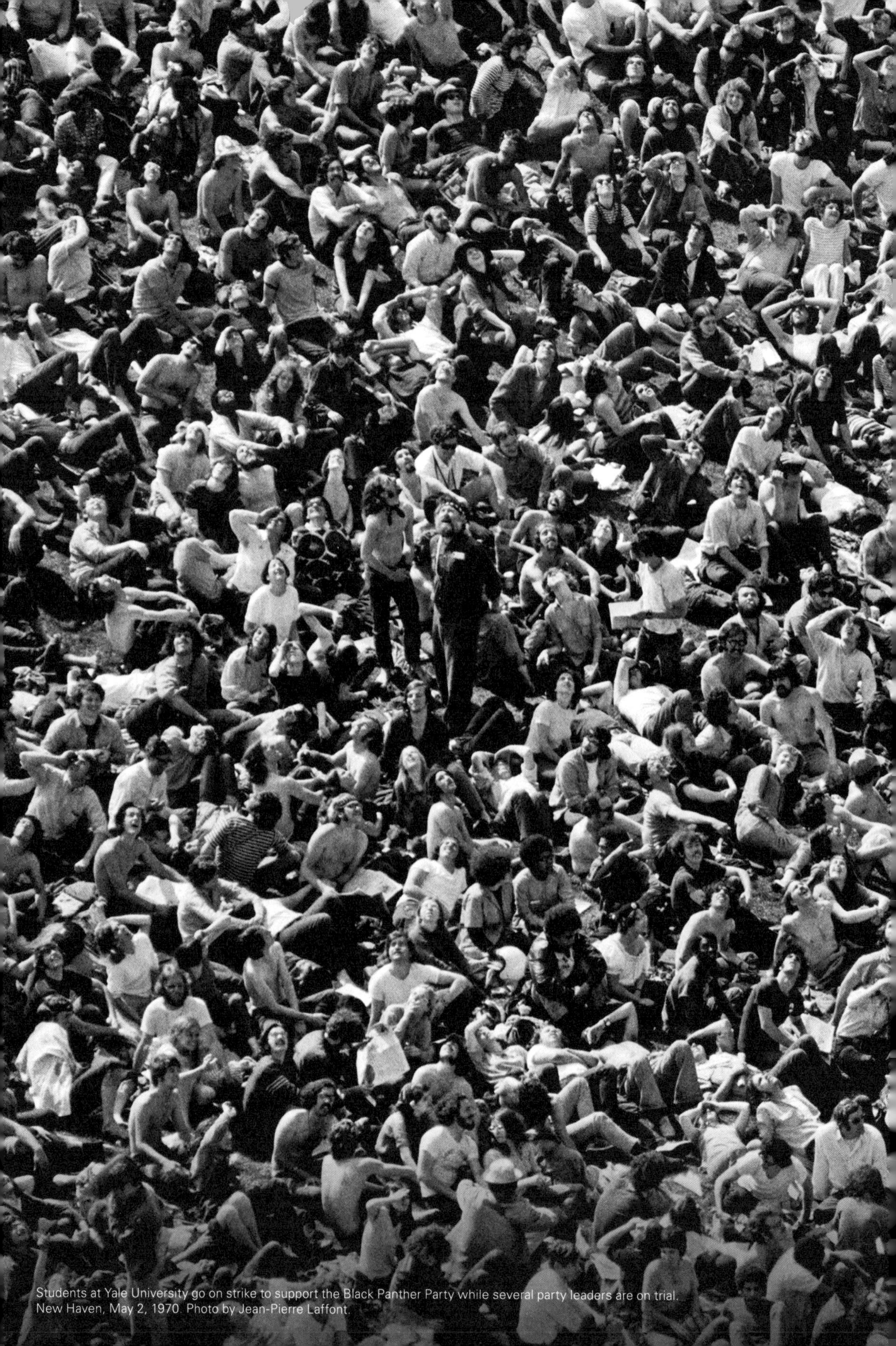

Students at Yale University go on strike to support the Black Panther Party while several party leaders are on trial. New Haven, May 2, 1970. Photo by Jean-Pierre Laffont.

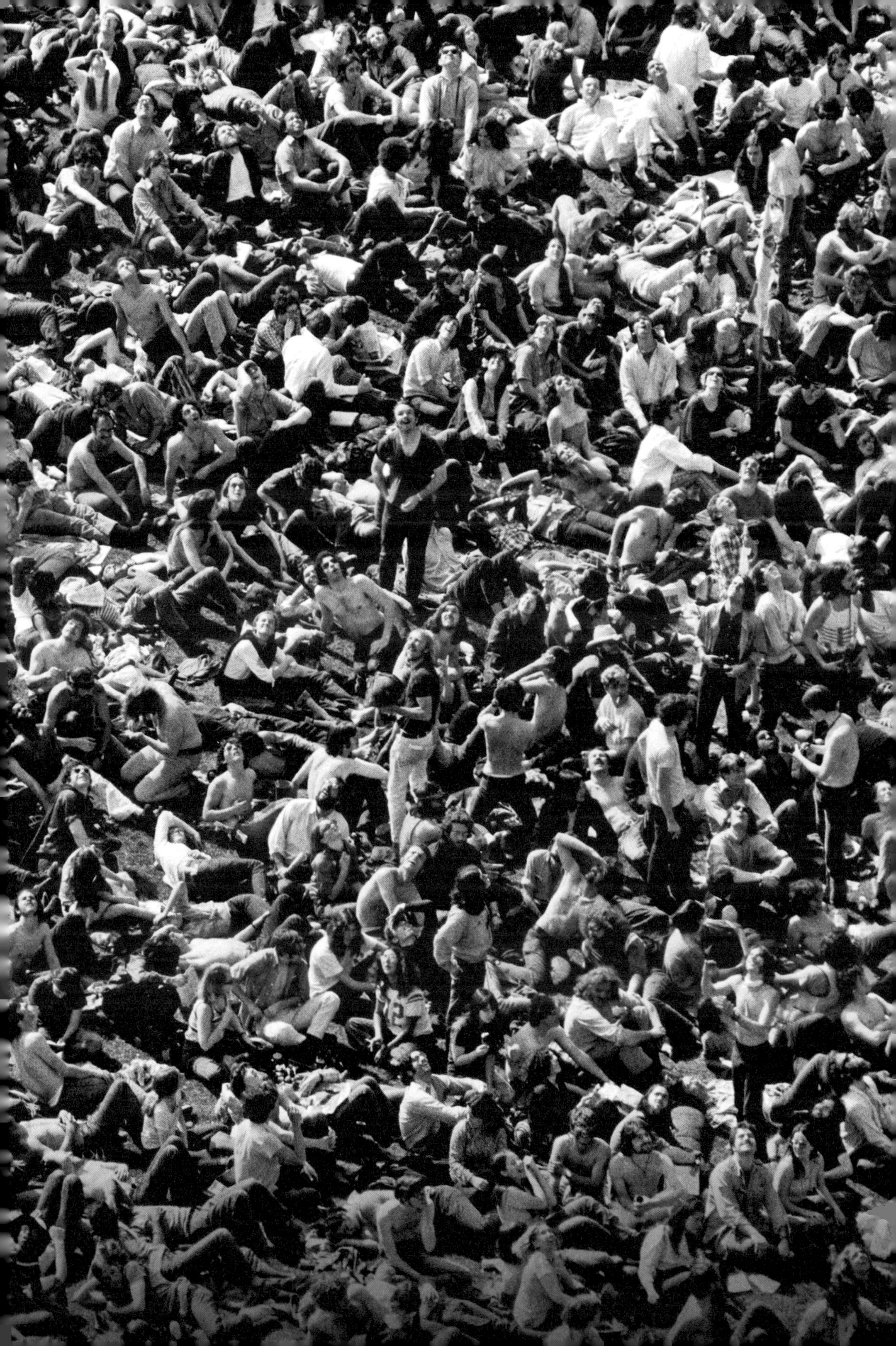

THE QUESTION OF REPRESENTATION AND EQUITY

The 1970s would prove a pivotal decade for feminism, as the movement would achieve significant gains in political representation and rights. In 1972 the United States passed the Equal Rights Act and the Equal Employment Opportunity Act, the latter making educational institutions subject to Title VII, whereby discrimination against minorities and women in the field of education was determined to be as impermissible as discrimination in any other area of employment. In June, Title IX of the Education Amendments of 1972 prohibited the gender discrimination rampant in U.S. colleges and universities at the time. It effectively promoted, for a period immediately following its passage, the hiring of women faculty nationwide in institutions of higher education—yet no woman secured access to tenure at the Yale School of Art until nearly two decades later.

At approximately the same time that Linda Nochlin published her canonical "Why Have There Been No Great Women Artists?" essay in *ARTnews*, in 1971, in which she identified systemic cultural bias against women as the basis for their exclusion from the ongoing history of art, the School of Art and Architecture transitioned into two separate schools. Neither the newly independent School of Art's leadership nor its senior faculty formally considered how to proactively include women within the broader governance, nor how to integrate related issues of feminism and the chronic underrepresentation of women artists into the general curriculum. In 1971 there were only three women on a faculty of thirty-two—Ch'ung-ho Chang Frankel, Jane Greenfield, and Polly Lada-Mocarski—all within Graphic Design. In 1972 Samia Halaby joined the School of Art as a Visiting Lecturer in Painting and was promoted to Associate Professor of Painting in 1973; in 1973 Gretna Campbell was hired as Assistant Professor of Painting and Inge Druckrey joined the faculty as Assistant Professor of Graphic Design; and in 1976 Winifred Lutz came to Yale as Assistant Professor of Sculpture. From 1973 through 1983, the total number of women faculty in any given year never exceeded eight with few in full-time positions.[34] No woman would be appointed Professor with tenure until 1990.

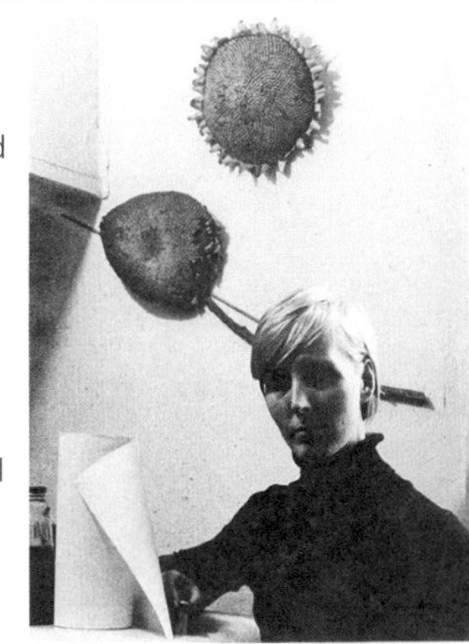

Inge Druckrey at the Philadelphia College of Art, around 1971. Photo by Christine Zelinsky. Courtesy Inge Druckrey.

34 For many of the faculty titles and dates of employment cited in this essay, see copies of the annual School of Art catalogue. Manuscripts and Archives, Yale University Library, New Haven.

  THE QUESTION OF REPRESENTATION AND EQUITY

FREE WOMEN at YALE

Sunday, March 1, marked the end of the "Free Women" conference called by the Yale Women's Alliance and held at the Yale Law School. The conference, which lasted four days and was attended by anywhere from 300-500 people, included movies, speakers, workshops, various media displays and literature. Thursday night, several hundred people attended a showing of *Salt of the Earth* and other films. Friday night was perhaps the most exciting event. Kate Millett of New York Women's Liberation spoke on patriarchy, not as simply a father-oriented family, but as a complete system of male dominance and ownership. In our society all authority is ultimately male and women therefore live in an alien culture that is not their making and that does not serve their needs. She rejected the notion that women could reform this system by changing laws here and there since this sophisticated patriarchal system that has evolved is only strengthened when its most notorious abuses are weeded out.

Following Kate Millett, Naomi Weisstein of Loyola University in Chicago recounted her experiences as a professional woman trying to 'make it' in a university system that systematically excluded women from anything but the most menial of academic chores. She suggested that the hope dies hard that if only women had enough qualifications they would be accepted and respected. They are not, no matter what their credentials, and won't be, until *all* women both within and outside the universities are freed from the degrading sex roles this culture forces on them.

On Saturday there were workshops on the Family, Alternative Lifestyles, Women and the Law, Employment, the Image of Women in Society, Abortion-Contraception-Health Care, Female Sexuality, Daycare, and Coeducation at Yale. These were attended by over 200 women from the New Haven area, most of whom were meeting each other for the first time. The workshops produced an exciting exchange of information, insights and experiences which in all likelihood will lead to the formation of more women's groups in and around New Haven.

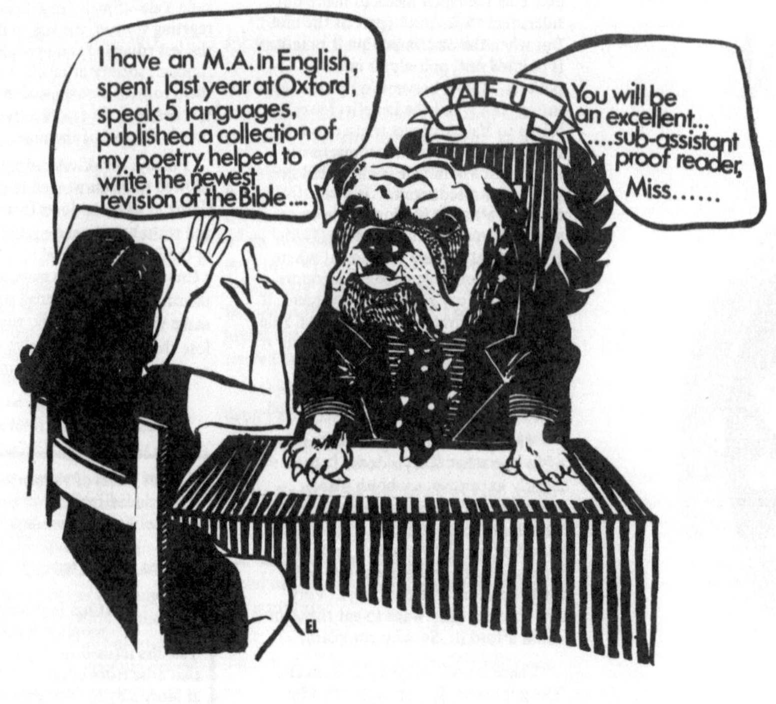

6

Page from <u>Yale Break: A Newspaper for and by Women</u>, vol. 1, no. 3, April 6, 1970. Employee Unions and Strikes, Yale University, Records (RU 105). Manuscripts and Archives, Yale University Library.

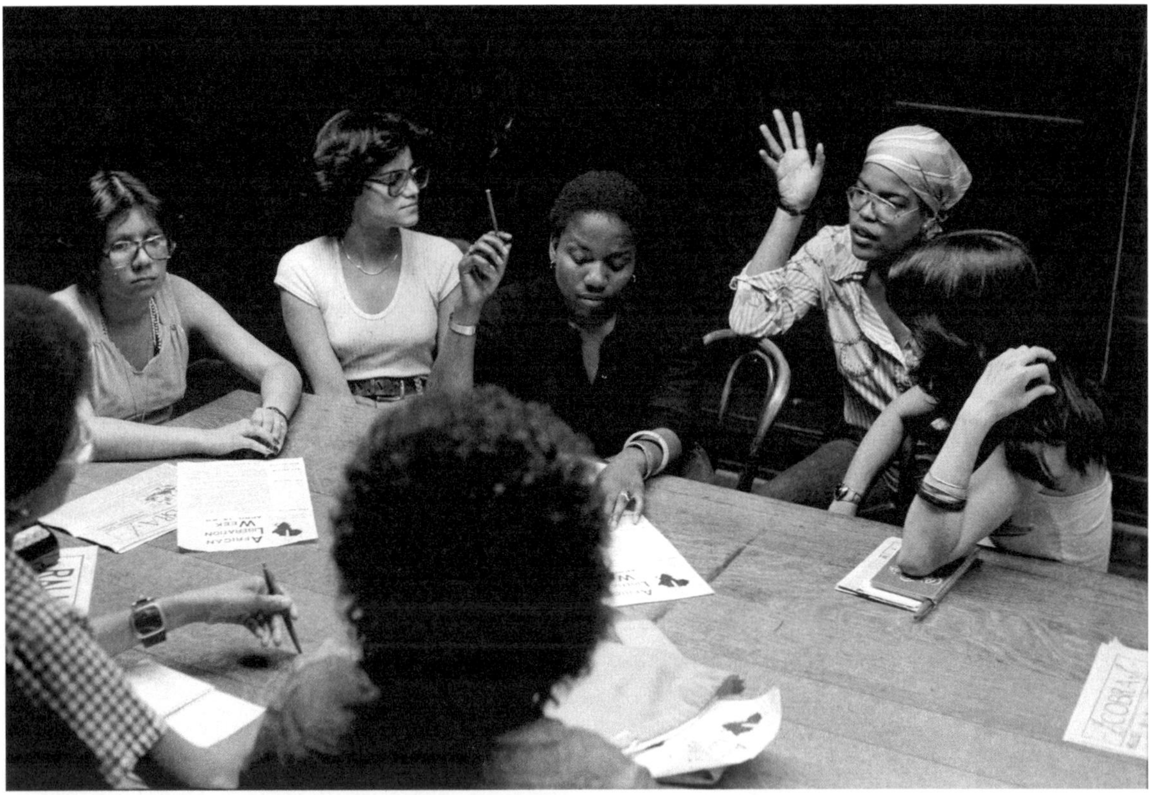

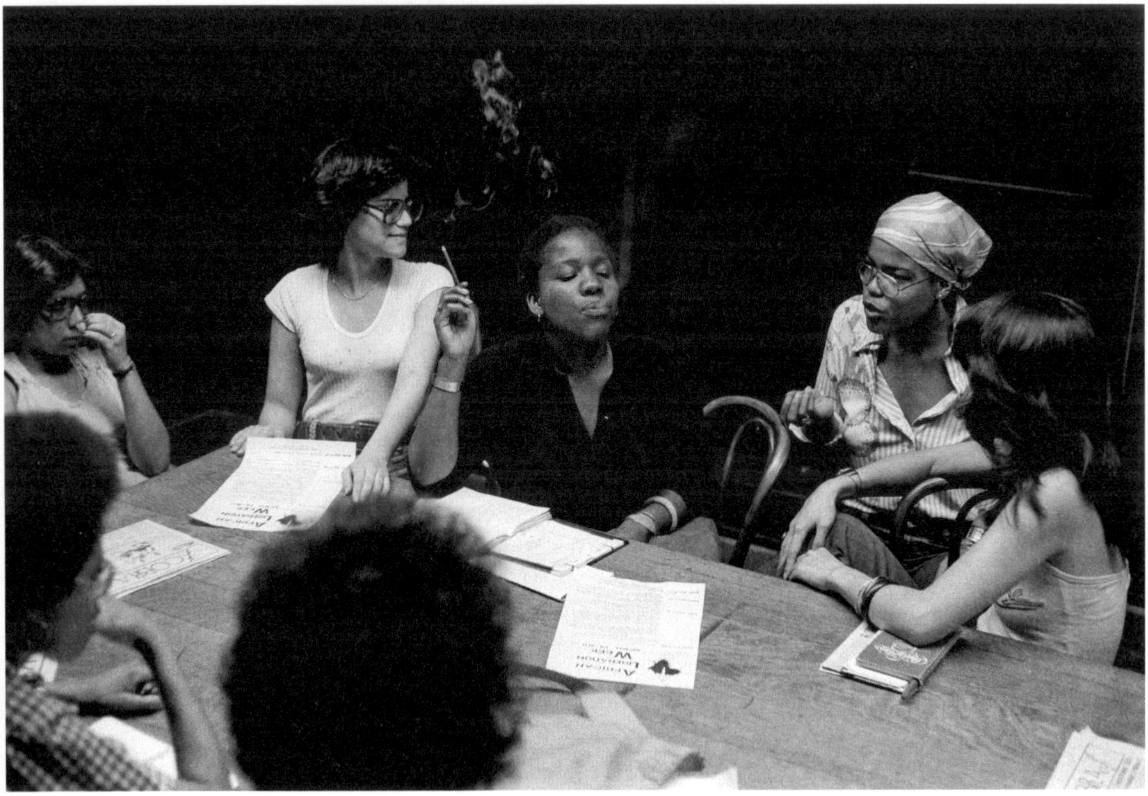

A meeting of the Council of Third World Women, spring 1977. Photo by Susan Meiselas.
© Susan Meiselas/Magnum Photos.

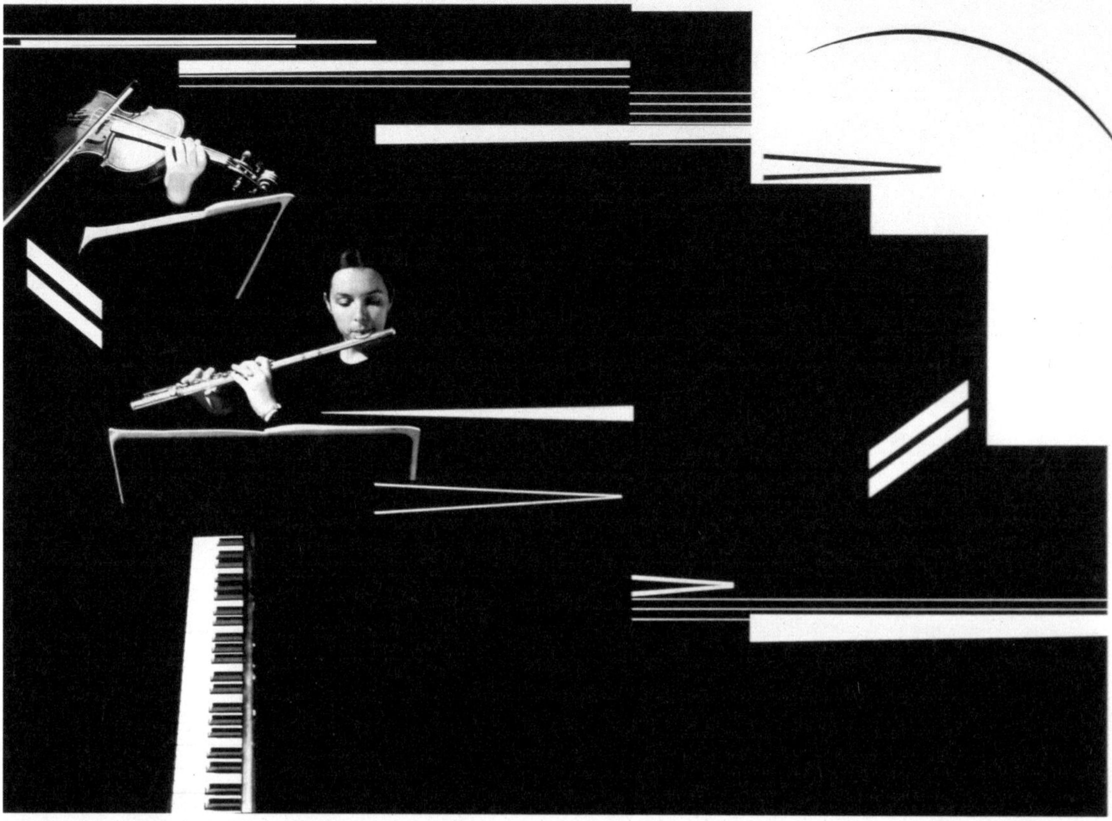

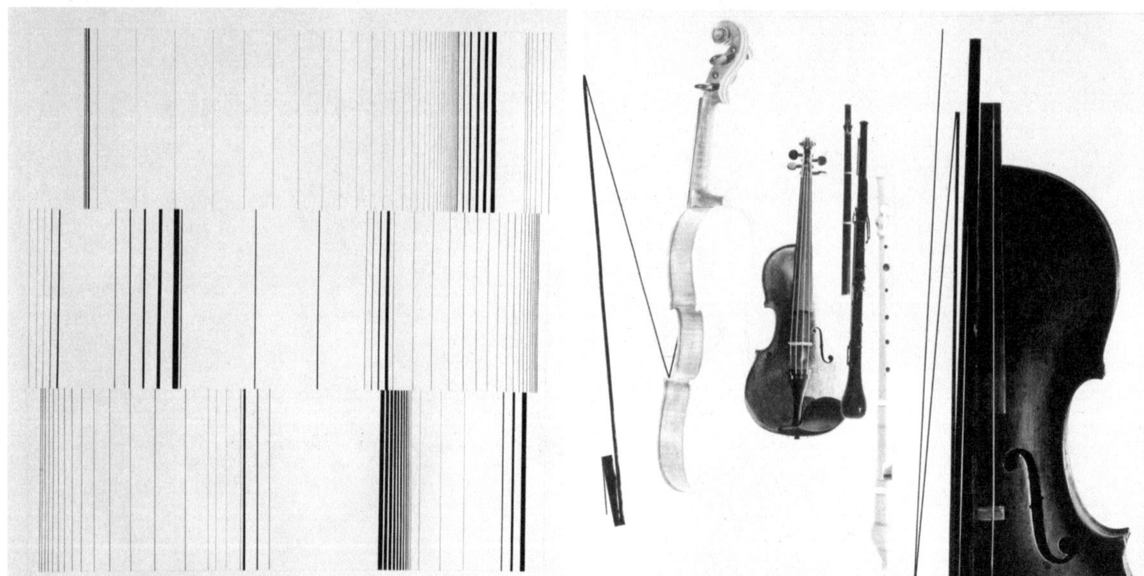

Inge Druckrey, Yale School of Music Brochure cover, ca. 1980s. Courtesy Inge Druckrey.

Left: Composition by Mike Zender for Inge Druckrey's "nine square grid" exercise given to Yale School of Art graduate students, ca. 1975–77. Right: Final composition by Mike Zender. Courtesy Inge Druckrey.

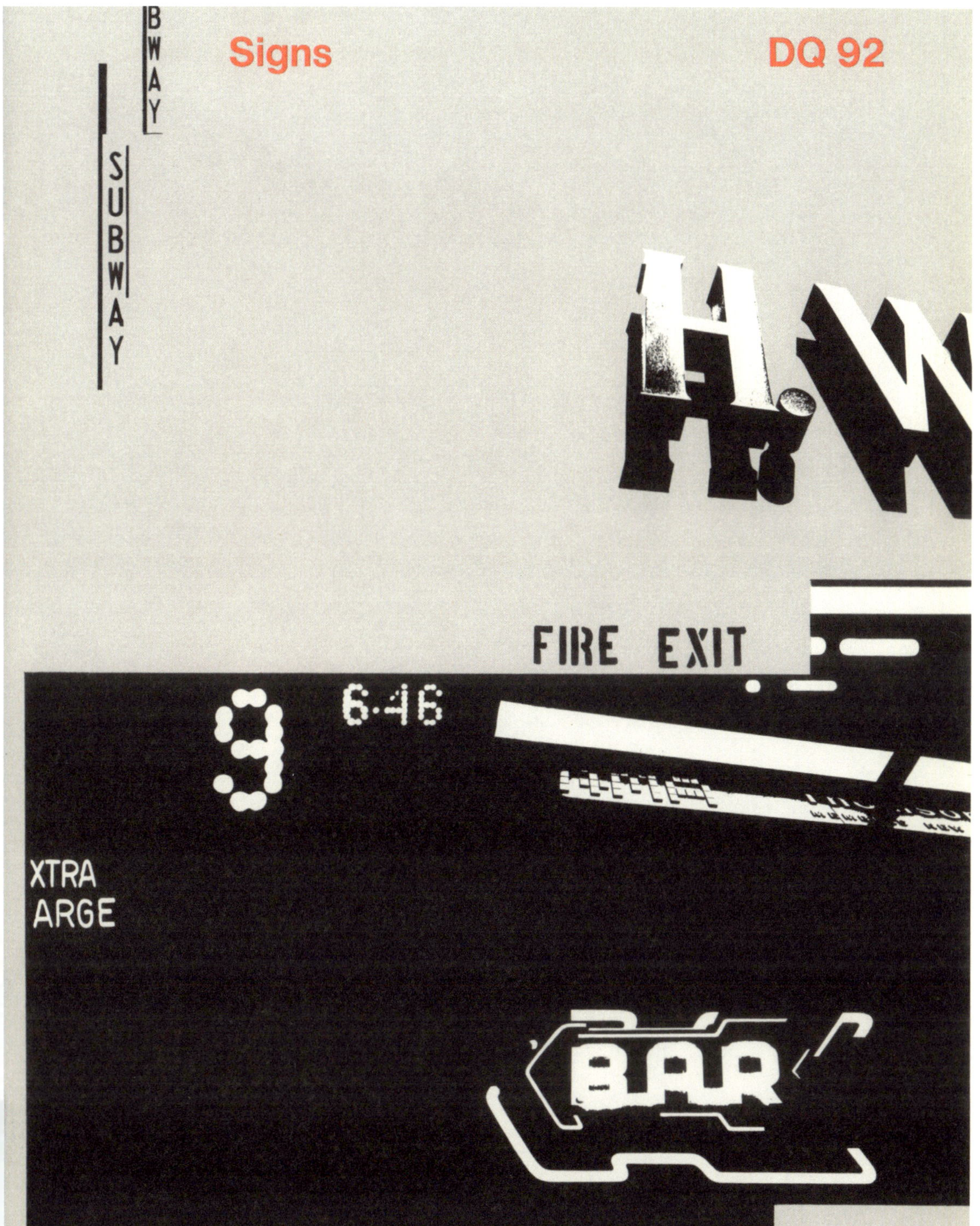

Inge Druckrey, cover of <u>Design Quarterly</u>, no. 92, 1974. Courtesy Walker Art Center, Minneapolis.

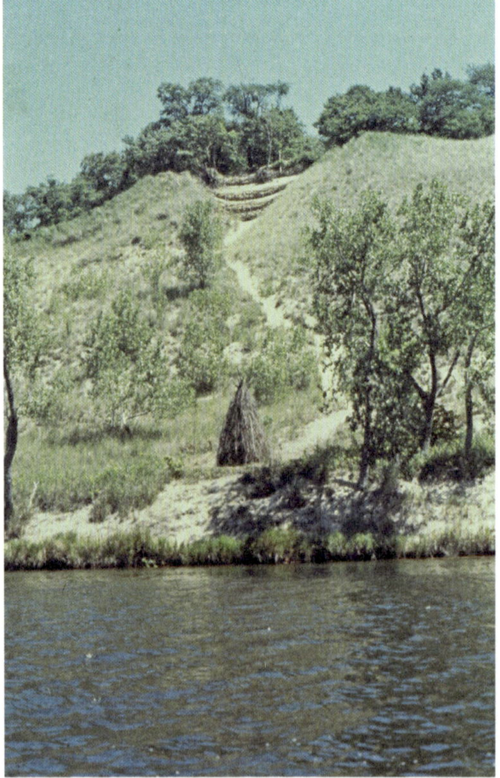

Winifred Lutz, Offshore view of <u>Blowout: The Accumulator Barriers and the Locator Cone</u>, 1976. Photo by Winifred Lutz. © Winifred Lutz.

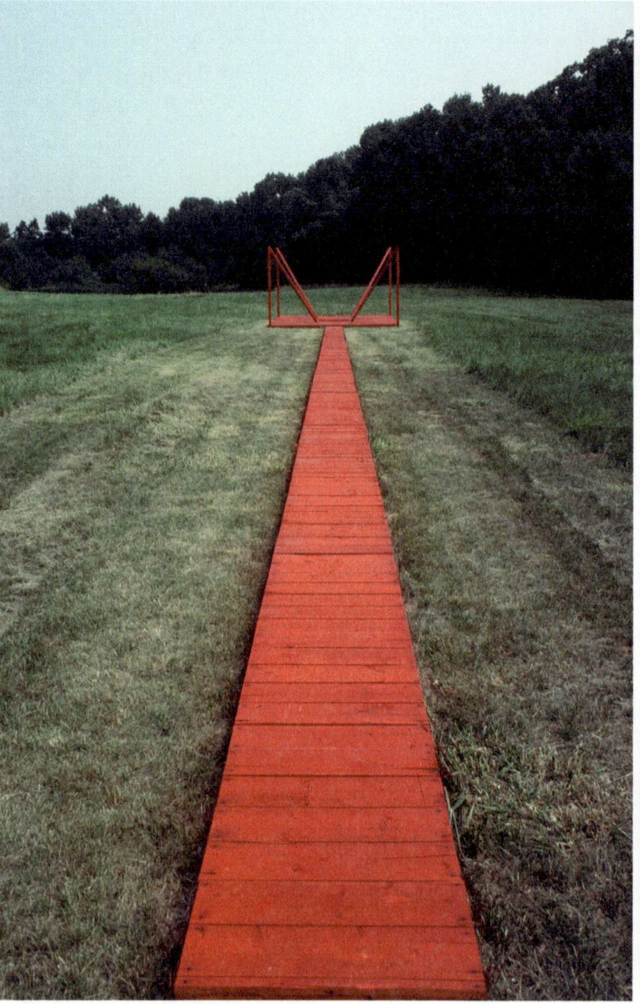

Winifred Lutz, <u>Hypotenuse</u>, 1977. View along axis of the boardwalk to the platform. Photo by Winifred Lutz. © Winifred Lutz.

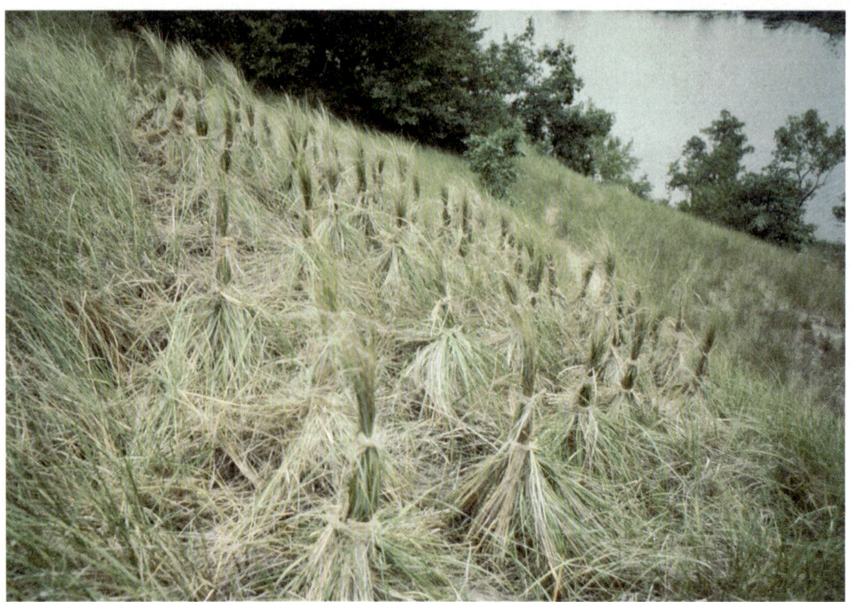

Winifred Lutz, <u>Blowout: The Accumulator Barriers and the Locator Cone</u>, 1976. Triangular area of bound grass from above. Photo by Winifred Lutz. © Winifred Lutz.

On July 21, 1975, nearly three years after Title IX was passed, the regulations it stipulated went into effect, mandating that "no person in the United States shall, on the basis of sex, be excluded from participation in, be denied the benefits of, or be subjected to discrimination under any education program or activity receiving Federal financial assistance."[35] Secretary ofHealth, Education, and Welfare, Caspar Weinberger, released a statement in June 1975, affirming that "much of the discrimination against women in education today exists unconsciously and through practices long enshrined in tradition. The regulations require that during the next year those in education begin a searching self-examination to identify any discriminatory policies or practices which may exist within their institutions and to take whatever remedial action is needed."[36] In October 1976, Yale University confirmed its completion of an "insurance of compliance" guaranteeing an educational self-evaluation.[37] That same year, a Yale Women's Studies Task Force (YWSTF) was formed through the lobbying efforts of Department of Germanic Languages and Literatures Professor Ingeborg Glier, the University's third tenured woman, appointed in 1973. The aim of the YWSTF was to draft recommendations for a "program of study about women."[38] The group's efforts led, in 1977, to a first course offering, *Feminism and Humanism*, taught within the Department of American Studies by Catherine MacKinnon, who was then a law student and PhD candidate in Political Science. In January of that same year, a Council of Third World Women [see p. 45] was formed to address sexism and racism faced by women from developing countries. In 1979, Yale University established a Women's Studies Program "to operate on an experimental basis for five years."[39]

Druckrey points out that her employment was prompted by the School's need to address Title IX and that, despite being engaged as Assistant Professor and later as Associate Professor, her position did not carry any real authority in the male-dominated governance structure that had long been in place. In just one example of gender dynamics at play during this time, Druckrey recalls a story regarding the hiring of a graduate student in the Department of Painting for a junior faculty position:

> The search had included several excellent women applicants whom the women faculty members in Painting and Sculpture preferred. The male faculty, who were probably not used to such strong resistance, became furious. When we informed one senior faculty member in Painting that any information on open positions known to him should be posted, he called us 'anti-American,' which was interesting, since two of us were foreign born. The male faculty was clearly used to getting their way.[40]

According to Druckrey, she was denied tenure when her contract was discontinued in the eleventh year of her employment. At the time, the School's faculty handbook stated that "no one on the Yale faculty may be employed in the ranks of instructor, assistant professor, and associate professor on terms longer than ten years."[41] Druckrey contested the decision, asserting her right to tenure and

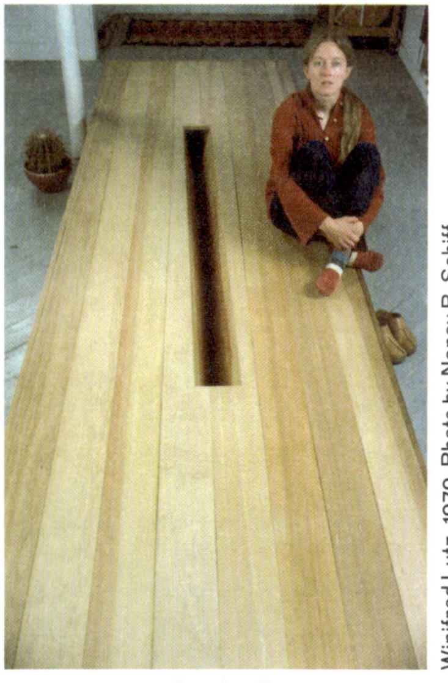

Winifred Lutz, 1979. Photo by Nancy R. Schiff. Courtesy Getty Images.

35   Peter E. Holmes, from the "Final Title IX Regulations Implementing Education Amendments of 1972," in "Memorandum for College and University Presidents, Chief State School Officers and Local School Superintendents," Department of Health, Education, and Welfare, Office for Civil Rights, June 1975.

36   Casper W. Weinberger, statement from U.S. Department of Health, Education, and Welfare, June 3, 1975.

37   Kirsten E. Lodal, "Engendering an Intellectual Space: The Development of Women's Studies at Yale University 1969–2001," (unpublished senior essay, History Department, Yale University, 2001), 14–15. wgss.yale.edu/sites/default/files/files/LodalEssayEngendering%20and%20Intellectual-Sapce.pdf.

38   Ibid, 28.

39   Ibid, 13.

40   Halaby is a Palestinian-born U.S. citizen, and Druckrey was born in Germany and not yet a citizen. Inge Druckrey, oral history interview by Laura Worden, April 17, 2019, transcript. Yale University Art Gallery archives.

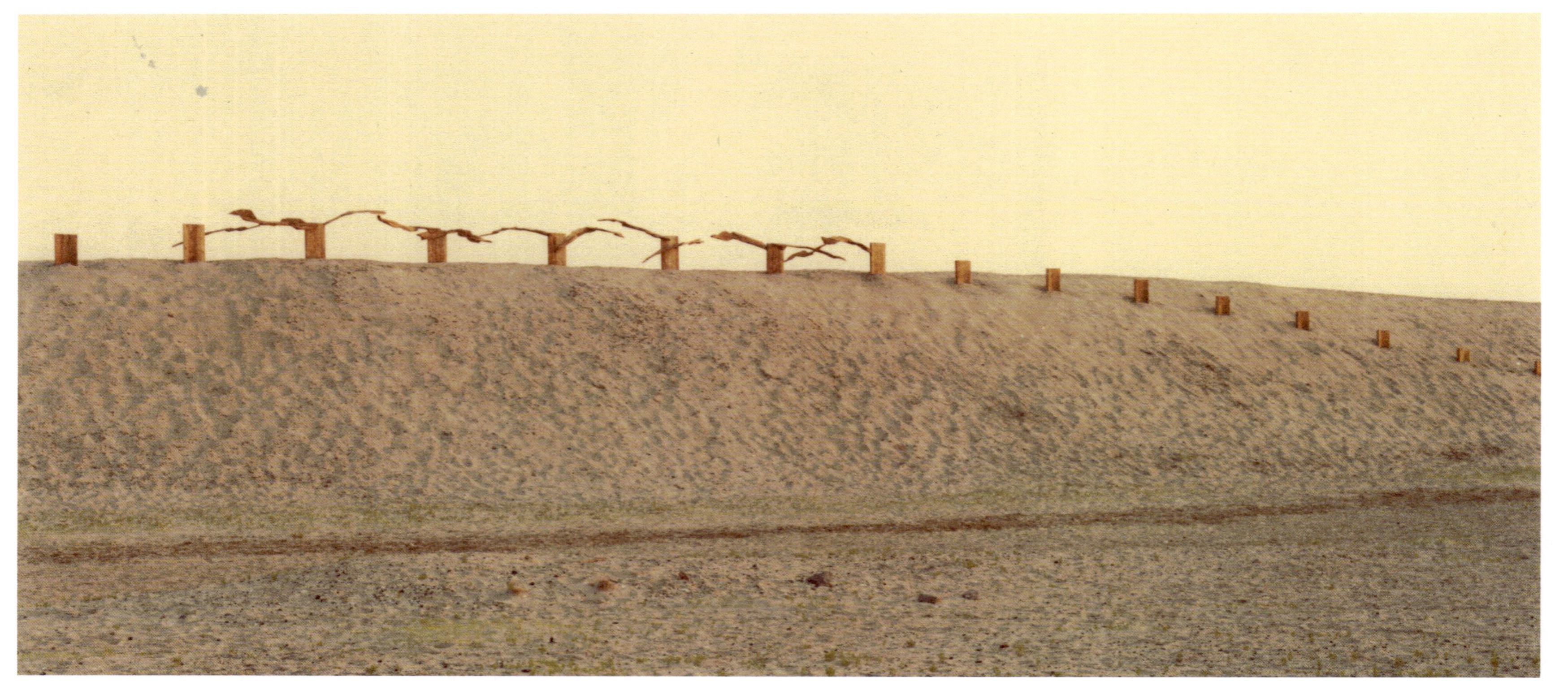

Ursula von Rydingsvard, _Saint Martin's Dream_, 1980. Courtesy Ursula von Rydingsvard.

extension of employment within rank for one additional year, an effort that resulted in her demotion to Senior Lecturer in 1982–83.

Over the decade following the formation of the autonomous School of Art in 1972, not one of the original nine women faculty members hired between 1971 and 1983 including Halaby, Campbell, Druckrey, and Lutz, was promoted by the School's all-male governance to a longer-term position with tenure. Though Lutz was promoted from Assistant to Associate Professor, she was denied reappointment in 1982. According to Lutz, she was told that "Yale had a quota on how many tenured faculty there could be in any year and … that [she] could not apply because the quota was full."[42] (While no documentation of such a policy is known to exist, relevant aspects of Yale's system of tenure and appointment procedures, which remained customary and informal at that time, were reviewed in 2005 and revised in 2007 with publication of The Report of the Faculty of Arts and Sciences Tenure and Appointments Policy Committee.) She cites the leadership of the School, composed solely of male senior faculty members from the Department of Painting, who attempted to parlay their influence within Sculpture, remarking, "They would insist on coming over [uninvited] to Hammond Hall [where the Sculpture department was then housed] to critique what the graduate students in Sculpture were doing … which we eventually diffused by creating Open Studios at Sculpture as a completely massive [event]," followed by several days of sanctioned critiques.[43] Although she did not receive tenure and was not reappointed, Lutz successfully demanded a seat on the selection committee for her successor, which resulted in the hiring of Ursula von Rydingsvard.

Halaby, who had a yearslong engagement with the Department of Painting, initially as a Visiting Lecturer, then Associate Professor, and later Associate Professor Adjunct, was also denied tenure and not reappointed, following a vote cast by an all-male faculty in the spring of 1981. Druckrey recalls that Halaby was asked to leave, "although a reappointment was supported by a cohort of junior faculty and by all the women faculty members."[44] In response to Halaby's departure, many Yale undergraduates, School of Art graduates, ex-faculty and students, as well as

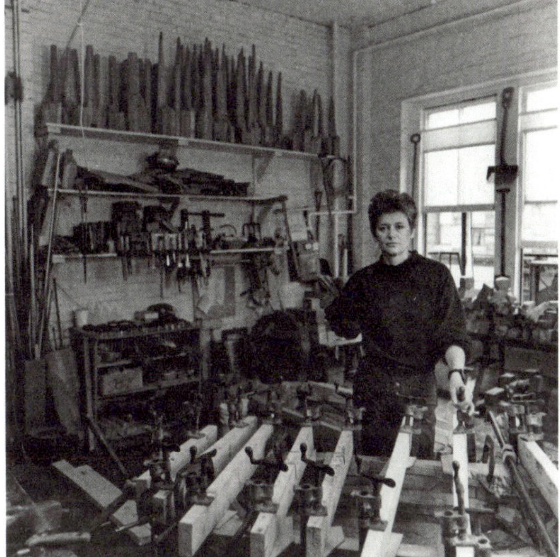

Ursula von Rydingsvard in her studio, New York, 1988. Photo by Allen Rokach. Courtesy Ursula von Rydingsvard.

Yale College students and alumni and Yale clerical and technical workers striving for unionization in Local 34, organized as "aesthetic dissidents," forming a coalition called The Committee for Art. The Committee curated *On Trial: Yale School of Art* [see pp. 54–55] at 22 Wooster Gallery in New York, in 1982, citing two basic grievances: that the School held a rigidly Eurocentric approach to art, and that it practiced institutionalized racism and sexism.[45] In a *Yale Daily News* article, Dean Andrew Forge was quoted as conceding the first point, saying, "This art school concerns itself with the art of Western culture. It makes no pretense of teaching Oriental art, African art, or any such thing."[46] Halaby, a Palestinian, said that in retrospect she felt that the School of Art had hired her in response to the social climate of the early 1970s. "I was hired at a time when society pushed the School to seem to have both men and women,"[47] she said. She recalls that Dean Weaver remarked to her shortly after her hire,

41 "Time to Tenure," *Faculty Handbook* (New Haven: Yale University, 1978; rev. February 1981). Manuscripts and Archives, Yale University Library, New Haven.

42 Winifred Lutz, e-mail conversation with the author, February 28, 2021.

43 Ibid.

44 Druckrey, interview 2019.

45 The exhibition was on view from December 29, 1982 to January 8, 1983. Jason Friedman, "Rebels Attack Yale School of Art Artists 'try' Art School." *Yale Daily News,* January 21, 1983.

46 Rob Glaser, "Art for Whose Sake?" *Yale Daily News,* January 28, 1983.

47 Friedman 1983.

     THE QUESTION OF REPRESENTATION AND EQUITY

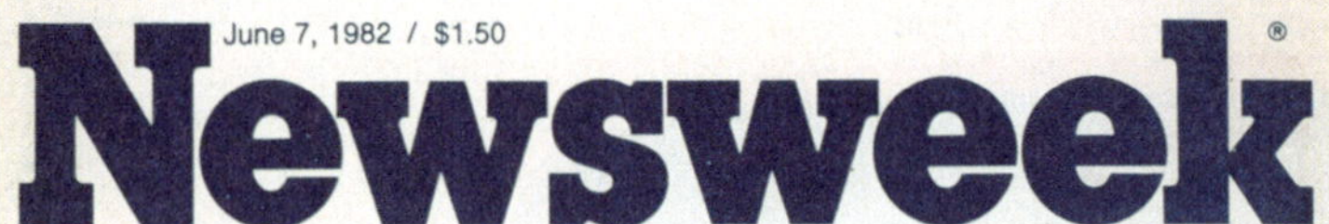

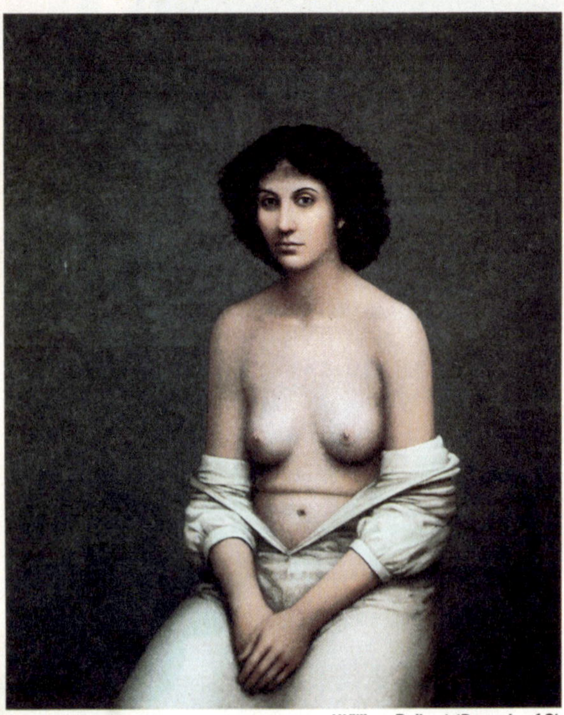

William Bailey's 'Portrait of S'

Newsweek featured William Bailey's Portrait of S on its cover in June of 1982, referring
to a feature authored by Mark Stevens titled "Revival of Realism," in which Stevens wrote
that "it is now possible to argue that, in the last twenty years, representational painters have
established an alternative tradition to the mainstream of late modernism." (Newsweek, June 7,
1982.) Stevens argued that Bailey's Portrait of S "has helped restore representational art to
a position of consequence in modern painting." Newsweek distributed nearly 3 million copies
before the issue was quickly removed from supermarket magazine racks and newsstands
in response to public outcry against the nudity depicted on the cover. According to William
Bailey's obituary in the New York Times, feminists described it as "something like bondage
in the dress straps that held the subject's arms close to her body." (William Grimes, "William
Bailey, Modernist Figurative Painter, Dies at 89," New York Times, April 18, 2020.) The cover
also became a subject of the exhibition On Trial, which took place from December 29, 1982,
to January 8, 1983, at 22 Wooster Gallery, New York.

48   Glaser 1983.

49   Friedman 1983.

50   Bird Brenner, telephone conversation with the author, April 10, 2021.

51   Bird Brenner, e-mail conversation with Edi Dai, June 15 and July 8, 2021.

"With you we kill two birds with one stone,"[48] an allusion to the fact that she is both a woman and a member of a minority ethnic community. Halaby noted that her concern for what she felt was prevalent racism and sexism influenced the School of Art not to reappoint her: "I spoke up for students, students who were grieved by faculty display of prejudice, both racial and sexual, amid those who experienced a rejection of their creativity."[49]

Bird Brenner (BA 1982), an undergraduate art major, attests to the influence of Samia Halaby and Winifred Lutz, whom she considered mentors. She recalls that both were marginalized as faculty members, however, within what Brenner referred to as a "boys' club" of senior male faculty. Brenner, who had been influenced by the work of Nam June Paik and applied to Yale with the intent of pursuing a transdisciplinary practice, recalls Dean Andrew Forge responding negatively to her requests for video equipment by saying, "Yale is not a trade school." While studying as an undergraduate in the Department of Painting, Brenner found the program "restrictive for those who did now follow the script, although deviance from the script was tolerated for male students."[50] Brenner, already an experienced activist, became involved with two student-led undergraduate groups—the Yale Mutants and The Sillimanders—to collaborate in organizing *On Trial*. She cites her primary motivation for organizing the exhibition as the suicide of fellow art student Maya Tanaka Hanway, "who jumped to her death from the Yale School of Art roof in 1982 … [and] was also marginalized in the art school. As women interested in interdisciplinary, non-traditional artistic projects, our concerns were never taken seriously by the administration. Many of us did our best to constructively articulate our marginalization, and actively sought acknowledgment and inclusion."[51]

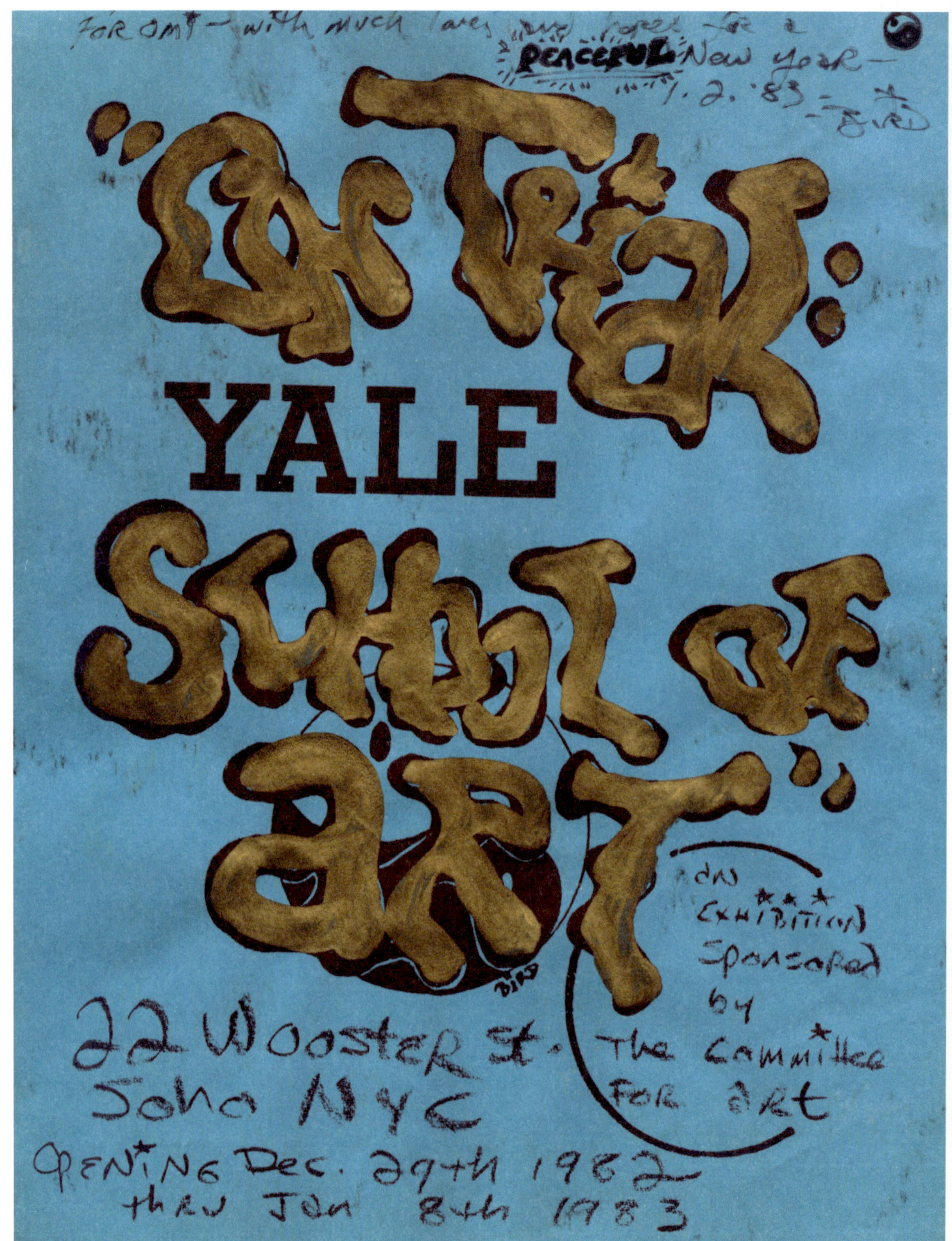

Poster for <u>On Trial: Yale School of Art</u> exhibition at 22 Wooster Gallery, 1982–83. Courtesy Bird Brenner.

THE COMMITTEE FOR ART

The Committee For Art is a group of students, faculty, and alumni whose disturbing experiences at the Yale School of Art have led them to action. These experiences include sexism and racism, an unbending Euro-centric approach to art and art history, and a controlling elite that redirects student creative energy towards its own purposes.

We present this exhibition and related publication entitled "ON TRIAL: Yale School of Art" as an optimistic endeavor. We intend it to be a high energy affair which generates esthetic experimentation. Through this effort and exhibit The Committee for Art intends to drive a wedge separating the administration of the School and of the University from everything that is good and creative at the School. The Committee wants to emphasize creative freedom and to stimulate the return of youthful energy and artistic daring. We wish to assert everyone's right to a good education. We invite your participation.

Students, alumni, teachers, ex-teachers, staff and workers of the School and their close relations and friends were all eligible to enter the show. Our Committee particularly urged workers at the University to make entries even though they have not had any opportunity to study art at the School because of present admissions policy

We want an end to the rigid barriers which divide the school from the workers, youth, and general population. We also want an end to the internal barriers which separate workers, students and teachers from each other.

We want a childcare facilty for children of workers, students and teachers.

We want an end to the tenure system (a system of privileges for a few). We demand job security for staff, students, and teachers. We demand security for all students and an end to the remedial course and probation techniques. We want written, clear descriptions of our positions.

We are against clique methods of running the School and the secrecy that promotes this non-democratic method. We want all the files and the budget opened.

We are against racist, chauvinist, and sexist methods. We demand an end to Euro-centric views of art, art history, and the world. We believe in the right of all groups discriminated against to have elected representatives on ALL decision-making committees.

We want an open intellectual atmosphere. We want an end to the stifling of creative student energy. We want past agreements to student demands honored.

We are for democratic worker-student-teacher control of education.

COMMITTEE REPRESENTATIVES: Imna Arroyo, Alix Baer, Nan Becker, Peter Bradley, Bird Brenner, Jeffrey M. Colón, Lisa Cortéz, Charles Denefeld, Stephen Fitch, Samia Halaby, Kevin Hylton, Ellen Irvine, Mariko Lockhart, Yvedt Matory,MD, Elizabeth J. Peak, Howardena Pindell, Susan K. Roecker, Paul Rutkovsky, Jean Schwinberg, Peter Siegel, Jack R. Smith, Ethan Spigland, Maurice Wilson, Michelle Wojcicki, Bill Coden, Michael A. Vuksta

I endorse this proposal and would like to have my name added to the list of Committee Representatives.

Signature_______________________________

THE COMMITTEE FOR ART   103 Franklin Street   New York, NY 10013

The Commitee for Art letter, from <u>On Trial: Yale School of Art</u> catalogue, 1982–83. Courtesy Bird Brenner.

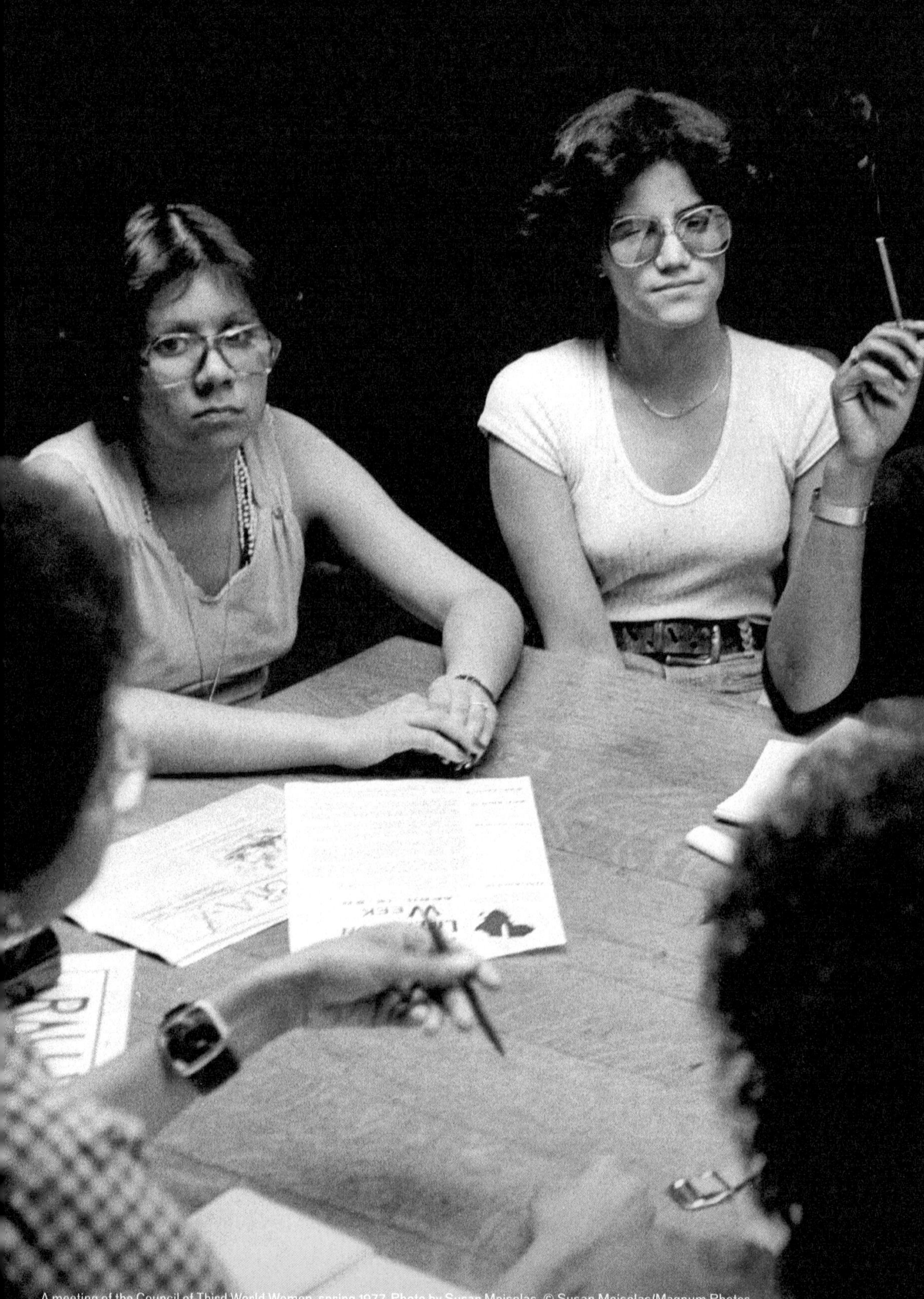

A meeting of the Council of Third World Women, spring 1977. Photo by Susan Meiselas. © Susan Meiselas/Magnum Photos.

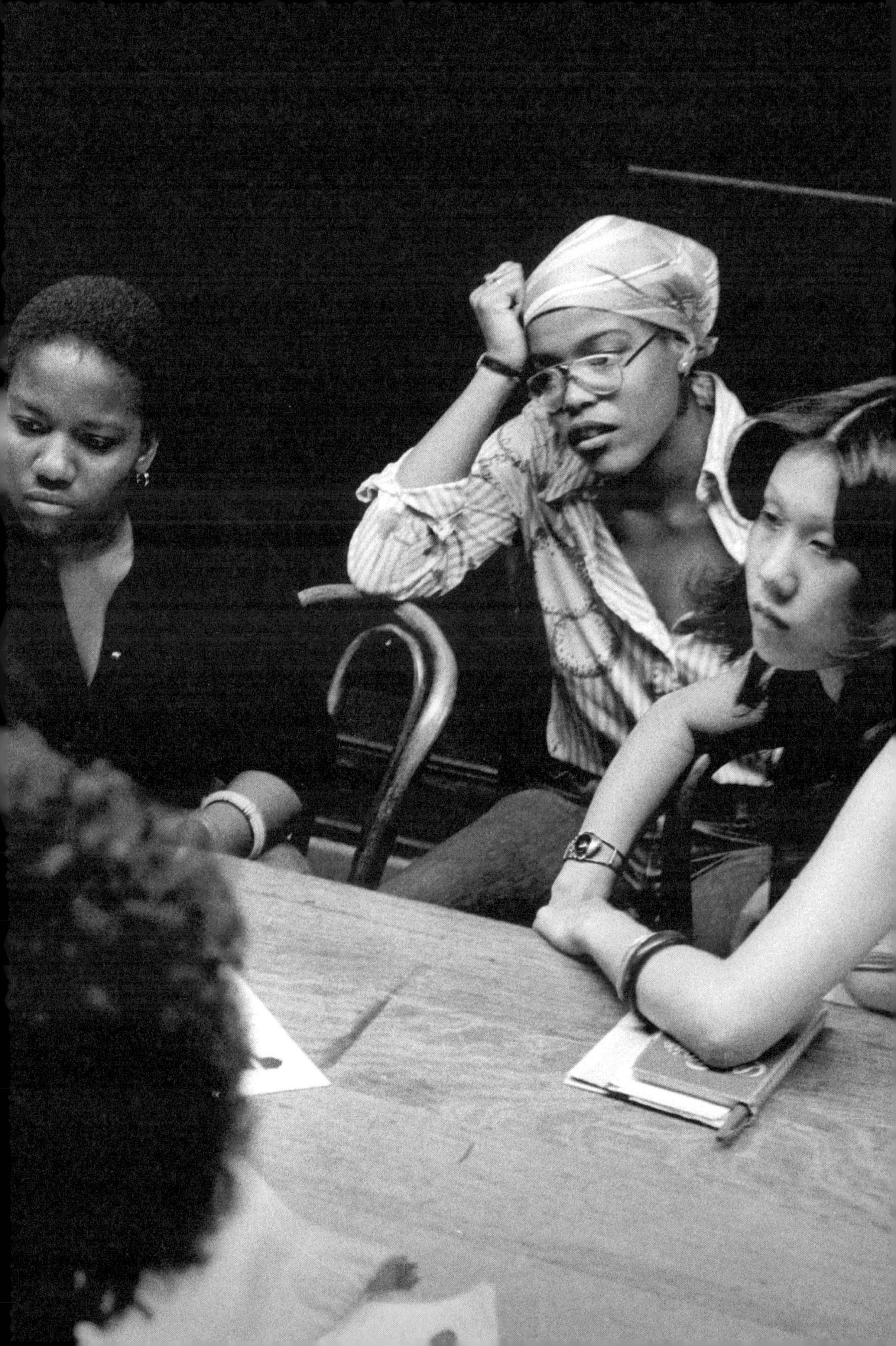

WOMEN GRADUATES IN THE POST-E.R.A. DECADE

52   Lumbard, Circuit Judge, U.S. District Court for the District of Connecticut. *Abele v. Markle, 342 F. Supp. 800 (D. Conn. 1972).* April 18, 1972.

53   Harry A. Blackmun and Supreme Court of The United States. *U.S. Reports: Roe v. Wade, 410 U.S. 113.* 1973.

In April 1972, an important feminist civil rights initiative was won in Connecticut when *Abele v. Markle* overturned the state's anti-abortion law in a U.S. district court, which ruled that the law was unconstitutional in "representing an over-reaching of the police power" by the state, which "trespasses unjustifiably on the personal privacy and liberty of its female citizenry."[52] Within a year, this opinion would inform the United States Supreme Court's landmark 1973 ruling in *Roe v. Wade* protecting a woman's right to legal abortion.[53] The period of feminism's second wave, marked by legal reforms banning sexual discrimination and enforcing gender equality in schools and workplaces, saw the release of several important publications, beginning in 1970, including Toni Cade Bambara's *The Black Woman*; Germaine Greer's *The Female Eunuch*; Carol Hanisch's *The Personal is Political*; Anne Koedt's *The Myth of the Vaginal Orgasm*; Kate Millett's *Sexual Politics*; Del Martin's *If That's All There Is*; Robin Morgan's *Sisterhood Is Powerful: An Anthology of Writings from the Women's Liberation Movement*; and Mitsu Tanaka's pamphlets, *Liberation from the Toilet* and *Declaration of the Liberation from Eros*. The proliferation of poetry, manifestos, and scholarly and personal essays constituted a feminist literary movement that galvanized a national conversation around consciousness-raising and other forms of activism, broadening and diversifying a canon to which Audre Lorde and Adrienne Rich were important contributors. Rich's *Diving into the Wreck* earned her the National Book Award in 1974 and solidified her status as a prominent cultural and political figure identified with feminism. Lorde's poem "Who Said It Was Simple," published in her 1973 book *From a Land Where Other People Live*, spoke out against conditional participation in feminism. Both poets helped to shape new understandings of gender and sexuality that would continue to develop over the next decades. As the School increased the number of women accepted as students and appointed as faculty, the institution was challenged to respond and adapt to the rapid structural changes underway in society at large.

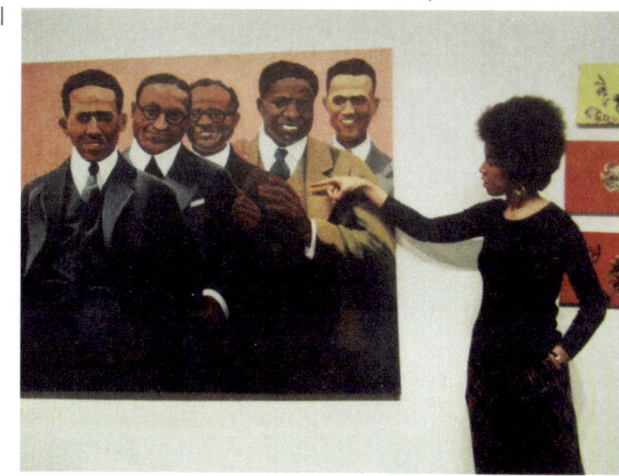

When Joyce Owens entered the MFA program in 1971, women graduates made up approximately one quarter of the student body. Owens (MFA 1973) was among the even fewer people of color and was the only African American graduate student in her class. She had been an undergraduate at Howard University, in Washington, D.C., where she studied art education with a great deal of hesitation:

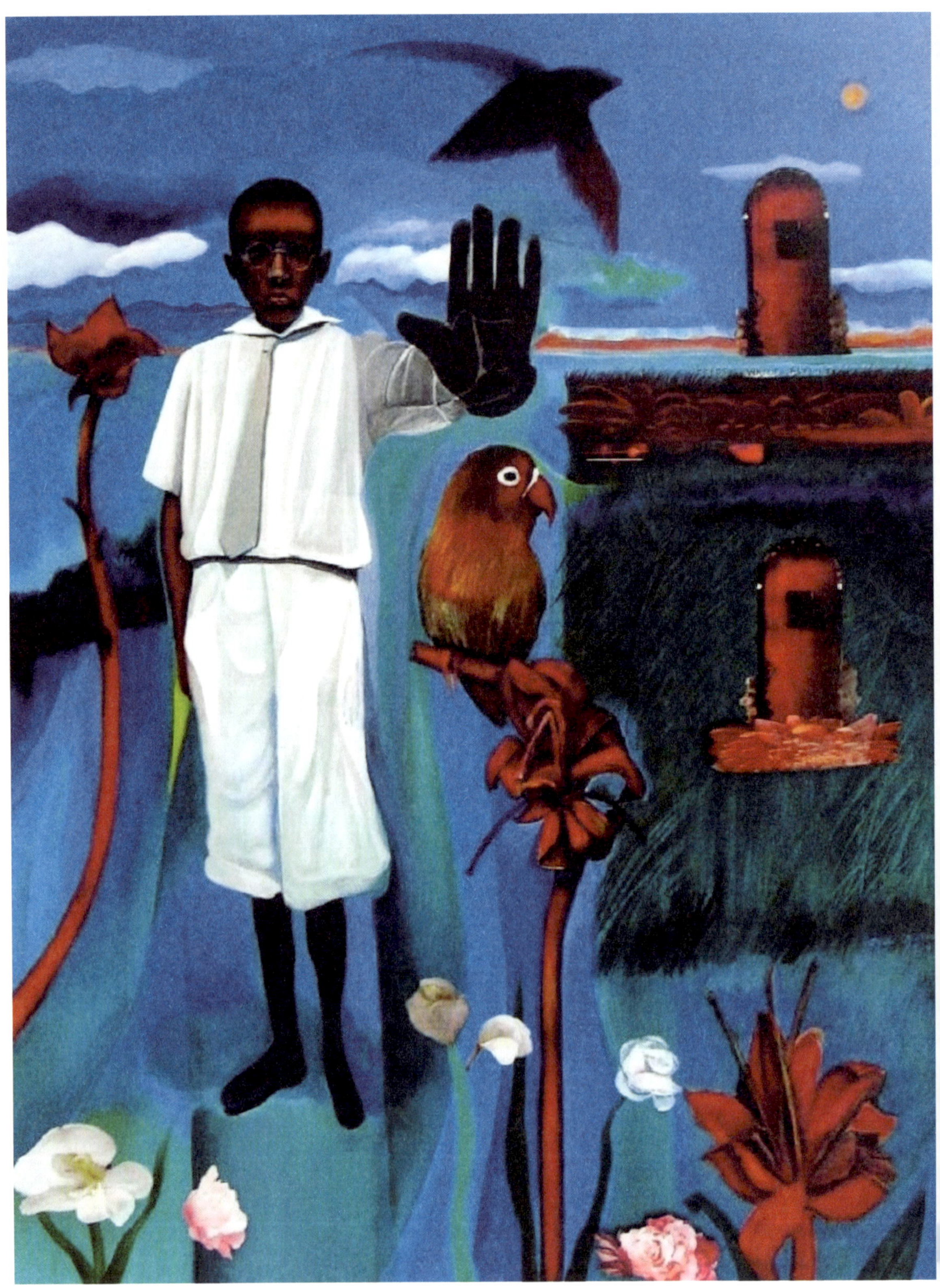

Joyce Owens, <u>Double Paradox</u>, 2009. Courtesy Joyce Owens.

54 Joyce Owens, telephone conversation with the author, January 27, 2020.

55 Ibid.

56 Ibid.

57 Ibid.

58 Ibid.

My mother, she said that I had to major in art education because she thought the only way I could make a living was to teach. So, being an obedient daughter, I did. For the final project, I wrote an essay about how I did not plan to continue in art education. I ended up seeking advice from an art professor at Howard, Leo Robinson, because I simply wanted to drop out of school. He said that I should switch my major to Painting. This was the first time I ever heard that you could major in Painting. And he said, "And then you teach it."[54]

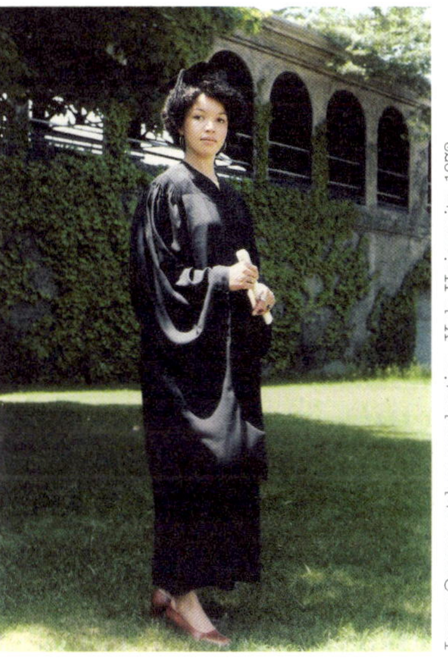

Joyce Owens at her graduation, Yale University, 1973. Photo by Jim Alexander.

Owens researched schools before applying to Yale. "In those days, you got a catalog. You would contact somebody and ask, 'Could you please send me a catalogue for your program?' So, I ordered all these catalogs and read through the material. Yale seemed the program for me, and I applied."[55] While employed as a teacher in Philadelphia, Owens received a letter of invitation from Yale. She wrote to the administration, explaining that she had no way of affording the cost of studies. She recalls that the administration was supportive, pledging that, "If we accept you, we will help you figure out a way to go."[56] While in graduate school, Owens taught at a local elementary school in New Haven, noting that she also viewed her studies at Yale like a job. "I went to my studio at 8:00 a.m., and I worked until 5:00 p.m."[57] She found the environment of the city peaceful and friendly, despite the turbulence and activism on campus in the preceding years:

I came from Howard University in the 1960s. My mother took me to my first civil rights marches. My uncle, Jack T. Franklin, was an acclaimed photographer of the civil rights movement for the *Philadelphia Tribune* and *Ebony*. … New Haven was quiet compared to D.C. … The only thing that upset me was that I was the only black person in my class. … I told Lester Johnson that if I was a token admittance, I was going to leave. He answered, "You have to see how it works." And I was introduced to this auditorium where second-year students were shown projected images of work by first-year students on the screen. The second years either booed or cheered. I guess it was a part of the admissions process, not the whole process, but part of the process. When I came to Yale, I remember someone asking, "Which work was yours?'" I described the painting that I think was called *We in The World Are One*, with faces emerging out of a tree hidden in plain view, and she responded, "Oh yeah, we liked that one. We liked your work."[58]

Seeking community, Owens attended classes in the broader University and cites as influential one at the School of Music on the migration of African polyrhythms, taught by the renowned jazz musician Willie Ruff.

Owens' female classmates included Nancy D. Lasar, who left the program before graduating, Louise L. Luthi (MFA 1973), and Judy Pfaff (MFA 1973). Owens forged important and lasting relationships with these peers, as well as others beyond the School:

[Judy Pfaff and I] would go out for walks around New Haven and pick up trash as material for our work. I suppose they might call this "found materials" now, but then, it was trash. … I considered myself a figurative artist, and I enjoyed life-drawing classes. Outside of school, I spent a lot of time at the Studio Museum in Harlem, as I was interested in Charles White and in Elizabeth

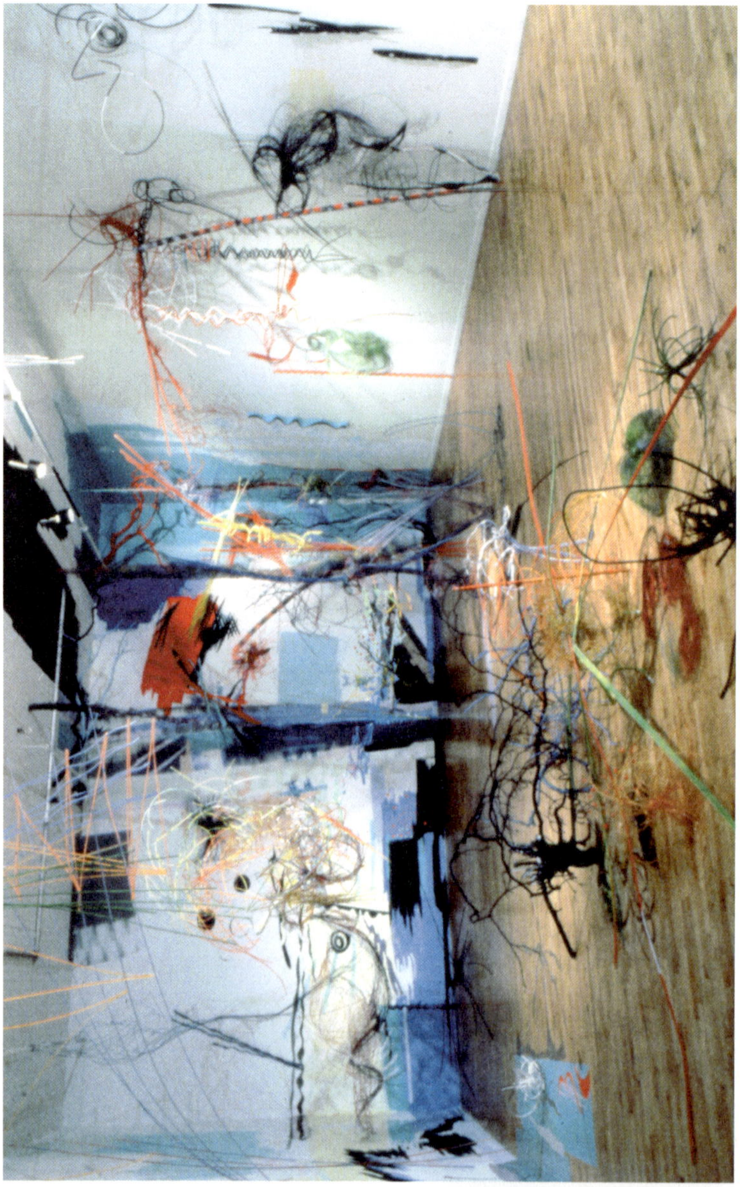

Judy Pfaff, _Deep Water_ at Holly Solomon Gallery, 1980. Courtesy Judy Pfaff Studio.

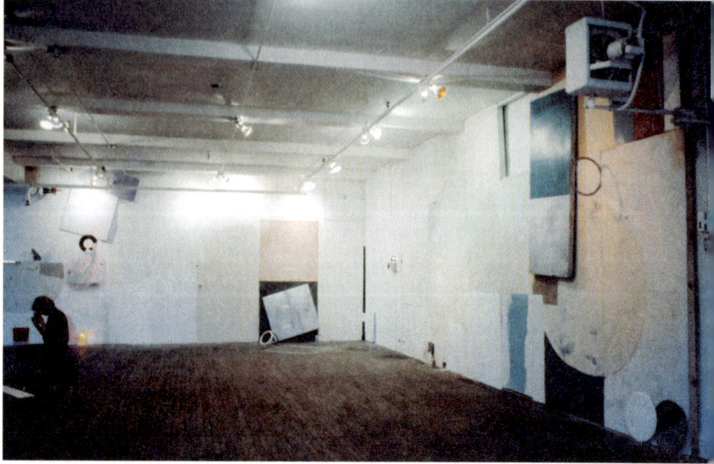

Judy Pfaff, Installation view of <u>J.A.S.O.N./J.A.S.O.N.</u> at Artists Space, 1975.
Courtesy Judy Pfaff Studio.

59   Ibid.

60   Judy Pfaff, conversation with the author, January 13, 2020.

61   Ibid.

62   Ibid.

Catlett. I just wasn't interested in Minimalism or Conceptual art. I had stories that I thought needed to be told, and I wanted to try to do that visually.[59]

Pfaff had decided to apply to the Yale MFA program on the recommendation of Robert Reed, then Assistant Professor of Art in the Department of Painting and Printmaking, after attending the Yale Summer School of Music and Art in 1970, where Reed had been her instructor. She recalls forging friendships with fellow students Don Gummer (BFA 1973; MFA 1973) and Haim Steinbach (MFA 1973) as well as Owens, but that that there were very few women in the program and that the climate was polarized in other ways, as well:

> My mentor throughout my graduate studies had been the painter Al Held, at a time when the painting program was dominated by the ruling opposites of William Bailey versus Al Held. The abstract painters [like Held] were on one side, and the figurative painters [like Bailey] on the other. They held positions like the Democrats and Republicans do today. … Bill Bailey had just been brought in, and there was a great deal of controversy around his being an intensely figurative painter at a time when that was not as accepted in contemporary circles.[60]

Pfaff has said that she believes the process-oriented approach to painting prevalent in the graduate program at the time was rooted in a very practical matter—the arrival of a significant supply of Rhoplex, a binder critical in paint formulations, and a component of all acrylic paint, from Philadelphia-based painting company Rohm and Haas:

> These guys from Philadelphia sent nearly fifty-five tubs of this acrylic medium to splash around with, and, so, the painting department developed into a process painting school, evolving techniques that were perhaps more radical than before but not really very radical. After all, we inherited the School of Art after the attempted burning down of the Rudolph building, after the Black Panther trials, the campus-wide student protests and strikes. And, so, the School of Art tucked itself back in and righted itself. I don't think we had any theory classes. Al wasn't going to think or talk about that, and Bill Bailey certainly wasn't.[61]

By the time Pfaff had arrived at the School, reluctance among graduate students in Painting toward "pit crits" was already legendary. Pfaff shares in this historical disdain for the critiques held in the atrium space between the third and fourth floors (the "pit") of the Rudolph building. She believes her very resistance to engage in those sessions motivated her venture into so-called installation format:

> I anchored all my work into the wall so it was not possible to bring the work downstairs. I was very uncomfortable with the nature of these crits, a panel looking and talking amongst themselves with the thumbs up, thumbs down approach. I decided that I wasn't going to … be part of that. … That panel was made up of all men, though Samia Halaby was there for a little while. … The artist-student was not allowed to speak, and the members of the faculty referred to the format as a way to take up old fights. It wasn't really about focusing on the work of the particular student. Rather, it was about the fight with one another. I never found it interesting, and, actually, I found it sort of scary. I asked myself, "This is the greatest [art] education in America, and this is what's going on?"[62]

Pfaff, like many other graduates, spoke of the isolation of the School's studio-based graduate studies from the rest of the University's academic offerings

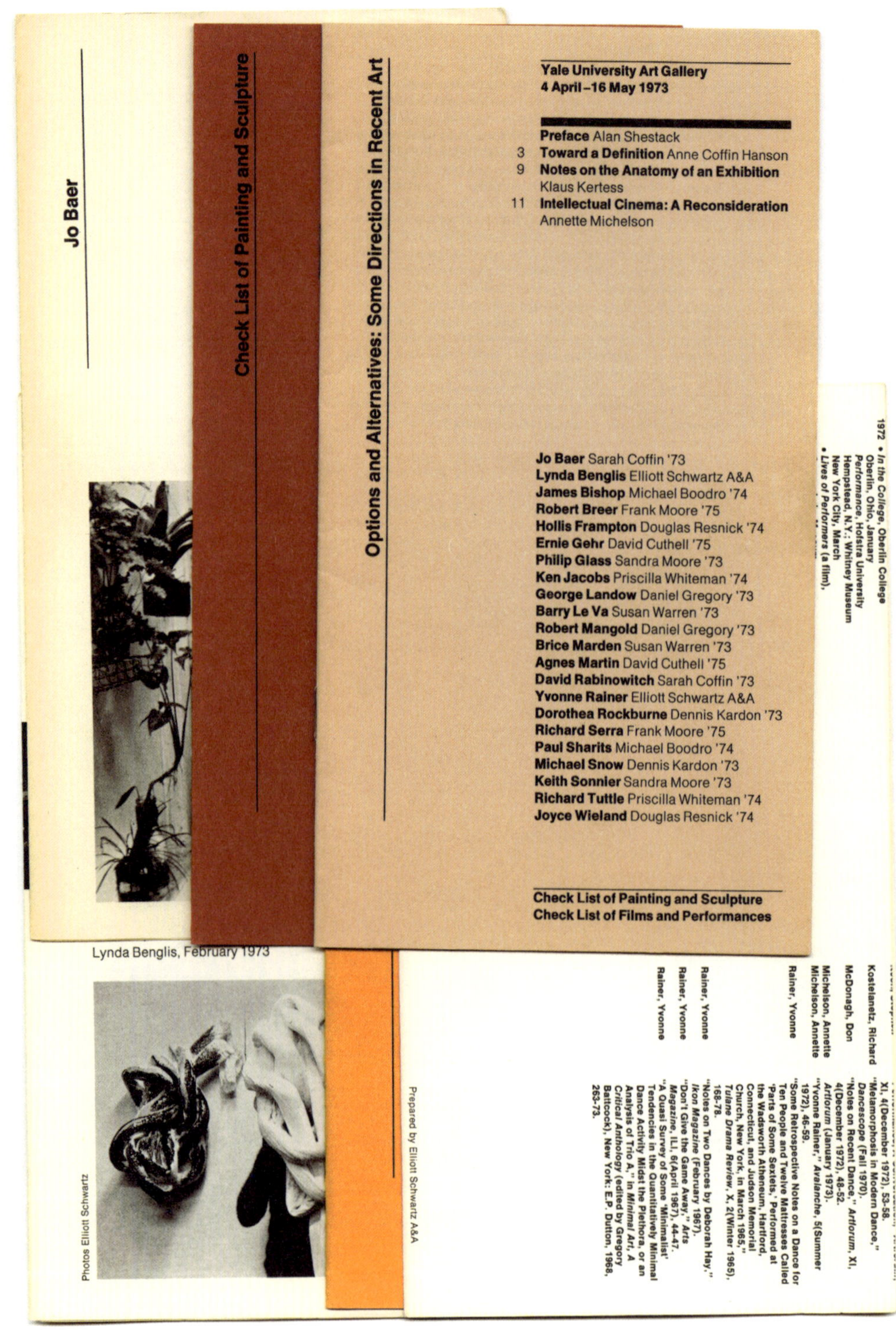

Pages from <u>Options and Alternatives: Some Directions in Recent Art</u>, published by the Yale University Art Gallery, 1973.
Courtesy Yale University Art Gallery.

and the absence of an institutional system to promote interdisciplinary exchange. She recalls, however, a "very prescient show" that opened in the spring of 1973. *Options and Alternatives: Some Directions in Recent Art,* held at the Yale University Art Gallery, was curated by the film critic and art writer Annette Michelson and critic Klaus Kertess, produced in cooperation with undergraduate students who had been assigned to interview the individual artists represented in the exhibition and to have that contribution become the catalogue. An initiative of the art historian Anne Coffin Hanson, the first woman to be hired as a fully tenured professor at the University, the exhibition, Pfaff says, was intended to "reflect on the many ways of collective thinking and feeling, which are not restricted to the arts, but extend to the many aspects of modern life."[63] In the exhibition catalogue, Hanson writes, "In the face of a rapidly expanding materialistic society, a sizeable proportion of Americans, young and old, are turning away from aggressive and rationalist activities and their immediate ends, to various forms of private exploration of sense and psyche that range from hallucination to contemplation."[64] The exhibition included works by Jo Baer, Lynda Benglis, Hollis Frampton, Yvonne Rainer, Paul Sharits, and Michael Snow, among others. Emphasizing open-ended processes that had not yet been integrated into the studio-based practices at the School of Art, it served as an inspiration for those students who had the opportunity to experience it.

Pfaff graduated in 1973, during an economic downturn, and although she quickly began exhibiting at museums and galleries, she struggled financially. About a solo exhibition at Artists Space, in New York, Pfaff recalls, "It was scheduled to open in twenty-four hours, and I had no money. I was not eating. It was, and I was, a mess. Al Held came to visit and lent me $200, and that's how I did the show."[65] After the exhibition at Artists Space, Pfaff participated in the 1975 Whitney Biennial, co-curated by John Hanhardt, Barbara Haskell, James Monte, Elke Solomon, and Marcia Tucker. While accepting many more exhibition invitations, Pfaff also took on various teaching engagements, at Ohio State University; Queens College of the City University of New York; the Tyler School of Art (now the Tyler School of Art and Architecture) at Temple University; California Institute of the Arts (CalArts); and, beginning in 1979, at Yale.[66] Teaching would provide her, and many other women artists, with a way in which to sustain her artistic practice. She credits the sudden nationwide demand for her as a teacher to the lack of professional women educators at the time and the significance of the Title IX movement. "I was among the few women graduating from my class at Yale," she says. "I became a commodity out of necessity. That degree rocketed me out of poverty and enabled me to get jobs because, before that, I had no legitimacy as a woman artist."[67] In fact, despite the challenges women artists faced within the School throughout the 1970s, numerous women graduates, like Pfaff, went on to important careers as not only practicing artists but also educators—a key role too often overlooked.

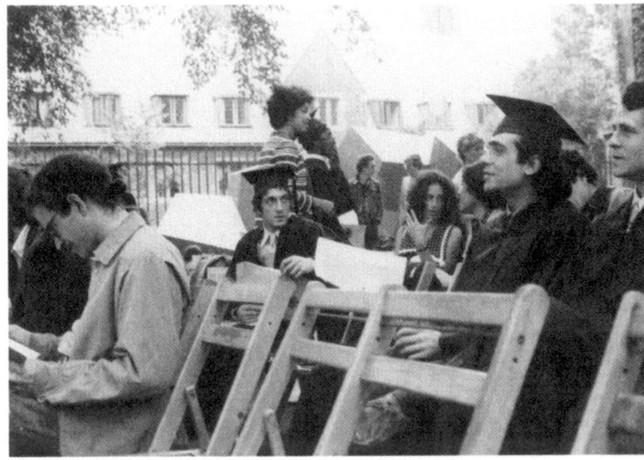

Haim Steinbach, Eric Holzman, and Joe Santore at Yale School of Art graduation, 1973. Courtesy Judy Pfaff Studio.

63   Ibid.

64   Anne Coffin Hanson, Klaus Kertess, and Annette Michelson, *Options and Alternatives: Some Directions in Recent Art.* Exh. cat. (New Haven: Yale University Art Gallery, 1973).

65   Pfaff conversation, 2020.

66   Ibid.

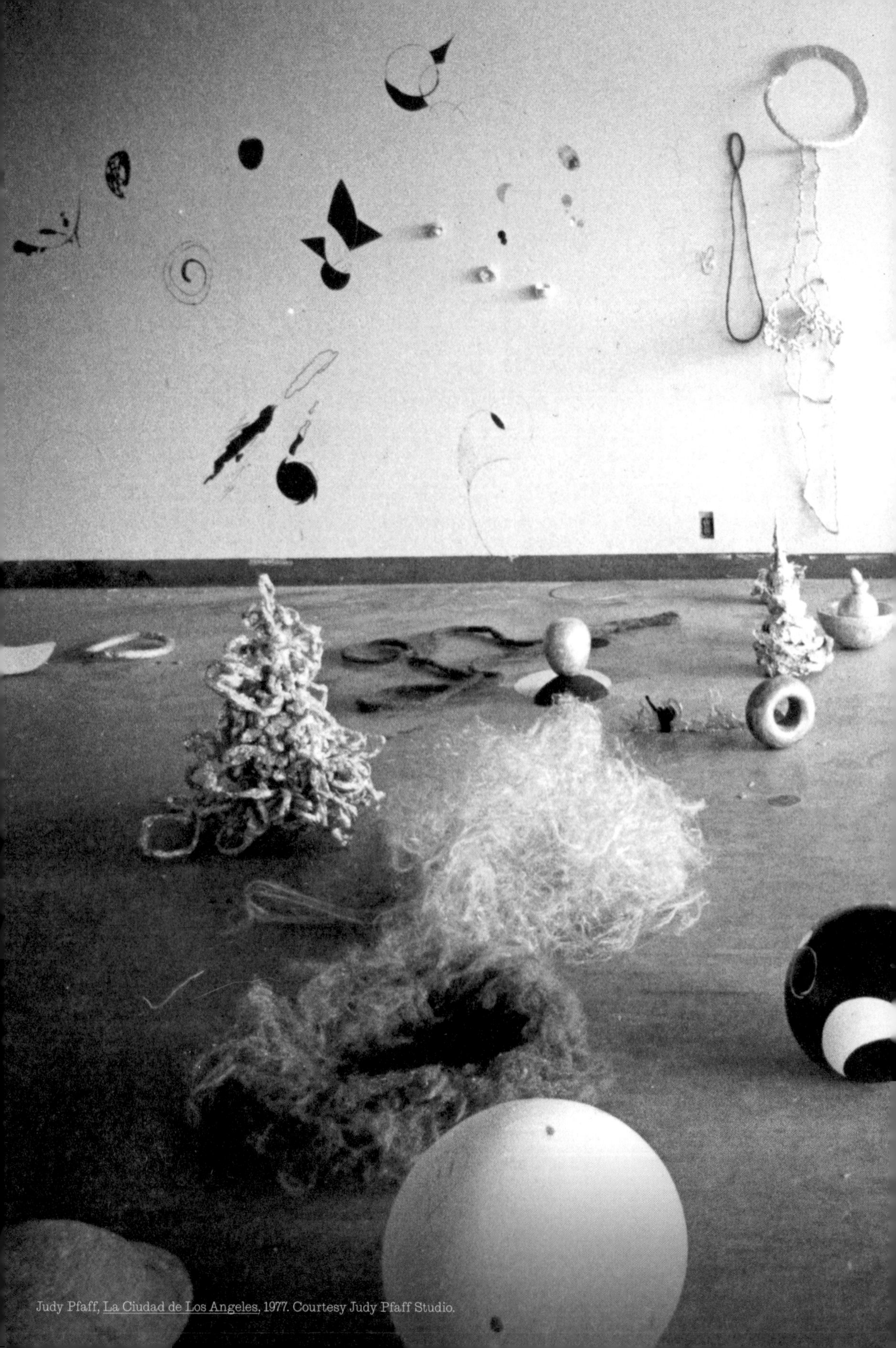

Judy Pfaff, <u>La Ciudad de Los Angeles</u>, 1977. Courtesy Judy Pfaff Studio.

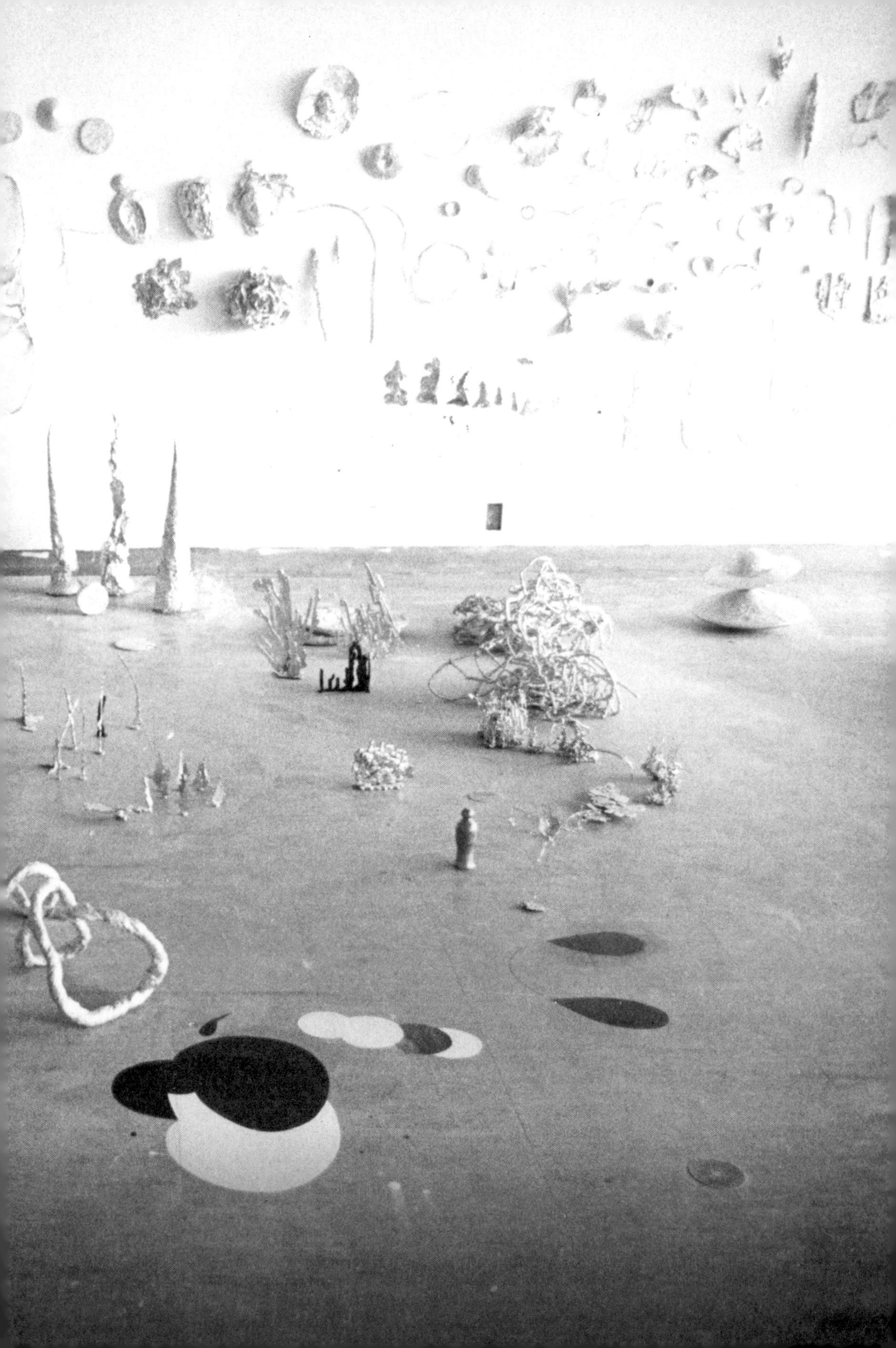

THE FOUNDING OF A DEPARTMENT OF PHOTOGRAPHY

The Department of Photography was not formally established at the School until 1979, though a handful of students, including several women, received MFA degrees in Photography before that date from a nascent program housed within Graphic Design. There, photography had long been part of the curriculum established by Herbert Matter, a Swiss-born photographer and graphic designer who had worked closely with Charles and Ray Eames before joining the School in the early 1950s with Josef Albers. Matter would spend twenty-four years on

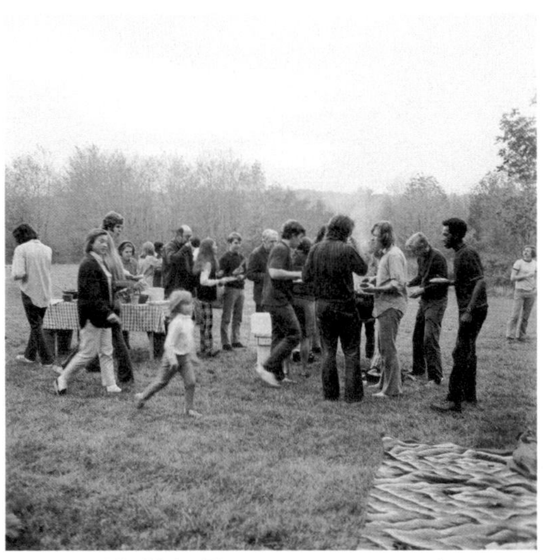

Walker Evans, *24 Views of Yale School of Art Barbecue*, 1968–72. The Metropolitan Museum of Art. The Walker Evans Archive, 1994 (1994.252.159.1) © Walker Evans Archive, The Metropolitan Museum of Art. Image copyright © The Metropolitan Museum of Art. Courtesy Art Resource, NY.

faculty, until 1976. In 1965, Matter, along with Alvin Eisenman, a typographer from Yale University Press who was brought on by Albers, and Jack Tworkov, invited the photographer and photojournalist Walker Evans to teach, in part because they were inspired by his approach to images as information. According to Eisenman, Tworkov had attended a lecture at the Century Club in New York City, at which Evans proceeded to show dozens of slides of images, of which only a few were his own, with "references to anatomical drawings, old prints, maps, postcards, and other kinds of images of interest to him. He talked about what each one meant to him and what he learned from them. ... he added the English language as an important part of recording images ... [maintaining that] one thing everybody needs to learn about is to read images, what information is contained in them. Learn about photography as information, use it as triable evidence, a universal and reliable kind of information."[68]

Evans joined the School of Art faculty as one of three principal teachers of photography in Graphic Design, together with Matter and John Hill, a graphic design and photography graduate. When the final faculty appointment was negotiated with Evans, Eisenman explained to him that he could not be called Professor of Photography but Professor of Graphic Design instead, to which Evans responded that he preferred the appointment, adding that *Let Us Now Praise Famous Men,* the canonical book co-authored with the writer James Agee and published in 1941, "was a reflection on his growing interest in graphic design."[69] According to Eisenman, Evans went on to say that "the idea of completely separating text and pictures was the right way to do it, that it should be nothing like the relationship of legend, caption, image, and text in the popular magazines of the day. It would be the presentation through the eyes of two different people, and they would be in different sections of the book."[70]

68   Eisenman and Thompson 2006.

69   Ibid. 131.

70   Ibid.

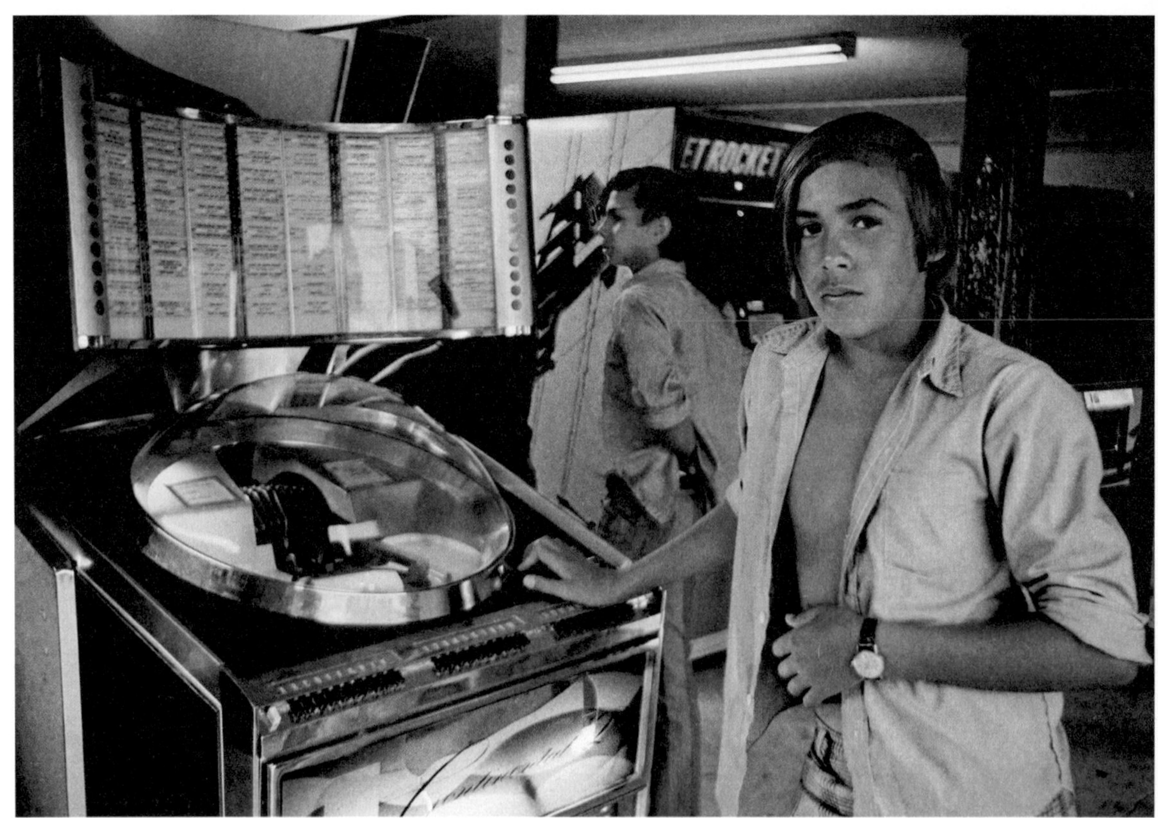

Christine Osinski, <u>Boy Near Jukebox</u>, 1971. © Christine Osinski.

Eisenman adds, "I do believe now that the layout of his book *Let Us Now Praise Famous Men* is the strongest statement on photographic books that's ever been made by anybody, and that it changed the design of photographic books."[71]

In a 1971 interview, Evans advocates for a photography with "the courage to present itself as what it is, which is a graphic composition produced by a machine and an eye and then some chemicals and paper. Technically, it has nothing to do with painting."[72] But he draws a distinction between documentary photography and documentary style, noting that, "I realized [my practice] established the documentary style as art in photography. … I use the word 'style' particularly because in talking about it many people say 'documentary photograph.' Well, literally a documentary photograph is a police report of a dead body or an automobile accident or something like that. But the style of detachment and record is another matter. That applied to the world around us is what I do with the camera, what I want to be done with the camera."[73] Eisenman writes that there was:

a wide belief here on the part of the faculty that the university was absolutely the wrong place for a photographer or an artist of any kind to be, because the practice of art was a separate track that ran alongside a university but shouldn't ever get mixed up with being in a university. … Robert Frank came [to the School of Art] in 1971 and he and Walker had a debate over whether it was possible for students from an Ivy League college to look at America and the world with the same kind of openness that he himself had about America.[74]

But according to Eisenman, Evans selected students for the program who understood what Evans believed—that "the secret of photography is that the camera takes on the character of the personality of the handler … the mind works on the machine, through it."[75]

Christine Osinski (MFA 1974), who entered the School of Art in 1972, was among the first graduates to receive a degree in Photography prior to the formal establishment of a department in 1979.[76] Osinski was motivated to apply to Yale after attending a lecture Evans gave while she was studying at the School of the Art Institute of Chicago. She submitted a portfolio of photographs taken in a campground in Old Lyme, Connecticut, which was occupied by teenagers hanging out among pinball machines. The images surprised the review committee, who accepted Osinski's application based on what they felt was a refreshing take on Old Lyme, the town in which Evans lived while working at Yale.

Osinski approached the prospect of attending Yale with some trepidation: "I came from a working-class background from the South Side of Chicago, and Yale represented such power, prestige, money, and tradition. [This] led me to develop a crisis of confidence with respect to navigating around the School and the University."[77] She recalls the program as highly unstructured, without assigned advisors, although "education in art at this juncture—not just at Yale but elsewhere—was like learning through osmosis."[78] She became interested in photographing a New Haven beauty parlor called the Artistic Salon— a place "where women went in looking one way and came back out looking altogether different. It was a project about … [women's] ideas around beauty and transformation." She was "met with reactions from male students and faculty who could not relate to the material. In the absence of female faculty members and peers, I moved away from photographing women to focusing on shooting interior domestic life devoid of figures."[79] Struggling to find the space within the School of Art for experimentation, she enrolled in classes at the University, including a course that read photography from a cultural perspective

71 Ibid.

72 Leslie Katz, "Interview with Walker Evans," in Vicki Goldberg, *Photography in Print: Writings from 1816 to the Present* (Albuquerque: University of New Mexico Press, 1981), 364.

73 (From 1971 interview with Paul Cummings, Oral History Interview with Walker Evans, 1971, October 13–December 23, American Art Archives). www.aaa.si.edu/collections/interviews/oral-history-interview-walker-evans-11721

74 Eisenman and Thompson 2006, 128.

75 Walker Evans, in Goldberg 1981, 364.

76 The first known woman graduate student to receive an MFA in Photography was Melinda Blauvelt Wells (BA 1971; MFA 1973).

77 Christine Osinski, telephone conversation with the author, February 9, 2020.

78 Ibid.

79 Ibid.

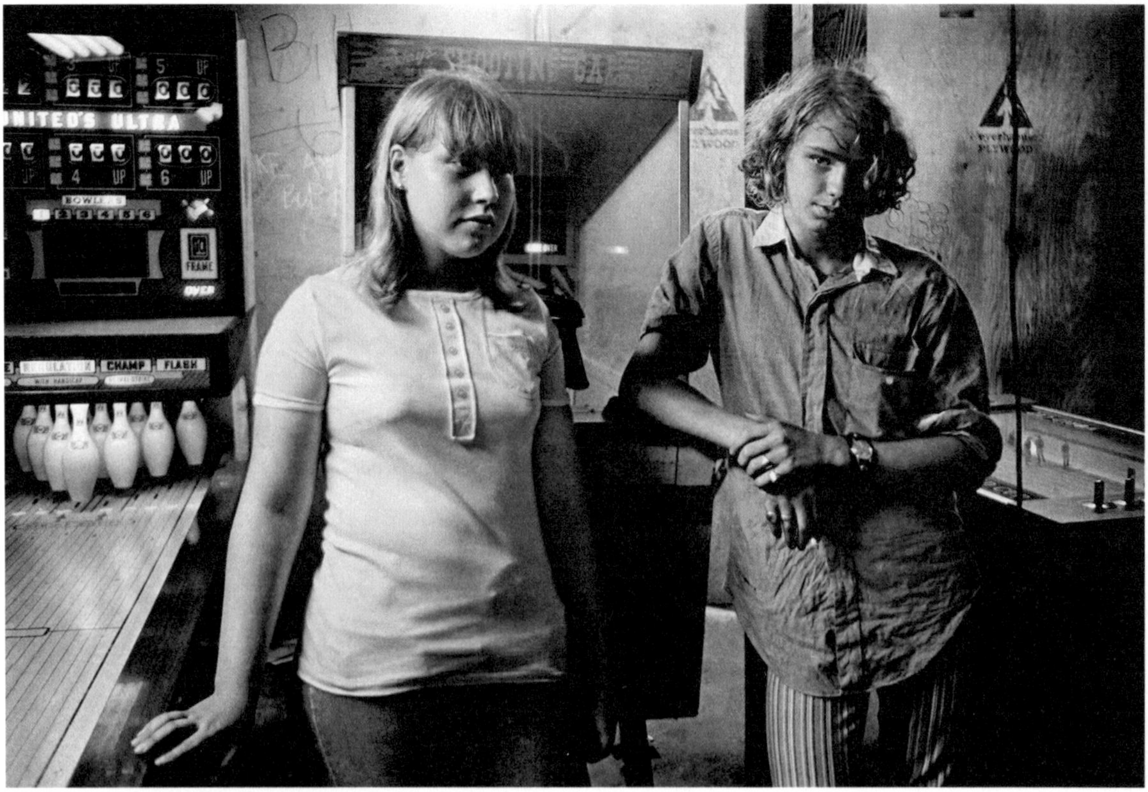

Christine Osinski, <u>Kids at an Arcade</u>, 1971. © Christine Osinski.

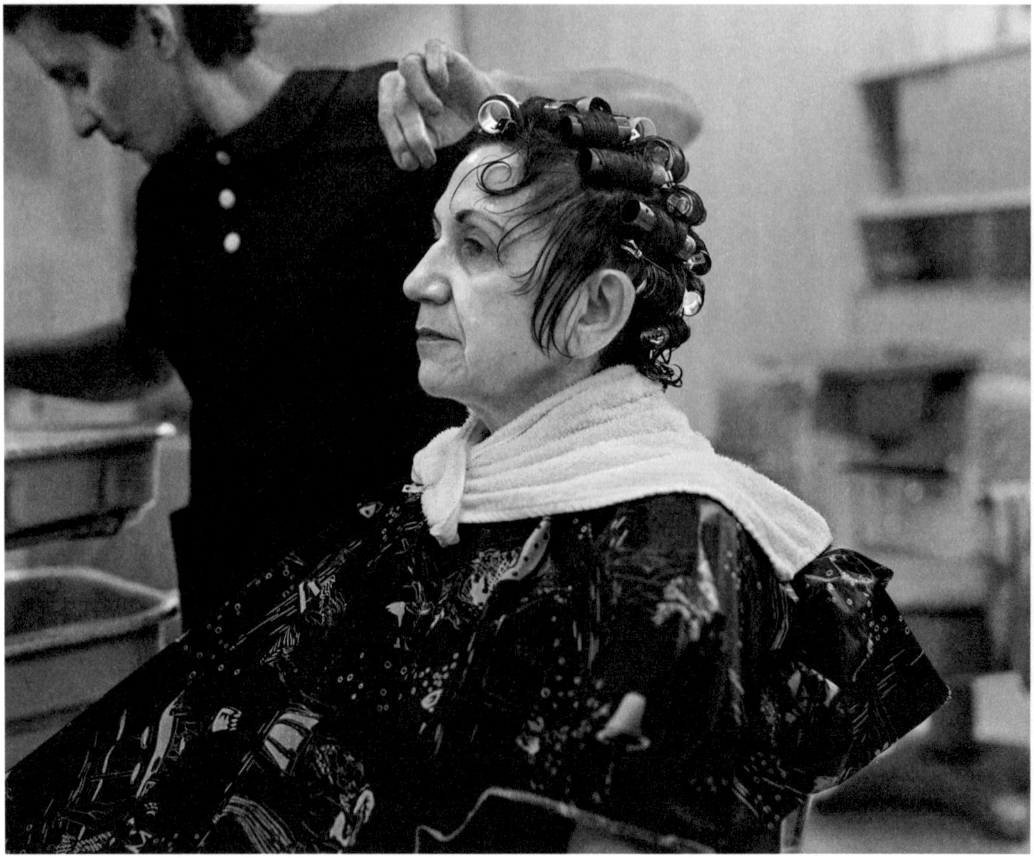

Christine Osinski, <u>Woman in Curlers</u>, 1972. © Christine Osinski.

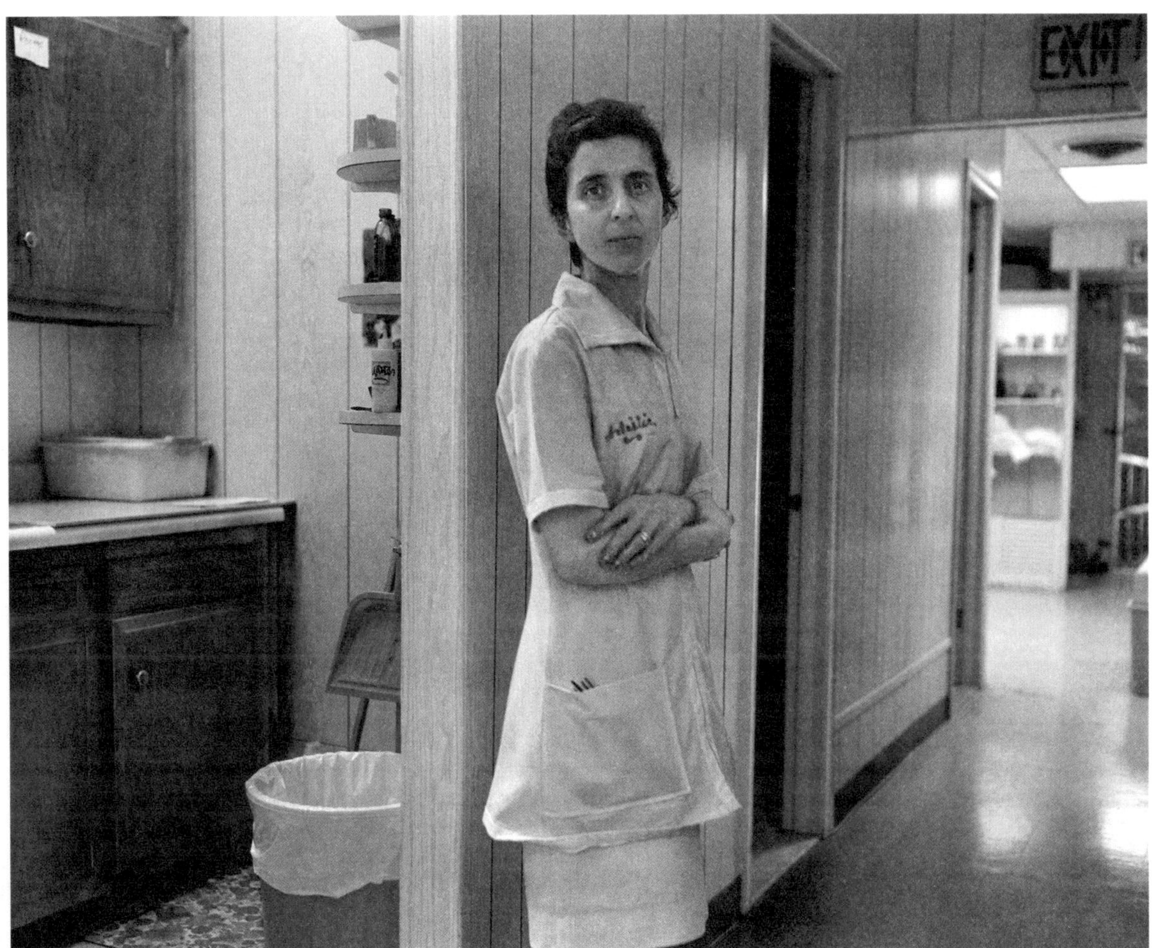

Christine Osinski, <u>Hairdresser at Artistic Beauty Salon</u>, 1972. © Christine Osinski.

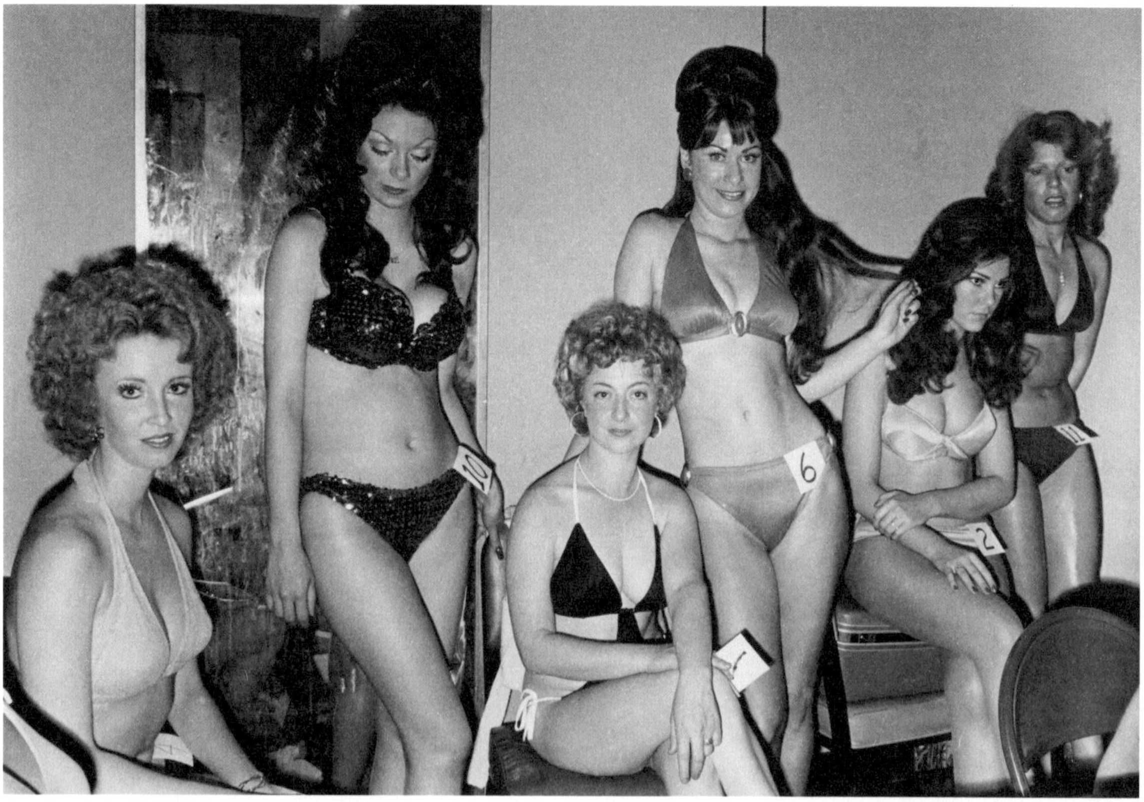

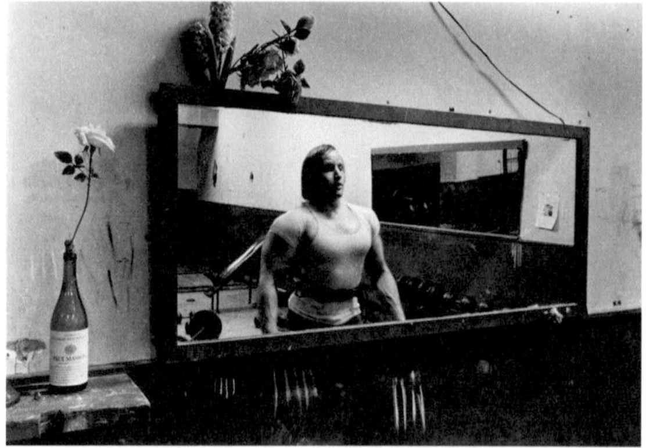

Joyce Baronio, <u>Untitled (Bathing Suit Contest)</u>, from her thesis portfolio, 1976. © Joyce Baronio. Courtesy Yale University Art Gallery.

Joyce Baronio, <u>Former Mr. Universe</u>, from her thesis portfolio, 1976.
© Joyce Baronio. Courtesy Yale University Art Gallery.

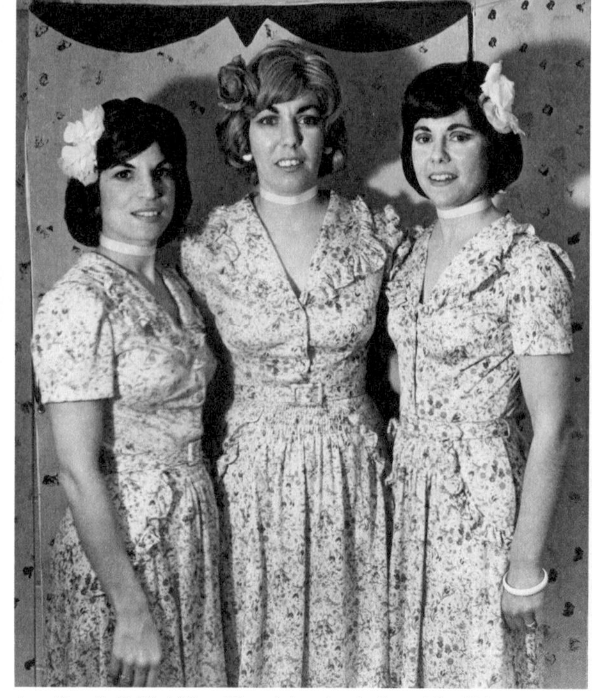

Joyce Baronio, <u>Untitled (Three Women)</u>, from her thesis portfolio, 1976.
© Joyce Baronio. Courtesy Yale University Art Gallery.

taught by Michael Lesy in the Department of American Studies; a literature class on William Faulkner taught by Cleanth Brooks; and a weekly film class taught by Annette Michelson in the Department of the History of Art, which was a particularly important resource for Osinski.[80] After graduating in 1976, Osinski taught at the Bedford Hills Correctional Facility for Women, in New York State, as well as C.W. Post College (now LIU Post), Long Island University; Parsons School of Design; and Pratt Institute, before being appointed Professor at Cooper Union, where she has taught photography since 1983.[81]

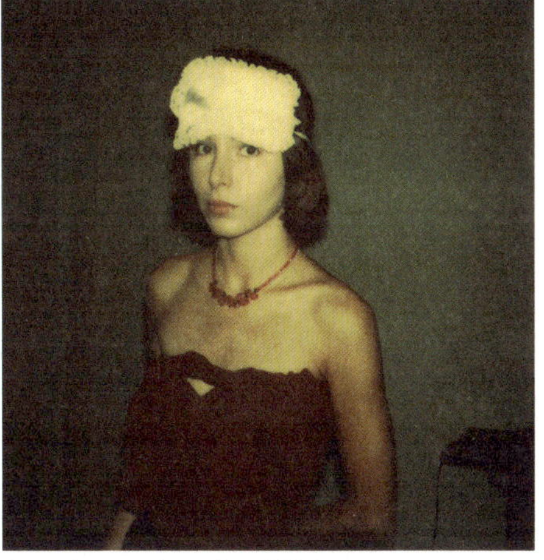
Walker Evans, Joyce Baronio, 1973–74. The Walker Evans Archive, The Metropolitan Museum of Art, 1994 (D.1994.262.150) © Walker Evans Archive, The Metropolitan Museum of Art. Image copyright © The Metropolitan Museum of Art. Courtesy Art Resource, NY.

Joyce Baronio (MFA 1976), who enrolled in 1974, was among the last students to have studied under Evans before his death in 1975. "Walker was interested in women," she remembers. "Looking for subjects to photograph with his SX-70 Polaroid, he asked me to sit for him in his studio. I saw him most days—he liked to drink a glass of white wine and to chat."[82] As an undergraduate, Baronio had been a Psychology student with a concentration in behavioral science:

> I was focused on fantasy, and I felt this [was] more a realm of women. … At some point, I went to a nude beauty contest in New Jersey somewhere, and I found out that many of the contestants worked in a variety of jobs in Times Square in New York City. Once I graduated in 1976, I went to New York and located this building called the Show World Center, that served as the headquarters for the Miss All Bare Beauty Contest. I promised those who modeled for me prints. I did not exactly blend in—I was in this "Yale" outfit with a long sleeve shirt and Abercrombie and Fitch pants, Walker Evans style. … I was able to keep my studio at Show World for $75 per month for rent. They called me J. J. and always kept an eye out for me. … I was asked if I could post my photographs of sex workers in the ground-floor window cases [of Show World]. The other places had tacky pictures of nude women with nipples covered over with XXX. … Those places got busted.[83]

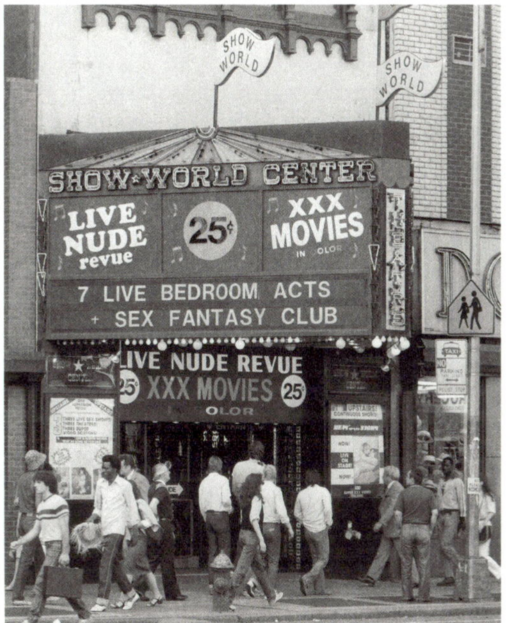
Show World Center at 669 Eighth Avenue and 42nd Street. © G. Paul Burnett/Shutterstock.

After their installation in the storefront windows of Show World, Baronio's photographs drew the attention of the American novelist and essayist Edmund White, who featured the images in the *Village Voice* with the header "Joyce Baronio on 42nd Street—Tripping the Light Fantastic."[84] [see pp. 134–37] Baronio eventually published the series, called *42nd Street Studio*, as a book of portraits of erotic entertainers, including famous porn

80 Ibid.

81 Osinski received a Guggenheim Fellowship in 2005.

82 Joyce Baronio, telephone conversation with the author, September 15, 2019.

83 Ibid.

84 Edmund White, "Joyce Baronio on 42nd Street—Tripping the Light Fantastic," *Village Voice*, August 6, 1979.

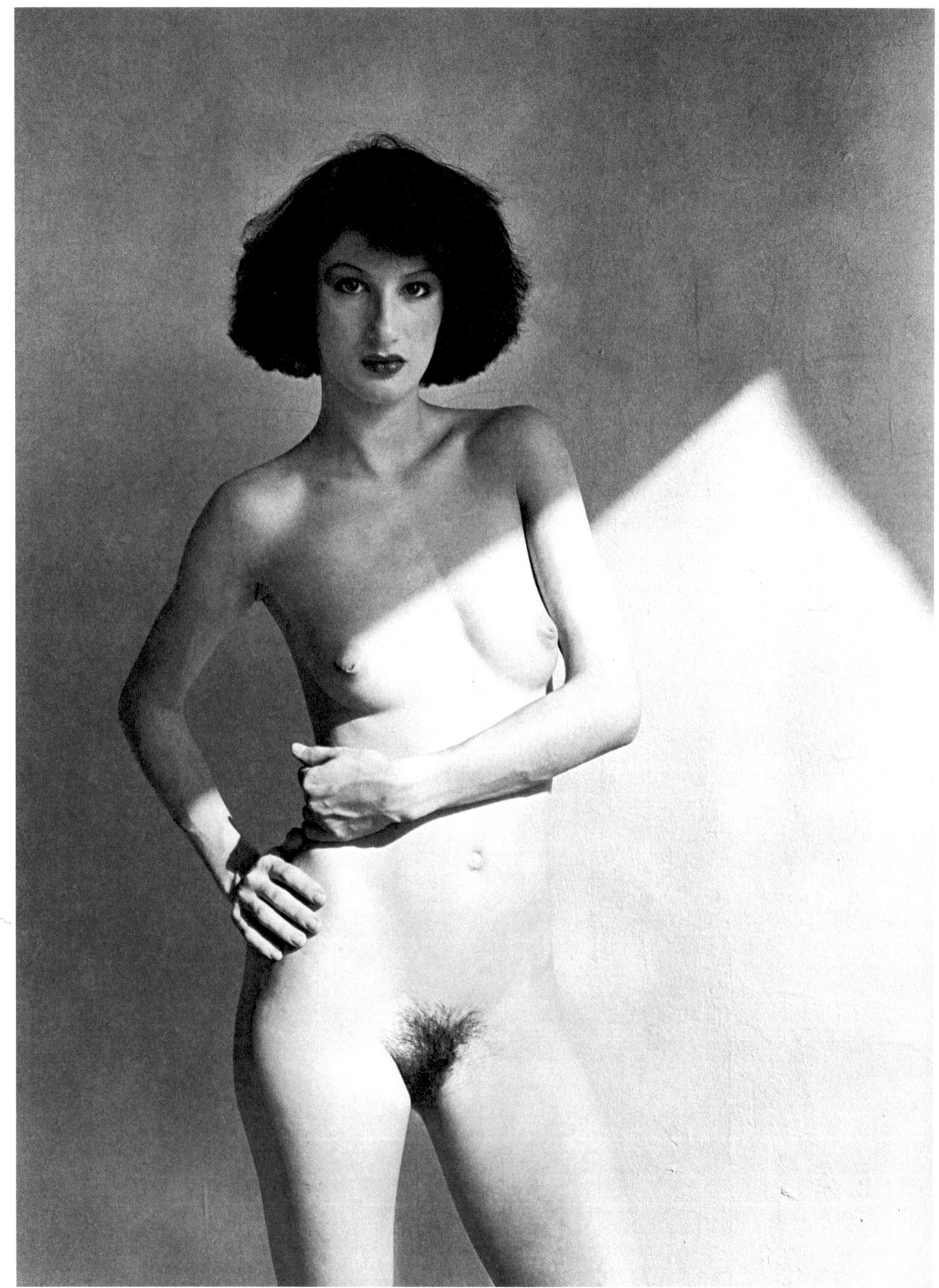

Joyce Baronio, <u>Untitled</u>, from the series <u>42nd Street Studio</u>, ca. 1980. © Joyce Baronio.

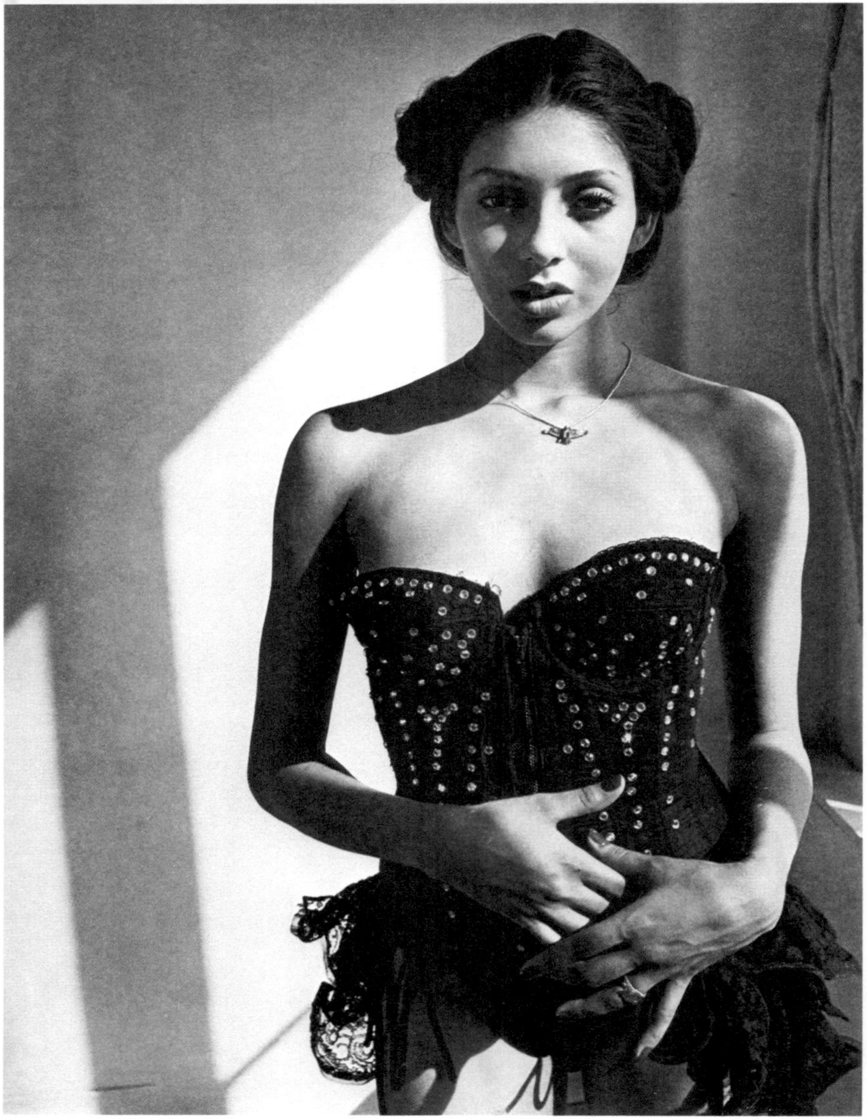

Joyce Baronio, Untitled, from the series 42nd Street Studio, ca. 1980. © Joyce Baronio.

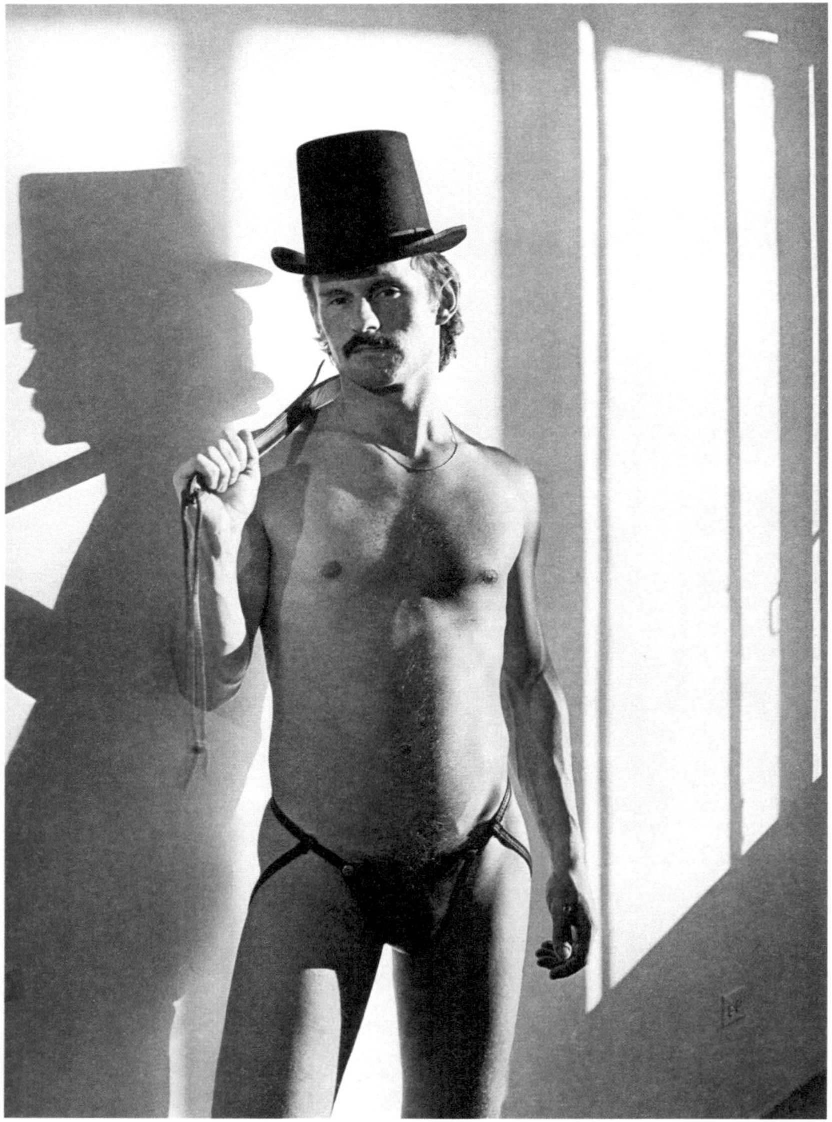

Joyce Baronio, Untitled, from the series 42nd Street Studio, ca. 1980. © Joyce Baronio.

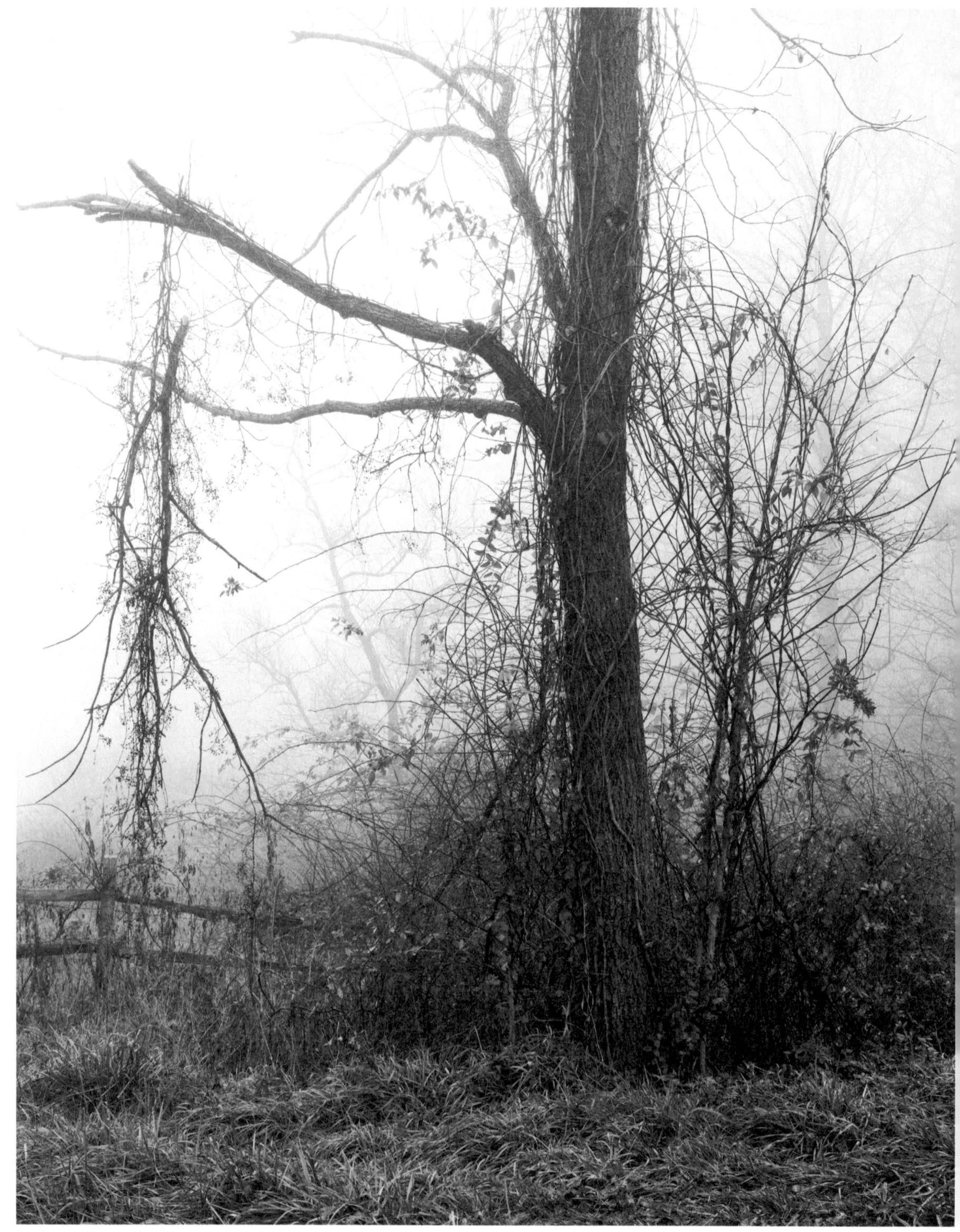

Lois Conner, <u>Brandywine River Valley</u>, 1979. © 2021 Lois Conner.

actors Beth Ann, Sharon Mitchell, Vanessa del Rio, Candida Royalle, and Joey Silvera. The book, released in 1980, included a lengthy introductory essay by Linda Nochlin, who wrote:

> Baronio is working with sex entertainers, not with prostitutes, and this seems to be a distinction that is as important to her as to her subjects. But even more important, Baronio is a woman photographing other women: her grasp of the subject may have more to do with empathy and identification than with capturing visual prey, no matter how delicately. … Baronio, however, focuses not on the universality of the erotic imagination but rather on the individuality and uniqueness of its manifestations in each of her subjects.[85]

By the late 1970s, the broader art world was gripped by a revised approach to the medium of photography, which hinged on questions of representation. In 1977 Douglas Crimp curated the influential exhibition *Pictures* at Artists Space, in which he identified a generation of artists pursuing a crucial shift in perspective regarding the relationship between "illusionism" and representation. In the catalogue for the show, Crimp wrote that representation "does not achieve signification in relation to what is represented, but in relation to other representations," thus illuminating "something absent to the condition of our apprehension of what is present."[86] That same year, Susan Sontag, already a well-known public intellectual, published a collection of essays, *On Photography*, as a reminder that "to photograph is to appropriate the thing photographed. It means putting oneself into a certain relation to the world that feels like knowledge—and therefore, like power."[87]

Following Evans' death in 1975, the School decided to create a Department of Photography. Eisenman writes that Diane Arbus had been Walker Evans' own candidate for a replacement, as she had been "the one Walker most closely identified himself with."[88] Eisenman, who visited Arbus to propose the idea, recalls that Arbus rejected it, saying, "There is no possibility that I would consider teaching anywhere in the world. … I have nothing to teach."[89] A lengthy recruitment process ensued, resulting in the eventual appointment of photographer Tod Papageorge in 1979 as the department's first Director of Graduate Studies. Papageorge's approach countered photography's "straightforward relationship to things in the world" with "young photographic artists as makers of visual fictions."[90] During Papageorge's thirty-five-year tenure, thirty-three graduates of the program earned Guggenheim Fellowships—twenty of them women, including Marion Belanger (MFA 1990), Lois Conner (MFA 1981), and Tanya Marcuse (MFA 1990). Two of those Guggenheim Fellows, Dawoud Bey (MFA 1993) and An-My Lê (MFA 1993), also received MacArthur Fellowships.

Lois Conner matriculated in 1979, immediately after formalization of the Department of Photography. She recalls a small program that included two women and three men, overseen primarily by Papageorge, along with Richard Benson and Jerry Thompson, a former student of Evans. The atmosphere of the department was "almost like a drawing room or living room," completely separated from the other disciplines.[91] Conner fulfilled the requirement to take electives outside the School by enrolling in courses in the Department of the History of Art, including one on the Ming Dynasty and another on British landscape painting, which informed her understanding of light and her own approach to light within photography. Upon graduation, she took on multiple part-time teaching engagements, including at the New School, the School of Visual Arts, and Cooper Union, in each case as an adjunct without possibility of tenure. Eventually, she applied for a full-time position as Assistant Professor at the Yale School of Art, and was appointed by Dean David Pease in 1991, later promoted to

85 Joyce Baronio, *42nd Street Studio* (New York: Pyxidium Press, 1980). Baronio's *42nd Street Studio* won the American Institute of Graphic Arts Award for Excellence in 1980.

86 Douglas Crimp, *Pictures* (New York: Committee for the Visual Arts, 1977), 5.

87 Susan Sontag, *On Photography* (New York: Picador, 1977), 4.

88 Eisenman and Thompson 2006, 130.

89 Ibid, 131.

90 Tod Papageorge, conversation with the author, January 16, 2020.

91 Lois Conner, telephone conversation with the author, April 5, 2021.

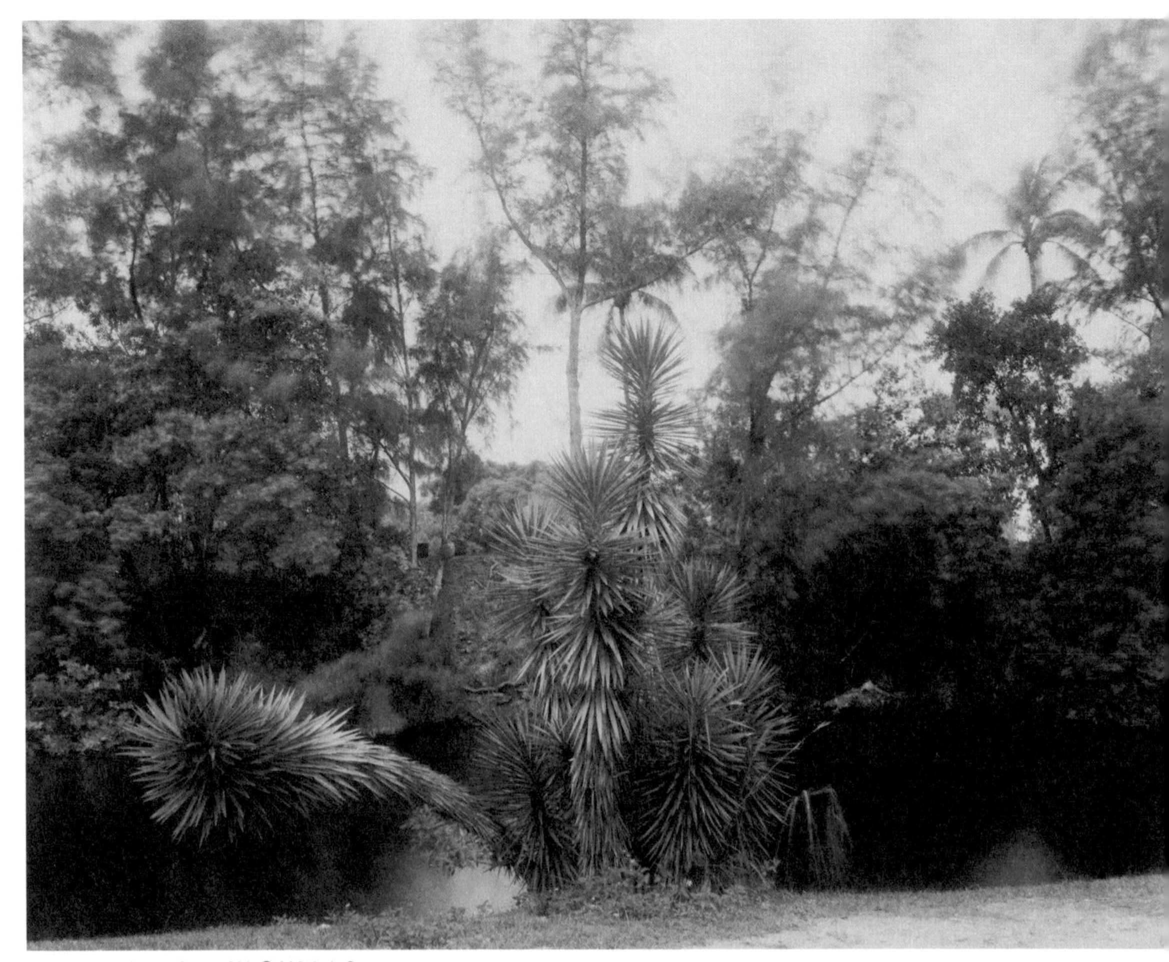

Lois Conner, <u>After Dr. Seuss</u>, 1980. © 2021 Lois Conner.

Associate Professor in 1994. She led under-graduate classes while participating in graduate critiques, which she found "intimidating and hard," recalling that, "In the beginning, I was very bold and outspoken. But you just feel kind of beaten down after a while."[92] Regarding her teaching assignments, Conner adds that she "had the 8:30 a.m. classes [every year]. No one else had the 8:30 a.m. classes—the people who lived locally didn't have the 8:30 a.m. classes; the men didn't have the 8:30 a.m. classes. But I did. I never missed a class, and I was never late. I told my students, 'If you are ever late, there is no excuse, because I'm coming in from New York City.'"[93]

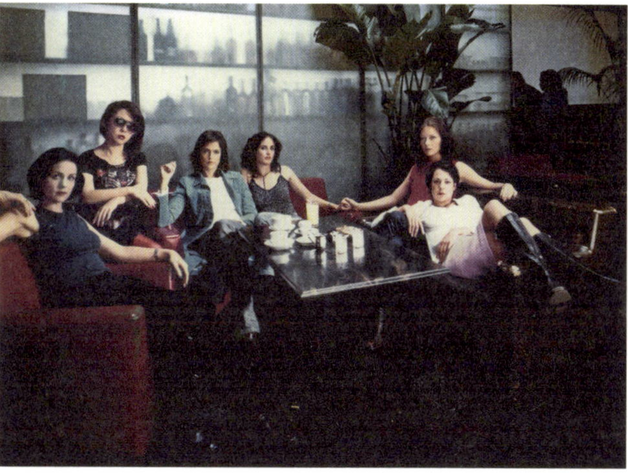

Jenny Gage (MFA 1996), Nikki S Lee, Dana Hoey (MFA 1997), Malerie Marder (MFA 1998), Kary Grannan (MFA 1998), Justine Kurland (MFA 1998), photographed by Catherine Opie for "Hot Shots," _Harper's Bazaar_, February 2000. © Catherine Opie.

92   Ibid.

93   Ibid.

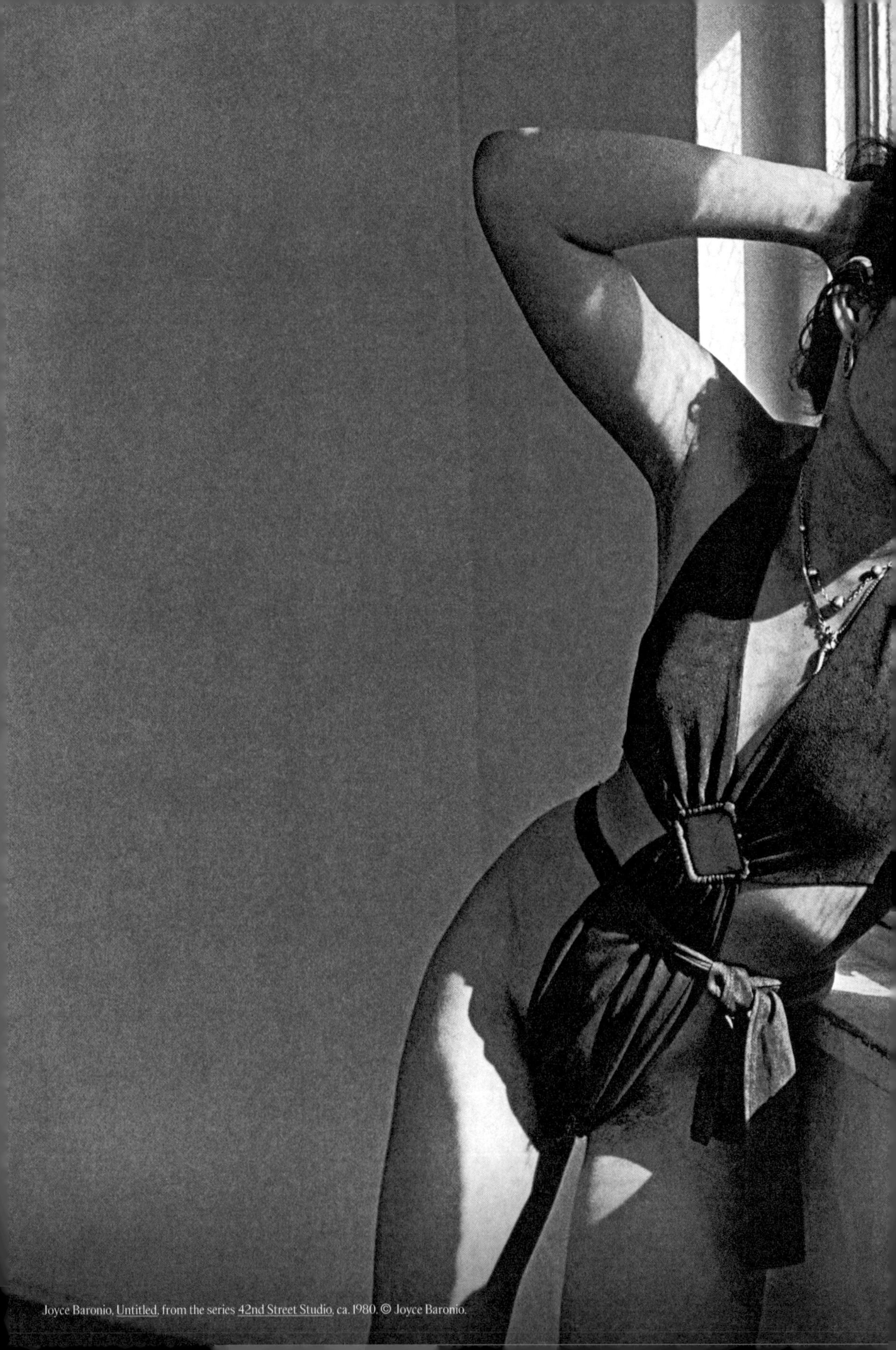

Joyce Baronio, <u>Untitled</u>, from the series <u>42nd Street Studio</u>, ca. 1980. © Joyce Baronio.

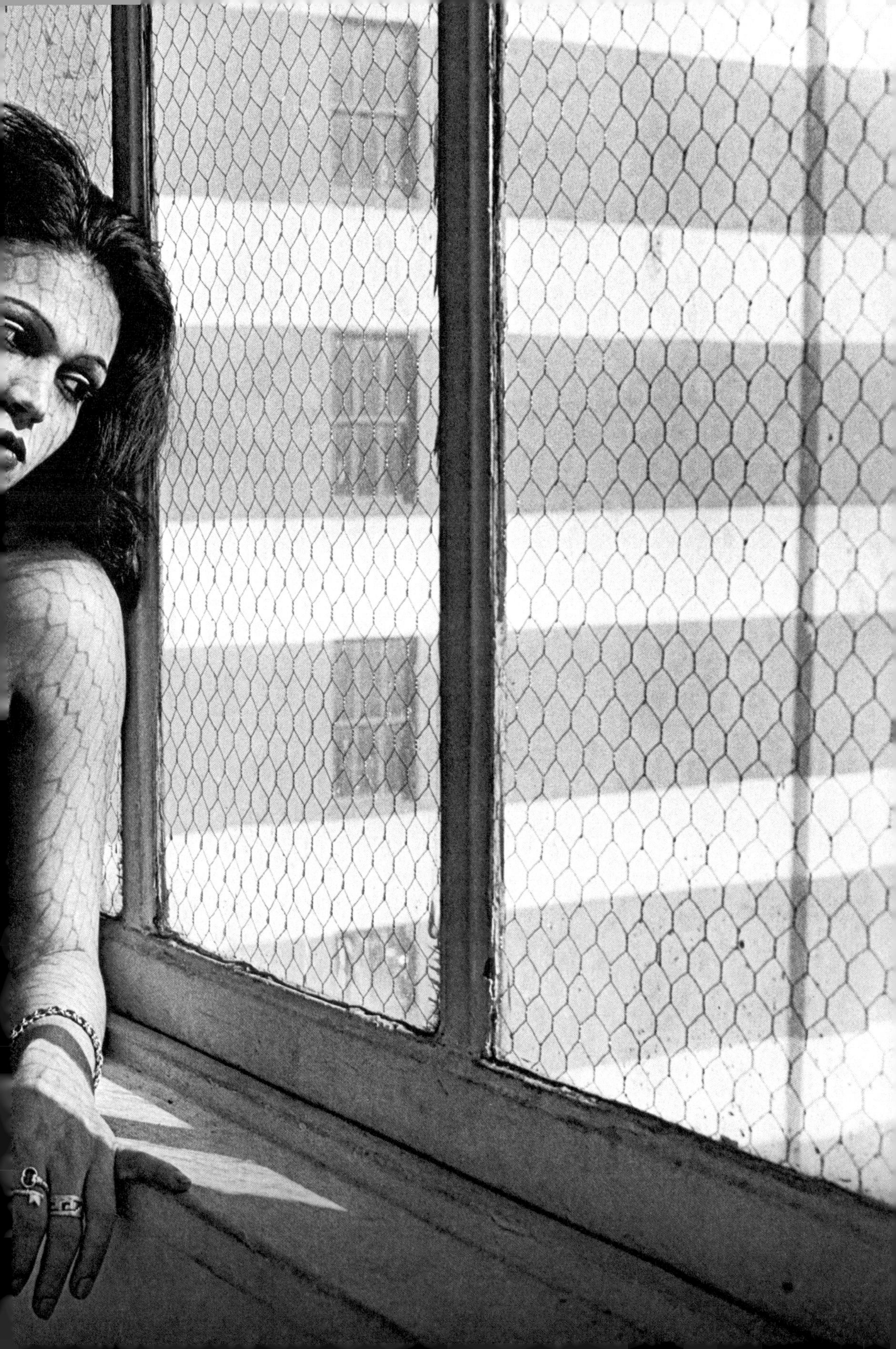

THEORY AND PRACTICE: THE RISE OF CRITICAL AND CULTURAL STUDIES

By the late 1970s, the concept of "criticality" had emerged as a primary framework for the interpretation and evaluation of the visual arts. Over the following decades, debate ensued within the field over art's "relation to the world"—more specifically, its relation to knowledge and power, to which Sontag had alluded. Concurrently, the Departments of French and English at Yale were earning a reputation as "a metonym for theory,"[94] where literary critics, theorists, and philosophers, including Paul de Man, Jacques Derrida, and, later, Fredric Jameson, set forth aesthetic education as a way of questioning historical objects and objectification itself. While the School of Art remained insulated from these developments, these influential theorists' ideas, particularly regarding the ongoing construction of power through common social forms, such as language, nevertheless constituted a foundation of cultural scholarship that profoundly affected art criticism, especially in its less market-bound reaches. *October*, for example, a break-off academic journal founded in 1976 by the art and film critic Annette Michelson and the art historian and critic Rosalind E. Krauss, commissioned in-depth essays of art criticism steeped in poststructuralism, deconstructivism, psychoanalysis, and feminism, thus presenting an alternative perspective to *Artforum*, which had been the primary monthly art publication of the era. In the United Kingdom, the cultural theorist Stuart Hall contributed to the conceptualization of "cultural studies," which entailed transdisciplinary critical analysis of contemporary conditions. "Critical studies," "critical practice," and "critical issues" had arrived in the art world, as critics and theorists began taking into consideration the social transformations of a multicultural society to address wide-ranging perspectives—feminist, queer, postcolonial, and more.

During the 1980s, as a neoliberal economic agenda proliferated in the United States and Europe, governmental protections for health, employment, and the environment steadily eroded. Against this backdrop, the art market boomed, consecrating what the art historian and curator Paul Ardenne described in his paper "The Art Market of the 1980s" as a "marriage" between art and the market, one that "established a new type of businessperson collector who used the market as a stock exchange … [and for whom] contemporary art was simultaneously a cultural alibi and a portfolio of stocks."[95] Critical studies and what came to be known as "research-based artistic practice" were attempts to distinguish art from the market and from the culture industry at large. Theorists demanded that the political resonance of all cultural artifacts be acknowledged. As Jameson wrote in *The Political*

94   Marc Redfield, *Theory at Yale: The Strange Case of Deconstruction in America* (New York: Fordham University Press, 2016), 3.

95   Paul Ardenne, "The Art Market of the 1980s," *International Journal of Political Economy* 25, no. 2 (Summer 1995): 116.

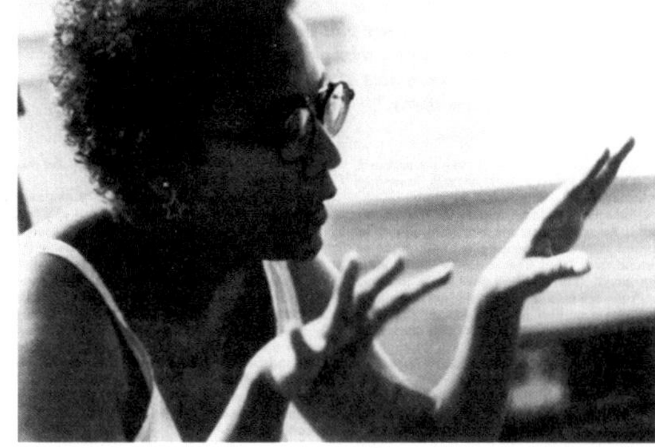

bell hooks in conversation with Helen Tworkov, 1992. Photo by Jeri Coppola. © Jeri Coppola.

   THEORY AND PRACTICE: THE RISE OF CRITICAL AND CULTURAL STUDIES

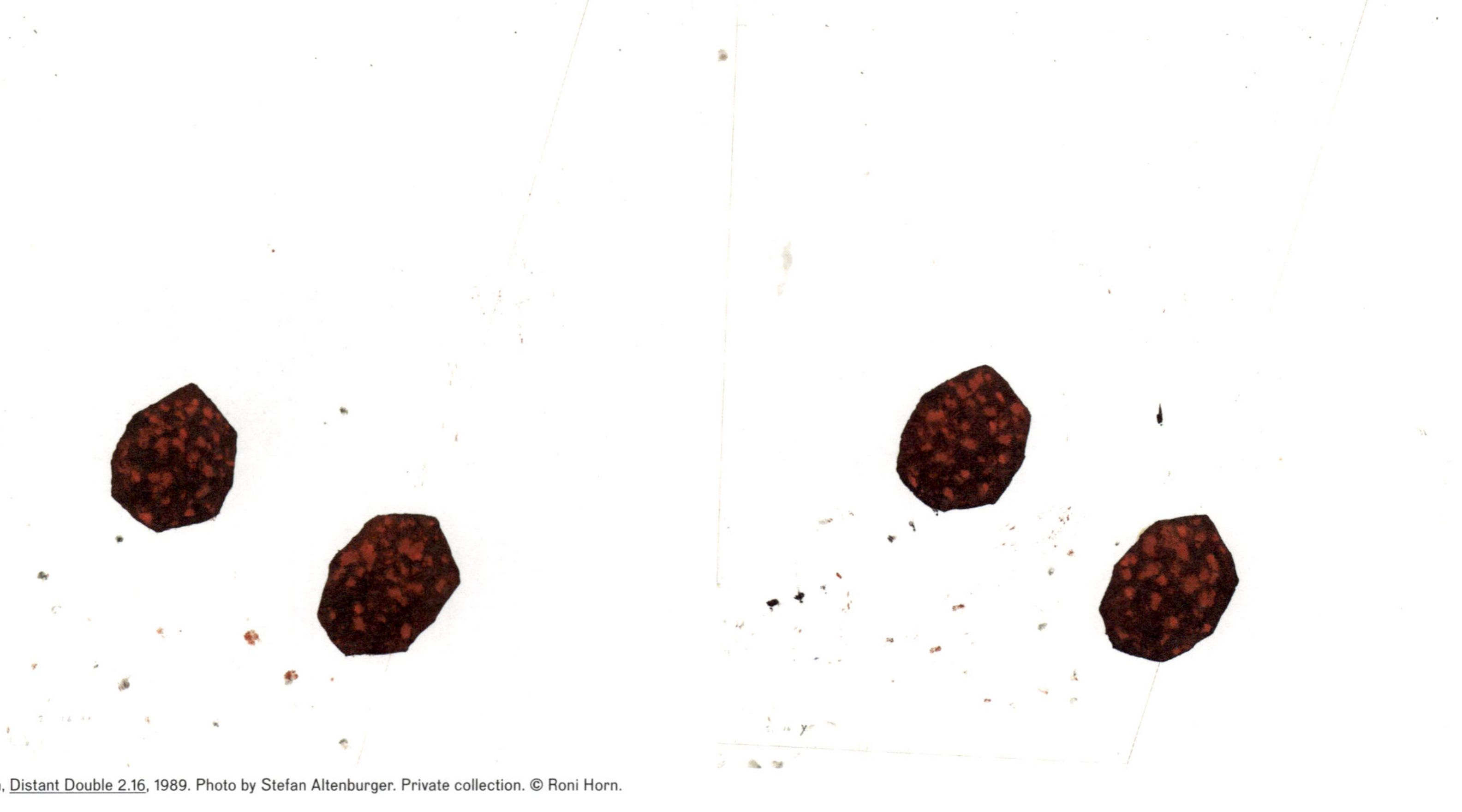

Roni Horn, _Distant Double 2.16_, 1989. Photo by Stefan Altenburger. Private collection. © Roni Horn.

96   Fredric Jameson, *The Political Unconscious: Narrative as a Socially Symbolic Act* (Ithaca, N.Y.: Cornell University Press, 1981), 20.

97   bell hooks, "The Oppositional Gaze: Black Female Spectators," in *Black Looks: Race and Representation* (Boston: South End Press, 1992), 126.

98   bell hooks, *Teaching to Transgress: Education as the Practice of Freedom* (New York: Routledge, 1994), 10.

Unconscious: Narrative as a Socially Symbolic Act, "The convenient working distinction between cultural texts that are social and political and those that are not becomes something worse than an error: namely, a symptom and a reinforcement of the reification and privatization of contemporary life."[96] Such a perspective, however, did not enter the School of Art, despite having been formulated literally right around the corner and despite Jameson's work having served as a primary touchstone for critical thought within the field of art from the 1980s onward.

Debates over criticality and the relationship of critique to the visual arts grew in tandem with the rise of feminism and the ascent of women to positions of authority beginning in the 1970s. Gloria Jean Watkins, better known by her pen name, bell hooks, was an Assistant Professor in the Departments of Afro-American Studies and English from 1985 to 1988. During this time, she began laying the groundwork for feminist theory by providing historical evidence of the sexism endured by Black female slaves and its effect on contemporary Black womanhood, publishing her pivotal works *Ain't I a Woman: Black Women and Feminism* in 1981, and *Feminist Theory: From Margin to Center* in 1984. In her essay "The Oppositional Gaze: Black Female Spectators," she wrote, "Given the context of class exploitation, and racist and sexist domination, it has only been through resistance, struggle, reading, and looking 'against the grain,' that black women have been able to value our process of looking enough to publicly name it,"[97] emphasizing the importance of "engaged pedagogy" as a mode of critical practice enabling the transformation of dominant narratives and the valuation of multiple, previously unacknowledged experiences.[98]

At the School of Art, graduate students, particularly those in the Department of Painting, contested what they felt to be the department's dominant concern with figuration and its formalist approaches to art as well as its marginalization of other conceptual frameworks—including the intersectionality that professors like hooks were exploring. They demanded that the curriculum be revised and new faculty added. As a result, students were granted the right to invite three outside lecturers, among them the American conceptual artist Mel Bochner, who arrived in 1979 as a Visiting Professor of Painting and who continued to teach at the School as a part-time faculty member through 2008. Bochner introduced the "Critical Issues" seminar in Painting, which was organized as close readings of critical perspectives regarding works of art, including, for example, Martin Heidegger's *The Origin of the Work of Art* (1935) and Derrida's *Restitutions of the Truth in Pointing* (1978). Bochner continued to lead seminars at the School over the following decades, with courses such as "When Language Enters the Studio," in which students investigated the relationship of language to contemporary art practice, both as a system of signs and as a social system.

Though discussions of poststructuralist theory did not pervade the School, some artists had begun to engage with related concepts in their work. Roni Horn (MFA 1978), for example, did not attend the courses at Yale given by either de Man or Derrida, but her practice evolved around the aesthetic function of language and the capacity of language to challenge the privileging of visual and haptic perception in aesthetic experience. When Horn applied to Yale in 1976, the selection jury for incoming students was, according to Winifred Lutz, comprised of faculty and enrolled students, mostly male, who partook in a communal review of applicants' work. Lutz vividly remembers Horn's submission, which consisted of two sets of slides—one addressing the identity of objects perceived in light, the other those same objects perceived in darkness. The reviewers responded raucously and dismissively to Horn's minimalist presentation. Lutz interrupted to contest, noting that if the School was requiring applicants to supply written statements along with their work the reviewers were obliged to read

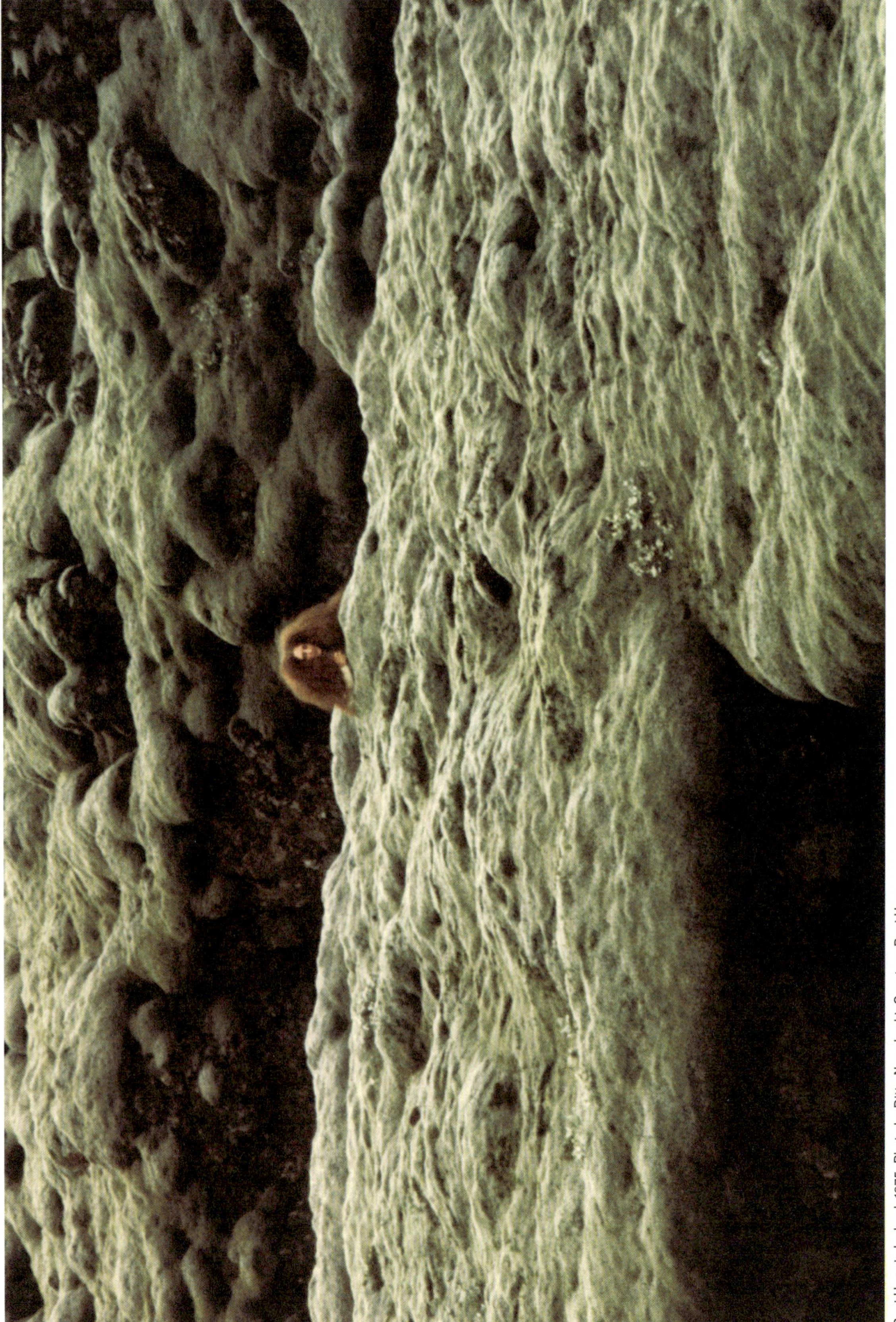

Roni Horn in Iceland, 1975. Photo by Ditto Nowakoski. Courtesy Roni Horn.

99   Winifred Lutz, telephone conversation with the author, February 11, 2020.

100   Mimi Thompson, "Roni Horn," *BOMB* 28 (July 1989).

101   Roni Horn, in "Roni Horn with Jarrett Earnest," *Brooklyn Rail* (December 2013–January 2014). brooklynrail. org/2013/12/art/roni-horn-with-jarrett-earnest.

those statements—at which point the group commenced to read Horn's text regarding the ambiguity inherent in any photographic depiction. Lutz's call for a consideration of Horn's work in the context of the artist's own writing led to the reevaluation and acceptance of her application.[99]

While at Yale, Horn says she felt estranged as an artist who was both gay and androgynous. She continued to develop a visual language around identity and difference and to explore the aesthetic function of language—work that evolved into her *Pair Object* series, reflecting her "acute awareness of circumstantial reality"[100] and ongoing concern with doubling. Horn's sexuality was not an explicit component of this work; nevertheless, she noted in a 2013 interview that:

> Coming from where I did, there is no question that that context was there. It was the early '80s. I think the AIDS crisis opened up people's willingness to engage sexuality publicly and it became more accessible, no longer something unspeakable. I remember the difference between what I was thinking and what people were seeing in that work and all the early *Pair Objects*. I don't know if I would have done those *Pair Objects* if I were a straight girl.[101]

Upon graduation, Horn received the Alice Kimball English Travelling Fellowship—Yale's oldest and largest endowed fellowship— and used the $5,000 grant to purchase and ship a motorbike to Iceland, where her travels through the country led to a long body of work exploring geology, spirituality, and indeterminacy. Horn's relationship to Iceland was the foundation for the *Library of Water* (*Vatnasafn*) (2007)

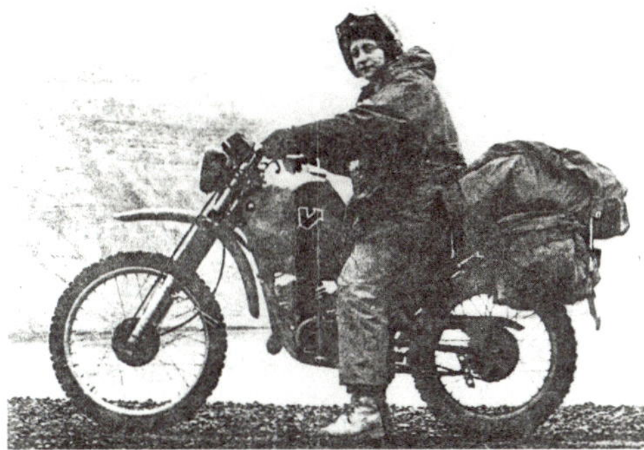

Roni Horn on a motorbike, Iceland, 1979. Photo by Harry Lieberman. Courtesy Roni Horn.

[see pp. 90–91], commissioned by London-based arts organization Artangel and realized in a converted mid-century library located in the small Icelandic town of Stykkishólmur, where Horn installed twenty-four floor-to-ceiling glass columns, containing water from different glaciers located around Iceland. Horn taught at Colgate University from 1978 until 1981, then actively began exhibiting in Europe.

Lorraine Wild (MFA 1982), entered the School of Art as a Graphic Design student after studying at Cranbrook Academy of Art under Katherine McCoy, in a program that was later considered a bastion of deconstructivist and poststructuralist thought. Ten years earlier, a notorious debate between Dutch graphic designers Wim Crouwel and Jan van Toorn had taken place in Amsterdam, setting terms of opposition between two schools of thought regarding objectivity and subjectivity in graphic design and the proper role of designers—as either supposedly neutral intermediaries striving for rationality or necessarily entangled subjects steering their work with unavoidably political consequences. Wild's interest in pursuing graduate studies grew from a desire to explore the history of teaching within the field, specifically as canonized at the Bauhaus in the 1920s and 1930s. Bauhaus faculty later immigrated to the United States, where they became influential pedagogues, seeking to dissolve hierarchies between the fine and applied arts while also focusing on function in design. By the time Wild arrived at Yale, the Bauhaus-influenced curriculum established by Albers had been adapted by the faculty, including American graphic designer Paul Rand,who combined his own corporate modernist formalism with his advocacy for typographic training imported from the Kunstgewerbeschule, in Basel, Switzerland. (For many years the School of Art ran a joint summer school in partnership with the Kunstgewerbeschule, led by Paul Rand and Swiss graphic designer

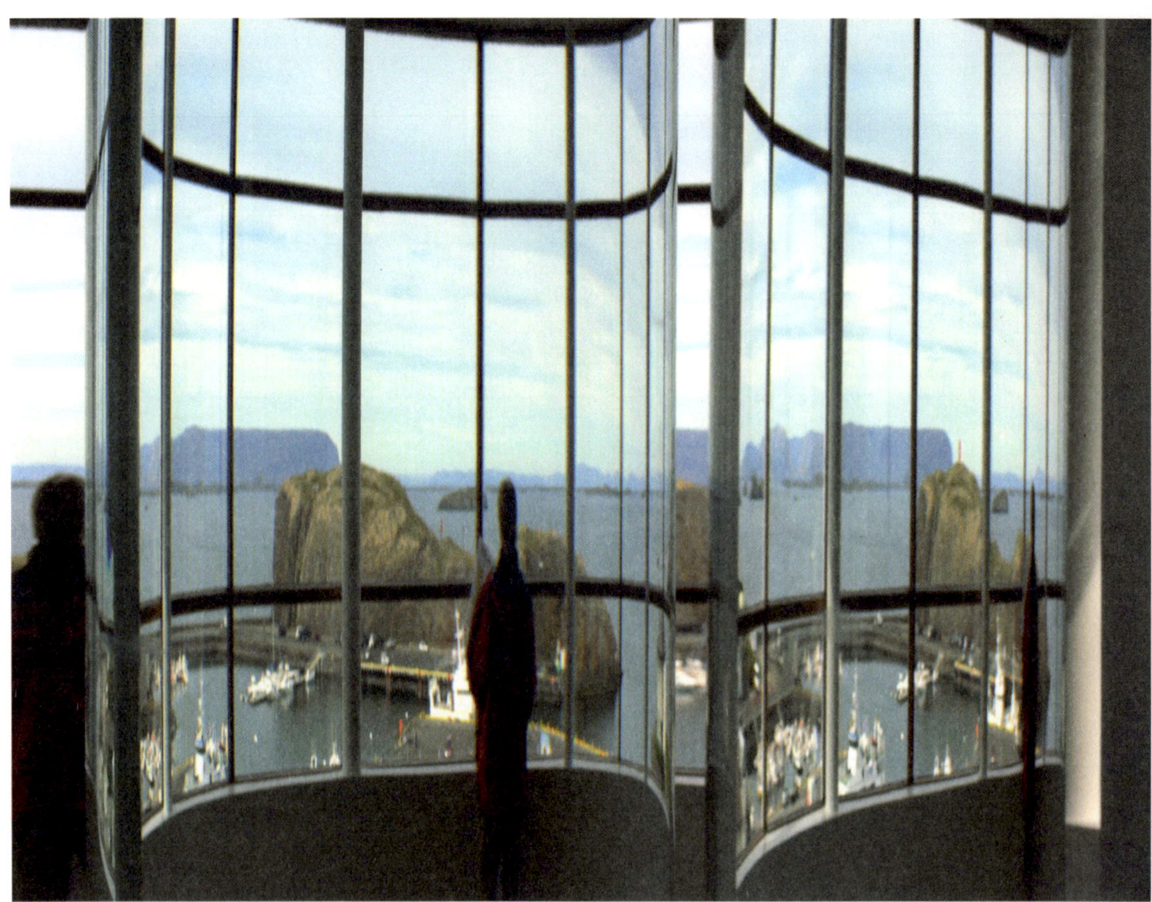

Christian Bickel, detail of Roni Horn's <u>VATNASAFN / LIBRARY OF WATER</u>, 2007.
© Christian Bickel/Wikimedia Commons/CC-BY-SA-2.0-DE.

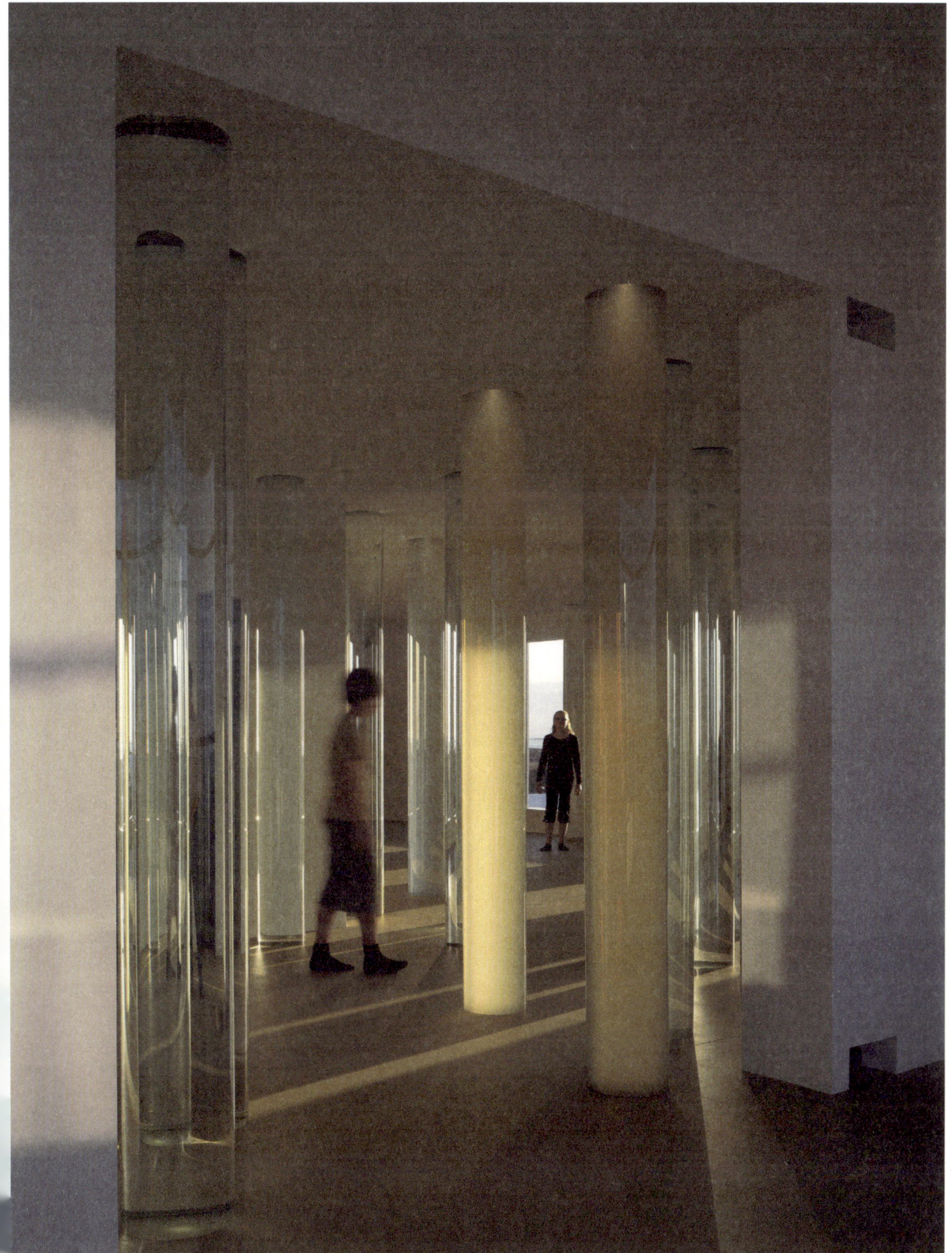

Roni Horn, <u>Water, Selected</u>, 2007. Permanent installation at <u>VATNASAFN / LIBRARY OF WATER</u>, Stykkishólmur, Iceland. Commissioned by Artangel. Photo by Stefan Altenburger. © Roni Horn.

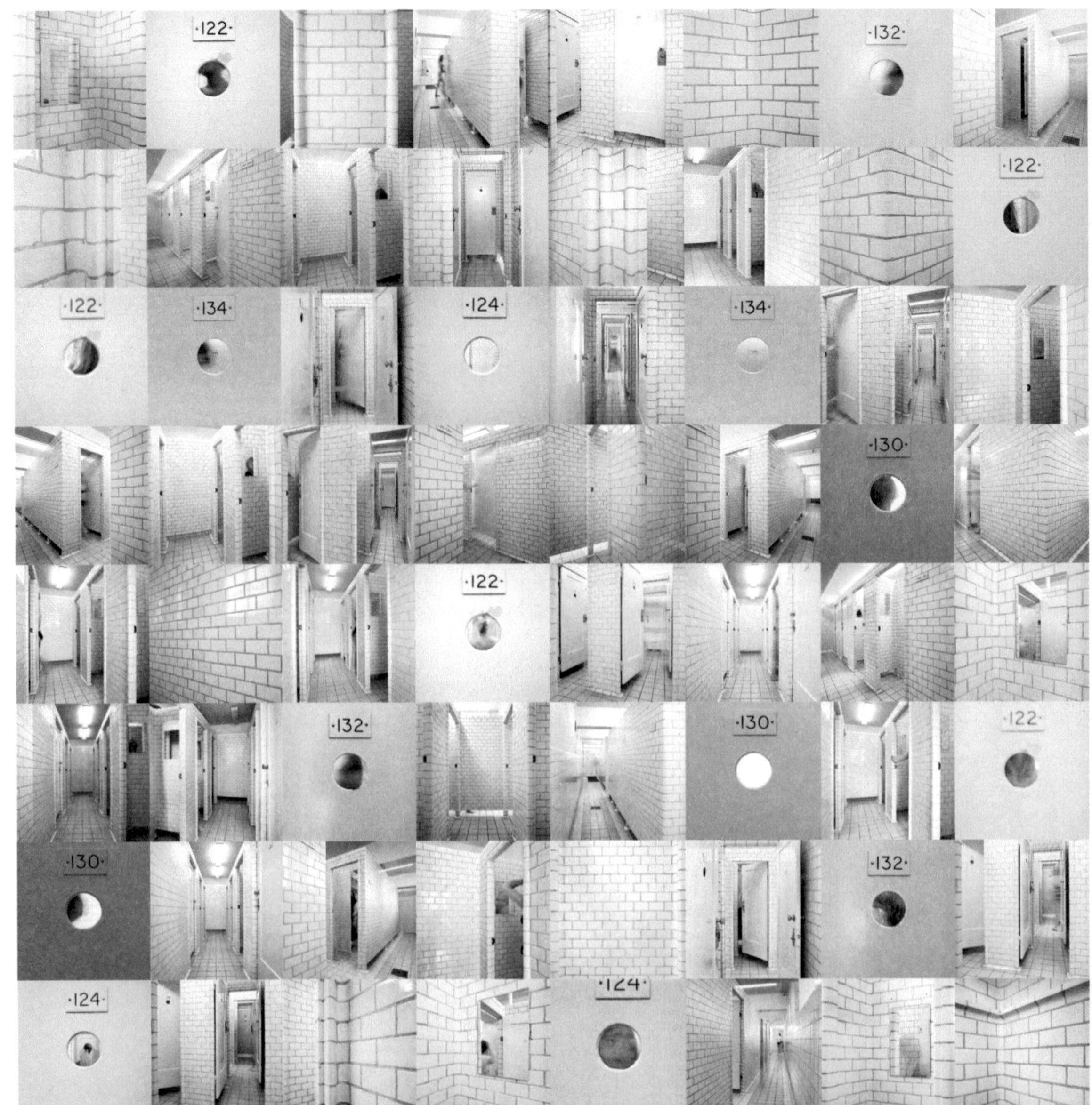

Roni Horn, <u>Her, Her, Her, and Her</u>, 2002–03. Solomon R. Guggenheim Museum, New York, gift Perry Wolfman, 2007. © Roni Horn.

Armin Hoffman.) Wild perceived the Rand curriculum as calculated and prescriptive in comparison with the earlier, more experimental style of working and thinking typified by Albers and Herbert Matter.[102]

Wild approached Rand and Bradbury Thompson—an American designer known for influential and often highly graphic typography that commented on the legacies of printing—as "historical artifacts," who, by the time she arrived at Yale, "represented a stultified formalist practice with no inclination to revisit some of the foundations of their earlier teaching." She says Rand was "rudely resistant" and Thompson "passive aggressive" in their adherence to the idea that modernism is timeless, noting, "The very philosophy of design that they had embodied was part of the reason they resisted speaking about how the work really came together or how they communicated their ideas to their clients."[103] After all, if a work is timeless and universal, then it needs no explanation, and, by the same token, if a work needs no explanation, it must be timeless and universal. The tools of critical discourse are anathema to such truisms.

Despite resistance from the faculty toward her research, which amounted to abandonment of supervision, Wild committed to writing an essay for her thesis project—an unconventional approach. Eventually, Dean Andrew Forge intervened on Wild's behalf, arguing that her proposed research was legitimate and helping to locate readers outside the design department.[104] There was no art or design school in the U.S. offering a graduate degree in design history that she was aware of at the time, and Wild found it necessary to conduct most of her research in the archives of the New York Public Library. She also sought inspiration in areas beyond the School, noting the "electricity" within the Departments of Comparative Literature and English, and adding that American Studies was a department with "many material culture people who were interested in speaking about visual culture and visual studies in … alternative ways." She continues, "They were not driven by those grand old men … in the Art and Art History Department[s]." Wild recalls a "classic Alvin Eisenman" story in which Eisenman, recognizing her particular pedagogical interests and her frustration, suggested: "You know, there's someone teaching over in Comparative Literature that I've heard people say is interesting, and he talks about something called postmodernism, which I don't understand." "Well, who is that?" Wild asked. She says Eisenman replied, "Oh, this Italian guy, Umberto Eco." Wild took Eisenman's advice to enroll in Eco's post-semiotic theory course, along with many other photographers and architects, discovering that Eco taught by way of vivid tales that were so engaging it was difficult to do anything but engage. When she returned to Eisenman to thank him for telling her about the course, he reportedly said, "Yeah, but it just makes no sense. How could there be any such thing as the postmodern?"[105]

Before graduate school, Wild worked with Massimo Vignelli at Vignelli Associates, one of the most highly respected offices at that time. There she focused on publications such as *Oppositions*, which had been produced by the Institute for Architecture and Urban Studies (IAUS) founded by Peter Eisenman in 1967. Wild was commissioned after graduation to design the 400-page monograph of the American architect John Hejduk, who directed the architecture program at Cooper Union. An article she wrote during this time, titled "More Than a Few Questions about Design Education," [see pp. 96–98] published in the Society of Typographic Art's *Design Journal*, captured the attention of Catherine Lord, the dean of the School of Art at CalArts. Lord turned Cal Arts' Graphic Design department over to Wild in 1985, when Wild was just thirty-two years old. Wild consolidated the faculty, built a curriculum, and revived the graduate program.

102   Wild also observed that Albers' legacy had migrated beyond the Department of Graphic Design to the Department of Painting. Toward the end of her studies, she recalls a daylong symposium in honor of the thirtieth anniversary of Albers' arrival at the School, which was organized by and composed almost entirely of painters and sculptors, without the participation of any design students or the remaining faculty members that Albers had originally hired; Lorraine Wild, telephone conversation with the author, January 28, 2020.

103   Ibid.

104   Wild also recalls that classmate Katy Homans (MFA 1982), chose to write an essay on British designer Robert Brownjohn and encountered the same amount of resistance to her thesis that Wild had. Ibid.

105   Ibid.

    THEORY AND PRACTICE: THE RISE OF CRITICAL AND CULTURAL STUDIES

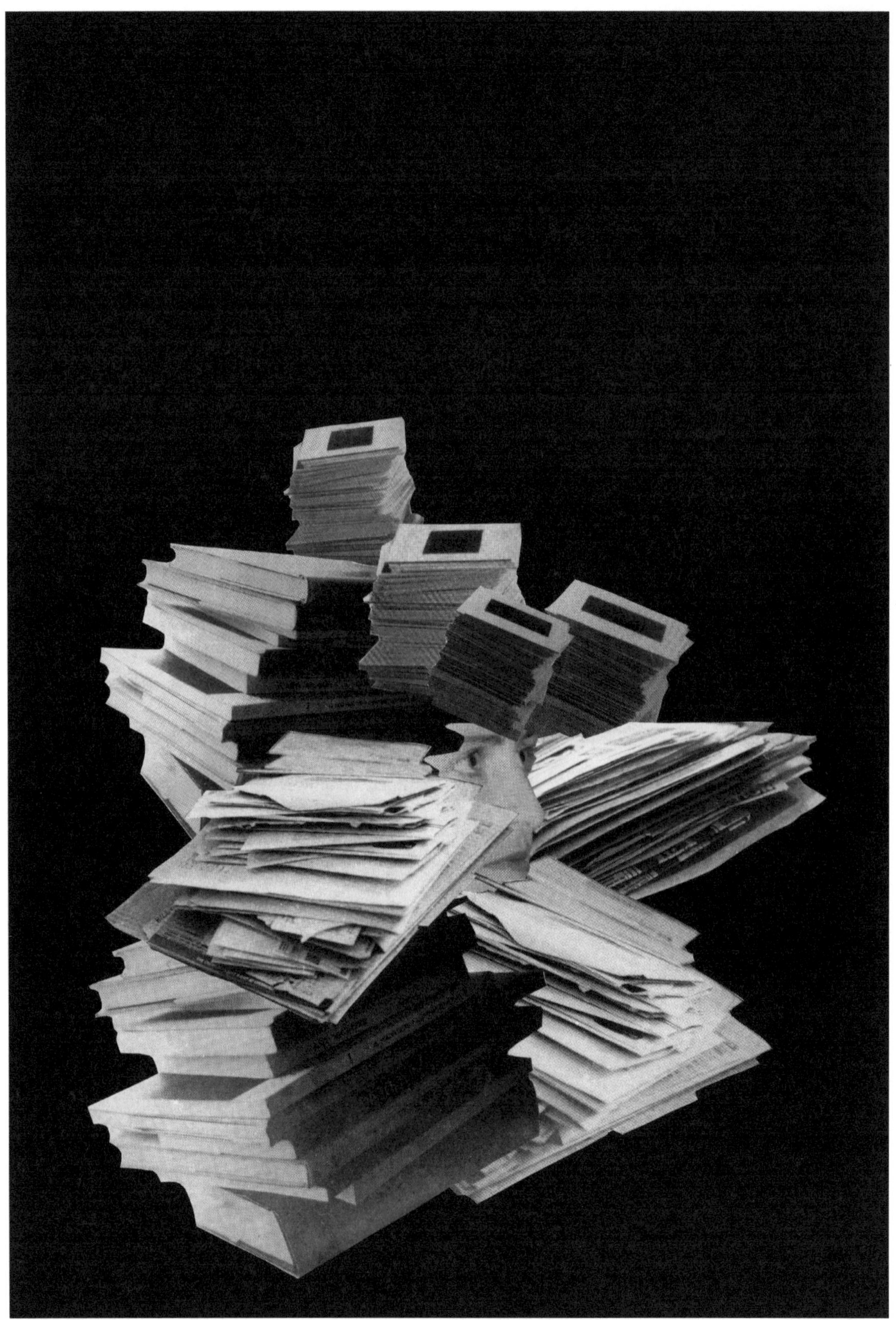

Lorraine Wild, self-portrait assignment from visiting artist Shigeo Fukada, Yale School of Art, 1981. Courtesy Lorraine Wild.

106 Ibid.

In looking back on her graduate studies, Wild notes that sexism was prevalent and went unquestioned, that "it was just there, and women kind of laughed about it, but there was no critical mass to somehow deal with it … It was always around the issue of feeling somehow not taken seriously and not treated as equal. That was the struggle one had to deal with."[106] Not until eight years after Wild's graduation from Yale would Sheila Levrant de Bretteville (BFA 1963; MFA 1964) become the first woman appointed as Director of Graduate Studies and tenured Professor in Graphic Design at the Yale School of Art.

More Than a Few Questions About Design Education

By Lorraine Wild

"How did you become a graphic designer?" Until recently this was one of the most interesting questions you could ask a graphic designer. Before the proliferation of professionally oriented BFA and MFA programs, designers received their training in all sorts of interesting ways. It seems that any academic or artistic discipline — art history, history, painting, physics, architecture, psychology, literature, education, writing — could provide a perfect background for the nascent designer. The common impulse shared by these designers of different backgrounds was their desire to translate thought and idea into a visual form; and in that process, to connect their personal knowledge with a larger world. The methods by which they could achieve this role in the communication of ideas were as varied as their backgrounds and as hard to define; thus all the jokes designers share about not being able to explain to inquisitive parents just what it is they do for a living. Methodology was sparse: the only general rule one could draw about craft or technique in graphic design was that a good sense of it would be necessary in order to successfully carry an idea through to its finished form. In its most basic sense, design is a conceptual project, and an idea is the catalyst for all subsequent action and results of that action. In other words, design is thought made manifest. "Problem solving," "asking the right questions," "making connections" — all of these phrases which we use to define the essential aspect of design activity are actually descriptions of the cause and effect of thought and energy; two very difficult things to teach.

But as our information based society needs (and produces) more and more designers to make visual sense out of its enormous output, the question of how to best prepare designers and what the ideal course of study would be becomes more intense. The lack of quantifiable evidence on the effect of specific design curricula condemns all opinions expressed about the topic to be just that — opinions. Mine are based on my experience as a student and practitioner of graphic design history, and not on my limited teaching experience. Like many other graphic designers, I had to invent my own course of study through a combination of schooling, working, and reading; and despite the fact that I have both BFA and MFA degrees in my chosen field, I, along with most of my peers, could not characterize my formal education as anything but "ad-hoc." This is a result of two conditions; the role of graphic design in the greater culture and the pedagogical "ad-hocism" of the 1970's. The former condition is a permanent one, a fact that any educator has to confront; that graphic design is an intimate reflection of its own time. "Ad-hocism" was temporary; the questions being raised now about the state of graphic design education are, in part, a reaction against an excessive preoccupation with the generalists' point of view that characterized so much schooling during the 1970's.

It has been noted in the pages of this journal that the design field is reaching a plateau of maturity (evidenced by the specialization of design practice and an increase in the body of knowledge about design) and that design programs are not responding to the growing sophistication of the field.[1] There is no doubt that design is in a growth period, and the advancement of knowledge that is the result of professional research can only be positive. But is the ongoing specialization of design practice a good thing? Should the specialization be institutionalized into the profession by its inclusion in undergraduate education? Should an 18-year-old be able to choose graphic design as a profession, and, within a year or two, be able to define a specialty within that discipline to further concentrate upon? These questions inevitably cause the design educator to define more closely just what he thinks design is — an art, a science, a branch of the humanities? History has shown us that the best graphic design is synthetic — it is the work that makes imaginative connections between different disciplines or modes of thought that we always admire. If we expect a student to "make form a meaningful thing"[2] then the student has to understand, in the first place, the importance of meaning, and secondly, the means by which meaning is conveyed. Finally, students must see themselves within the historical continuum of visual and verbal communicators.

It is my opinion that while specialization may be appropriate to graduate work, undergraduate study should remain a bastion of generalism, but not in a way which translates into mediocrity or the lack of a plan. The generalism that is desirable is not in terms of design technique or theory, but is something external that will supplement design studies. For instance, there are many undergraduate programs that offer a BS or BA with a major in architecture. These programs insist that a student complete a full schedule of academic classes along with studio courses — and it is assumed that students who are serious about becoming architects will continue their professional training in graduate school. If the graphic design profession is ever to reach maturity, not only in the minds of its own members, but in those of the outside world as well, it has to rid itself of the idea that majoring in design is less demanding on a student's literacy.

To "major in design and minor in (some other discipline)" could actually

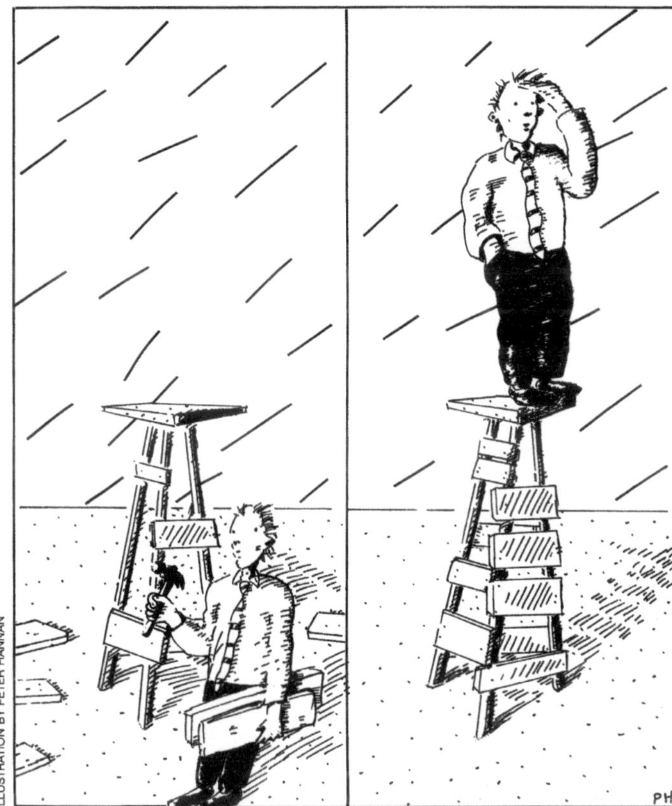

strengthen the undergraduate design degree, because the experience gained in the pursuit of a minor would add to the student's conceptual baggage — the most valuable possession a designer walks out of college with (along with a portfolio).

So what actual design training should an undergraduate receive? The obvious basics of drawing, typography, and photography are unchallenged, but they should be supplemented with classes on design methodology, design history and communications theory. The studio courses should concentrate on building a foundation of skills and approaches that the student will be able to depend on to guide them through the tough problems and changing technologies they will encounter after they leave school. A curriculum that builds upon a specific philosophy or point of view is preferable to one that exposes the student to conflicting, indefinite points of view. Again, the goal is to build a foundation for further growth.[3] It is true that students can pursue this variation independently through an interdisciplinary program; but it would be much better if the studies were directed and supported by the design department. There is no reason why this sort of program could not be implemented at an art school as well — in fact, it is important that the standards for a BA or BFA in graphic design be the same, whether from a university or an art school, for it has its ultimate effect on the credibility of the profession itself.

If this idealized undergraduate education sounds a little light on the studio side — and it would be (a student would probably spend most of their first two years completing the academic requirements), then graduate school becomes a more important step for the student who is seriously committed to becoming a professional. If a student chose to stop their education with the undergraduate degree, at least they would be armed with a legitimate education and the basic skills necessary to handle an entry-level job with competence.

Graduate school is the place where specialization in design education belongs. The graduate departments of many universities have definite philosophies, usually formed by the interests of their strongest faculty, and they attract students based on those areas of emphasis. The student who goes to study at a particular department usually knows exactly what they are going to be concentrating on and why. There is no reason why this would not work in graphic design education. As the body of knowledge about graphic design grows, it becomes clear that there are specific areas of study that deserve (in fact, desperately need) departments devoted to advanced research.

If a greater consensus could be reached on the standards for a BA or BFA, graduate schools would be freer to pursue more advanced levels of aesthetic, theoretical, or methodological research. The problem with many graduate programs in graphic design now is that even the best schools cannot count on building a program for a pool of qualified students with a common level of skills. Too much time out of the precious two years of an MFA program is spent building a shared level of competency before students are able to approach the more complex issues appropriate to graduate study.

It has been said that one of the reasons more students are attracted to design schools and departments is because they perceive design to be a more pragmatic field in these years of severe job insecurity. It is ironic because the design profession is at the threshold of a time, as are so many other professions, when technology will eliminate many entry-level jobs. The best way to insure a vital role for designers is to prepare them for the complexity of social conditions which will form the context of their work. Sophistication of tools or facilities in a design department is irrelevant. Four years of "textural studies" at a drawing board *or* a computer terminal are not going to prepare anyone to face the challenge of being a communicator in the 1980's or 1990's.

To sum up, the course of undergraduate and graduate study in graphic design should reflect the dual nature of graphic design itself. It is a generalist's discipline in that it provides a pivot by which the great mass of graphic communication is transformed, perceived, and understood. It is a specialist's discipline in that certain very specific bodies of knowledge are required to develop in order for the individual designer and the entire profession to continue to thrive. To lose sense of either of these qualities of design would distort the definition of graphic design itself.

But what about that ineffable step in anyone's education, what Alvin Lustig called the "transforming experience, this sudden opening of the eye"?[4] What information suddenly bonds the student to the subject, driving him to carry on his education in a self-directed manner, beyond the years spent in school? The design profession can legislate educational standards, but not innovation or excitement. We can only hope that inspired professionals devote their energies to teaching, and that each committed student be lucky enough to encounter one of those teachers some time between freshman year and graduation day. ∎

Notes

1. Patrick Whitney. "Why Design Education Is Not Working" *The Design Journal*, vol. 1, no. 1, 1983. Chicago, IL, 1983. Pg. 31.

2. Alvin Lustig. "Designing, a Process of Teaching" *The Collected Writings of Alvin Lustig*, New Haven, CT, 1958. Pg. 15.

3. Gordon Salchow. "Two Myths about Design Education" *Print*, vol. 35, no. 6, November-December 1981. Pg. 74.

4. Alvin Lustig. "Designing, a Process of Teaching," Pg. 15.

Lorraine Wild is an assistant professor at the University of Houston and teaches graphic design within the School of Architecture. She combines her teaching with an ongoing design practice and design history research. Ms. Wild holds an MFA from Yale University and a BFA from Cranbrook Academy of Art.

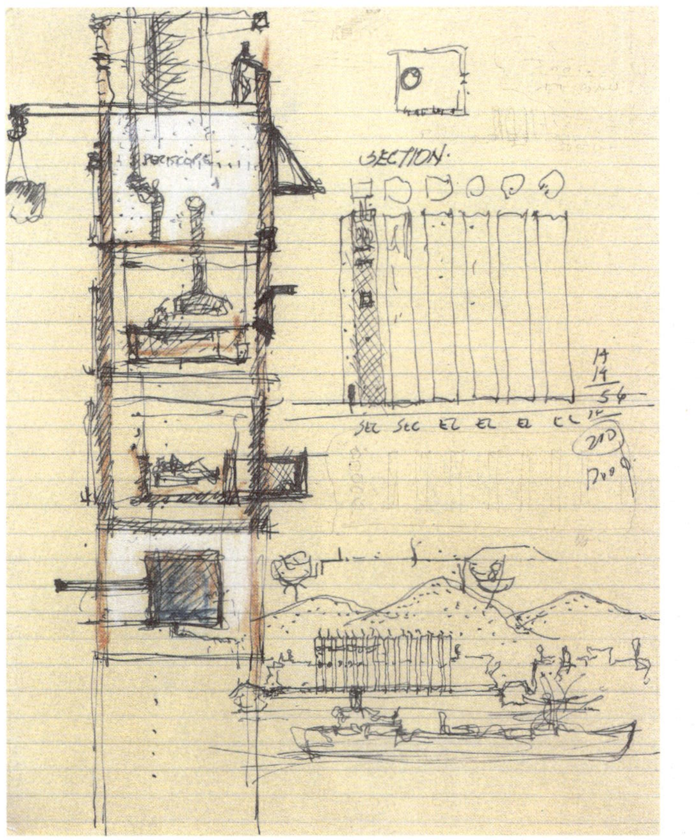

Lorraine Wild, page from John Hejduk: Mask of Medusa, 1989. Courtesy Lorraine Wild.

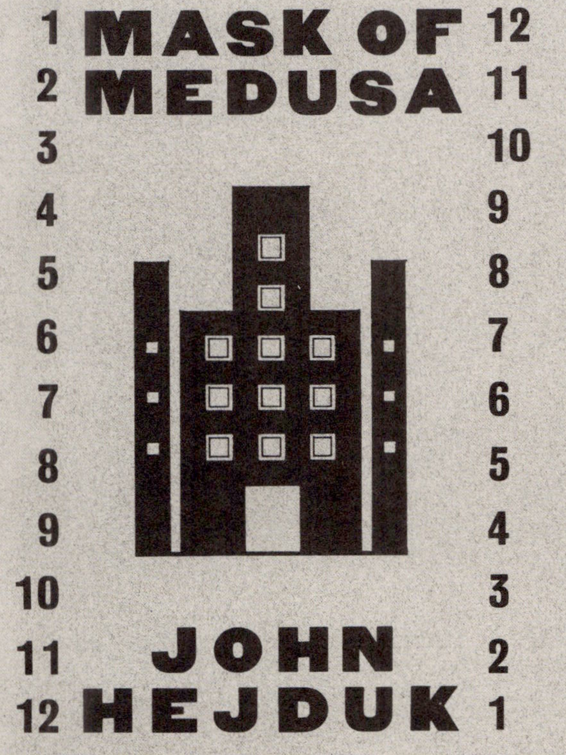

Lorraine Wild, cover of John Hejduk: Mask of Medusa, 1989. Courtesy Lorraine Wild.

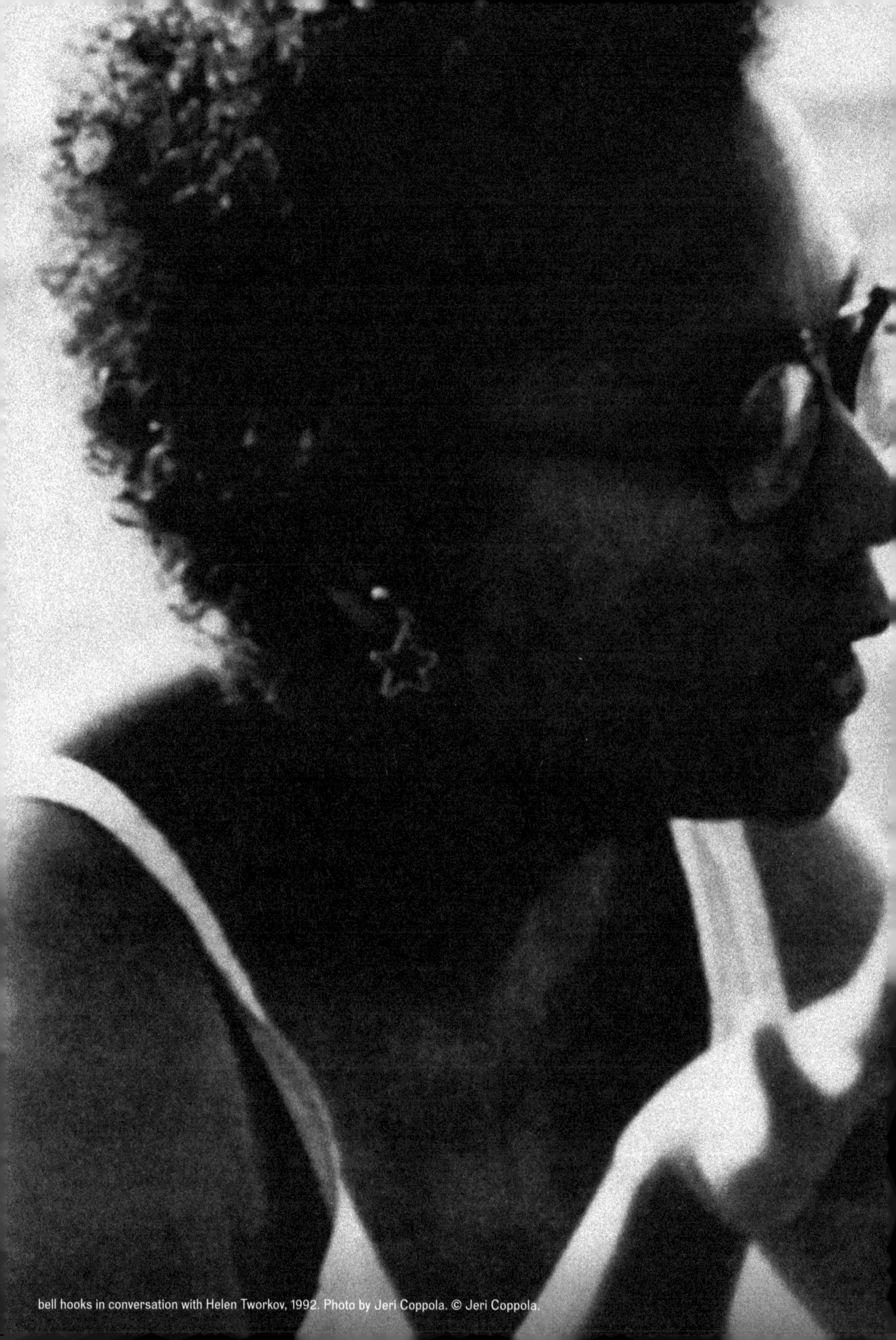

bell hooks in conversation with Helen Tworkov, 1992. Photo by Jeri Coppola. © Jeri Coppola.

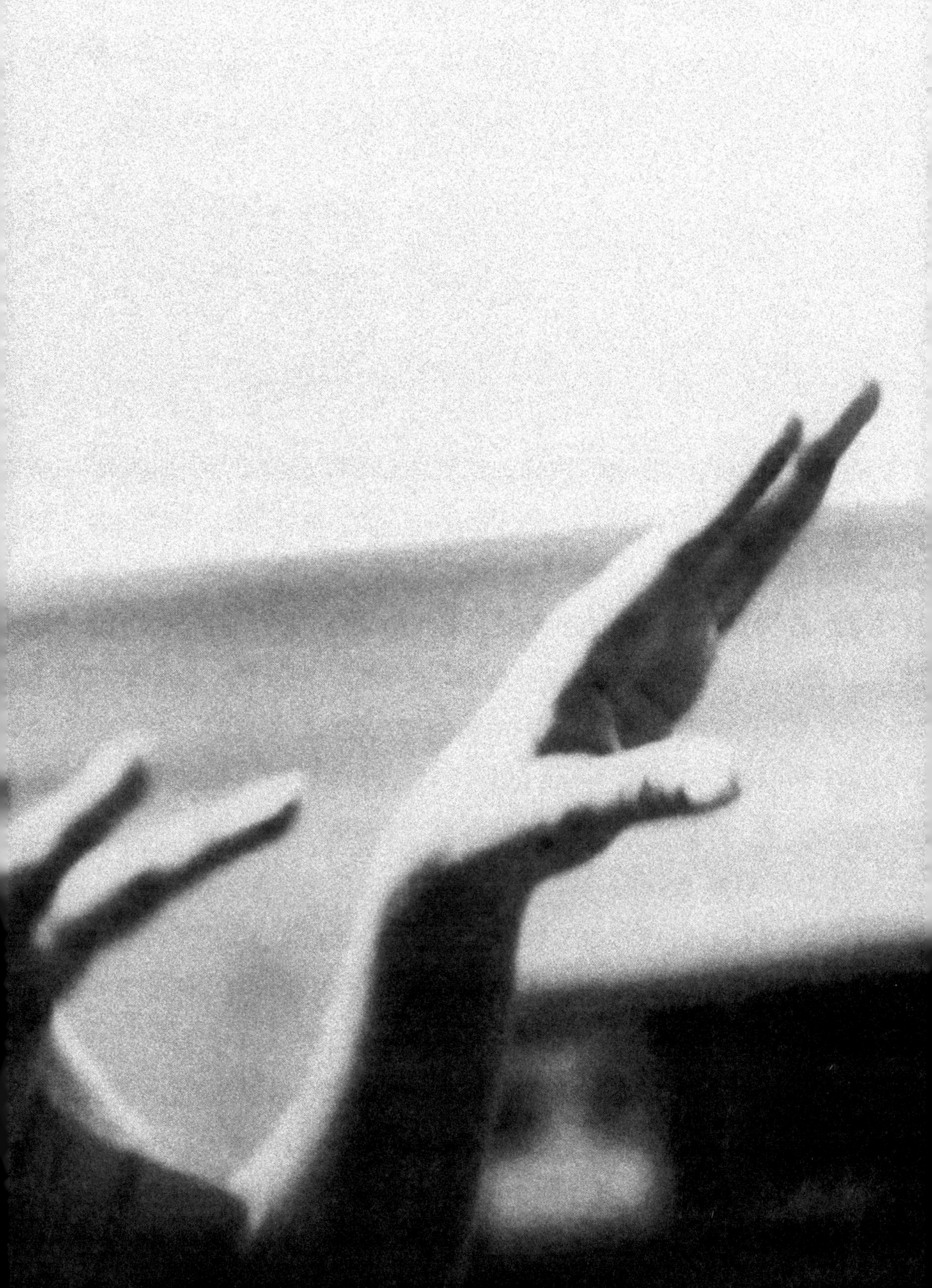

OCCUPYING SPACE
AS AN ACT OF AGENCY

National and international recognition of women graduates and undergraduates from and affiliated with the School of Art continued to grow as their enrollment increased and they developed networks of mutual support both within and beyond the School. The 1982 commission of Maya Lin's winning proposal for the Vietnam Veterans Memorial in Washington, D.C., granted while she was still an undergraduate at Yale, marked a milestone achievement for women in the fields of art, architecture, and design. Selected during her senior year of studies as the winner of a national competition, Lin became not only the creator of one of the most significant monuments in the nation's history but also the first woman to design a federal monument for the National Mall. The requirements for the D.C. memorial indicated that all 57,000 names of those missing and killed be included in the final design, and that the design be apolitical.[107] In thinking about her proposal [see p. 104], Lin recalled that in the Memorial Rotunda at Yale's Woolsey Hall are engravings of all the names of the Yale alumni killed in previous wars, inviting those passing by to "feel" the individual inscriptions. Lin visited the site where the memorial would be erected and imagined "taking a knife and cutting into the earth, opening it up, an initial violence that in time would heal."[108] The remaining challenge was to "find the chronology for the names of the dead." She recalls, "Between the first and second crit, my professor [Andy Burr] advised me that the apex was very important, at which point I switched the chronology from starting on the left side."[109] On the finished memorial, the names are in chronological order beginning at the apex of the wall, then circling back to the far left end and rejoining the apex.[110]

107 Maya Lin, *Boundaries* (New York: Simon and Schuster, 2000), 4:10.

108 Ibid., 4:11.

109 Maya Lin, telephone conversation with the author, January 20, 2020.

110 "Frequently Asked Questions," National Park Service, Vietnam Veterans Memorial, updated November 9, 2017, www.nps.gov/vive/faqs.htm.

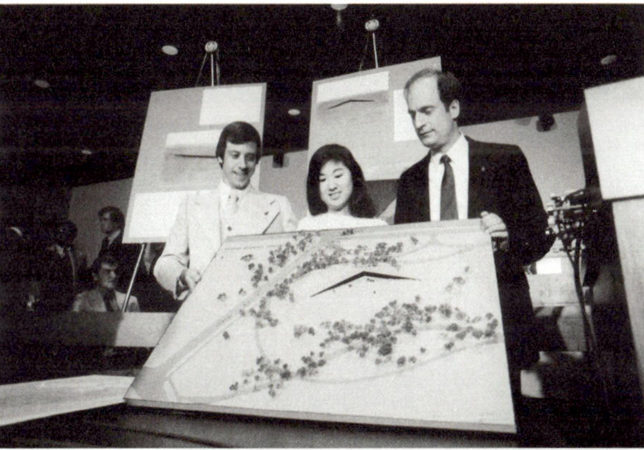

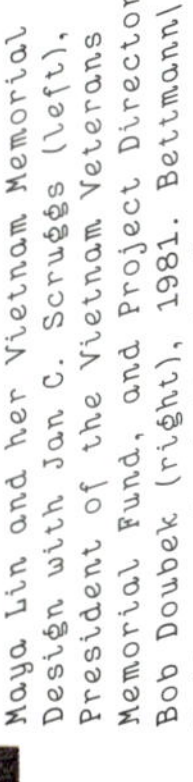

Maya Lin and her Vietnam Memorial Design with Jan C. Scruggs (left), President of the Vietnam Veterans Memorial Fund, and Project Director Bob Doubek (right), 1981. Bettmann\Bettmann via Getty Images.

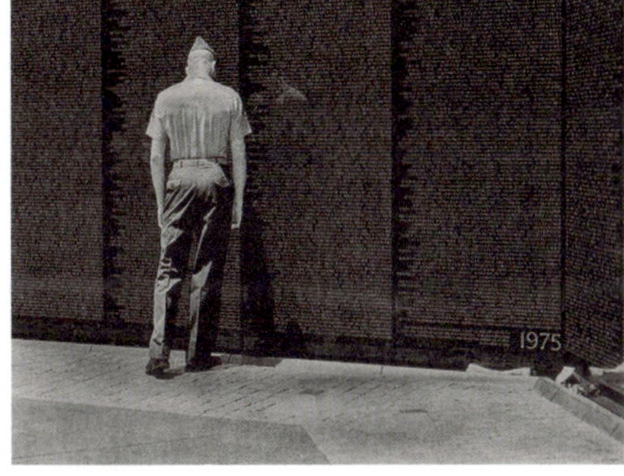

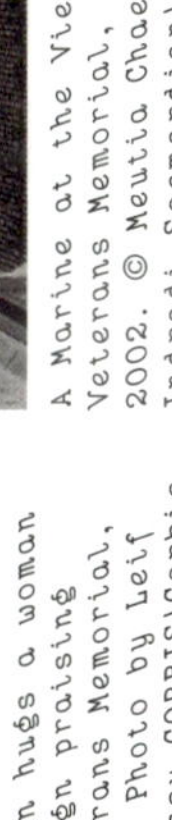

A Marine at the Vietnam Veterans Memorial, July 4, 2002. © Meutia Chaerani – Indradi Soemardjan\Wikimedia Commons\GNU FDL.

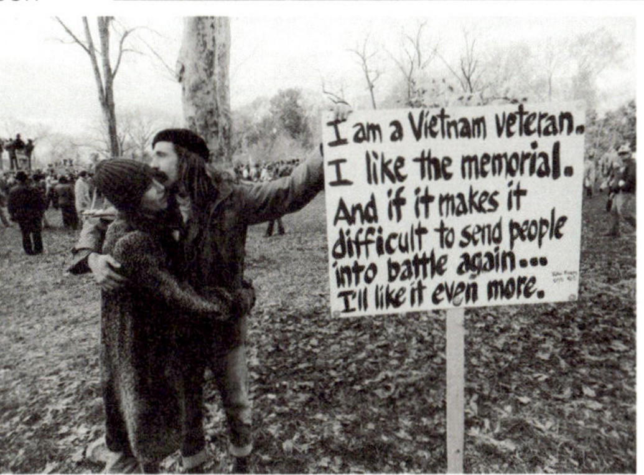

A Vietnam veteran hugs a woman as he holds a sign praising the Vietnam Veterans Memorial, January 1, 1983. Photo by Leif Skoogfors. Courtesy CORBIS\Corbis via Getty Images.

Walking through this park-like area, the memorial appears as a rift in the earth—a long, polished black stone wall, emerging from and receding into the earth. Approaching the memorial, the ground slopes gently downward, and the low walls emerging on either side, growing out of the earth, extend and converge at a point below and ahead. Walking into the grassy site contained by the walls of this memorial we can barely make out the carved names upon the memorial's walls. These names, seemingly infinite in number, convey the sense of overwhelming numbers, while unifying these individuals into a whole. For this memorial is meant not as a monument to the individual, but rather as a memorial to the men and women who died during this war, as a whole.

The memorial is composed not as an unchanging monument, but as a moving composition, to be understood as we move into and out of it; the passage itself is gradual, the descent to the origin slow, but it is at the origin that the meaning of this memorial is to fully understood. At the intersection of these walls, on the right side, at this wall's top is carved the date of the first death. It is followed by the names of those who have died in the war, in chronological order. These names continue on this wall, appearing to recede into the earth at the wall's end. The names resume on the left wall, as the wall emerges from the earth, continuing back to the origin, where the date of the last death is carved, at the bottom of this wall. Thus the war's beginning and end meet; the war is "complete", coming full circle, yet broken by the earth that bounds the angle's open side, and contained within the earth itself. As we turn to leave, we see these walls stretching into the distance, directing us to the Washington Monument to the left and the Lincoln Memorial to the right, thus bringing the Vietnam Memorial into historical context. We, the living are brought to a concrete realization of these deaths.

Brought to a sharp awareness of such a loss, it is up to each individual to resolve or come to terms with this loss. For death is in the end a personal and private matter, and the area contained within this memorial is a quiet place meant for personal reflection and private reckoning. The black granite walls, each 200 feet long, and 10 feet below ground at their lowest point (gradually ascending towards ground level) effectively act as a sound barrier, yet are of such a height and length so as not to appear threatening or enclosing. The actual area is wide and shallow; allowing for a sense of privacy and the sunlight from the memorial's southern exposure along with the grassy park surrounding and within it's wall contribute to the serenity of the area. Thus this memorial is for those who have died, and for us to remember them.

The memorial's origin is located approximately at the center of this site; it legs each extending 200 feet towards the Washington Monument and the Lincoln Memorial. The walls, contained on one side by the earth are 10 feet below ground at their point of origin, gradually lessening in height, until they finally recede totally into the earth at their ends. The walls are to be made of a hard, polished black granite, with the names to be carved in a simple Trajan letter, 3/4 inch high, allowing for nine inches in length for each name. The memorial's construction involves recontouring the area within the wall's boundaries so as to provide for an easily accessible descent, but as much of the site as possible should be left untouched (including trees). The area should be made into a park for all the public to enjoy.

111 Maya Lin, telephone conversation with the author, January 20, 2020.

112 Ibid.

113 Ibid.

114 Ibid.

115 Ursula von Rydingsvard, telephone conversation with the author, January 31, 2020.

116 Ibid.

Lin, an Architecture major, aspired to study art as well, and had applied for a double major in Architecture and Photography, but her request was denied by the senior faculty of the School of Art. The committee used Lin's request to spend part of her undergraduate studies abroad as justification for its denial. As she explains, they believed that "if you were serious about entering a double major—the art major—you would not be going away. And if you [decided] to go away, you [would] never amount to anything more than a second-rate draftsman."111 Despite this, Lin attended courses led by Richard Benson and Tod Papageorge, pursuing what she considered an "obsessional" interest in photography. "I might have double-majored in Photography," she says, "but if I had, I wouldn't have designed the Vietnam Memorial."112

Lin spent a year in Washington, battling for the validity of the monument before a Senate subcommittee while working to complete it. Later, she returned to Yale for her master's degree in Architecture, following a short stint at Harvard. Of her postgraduate studies at Yale, Lin says, "I arrived labeled within Architecture when I felt myself more an artist. So, I drifted over to the art department." She continues:

> When I was an undergraduate student in architecture, I was pretty much supported, but when I returned to graduate school, the faculty's expectations of me were different. There was an expectation that if I wanted to be an architect, I would have to be a different person. But I was still trying to figure out my voice in art. At one point, some architectural critics said, "We have no way to respond to your work. It's too intuitive." They thought I was rebelling, but I wasn't. It didn't matter to me; I was hanging out in Hammond Hall [where the Department of Sculpture was housed after the 1969 fire]. Ursula von Rydingsvard was amazing. She was very supportive, and I started making art.113

At Hammond Hall [see pp. 116–17], Lin noticed that "the boys got enormous studios." She added, "They just decided, 'Well, these artists are working on a bigger scale, and so they require the bigger space.' It opens the question then, if we as women had been given a bigger space, would our work have been different?"114

While the dearth of women among tenured faculty at the School of Art persisted through the 1980s, von Rydingsvard has been referred to by many graduates of that period as a revered mentor. Von Rydingsvard had been hired to join the Sculpture department under the direction of David von Schlegell, following the recommendation of a hiring committee that included Winifred Lutz, who wanted to ensure that her own position would be filled by a woman. She was promoted to Associate Professor in 1985, but eventually left to pursue a full-time practice as an artist, noting that the School's leadership seemed to have "a narrow idea with respect to the fact that good educators could and should be active practicing artists."115 She describes her teaching methodology as "looking at and following a student's work carefully as to what could be added or substituted, or how one could go about one's work to carry more depth. It required me to get into the student's mind and to understand how they changed over time. I felt very strongly my teaching was not about putting my own wants onto the project or defining who they should be. And I understood if, at times, what was articulated by the work might not be expressed verbally by the artists."116 Recalling the courses in which she taught Architecture students, including Maya Lin, von Rydingsvard says, "I wanted to push them toward [other]

Maya Lin working on the Civil Rights Memorial, 1988. Photo by Adam Stoltman.

     OCCUPYING SPACE AS AN ACT OF AGENCY

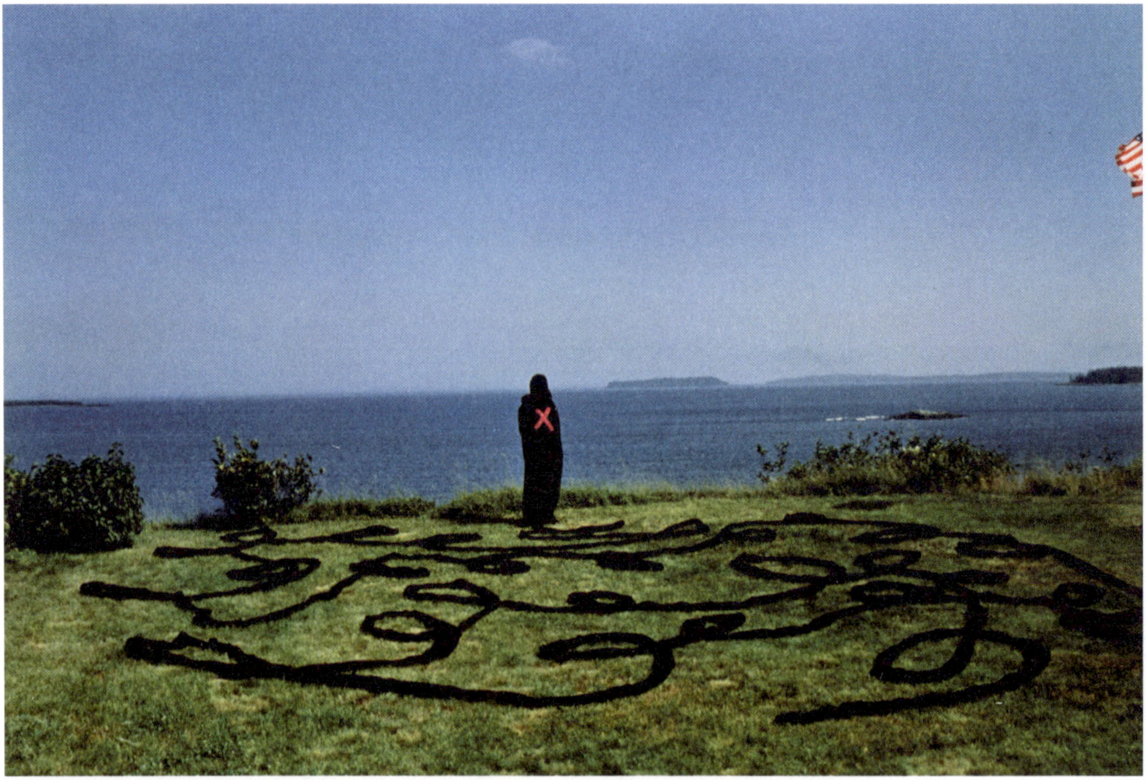

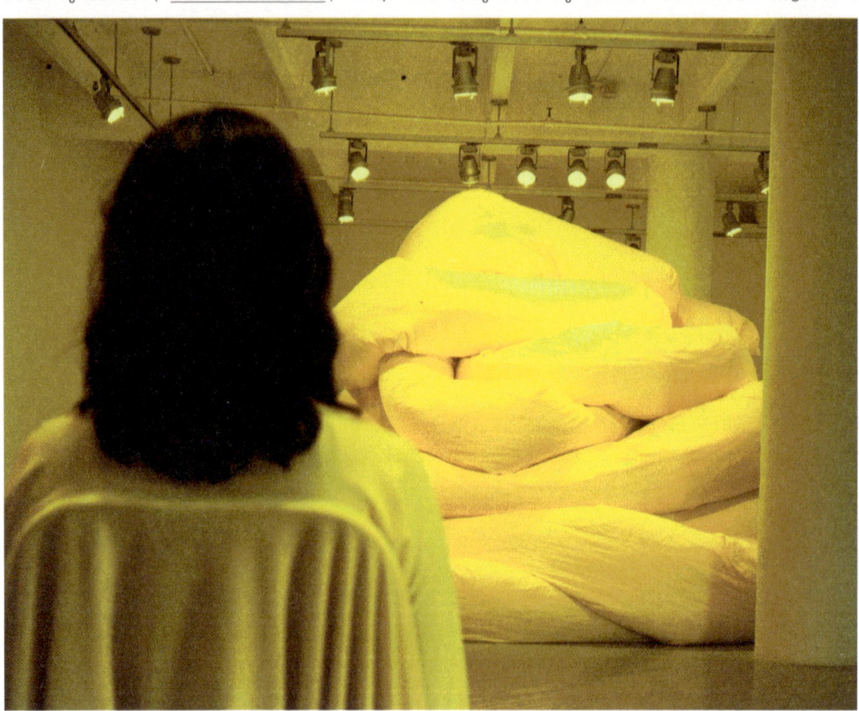

Beverly Semmes, <u>Buried Treasure</u>, 1994. Courtesy Beverly Semmes and Susan Inglett Gallery, New York City.

Beverly Semmes, <u>Watching Her Feat</u> at the Fabric Workshop and Museum, Philadelphia, 2000.

materials instead of concentrating on their usual medium of cardboard. I had them build things with alternative materials uncommon to architectural draftsmanship and model building, and install their projects around an old defunct railroad in New Haven."[117] She was mentor to, among others, Jessica Stockholder (MFA 1985): "I loved her sense of humor, which was not at all humorous." She also mentored Ann Hamilton (MFA 1985), who, she says, "took things that no one else did to reach into places that were psychologically oriented, such as putting her head through a hole in a table." She recalls teaching Beverly Semmes (MFA 1987), and Meg Webster (MFA 1983), who she notes "held a special relationship to nature, to earth," as well as Ritsuko Taho (MFA 1985), whose work "spared nothing and was so labor oriented."[118]

Scale figured into the work of many Sculpture students as a direct effect of their studios being located in Hammond Hall, a remote building on the edge of campus some fifteen minutes' walk from the rest of the School. By virtue of its vast size and informal relationship to codes and regulations, the building fostered a sense of experimentation. "It was spectacular," von Rydingsvard notes of the building. "We could screw up the floors, studios were plentiful, the ceilings were forty feet in height. It was a building made entirely of stone [and] had once been used for ROTC."[119] Semmes, who entered the MFA program in 1985—and credits it with creating synergy around an intense work ethic, an emphasis on production, energetic critiques, and a close peer structure—feels similarly. Of the experience of working in a space like Hammond Hall, she says, "It was a provocation to my own feelings about scale, it served as an invitation to make pieces that take up a room." Semmes' further analysis provides an answer to Lin's question above: "That impulse to take up space conveyed a sense of strength and empowerment, and for me, represented a feminist gesture."[120] (Semmes, like her peers Hamilton and Stockholder, went on to teach, joining the faculty of New York University in 1995, where she stayed until 2015.) Many graduates felt the location of Hammond Hall contributed to the "outsider" status of the School in relation to the larger University. Pfaff says, "As no one cared very much about the School within the University, it was left up to us to be accepted and regarded by the art world and by those who graduated from it, to help uphold it … to recognize the long history of challenge that women faced within the school, either as graduates or as leaders and teachers."[121]

Stockholder entered the MFA program at Yale as a Painting student in 1983, having studied with Mowry Baden, who, according to the artist, "was very involved with thinking about how art objects function politically within the economy."[122] She recalls that the faculty in Painting were suspicious of her practice because she did not work with materials or processes that had traditionally been accepted within that department. Regarding the structure of group critique in Painting, Stockholder felt that some faculty members had a disrespectful approach, recalling the painter Lester Johnson, Director of Studies in the Department of Painting from 1969 to 1974, commenting, "Well, you look lovely standing there, but beyond that, I have nothing else to add to your work."[123] So, she frequented Sculpture critiques at Hammond Hall instead, eventually transferring to that department in 1984, with the assistance of painter David Pease, who was Dean at that time.[124] After moving to the Sculpture department, Stockholder found that von Rydingsvard and Pfaff had a significant impact on her evolving practice, one routed through painting but with a spatial sensibility that aimed to include "an experience of material, objects, and environment"—something Pfaff herself had pursued in the early 1970s, before installation art arrived as a category. She notes that Jake Berthot, Visiting Professor in the Painting Department, continued to support her work after she transferred to Sculpture. Stockholder maintains the "most important aspect of my education had been the processing of ideas through the conversation

117 Ibid.

118 Ibid.

119 Ibid.

120 Beverly Semmes, telephone conversation with the author, February 6, 2020.

121 Judy Pfaff, conversation with the author, January 13, 2020.

122 Jessica Stockholder, quoted in "There Are No Words for What I'm Going to Do: An Interview with Jessica Stockholder," Artspace, June 14, 2018, www.artspace.com/magazine/interviews_features/qa/there-are-no-words-for-what-im-going-to-do-an-interview-with-jessica-stockholder-55484.

123 Jessica Stockholder, telephone conversation with the author, January 8, 2020.

124 Ibid.

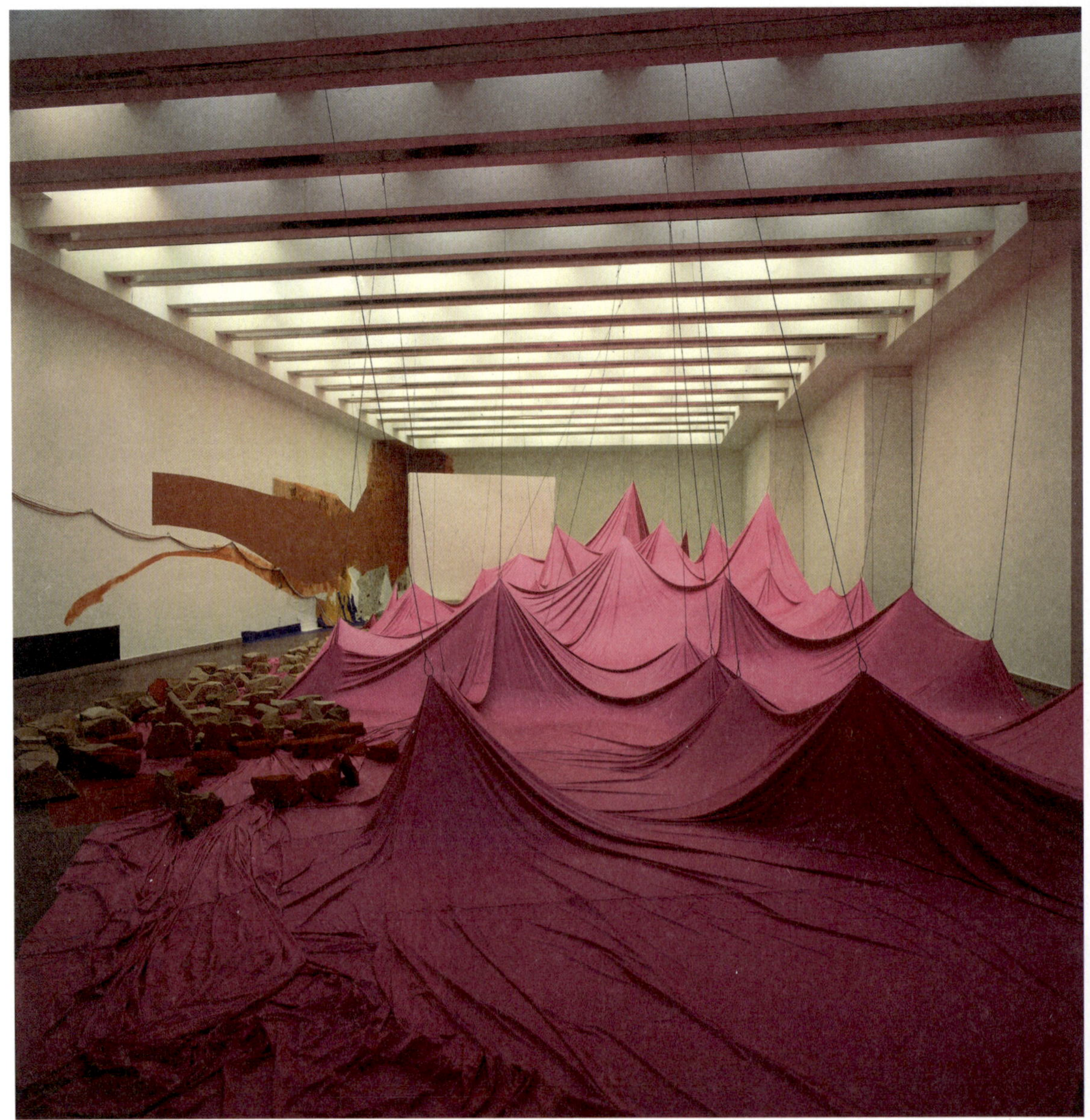

Jessica Stockholder, *Inventory #JS171: Growing Rock Candy Mountain Grasses in Canned Sand*, 1992.
Courtesy Jessica Stockholder and Mitchell Innes & Nash Gallery.

with my peers—with artist-classmates Ann Hamilton, Carolyn Ginsberg (MFA 1985), Jan Cunningham (MFA 1985), Mark Holmes (MFA 1985), and Jack Risley (MFA 1986)."[125] She supplemented her studio-based education by attending the lectures of the art historians Vincent Scully and Karsten Harries and the philosopher George Schrader. Within the School, she says, there were "few mechanisms to bring people together from other departments," but there were some all-School critiques.[126] Though Stockholder does not consider her work to have been influenced by the community of theorists at Yale, her artistic practice addresses controlled chaos, fragmentation, and ideas related to the parergon—a detachable part not quite separate from the whole—which had been discussed by Derrida. As Hamilton notes, "I don't think we were consciously aware of the theoretical debates going on in the University, but perhaps it's like growing up in a context where you might not go to church, but it is in the culture and you absorb its customs and values."[127]

When interviewed for a place in the Yale Sculpture department, Hamilton was asked, "You don't do this weaving stuff anymore, do you?"—a question that disarmed the artist, whose practice included woven elements and was informed by the medium of textiles.[128] "It was such a different time, with a different attitude towards what [weaving] might even mean socially, and the judgment around those histories, with a much more hierarchical attitude about the relationship between what is art and what is craft," she says.[129] The denigration of a process intrinsic to Hamilton's work—one that she considered related to some understanding of women's bodies—negated what she felt were "the meaning of the processes fundamental to textiles. Weaving, sewing, knitting, and netting are constructions in which individual elements forge a mutual whole and, in their coordination, become metaphors for social structures and relations."[130] In discussing her time at Yale, Hamilton emphasizes the tremendous importance of strong, female professors like von Rydingsvard, Pfaff, and others.[131] Lauren Ewing, for instance, a Critic in the Department of Sculpture at the time, "was perceptive and articulate in leading the conversation in group critiques." She continues, "Rydingsvard, Pfaff, and Ewing were faculty members I really admired and respected. … They made a life in art seem possible and were incredibly generous to us as students."[132]

Hamilton has noted how much the architecture of Hammond Hall helped to create a culture around space, inspiring a sense of freedom and a spatial broadening of one's work: "Hammond Hall had beautiful, tall windows and light, and it served as a studio as well as a forum and a conversation for the presentation of work during twice-a-semester open studios. … I started to place my own body into the work, and without the context of the open studios in a former industrial building I probably wouldn't have had a forum for these early experiments."[133] Hamilton's project *tropos* (1993) [see pp. 114–15], a genre-breaking work that blanketed a 5,000-square-foot floor of the original Dia Art Foundation in Chelsea with horsehair, followed a direct line from Hammond Hall:

Working in response to the architecture began at Yale. The duration of the several-hour open houses raised, for me, the question of time. Were these performances, are these live works, is this a tableau, is this meant to be photographed? I really didn't know what to call it, but the impulse to make the work live came from my interest in carrying forward the attention, focus, and energy of *making* into the ongoing life of the work, instead of thinking about presenting the work as the funeral when [the making is] over.[134]

Hamilton actively drew from resources offered by the larger University, recalling, "What I loved about the program is that I felt we could venture into other areas

125   Ibid. Similarly, Semmes recalls the Sculpture program as being a "functional community," with people who were supportive of one another; Beverly Semmes, telephone conversation with the author, February 6, 2020.

126   Jessica Stockholder, telephone conversation with the author, January 8, 2020.

127   Ann Hamilton, telephone conversation with the author, February 5, 2020.

128   Hamilton had received a BFA in Textile Design from the University of Kansas in 1979.

129   Ann Hamilton, telephone conversation with the author, February 5, 2020.

130   Ibid.

131   Ibid.

132   Ibid.

133   Ibid.

134   Ibid.

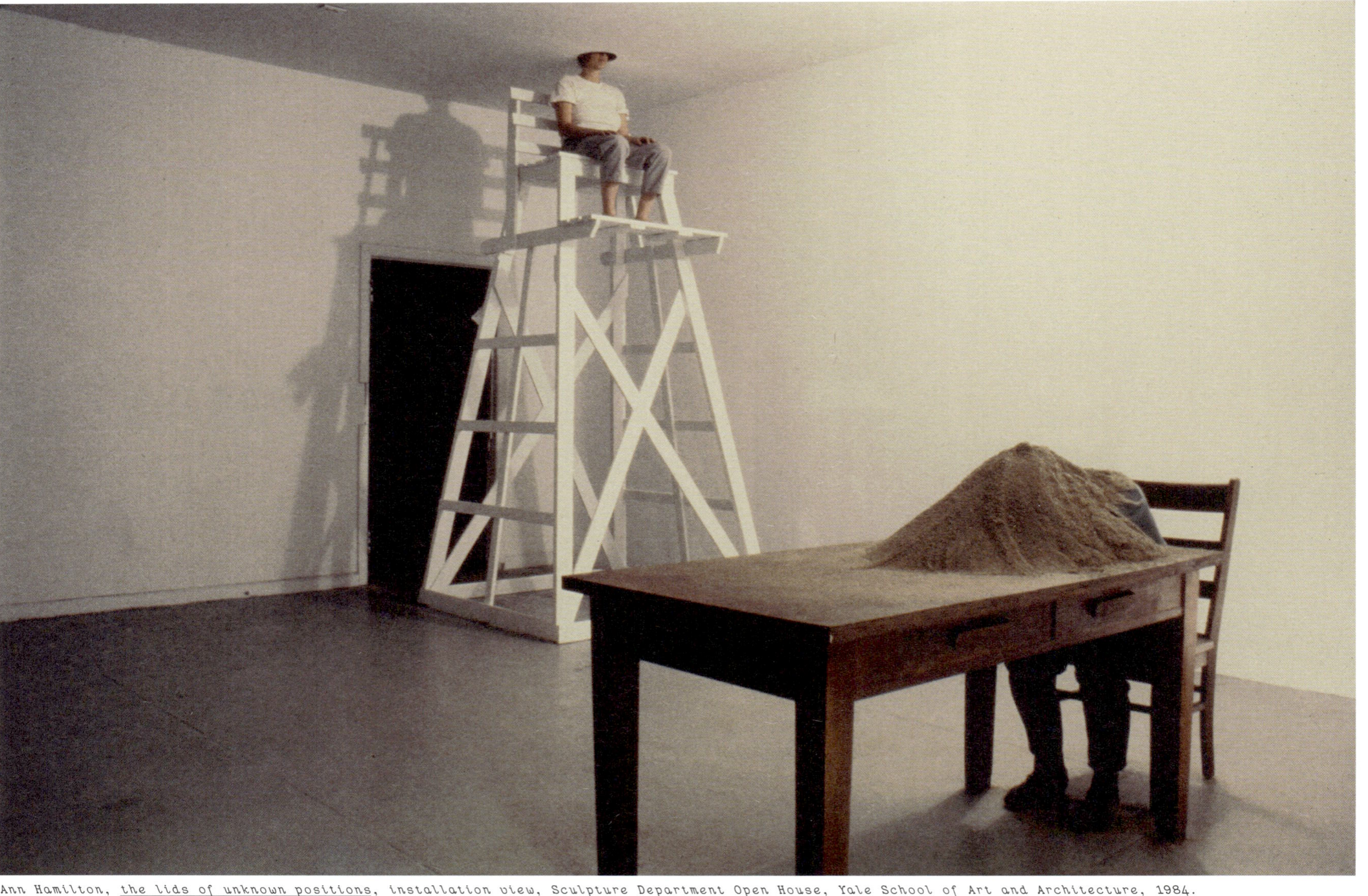

Ann Hamilton, _the lids of unknown positions_, installation view, Sculpture Department Open House, Yale School of Art and Architecture, 1984. Photo by Bob McMurty. Courtesy Ann Hamilton Studio.

and study other disciplines. … It's an incredible university to do that within."[135] She adds that she longed for more theoretical conversation, which she felt was lacking in the program, and she notes this desire was shared by her peers, who also recognized there was no structure for it within the School. In American Studies, however, Hamilton discovered Leslie Rado, who taught a class in the cultural construction of the body called "The Body: Gender, Symbol, and Society," which was described in the course catalog from the time as "an exploration of the social, ritualistic, and symbolic aspects of the human body with emphasis on gender differences," with topics including "the language of dress and style, body expressiveness, cultural images of the body, and body stigma, including illness and aging."[136] Hamilton remembers that she was the only student in Rado's seminar without any theoretical background. The class required weekly short essays in response to assigned readings, and it generated discussions that engaged Hamilton as an analytical thinker, enabling her to trust her own intelligence. Rado made a point of supporting Hamilton's thinking as an artist, and her mentorship became a foundation of Hamilton's education. Of the class she says:

> It helped give me a vocabulary to think about what I was doing. I made a suit covered in a dense hide of toothpicks painted black with white tips. I was thinking about camouflage, surface, and skin, and the ways in which a membrane can be protective in one context but make one vulnerable and exposed in another. I didn't know what to do with it or how to present the suit. A fellow sculpture student, Melinda Hunt (MFA 1985), looked at the work and said to me, "Ann, you are an armature. Why don't you just wear it?" It was a casual comment, but it was like the bells went off. And, of course, I wore it, and the experience of wearing it changed everything. … Leslie's class helped me to think about the experience of standing still as an active experience. … Her class was the most important class I took as a student.[137]

After graduation, Hamilton was hired by the University of California, Santa Barbara, where she stayed until 1991, when she left teaching to pursue her art-making practice full time. Soon thereafter she produced *tropos*. In the catalogue for the *tropos* exhibition, Dia's curator and director Lynne Cooke wrote, "The significance of crossing the threshold into one of Hamilton's works thus bears less upon issues of art per se than it heralds a coming into a special place, a site with a character of its own. The spaces she transforms are cast into a unity as spatial, sentient, and social places, as worldlike but not worldly. Inhabited by humans and/or animals, they appear at first encounter as spaces set apart, virtual sanctuaries, or preserves."[138] In this same essay, Cooke remarked upon Hamilton's graduate education at Yale: "Fundamental to Hamilton's fusion of installation and performance modes at this time were the requirements and restrictions attendant on presenting work as a student in a studio situation at the Yale School of Art."[139]

135 Ibid.

136 "Yale College Programs of Study: Fall and Spring Terms, 1983–84," *Bulletin of Yale University*, ser. 79, no. 8 (August 15, 1983), 55, Manuscripts and Archives, Yale University Library, New Haven.

137 Ann Hamilton, telephone conversation with the author, February 5, 2020.

138 Lynne Cooke and Karen Kelly, eds., *Ann Hamilton: tropos* (New York: Dia Art Foundation, 1993), 61.

139 Ibid, 62–63.

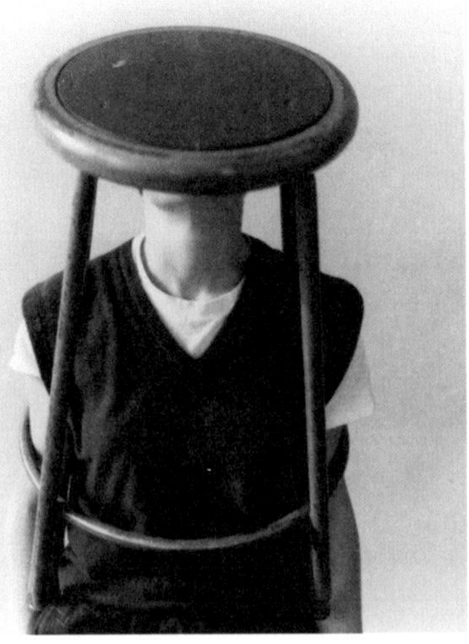

Ann Hamilton, <u>body object series #2, stool</u>,
1984–91. Courtesy Ann Hamilton Studio.

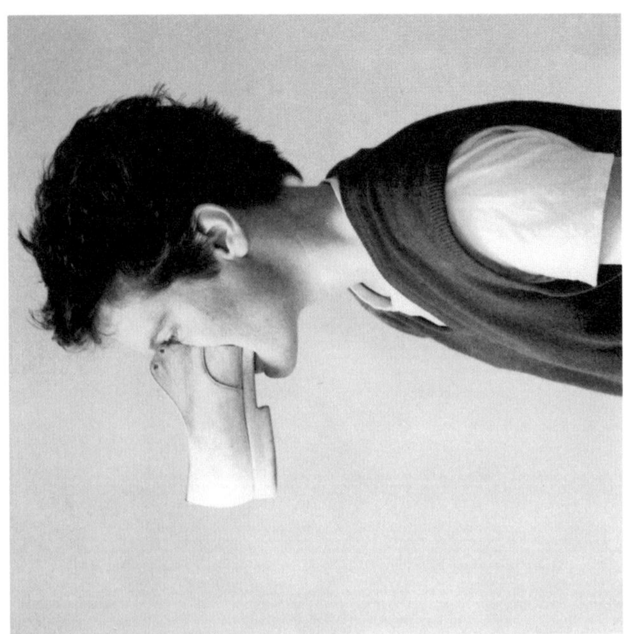

Ann Hamilton, body object series #3, shoe, 1984–93.
Courtesy Ann Hamilton Studio.

Ann Hamilton, <u>body object series #1, chair</u>, 1984–93. Courtesy Ann Hamilton Studio.

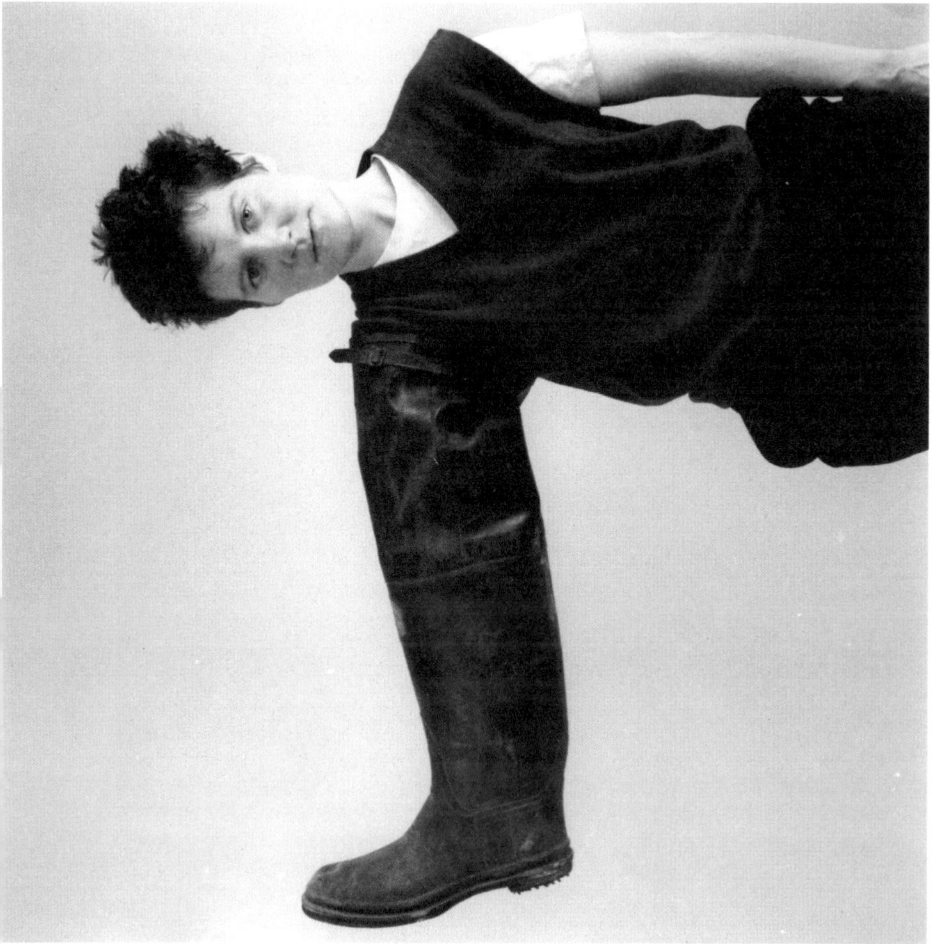

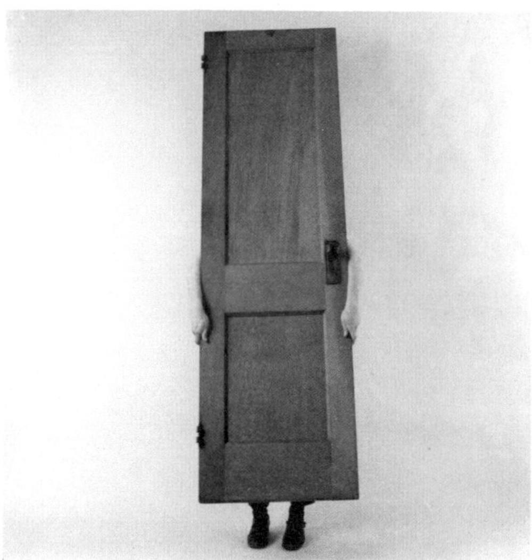

Ann Hamilton, *body object series* #11, boot, 1984–93. Courtesy Ann Hamilton Studio.

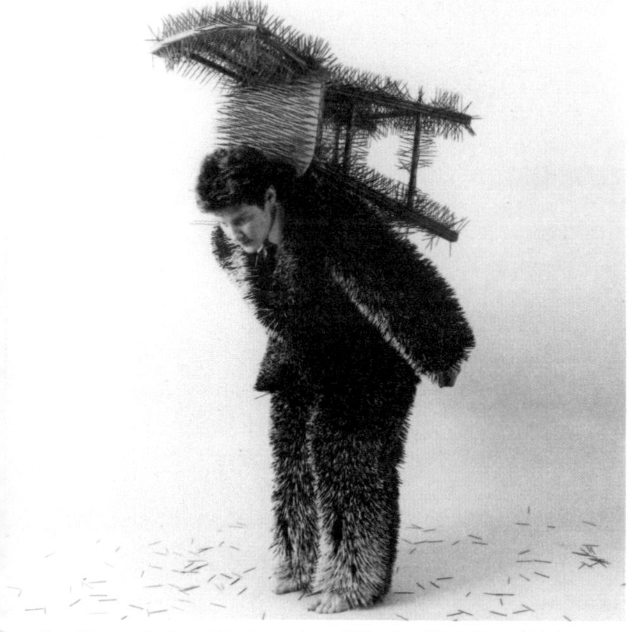

Ann Hamilton, *body object series* #13, toothpick suit/chair, 1984–93. Courtesy Ann Hamilton Studio.

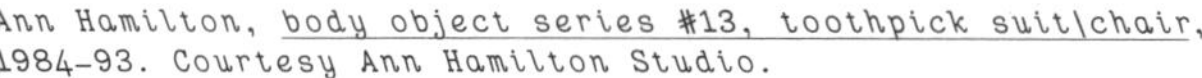

Ann Hamilton, *body object series* #12, door, 1984–93. Courtesy Ann Hamilton Studio.

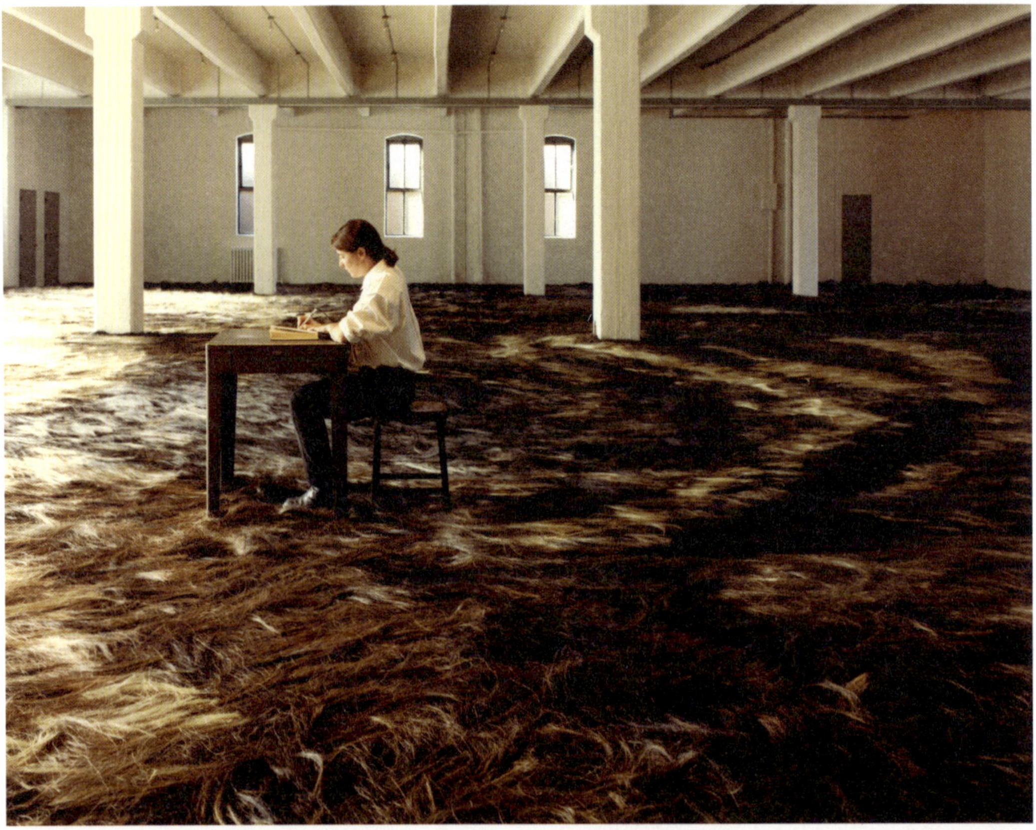

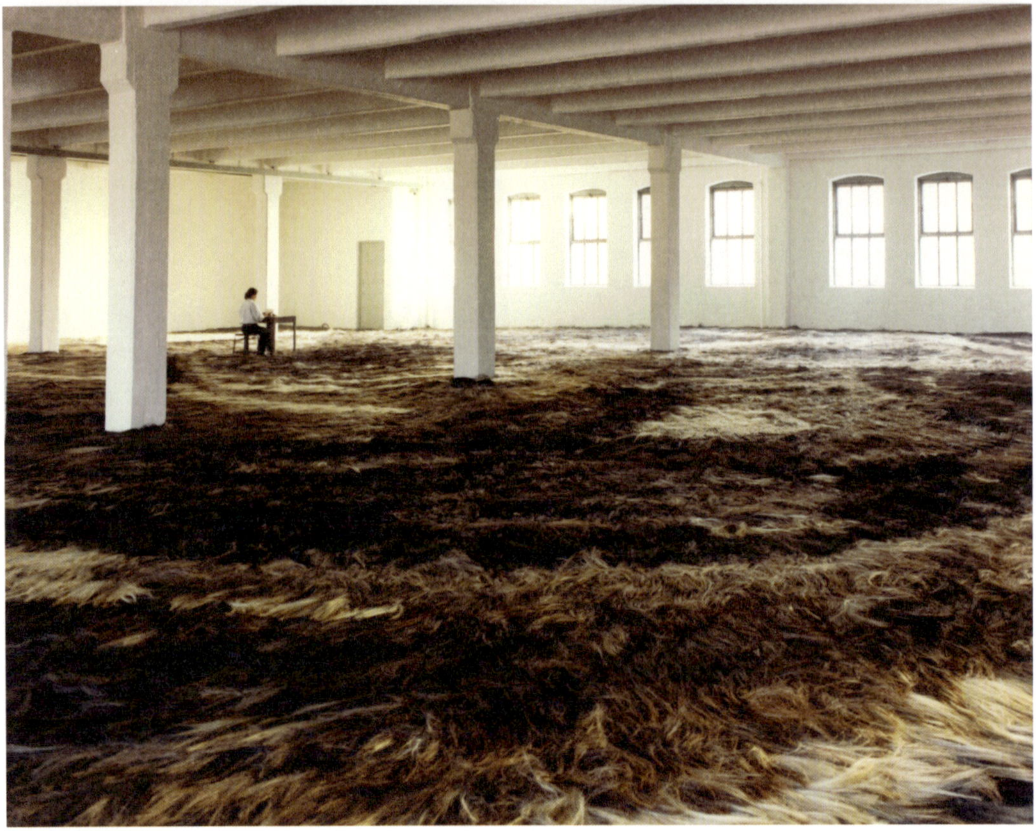

Ann Hamilton, installation view, _tropos_, Dia Center for the Arts, New York, 1993-94.
Photo by Thibault Jeansen. Courtesy Ann Hamilton Studio.

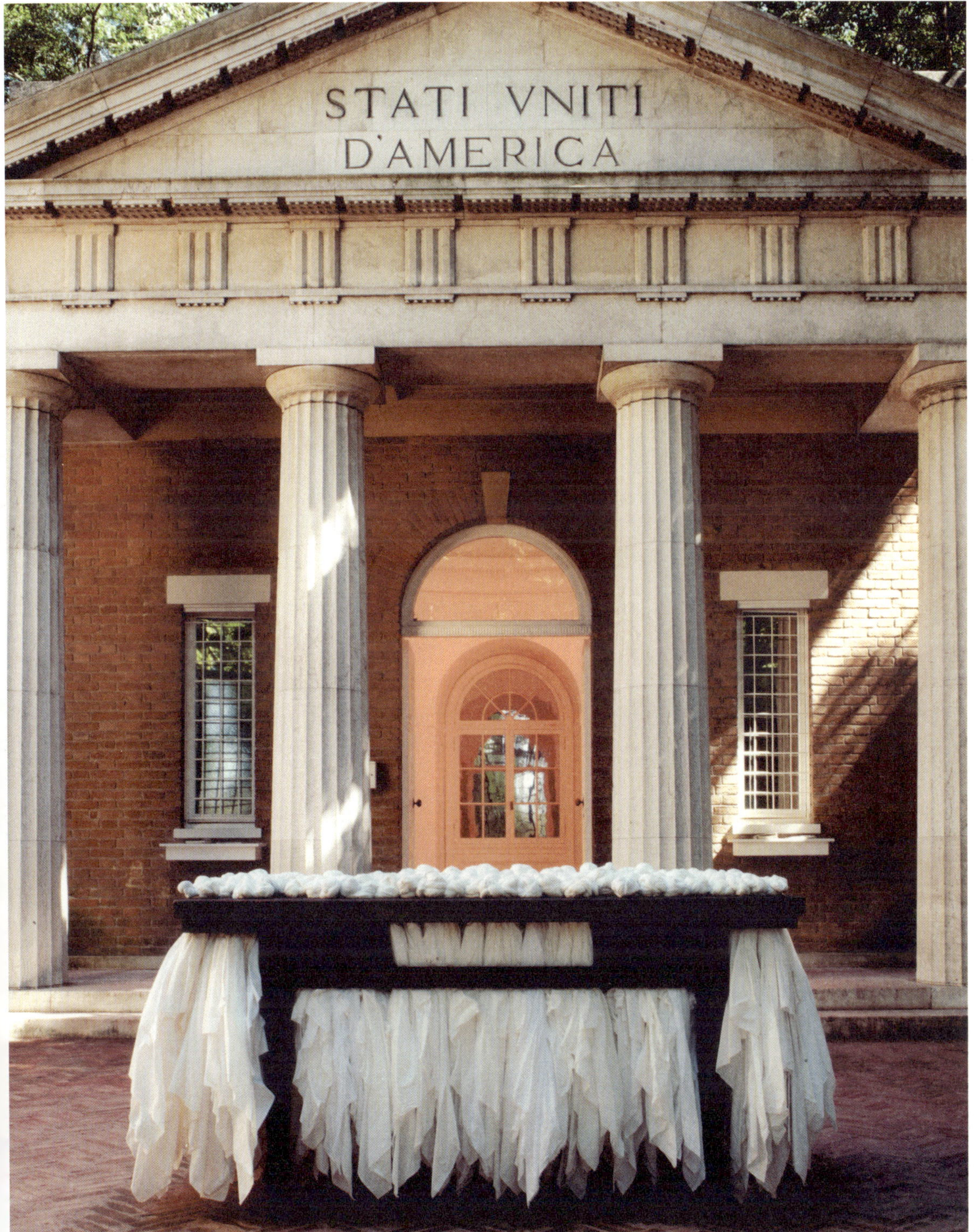

Ann Hamilton, <u>myein</u>, the United States Pavilion, 48th Venice Biennale, 1999.
Courtesy Ann Hamilton Studio.

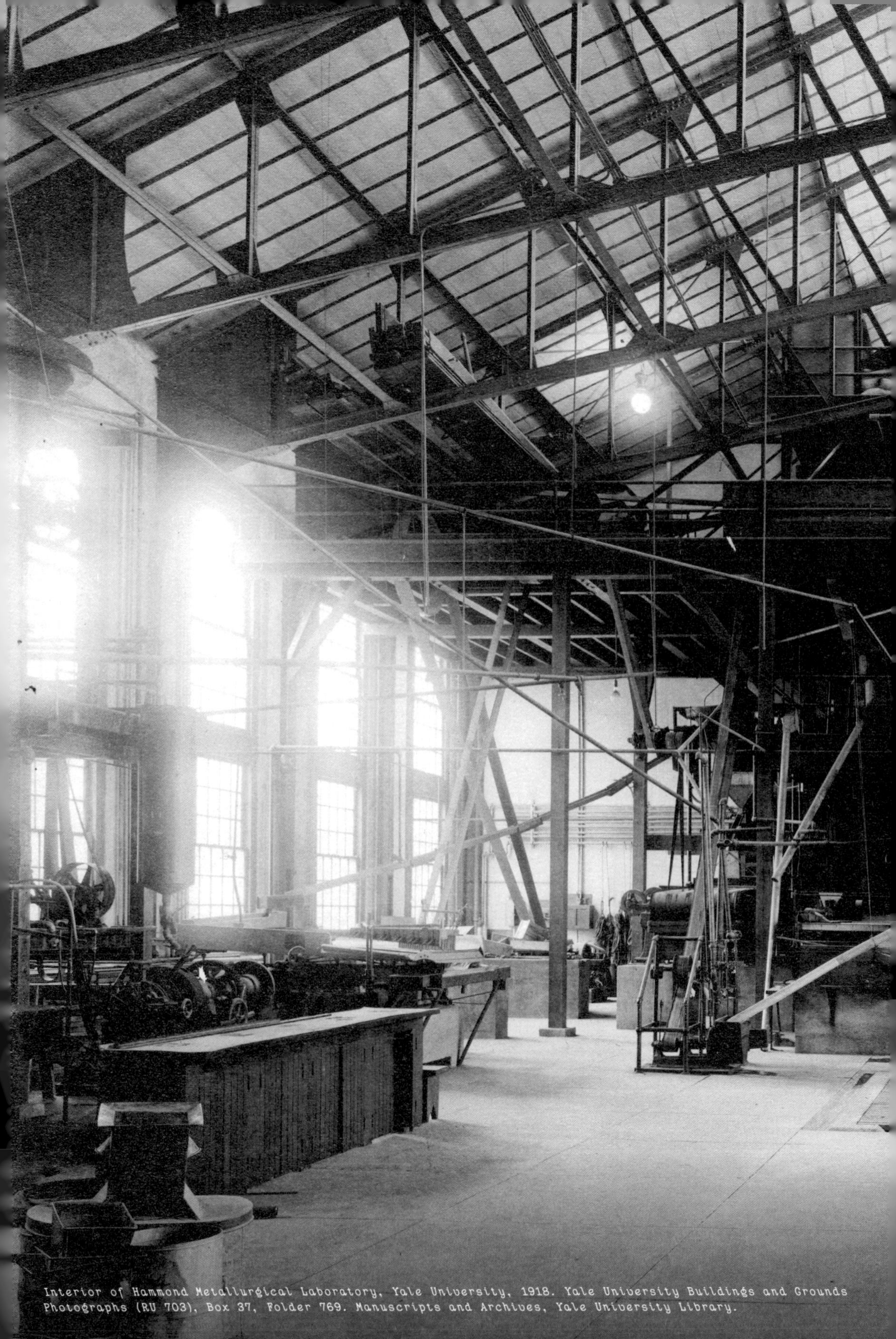

Interior of Hammond Metallurgical Laboratory, Yale University, 1918. Yale University Buildings and Grounds Photographs (RU 703), Box 37, Folder 769. Manuscripts and Archives, Yale University Library.

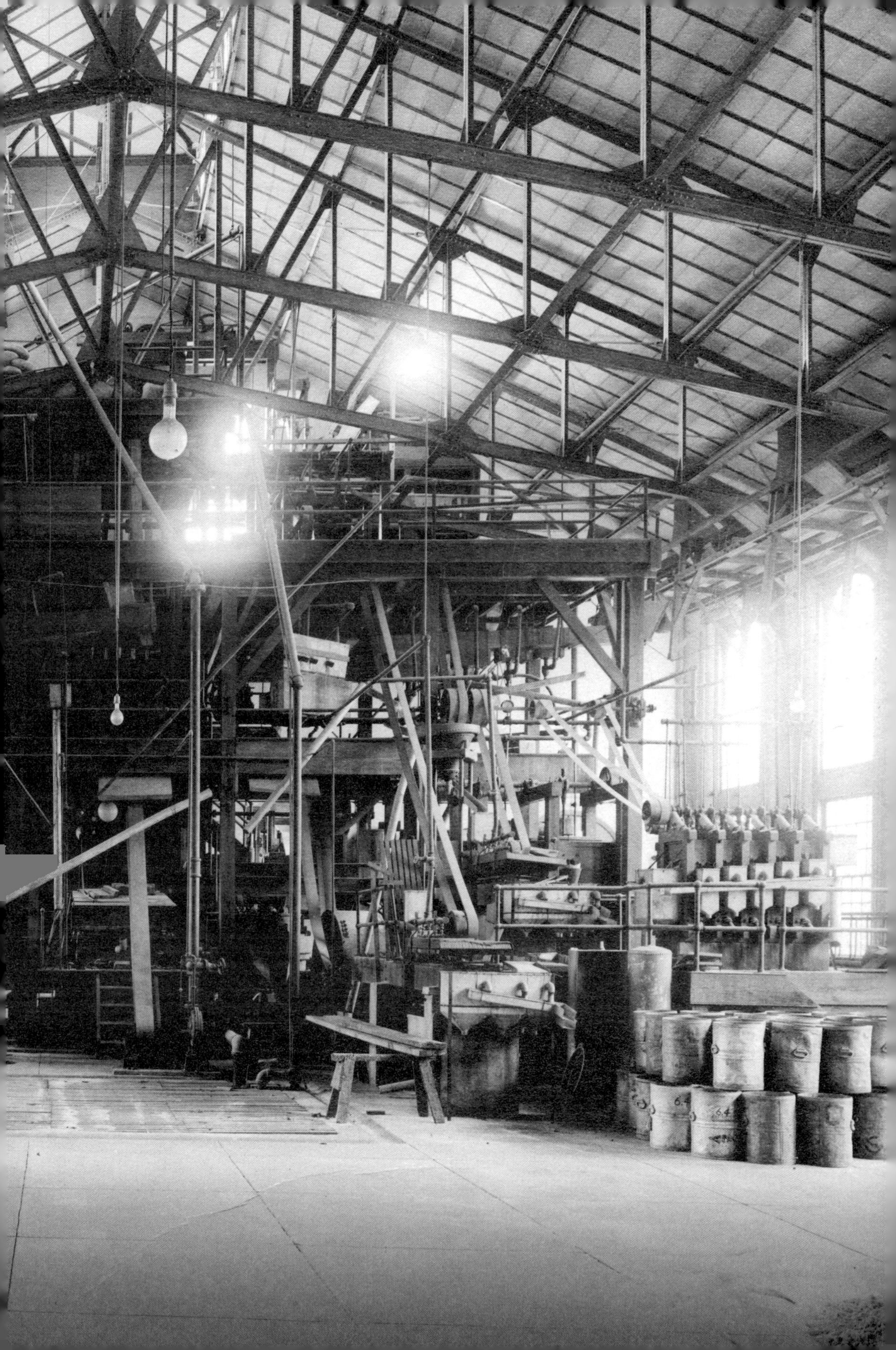

WOMEN ASCEND TO LEADERSHIP IN THE YALE SCHOOL OF ART

From the late 1980s into the 1990s, as the AIDS crisis accelerated, a conservative U.S. government led a campaign to censor the arts, provoking what came to be known as the "culture wars." Funding for the National Endowment for the Arts was drastically cut as public controversy ensued around various exhibitions, including Nan Goldin's group show *Witnesses: Against Our Vanishing* at Artists Space, in New York (1989), and Robert Mapplethorpe's *Perfect Moment* at the Corcoran Gallery of Art, in Washington, D.C. (1989). In 1986, at the initiative of the medievalist John Boswell, a committee comprised of students and faculty was formed in to establish the Lesbian and Gay Studies Center at Yale (LGSCY), which held its inaugural conference in October 1987 [see pp. 120–21].

Craig Owens, a Visiting Professor in the Department of the History of Art and author of *The Allegorical Impulse: Toward a Theory of Postmodernism* (1980), *The Discourse of Others: Feminists and Postmodernism* (1983), and *Outlaws: Gay Men in Feminism* (1987), had participated the same year in a conference held on campus in February 1987 called "Postmodernisms: Politics, Practices, Performance." The conference included the artist Barbara Kruger, the philosopher Edward Said, the choreographer and filmmaker Jo Andres, the performance artist John Kelly, and the choreographer Yvonne Rainer.[140] The following year, Owens worked with an undergraduate student, Richard Meyer (BA 1988), now an art historian, to organize a film series called *Visualizing AIDS*, which included work by Gregg Bordowitz and Maria Maggenti, core members of the AIDS Coalition to Unleash Power (ACT UP).[141] Owens himself succumbed to AIDS in 1990 at age thirty-nine.

Laura Wexler, then Associate Professor of Women's Studies, wrote a memorandum in 1988 with the Chair, Margaret Homans, proposing that the name of the program, founded in 1979, be changed to Women's and Gender Studies due to changes in the field, centering "the study of gender as a primary mode of social differentiation that is both historically constructed and active in producing patterns of power."[142] As stated in the *Yale College Programs of Study, 1998–1999*, Women's and Gender Studies (later to become Women's,

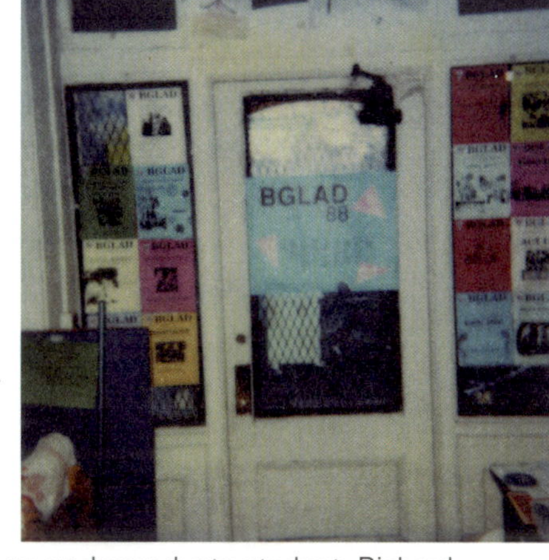

Door with posters for BGLAD week events, 1988. Lesbian, Gay, Bisexual, Transgender Cooperative at Yale Records (RU 1059). Manuscripts and Archives, Yale University Library.

140 Richard Meyer, "Postmodernisms at Yale," *Yale Daily News*, February 20, 1987.

141 Stephen Heuser, "Films and Producers Help Visualize AIDS Epidemic," *Yale Daily News*, March 2, 1988. The series was a four-hour program that included the work of Maria Maggenti and Gregg Bordowitz. The film series also screened *Snow Job: The Media Hysteria of AIDS* by Barbara Hammer.

142 Margaret Homans and Laura Wexler, Memo to Course of Study Committee, February 27, 1998 in Kirsten E. Lodal, "Engendering an Intellectual Space: The Development of Women's Studies at Yale University 1969–2001," (unpublished senior essay, History Department, Yale University, 2001), 57, wgss.yale.edu/sites/default/files/files/LodalEssayEngendering%20and%20IntellectualSapce.pdf.

LESBIAN/GAY STUDIES '87
Definitions and Explorations

Sponsored by The Center for Lesbian and Gay Studies at Yale and by the Whitney Humanties Center

October 30-31, 1987

The Whitney Humanities Center
Yale University
53 Wall Street
New Haven, Connecticut

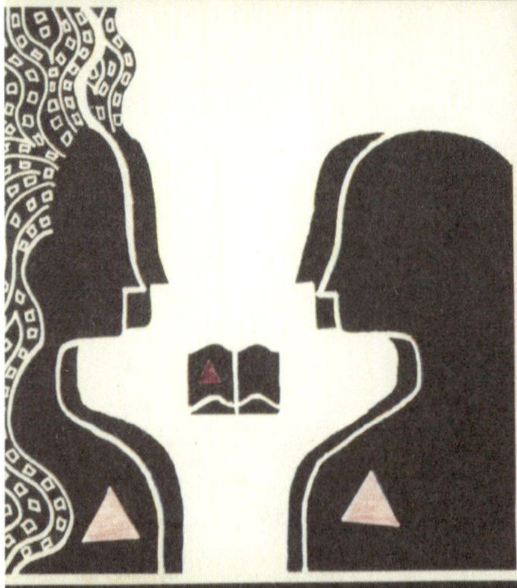

Friday October 30

12:00 p.m.	Registration	Whitney Humanities Center
1:00-2:00 p.m.	Words of Welcome	John Boswell Beth Povinelli
2:00-3:30 p.m.	Gay People and the Constitution	Harlon Dalton Arthur Leonard Benno Schmidt Tom Stoddard
4:00-5:30 p.m.	Do Lesbians and Gay People Constitute a Minority?	Jeffrey Levi Richard Mohr Martha Nussbaum Nancy Cott

Saturday October 31

9:00-10:30 a.m.	Perspectives on AIDS	Carol Levine Al Novick Mark Senak Richard Selzer
	Lesbians and Gay People Cross-Culturally	Evelyn Blackwood Susan Cavin Micaela di Leonardo
	The Canon and the Closet	Adrienne Donald Michael Moon Eve Kosofsky Sedgwick Margaret Homans
11:00 a.m.-12:30 p.m	The Histories of Lesbian and Gay People	George Chauncey Liz Kennedy Madeline Davis Michael Lynch Regina Kunzel
	Can There Be a Gay Criticism?	Michael Cadden Robert K. Martin Lee Edelman Jill Campbell
	Making it Gay: Homosexual Representations in Contemporary Art	Nancy Fried Wendy Kuppermann William Olander Craig Owens Jonathan Weinberg
2:00-3:30 p.m.	Differences Within Differences: Issues of Lesbian and Gay People of Color	Gloria Anzaldúa Juanita Ramos Migdalia Reyes Rhonda Williams
	Frames, Images and Case Studies	Wayne Koestenbaum Vito Russo James Saslow Larry Kramer
	Limerence, Lust and (maybe) Agape: A New Biologically Based Model of the Sexual Orientations	James Weinrich John Gonsiorek John Boswell
4:00-5:00 p.m.	The Future	Open Discussion

design: Sean Tavizonée

Poster for the inaugural conference of the Lesbian and Gay Studies Center at Yale, 1987. Larry Kramer Initiative for Lesbian and Gay Studies, Yale University, Exhibit and Research Materials from <u>The Pink and the Blue</u> (RU 963). Manuscripts and Archives, Yale University Library.

Lesbian/Gay Studies '87: Definitions and Explorations

Sponsored by the Center for
Lesbian and Gay Studies at Yale
and by the Whitney Humanities Center

October 30-31, 1987

The Whitney Humanities Center
Yale University
53 Wall Street
New Haven, Connecticut

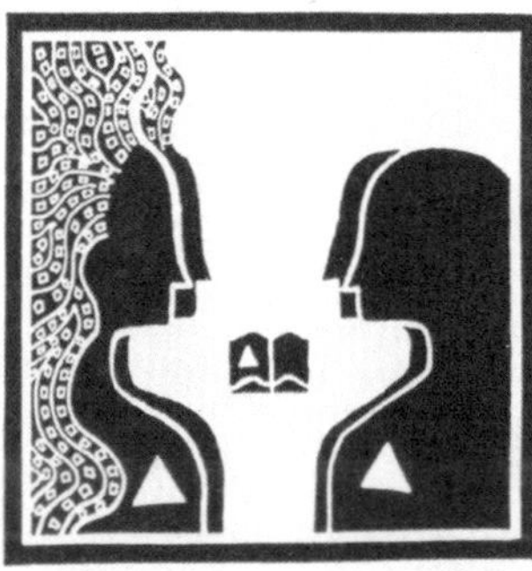

graphic: Sean Tavizonée

Program for the Lesbian/Gay Studies '87: Definitions and Explorations conference, held at the Whitney Humanities Center, Yale University, October 30-31, 1987. Lesbian and Gay Studies Center at Yale Records (RU 1013). Manuscripts and Archives, Yale University Library.

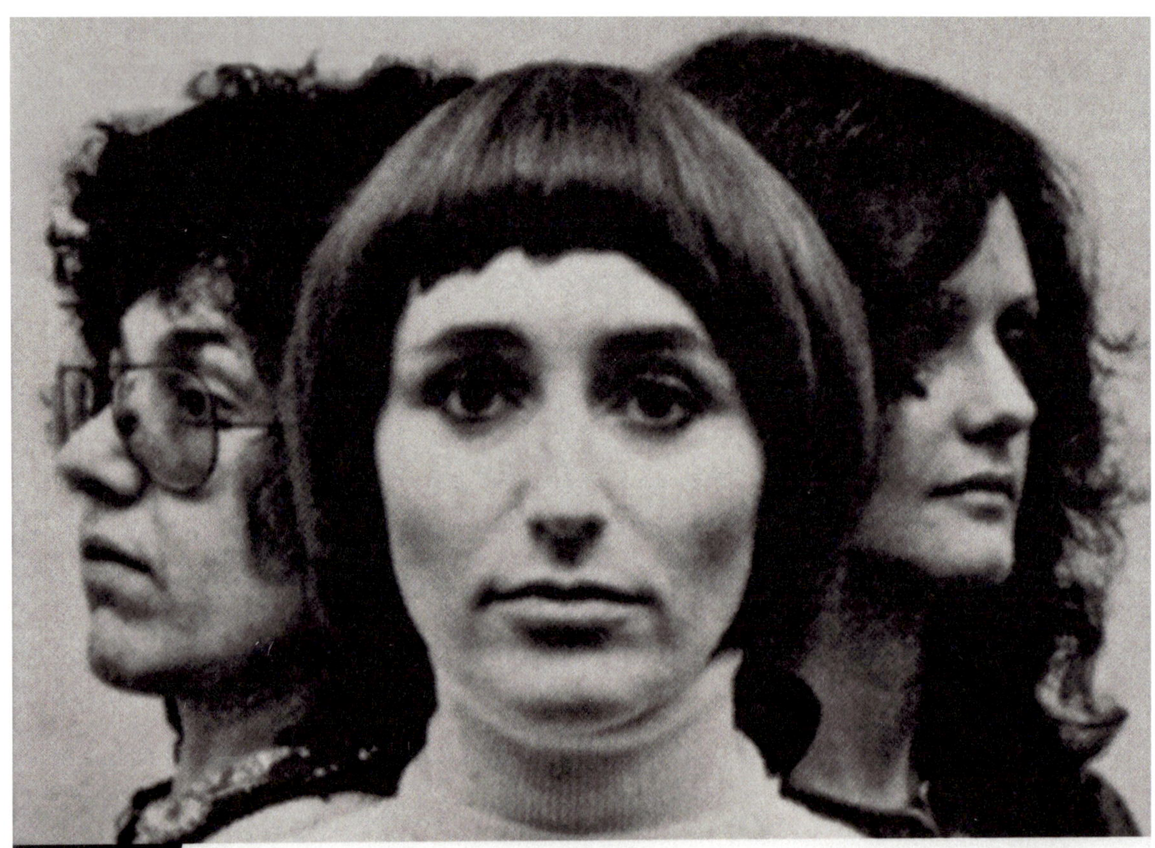

Cover of From Site to Vision: The Woman's Building in Contemporary Culture, edited by Sondra Hale and Terry Wolverton, 2011. Ben Maltz Gallery, Otis College of Art and Design and the Woman's Building. Courtesy Woman's Building Image Archive, Otis College of Art and Design.

Gender, and Sexuality Studies) established gender and sexuality as "fundamental categories of social and cultural analysis and [offered] new critical perspectives from which to study the diversity of human experiences."[143] Wexler equated the shift with the new inquiries into sexuality, noting that, "We're now being led by lesbian and gay civil rights" as a "reflection of what's changing in the world outside the academy."[144]

Critical discourses that continued to evolve during the 1990s directly impacted the School, making its continued isolation untenable. The 1993 Whitney Biennial, curated by Thelma Golden, John G. Hanhardt, Lisa Phillips, and Elisabeth Sussman, engaged head-on with some of the most divisive issues in U.S. cultural politics, including racism, the AIDS crisis, feminism, and economic inequality. It was famously the first Whitney Biennial exhibition in which white male artists were in the minority (a fact memorialized by a poster from the artist group the Guerilla Girls), and it introduced to the world a new generation of artists who had not previously been shown in major museums, some of whom began to arrive at the School as influential critics and lecturers.[145] The fall of the Berlin Wall, the collapse of historical Communism in Eastern Europe, the dissolution of the former East-West divide, the emergence of global capitalism—these, too, were important developments impacting discussions around art. In 1995, the first Johannesburg Biennale was held in postapartheid South Africa. And, in 1997, Documenta X, in Kassel, Germany, was curated for the first time by a woman, Catherine David. David presented an expansive international project that included critical and political perspectives toward neoliberalism, global capitalism, privatization, global migrations, and the rise of populism.

Within this context, the School of Art's all-male governance, which structurally privileged white male perspectives, was soon challenged.[146] In the twenty years since the arrival of feminism's second wave, the School had not yet integrated tenured women faculty. This changed in 1990, when Pease recruited and appointed Sheila Levrant de Bretteville, a pioneer in the field of feminist design, as Director of Graduate Studies in Graphic Design and a tenured Professor, making her the first woman with tenure in the School's 120-year history. This appointment came nearly two decades after de Bretteville founded the first feminist design program at CalArts.[147] She recalls her interview

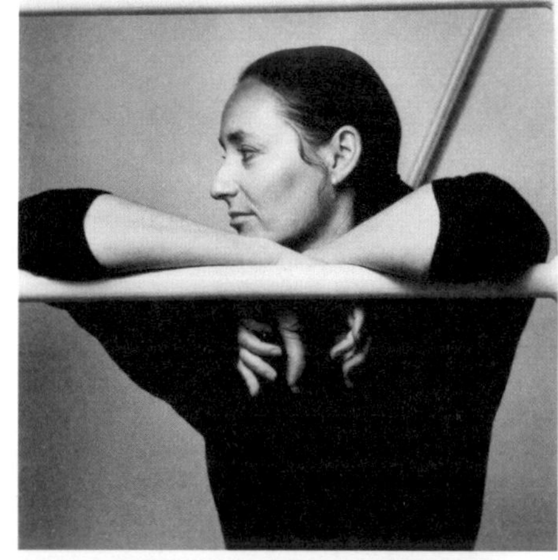

Sheila Levrant de Bretteville, 1985. Photo by Bradford Fowler. Courtesy Sheila Levrant de Bretteville.

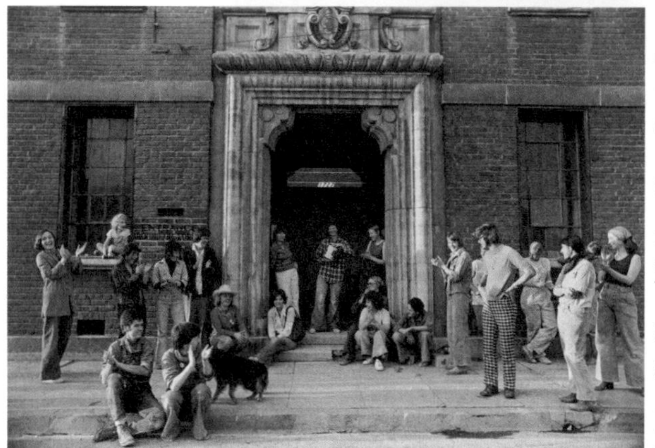

Exterior of the Woman's Building at Spring Street, with Sheila Levrant de Bretteville on the far left, 1975. Photo by Maria Karras. © Maria Karras. Courtesy Getty Research Institute, Los Angeles (2018.M.16).

143 "Yale College Programs of Study, 1998–1999," 543, quoted in ibid., 59.

144 Ibid., 59–60.

145 These included Donald Moffett (Lecturer in Graphic Design, 1993–95), Fred Wilson (Critic in Sculpture, 1994–95), Gary Simmons (Critic in Sculpture, 1998–99), Suzanne McClelland (Senior Critic in Painting/Printmaking, 1999), and Byron Kim (Senior Critic in Painting/Printmaking, 1999–2000, 2001–02, 2009–10, 2012–present).

146 Women served as Directors of Undergraduate Studies in Art as early as 1987 with Susana Jacobson. Since then, JoAnn Walters, Janice Murray, Lois Conner, and Lisa Kereszi have also held this position. None of them were tenured. "Directors of Undergraduate Studies in Art, 1967–Present," Undergraduate Studies in Art, Yale School of Art archives, New Haven.

147 De Bretteville also co-founded the Woman's Building and the related Women's Graphic Center at CalArts and was a founding member of the first independent feminist art school in the United States, the Feminist Studio Workshop, in Los Angeles.

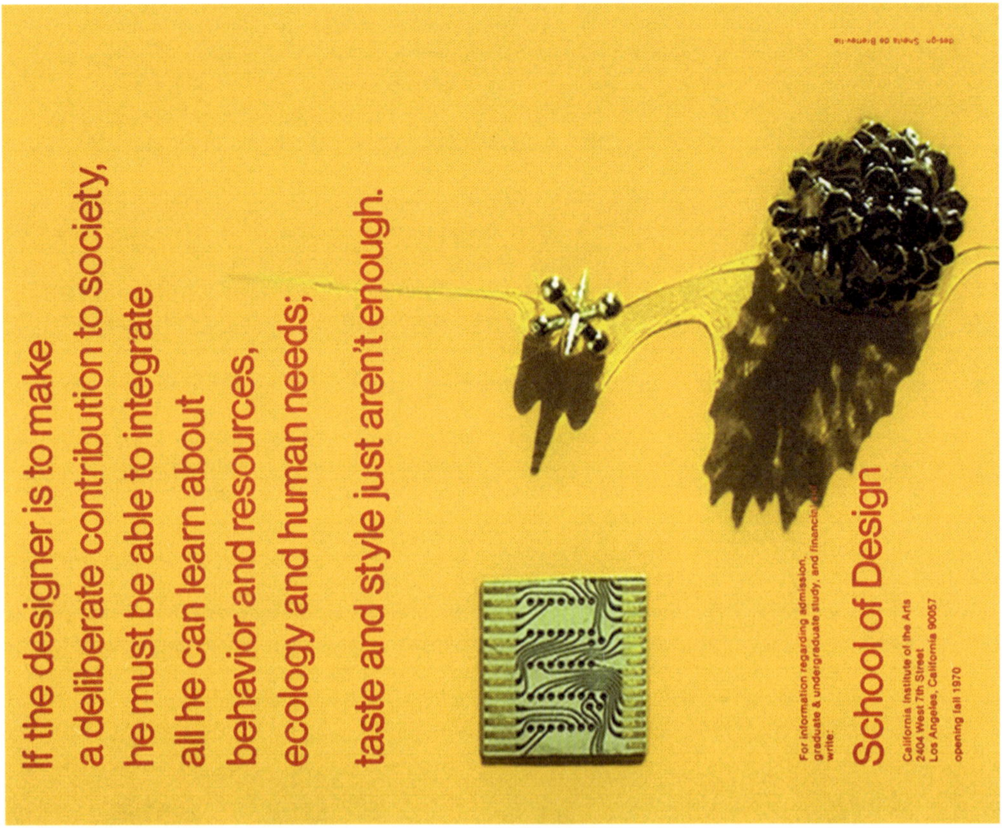

Sheila Levrant de Bretteville, three-dimensional poster for the School of Design at the California Institute of the Arts, 1970. Courtesy Sheila Levrant de Bretteville.

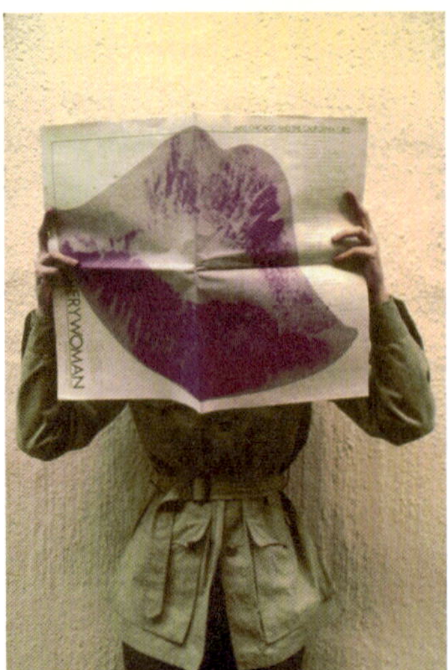

Special edition of the feminist newspaper <u>Everywoman</u> designed by Sheila Levrant de Bretteville (pictured), 1970. Photo by Peter de Bretteville. Courtesy Sheila Levrant de Bretteville.

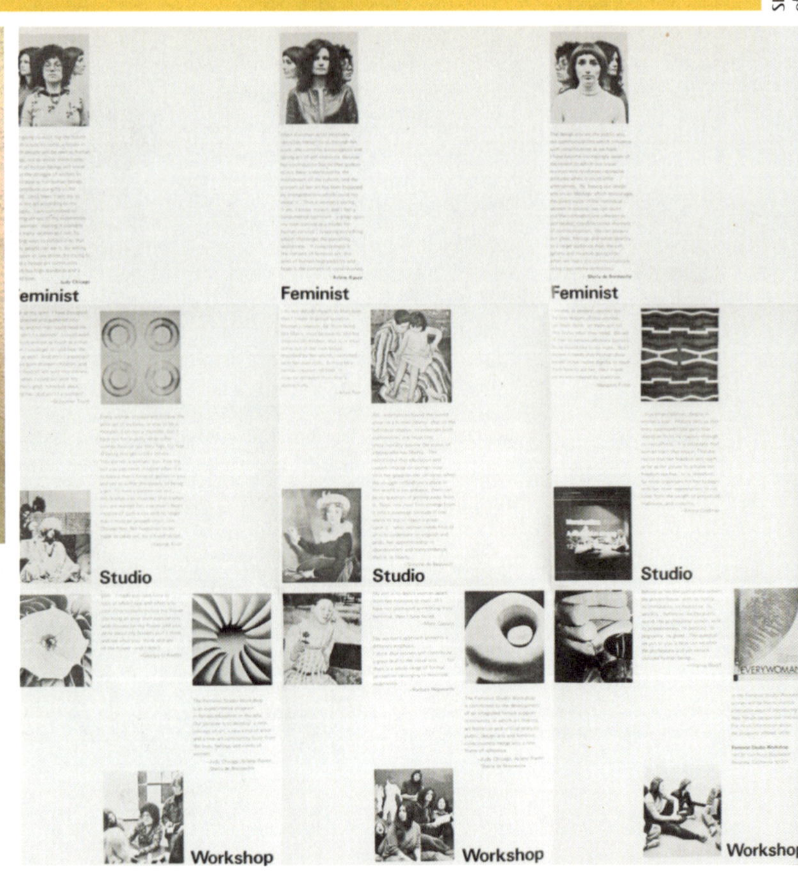

Sheila Levrant de Bretteville, Feminist Studio Workshop brochure, 1973. Courtesy Sheila Levrant de Bretteville.

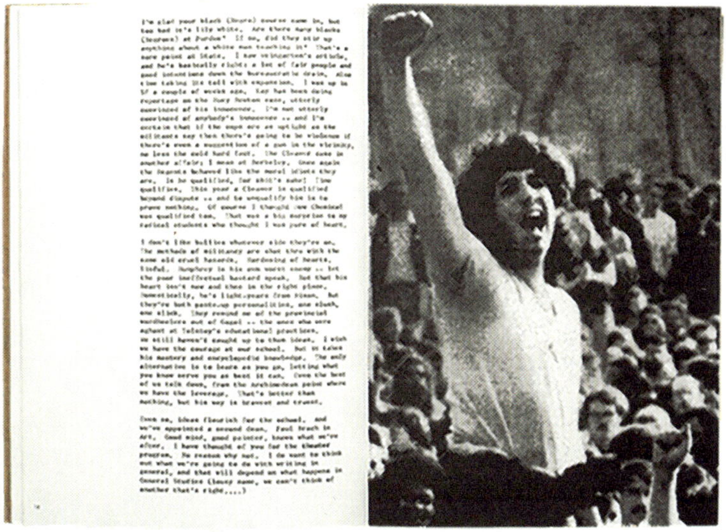

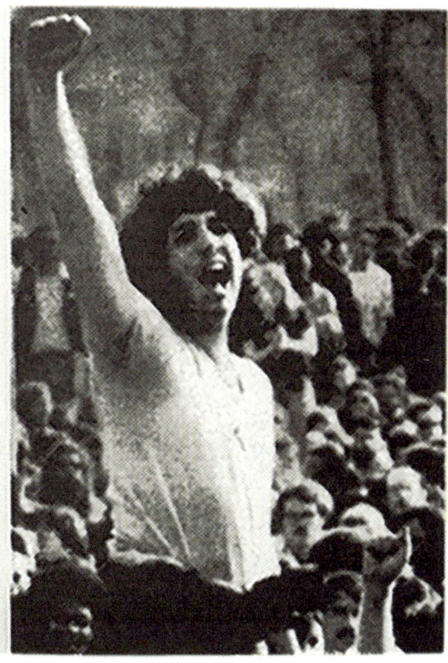

Sheila Levrant de Bretteville, special issue of <u>Arts in Society</u> about the formation of California Institute of the Arts, 1970. Courtesy Sheila Levrant de Bretteville.

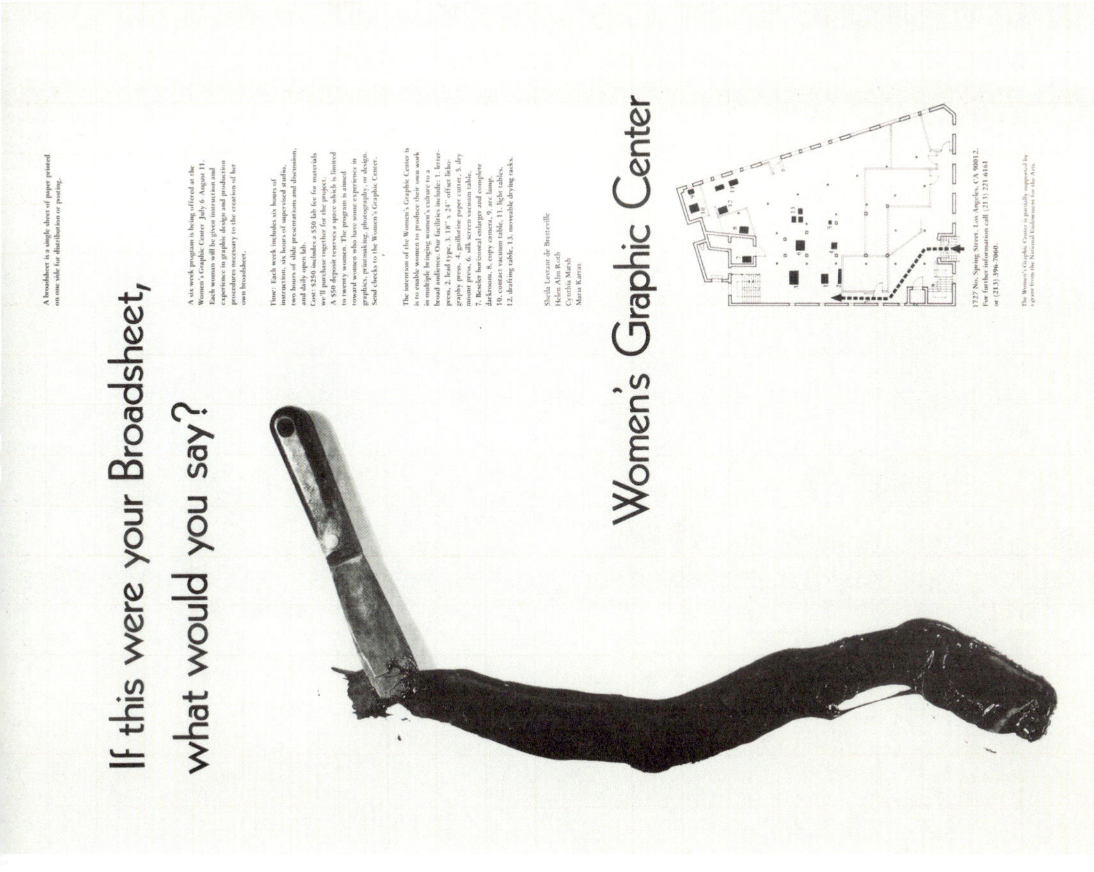

Sheila Levrant de Bretteville, poster invitation to the Women's Graphic Center at the Woman's Building, ca. 1980.
Courtesy Sheila Levrant de Bretteville.

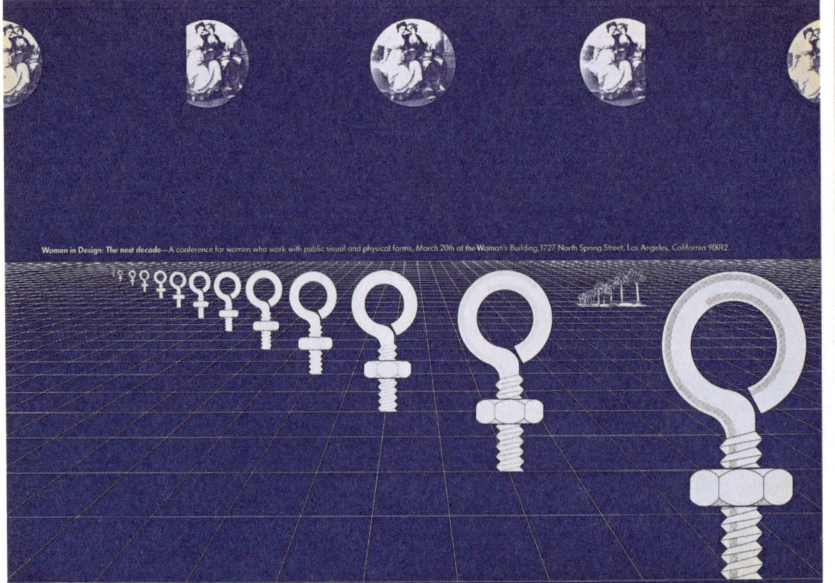

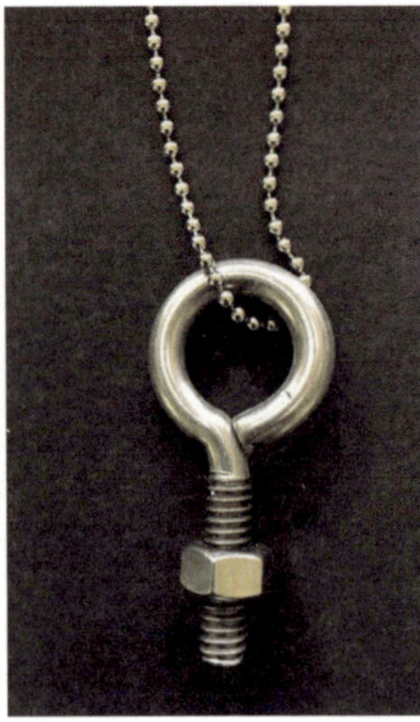

Keychain necklace with eyebolt pendant designed by Sheila Levrant de Bretteville and given to everyone who attended the Women in Design conference she organized in 1974. Courtesy Sheila Levrant de Bretteville.

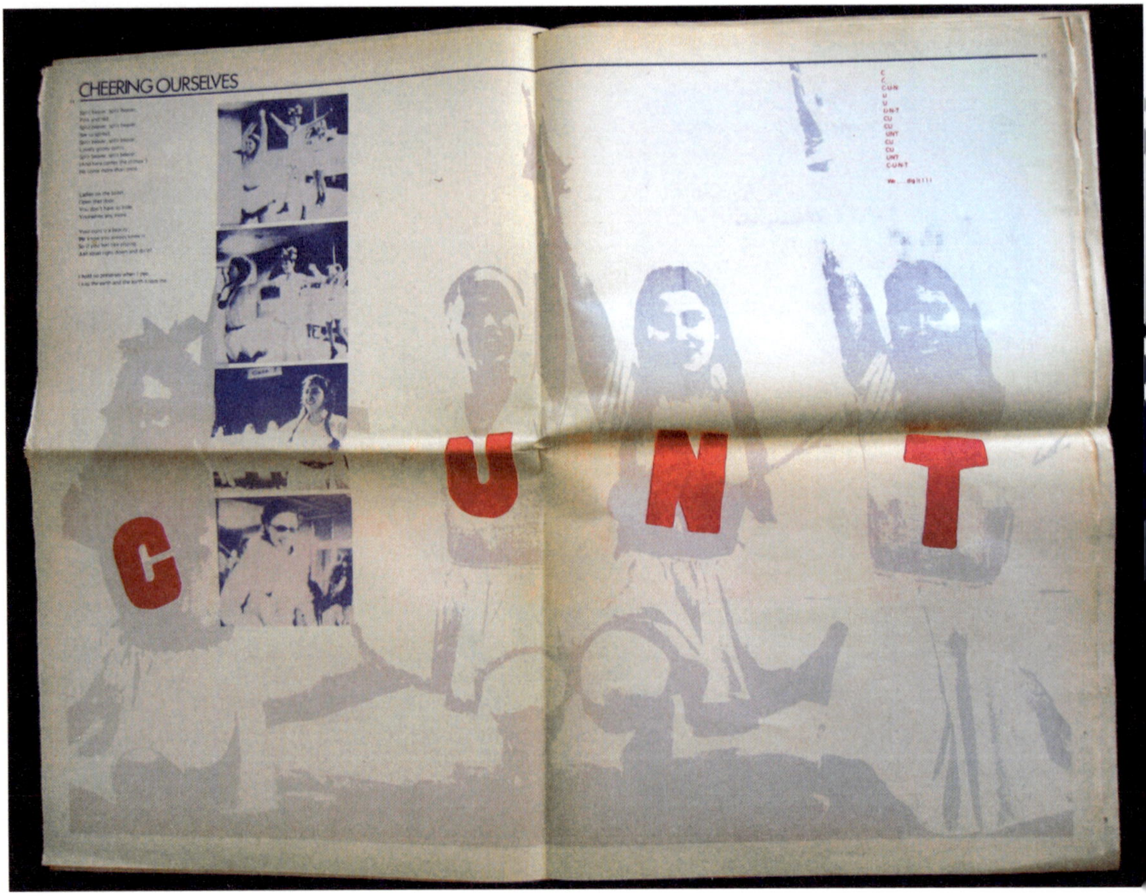

Sheila Levrant de Bretteville, Women in Design conference poster, 1974. Courtesy Sheila Levrant de Bretteville.

Sheila Levrant de Bretteville, _Everywoman_ newspaper centerfold, 1970. Courtesy Sheila Levrant de Bretteville.

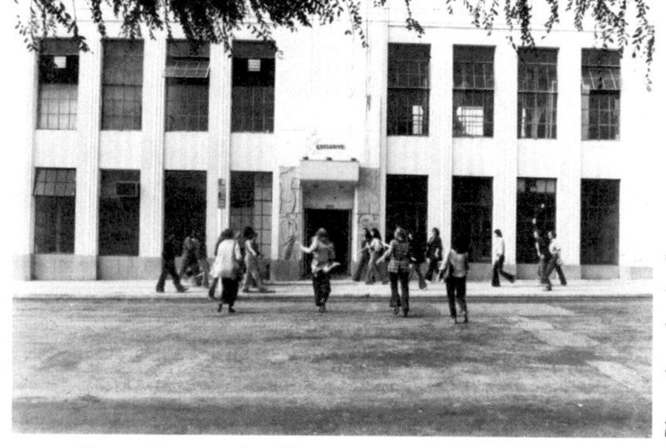

with Yale's all-male review committee and teaching staff, who asked what she felt the School of Art had not yet done that they should do. "Bring more women!" she answered.[148]

Significantly influenced by the Brazilian philosopher Paulo Freire's critical pedagogy, de Bretteville endeavored to rethink the Graphic Design curriculum, revising that which had been adopted nearly forty years earlier to instead reflect an explicitly feminist pedagogical agenda, with the idea that feminist design respects forms of public life rather than privileging a corporate client. She introduced a "person-centric" curriculum in which students, for the first time, were asked to pull ideas and inspiration from their own experiences—a radical shift from the standard "design-as-problem-solving" model championed by her predecessors, who had conceived of design education as preparation for corporate vocations. De Bretteville remembers feeling that some of the men who preceded her at the School were worried that she was going to let the outside world in, which of course was exactly what she planned to do. "Feminist design," she stated at the start of her tenure, "is an effort to bring the values of the domestic sphere into the public sphere; feminist design is about letting diverse voices be heard through caring, relational strategies of working and designing. Until social and economic inequalities are changed, I am going to call good design feminist design."[149]

As a result of the autonomy with which de Bretteville set out to revise the department, the beginning of her tenure was characterized by a rally of dissent from other tenured faculty. Her inclusive definition of design and her leadership of the department enraged Paul Rand, in particular. A member of the School's faculty since the 1950s, Rand felt himself very much the embodiment of the Yale graphic design profile. In his essay "From Cassandre to Chaos," which appeared in his 1993 book *Design, Form, and Chaos*, Rand directly criticized de Bretteville's approach to the department: "Both in education and in business graphic design is often a case of the blind leading the blind. To make the classroom a perpetual forum for political and social issues, for instance, is wrong; and to see *aesthetics as sociology*, is grossly misleading. A student whose mind is cluttered with matters that have nothing directly to do with design, whose goal is to learn *doing* and *making* … and who is overwhelmed with social problems and political issues is a bewildered student. This is not what he or she bargained for nor, indeed, paid for."[150] De Bretteville's pedagogy shifted the direction of a department that, as Lorraine Wild notes, had become stultified.[151] In the three decades since de Bretteville's arrival at the School, the Graphic Design program has generated a cadre of successful women designers.[152]

De Bretteville's appointment in 1990 as the School's first

148   Sheila Levrant de Bretteville, oral history interview by Edi Dai, October 12, 2018, transcript, Yale University Art Gallery archives, New Haven.

149   Sheila Levrant de Bretteville, in Ellen Lupton, "Reputations: Sheila Levrant de Bretteville," *Eye* 2, no. 8 (Fall 1993).

150   Paul Rand, "From Cassandre to Chaos," in *Design, Form, and Chaos* (New Haven: Yale University Press, 1993). Italics are Rand's.

151   Lorraine Wild, telephone conversation with the author, January 28, 2020.

152   Since de Bretteville assumed the directorship of the department in 1990, women graduates have included: Lucinda Hitchcock (MFA 1994), head of the undergraduate Graphic Design department at the Rhode Island School of Design, Providence; Miko McGinty (BA 1993; MFA 1998), who runs an eponymous design studio in New York; Alicia Cheng (MFA 1999) and Sarah Gephart (MFA 1999), who founded the design studio MGMT; Tamara Maletic (MFA 2001), partner and co-founder with Dan Michaelson (MFA 2002), of Linked by Air; Juliette Cezzar (MFA 2002), former president of AIGA/NY and former director of the BFA program in Communication Design at Parsons; Sulki Choi (MFA 2003), who runs an independent studio located in her native South Korea; Danielle Aubert (MFA 2005), co-founder of a three-woman studio based in Detroit, as well as a labor activist and board member of Metro Detroit DSA; Yoonjai Choi (MFA 2006), who runs a studio in New York; Rachel Berger (BA 2003; MFA 2009), chair of the Design department at the California College of the Arts; Julia Novitch (BA 2006; MFA 2013); and Jessica Svendsen (BA 2009; MFA 2013), Design Director, Work & Co., Lecturer at the Yale School of Art, and Assistant Professor Adjunct at Pratt Institute.

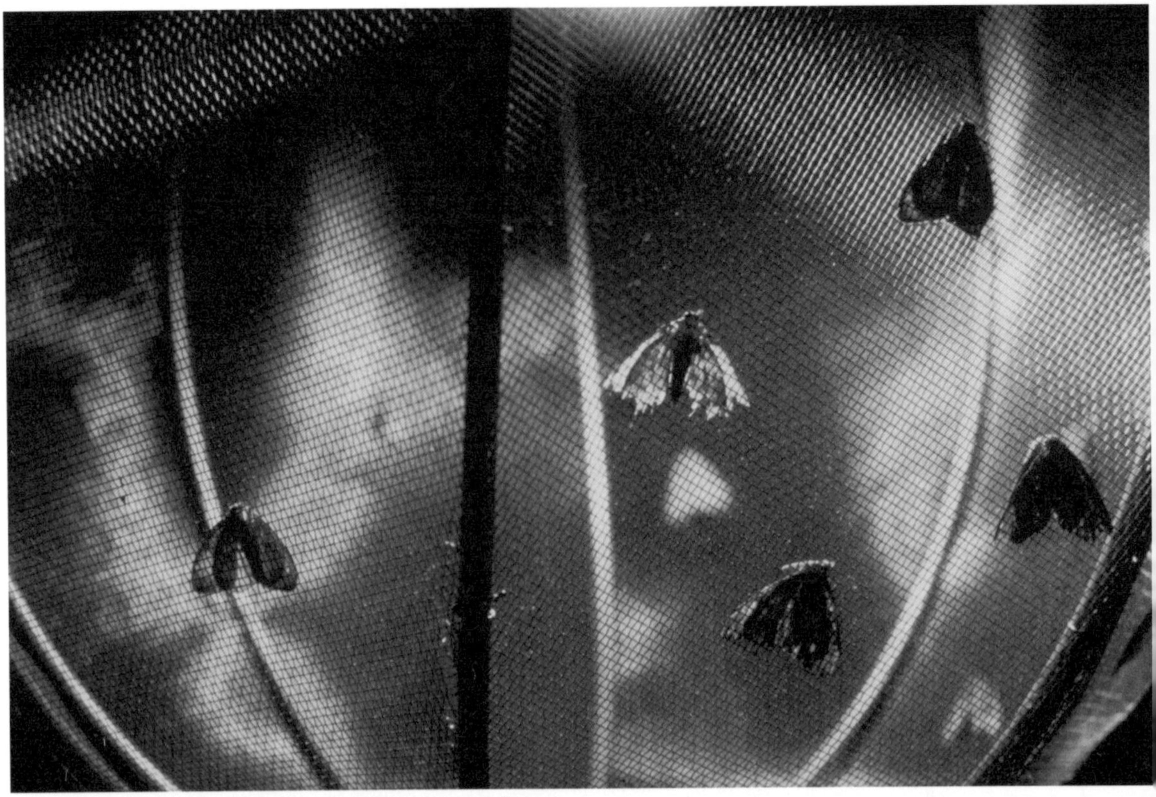

Rachel Berwick, <u>The Economy of Desire</u>, 1990 (detail). Courtesy Rachel Berwick.

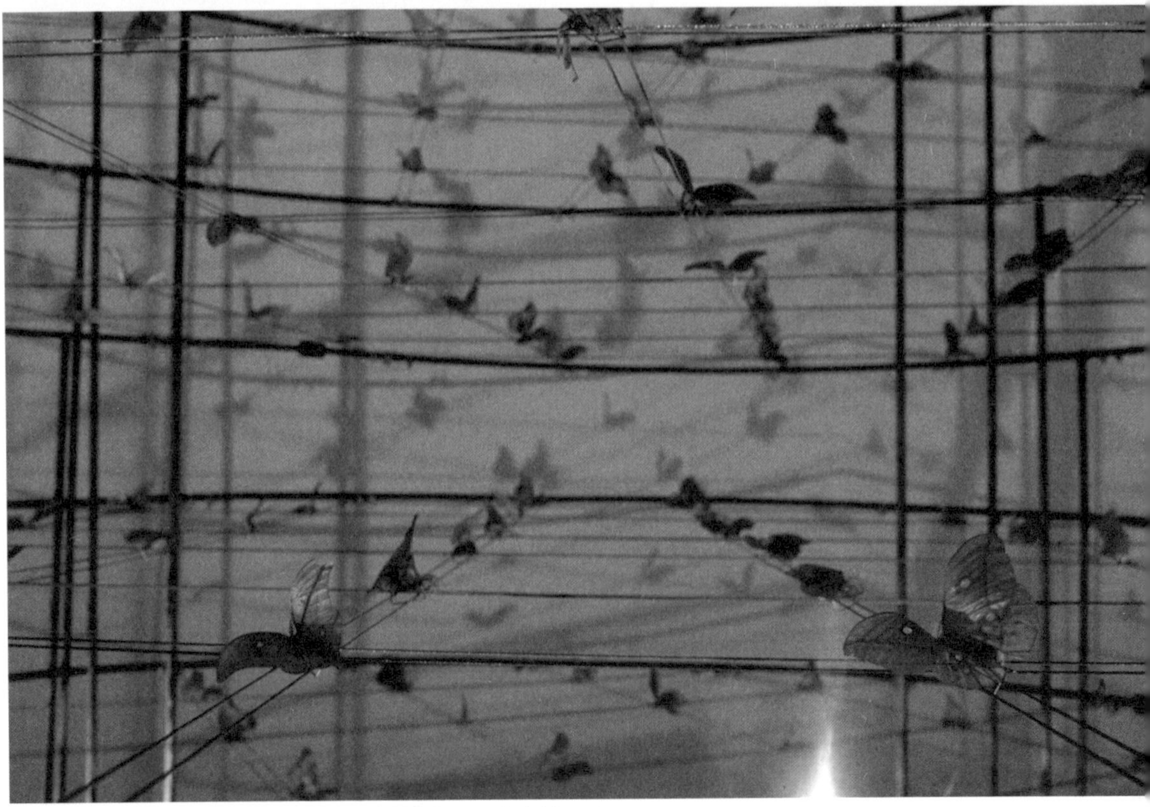

Rachel Berwick, <u>Willing Suspension of Disbelief</u>, 1992 (detail). Courtesy Rachel Berwick.

female tenured Professor under Pease's deanship was followed by Pease's appointment of Alice Aycock to Director of Graduate Studies in Sculpture and tenured Professor in 1991, making Aycock the second woman with tenure in the School's history. Aycock assumed the directorship after David von Schlegell, who had served nearly twenty years, retired from the position. An internationally recognized artist who had participated in Documenta VI and VII, Aycock had arrived at the School in 1989 as a Senior Critic in Sculpture, becoming a mentor to Matthew Barney (BA 1989), Rachel Berwick (MFA 1991), Leo Villareal (BA 1990), and others. As director, Aycock introduced the "Critical Studies" course in the department, noting, "I had wanted to make a think tank. If I was going to do it, then let's all let our guard down, let's have a great graduate moment where we are all exchanging ideas, we're talking about our work, we're experimenting, and we are not worried whether we are going to be famous or not."[153] Her attempts to widen the conversation around artistic practice were resisted by a group of students who were only "interested in meeting whatever critic was hot at the moment" and who she felt prioritized career-building over experimentation. She decided to leave the School after just one year as director, citing the need to focus on her own practice and the death of a student from AIDS as determining factors: "The [AIDS] crisis was full-blown, and it was hitting really young people. There were three graduate students in my class, each of them gay. … Each got AIDS, and each was dying. I remember it was in February that I went to visit one of the students in the hospital, where he was comatose. I watched this young man die. I think it was a kind of coup de grâce for me."[154]

Aycock's former student Rachel Berwick, who had recently graduated, was hired as a Lecturer in 1991, under the temporary directorship of John Newman, with the expectation that she would oversee the day-to-day operations of the department.[155] Berwick's hire was intended as a two-year engagement, but after von Schlegell's retirement and Aycock's quick departure left the Sculpture department with no director and with two main faculty members—Newman and Ronald Jones—who both lived two hours away in New York, she stayed on, becoming Critic in 1996 and Acting Director of Sculpture in 1998, following the departures of Newman and Jones. According to Berwick, she was an equal partner for the duration of her time as faculty, "selecting, inviting, and interacting with the visiting lecturers, visiting faculty, and visiting critics year to year." She "taught both undergraduate and graduate students and participated, along with [her] colleagues, in the admissions process and in critiques of all graduate student work, without exception."[156] Like Pfaff ten years earlier, Berwick notes that there had been an economic downturn at the time she began teaching; students moved toward immersive installations that explored metaphors aligning personal experiences and perspectives. She recalls that Trisha Donnelly (MFA 2000) brought a trampoline into her studio, on which she performed as an artwork.

Echoing the perceptions of Alice Aycock in the Sculpture department, Mary Berridge (MFA 1991), who entered the Department of Photography in 1989, recalls a program that acknowledged neither the raging culture wars nor the AIDS epidemic, but focused on the formal aspects of photography. Critiques were led by Tod Papageorge and Susan Kismaric, a Visiting Artist (1988–89), Senior Critic (1990–94), and curator in the Department of Photography at the Museum of Modern Art, joined by Professor (Adjunct) Richard Benson and Assistant Professor Joanne Walters. According to Berridge, the individual departments within the School were isolated from each other, and the School was isolated within the larger University, with faculty sometimes explicitly discouraging students from pursuing courses outside of studio art, though she notes that she was not aware of this occurring within the Photography department. Berridge recounts that, after graduating, she "was working very

153   Alice Aycock, telephone conversation with the author, September 30, 2020.

154   Ibid.

155   Rachel Berwick, telephone conversation with the author, September 9, 2020.

156   Rachel Berwick, e-mail conversation with the author, March 5, 2021.

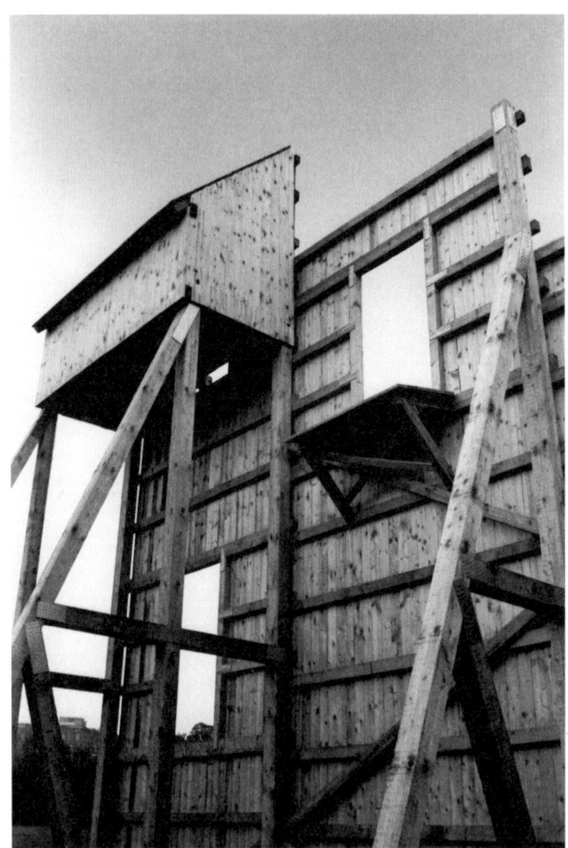 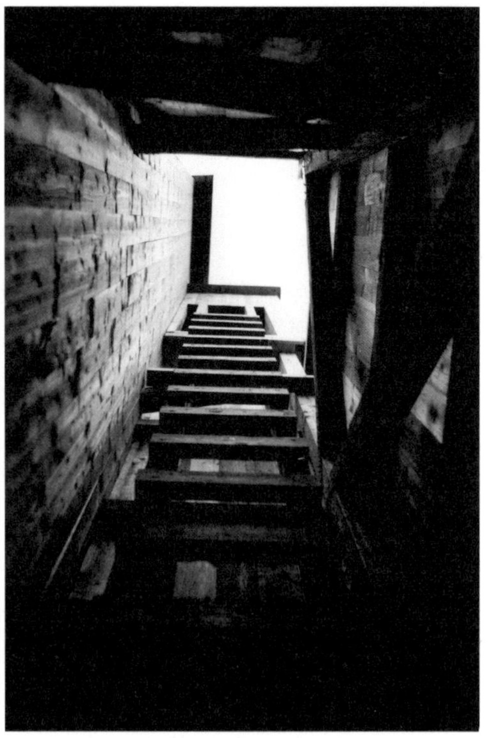

Alice Aycock, installation view, <u>Project Entitled "The Beginnings of a Complex..." (for Documenta)</u>, 1977, Documenta 6, Kassel, Germany. Photo by Alice Aycock. Courtesy Alice Aycock.

Alice Aycock, installation view, <u>Project Entitled "The Beginnings of a Complex..." (for Documenta)</u>, 1977, Documenta 6, Kassel, Germany. Photo by Alice Aycock. Courtesy Alice Aycock.

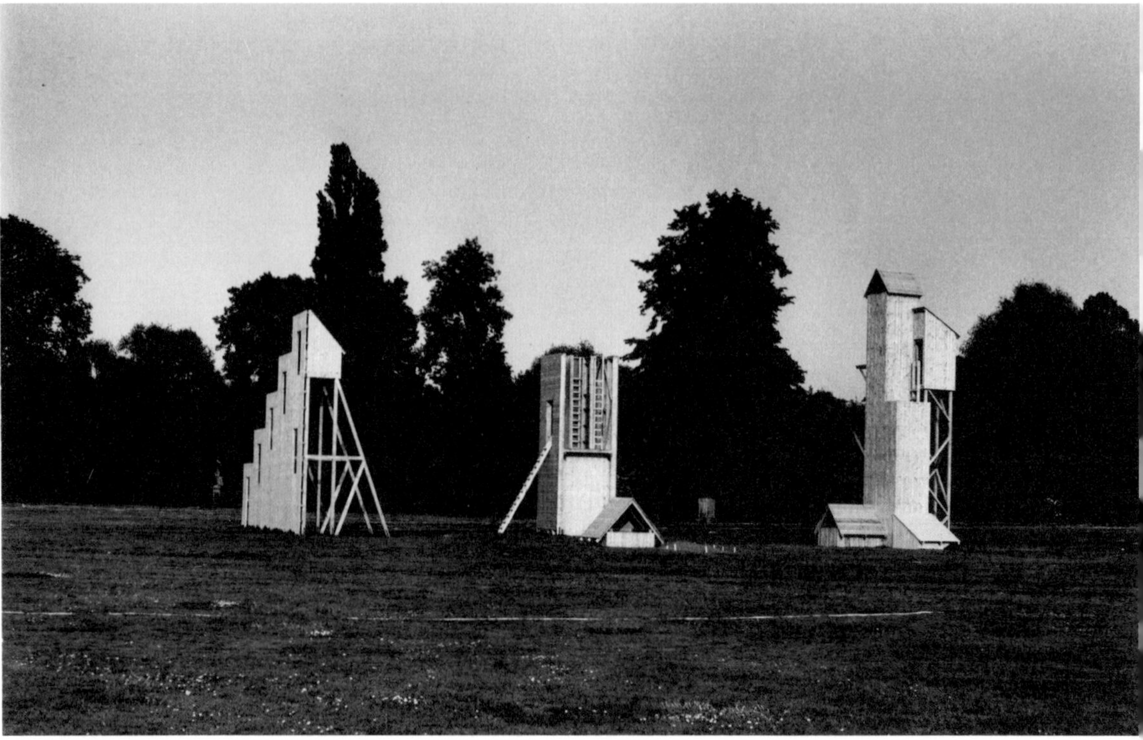

Alice Aycock, installation view, <u>Project Entitled "The Beginnings of a Complex..." (for Documenta)</u>, 1977, Documenta 6, Kassel, Germany. Photo by Alice Aycock. Courtesy Alice Aycock.

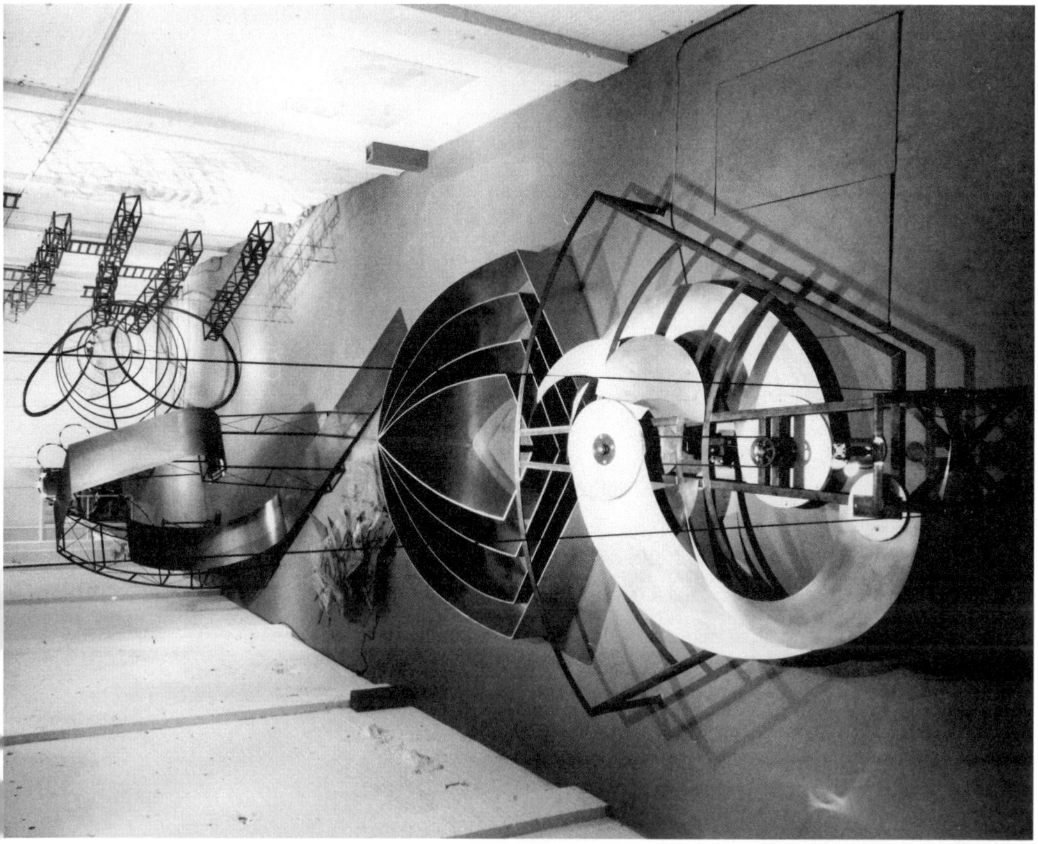

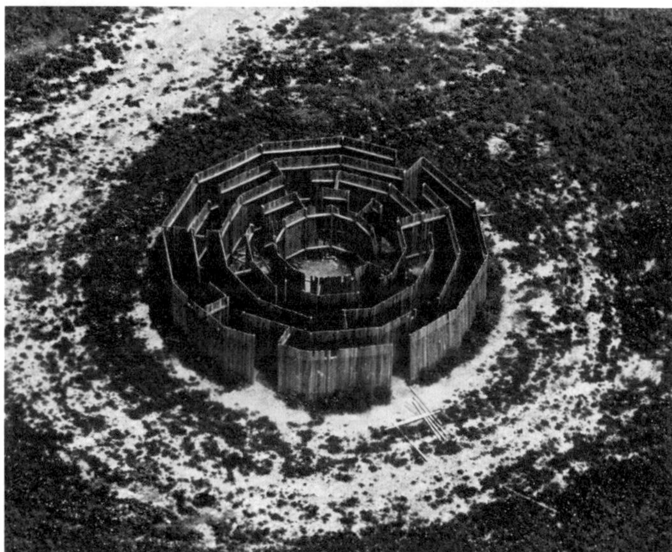

Alice Aycock, installation view, The Thousand and One Nights in the Mansion of Bliss, 1983, Protetch McNeil Gallery, New York. Photo by Wolfgang Staehle. Courtesy Alice Aycock.

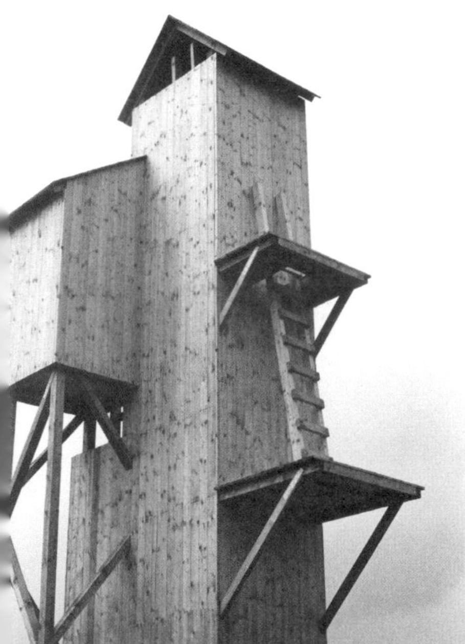

Alice Aycock, installation view, <u>Project Entitled "The Beginnings of a Complex..." (for Documenta)</u>, 1977, Documenta 6, Kassel, Germany. Photo by Alice Aycock. Courtesy Alice Aycock.

Alice Aycock, <u>Maze</u>, 1972. Photo by the Silver Spring Township Police Department. Courtesy Alice Aycock.

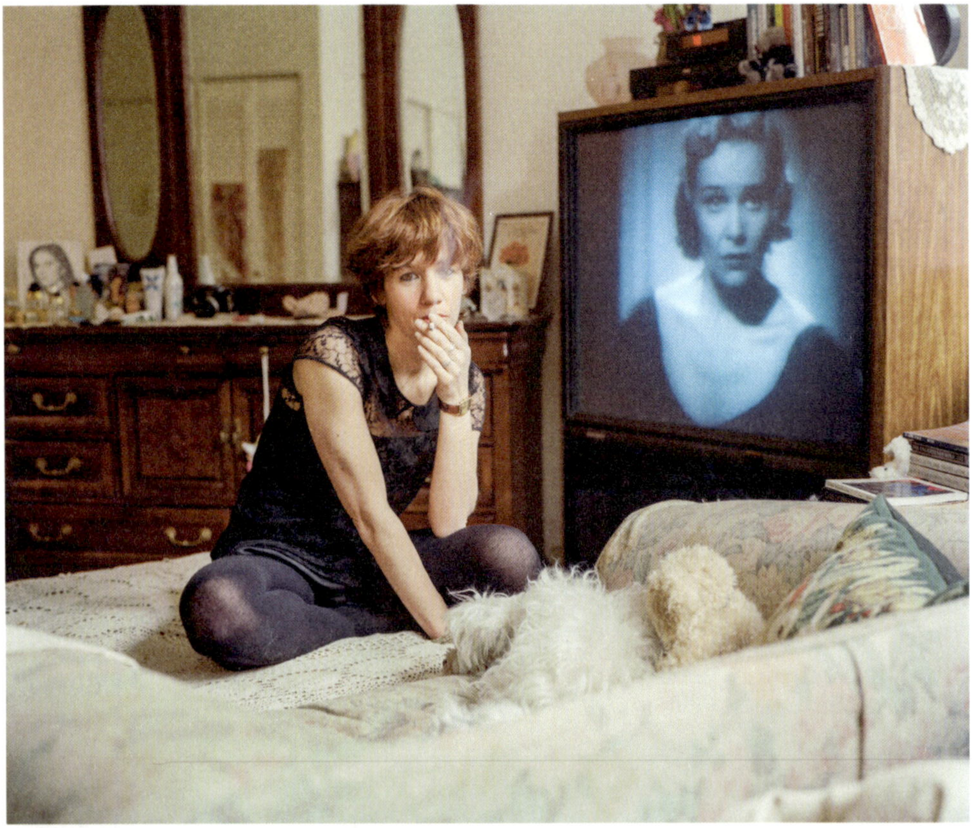

Mary Berridge, <u>Robin</u>, 1995, from <u>A Positive Life: Portraits of Women Living With HIV</u>. © Mary Berridge.

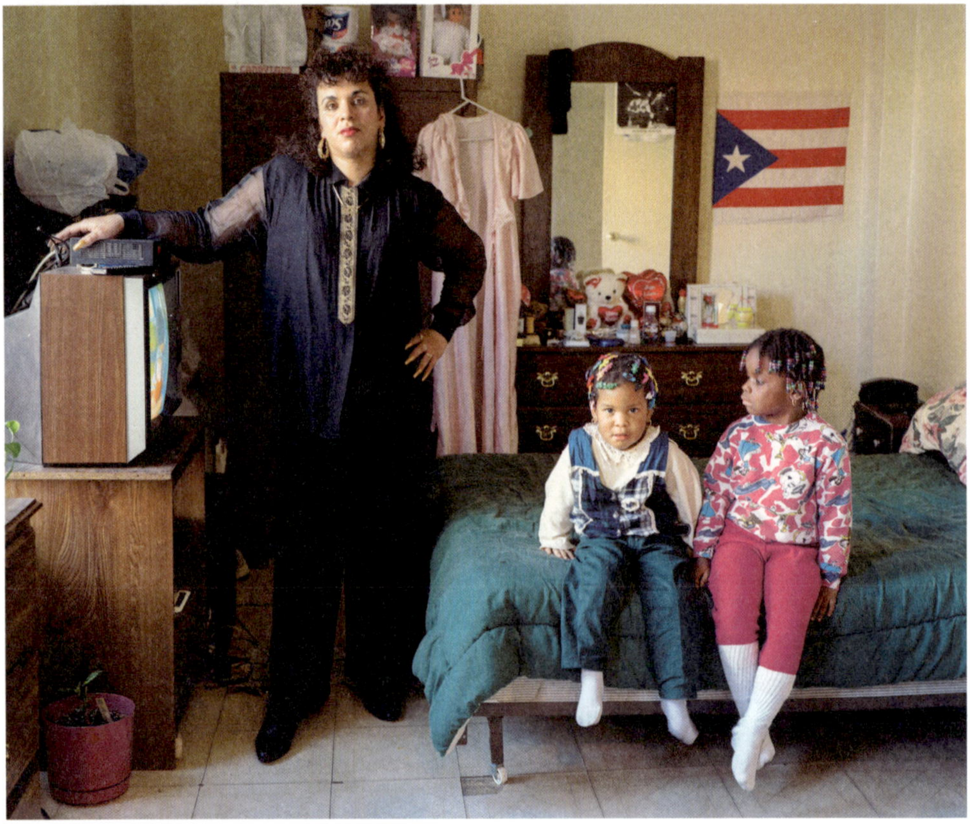

Mary Berridge, <u>Sugar</u>, 1996, from <u>A Positive Life: Portraits of Women Living With HIV</u>. © Mary Berridge.

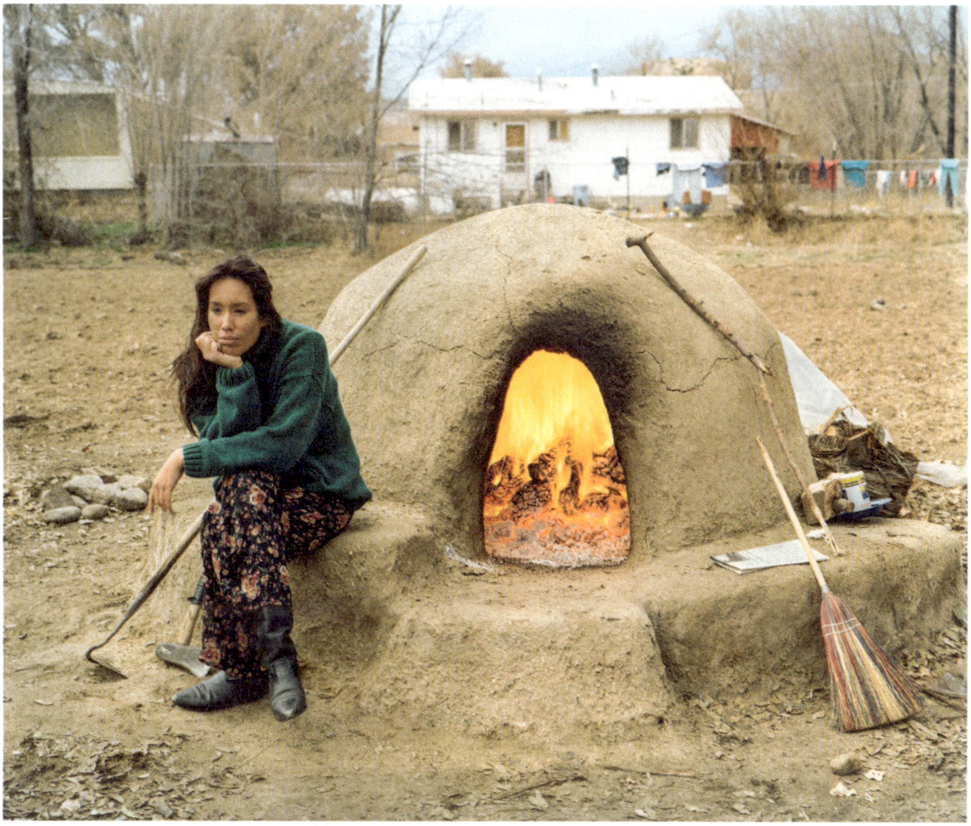

Mary Berridge, <u>Shana</u>, 1996, from <u>A Positive Life: Portraits of Women Living With HIV</u>. © Mary Berridge.

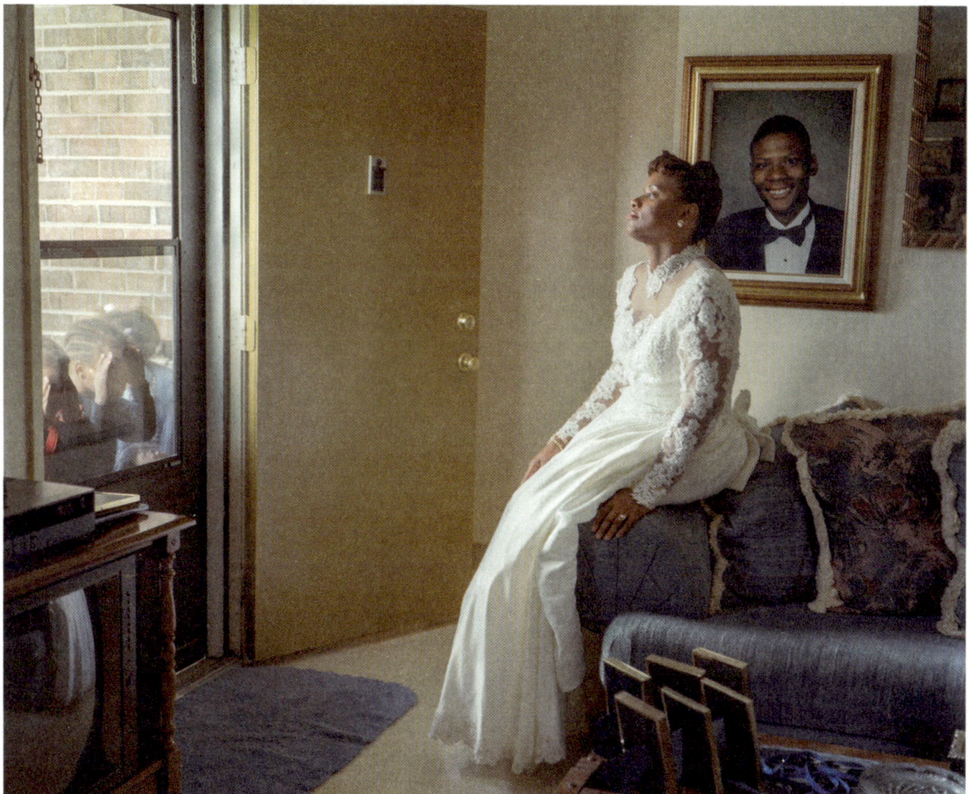

Mary Berridge, <u>Tracie</u>, 1996, from <u>A Positive Life: Portraits of Women Living With HIV</u>. © Mary Berridge.

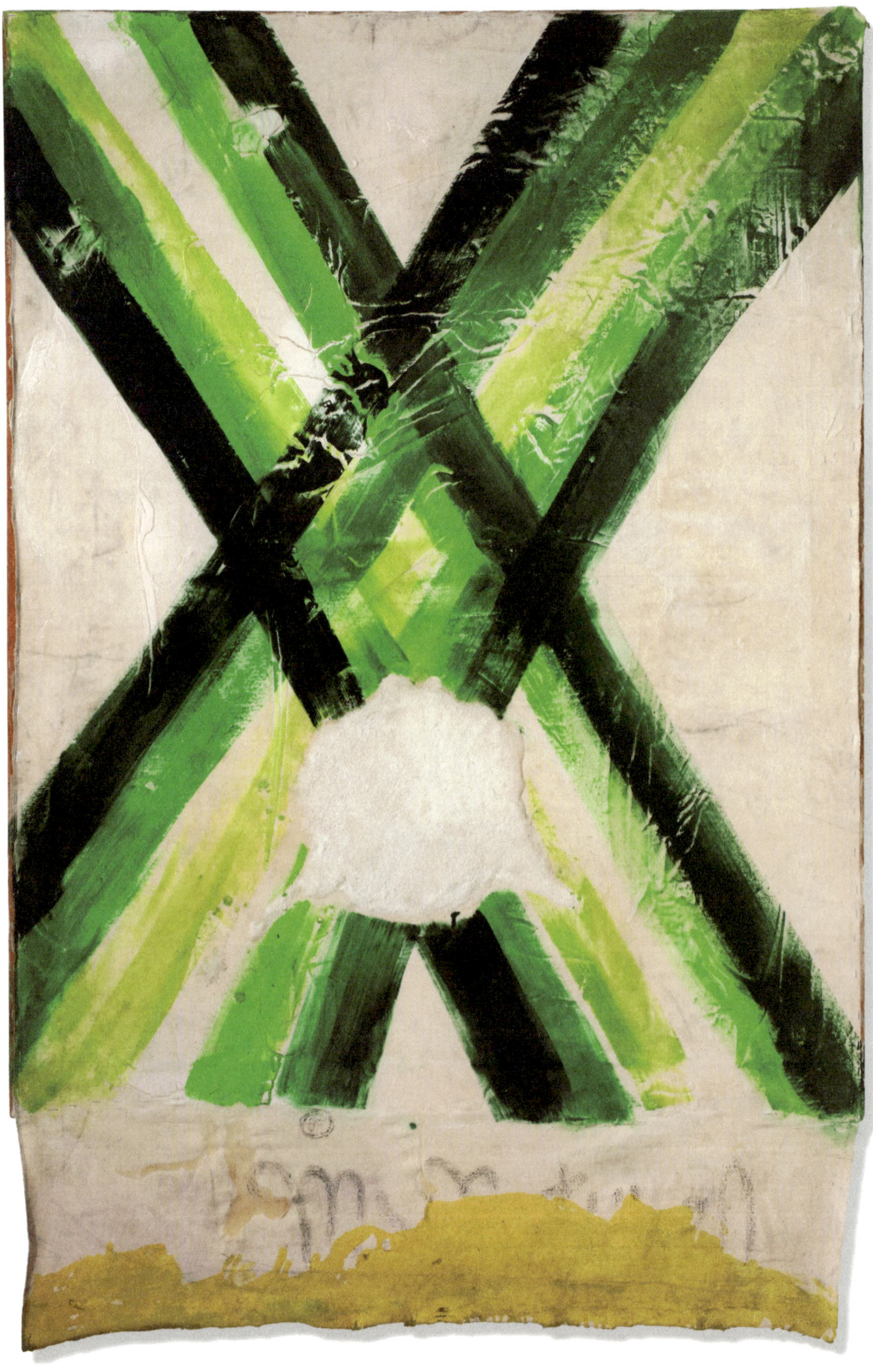

Rochelle Feinstein, <u>Mr. Natural</u>, 2009. Photo by Adam Reich. Private collection.

low-paying, adjunct-level, part-time teaching jobs at various colleges and universities and always seeking other work." She continues:

> I heard about employment as a researcher available through the Columbia University Department of Psychology, studying the impact of a mother's illness from AIDS on teenage children. I would interview the subjects either over the phone or at their homes and ask them hundreds of questions, many of which were incredibly personal and intimate, about what kind of sex they had or what kind of drugs they were using—whatever. It was in the poorest of the poor areas of New York City, and it was an eye-opening experience for me. AIDS, up until that time, at least in the media, was completely associated with men—gay men, men using drugs. That was the picture the media presented, and yet the women had the fastest growing rates of infection at the time. I just thought, "This is something that really needs to be seen."[157]

Berridge did not photograph the women engaged in the studies, but she located other women who were willing to go public, one of whom was the writer River Huston, who collaborated with Berridge on the book *A Positive Life: Portraits of Women Living With HIV* [see pp. 132–33], which received the Dorothea Lange-Paul Taylor Prize in 1996. Berridge went on to join the faculty at Princeton University as Lecturer in the Department of Art and Archaeology.

Lois Conner (MFA 1981) was hired in 1991 as Assistant Professor and promoted to Associate Professor on term in 1994, becoming the first woman within the Department of Photography to hold a full-time senior faculty position. Conner recalls that, by the time of her appointment, AIDS had become an important part of the conversation within the Department. In the following years, according to Conner, Tod Papageorge often cited David Hilliard (MFA 1994), whose early work centered upon homosexuality and AIDS. But Conner also recalls an environment of intimidation within the department: "There was an underlying level of intimidation during critiques that never wavered. The last few years, I was always made to feel that my opinions and views were less relevant than the male faculty's, though they would quote me verbatim. … Often, I was placed in the 'woman's role' and even recall being asked to get coffee."[158] Conner fulfilled the nine years of her contract, attending to a demanding schedule of undergraduate and graduate teaching. Though qualified for tenure at that point, she was told there were no available tenure positions to accommodate her, and thus she was forced to leave her full-time position when the term of her appointment concluded at the end of the 1999–2000 academic year under Dean Richard Benson. She returned to the School in later years as a part-time Critic.

Following a national search, Dean David Pease appointed Rochelle Feinstein as Director in Printmaking and tenured Associate Professor in Painting

157 Mary Berridge, telephone conversation with the author, April 6, 2021.

158 Lois Conner, telephone conversation with the author, April 5, 2021.

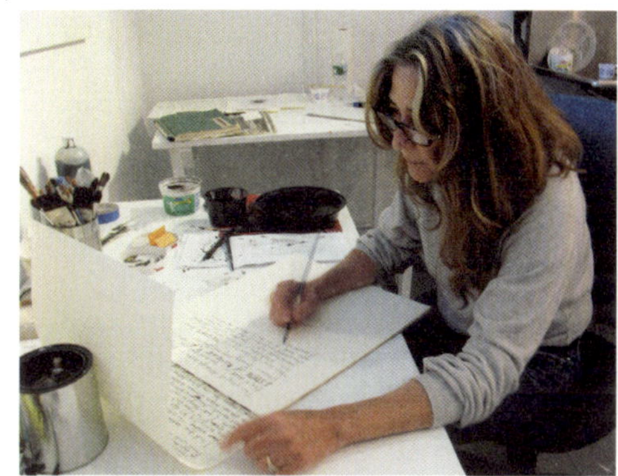

Rochelle Feinstein at the Yaddo Residency, August 21, 2010. © BTG Productions/Bari Pearlman.

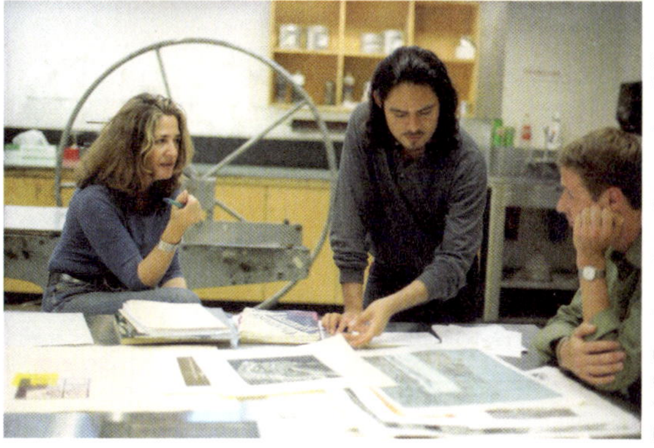

Rochelle Feinstein with graduate students William Cordova and Bryan Stryeski at the Gabor Peterdi Print Studio, Yale School of Art, 2004. Courtesy Lisa Kereszi.

   WOMEN ASCEND TO LEADERSHIP IN THE YALE SCHOOL OF ART

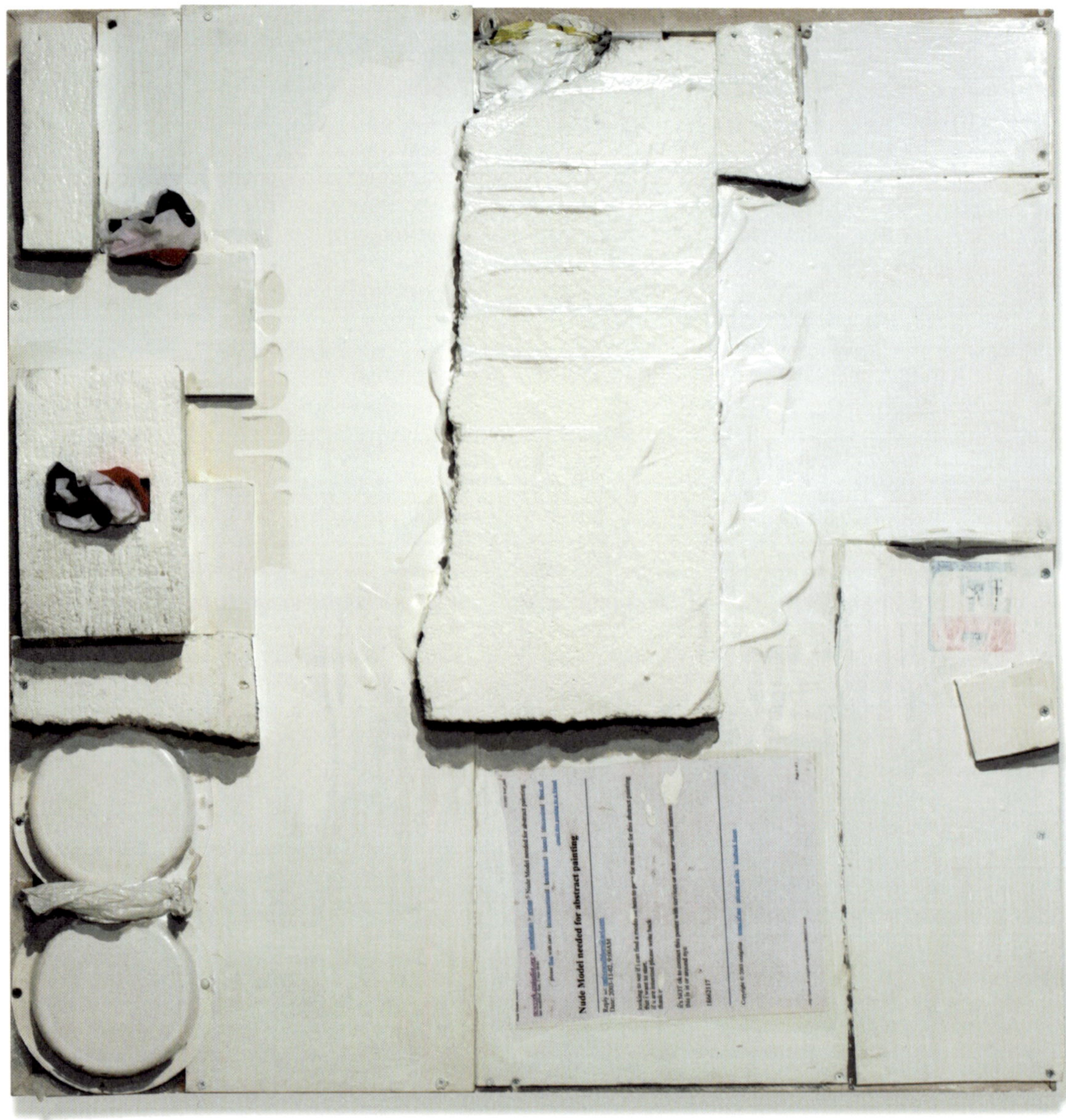

Rochelle Feinstein, <u>Nude Model</u>, 2009. Photo by Adam Reich. Courtesy Rochelle Feinstein.

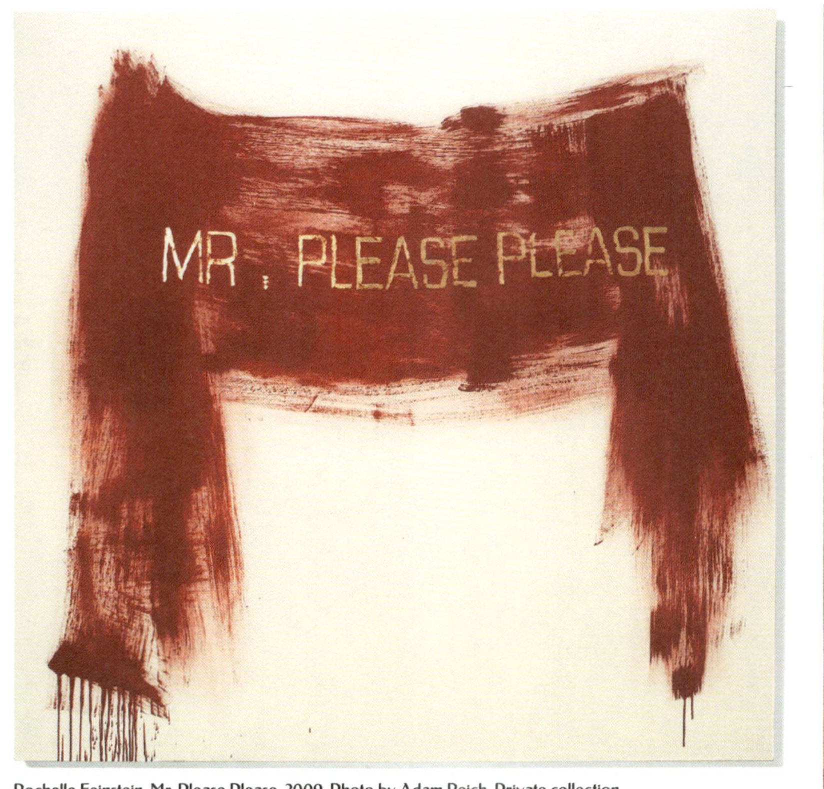

Rochelle Feinstein, <u>Mr. Please Please</u>, 2009. Photo by Adam Reich. Private collection.

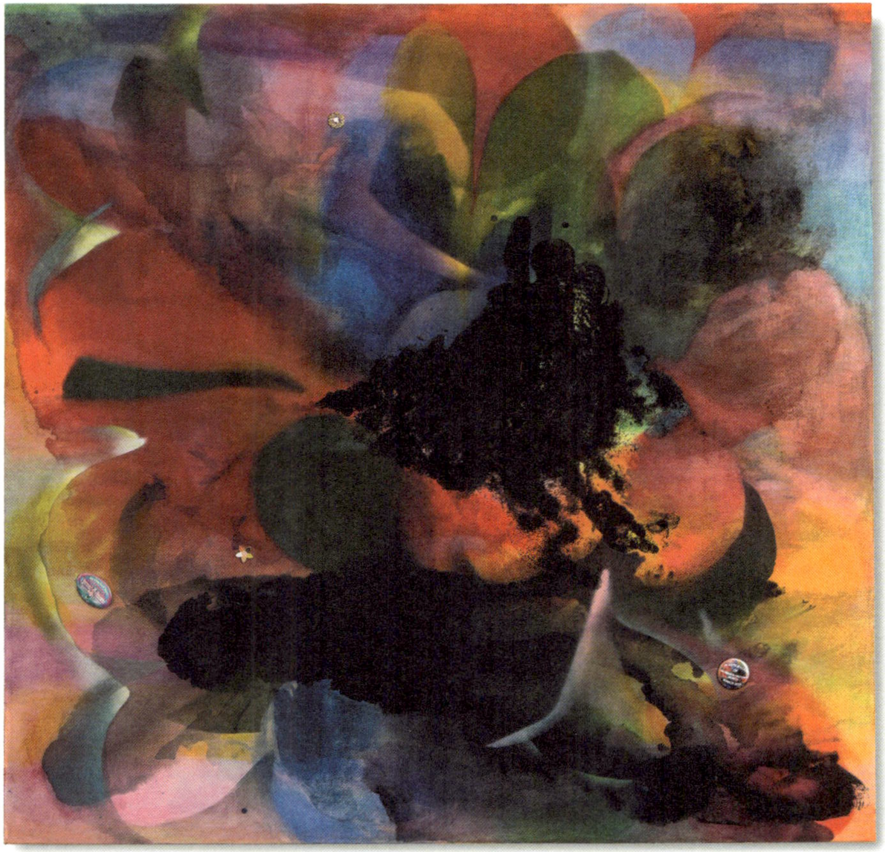

Rochelle Feinstein, <u>In Anticipation of Women's History Month</u>, 2013. Photo by Adam Reich. Private collection.

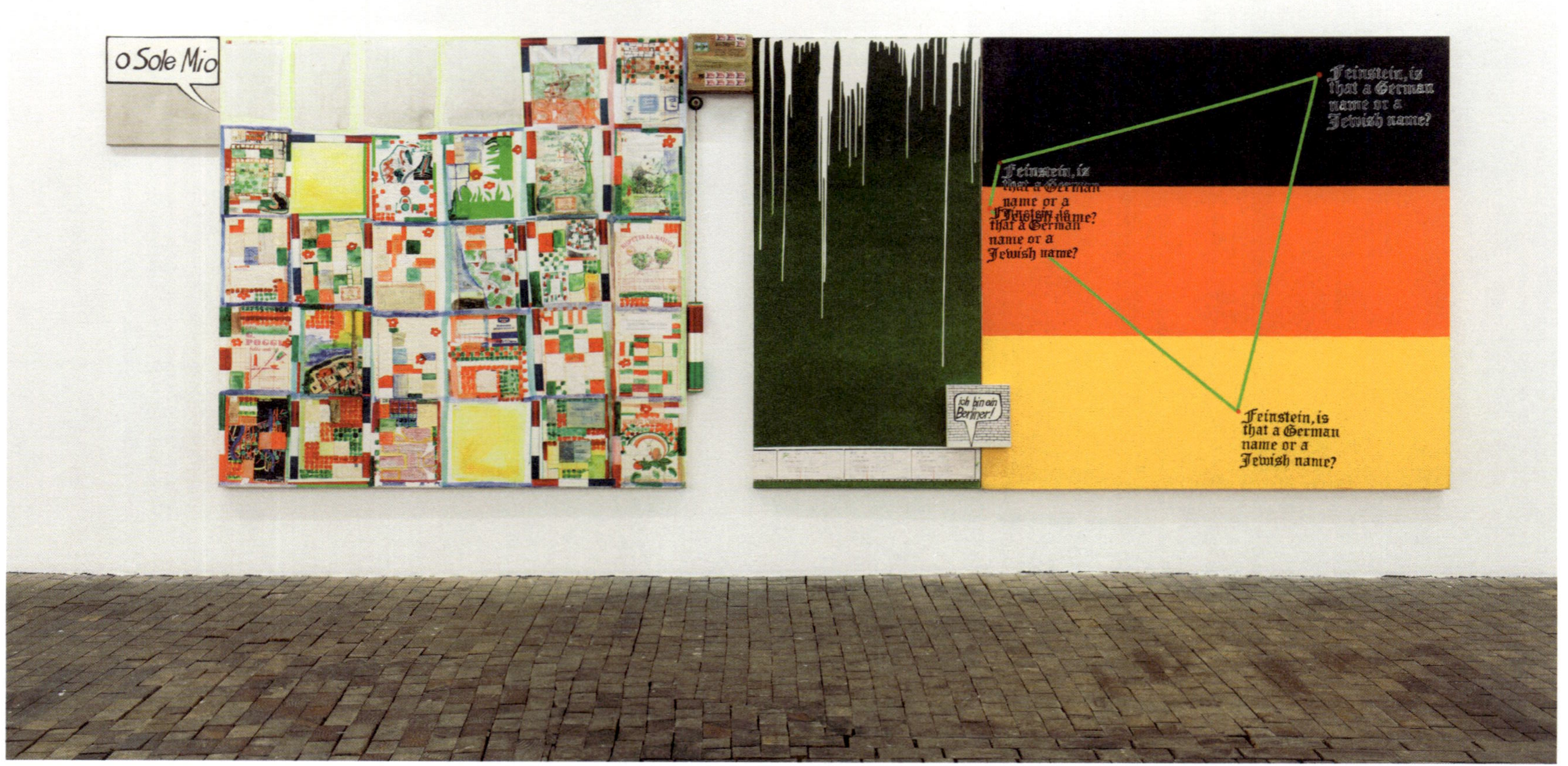

Rochelle Feinstein, _Travel Abroad_, 1999. Photo by Gunnar Meier. Courtesy Rochelle Feinstein.

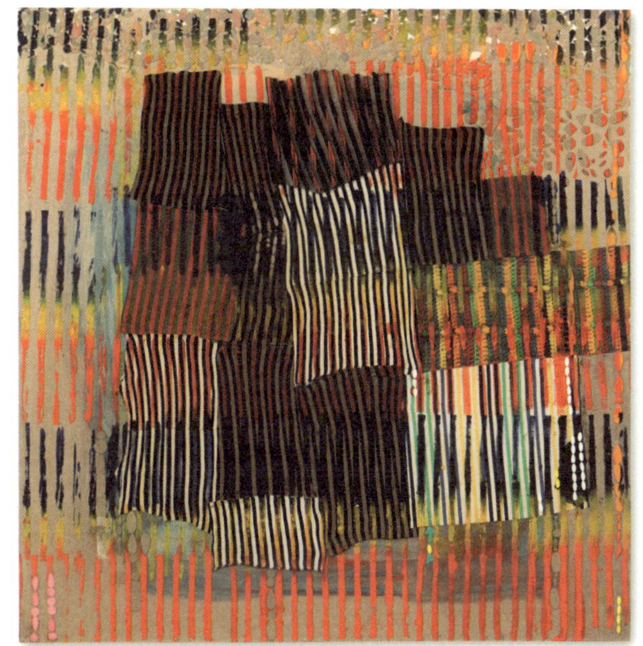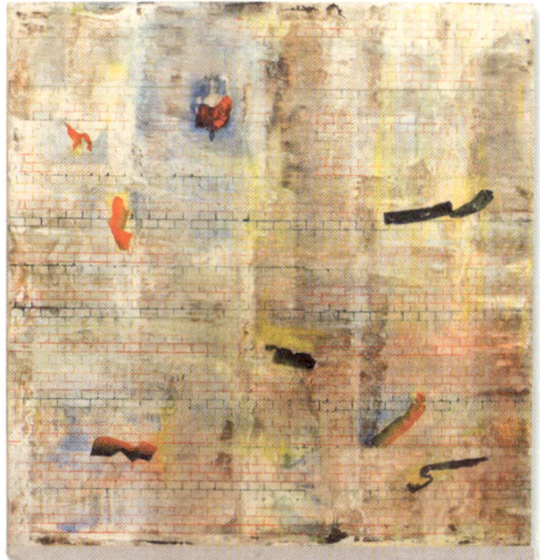

Rochelle Feinstein, <u>Mother and Child</u>, 1994. Photo by Adam Reich. Courtesy Rochelle Feinstein.

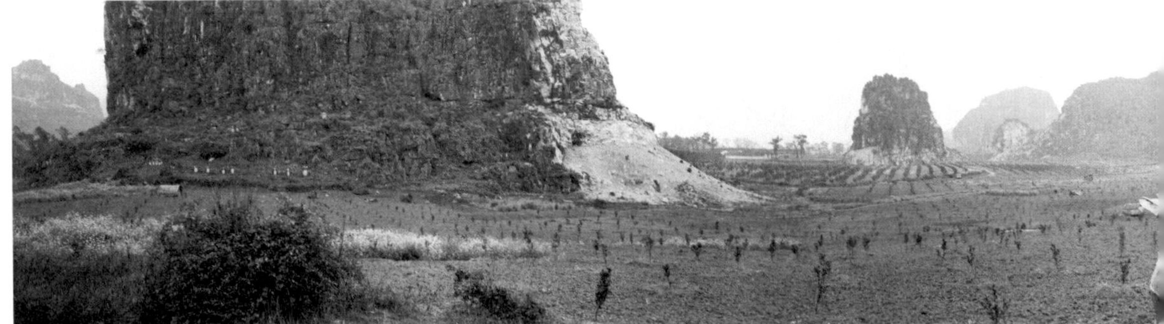

Lois Conner, <u>Triptych, Yangshou</u>, 1991. © 2021 Lois Conner.

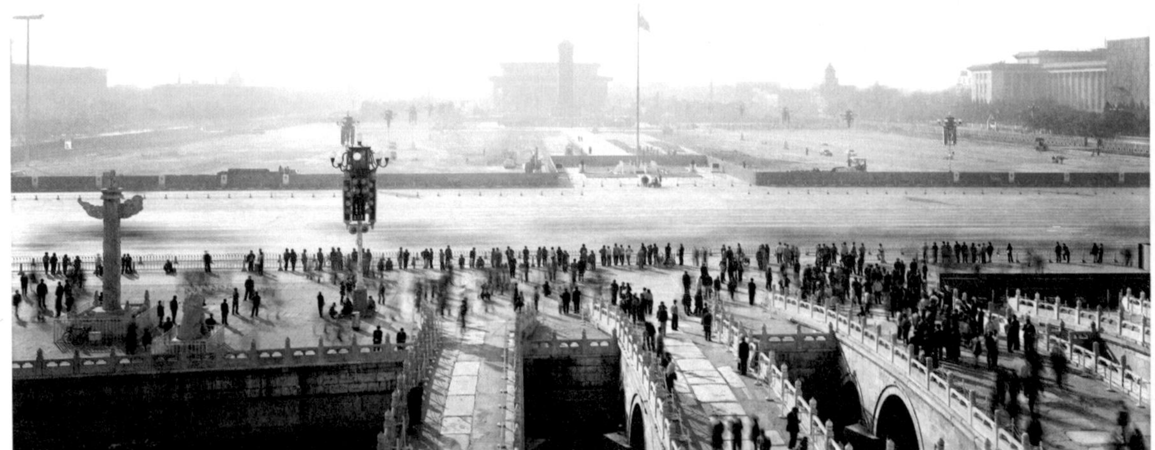

Lois Conner, <u>Tiananmen Square, Beijing</u>, 1998. © 2021 Lois Conner.

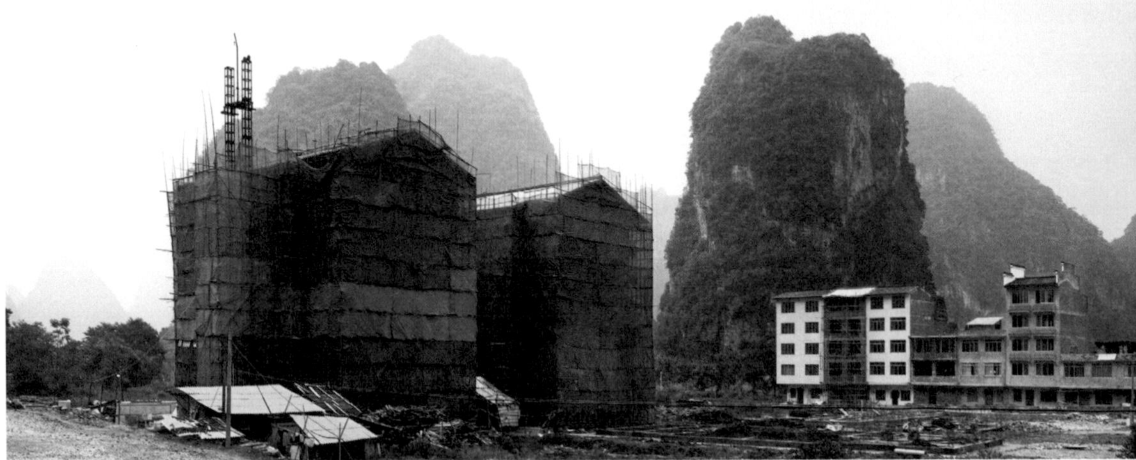

Lois Conner, <u>Construction, Yangshuo</u>, 2002. © 2021 Lois Conner.

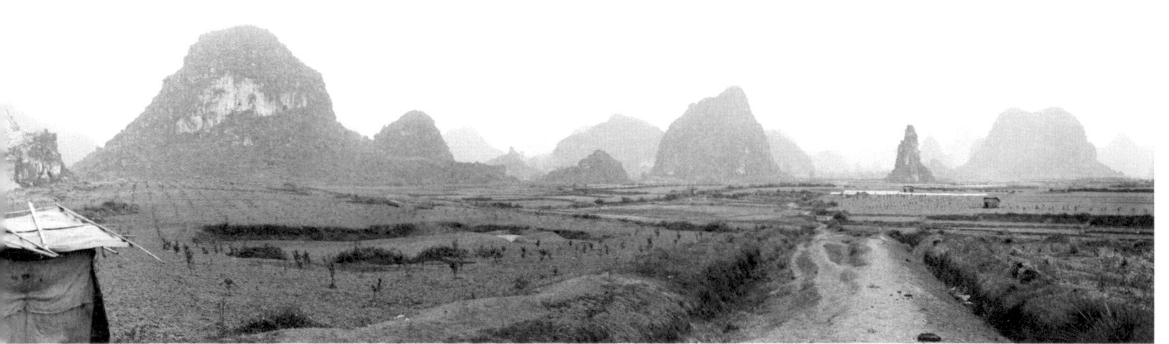

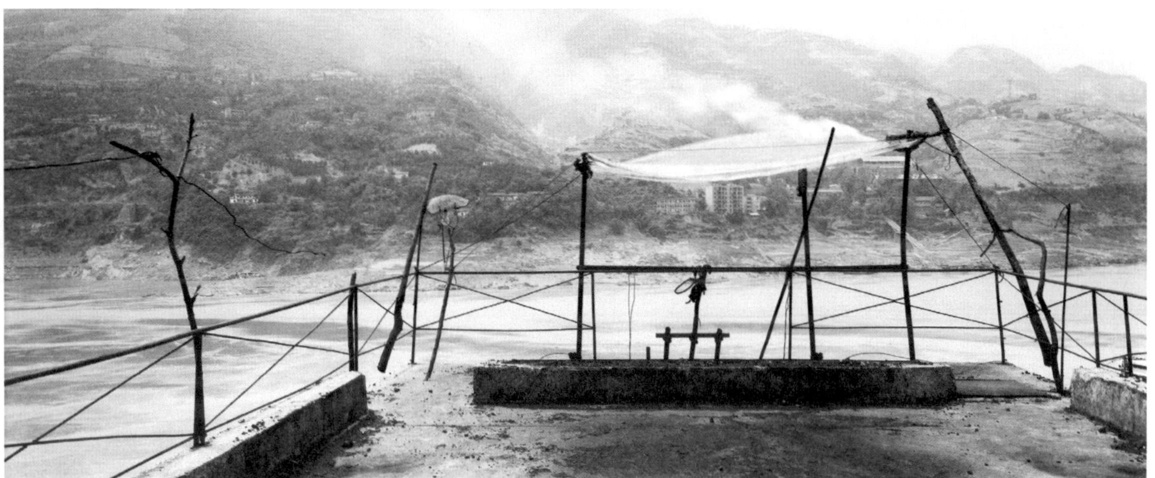

Lois Conner, <u>Yangtze River, China</u>, 1997. © 2021 Lois Conner.

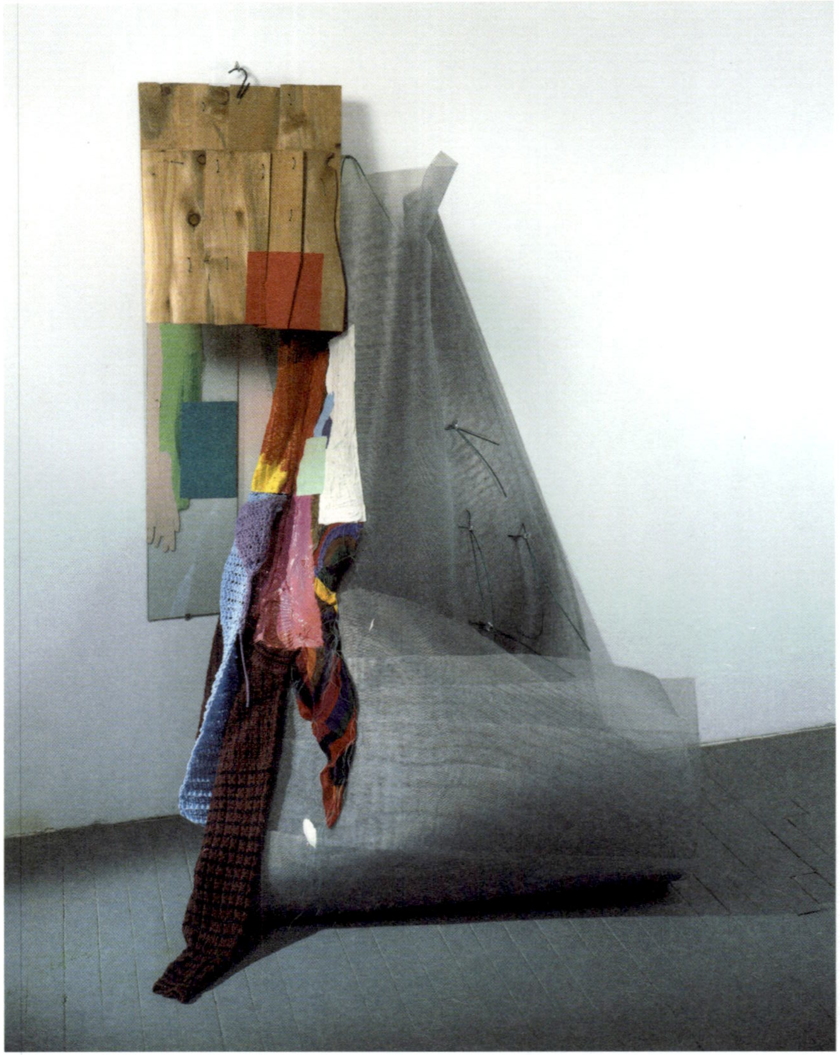

Jessica Stockholder, Inventory #JS317, 1999. Courtesy Jessica Stockholder and Mitchell Innes & Nash Gallery.

Jessica Stockholder, Inventory #JS264, 1996. Photo by Stefan Rohner. Courtesy Jessica Stockholder and Mitchell Innes & Nash Gallery. In the collection of the Art Institute of Chicago.

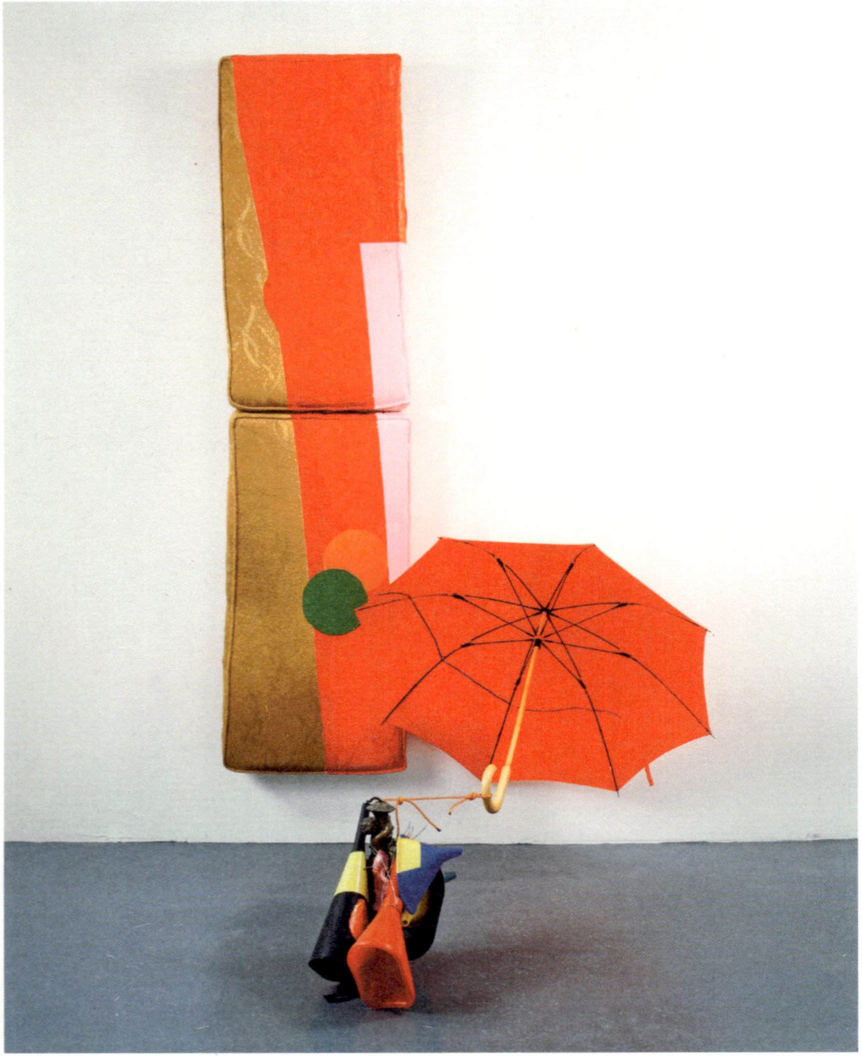

159 Women have served as Directors of Undergraduate Studies in Art since 1987 when Susana Jacobson was appointed. Since then, Jo Ann Walters, Janice Murray, Lois Conner, and Lisa Kereszi have also held this position. "Directors of Undergraduate Studies in Art, 1967–Present."

160 Rochelle Feinstein, conversation with the author, February 9, 2020.

161 Ibid.

162 School of Art Bulletin of Yale University (2004), 29.

163 Rochelle Feinstein, telephone conversation with Edi Dai, October 18, 2018.

164 Jessica Stockholder, telephone conversation with author, January 8, 2020.

and Printmaking in 1994, making her the third woman in the School's history to serve in a full-time tenured faculty and leadership position.[159] Feinstein was a highly accomplished artist whose practice extended beyond painting and drawing into photography and video and related to the legacy of a largely male-dominated modernist tradition through works characterized by vibrant color fields, bold brushstrokes, and fragmented slogans that conveyed a slapstick feminist sensibility. She had fourteen years of experience teaching at Bennington College, in Vermont, where she had also held tenure. Despite this, her appointment at Yale was contested by many of the all-male faculty, who challenged her credentials. During her third interview, she says, William Bailey asserted that she was "not a part of painting culture."[160] At the time, Feinstein perceived Bailey's motive as protecting the Painting program from the incursion of political or social concerns into a discourse mainly concerned with the formal conventions and operations of painting as a two-dimensional space. She became the singular woman in a traditionally paternalistic Painting and Printmaking department. Once at Yale, she worked within what she found to be a "toxic" environment, requiring "a rope to pull through the trenches."[161]

Feinstein continued to teach at the School for twenty-three years, offering diverse perspectives on painting and printmaking. In her later role as Director of Graduate Studies in Painting and Printmaking, she revised the graduate curriculum and implemented a rotating program of "Core Critics" to bring emerging, diverse, and urgent conversations to the School. When the School moved from Rudolph's Art and Architecture Building to its current location in Holcombe T. Green, Jr. Hall (on Chapel and Crown Streets) in 2000, Feinstein designed an expanded printmaking area that not only embraced traditional media but also made room for the new. In 2004 she introduced "LABoratory," a graduate seminar focused on contemporaneous artworks from the mid-twentieth century to the present through periodicals, essays, reviews, and criticism, to encourage students to engage with new work outside their individual studio practices.[162] The objective was "to think through a problem, discover capacities not yet unearthed, and understand the historical context that informs how objects are made and what they might have meant in relation to their own moment of making."[163]

In 1999, following Berwick's departure from the Sculpture program, Jessica Stockholder was appointed Director of Graduate Studies in Sculpture and tenured Associate Professor. "When I came into the School as faculty," Stockholder notes, "I understood that to arrive with tenure was a very privileged and secure position. Yet I realized that those who had retired into emeritus positions—such as William Bailey, Lester Johnson, David Pease— continued to put pressure on Chip [Dean Richard Benson] and still seemed to have some influence."[164]

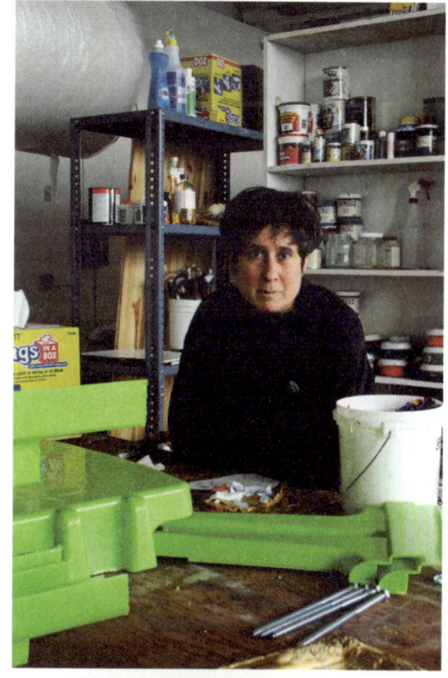

Jessica Stockholder, self-portrait in her studio at Erector Square, New Haven, 2004. Courtesy Jessica Stockholder.

Joe Scanlan, Alex Da Corte, Daphne Fitzpatrick, Michel Auder, Kate Levant, Meredith James, and Ryan Wolfe at a critique in Hammond Hall, 2009. Photo by Jessica Stockholder.

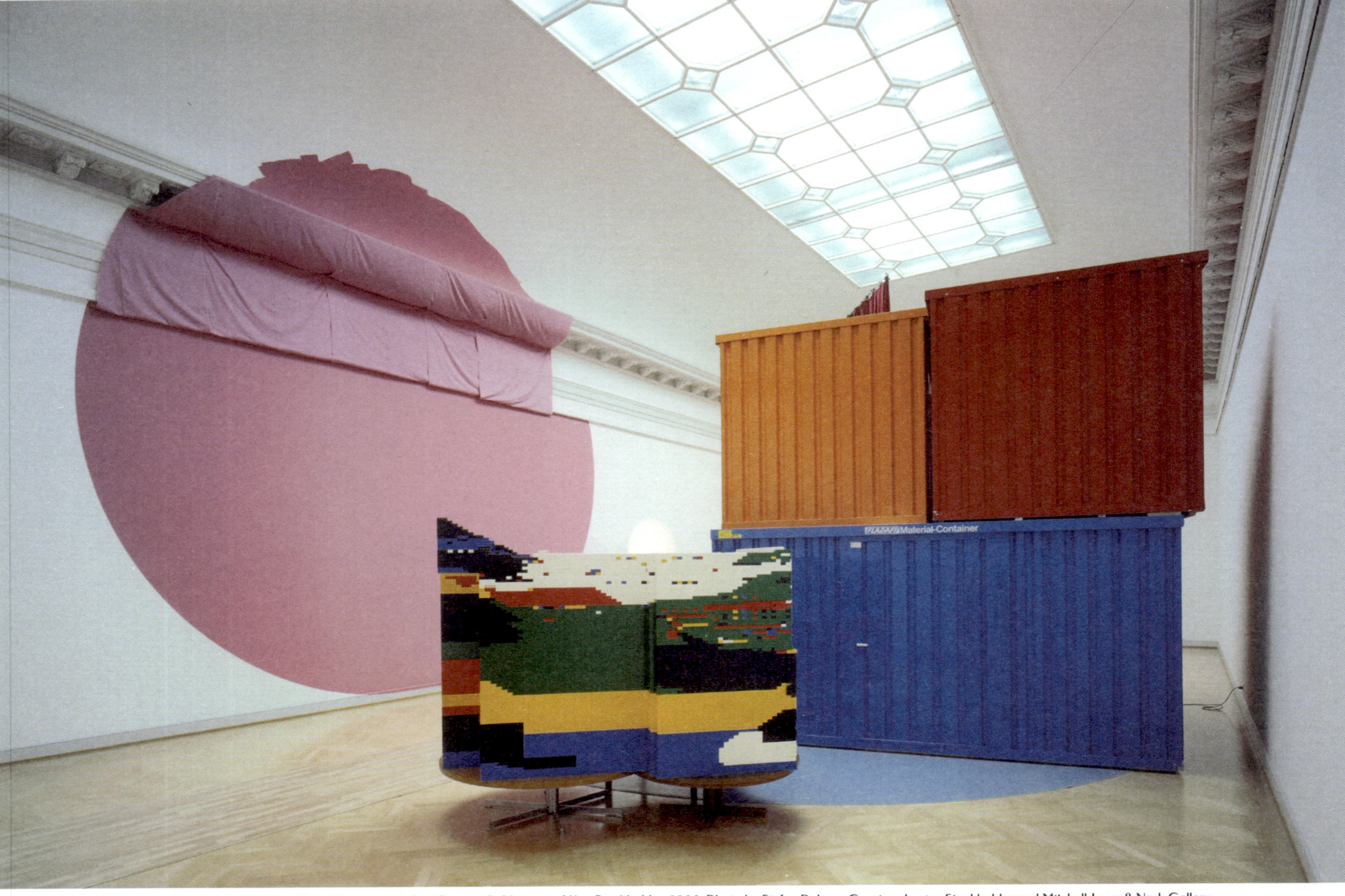

Jessica Stockholder, Inventory #JS222: Vortex in the Play of Theater with Real Passion. In Memory of Kay Stockholder, 2000. Photo by Stefan Rohner. Courtesy Jessica Stockholder and Mitchell-Innes & Nash Gallery.

Stockholder built upon the structure David von Schlegell had established for the Sculpture program, appointing faculty whom she believed balanced an interest in conceptual, political, racial, and gender issues with an emphasis on how processes and forms of making generate meaning. During Stockholder's tenure, the department moved from Hammond Hall, where it had resided for almost forty years, to a newly constructed building at 36 Edgewood. The building was considerably closer than Hammond Hall to the rest of the School, but the departments remained fairly siloed, although students were able to attend critiques in other departments. Conversations, often fraught, ensued over the possibility of establishing more formal channels for cross-disciplinary encounters, as well as exchanges within the larger University. Stockholder, attempting to address the disconnection, proposed a collaboration with the Yale Law School, but this was not met with support by the School's leadership. After a twelve-year engagement with the School, she decided to leave her tenured position in 2011. She accepted a tenured Professorship in the Department of Visual Arts at the University of Chicago, a position she still holds.

Seventeen years would pass after Stockholder's 1999 appointment before women faculty would again enter the School's governance, with the appointment in 2016 of this author as the first woman dean in the School's 150-year history.

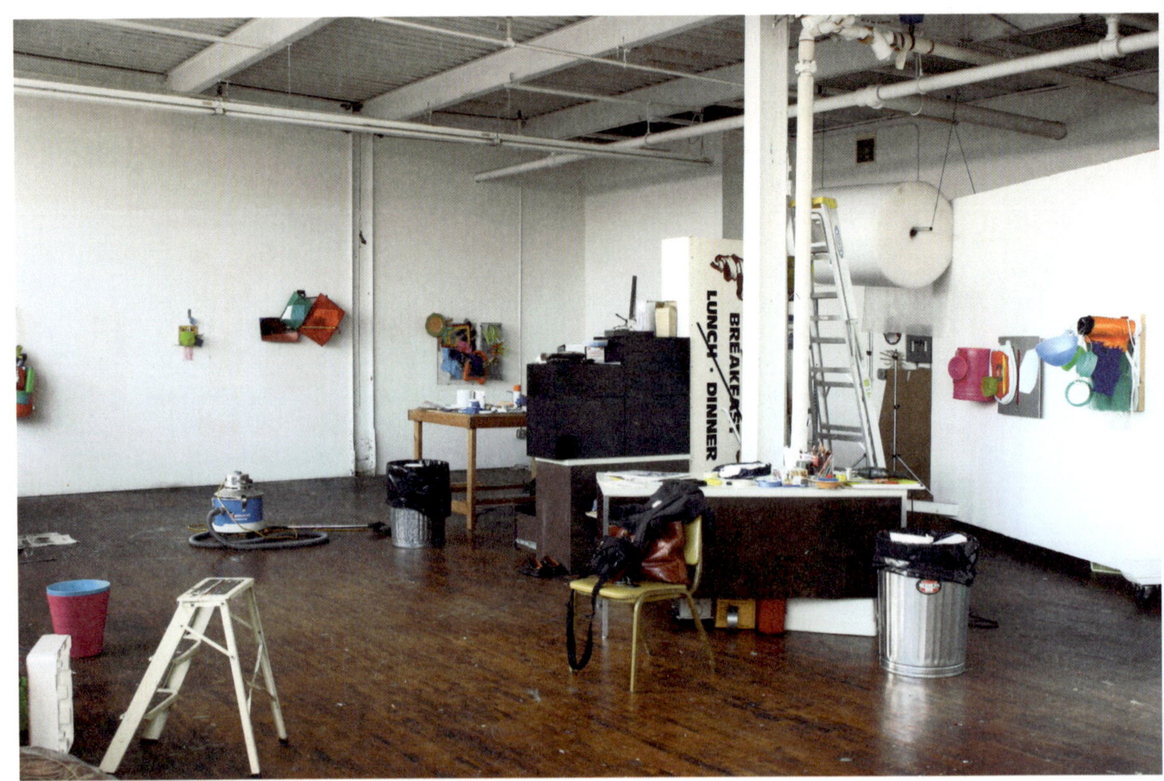

Jessica Stockholder's studio at Erector Square, New Haven, 2004. Courtesy Jessica Stockholder.

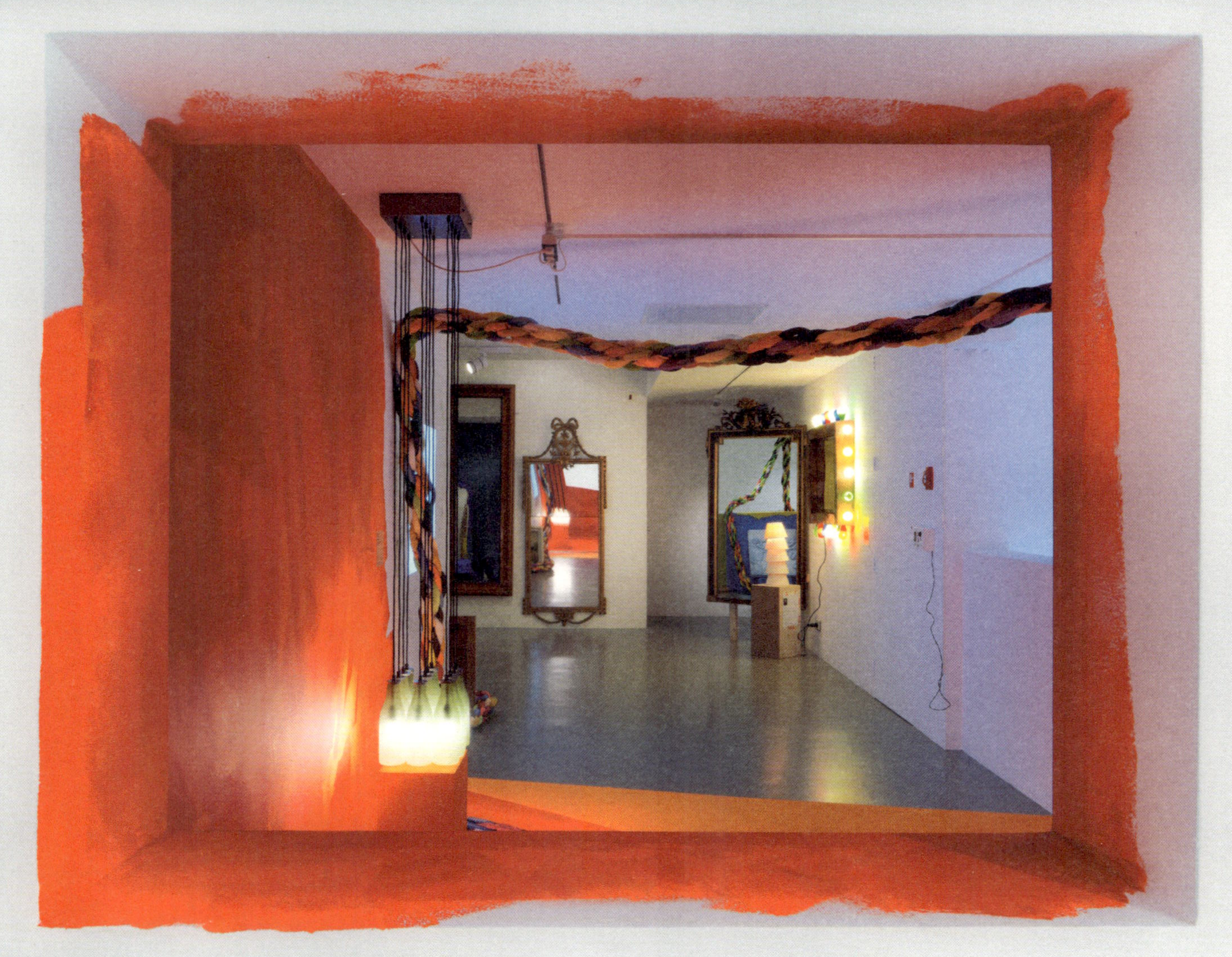

Jessica Stockholder, _Inventory #JS867: In the Face of Drifting Eye,_ 2019 (detail), from the exhibition _Stuff Matters._ Photo by Gert Jan van Rooij. Courtesy Jessica Stockholder and Mitchell Innes & Nash Gallery.

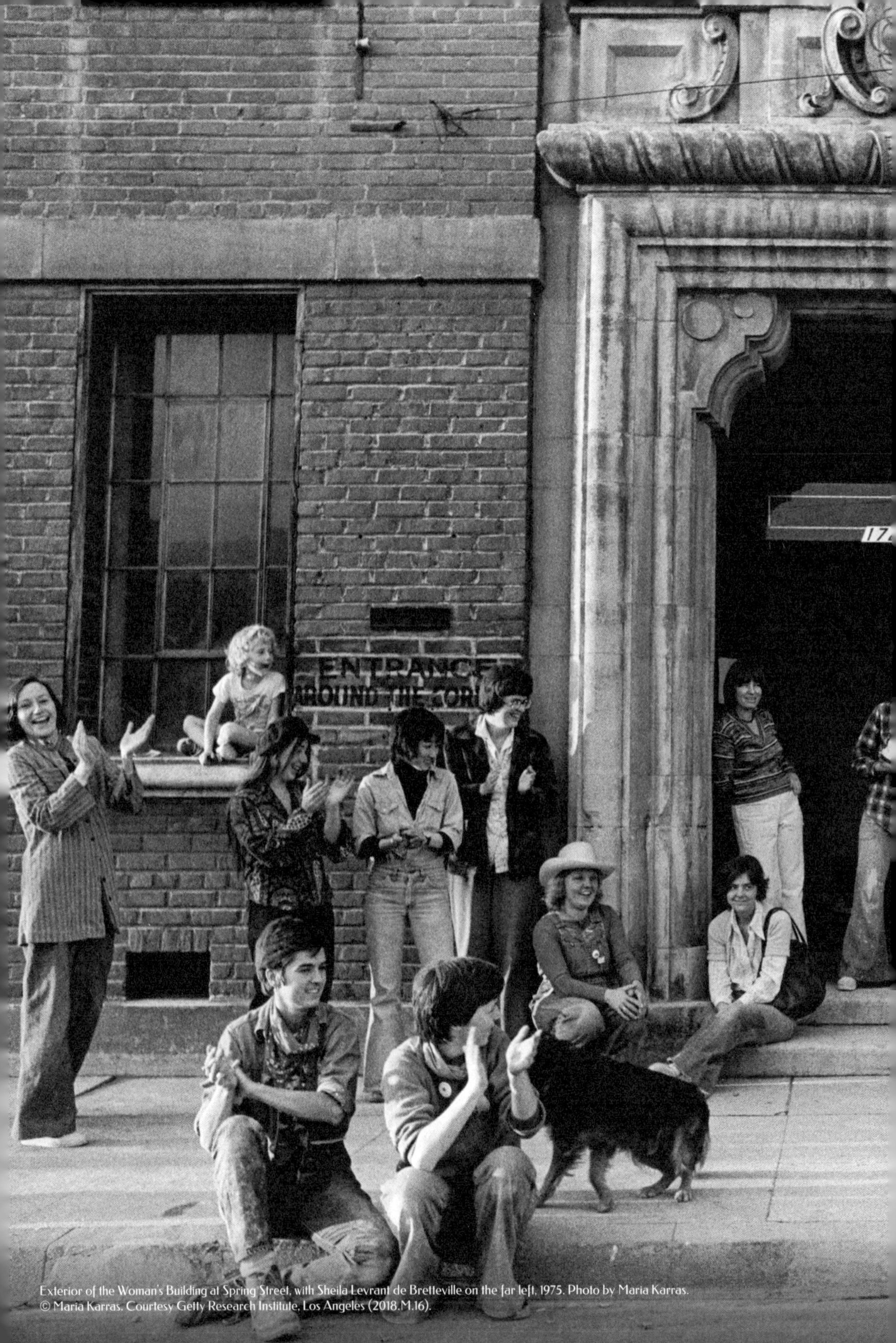

Exterior of the Woman's Building at Spring Street, with Sheila Levrant de Bretteville on the far left, 1975. Photo by Maria Karras.
© Maria Karras. Courtesy Getty Research Institute, Los Angeles (2018.M.16).

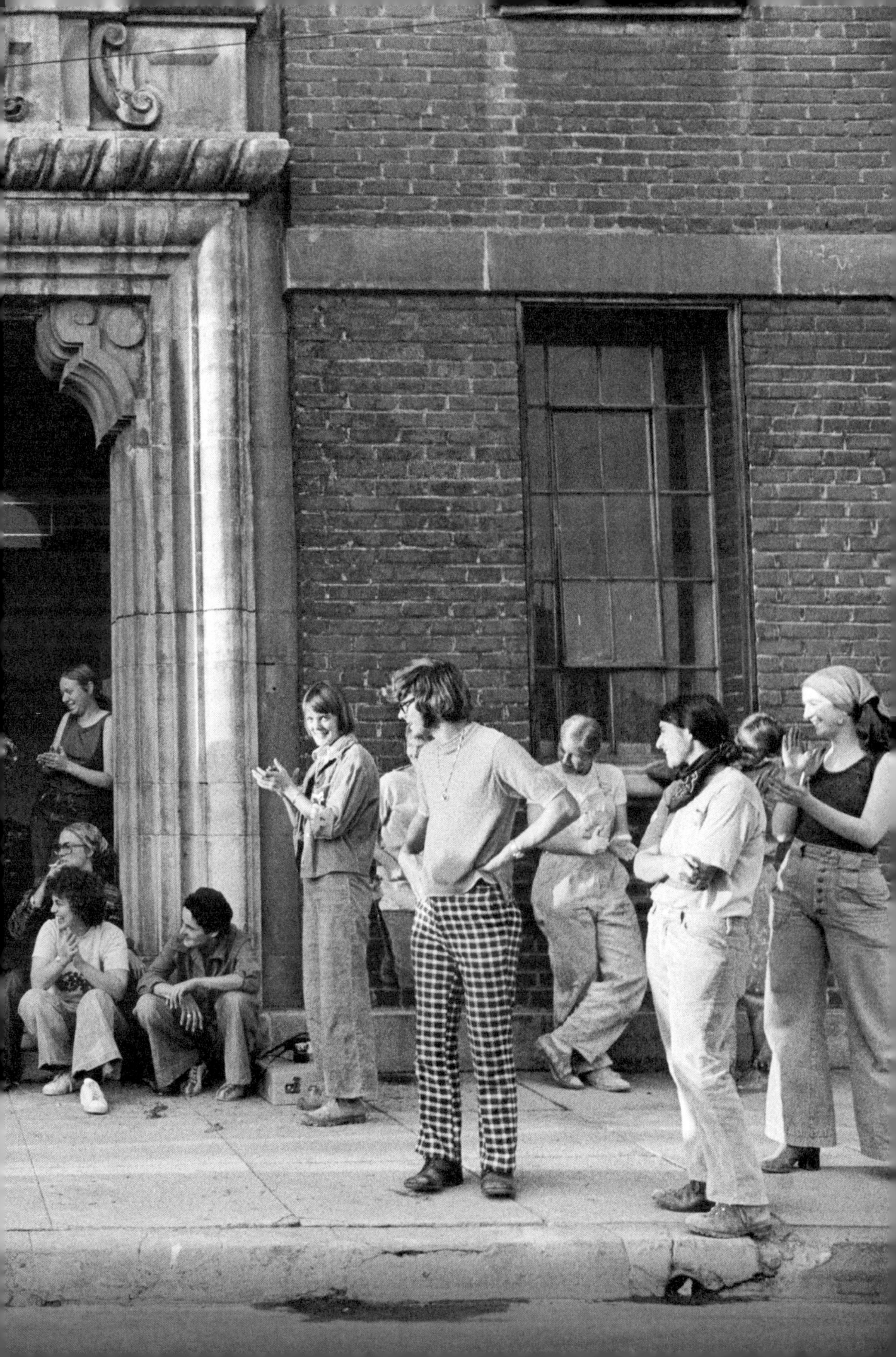

CRITIQUE AS A MODE OF REFLEXIVITY AND REFLECTION

In 2016 the School's Critical Practice course was revised to a weekly lecture and seminar called "Diving into the Wreck: Revisiting Critical Practice"—a title borrowed from a 1973 poem by Adrienne Rich—thus formalizing critical study as part of the curriculum and expressing a decanal perspective in direct contrast with that of the preceding deans who maintained that artists should be makers, not thinkers.[165] As a Hayden Distinguished Speaker addressing the "Diving into the Wreck" course in fall 2020, the scholar and activist Angela Y. Davis cited the description of the course, noting its stated intent to provide "space for a cultivation of consciousness that extends self-knowledge outwards into a sense of community, through the act of critical reflection."[166] In her lecture, Davis emphasized that creative existence is based on the ability to hold contradictions, "to form new knowledges, to critically engage with the world."[167] Yet, over several decades, the sequestration of critical practice within the domain of theory, rather than its integration into a system of inquiry endemic to artistic practice, had largely come to characterize education at the School, while students and faculty mused over the issue, expressing a wish to transcend the format of group critiques.

During her tenure as Director of Graduate Studies in Sculpture, Stockholder had introduced her own structure for group critiques, one that aimed to place viewers and artists on equal footing in a process of generating dialogue regarding a work:

> The student was asked to present their work and everything that they felt was important for us to know about it. After that, they were asked not to speak for the first half of the critique. The onus was on the rest of us, faculty and students, to put words to the work and to articulate where our questions came from. Midway through their crit, we brought the student into the conversation. This mode of critique privileged the work over language, and proposed that as viewers, our reception of the work, and how we articulate what we care about, is of equal importance to the subjectivity of the artist who made the work. It also eliminated the need for the student to be defensive, leaving room for layered conversations to develop. At its best, we, as a group, would create a very rich dialogue.[168]

Sarah Oppenheimer (MFA 1999) offers a different perspective on critique structures, rooted in her experiences within the Department of Painting and Printmaking as a student and, shortly thereafter, as a faculty member. When she arrived at the School in 1997 with an undergraduate degree in semiotics from Brown University, she found that semiotic theory was largely absent from the program. However, Oppenheimer did encounter "alternative frameworks and conceptual tools that empowered students to decode the formal play of abstraction into strategic games of historical meaning."[169] She studied at the

165   Photographer Dawoud Bey recalls from his conversations with Dean Richard Benson that "[Benson's] opinion [was] that as artists we think by making things, that the act of making is the thinking that makes the physical object," and that any interest that extends beyond studio-based practice would be up to the individual to seek from the wider University. Dawoud Bey, speaking at the Richard "Chip" Benson memorial, October 7, 2017, Yale University Art Gallery.

166   Angela Y. Davis, "Diving into the Wreck: Rethinking Critical Practice."

167   Ibid.

168   Jessica Stockholder, telephone conversation with the author, January 8, 2020.

169   Sarah Oppenheimer, telephone conversation with the author, March 15, 2021.

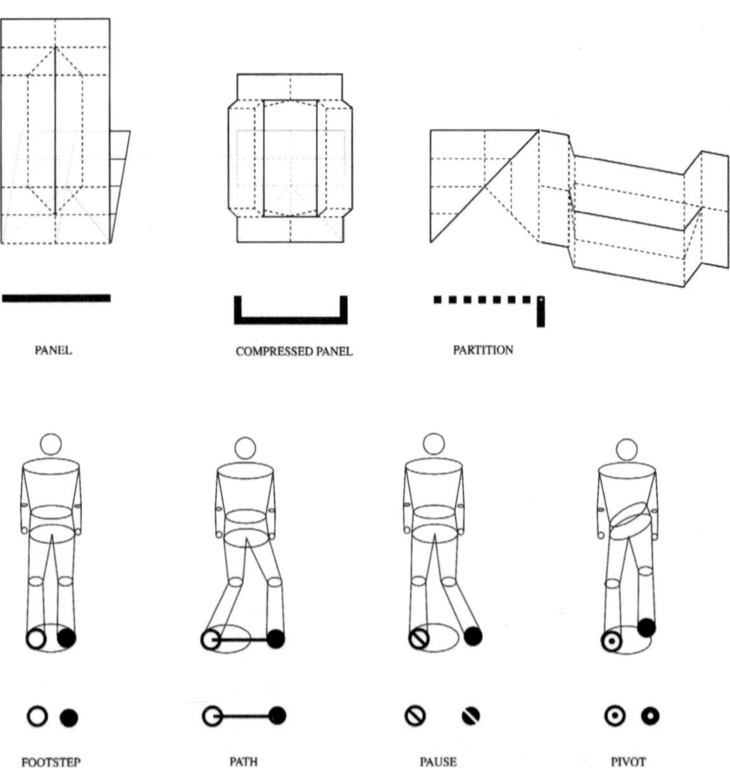

Like the mean test subject, the drywall panel is a standard unit within a larger structure. The hallway tests illustrate how alterations to a standard wall unit affect human movement and thus create standardized behavior. The controlled study allows for inferences to be drawn from the specific site of the Drawing Room to hallways in general, in the sense that they imply an architectural program.

Hallway is as much a research investigation as an art project. The design of the panel allows for the implementation of the test anywhere. Prepackaged units can be shipped to any site and assembled in any configuration. The standardization of the panel allows identical tests to be conducted in multiple locations and communities. Test results are amassed and analyzed, and data is then posted at www.foldingenterprises.com. Results of completed tests include maps, video footage, and theoretical conclusions based on analysis of the data.

Designs derived from such analysis alter the relationship between the wall and the footstep, which is the articulation of human behavior most easily mapped as a representative mark. The accumulation of footsteps now becomes a primary drawing tool, a tool that continually sketches the possibilities of space. Thus walls can be designed and reconfigured to respond to the footstep. In fact, they become a final and usable drawing until a new circulation pattern forces a new change.

Sarah Oppenheimer, from the Drawing Center's <u>Drawing Papers</u> 30, 2002.
Courtesy Sarah Oppenheimer and the Drawing Center.

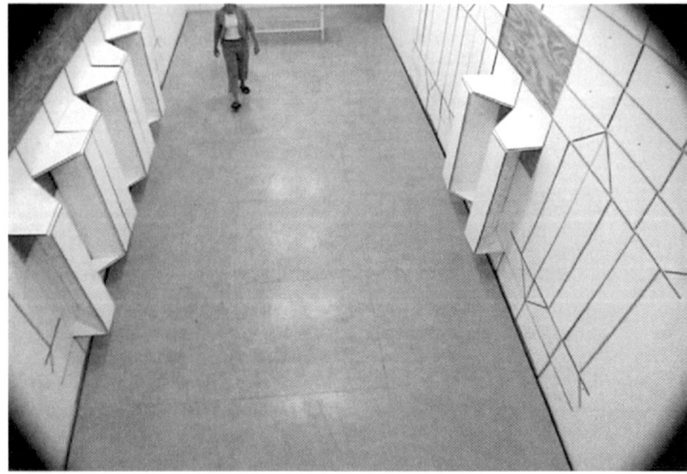

Sarah Oppenheimer, video footage of test subject exploring <u>Hallway</u>, Drawing Center, 2002.
Courtesy Sarah Oppenheimer.

170 Sarah Oppenheimer, telephone conversation with the author, January 9, 2020.

171 Ibid.

172 Ibid.

173 Carol Vogel, "Warhols of Tomorrow Are Dealers' Quarry Today," New York Times, April 15, 2006.

174 Rochelle Feinstein, conversation with the author, February 9, 2020.

175 Sarah Oppenheimer, telephone conversation with the author, January 9, 2020.

School during the last year that the Department of Painting and Printmaking inhabited the Rudolph building, noting that "hammered concrete walls and limited daylight intensified the atmosphere of social pressure. The tone of the pit crit was inflected by the surrounding Brutalist architecture."[170] In 2000, when the School of Art moved into Holcombe T. Green, Jr. Hall—the "more polite" building on Chapel and Crown Streets—it also "affected the tone of the review," she says, explaining that "criticism transformed into a descriptive exercise. There was a substitution of collegiality for criticality, with an emphasis on an antihierarchical, egalitarian structure."[171]

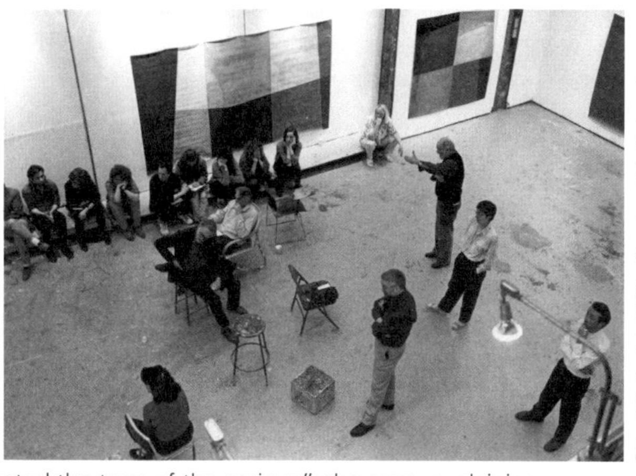

Pit crit in the late 1980s. Courtesy Yale University Art Gallery Archives.

Oppenheimer, who joined the faculty in 2003 as Lecturer in the Department of Painting and Printmaking, noticed that a change had also taken place during the early aughts in the relationship between the School and the art market. She recalls that, as a graduate student, she did not visit commercial art galleries. "I did not read trade magazines," she continues. "I was unaware of a professional world outside of the program I inhabited. When I [returned to join the faculty], I somehow felt as though the School of Art had done a 180-degree turn—becoming entirely oriented toward the rapidly evolving art market. It was a major shift."[172]

Feinstein agrees, noting that, in the early 2000s, the market entered the studios. She remembers a 2006 *New York Times* article written by the art critic Carol Vogel with the headline "Warhols of Tomorrow Are Dealers' Quarry Today," that proclaimed the status of the art world as a "numbers game" and said that "as collectors, art fairs and galleries keep growing … dealers and collectors are scouring the country's top graduate schools looking for the Warhols of the future."[173] Feinstein had expressed concern at the time that this market pressure impinged on the students' "freedom to fail"—an important need for any artist in the process of developing new work.[174] Recognizing that the aims of a critically driven practice and an economically viable one may be contradictory, Oppenheimer acknowledges that students face tremendous pressure to develop their work according to market-driven priorities: "Currently, the debt students leave with is so onerous, it's unsurprising that people are not looking toward the theoretical or the experimental, when the aim is to get work out there, to hustle—all of which leads to more conservative work."[175]

The beginning of the millennium was marked by a global expansion of the art market and the arrival of art as an asset class, with artworks as portable and transferrable assets detached from fiat currencies, which fueled interest in art as a highly desirable financial investment. As the art critic Holland Cotter observed in a 2009 *New York Times* article, this market growth also brought to greater awareness movements and histories previously unknown to Western audiences while simultaneously discouraging political engagement. He writes that:

> The 2000s really started in the late 1990s. In the early years of that decade the American economy was in woeful shape, the art market a shambles. AIDS and the culture wars raged. At the same time multiculturalism and a budding globalism were opening doors. Not only were we seeing African-American, Latino and Asian-American artists stepping onto the stage in

     CRITIQUE AS A MODE OF REFLEXIVITY AND REFLECTION

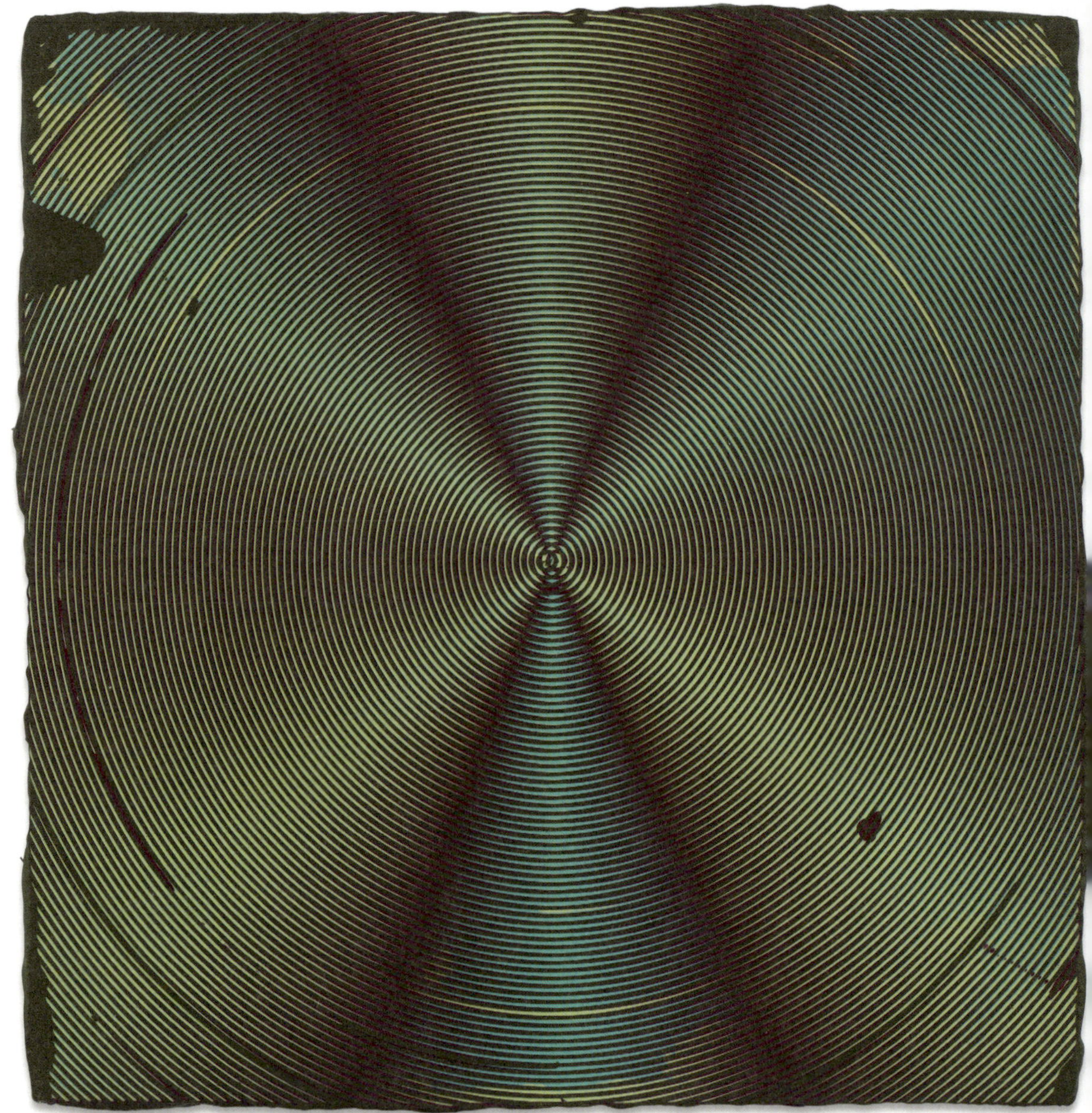

Anoka Faruqee, <u>2017P-28 (Circle)</u>, 2017. Photo by Jeffrey Sturges. Courtesy Anoka Faruqee.

176 Holland Cotter, "Depending on the Culture of Strangers," *New York Times*, December 31, 2009.

177 Ibid.

178 Sarah Oppenheimer, e-mail correspondence with the author, April 3, 2021.

New York in unprecedented numbers, but we were getting news from art centers in Africa, Latin America and Asia. … By 2000 the economy was a few years on the rebound. … Politics, viewed by the New York market as yesterday's news, seemed distanced, or disguised or put on the shelf. … As the 2000s progressed, we got acres of well-schooled paintings and drawings. … Art fairs grew on top of art fairs. Did I mention that United States had started a war in Iraq? The art world didn't mention it either."[176]

He continues:

During the 2000s what began as a contemporary art boom in China grew into a colossal industry. … Thanks to a flourishing Asian economy, the decade also saw the exponential growth of the contemporary art scene in India. … we were given an extraordinary historical exhibition on the subject of African modernism in *The Short Century: Independence and Liberation Movements in Africa, 1945–1994* … organized by the Nigerian-born curator Okwui Enwezor … [as well as] 'Inverted Utopias: Avant-Garde Art in Latin America,' … which cast comparable illumination on Latin American modernism.[177]

In other words, as capitalism achieved global hegemony, an expanding art market saw what had been a narrative of one, centrally anchored modernity replaced by a story of many modernities. This resulted in the gradual erosion of art institutions as privileged sites for art and the emergence of art as constitutive of a site in itself. Oppenheimer notes:

The financial structure shifted the role of the institution from one of post-production distribution to producer and collaborator, creating a strange new creative bedfellow for the artists. The interests and agendas of curators and their respective institutions (biennials, art fairs, museums, universities, etc.) has radically changed over the past twenty years … This demands a critical new relation to 'site,' one that upends and makes apparent the complex fields and forces at play in each location. Pedagogically, these social systems change the art we are looking at and therefore require a new analysis—not only of the work itself, but of the context in which and for which the work was made.[178]

Anoka Faruqee (BA 1994) joined the faculty in 2011 as Associate Professor of Painting and Printmaking, was promoted to Director of Graduate Studies in Painting and Printmaking in 2015, and again to tenured Professor in fall of 2016 during my appointment as Dean. Faruqee says that her greatest challenge as Director has been "to reform longstanding norms within Yale that reinscribe authoritarian and ego-driven structures that exist in the broader culture outside of Yale." She has worked to implement an inclusive critique structure based even more explicitly than Stockholder's on a spirit of co-teaching between faculty and students. Faruqee continues, "In an intensely market-driven art world, and with authoritarianism on the rise here and all over the world, how do we challenge a competitive and top-down learning environment in order to deepen rigor and critique? Because the diversity of our student populations has been steadily increasing over the last five or so years, we constantly work to establish a collective vocabulary, mission, and

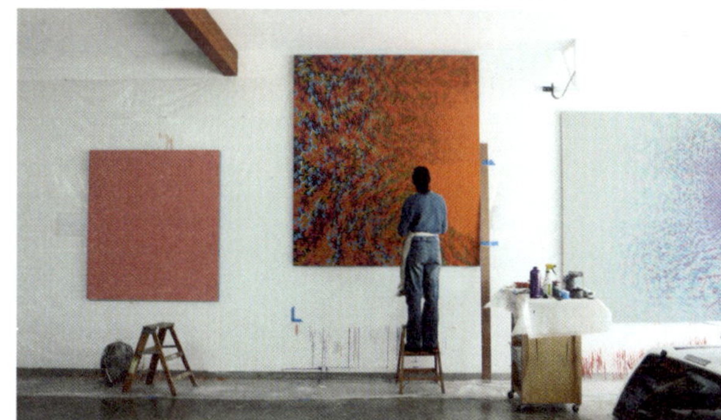

Anoka Faruqee in her studio, 2010. Photo © Clarissa Tossin. Courtesy Anoka Faruqee.

   CRITIQUE AS A MODE OF REFLEXIVITY AND REFLECTION

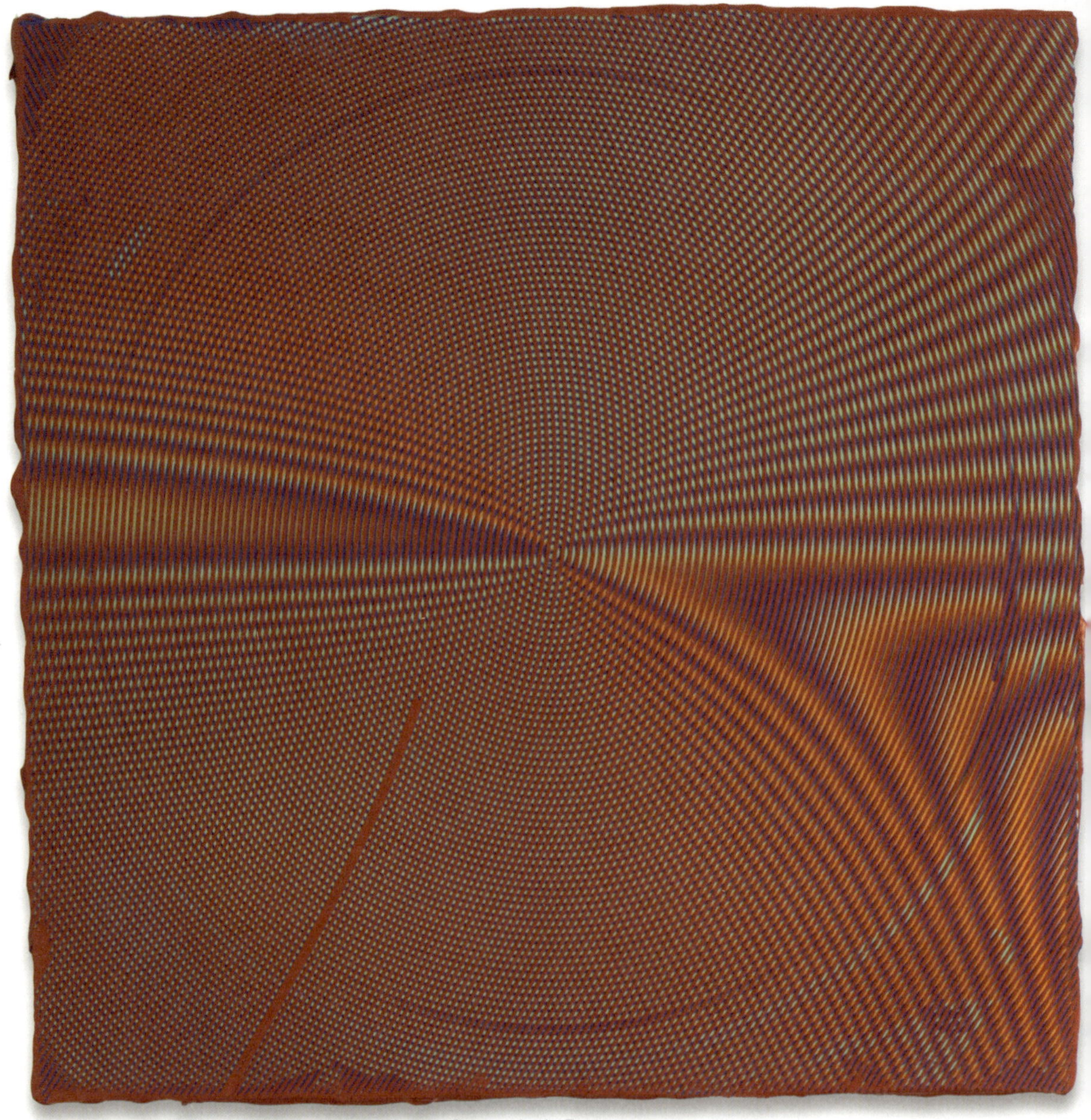

Anoka Faruqee, <u>2017P-05</u>, 2017. Photo by Madelyne Harmon. Courtesy Anoka Faruqee.

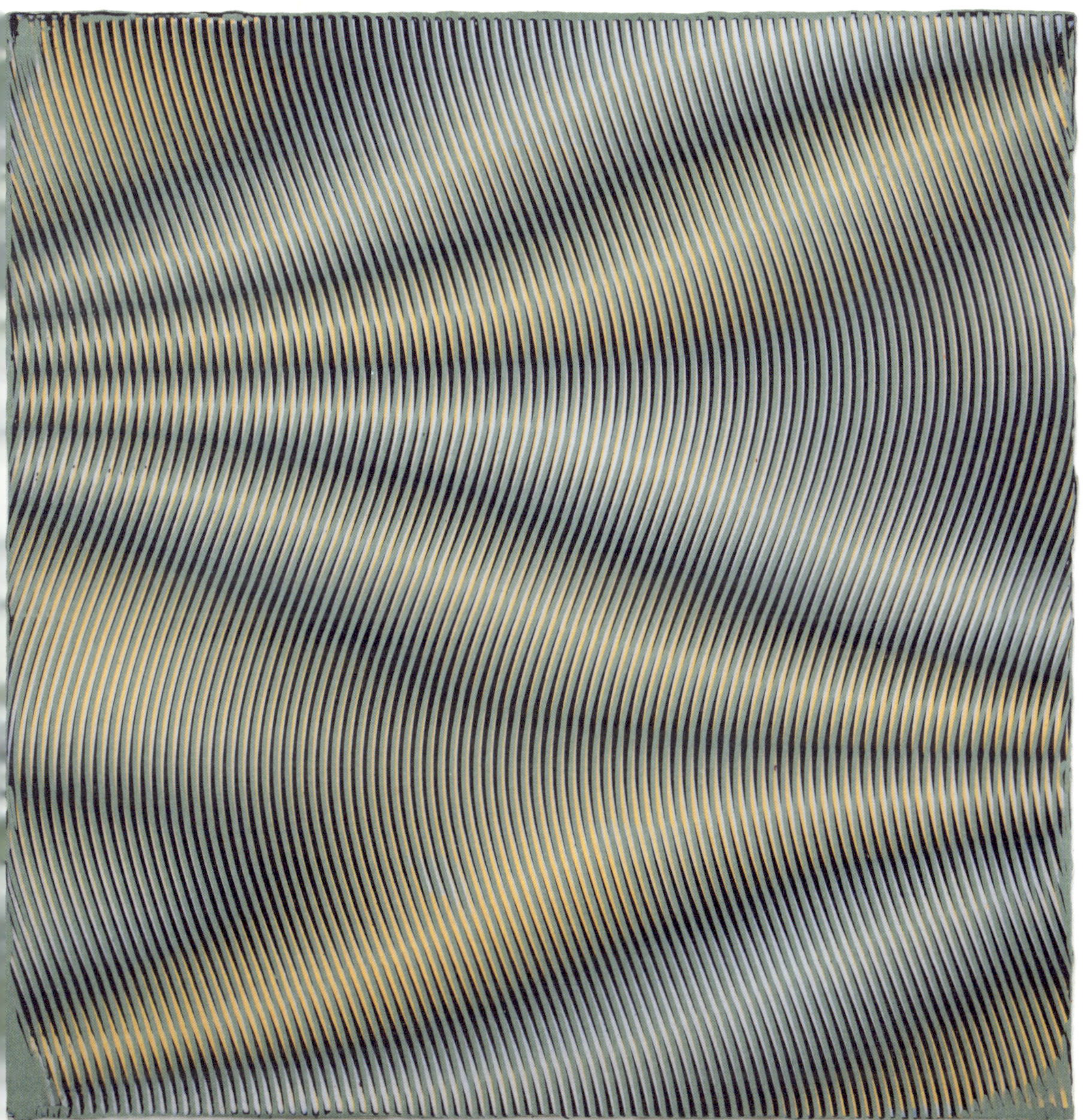

Anoka Faruqee, <u>2013P-79 (Wave)</u>, 2013. Photo by Evan Whale. Courtesy Anoka Faruqee.

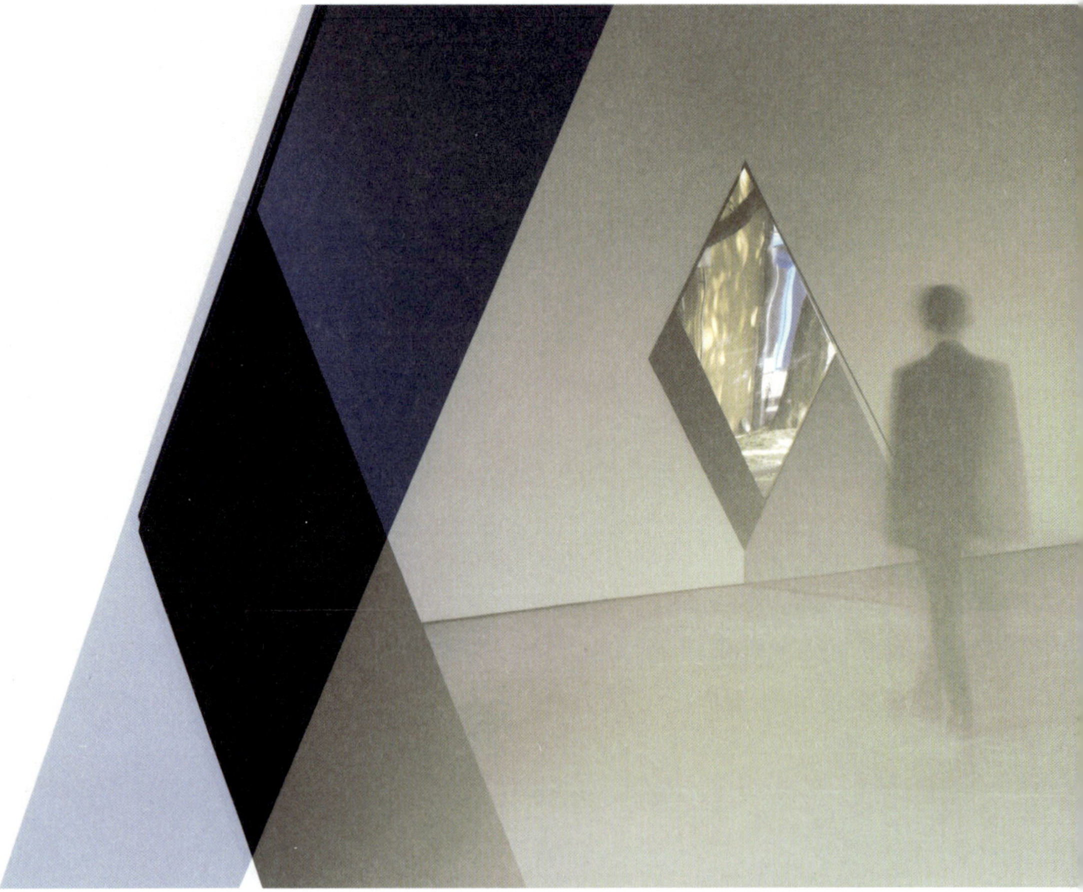

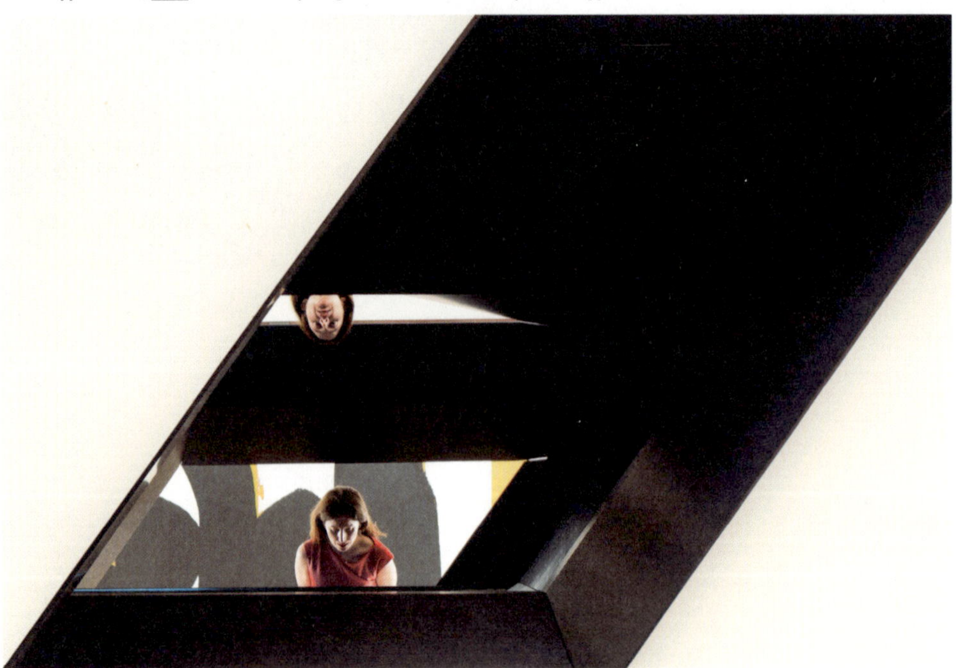

Sarah Oppenheimer, <u>33-D</u>, 2014. Photo by Serge Hasenböhler. Courtesy Sarah Oppenheimer.

Sarah Oppenheimer, <u>W-120301</u>, 2012. Photo by James Ewing. Courtesy Sarah Oppenheimer and the Baltimore Museum of Art.

179   Anoka Faruqee, email correspondence with the author, February 11, 2020.

180   Sarah Oppenheimer, telephone conversation with the author, March 15, 2021.

ethos to have the most in-depth and difficult conversations about art-making, pedagogy, and culture. The curriculum is and should remain a work in progress."[179]

Oppenheimer concurs on the importance of bringing increased awareness of political and economic contexts to the dialogue of group critiques, while emphasizing that graduates will nevertheless emerge from the School into a professional world that is typically less collegial and inclusive: "Although I respect the integrity of [an antihierarchical] model, it's a bit of a contradiction … to be fostered within a fictional sense of democracy, understanding that upon graduation, one will enter into an art market which is anything but neutral."[180]

During her time in graduate school, Oppenheimer sought elective courses outside of the School, extending her practice into research-based methods informed by studies in architecture and the social sciences. Her 2002 exhibition, *Hallway*, held at the Drawing Center in New York, explored the lived environment as a socially constructed space in which the categories of "research" and "exhibition" become entangled through the live construction of an artwork and an audience's varied encounters with that artwork over the duration of the exhibition. For *Hallway* [see p. 152 bottom right], Oppenheimer created sixteen modular wall panels that were repeatedly reconfigured in the gallery space, according to research conducted on test subjects monitored under controlled conditions. Oppenheimer's work has continued to focus on the shifting spatial and temporal paradigms impacting human behavior that evolve along with changes in capital and information flows and the development of new technologies and organizational structures.

The financialization of art did not impact all departments within the School equally. Rachel Berger (BA 2003;

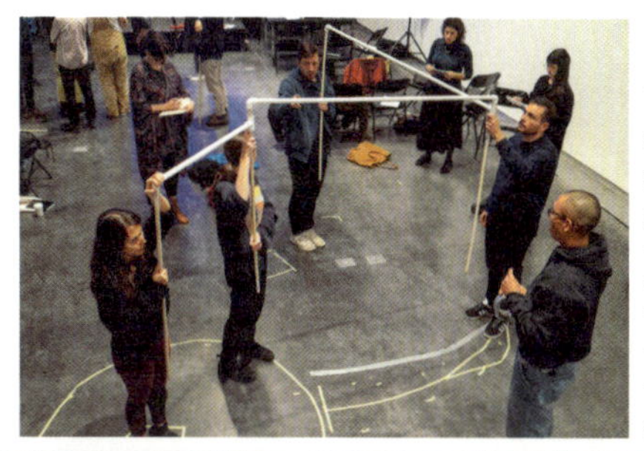

Graduate students Emilie Gossiaux, Nicki Cherry, Emma Gregoline, Alexander Zak, Efrat Rachel Lipkin, Simone Cutri, Catalina Ouyang, and Evan Chang at the Sensitive Machine workshop co-taught by Sarah Oppenheimer and Joseph Zinter, E.I.K., 2018. Photo by Sara Abbaspour.

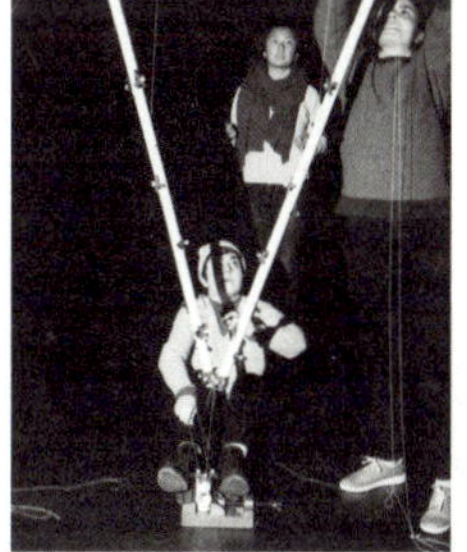

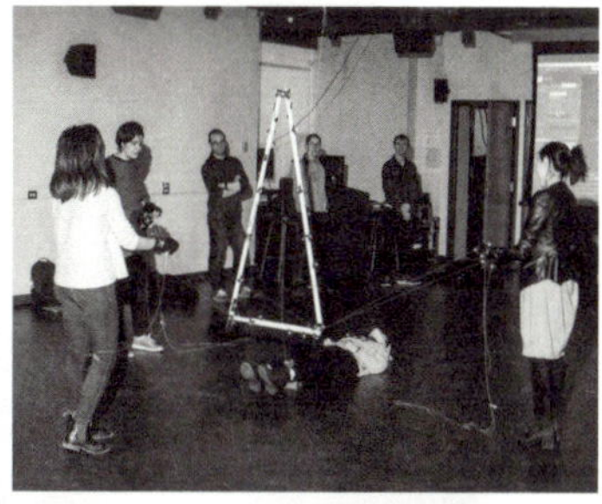

Graduate students at the Sensitive Machine workshop. Photo by Brian Galderisi.

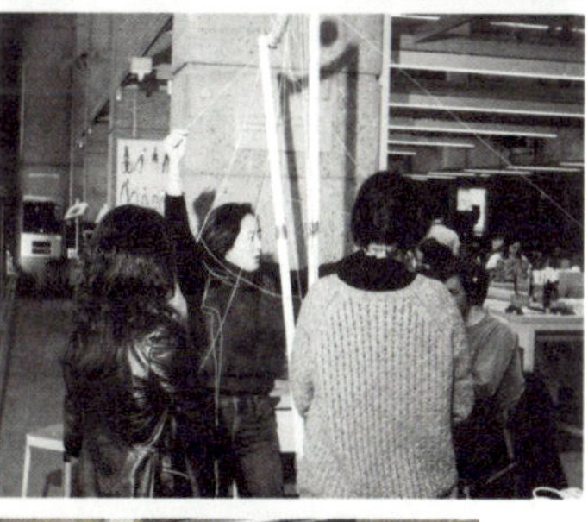

Graduate students at the Sensitive Machine workshop, co-taught by Sarah Oppenheimer and Joseph Zinter, Yale Center for Collaborative Arts and Media, 2019. Photo by Brian Galderisi.

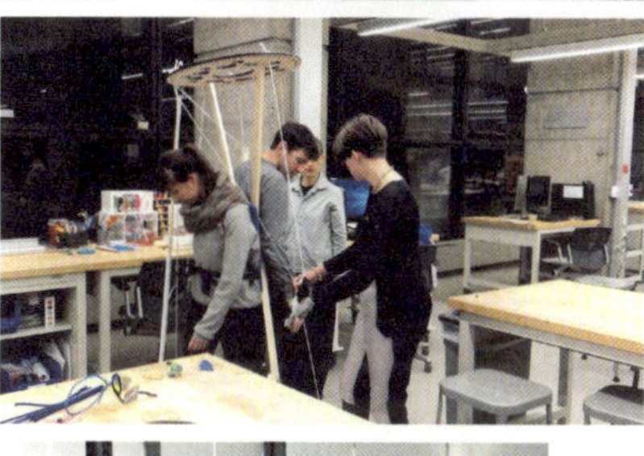

Graduate students Nicki Cherry, Elena Tilli, and Alex Zak with Professor Sarah Oppenheimer at the Sensitive Machine workshop, co-taught by Sarah Oppenheimer and Joseph Zinter, Yale Center for Engineering Innovation and Design, 2018. Video still by Evan Chang.

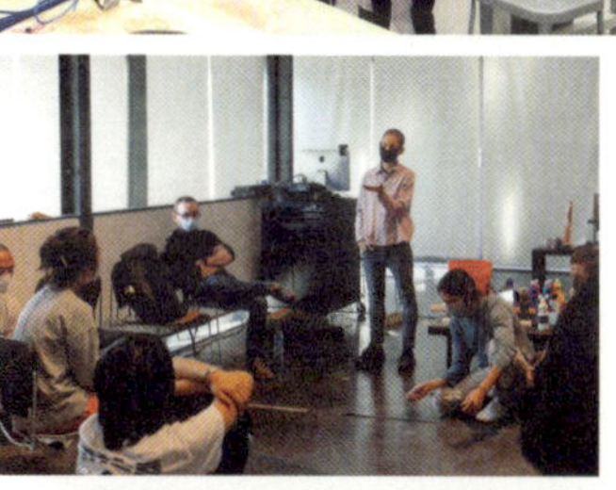

Graduate students Jeenho Seo, Stella Zhong, Mianwei Wang, Lucas Yasunaga, and Riley Duncan with Professors Joseph Zinter and Sarah Oppenheimer at the Frequency *II* Apparatus workshop co-taught by Joseph Zinter and Sarah Oppenheimer, E.I.K., 2020. Photo by Emily Barresi. © Emily Barresi.

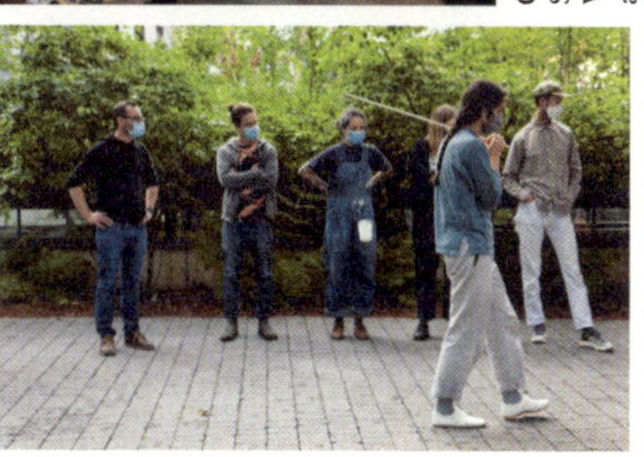

Professor Joseph Zinter and graduate students David Craig, Luiza Dale, Anna Sagström, Lucas Yasunaga, and Nick Massarelli at the Frequency *II* Apparatus workshop. Photo by Emily Barresi. © Emily Barresi.

159   CRITIQUE AS A MODE OF REFLEXIVITY AND REFLECTION

in the United States between 1871 and 1945: "Because the technology of publishing required many skilled printers, because commercial print shops often rejected anarchist materials, and because of a general anarchist reverence for the written word, printing was one of the most common occupations of anarchists."[19] In writing about the role of the printer in the development of socialism, French philosopher Régis Debray describes the printer as "quintessentially a 'worker intellectual or an intellectual worker,' the very ideal of that human type who would become the pivot of socialism: 'the conscious proletarian.'"[20]

While the Perlmans did not explicitly identify as anarchists or socialists (or any "-ist," for that matter), they followed in the tradition of radical left printers. As Ferguson writes, the anarchists of the late nineteenth and early twentieth centuries had "less money to spend on new technology, and thus were more likely to stick with the older machines, even after the new became available."[21] Similarly, Co-op users had little money and made do with old equipment.

The Revolutionary Printing Cooperative, which predated the Detroit Printing Co-op, used two different marks, which functioned similarly to a union bug. The first has the name of the cooperative encircling a red and black flag. It appears on at least two publications and their 1969 price list. The two flags represent anarchism (black) and communism (red). They began using an actual union mark when several Co-op users became dues-paying members of the IWW (Industrial Workers of the World). A version, with the words Revolutionary Printing Cooperative encircling the IWW logo, appears on some publications from early 1970.[22]

In 1968, Fredy and Lorraine Perlman had visited the IWW headquarters in Chicago, where they were impressed with the level of activity and engagement. The Wobblies, as IWW members are called,

Detroit Printing Co-op union bug designed by Fredy Perlman, 1970.

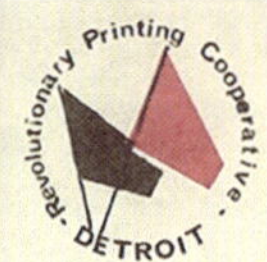

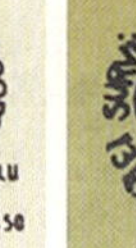
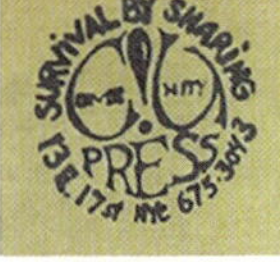

Above: printer's marks for the Revolutionary Printing Cooperative from 1969 (left) and 1970 (right).

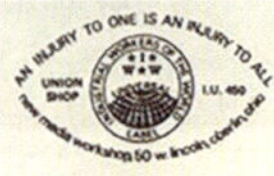

Above: unions bugs for the IWW print shops Come!Unity Press and New Media Workshop.

had been in the same office in Chicago since the 1920s and the space was full of literature and materials that dated back to those days. Members included older Wobblies who tended toward democratic socialism, and younger activists who leaned toward anarchism.[23] At some point in the spring of 1970, Fredy Perlman designed a mark for the Detroit Printing Co-op. The language around the bug—"Abolish the wage system / Abolish the state / All power to the workers!"—is part of the preamble to the IWW constitution. The Perlmans had a copy of Joyce Kornbluh's 1964 graphic history of the IWW, *Rebel Voices*, which may have provided inspiration for the label.[24]

The Co-op bug communicates both information about the print shop and an idea for system change. The IWW is a radical union, and in calling for the abolition of the state and the wage system, the Co-op bug demonstrates the ways in which the aims of the IWW (e.g., "One Big Union") are different from traditional labor unions that seek primarily to negotiate fair wages and working conditions for the workers they represent.

Unlike some other IWW union bugs from this time period, such as New York City's hand-drawn badge for Come!Unity Press (with the tagline "Survival by Sharing") or even the Oberlin, Ohio New Media Workshop's "An injury to one is an injury to all," the Detroit Co-op's bug directly commands the reader to act ("Abolish the state!"). It eschews cuteness or any romanticizing of what it means to upend the wage system. It isn't hand-drawn—it isn't something you can do at home—it is machine made, all caps, insistent.[25]

Printing at the Co-op

The Harris offset press was an enormous, ancient, cast-iron machine with wooden wheels. One Co-op user, Ralph Franklin, recalled, "There were open gears that you were certain would grab your elbow at some point." (At least one person, Peter Allen, did get his shirt caught in the gears while printing and narrowly avoided serious injury.) In addition to the large Harris press, the Co-op had a smaller Davidson 863 two-cylinder offset press that could print 16 × 18 inches and a smaller Multilith 1250 offset duplicator that could do 11 × 14 inches, a large sheet folder for folding book signatures, a

19 Kathy E. Ferguson, "Anarchist Printers: Material Circuits of Politics" *Political Theory* 42, 4 (August 2014), p. 393. One example of an anarchist printer is Joseph Labadie. Ferguson writes, "Labadie, whose collection of anarchist materials forms the basis of the University of Michigan archive of radical literature bearing his name, was one of the tramp printers who crisscrossed the U.S., working as a freelance artisan as well as organizing unions and spreading anarchist practices, before later settling in his home town of Detroit. Labadie printed a series of labor papers and wrote articles and verse for anarchist journals. He and his colleague Judson Grennell printed over 200,000 pamphlets explaining socialism and anarchism (which were often considered interchangeable) to working class readers." Ferguson 2014, p. 392.

20 Régis Debray, "Socialism: A Life-Cycle," *New Left Review* 46 (July-August 2007).

21 Ferguson 2014, p. 396.

22 This mark was used on *Radical America* vol. 4, nos. 2 and 3 (Feb. and Apr. 1970), *A Child's Garden of Perverse* (ca. 1970), and *The Gnomon* (June 1970).

23 Conversation with Bernard Marszalek, January 20, 2018. Lorraine wrote in *Having Little, Being Much*, "for several years we pasted the dues stamps into our little red membership books." L. Perlman 1989, p. 64.

24 Conversation with Lorraine Perlman, September 19, 2015. Joyce Kornbluh, *Rebel Voices: An IWW Anthology* (Ann Arbor: University of Michigan Press, 1964).

25 Ironically, given how unusual it is, the Detroit Printing Co-op mark is the one that appears on the Wikipedia page for "union bugs." A typical union bug does not call for the abolition of wage labor or the state.

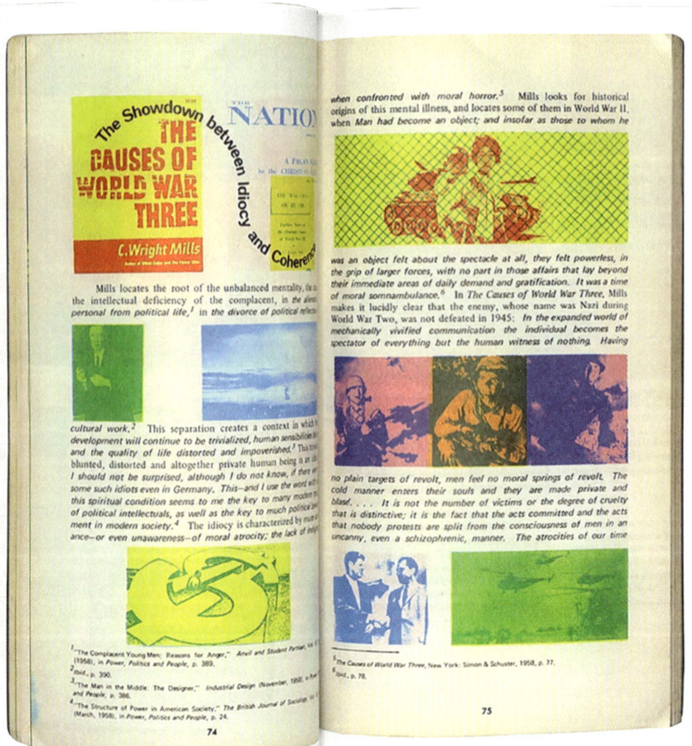

The Causes of World War Three, New York: Simon & Schuster, 1958, p. 77.

Spread from Danielle Aubert's <u>The Detroit Printing Co-op: The Politics of the Joy of Printing</u>, 2019. Courtesy Danielle Aubert and Inventory Press.

181 Rachel Berger, telephone conversation with Edi Dai and Willis Kingery, February 10, 2020.

182 Danielle Aubert, conversation with Willis Kingery, February 13, 2020.

183 Ibid.

184 "Yale's Labor Troubles Deepen as Thousands Go on Strike," *New York Times*, March 4, 2003.

185 Danielle Aubert, conversation with Willis Kingery, February 13, 2020.

186 Ibid.

MFA 2009), who began her studies in the Department of Graphic Design in 2006, recalls, "The market was not acknowledged when I was in graduate school. We didn't talk about jobs or money. There wasn't career counseling. I think that would have been anathema to the Graphic Design program. But these are things that, because the cost of education is so high, we had to think about."[181] Danielle Aubert (MFA 2005) recalls feeling immersed during her studies in a sense of solidarity and political action that were new to her practice: "One of the things that really made me want to become a graphic designer was the AIDS crisis, learning about ACT UP and Gran Fury. I got a chance to meet Marlene McCarty, who was a member of Gran Fury. She had co-taught a workshop titled "Community Action" with Donald Moffett at Yale in the early 1990s on Sheila's invitation after [Sheila] saw an ACT UP campaign on the side of a bus in New York City."[182] At Yale, Aubert joined the graduate student union Local 33 as a representative for the Department of Graphic Design, and took part in the campus-wide strike of 2003, which included students, sanitation

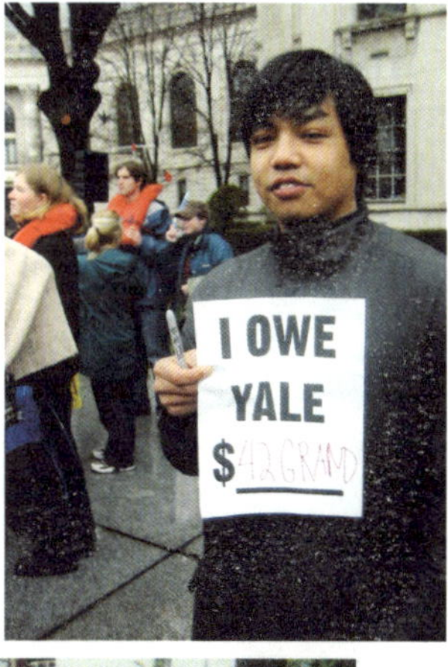

Manuel Miranda at the debt strike in Beinecke Plaza, 2004. Courtesy Danielle Aubert.

workers, and teamsters,[183] and was reportedly the broadest walkout at a university since 1968.[184] "What was so powerful to me," Aubert recalls, "and confusing, was that I was a [teaching assistant], but I didn't identify as a worker, yet I could recognize that the cost of tuition was so high, and Yale's got all this money—they've got this giant endowment—so why are they fleecing their students? We're all taking on debt … there was this kind of combined argument around teaching labor, then the tuition, contrasted with people feeling like they need an MFA in order to enter the profession …"[185] Aubert currently teaches at Wayne State University in Detroit, Michigan, where she encourages undergraduates to approach the history of graphic design by taking into account the problematics accompanying that legacy: "It's important to convey the big players like the Bauhaus and Paul Rand so students can be conversant, but also to break away from that and include moments like the International Typographical Union and labor history, or Tadanori Yokoo and Japanese psychedelia." Aubert has returned to Yale as a Visiting Critic since graduating and been surprised by the conversations taking place there, remarking, "You [students] have all the skills … You can do whatever you want, it's just about ideas at that point."[186]

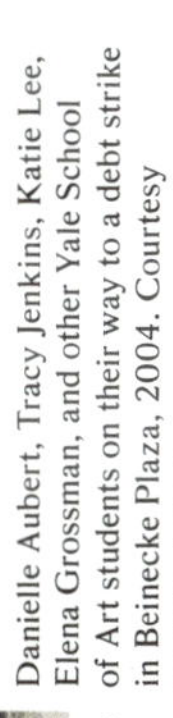

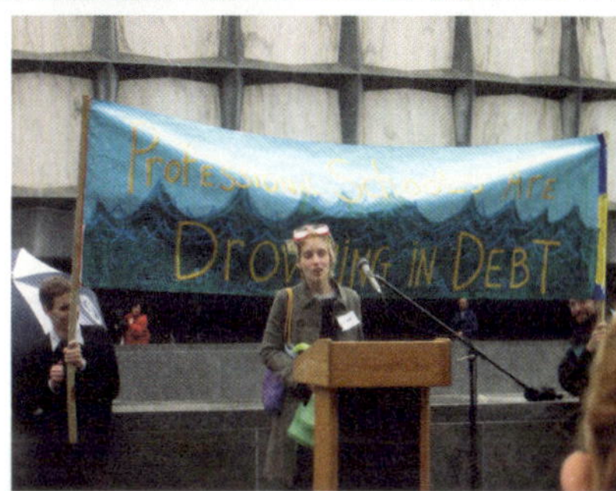

Danielle Aubert, Tracy Jenkins, Katie Lee, Elena Grossman, and other Yale School of Art students on their way to a debt strike in Beinecke Plaza, 2004. Courtesy Danielle Aubert.

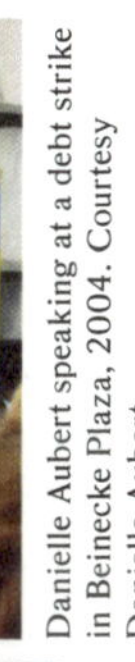

Danielle Aubert speaking at a debt strike in Beinecke Plaza, 2004. Courtesy Danielle Aubert.

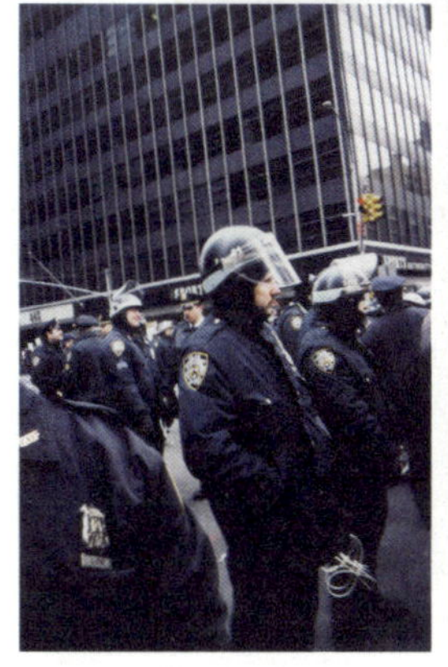

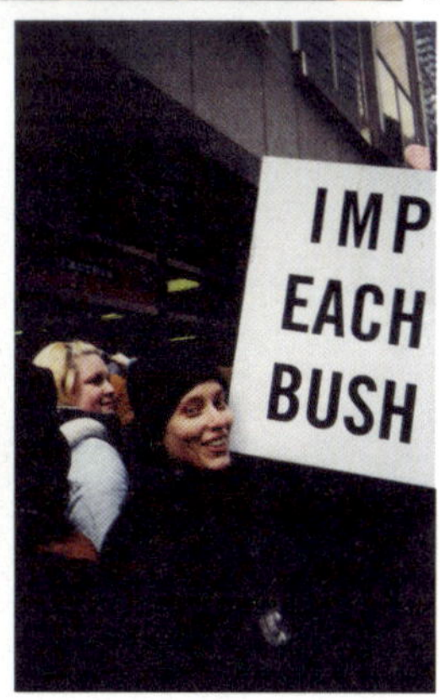

Danielle Aubert at an Iraq War protest, New York City, 2004. Courtesy Danielle Aubert.

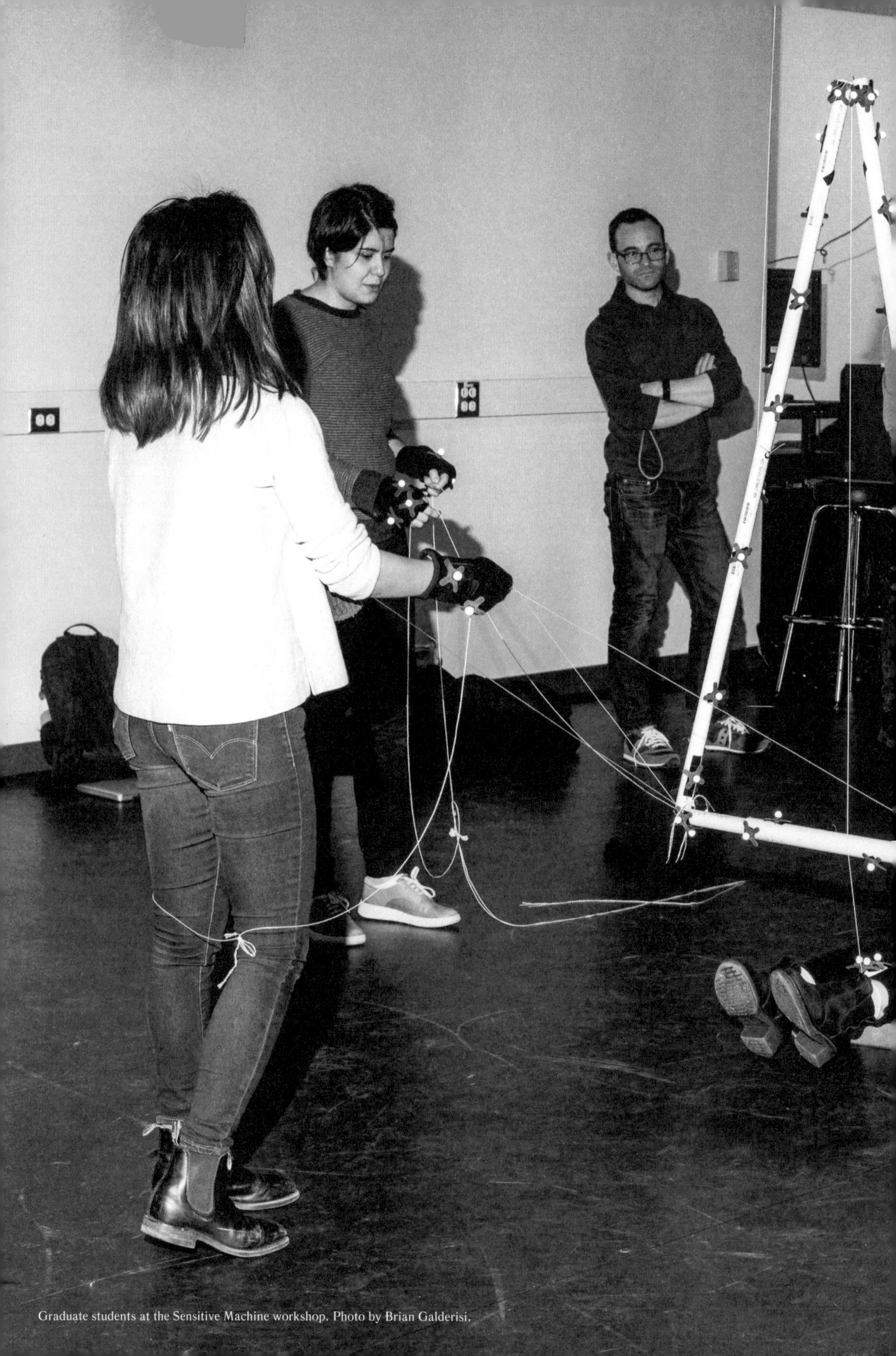

Graduate students at the Sensitive Machine workshop. Photo by Brian Galderisi.

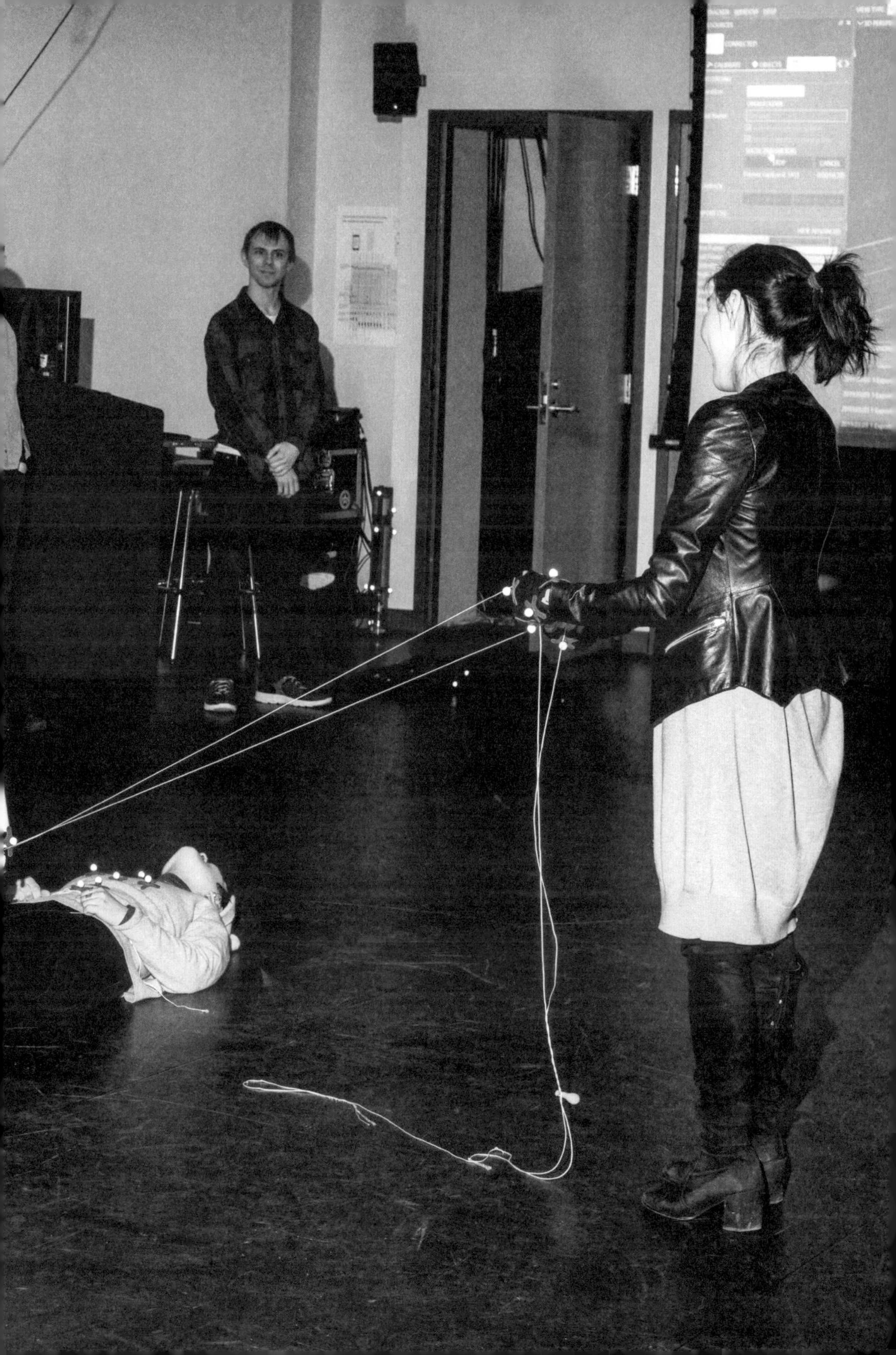

EMBODIED PERSPECTIVES

As critical practice and critique have increasingly become flashpoints in a school where women increasingly serve in both formal and informal leadership roles, the gradual but deliberate transformation in the demography of the student body also continues to transform the pedagogical perspectives of the School. While statistics are only ever insufficient indices of complex realities, they can be valuable signposts. Beginning in the 1990s and continuing to the present day, the student body has become increasingly diversified, with more than half the students at the Yale School of Art identifying as women and roughly a third of students identifying as international in 2019.[187]

Oppenheimer was promoted to Assistant Professor in the Department of Painting and Printmaking in 2006. Though she opted to step back from full-time engagement the following year to focus more energy on the development of her practice, she continues as Senior Critic and has remained dedicated throughout the past two decades to fostering interdisciplinary, interdepartmental discussions regarding art production. This led her to develop "Screen Space," a course at the intersection of art and engineering, that she has taught since 2016. She recalls that, even as recently as the late 1990s, "it was far more complicated to be out and queer than to be a woman graduate student. There was no language within the school, nor within the living environment, around how I identified—neither institutionally nor publicly."[188] As a member of the faculty of the Department of Painting and Printmaking for the past eighteen years, however, Oppenheimer notes that "the theoretical development around non-dominant subject positions has given students a place from which to speak. At the time of my graduate studies, there was no theoretical resource and no way to intellectually hook onto a publicly sanctioned discourse. I believe that has changed."[189]

Laura Wexler joined the Women's Studies program at Yale in 1988 as an adjunct, which formalized in a joint appointment with the Department of American Studies as Assistant Professor in 1992, during which time she taught a course on feminist theory with a prominent focus on the work of artist Mary Kelly, and courses on the history of photography that centered feminism. Wexler, along with Margaret Homans, changed the program's name from Women's Studies to Women's and Gender Studies. Wexler notes, "The term 'woman' was being used in extremely conservative ways and had to be challenged by gender," adding that her ambition for the revision was informed by her own understanding of herself as a feminist.[190] When Wexler became Chair in the early 2000's, she and Homans broadened the program to Women's, Gender, and Sexuality Studies, and the department was divided into a number of different tracks, including a Women's Studies track, a Gender Studies track, and a Lesbian, Gay, Bisexual, Transgender studies track. Asked whether she ever reached out to the School of Art for cooperation, Wexler reflects, "It's taken me a long time to grow out

187 "Yale University Race/Ethnicity, Gender and International Student Enrollment by School 2014-15 to 2020-21" (Office of Institutional Research, Yale University, November 2020), February 15, 2021, oir.yale.edu/sites/default/files/w010_enroll_race_gender_2021.pdf. Race/ethnicity categories are established by the federal government, as reported to the National Center for Education Statistics (NCES) in the Integrated Postsecondary Education Data System (IPEDS). All U.S. citizens and permanent residents are reported in their respective race/ethnicity categories, while all temporary residents are reported in the International category. 2019-2020 U.S. Citizens and Permanent Resident Students at the Yale School of Art: 17 "Hispanic of Any Race"; 18 "Black or African American"; 0 "American Indian or Alaskan Native"; 13 "Asian"; 0 "Native Hawaiian or Other Pacific Islander"; 36 "White"; 6 "Two or More Races" *U.S. students groups together U.S. citizens and Permanent Resident Students

188 Sarah Oppenheimer, telephone conversation with author, January 9, 2020.

189 Sarah Oppenheimer, telephone conversation with author, March 15, 2021.

190 Laura Wexler, telephone conversation with the author, April 5, 2021.

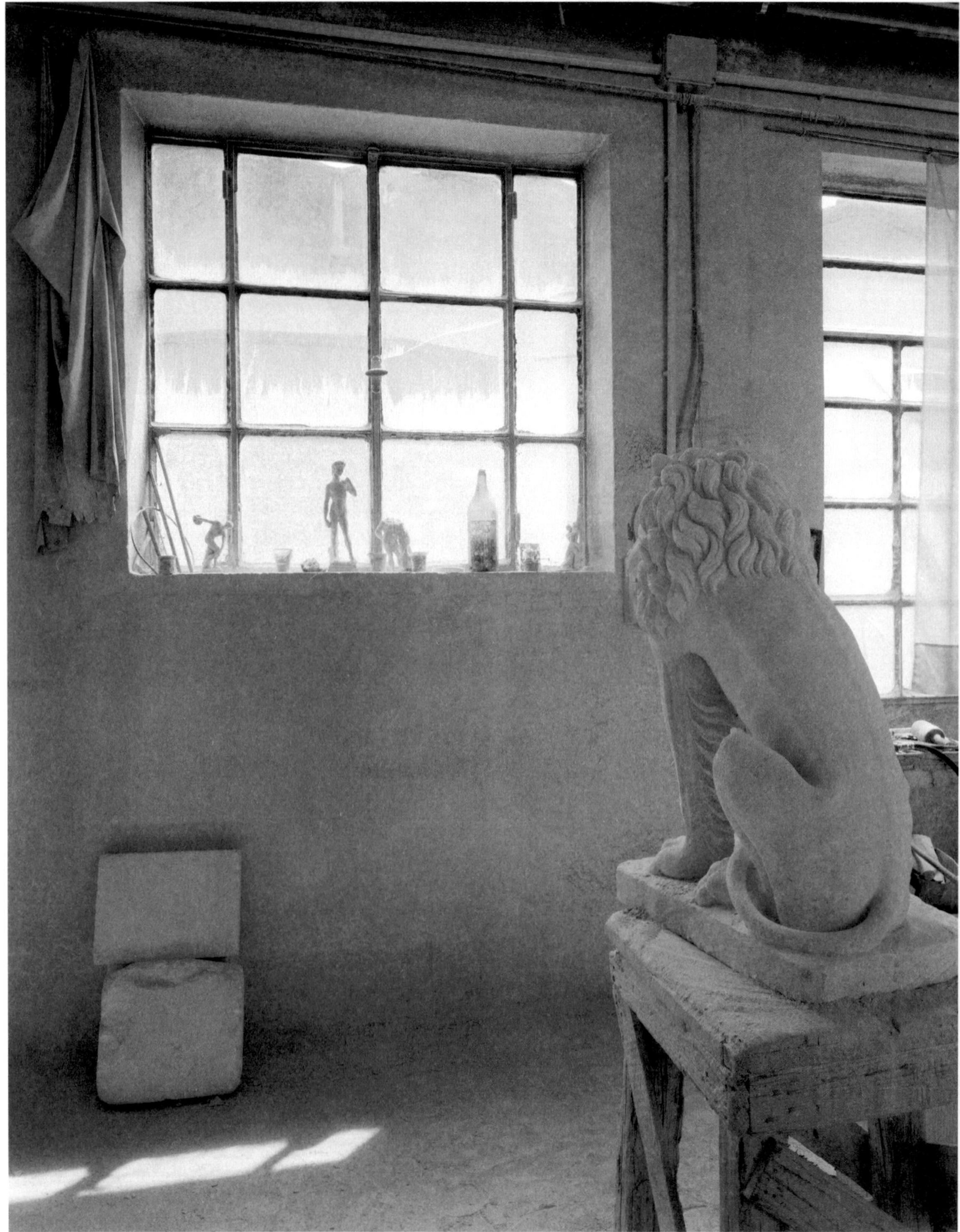

An-My Lê, <u>Milani Studio, (Leo), Vicenza, Italy</u>, 1991. © An-My Lê. Courtesy the artist and Marian Goodman Gallery.

of the idea that I'm an illegitimate presence with respect to the School of Art. Even though I'm an honored senior faculty member, I would have had trepidation to reach out and ask to cooperate. Actually, it never occurred for me to ask despite my immersion in visual culture and feminism. I guess I felt I was there on sufferance. I knew I could teach the School of Art students and that I could help them bloom, which I have. But I didn't have any other sense of a place there for myself [professionally]."[191]

An-My Lê (MFA 1993), who entered the program in Photography in 1991, was born in Saigon and left with her family after the Fall of Saigon in 1975, when she was fifteen. She received a BASC and an MS in biology from Stanford University, where she was also mentored in photography by Laura Volkerding, who suggested that she apply to graduate school. While she was studying at Yale, an important influence for Lê outside of the photography program was Huỳnh Sanh Thông, a preeminent translator of Vietnamese poetry and literature who was also Director of Vietnamese Studies and Director of the Southeast Asian Refugee Project at Yale, but it was not until 1994—one year after her graduation and the year the U.S. economic embargo was lifted—that Lê was able to return to Vietnam to produce work. She recalls that, "Without access to revisit Vietnam during the time I was at Yale, I produced still-lifes that incorporated images of Vietnam and the Vietnamese people from the colonial era as part of my graduation portfolio."[192]

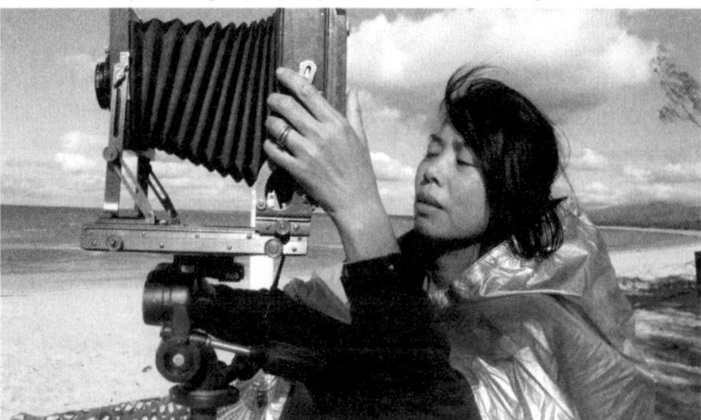

Over the following years, Lê produced a major body of work, realizing that "war was something I had to tackle."[193] She had heard about American Vietnam War reenactors, and she located a group in Virginia with whom she could work, beginning in 1999. As this project was concluding, the U.S. invaded Iraq, which added another degree of complexity to her military-focused research; the artist had intended for the reenactments to reflect on lessons learned or not learned from Vietnam, but, with the invasion of Iraq, new questions were raised as to how war is perpetuated in the American cultural imagination. Lê eventually worked with active military, though she was never embedded. She explains:

I had a very complex relationship with those I engaged with. I realized that these photographic inquiries provided ways to explore my paradoxical feelings about the American military. Thanks to the military, and by extension American foreign policy, I was given a life with many more opportunities when we were evacuated to the U.S. at the end of the war, but at the same time, twentieth-century American hegemony devastated my country.[194]

As a landscape photographer using a large format camera, Lê turned to the work of early war photographers Timothy O'Sullivan and Roger Fenton for inspiration, noting:

I initially looked at their work because of their use of scale. I think studying their work also showed me that photographing before and after can be more compelling than photographing during the event itself in the sense that you could suggest so much more … not having access to the real thing at the immediate moment. To have to re-set the possible before or after forces the imagination to work harder. I watched many war films which led me to think

191   Ibid.

192   An-My Lê, telephone conversation with the author, January 16, 2020.

193   Ibid.

194   Ibid.

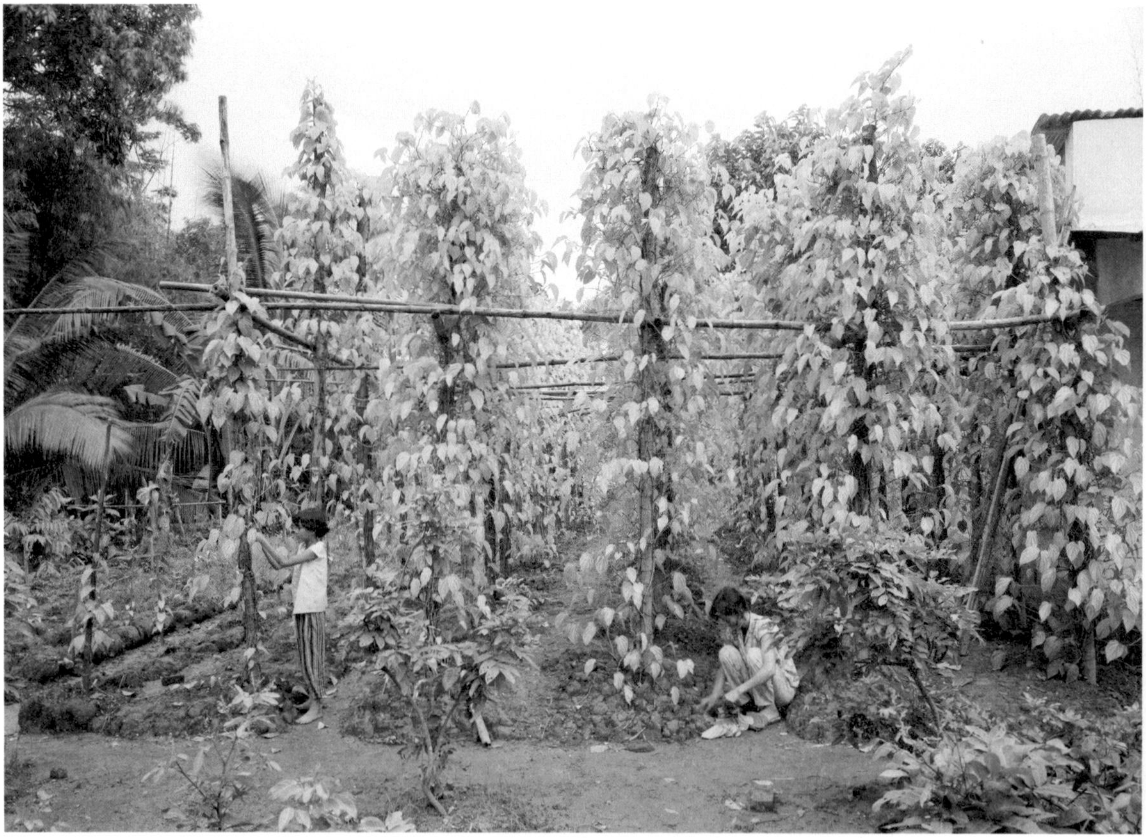

An-My Lê, <u>Viet Nam: Untitled, Mekong Delta</u>, 1995, from the series Viêtnam. © *An-My Lê. Courtesy the artist and Marian Goodman Gallery.*

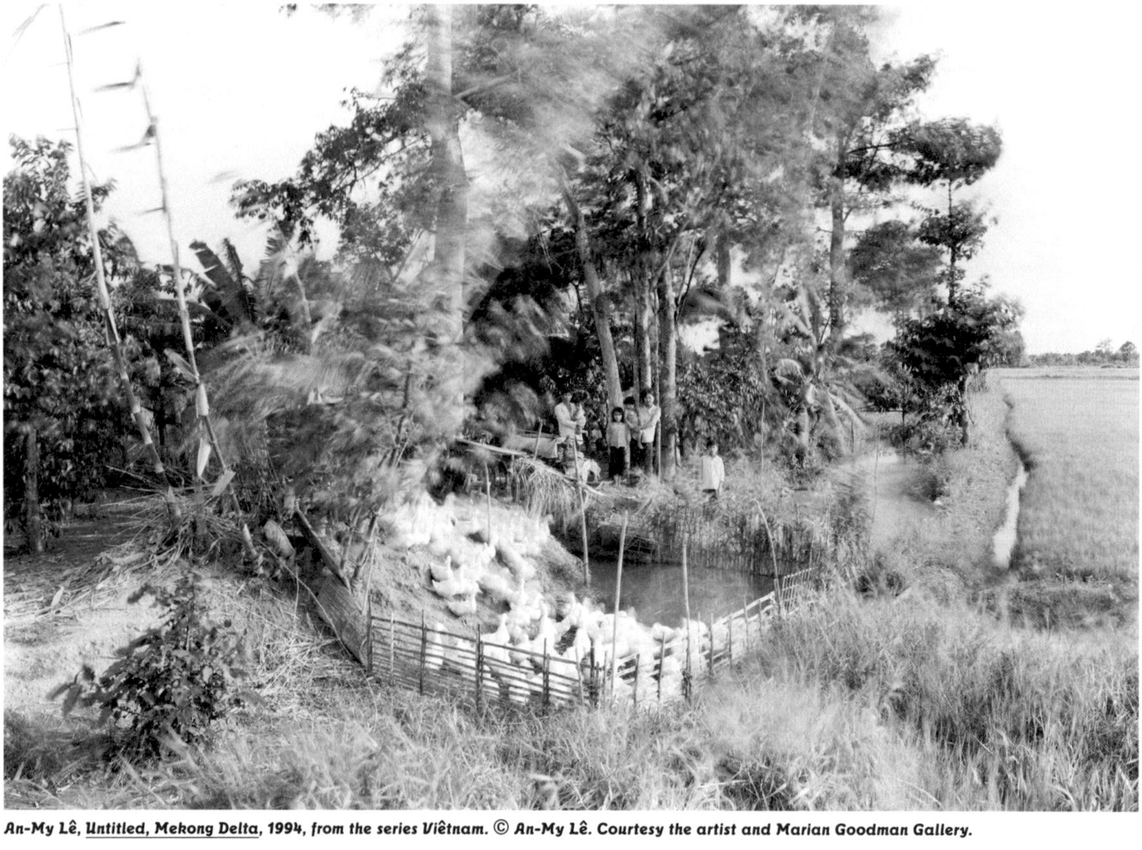

An-My Lê, <u>Untitled, Mekong Delta</u>, 1994, from the series Viêtnam. © *An-My Lê. Courtesy the artist and Marian Goodman Gallery.*

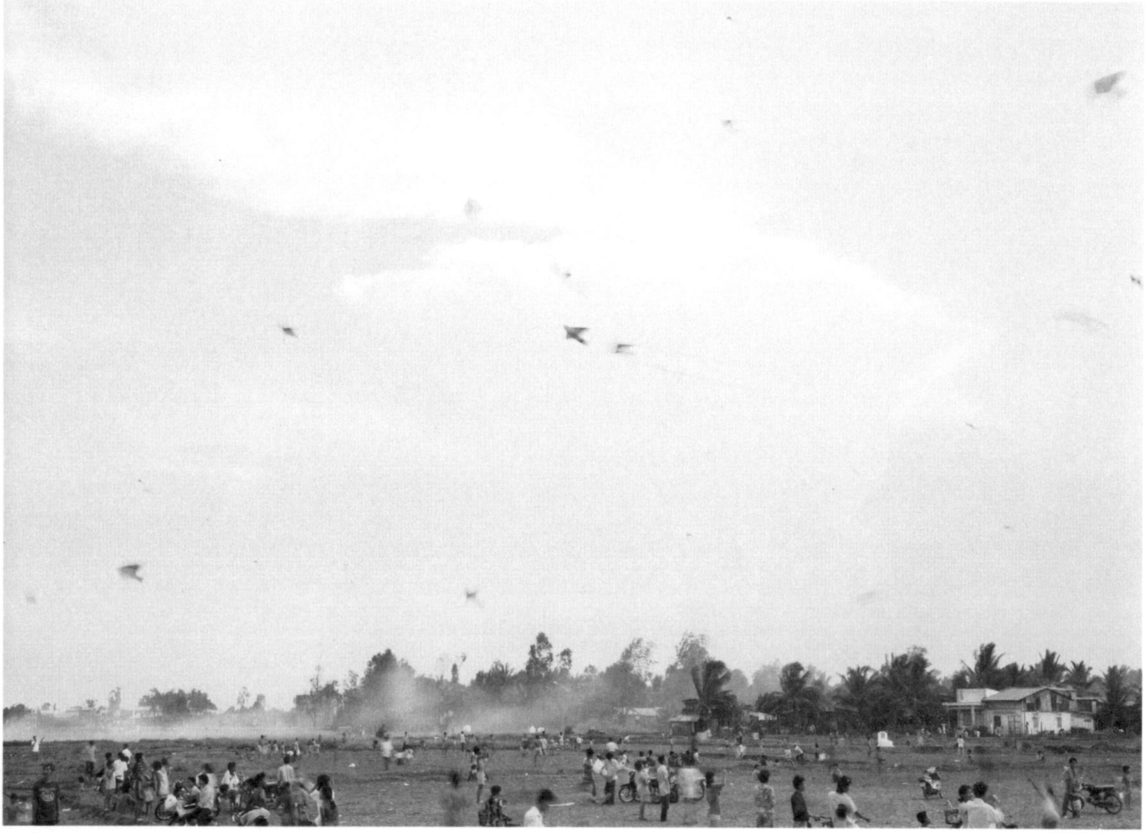

An-My Lê, _Untitled_, Ho Chi Minh City, 1998, from the series _Viêtnam_. © An-My Lê. Courtesy the artist and Marian Goodman Gallery.

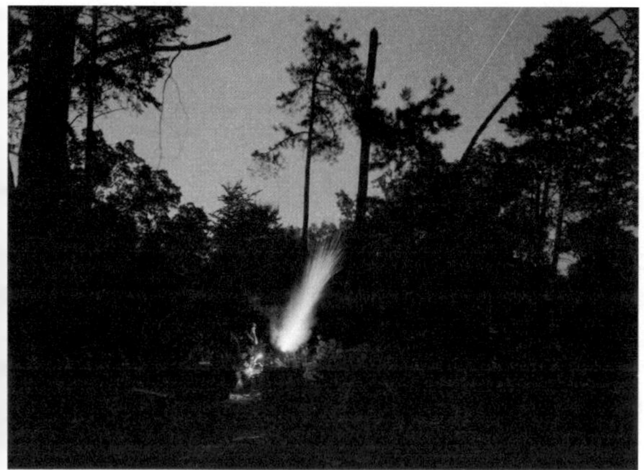

An-My Lê, _Mortar_, 1999–2002, from the series _Small Wars_.
© An-My Lê. Courtesy the artist and Marian Goodman Gallery.

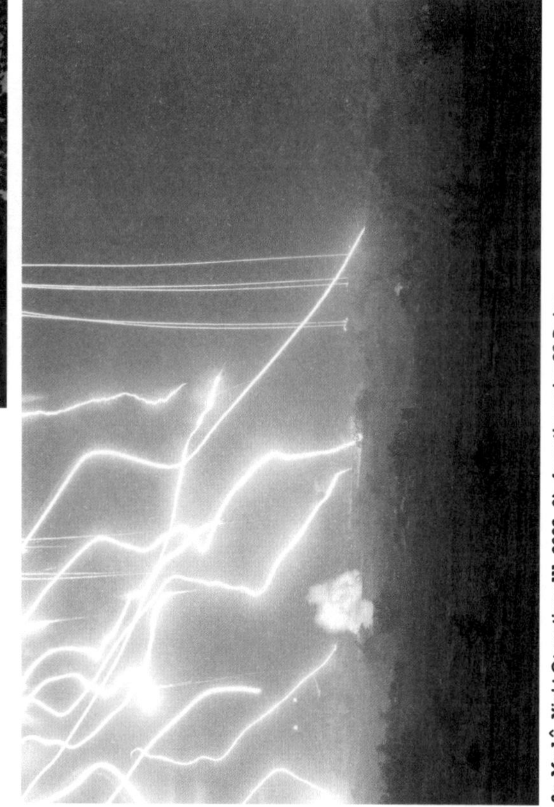

An-My Lê, _Night Operations III_, 2003–04, from the series _29 Palms_.
© An-My Lê. Courtesy the artist and Marian Goodman Gallery.

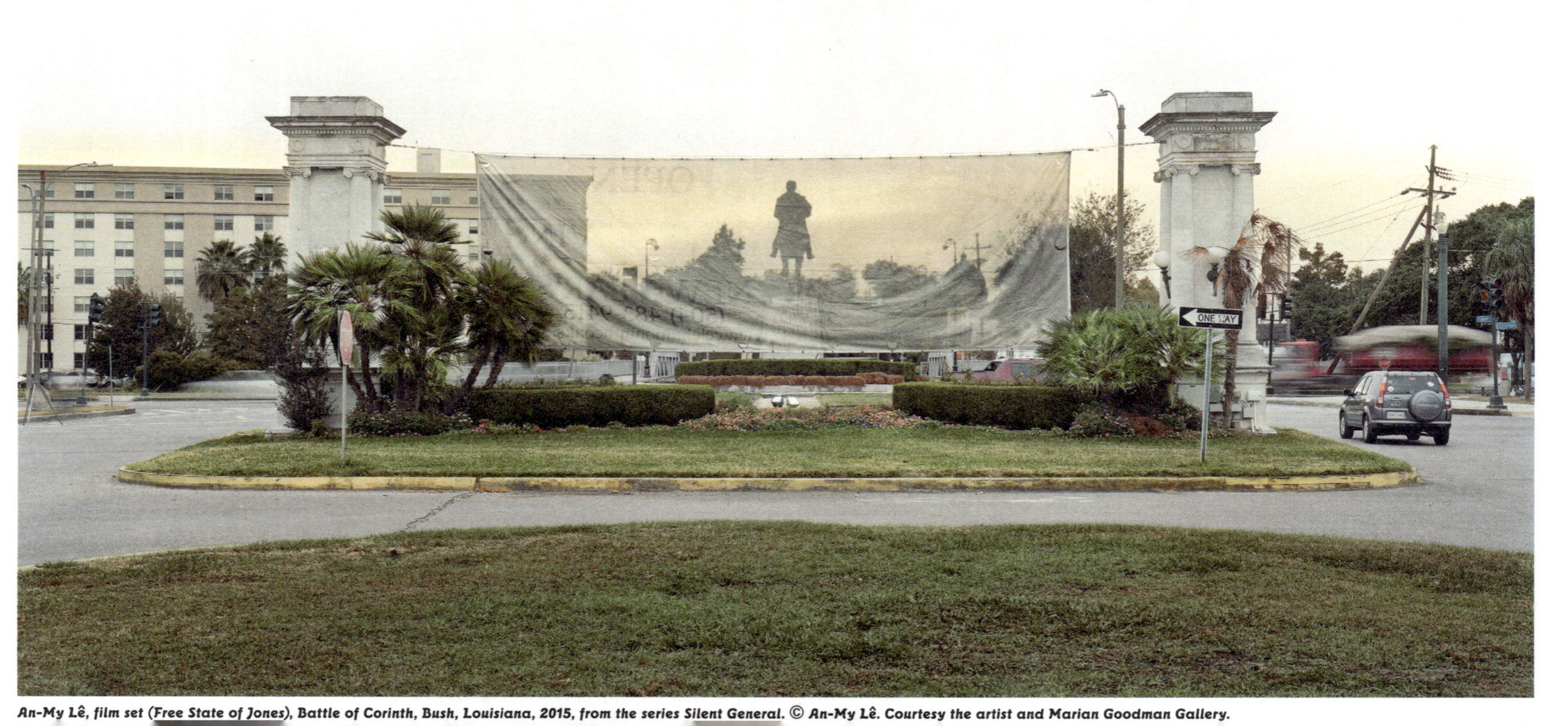

An-My Lê, film set (Free State of Jones), Battle of Corinth, Bush, Louisiana, 2015, from the series Silent General. © An-My Lê. Courtesy the artist and Marian Goodman Gallery.

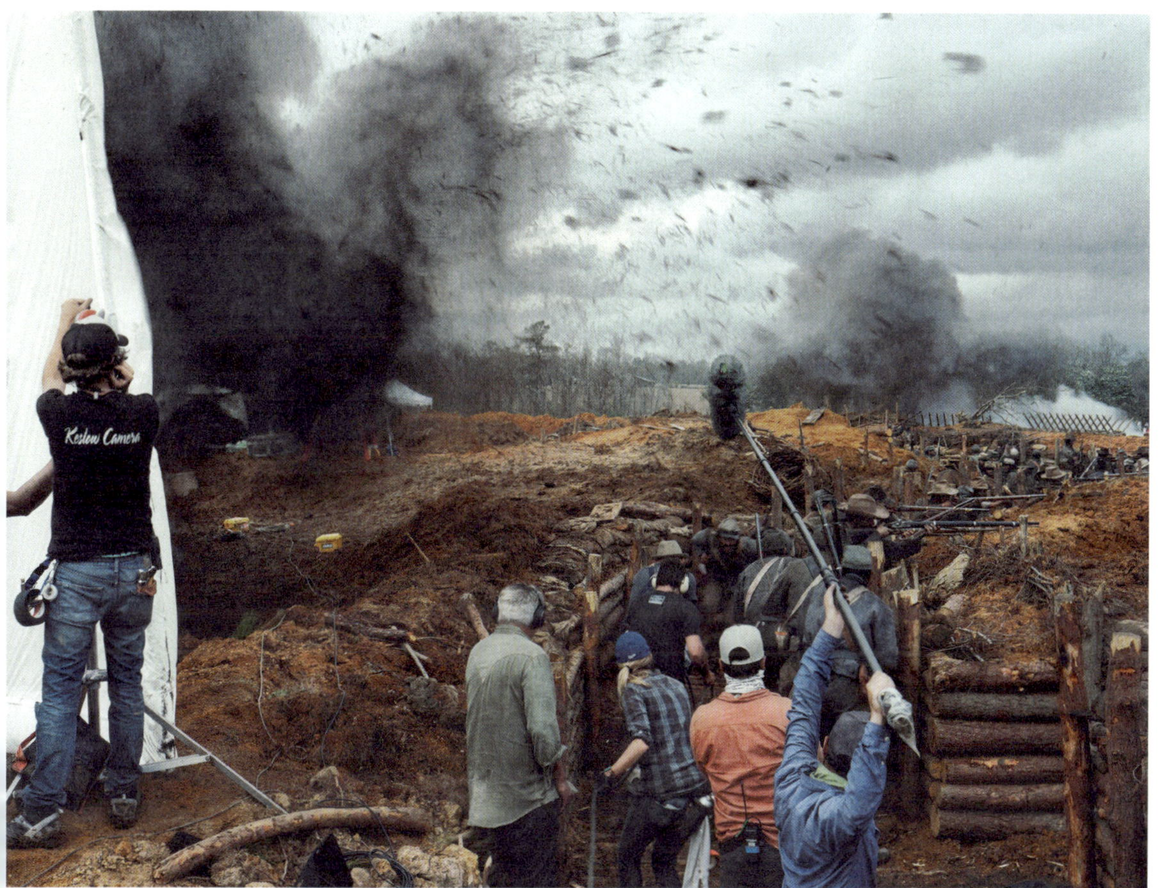

An-My Lê, film set (*Free State of Jones*), Battle of Corinth, Bush, Louisiana, 2015, from the series *Silent General*.
© An-My Lê. Courtesy STX Entertainment, the artist and Marian Goodman Gallery.

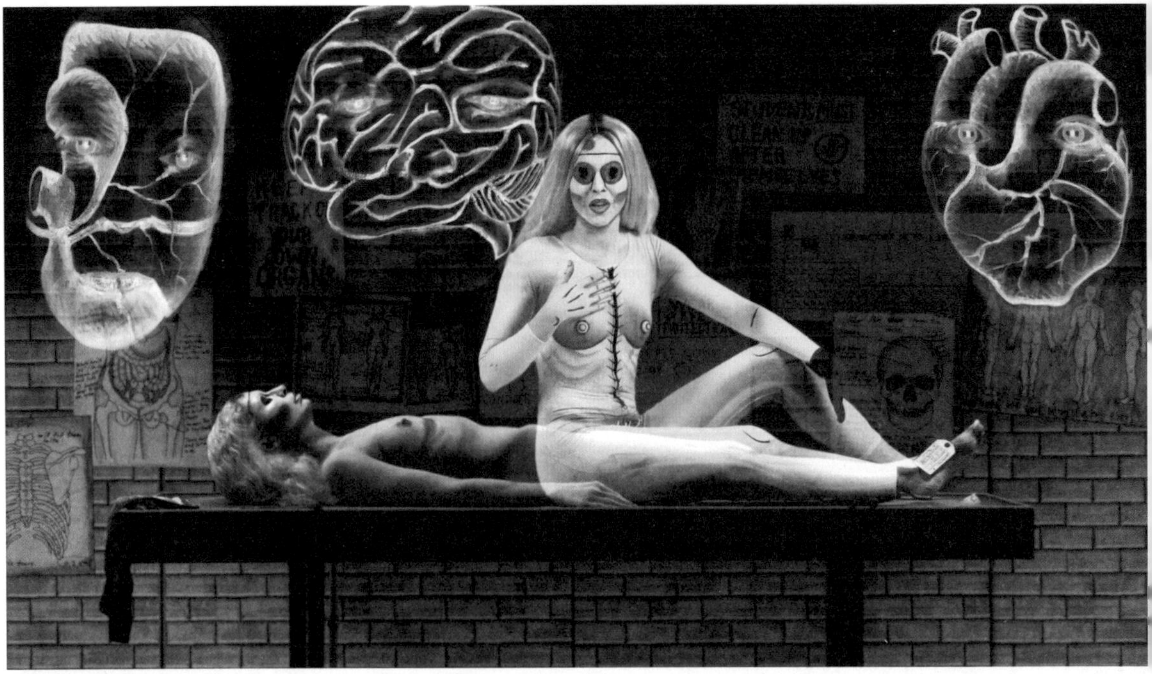

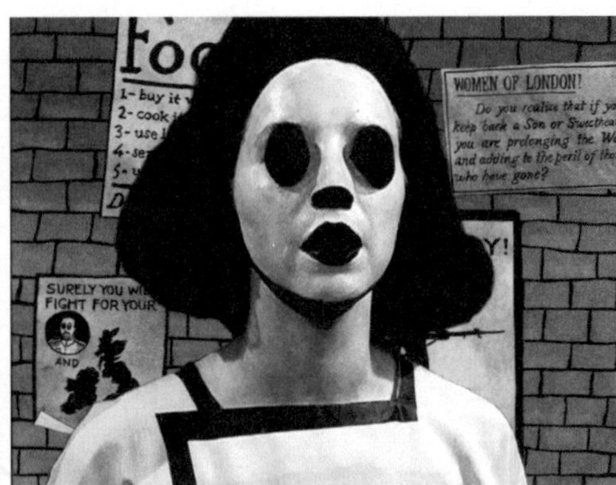

Mary Reid Kelley and Patrick Kelley, still from *This Is Offal*, 2016. Courtesy Mary Reid Kelley and Patrick Kelley; Fredericks & Freiser; Vielmetter Los Angeles; and Pilar Corrias.

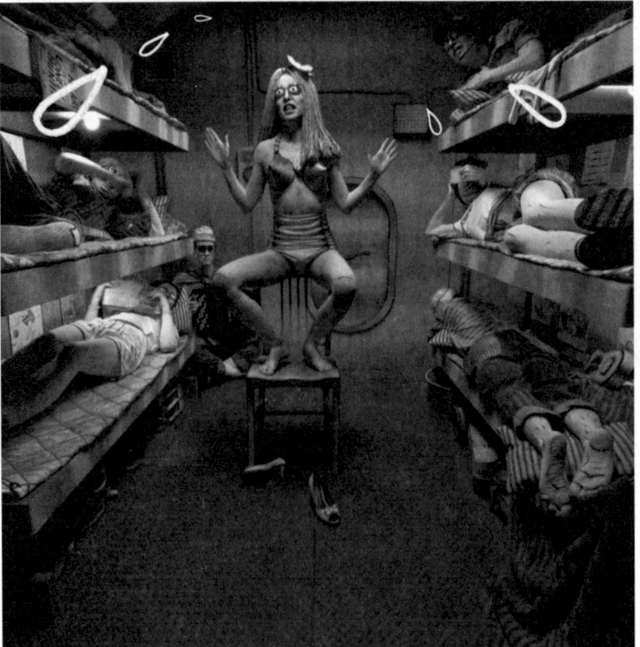

Mary Reid Kelley and Patrick Kelley, still from *In The Body of The Sturgeon*, 2017. Courtesy Mary Reid Kelley and Patrick Kelley; Fredericks & Freiser; Vielmetter Los Angeles; and Pilar Corrias.

Mary Reid Kelley, still from *Sadie, The Saddest Sadist*, 2009. Courtesy Mary Reid Kelley; Fredericks & Freiser; Vielmetter Los Angeles; and Pilar Corrias.

about production and set-ups, and so Jeff Wall's approach to photography comes into play. That is, how do you construct something, how seamless should it be, or is it important to show the disjunction? I had the opportunity to meet him during my early teaching years at Bard College, and we had interesting discussions about his working methods at a time when I was still grappling with mine.[195]

With the U.S.-led war in Afghanistan and Iraq underway, Tala Madani (MFA 2006), who had emigrated from Iran ten years earlier, entered Yale's MFA program in Painting and Printmaking in 2004. There she discovered "generational attitudes" regarding what was and was not valuable, "with a reliance on a formalist history, but one rooted in American minimalism or American abstraction."[196] She continues, "I realize that at one point in its history, the School had been tied to realism, as in the work of Lisa Yuskavage, but we were the ones that came out with all the squares. My thought was, 'How can I put myself in a subversive position in relation to this?'"[197]

Prior to enrolling at Yale, Madani held an internship within the German Council of Foreign Affairs in Berlin, which focused on issues of integration and immigration. She met regularly with experts, political analysts, and members of the World Bank, concentrating on the political affairs of Iran, Iraq, and the Middle East. Madani maintains that this experience subsequently influenced her artistic practice, as she reacted against "the world of administrative political analysis" in favor of "the immediacy and imagination of painting."[198] She took classes at the University, including "Constitutional Change in the Islamic World," taught by Noah Feldman from the Yale Law School, and "Schopenhauer's The World as Will and Representation," taught by Karsten Harries, which was cross-listed in the Comparative Literature and Philosophy Departments. In the School of Art, Madani studied closely with Catherine Murphy, a Senior Critic, whom she found "beyond extraordinary in her temperament and in the way she could understand things."[199] Like many recent alumni, she notes the importance of Murphy within the Painting faculty. Madani later learned that it was Murphy who had advocated for her to be accepted to the School.

Mary Reid Kelley (MFA 2009) entered the program in Painting and Printmaking in 2007 during a troop surge in the Iraq War that was part of a plan President George Bush had called "The New Way Forward in Iraq."[200] Reid Kelley recalls how Yale's Woolsey Hall rotunda presented the subject of memorial, prompting her to connect the past World Wars with the war in Vietnam and the war that was then ongoing in the Middle East:

[Woolsey Memorial] is the one that supposedly inspired Maya Lin when she was an undergraduate at Yale—with a little under 2,000 names of Yale students and faculty who had died. I started making rubbings [of it] with newsprint and crayon … I knew when I came to campus that I was very interested in text and in writing, but I didn't have very much confidence in what I was going to do or if I was going to make anything of that. … I eventually ended up transcribing the entire memorial into a document, and I would use the word search function to search for letter combinations by which I was able to make little verse forms. I, of course, was thinking about Dada and Surrealism and the chance-based techniques that were so connected to an era of upheaval in the early twenty-first century. … War [was] a big part of that, and so that got me really into the First World War and working specifically with [the inscribed names of] about 200 Yale men— I don't think there was a single female student on the memorial. I used the Alice Kimball [English Travel] Fellowship to go visit the men's graves in Europe. … It was common to bury students abroad, because the feeling back then was there was value in burying the soldier with his men—with his fellow

195 Ibid.

196 Tala Madani, telephone conversation with the author, January 24, 2020.

197 Ibid.

198 Tala Madani, email correspondence with the author, March 22, 2021.

199 Ibid.

200 President George W. Bush (January 10, 2007). "President's Address to the Nation". Office of the Press Secretary. Retrieved on January 13, 2021.

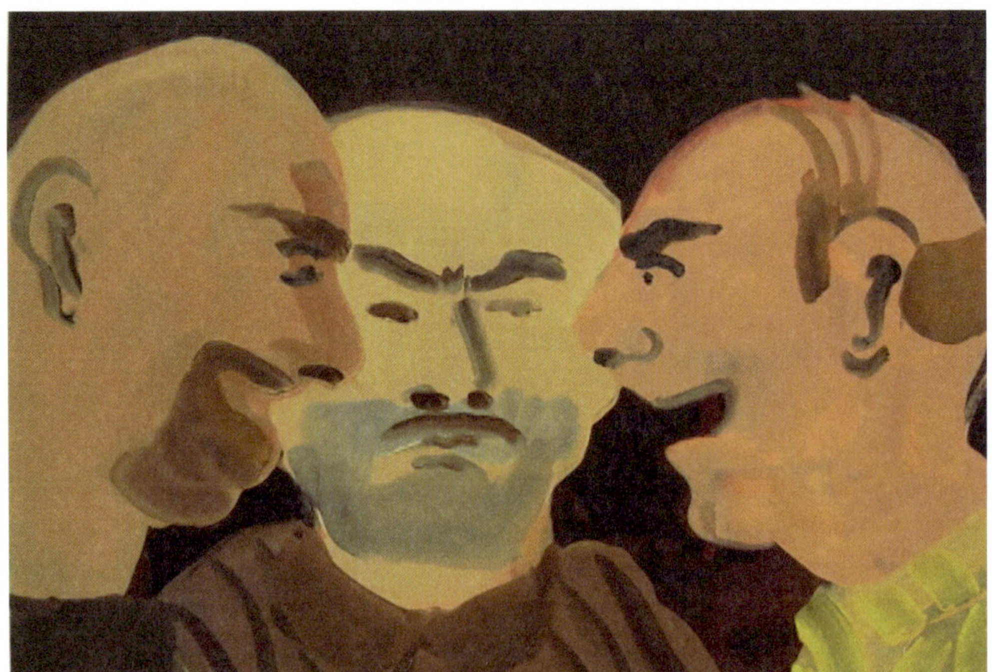

Tala Madani, still from Chit Chat*, 2007. Courtesy Tala Madani.*

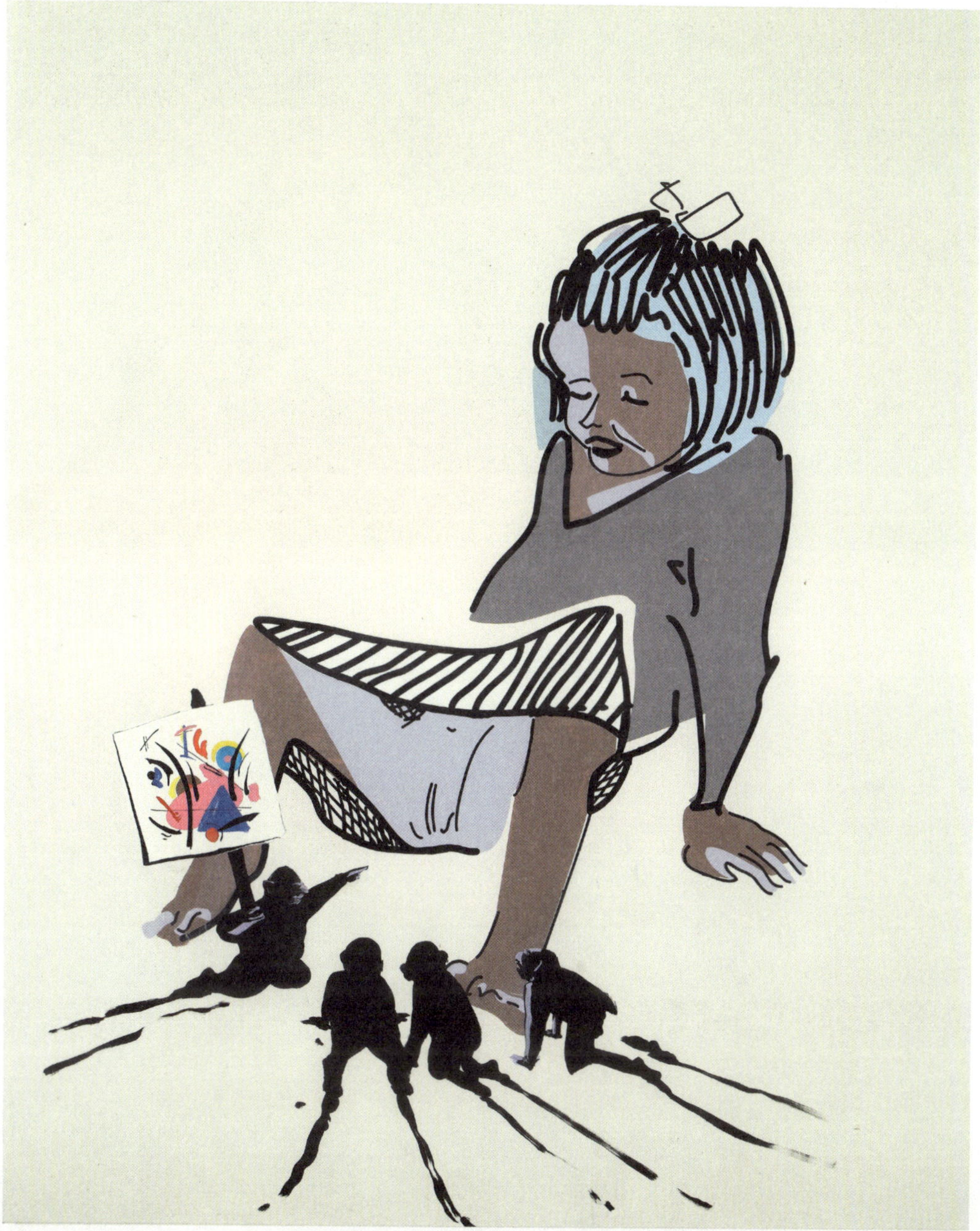

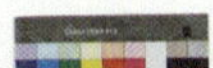

Tala Madani, _Abstract Pussy_, 2013. Courtesy Tala Madani.

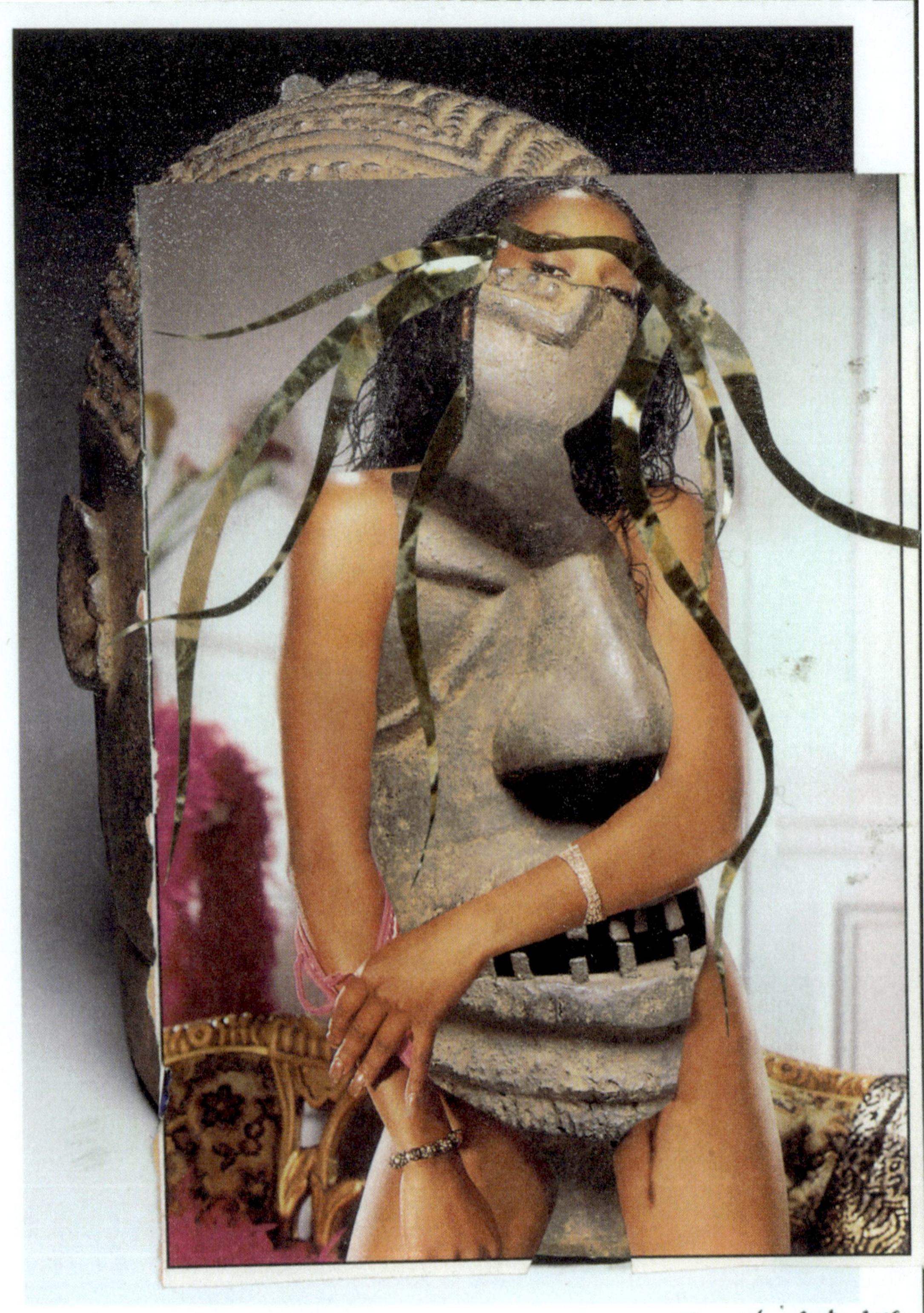

Wangechi Mutu, *Mask*, 2006. © Wangechi Mutu.

201   Mary Reid Kelley, oral history interview by Edi Dai, March 7, 2019, transcript, Yale University Art Gallery archives, New Haven.

202   Wangechi Mutu, telephone conversation with the author, January 15, 2020.

203   Ibid.

soldiers—and making it very explicit what this young person died for. So, this was at the peak of our involvement in Iraq, and I felt like I had several different groups to guide me through what this kind of spasm of national and international violence meant.[201]

Wangechi Mutu (MFA 2000), who was born in Kenya, enrolled as a graduate student in the Department of Sculpture in 1998, having spent part of her undergraduate studies at Parsons School of Design and the New School for Social Research, focusing on anthropology and cultural studies, before transferring to Cooper Union, where she was advised by the artist Robert Bordo and taught by Dennis Adams, Doug Ashford, Julie Ault, Hans Haacke, Faith Wilding, and Fred Wilson. She arrived at Yale with a rigorous grounding in institutional critique, criticism, art theory, and modernist histories, but her plans for graduate studies were to pursue figuration. Mutu explains, "The body could be an extension of my voice, a tool of empowerment and means of rebellion, a gender-switching device. … I understood the capacity for the body to twist and transform the conditions around which it exists."[202] Mutu recognized the body as "a mechanism with which to move the mind around issues of otherness, of transplanted-ness as a young woman, of blackness as an African-raised Black woman in New York City." Since she was interested in a multidisciplinary approach to art-making from a non-European perspective, she sought out academic classes within the University on film theory and music. Mutu recalls of her first year in the Sculpture program at Yale:

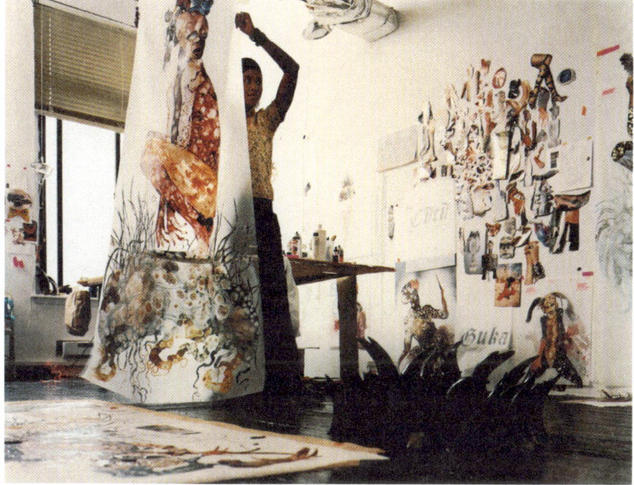

Wangechi Mutu in her studio, New York City, June 22, 2004. Photo by Jason Schmidt. © Jason Schmidt.

There were ten new students, and five of them were non-U.S. citizens. There were a few Black students at Yale … But there was a stench of entitlement in the rooms of the department and the critiques. I learned to be even more resourceful, more independent than I thought was even possible. I had no choice. I needed to carry myself along and hold up my side of the arguments coming from my incredible experiences traveling through Europe and being raised in East Africa, a place which had been colonized but not experienced slavery in the way Americans understood. Many of the American students in class did not know (or care to know) where Kenya or Korea or anywhere outside of the United States was. This taught me much about the Art World and the United States and thickened my skin.[203]

Mutu's initial insight about the capacity of the body and its potential importance for her work followed from a vivid experience watching television coverage of a protest in Nairobi that took place in the early 1990s, led by the late Wangari Maathi and mothers of students who were detained as political prisoners, together with activists calling for the release of the students. Mutu relates that:

The women were sitting in front of the parliament buildings refusing to leave, the riot police were ordered to disperse the seated, instead they went and

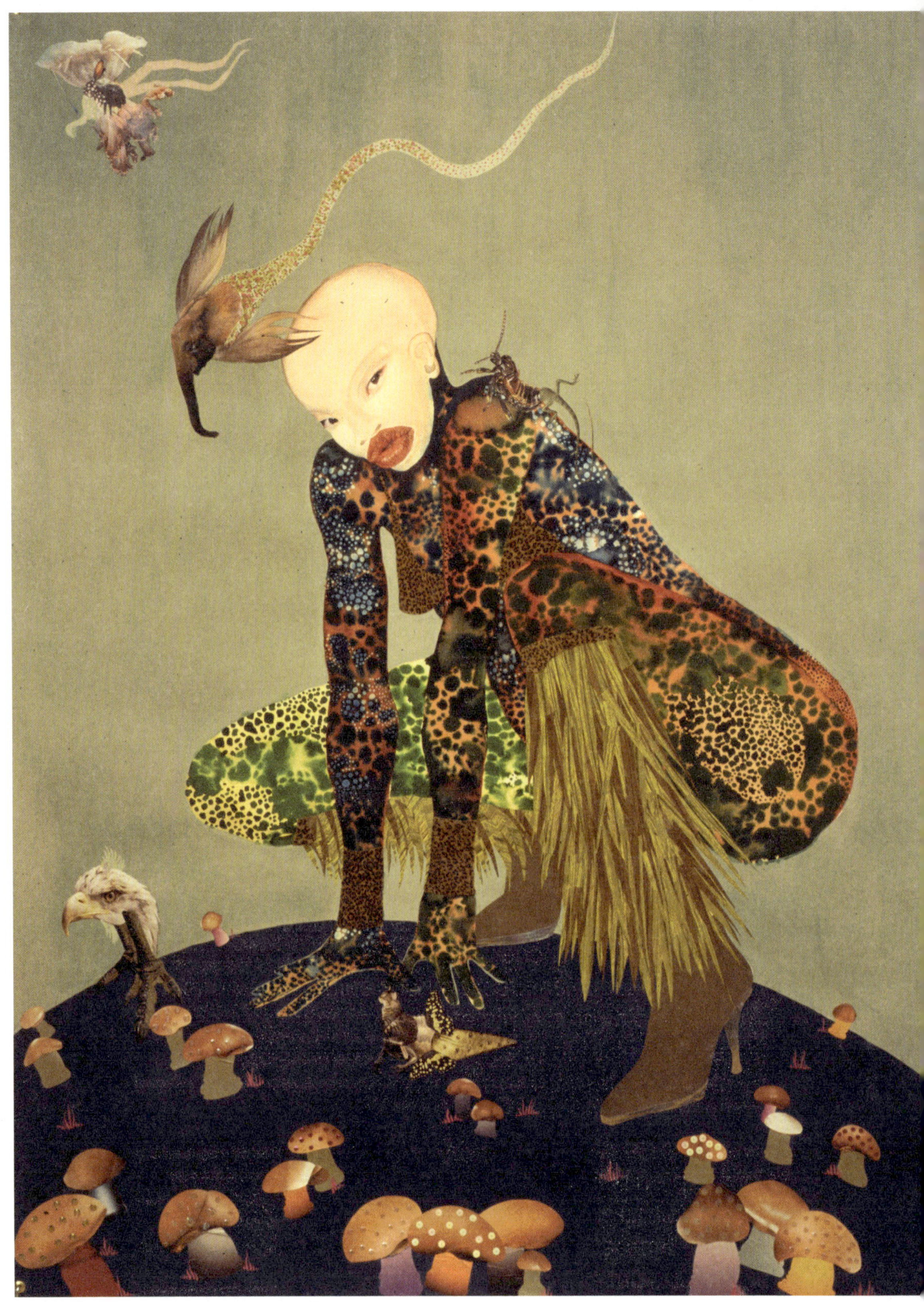

Wangechi Mutu, Riding Death in My Sleep, 2002. © Wangechi Mutu.

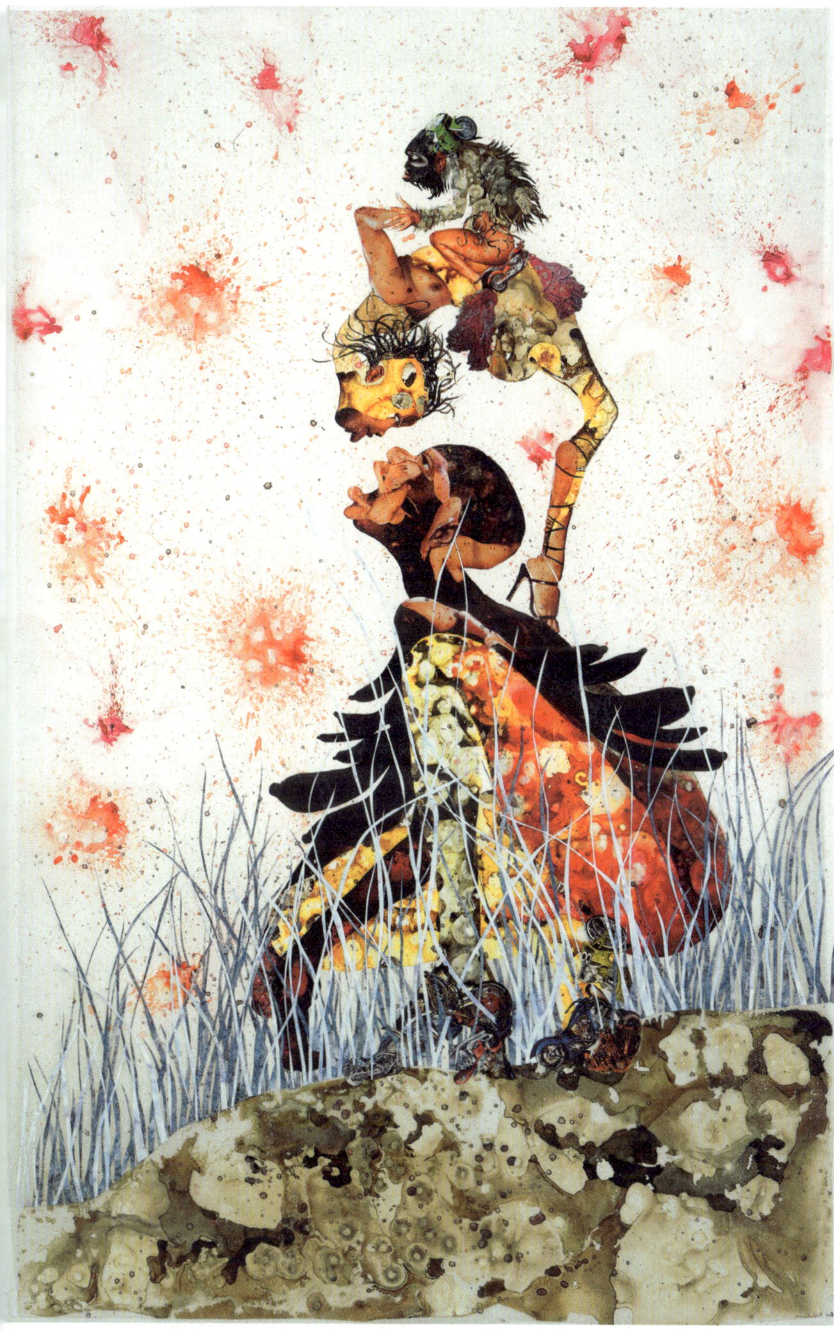

Wangechi Mutu, _Misguided Little Unforgivable Hierarchies_, 2005. Photo by Joshua White.
© Wangechi Mutu.

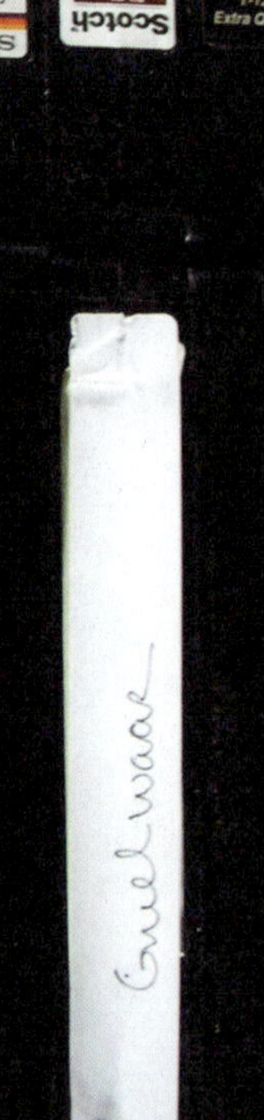

Leslie Hewitt and William Cordova, 1 Wish It Were True, *2004 (detail). Courtesy Leslie Hewitt.*

began to beat the women with their rungus and threatened and yelled insults and kicked them out of their way … The confrontation became quite serious, and, before long, these desperate, courageous women began to disrobe and show their pendulous breasts and their hanging bellies. The riot police began to back off and flee, and … all hell broke loose. The bodies of these Mamas had frightened and unnerved the men. These women were in fact releasing an ancient curse upon the cowardly men. Years later, when I arrived in New York, I remember obsessing on what I had witnessed that day on TV in Nairobi, and I remember how it impacted me slowly, the strength of these women's powerful African bodies, their courage, and their loud skin. This led me to research and ask about other stories like this … where many African women had stood in front of men, police, armed British soldiers, yelling abuses and unleashing curses whilst powerfully advocating for change.[204]

Mutu acknowledged that it would be "crucial to me to use the figure as a pivot, but also to recognize it as a trap. There is something about the body that confines us, that disables, that prevents us from being immaterial, being invisible, being all these things that maybe you want to be, because you don't want to stand out."[205] Mutu eventually turned toward configuring the Black female body as a hybrid that borrows from mythical and historical sources, as well as from the cultural imagination around otherness, in the spirit of writer Octavia Butler and the Afrofuturist vision that developed from Butler's work.

Leslie Hewitt (MFA 2004) enrolled in the Department of Sculpture in 2002, while completing a Clark Fellowship in Africana and Visual Cultural Studies at the Department of Social and Cultural Analysis at New York University from 2001–03, under photo historian Deborah Willis. There, Hewitt also studied under the Malian cultural theorist Manthia Diawara, enriching her knowledge about Black conceptual art traditions from an international perspective. It had been the intervention of Martinique artist Marc Latamie that steered Hewitt toward Africana and Visual Cultural Studies when she was still an undergraduate at Cooper Union. The fellowship helped to focus Hewitt's development of a critical writing practice while reaffirming her desire to cultivate an artistic practice that could "make an argument in a tangible, physical way."[206] Her decision to apply to the Yale School of Art was informed by Tony Gonzalez (MFA 1989), Margaret Morton (MFA 1977), and Irwin Rubin (BFA 1953; MFA 1956), three of Hewitt's professors at Cooper Union, as well as Mutu, who had recently graduated. Hewitt was interested in the Yale MFA program, moreover, because it was located within a leading University renowned for its programs in the humanities. Although Hewitt recalls a rigid separation between individual departments within the School of Art and the absence of intercurricular classes, she found that possibilities for interdepartmental conversations existed if one sought them out. Hewitt attended several courses with Kellie Jones, who was an Assistant Professor in African American Studies and History of Art and is known as both an academic and a highly regarded curator of exhibitions, including *Energy/ Experimentation: Black Artists and Abstraction, 1964–1980* (The Studio Museum, 2006) and *Now Dig This! Art and Black Los Angeles, 1960–1980* (Hammer Museum, 2011). Hewitt recalls Jessica Stockholder, then Director of the Department of Sculpture, for her "strength of leadership, her respect of different registers of being, encouraging that each person was bringing in their own modality." She notes that it "sometimes felt frustrating, but I think it did create more autonomy for the artist to seek and build their own support structure. In the end, I see it as extremely important to my development and to the development of my peers at the time."[207]

Hewitt cooperated closely with her peers at the School, including William Cordova (MFA 2004), Martha Friedman (MFA 2003), Emi Okubo (MFA 2003), Mamiko Otsubo (MFA 2004), and Aaron Young (MFA 2004), to organize

204 Ibid.

205 Ibid.

206 Leslie Hewitt, telephone conversation with the author, April 2, 2021.

207 Ibid.

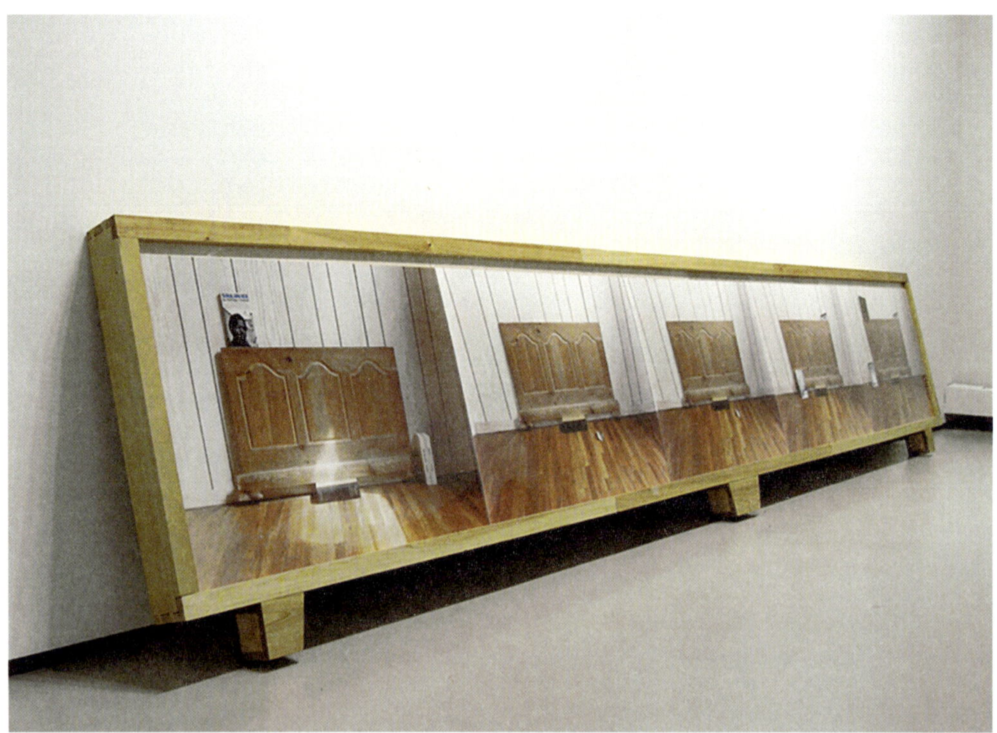

Leslie Hewitt, *Like It Is*, 2004. Courtesy Leslie Hewitt.

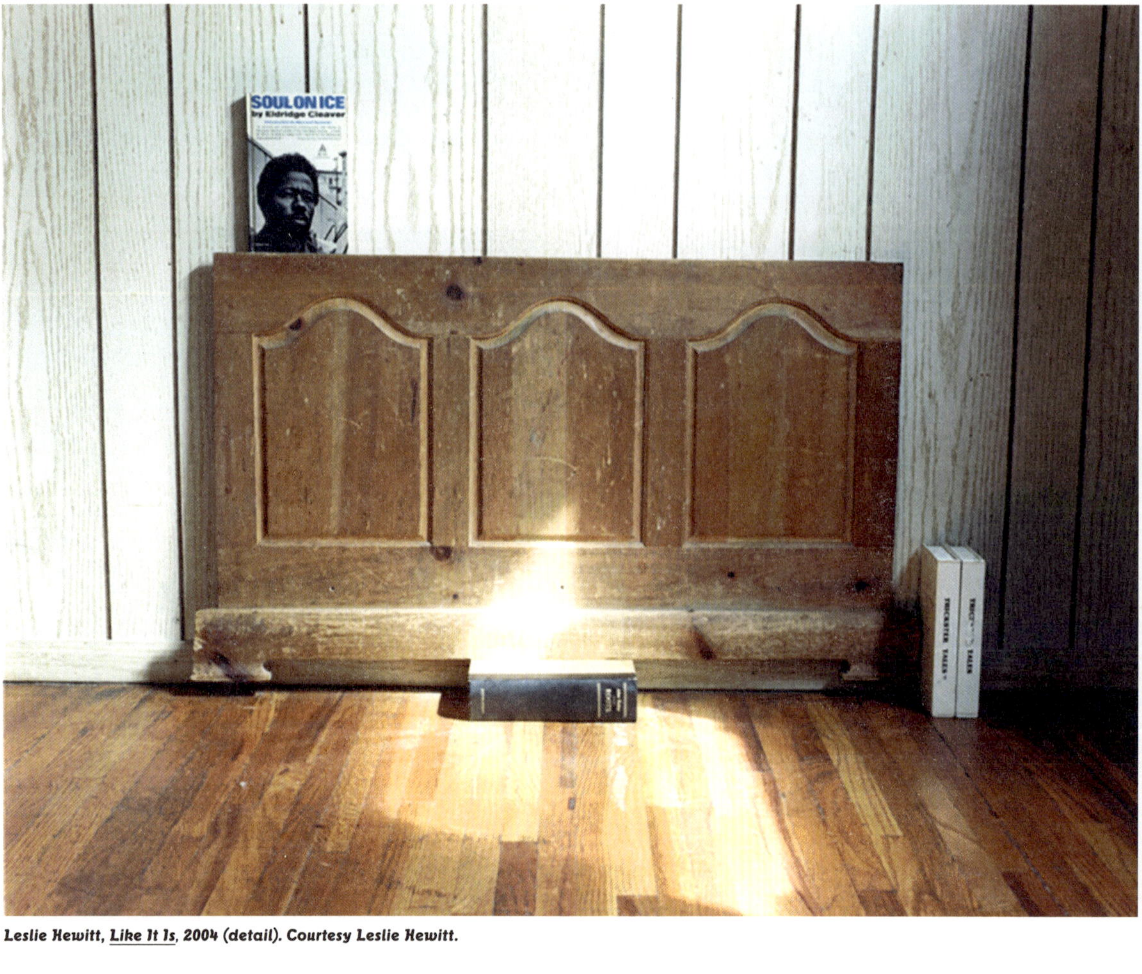

Leslie Hewitt, *Like It Is*, 2004 (detail). Courtesy Leslie Hewitt.

208 Ibid.

209 Ibid.

210 Ibid.

211 Elle Pérez, conversation with the author, January 11, 2020.

212 Ibid.

213 Ibid.

visiting lecturers and develop an enduring community. These relationships led to cooperative work extending into projects with former visiting faculty of the School, including Walid Raad, Coco Fusco, and Doug Ashford. Hewitt continued to work collaboratively with Cordova beyond graduation on a project called *I Wish It Were True*, which began in 2004, and was included in the Whitney Biennial (2008) in the form of a working library of Third Cinema-influenced and Third Cinema films."[208] Hewitt describes her interest in historical narrative and historical materialism as "embedded within a corporeal treatment of photography" that sympathizes with Ariella Azoulay's ideas around how a work can "reconfigure the way in which the gaze for introspection can be extrospective."[209] Hewitt, currently an Associate Professor at Cooper Union, often returns as a Visiting Critic to the Department of Photography. Regarding her role as an educator, she notes, "I enjoy being with artists. I am committed to encouraging [a laboratory] of understanding art and to creating a space where students determine where art lives and rests in their psyches. It's not for me to overdetermine that for them. But it is my responsibility, I think, to protect that space and to make it as large as it needs to be and as porous as it needs to be."[210]

Elle Pérez (MFA 2015), entered the School of Art in 2013. Their application to the Photography department consisted of images made on a queer farm in rural Tennessee that they visited annually, as well as some images of their family in Puerto Rico. At the time, transgender and gender nonconforming space were not part of the national conversation. According to Pérez, "As a photographer, my earlier, pre-graduate work addressed transgender people's experiences in relation to those who were not adhering to a particular or straightforward transition narrative, either because they didn't want to, or because their circumstances didn't allow for it—everything from nineteen-year-old radicals in the Bay area, to the fifty-three-year-old social worker who worked with single-sex populations, built an entire career within that structure, and could not transition because that would affect their job and their ability to do their job."[211]

Since graduating in 2015, Pérez has continued to return to Yale as a Critic, commenting that, "Since coming back to the School in a different capacity, it's been really clarifying of my own graduate education, and then it has also made me think about how much the school has changed in the seven years."[212] Pérez still relates to the anxiety that a graduate student goes through, and the importance of having interlocutors and mentors who can perceive the stakes in one's work and foster its development: "As a student, it's always so hard, because you are always in this mental space of wanting something so badly that is difficult to actualize. I remember being in a crit, and I gave some vague introductory statement about resilience in relation to a series of images of wrestlers in the Bronx. Someone in the crit shouted out, 'Did anyone understand what they meant?' and Roni Horn, who had been on the review panel that day answered, 'Yes, I understood what they meant'—an affirmation that stayed with me ..."[213]

In a discussion on the role of realism in the photography department, Pérez agreed that one could say the Yale department has a traceable documentary style, though they supposed that idea "might not hold water once pressured"— that the effect may have more to do with the legacy of photography and how the work of Walker Evans or Todd Papageorge relate to that. Pérez cites a recent crit of work by a student, Robert Andy Coombs (MFA 2020), adding:

> The stakes in that work include a kind of reclamation of autonomy. That is, in the best moments, it flips the value structure of society away from an independent, able body. The work restates the value structure as being rooted in interdependence, as that being the most beautiful thing that could exist in the world. I think that really does something that is so exciting as a human being. When I think about the ethos of the photography department or the kind of work of lineage and legacy and what that does or what it looks

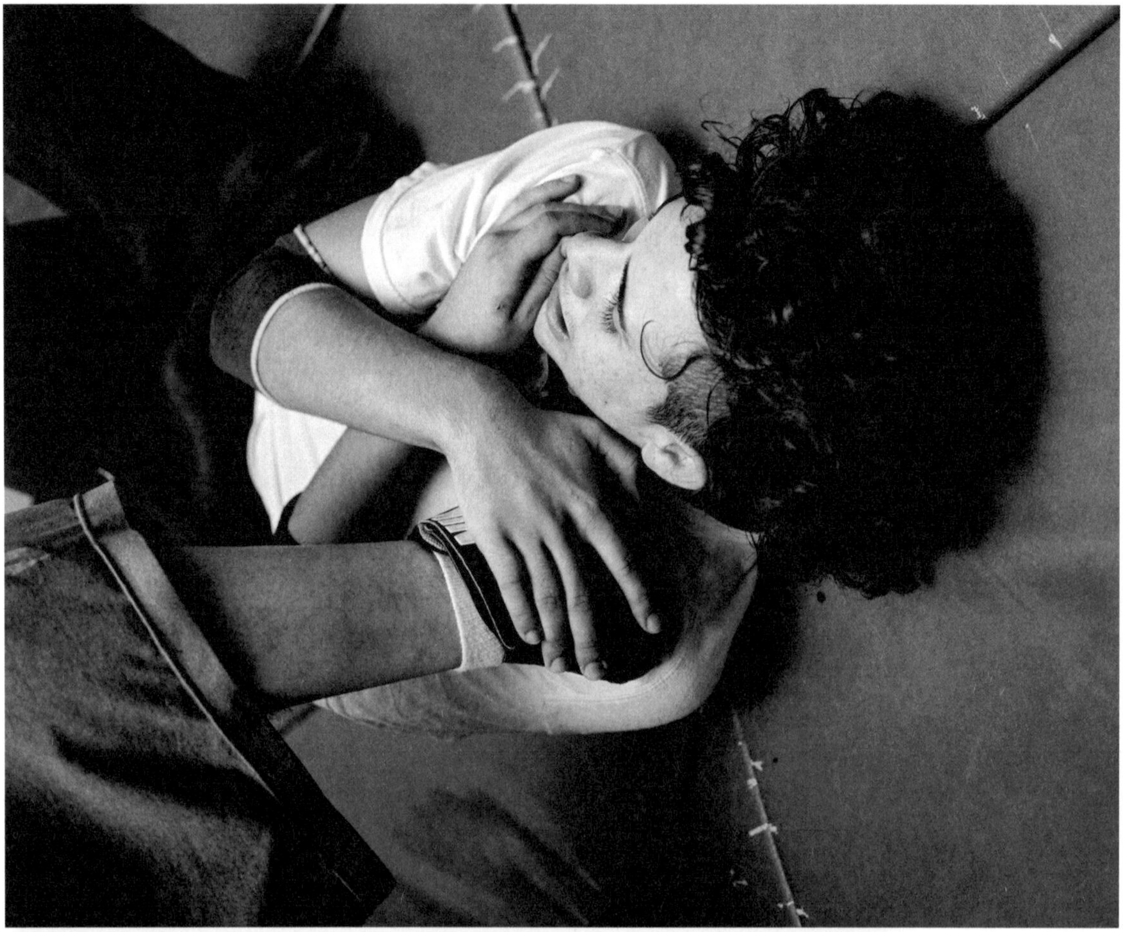

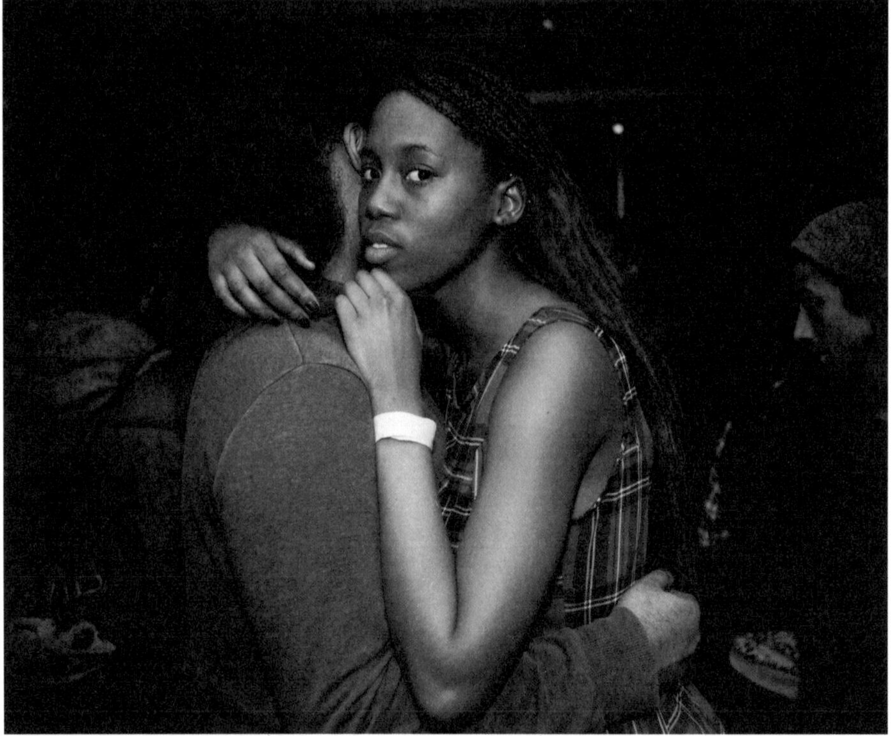

Elle Pérez, <u>untitled (Kirsten)</u>, 2015/2019. Courtesy Elle Pérez and 47 Canal, New York.

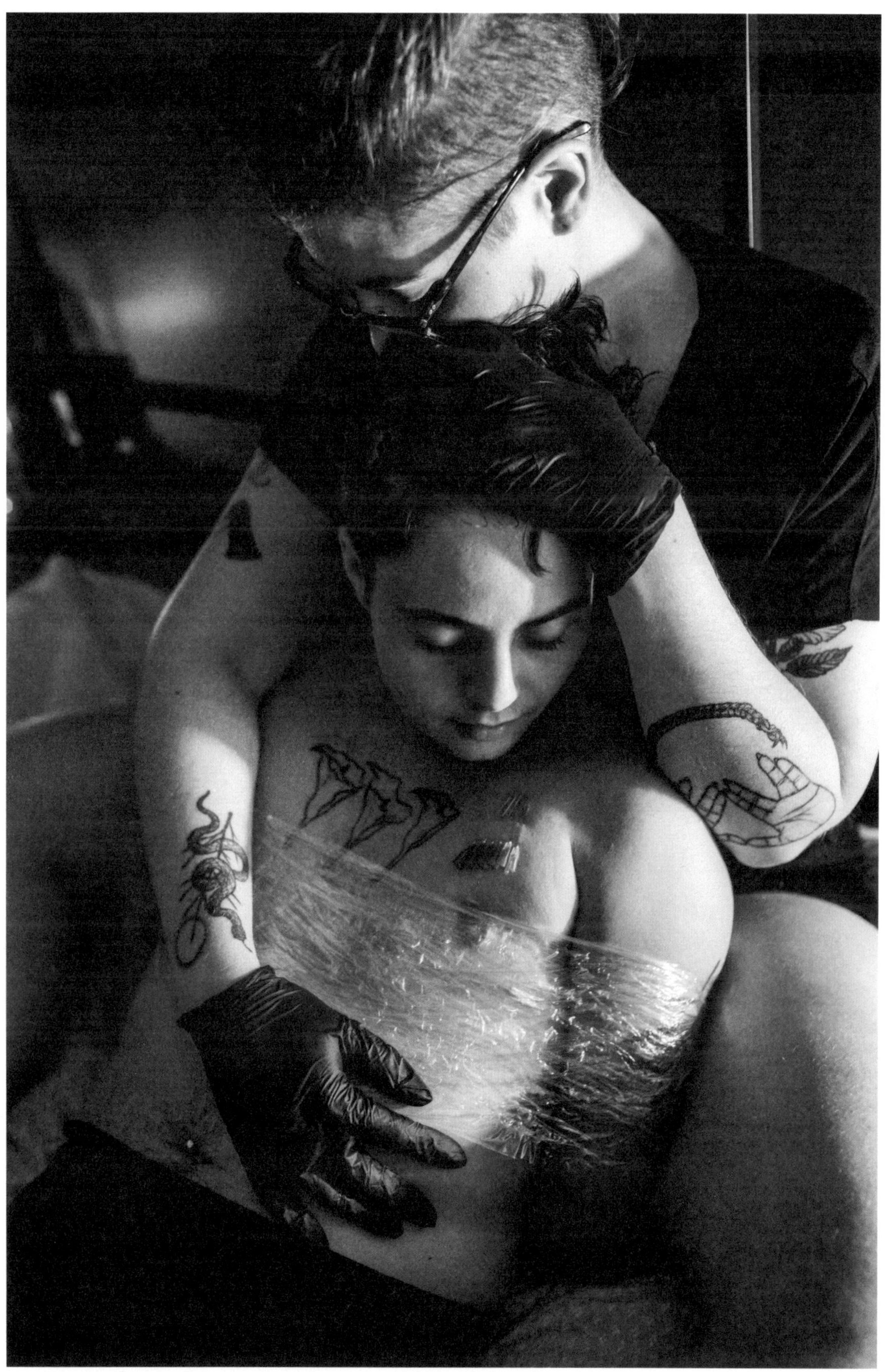

Elle Pérez, _Wilding and Charles_, 2019. Courtesy Elle Pérez and 47 Canal, New York.

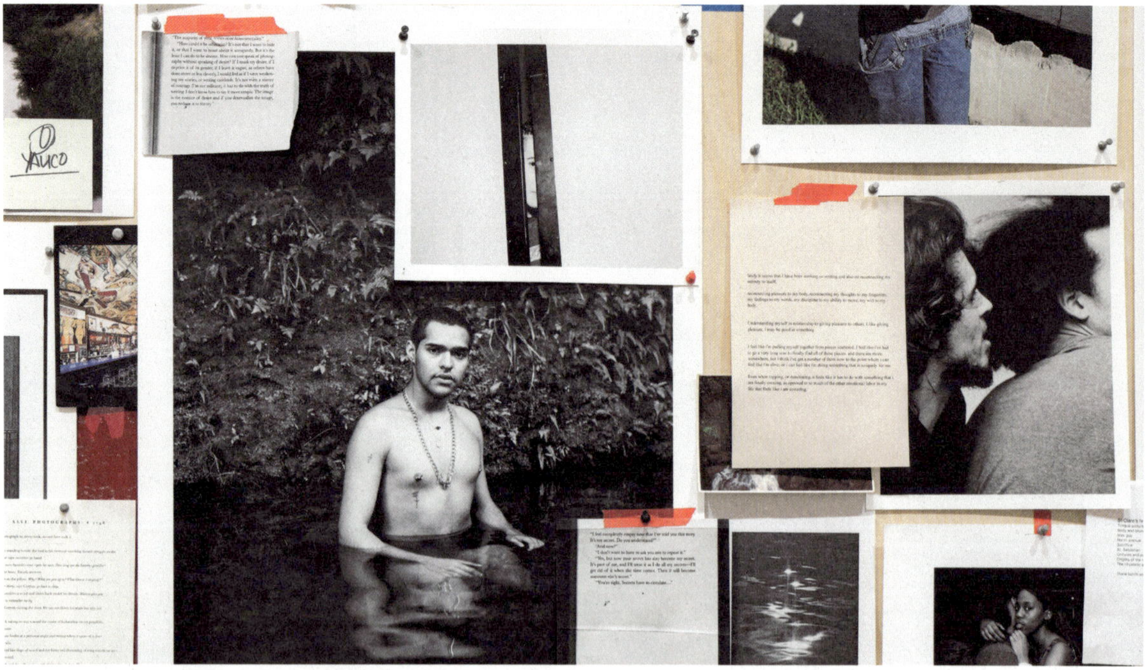

Elle Pérez, <u>Diablo</u>, 2018 (detail). Courtesy Elle Pérez and 47 Canal, New York.

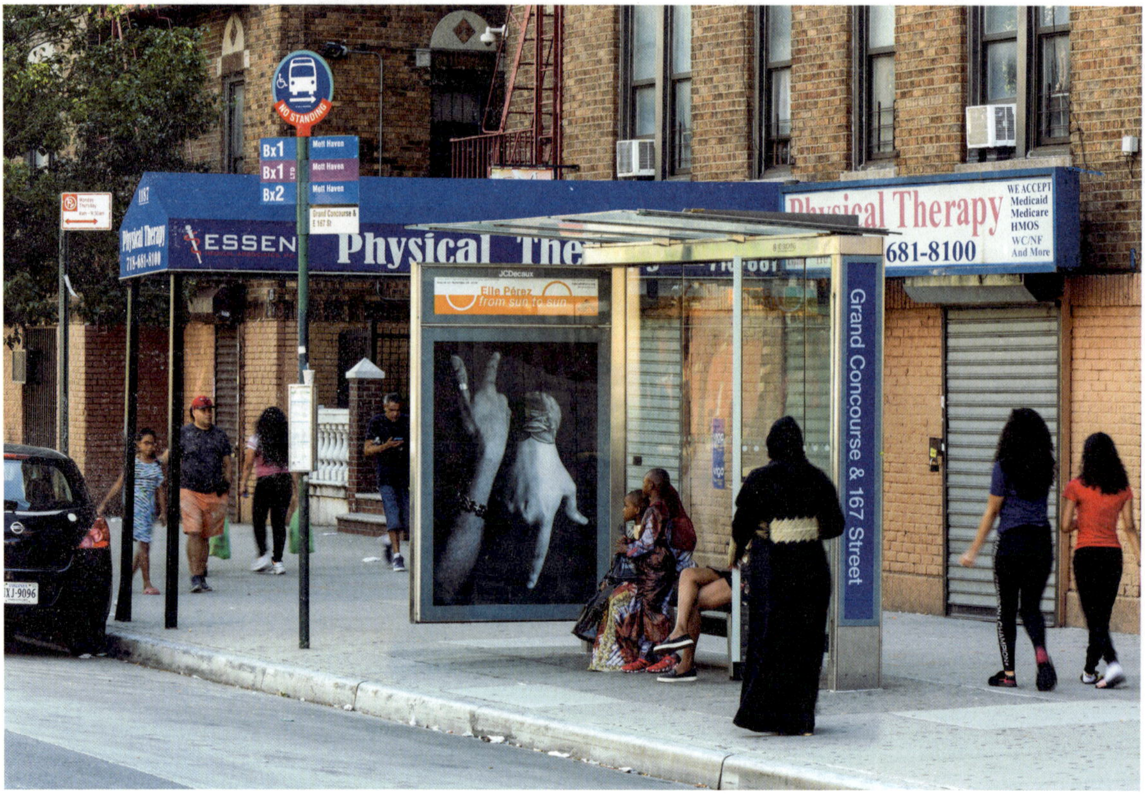

Elle Pérez, installation view of <u>from sun to sun</u>, Public Art Fund, New York, 2019. Photo by Nicholas Knight.
Courtesy Elle Pérez; 47 Canal, New York; and Public Art Fund, New York.

like, I think about Robert's work, and how that pushes the boundary …
I think what the camera can tell us about being a human is maybe one of
the fundamental questions of the Department of Photography over time.[214]

Pérez concludes:

I guess what I've been trying to figure out for myself in returning to these
spaces and participating in them … now as opposed to then, is how to move
through them and where the line between an external and internal conflict
lies in existing in these spaces. So, for example, I identify as a person of
color—being a person of color in that space, being someone who is gender
nonconforming in that space, what I thought was possible for me in that
space, and what was actually possible for me in that space, and then
what was actually externally happening, or how I was reading people's
motivations … As a student, I think I brought my own baggage or my
own expectations to the space that had to do with what I thought was
possible for me there, or how I thought I was going to be treated.
I saw what I wanted to see in a way. Now that I'm back in the space in a
different way, at a different time, in a different role, and watching people
go through it, I'm teaching myself how to recognize that struggle.[215]

214   Ibid.

215   Elle Pérez quoted
in an abridged version of
the current text published
as "The Yale School of
Art: A Legacy Revisited,"
in On the Basis of Art:
150 Years of Women at
Yale. (New Haven, Yale
University Art Gallery,
2021. 151).

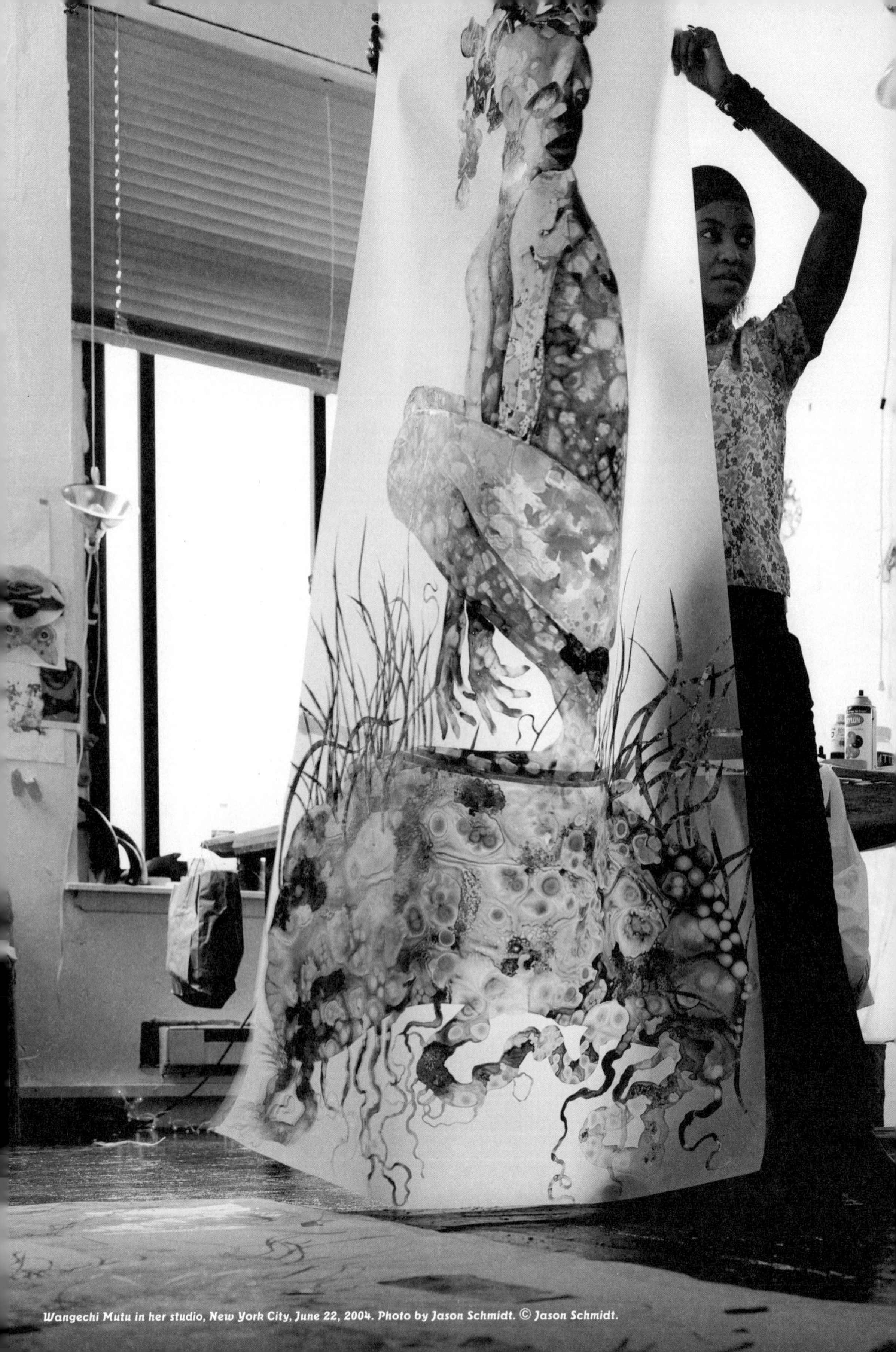

Wangechi Mutu in her studio, New York City, June 22, 2004. Photo by Jason Schmidt. © Jason Schmidt.

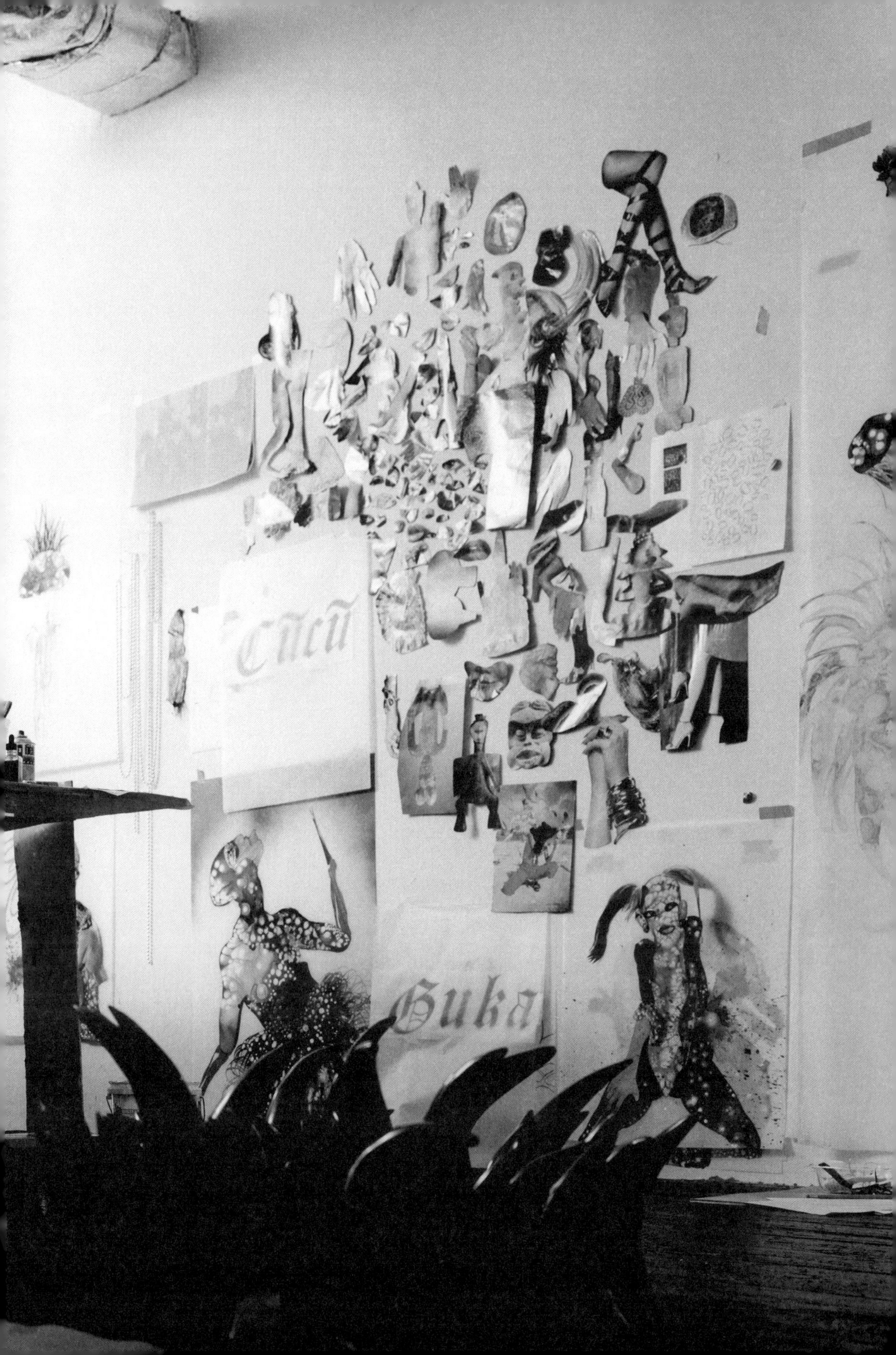

A FORTHCOMING HISTORY OF INCLUSIVITY

The year 2016 proved pivotal for the School of Art and moreover for graduate programs throughout the country. Months prior to my arrival as the new, female dean in August and a fall 2016 election season that culminated in the defeat of the first major-party ticket to feature a woman candidate for the office of President of the United States, students at the School self-organized to demand that the institution become more diverse and inclusive. Student-driven pressure for institutional change only increased following the election. Farah Al Qasimi (MFA 2017) recalls a dramatic change from one year to the next. According to Al Qasimi, the atmosphere at School became more contentious as "the election [of Donald J. Trump] brought up a lot of instances of racial tension that felt immediate to some and not to others." She continues:

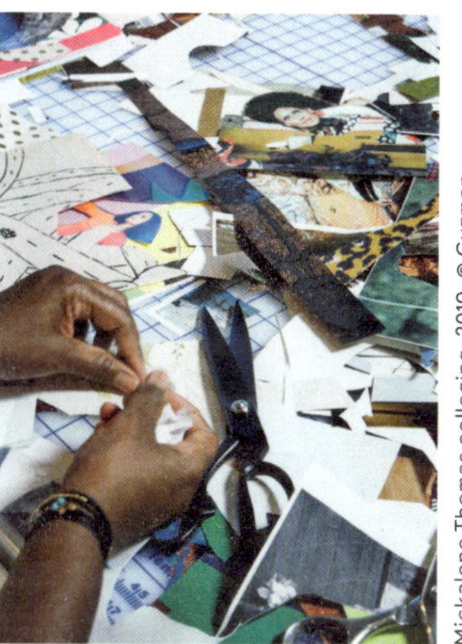

> I think graduate school is a tense place already. Most people have given up a lot to be there. Everyone is going through some sort of magnificent transformation, and battling their respective demons in different ways. Critiques can become charged and personal, especially in discourse around identity politics. And then, the frantic energy around the 2016 election heightened the inherent tension.[216]

216 Farah Al Qasimi, telephone conversation with the author, March 31, 2021.

Al Qasimi recalls that, in early 2016, during her first year as a student, a diversity committee was formed to serve as "an intermediate body between the administration and the students," necessitated by "what was unfolding nationally … [but precipitated by problems with] the process of signing up for studio visits with visiting artists." She explains that students "ended

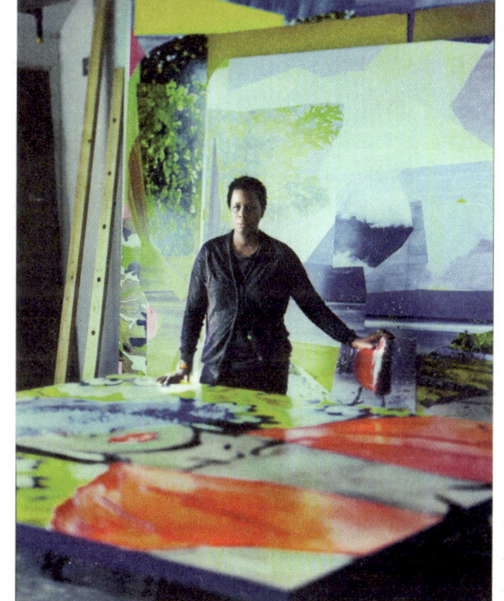

up with bi-weekly meetings … overseen by Mark Gibson [Assistant Dean from July 1, 2017 to June 30, 2018] and Anoka Faruqee as a way to air grievances."[217] Al Qasimi recalls that students successfully placed demands on new hires, resulting in the Dean's 2017 appointment of Gibson, as well as the appointment that same year of A. L. Steiner as 2018 Presidential Visiting Fellow in the Department of Photography, followed by further appointments of Mickalene Thomas (MFA 2002) in 2020, and Sondra Perry in 2021. Steiner had previously

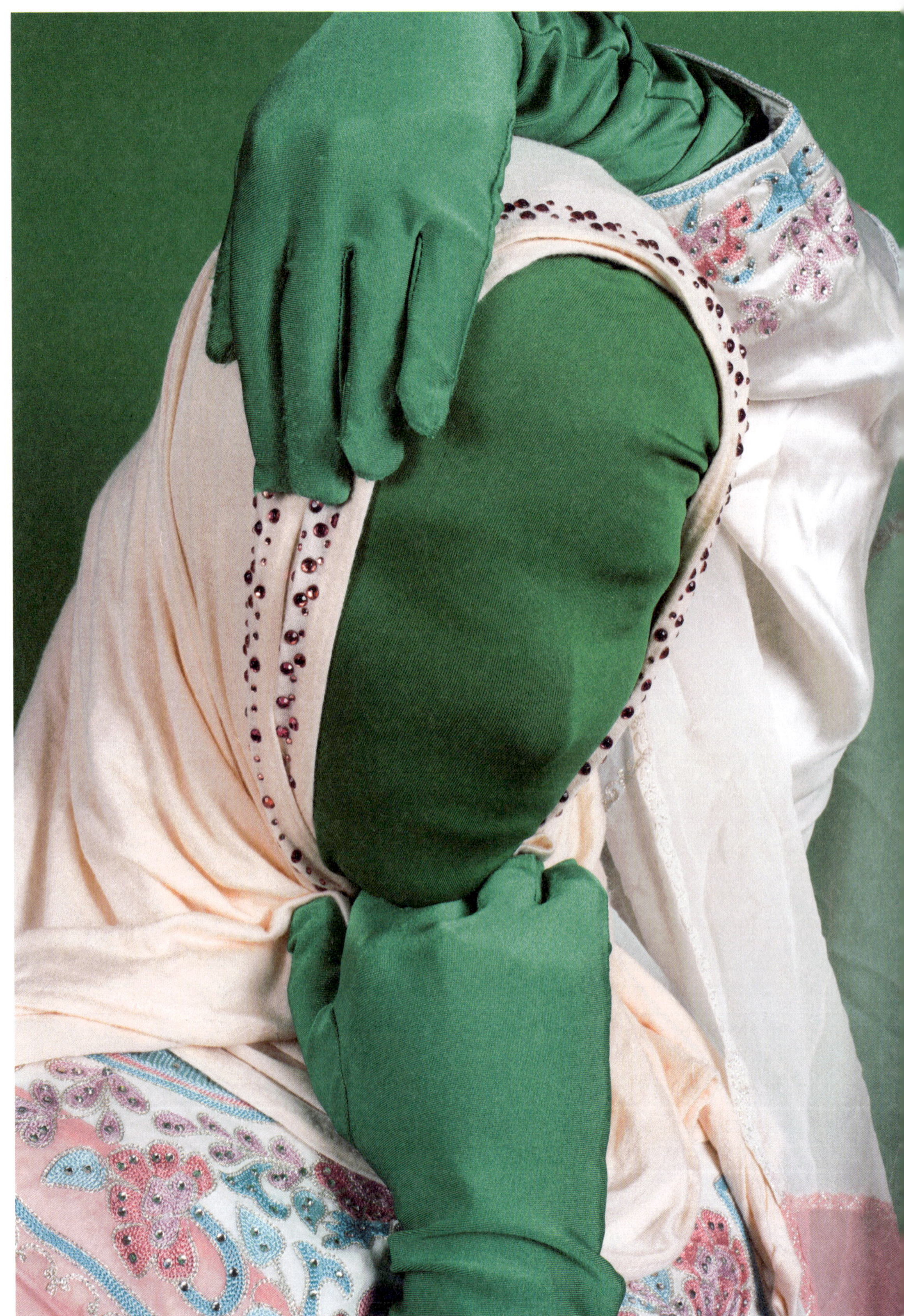

Farah Al Qasimi, <u>It's Not Easy Being Seen 2</u>, 2017. Courtesy Farah Al Qasimi; Helena Anrather, New York; and the Third Line, Dubai.

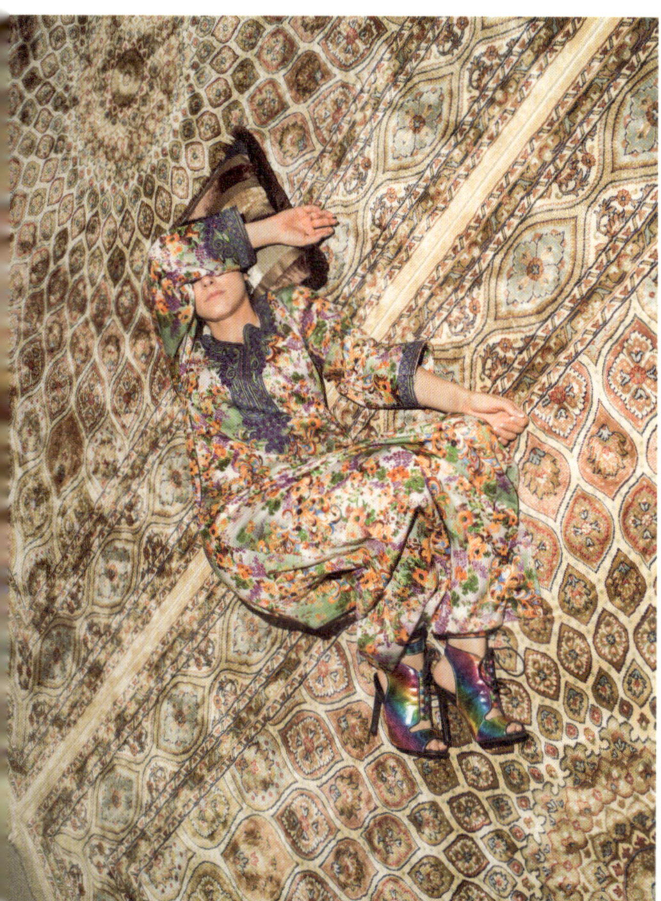

Farah Al Qasimi, <u>M Napping on Carpet</u>, 2016. Courtesy Farah Al Qasimi; Helena Anrather, New York; and the Third Line, Dubai.

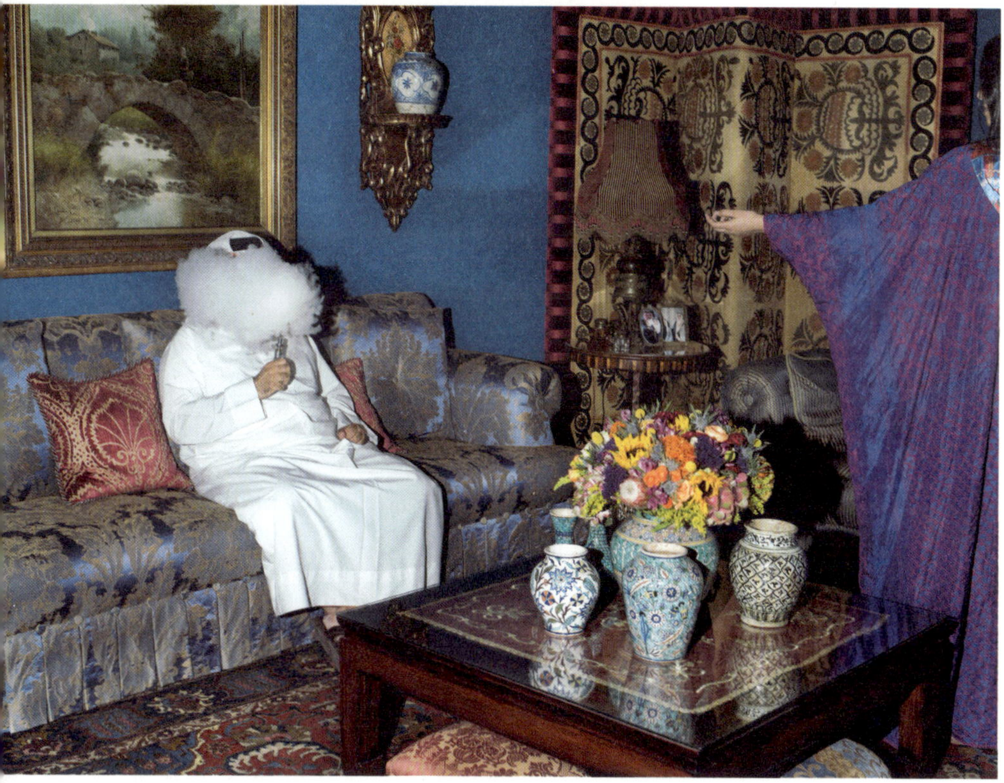

Farah Al Qasimi, <u>Living Room Vape</u>, 2017. Courtesy Farah Al Qasimi; Helena Anrather, New York; and the Third Line, Dubai.

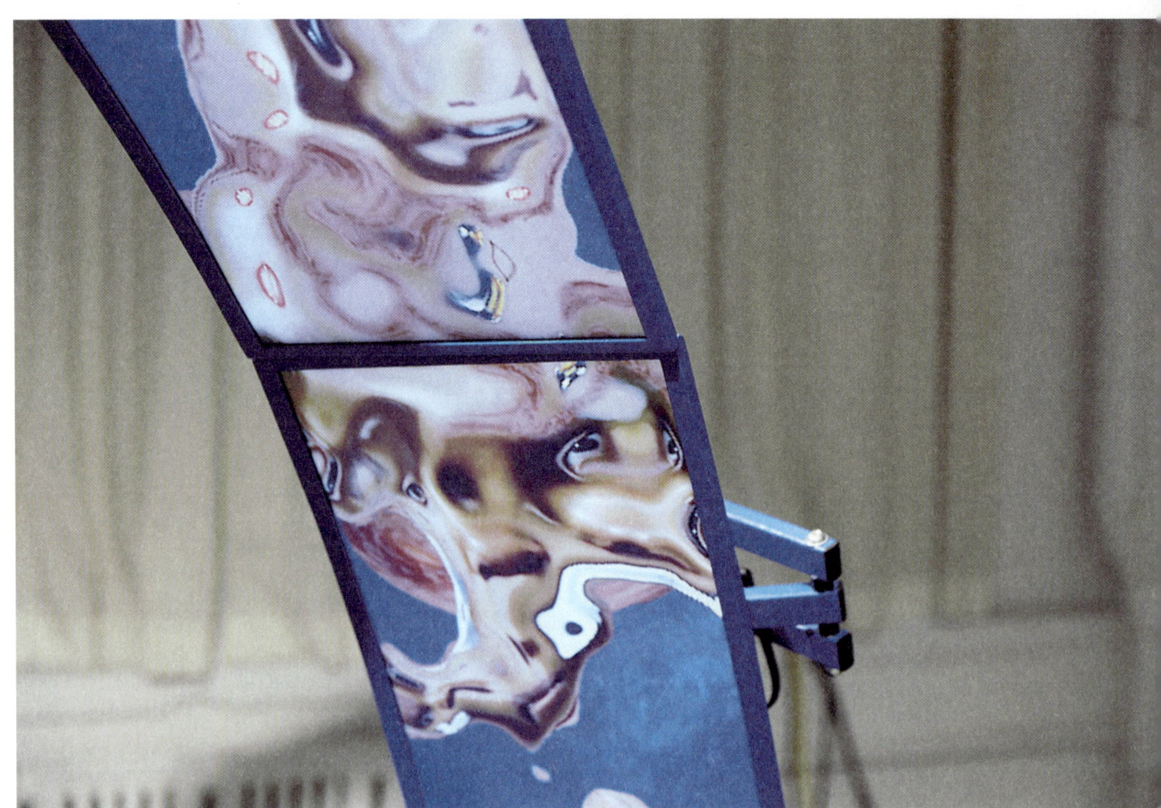

Sondra Perry, ffffffffffffoooooooooooouuuuuuuuuurrrrrrrrrrrrrrrrrrrrrrrrrrrrr, 2017 (detail). © Sondra Perry. Courtesy the artist and Bridget Donahue, New York.

been a Critic who, according to Al Qasimi, adeptly negotiated otherwise fraught environments, effectively dissipating tension and redirecting students' energy. Al Qasimi, who currently teaches at the Bard College Department of Photography and at the Pratt Institute Graduate School of Art, noted that these moments helped to prepare her as an educator:

> So many academic communities are not equipped to redirect and focus conflict in productive ways. … [W]e can and should have disagreements—it's wrong to assume that everybody operates within the same moral framework—but we should be able to arrive at a place of mutual understanding. When I was a graduate student at Yale, there was a lot of, "You should believe in this," or, "You should not believe in that." But it's not that simple for a lot of people. I think there were not enough outlets for deeper conversations.[218]

Al Qasimi also recalls the difficulty of personally grappling with increasingly dramatic national political events and related news coverage:

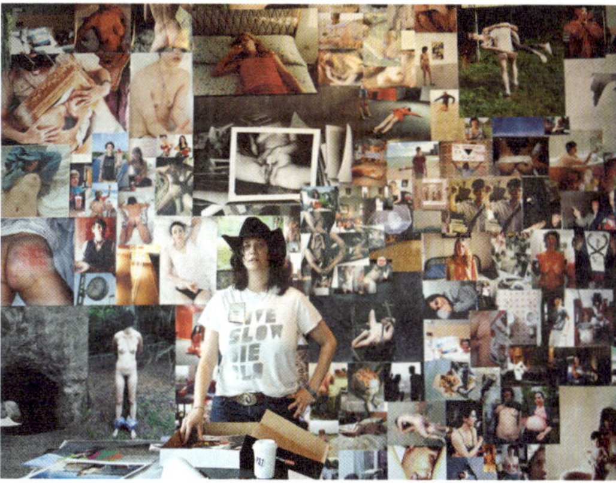

> I became acutely aware of the fact that I was suddenly a highly visible minority. It was a year of loud anti-Muslim rhetoric. I remember trying to make work for a critique and having the shoot derailed by a passerby who stopped his car to record me on his phone while calling me by racial slurs. I felt I needed to suspend my own emotional reaction, to remain research-driven and steadfast in my approach to the work. I took an amazing class called Islam in the American Imagination, taught by Zareena Grewal in American Studies [cross-listed in Women's, Gender, and Sexuality Studies; and in Ethnicity, Race, and Migration]. It supplemented my knowledge about what I was dealing with on a personal level, and it contributed to my thesis work. [219]

Laura Coombs (MFA 2017) also recalls a contentious environment among students related to the election, as well as heightened concern over the newly elected administration's intention to repeal women's rights, including reproductive rights and access to healthcare. According to Coombs, "We were honestly scared—*are they really going to roll back our rights?*"[220] As a reaction, Coombs, who was studying in the Department of Graphic Design, produced a series of books related to contraception issues. She lobbied for more women to teach workshops at the School, more women to design the posters featured in the School's hallways, and more people of color to be invited as guest lecturers. Recognizing design as an embodiment of ideological perspectives, she felt a sense of urgency to bring issues of political concern to the fore of her work.[221]

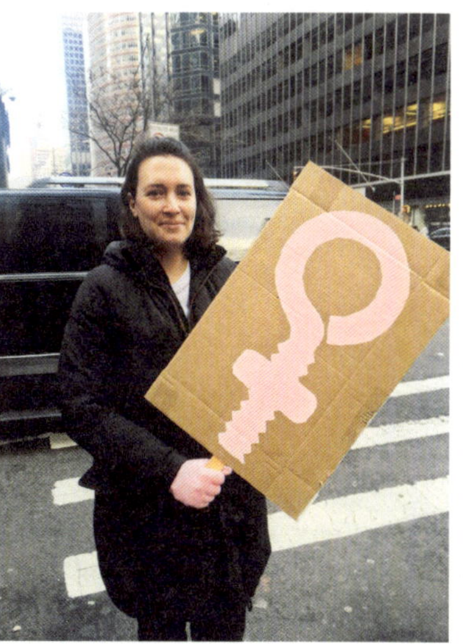

218   Ibid.

219   Ibid.

220   Laura Coombs. Telephone conversation with the author, April 11, 2021.

221   Ibid.

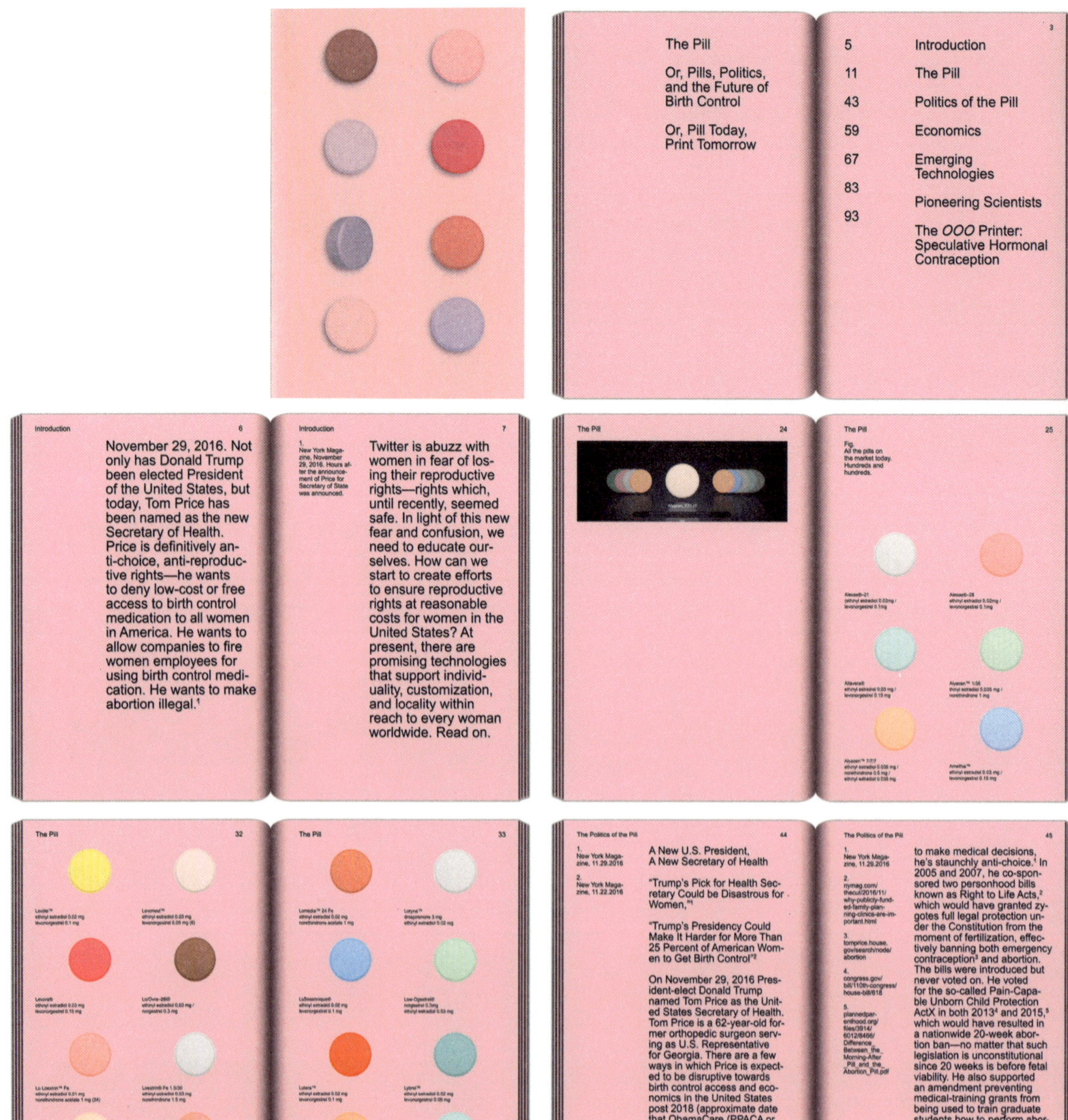

Laura Coombs and Anastasiia Raina, pages from The Pill, 2016. Courtesy Laura Coombs.

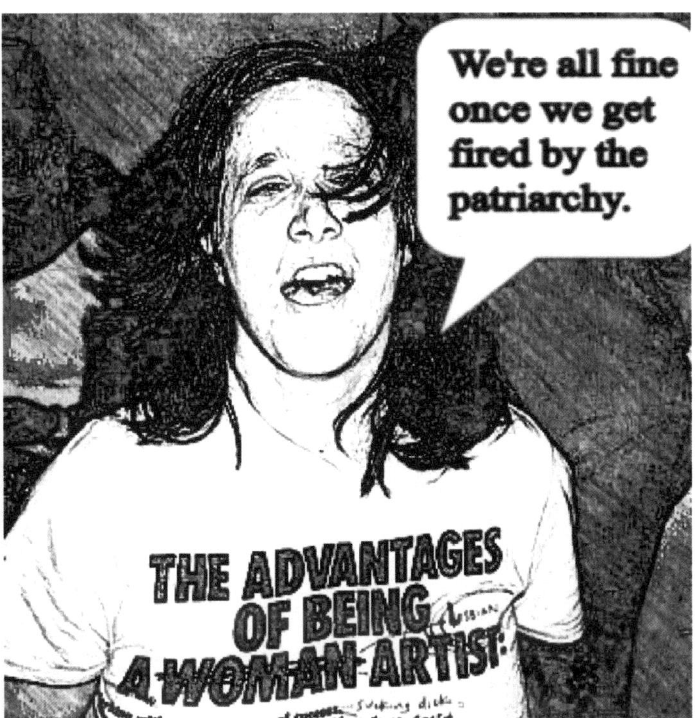

Russell Brown @gorgeousladiesofwisdom, <u>A. L. Steiner: We're all fine once we get fired by the patriarchy</u>, 2014. Courtesy Russell Brown.

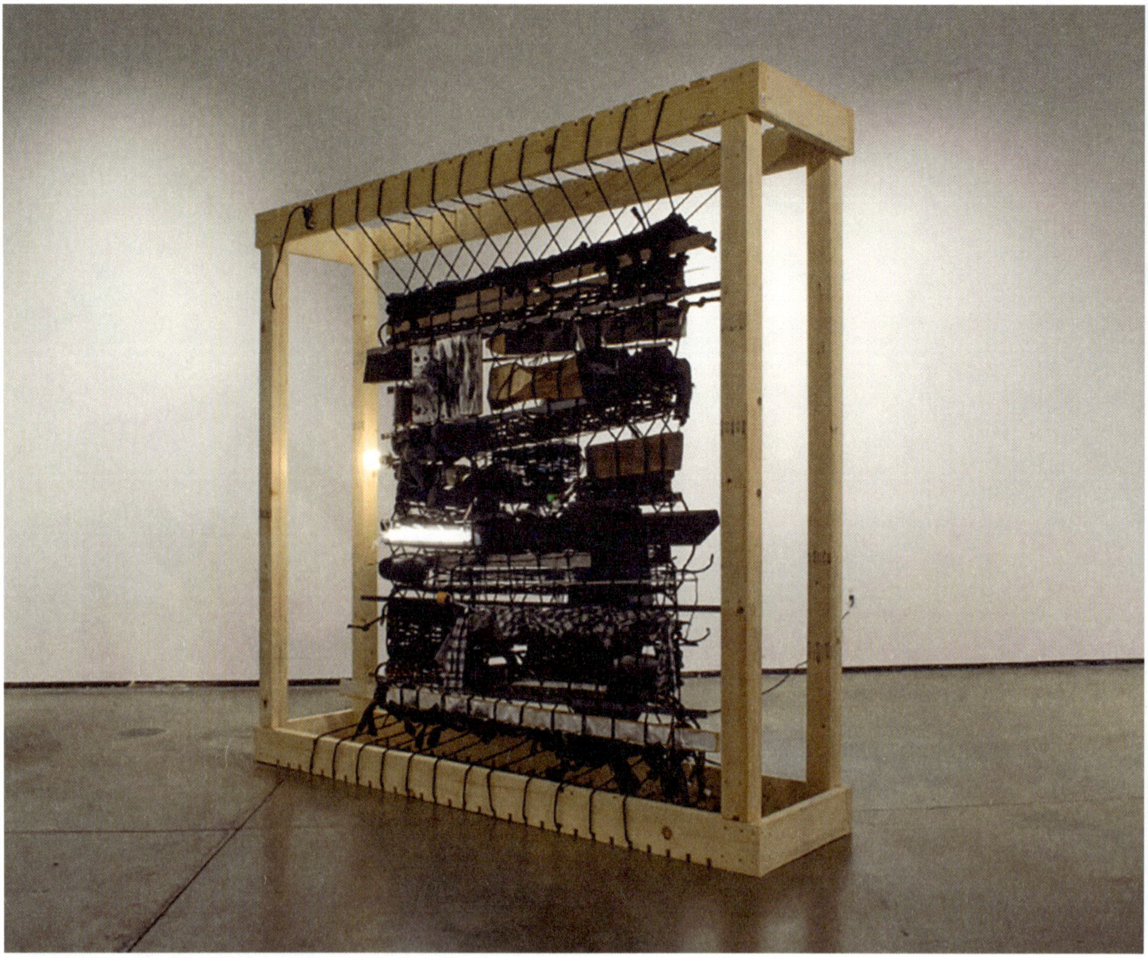

Kenturah Davis, <u>Interface II</u>, 2017. Courtesy Kenturah Davis.

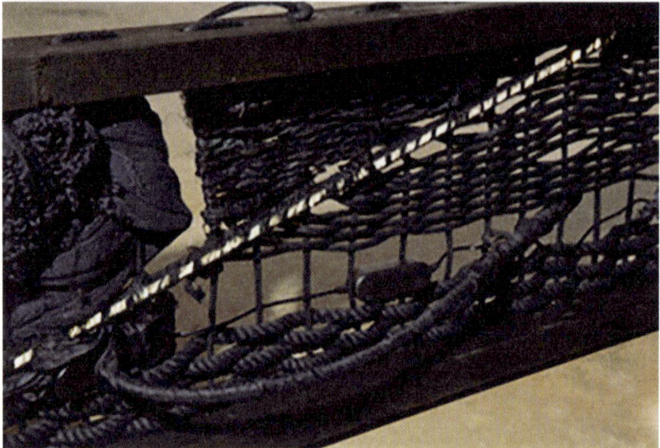

Kenturah Davis, <u>Interface III</u>, 2018 (detail). Photo by Bek Andersen.
Courtesy Kenturah Davis.

In direct response to the devolving
political context, Critical Practice
took as its course title "Diving
into the Wreck: Rethinking Critical
Practice," quoting the title of
Adrienne Rich's poem, "Diving
into the Wreck," which she
wrote in the midst of feminism's
second wave, in the wake of the
civil rights movement, and amid
student protests against the
Vietnam War as a reflection upon
her own process of self-discovery
and personal emancipation. The

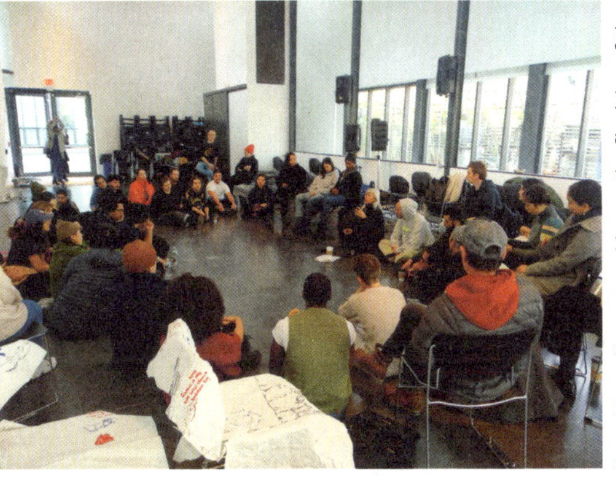

poem focuses on the experience of isolation as well as community. Al Qasimi,
a Teaching Assistant appointed in fall of 2016 for the first semester of the newly
conceived course, noted:

> It was exciting to be part of re-imagining of such an important class, especially
> having experienced it in its previous iterations, which felt a bit siloed-off with
> regard to subjects that were intersectional. For me, it was exciting to see
> how a class could be a living, breathing thing that could shift with the needs
> of the students and follow the trajectory of the world. I'll never forget the day
> when Walid Raad came to visit. It was the morning after the 2016 election
> and … there was this mood in the room, as if everyone wanted to be there
> because we needed to be together in a community. Raad ended up—instead
> of giving a traditional artist's talk—giving a talk about the civil war in Lebanon.
> And it became this real "here and now" moment—as in, let's stop, let's take
> stock, let's process. I think it was important for there to be room for that in the
> School, where it felt like there had not been room previously.[222]

Over the following years, Critical Practice was confounded by debates regarding
its legitimacy within an art school. The course was characterized by its detractors
as a foil, at best, or as an outright hindrance to a concept of "practice" construed
as material production. Yet, as the matters of critical practice and critique
have increasingly become flashpoints in a school where women increasingly
serve in both formal and informal leadership roles, the gradual and deliberate
transformation in the demography of the student body *has* transformed the
pedagogical perspectives of the School in kind. After all, as
a student, Elle Pérez, now a teacher, found a receptive audience
in Roni Horn, who had once, decades earlier, been supported
as an applicant by Winifred Lutz. Inevitably, status quo is reshaped
over time as generations of previously excluded students and
educators enter the institution, form ties, and together grapple
with complex experiences of marginalization. Along with the
increase in enrollment of students who identify as female or
gender-nonbinary, racial diversity among U.S. students has also
increased in recent years, as well as international enrollment.[223]

Kenturah Davis (MFA 2018) entered the Department of Painting and Printmaking hoping to "squeeze in as much as possible." Anticipating the opportunity
to study at Yale, she felt that "it was less about Yale as the place where artists
might get 'discovered' and more like, 'This is the place where I can get into
the nitty-gritty of any given topic that I want to think about.' It was about using
two years to experiment and to expand my practice." While at Yale, Davis took
a class called *Language and Power* taught by Jason Stanley in the Philosophy
department and an Anthropology course on the invention of writing. She recalls

222   Farah Al Qasimi,
telephone conversation
with the author, March
31, 2021.

223   "Yale University
Race/Ethnicity, Gender and
International Student Enrollment
by School 2014–15 to 2020–21,"
Office of Institutional Research,
Yale University, November 2020,
February 15, 2021, oir.yale.
edu/sites/default/files/w010_
enroll_race_gender_2021.
pdf. Race/ethnicity categories
are established by the federal
government.

        A FORTHCOMING HISTORY OF INCLUSIVITY

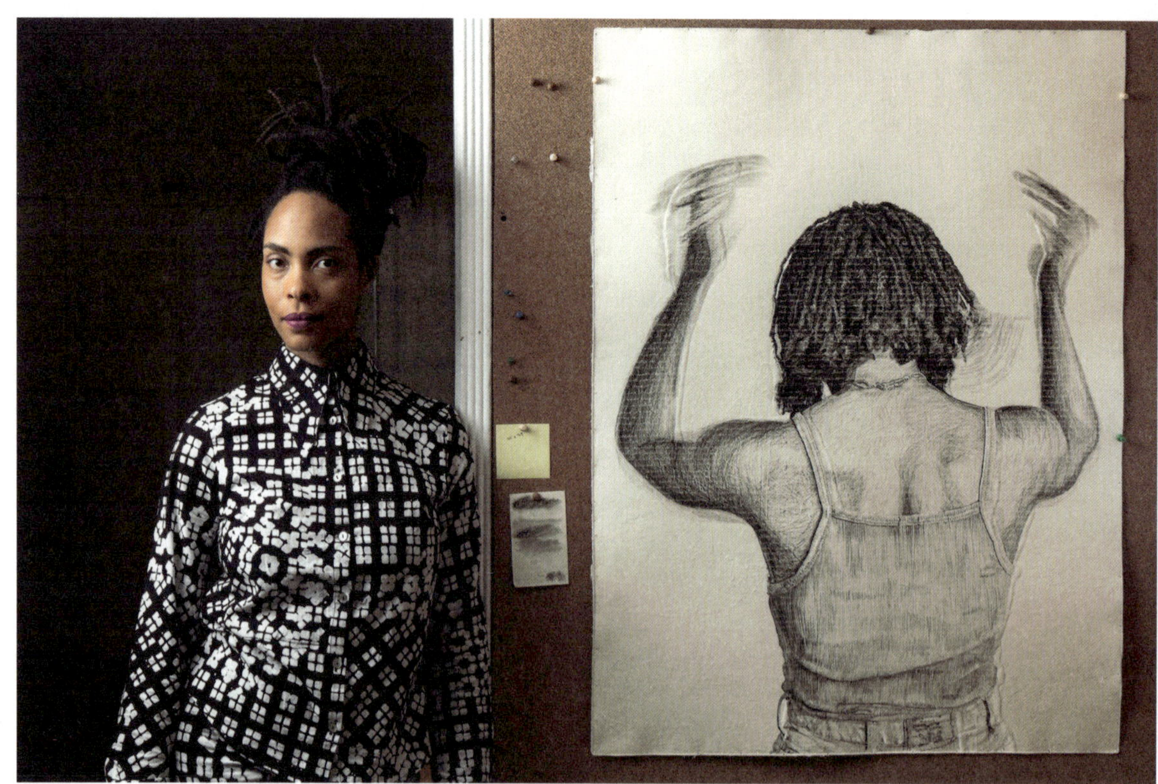

Kenturah Davis at her studio in Los Angeles, California, 2020. Photo by Marc Campos.

224 Kenturah Davis, telephone conversation with the author, February 1, 2020.

225 bell hooks, *Theory as Liberatory Practice, Yale Journal of Law & Feminism* 4, nos. 1/2 (1991), 5. https://digitalcommons.law.yale.edu/yjlf/vol4/iss1/2.

226 Ibid., 6.

that, "It took me a while to figure out what kind of studio visits were most productive for me, which was not so much about the work I had in the studio, more about asking questions around what I wanted to think about in making that work—seeking out or figuring out where my interest might overlap with whoever it was I was talking to, and how to generate a conversation that was cerebrally interesting for me, perhaps not by focusing on explaining what was being looked at." Davis remembers "a couple instances when comments were made by male faculty—something about a combination of me being a woman making figurative work. It seemed to just roll off the tongue, and to be a way to try to embarrass me. It just opened the door for people to say some really messed up shit." According to Davis, she found it "difficult as a Black woman to have conversations about making figurative work that become cornered in patronizing analysis around body types, especially with some of the male faculty. But such challenges led me to focus more on perception and the flaws in how we draw conclusions about our visual experience."[224]

In a 1991 essay, "Theory as Liberatory Practice," published in the *Yale Journal of Law and Feminism*, bell hooks addresses the potentially healing, liberating effect of theoretical discourse and the potentially undermining impact of drawing false boundaries between theory and practice, writing "many women have responded to hegemonic feminist theory that does not speak clearly to us by this hegemonic trashing theory, and as a consequence, further promoting the false dichotomy between theory and practice. Hence, they collude with those whom they would oppose. By internalizing the false assumption that theory is not a social practice, they promote the formation within feminist circles of a potentially oppressive hierarchy where all concrete action is viewed as more important than any theory written or spoken."[225] In her essay, hooks maintains that the devaluation of intellectual work subverts the possibility of "oppositional political dialogue," and that working to understand "our contemporary predicament" is "the means by which we might collectively engage in resistance struggle" to "transform our current reality."[226] Angela Davis concurred with hooks' point of view in her aforementioned 2020 Critical Practice lecture (transcribed and published in this volume), rejecting the idea that art is polluted by political claims and questioning the philosophical segregation of the field of aesthetics from the field of epistemology. While Linda Nochlin's "Why Have There Been No Great Women Artists?" was rooted in the so-called woman question, her astute analysis of structural oppression applies equally to the "intersectional question," as one can easily imagine by reading the following

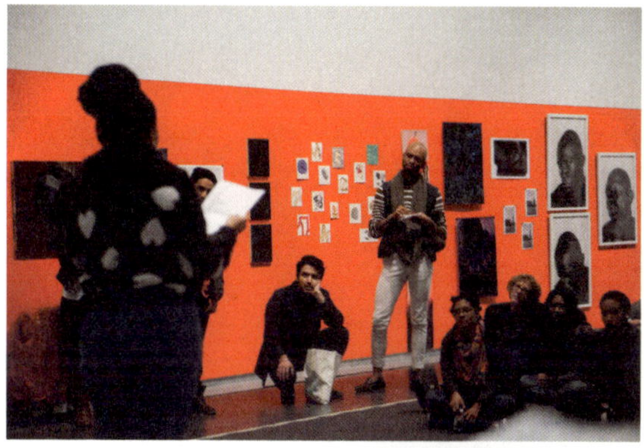

Black Joy, a community event celebrating and exploring joy and wellness within the Black Diaspora curated by Yale School of Art graduate students Shikeith, Kenturah Davis, Vaughn Spann, and Jonathan Payne, 2016. Photo by and courtesy Shikeith.

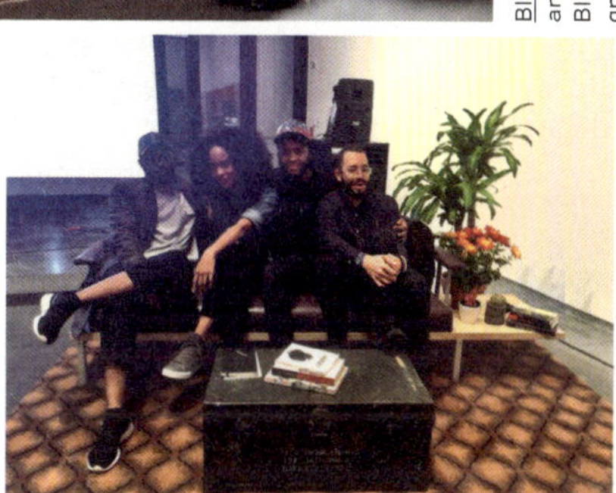

Curators of Black Joy, 2016. Courtesy Kenturah Davis.

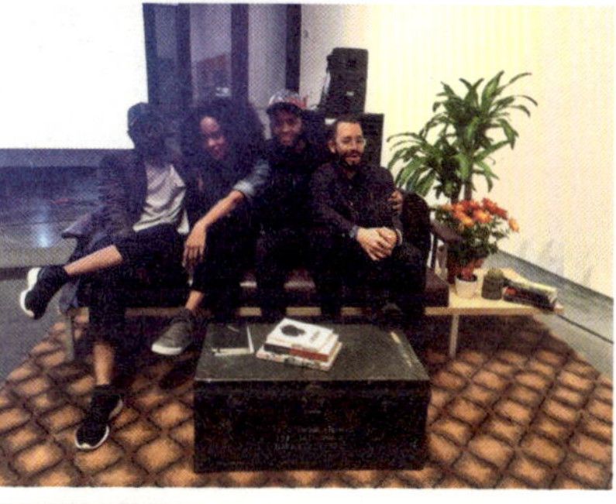

Tschabalala Self speaking with art critic and writer Antwaun Sargent at Black Joy, E.I.K., 2016. Courtesy Kenturah Davis.

BLACK JOY

SATURDAY, NOVEMBER 12TH

LACEY LENNON
GERALD SHEFFIELD
SULA BERMUDEZ-SILVERMAN
MICHELLE KEMEI
ANNA WANE
VAUGHN SPANN
SHIKEITH
KENTURAH DAVIS
JOHNATHAN PAYNE
MICHAEL DEMPS

SARAH HEARDE
JEREMY O. HARRIS
SAKINA ABDUSSHAKUR
COREY STAGGERS
JULIANNA SIMS
ASHIA AJANI
JOSH WILDER
YONAS TAKELE
WILL WHEELER
AND MORE!

E.I.K., 32 EDGEWOOD AVE.

LIBERATION LOUNGE
SPIRITUAL WELLNESS AND MEDITATION WITH PAUL DANIELS, II.
12PM–1:30PM

LISTENING SESSION WITH KENTURAH DAVIS
1:30PM–3PM

THE TURN-UP
A CELEBRATION OF ARTS AND CULTURE
6PM–9PM

#BLACKJOYATYALE

SPONSORED BY THE AFRO-AMERICAN CULTURAL CENTER AT YALE

Black Joy, curated by Yale MFA students Kenturah Davis, Vaughn Spann, Johnathan Payne, and Shikeith, took place on November 12, 2016, at 32 Edgewood Gallery, which had been "recontextualized as a conceptual satellite space called Expropriated Investigatory Kabinett. E.I.K.," following the November 8, 2016 U.S. Presidential election, to serve as "a platform for Yale School of Art students to produce programming that is free and inclusive to all publics and respectful of human rights," according to the description posted on the event calendar of the Afro-American Cultural Center at Yale, which was a co-sponsor. The poster was found burned on a kiosk outside of Sterling Memorial Library on Thursday, November 10. (Jingyi Cui and Britton O'Daly, "Poster for Black Joy event burned," Yale Daily News, November 14, 2016.)

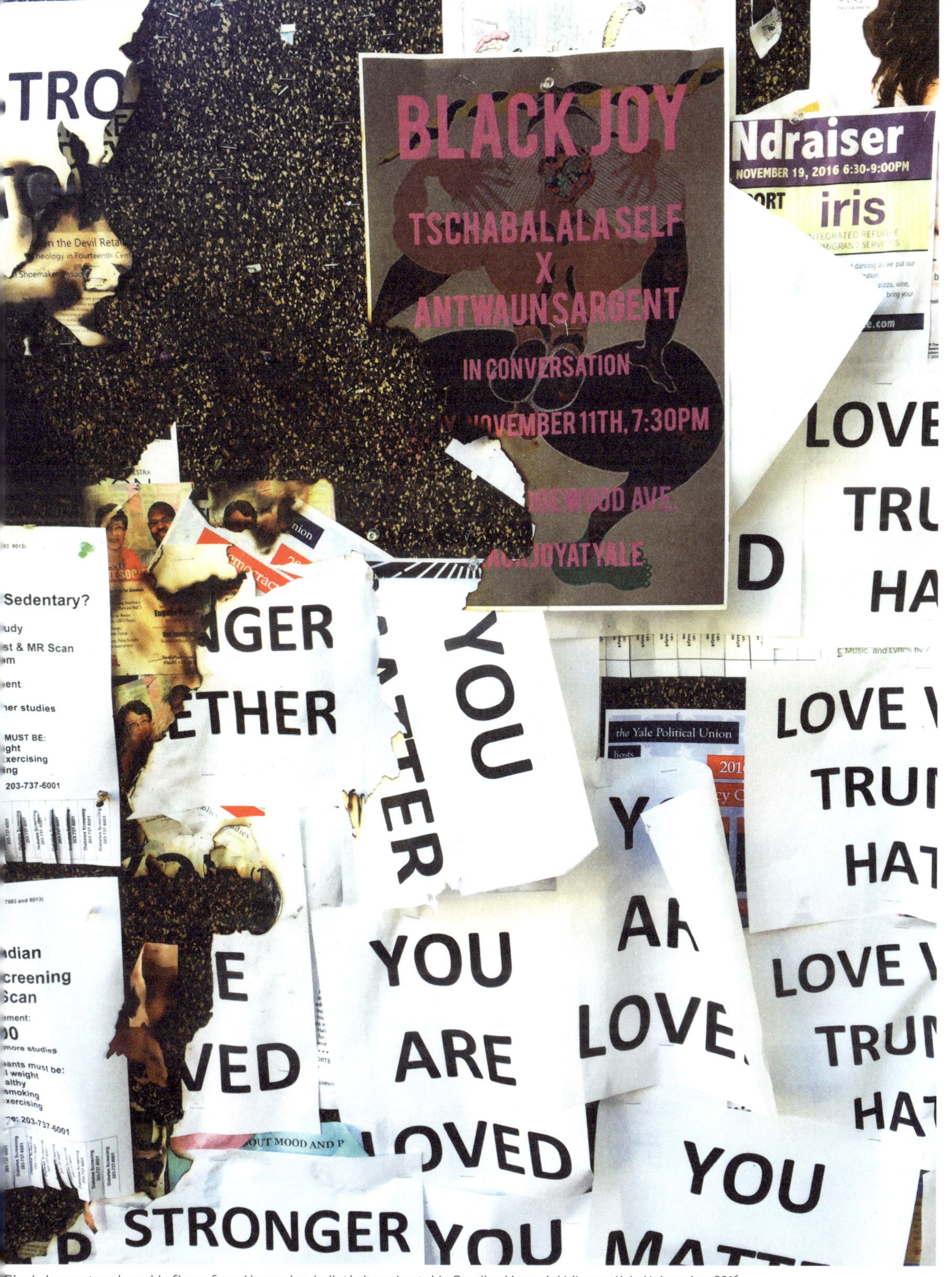

Black Joy poster alongside flyers found burned on bulletin board outside Sterling Memorial Library, Yale University, 2016. Photo by and courtesy Shikeith.

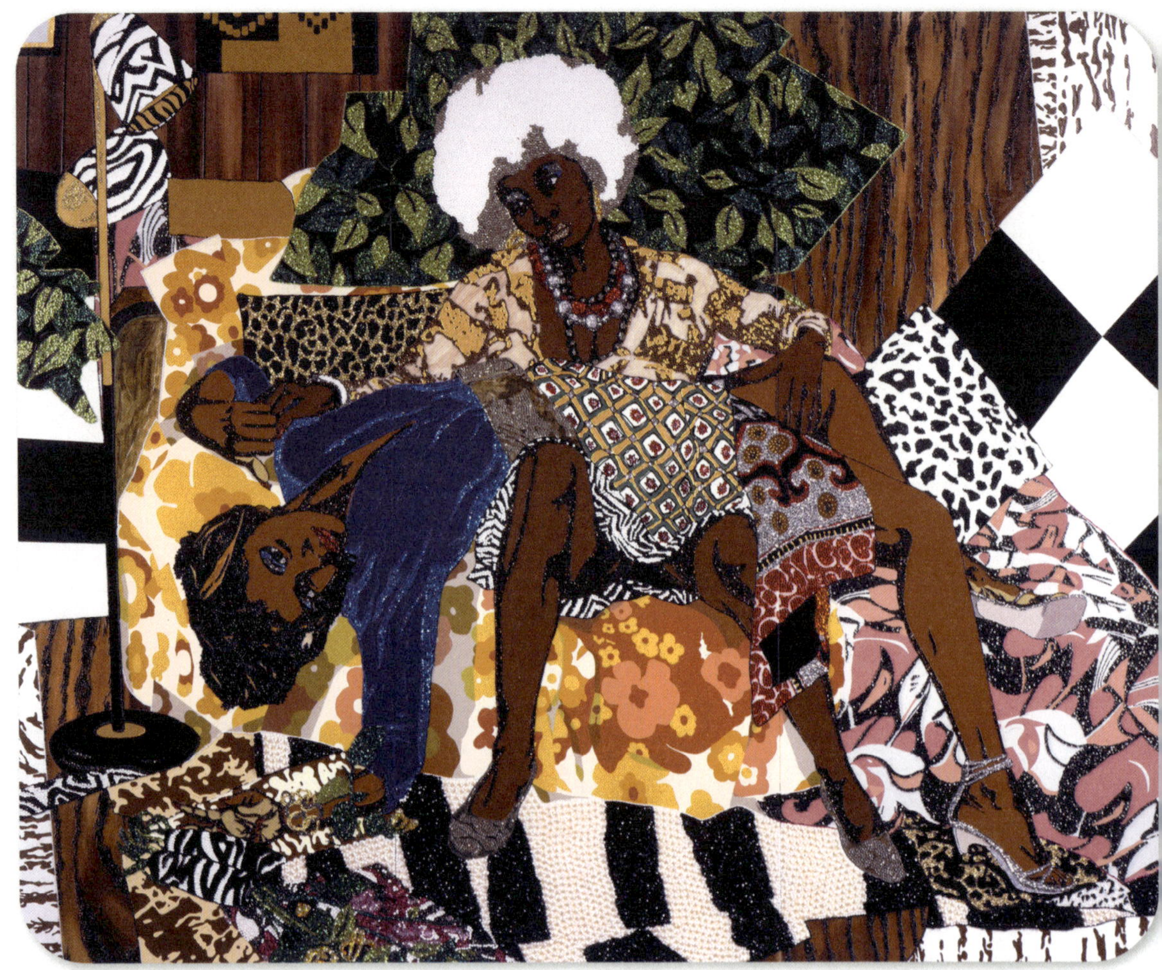

Mickalene Thomas, <u>La leçon d'amour</u>, 2008. © Mickalene Thomas.

excerpt while substituting for "women artists" many other designations from a spectrum of marginalized racial, ethnic, gender, or ability-based categories:

> Even a simple question like "Why have there been no great women artists?" can, if answered adequately, create a sort of chain reaction, expanding not merely to encompass the accepted assumptions of the single field, but outward to embrace history and the social sciences, or even psychology and literature, and thereby, from the outset, to challenge the assumption that the traditional divisions of intellectual inquiry are still adequate to deal with the meaningful questions of our time, rather than the merely convenient or self-generated ones.[227]

Nochlin's insight may be stated simply, "A story reflects those who tell it."

As the first woman Dean in the School's long history, it has been my responsibility to raise the question and my aim to help bring to light, as a form of contingent response, the experiences of the many former students and faculty who contributed their time and their testimony to this book. It is my hope and expectation that the story begun here will be continuously reformulated in the years to come, until the day arrives when the question Nochlin posed is no longer sensible because the premise is no longer appreciable.[228]

[227] Nochlin 1971.

[228] Upon the printing of this book and the conclusion of the author's tenure as Dean (2016–21), Dr. Kymberly Pinder was appointed in June 2021 as the first Black woman Dean in the history of the School of Art and the first Black woman to become a tenured Professor in the School of Art.

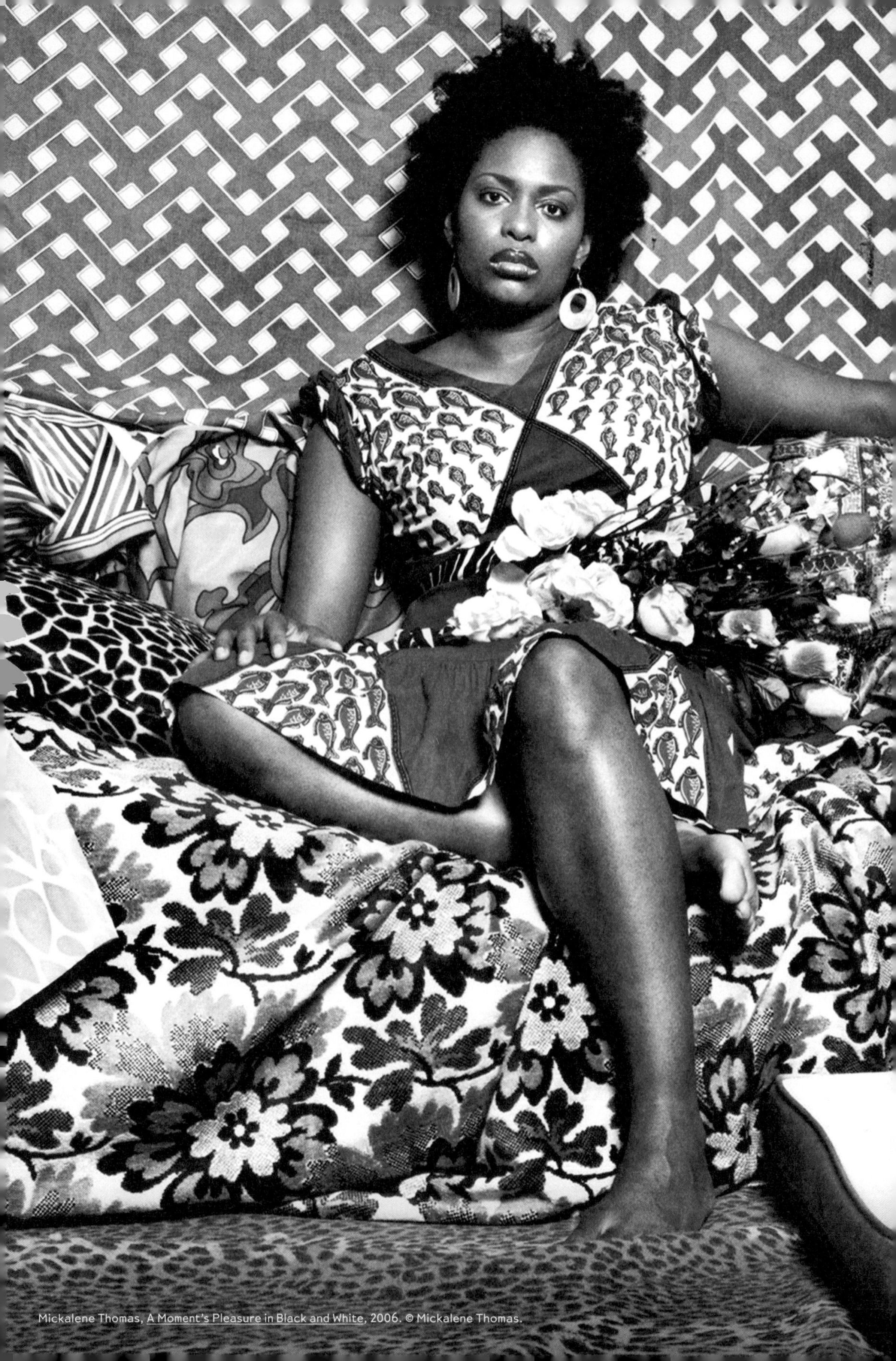

Mickalene Thomas, *A Moment's Pleasure in Black and White*, 2006. © Mickalene Thomas.

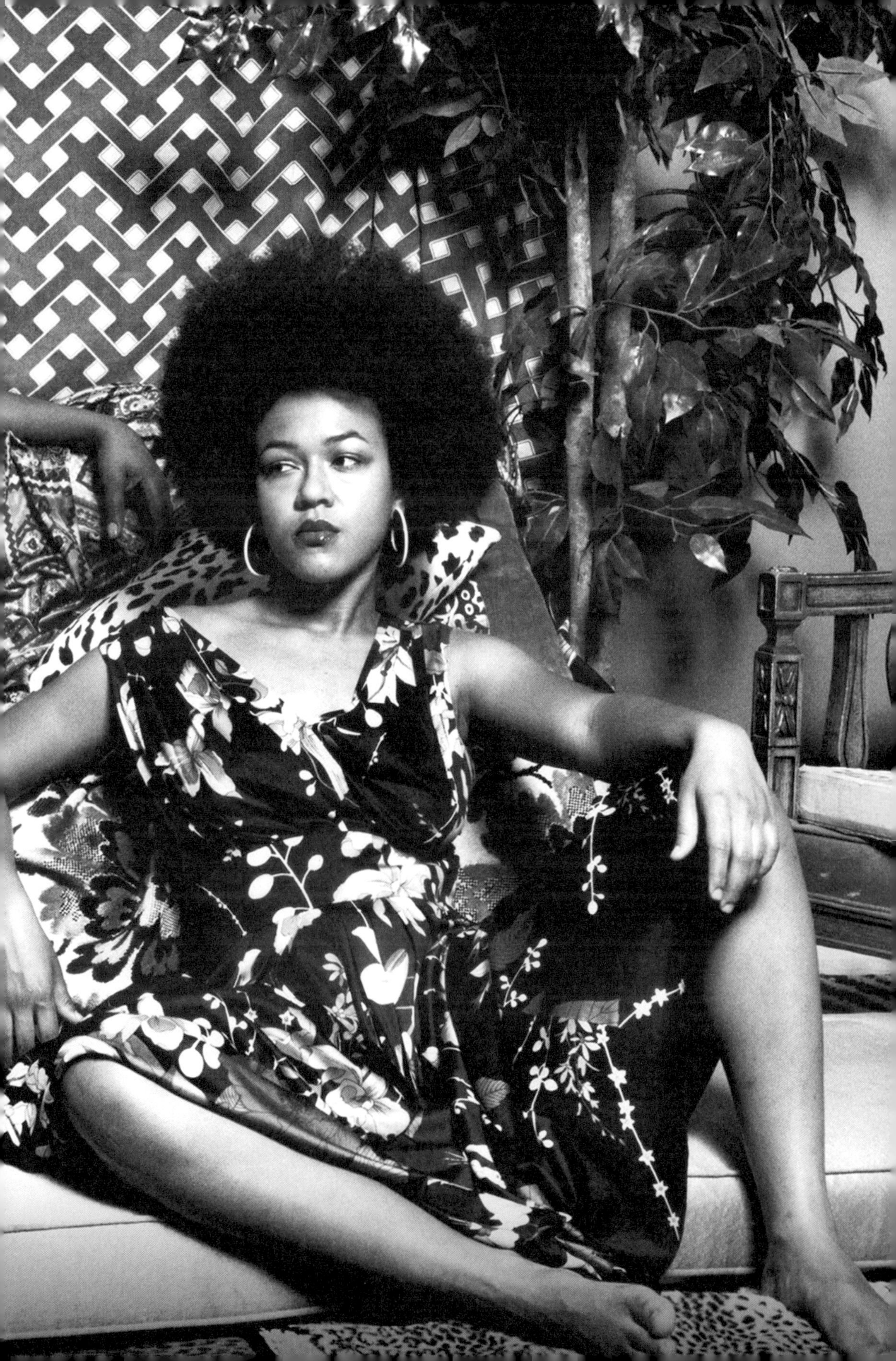

[see p. 17]

THE FINE ARTS.

The Exhibition at Yale College.

Correspondence of the New-York Times.

NEW HAVEN, Friday, July 19, 1867.

Among the many pleasant features of the Commencement season at Yale College this year, none is of more general interest than the first annual exhibition in the new school of Fine Arts, which may be regarded as the inauguration of an institution that, for fifty years or more, has been a necessity in this country. The fact that no such institution has existed before, is something we have reason to be ashamed of. Such of our young men as were ambitious of artistic success, or anxious to acquire a knowledge, theoretical as well as practical, of the more scientific branches of high art, have been compelled to seek even the rudiments of such an education in Europe. A few attempts have been made in this country, it is true, to found an institution supplying this great need, but they either failed entirely or came short of accomplishing results in the least degree adequate to the existing necessity. Most of them have been private enterprises, imperfectly planned and badly conducted, while such as have been under the control of corporations, have been ruined by the infusion of an amateur spirit into both means employed and results accomplished. We have never had a school of high art where young men could receive an artistic training that would fit them for the actual work of their profession, and we congratulate the authorities of Yale College on having so far succeeded in their efforts to add this new department to their already extensive university. It is to be hoped that the time is not far distant when the original plan of its founder may be carried out to the fullest extent.

The Yale School of the Fine Arts was founded in 1864 by the late AUGUSTUS R. STREET, Esq., of New-Haven. This gentleman generously offered to furnish the Corporation with funds sufficient for the erection of a suitable building for the proposed school, so that the long-needed department might be added to the College. Operations were at once commenced, and the edifice was nearly completed in the Summer of 1866. The building is not yet quite finished, according to the original plan, as the main tower and five smaller turrets are still to be raised and finished

CHURCH. "The Inheritance," by LOUIS LANG, is much admired by young ladies and old people, who are more sentimental than critical. The conception is very pleasing and the painting good, but its merits as a picture would have been improved if the artist had more carefully regarded the eternal fitness of things as regards the drawing. A very large baby, with a very small mother, is lying in a very short cradle, playing with a very long sword. We do not wish to be hypercritical in judging this work, for it undoubtedly affords many who see it much pleasure—of a sad kind, it is true; but why the various objects should be so disproportionate to each other is something to be wondered at. The chief merits of Mr. LANG's picture is its strength of coloring, all the light and flashy tints so popular now-a-days being wisely omitted. If Mr. LANG would paint this picture over again, and give more care to the drawing, he would make it much better, if not really good. There are also in this gallery about twenty-five characteristic pictures by artists of what is commonly considered the modern pre-Raphaelite school, FARRER and MOORE. As it is pretty hard to define what the principles of this school really are—for no two men agree perfectly on the subject—we adopt the popular idea as applying to these realistic painters, who sacrifice effect to accuracy, and prefer elaboration of detail to the sketchy and suggestive style now so generally popular. Of this school, which is generally considered pre-Raphaelite, as it is an elaboration of details for the sake of the subject rather than for the sake of finish, FARRER and MOORE are creditable representatives. Their pictures, in most instances, fail, and do not accomplish the results their painters desire, it is true, for they "o'erstep the modesty of nature" in each and every instance, and fail to imitate because too truthful. Many of Mr. FARRER's little pictures were shown at the Academy last season, and are quite well known. Some of his studies of wild flowers and grasses, that have no background, as everything is crowded to the front, are exceedingly good and natural, but his landscapes, without exception, are far from pleasing, if not positively bad.

We fully appreciate the amount of care and hard work necessary to the production of one of those so-called pre-Raphaelite studies of nature, but they seem to fall short of high art and to fail in giving that real satisfaction that we derive from a good picture. The attention is detracted from the effect of the whole by the lesser details that are of little or no real consequence; as a mole or a spot of black court-plaster on the face of a beauty distracts from the effect of her expression by fixing the attention on the one blemish. This illustration is not very elegant, but it seems to express the idea. To those who are but slightly acquainted with art, FARRER's and MOORE's pictures seem wholly bad, and it is only by experienced amateurs or critics that such merits or beauties as they may possess are discussed and appreciated—which seems a sufficient proof of itself that they fail in their attempts to imitate nature accurately.

In the corridor are many good and more bad water-color sketches and pen drawings, principally by FARRER, MOORE, Miss McDONALD, R. NEWMAN and Miss NIMS. Miss ELIZABETH MURRAY, of Boston, has contributed four or five of her magnificent water-color drawings, which have all been exhibited in the National Academy in this City. Beside these and a few small marbles, there is little of interest in the corridor. In the centre of the large gallery is LOMBARDI's statue of Ruth, which is generally admired. The other marbles are small and rather uninteresting. The exhibition opened on the evening of Thursday, the 11th inst., with a dress reception, which was repeated last Thursday evening. Since the 11th it has been open day and evening for visitors and students, and has been well patronized. The collection is not superior to the Annual Academy Exhibitions, but among the pictures are representations of almost all the modern schools of art.

The object of this school of the fine arts that has opened under such favorable auspices, is to cultivate, not only a critical taste for art on the part of all the students, but to supply the want that has so long existed in this country. The annual exhibitions are intended to facilitate this object, by bringing together good pictures by good painters of each style and school of art. The legacy and donations of Mr. STREET having been expended on the building, there now remains no money to found a professorship and consecrate a school for practical instruction in painting and the principles of high art. For the present

was made by Mr. F. D. WHITE, of this city, who was also the architect of the National Academy of Design in Twenty-third-street, and the building was erected by a well-known firm in New-Haven. The material used is a light brown sand-tone from New-Jersey, and the porch over the main entrance is supported on columns of white and variegated marble. Its exterior is highly ornamented, and it will greatly add to the wants of the college grounds. Its interior arrangements are very similar to the National Academy, and it will compare favorably with that building in point of convenience and beauty. The woodwork is principally oiled black walnut, and the floors are inlaid with white and dark stripes. The sky-lights and gas-burners are skillfully placed, and the arrangements are in every way perfect and complete.

The school, as it is called—although not yet devoted to the practical instruction of the students—is under the management of a council composed of President WOLSEY, Profs. SALISBURY and PORTER, HUNTINGTON, of the National Academy, and D. G. MITCHELL, of literary fame. It was decided by these gentlemen that the most suitable way of inaugurating the new school was by an exhibition of paintings and statuary; and all, or nearly all, of our best artists were invited to contribute such works as were at their disposal. The invitation was liberally responded to, not only by artists, but by the owners of valuable paintings. Several of our New-York picture dealers, including SCHAUS, and GOUPIL & Co., also loaned choice works of art, which is particularly generous, considering the length of time they would be on exhibition. The collection presents very few novel features to a New-Yorker, as a large portion of the paintings have been transferred from the National Academy, where they remained through the late exhibition; but in itself considered, it is very fair.

The chief feature of the Yale exhibition is a portion of the Trumbull Gallery, which is owned by the College. Many of his largest and best pictures are placed in the new school building, including "The Woman Accused of Adultery," "Lamberg and Gelchossa," "Knighting of De Wilton," "Christ Blessing Little Children," the life-size portrait of WASHINGTON, and many smaller battle pieces and portraits. This collection, some thirty in all, occupies a portion of the main gallery, at the other end of which hangs WASHINGTON ALLSTON's "Jeremiah;" that, like the most of Col. TRUMBULL's pictures, are more valuable as historical relics than as works of art. "Jeremiah" is also owned by the College, and if not very ornamental, will be useful in the art school. The two main galleries are will filled with good pictures. Prominent among the names on the catalogue are those of Huntington, Wust, Gray, Bierstadt, Church, Eastman Johnson, Beard, Kensett, Whittridge, S. Coleman, McEntee, Edwin White, James M. Hart, Weir, Lang, and M. F. L. DeHaas; and among the foreign artists represented are Achenbach, Verbeckhoven, Meyer, Von Bremen, Hiddeman, Bosch, and Van Scheudel. A large landscape, by GUSTAVE DORE, is also expected, but has not yet arrived. The collection is constantly receiving additions from various sources, and new pictures are arriving every day. The hanging committee have performed their work with much better taste and judgment than was displayed at the National Academy, and the artists represented have much more reason to feel satisfied with the disposition made of their pictures than on that occasion.

It is hardly necessary for us to notice the pictures in detail, particularly as few of them are new to our readers. In the north gallery the pictures chiefly worthy of special mention are, "The Meadow Brook," by SHATTUCK; "Mild River," by SONTAG; "Chucorua Peak," by HUNTINGTON; "Sunlight and Shadow," by BARNSTADT, (which is one of the best pictures ever painted by an American artist, and accomplishes the almost impossible effect of actual light;) "The Watzman on the Konigsee," by LEU; "The Iceberg," by GEORGE CURTIS; "The Brook," by JAMES M. HART; "Sunrise on the Sea-shore," by L. R. GIFFORD; "Approaching Storm," by ACHENBACH; "Genevieve," by HARRY PETERS GRAY; "The Claim Agent," by EASTMAN JOHNSON; "Before the Prison Door," by GALLIAT; two or three little studies of animals, by BEARD; "Moses Preparing for the Fair," by RITCHIE; "On the Androscoggin," by FAIRMAN; and "Morning in the Tropics," by F. E.

diplomas and degrees are honored everywhere. We commend it to the attention of all liberal and wealthy patrons of art, as an object worthy of their benevolent donations, and trust that within a few years at furthest, we shall have a school of high art that will rival the best of European academies.

The exhibition at Yale College will continue until the end of September, and will be an attractive feature of New-Haven during the Summer months. Should it prove a success, it will be repeated annually; and it is hoped that they will be largely beneficial in diffusing a knowledge of, and a critical taste for art. We hope that every aim of the council may be more than realized, and that it will soon become a school of the fine arts in reality, as well as in name.
OSCURO.

A & A Protesters Hold Mock Burial

By Tom Warren

Art and Architecture students employed "guerrila theatre" tactics on the Yale campus yesterday to further dramatize their demand that the University institute financial equity for all graduate students.

Protesting students of the Art and Architecture School voted shortly after midnight this morning to hold a public auction of the paintings in the Yale Art Gallery in order to raise money in their behalf.

The students said they planned to enter the building peaceably around 11 this morning, and would not touch the paintings. They said they would stay past the closing time of 5 if necessary.

The students want the University to provide more scholarship and budgetary aid to the Art and Architecture School.

Protesting students began with an elaborately staged mock funeral in Beinecke Plaza at noon, then marched to the Yale Art Gallery and gained admission to the sculpture court behind Weir Hall.

In the evening a smaller group, numbering about 30 students, entered the Law School dining room and attempted to eat without paying.

Financial Situation

Finally, the A & A students demonstrated at the opening night performance of the Yale Repertory Theatre's

Yesterday's demonstrations followed one at Woodbridge Hall and the Art Gallery Wednesday. [see p. 23]

"We hope to embarrass Brewster and the administration with acts of guerrila theatre," said architecture student Henry Stone. "Begging at the opening of 'Greatshot,' for example, was an attempt to point up the poverty of the arts at Yale."

In a letter released Wednesday responding to the student demands, President Kingman Brewster Jr. acknowledged the financial problems of the A & A, Drama, and Music Schools, but stated the demands for equity by next year could not be met.

Yesterday's demonstrations were light-hearted in tone particularly the mock funeral staged in Beinecke Plaza. The procession began when the students loaded a coffin labeled "the Unknown A & A building."

With a motorcycle escort, the hearse proceeded to Beinecke Plaza followed by a train of wailing mourners. The students then unloaded the coffin and, with great solemnity, lowered it down gently into the Beinecke sculpture court.

'Beautiful Performance'

A eulogy by architecture student Tom Carey completed the ceremony. "The whole thing was a beautiful performance, done with great style," said History of Art professor Vincent

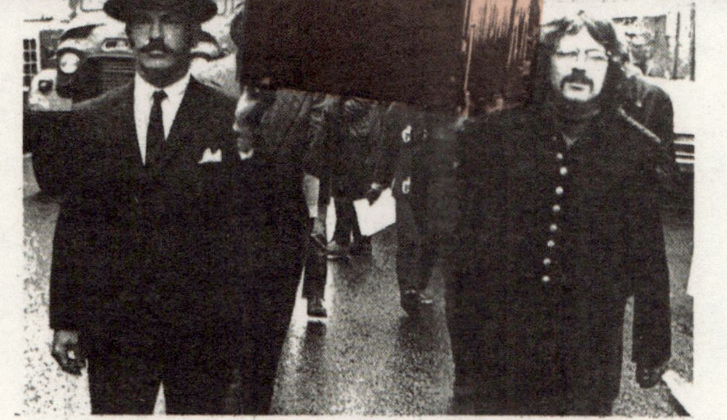

Art and Architecture students carry coffin containing "The Unknown A & A Student" on their way to mock funeral in Beinecke Plaza. The funeral was one of several demonstrations yesterday protesting "financial inequity" in the A & A School.

Tom Warren, "A&A Protesters Hold Mock Burial," *Yale Daily News*, May 9, 1969. © Yale Daily News Publishing Company, Inc. All rights reserved. Reprinted with permission.

A & A Faculty Agrees To Suspend Academics

By Tom Warren

The faculty of the Yale Art and Architecture School agreed yesterday to suspend academic course work for the rest of the semester to allow students and faculty "to discuss the programs and objectives of the School."

The faculty decision was made in a closed three-hour meeting attended by President Kingman Brewster Jr. and Provost Charles Taylor.

The faculty essentially affirmed a resolution adopted Wednesday by an open meeting of the A & A School at which several faculty members were present.

That resolution called for the suspension of courses in the interests of discussion ane evaluation of the present organization of the Art and Architecture School.

The faculty voted yesterday "to encourage the scheduling of general meetings of faculty and students during the next two weeks to discuss the programs and objectives of the School."

The decision, which was read to the assembled A & A students by Dean Howard Weaver, added, "Regular academic work begun in this term can be completed at a later date according to arrangments between each student and his individual instructors."

The original proposal to suspend course work for a discussion of the problems in the A & A School was advanced by students following Monday's meeting with President Brewster concerning their demands for increased financial aid.

(Following that meeting Brewster wrote a letter to students in the Art and Architecture Drama, and Music Schools informing them of his intention to raise scholarships in the three schools to the subsistence level.)

"Our financial complaints led us to vent our dissatisfaction with other aspects of the school," said architecture student Tom Carey. "At the open meeting Wednesday we decided to suspend the normal exam routine and try to get at what is wrong with the educational structure here."

The students interpreted Brewster's presence at yesterday's faculty meeting as an attempt to have the faculty repudiate the resolution of Wednesday's open meeting.

Charles Brewer, professor of architecture, said the president

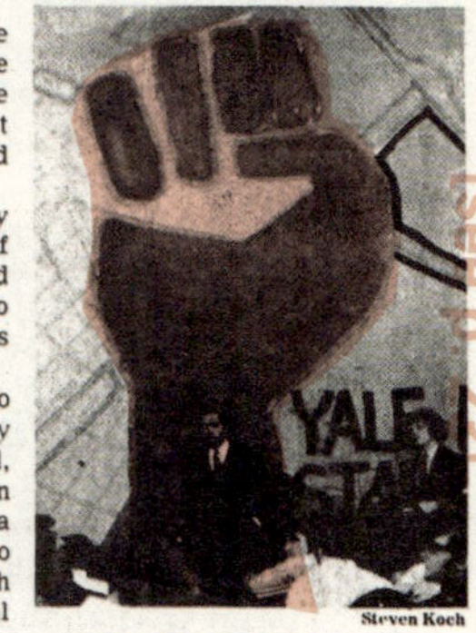

KINGMAN BREWSTER JR.
Promises "Subsistence"

had questioned any faculty move toward a "moratorium" on course work. "He warned against intimidation by the students," said Brewer. "I told him his presence at the meeting was in a sense an attempt to intimidate."

Brewster stated his purpose at the meeting was simply "to warn the faculty members against abdicating their academic responsibilities. I had the impression that the faculty of the Art and Architecture School was considering excusing students from the remainder of its academic requirements," he said.

"Before they did this in any precipitate manner, I wanted to remind them of two functions which cannot be delegated to students — the establishment of requirements for the granting of a degree and the appointment of faculty."

When the faculty finally adjourned their statement was read to the waiting students and Dean Howard S. Weaver.

Tom Warren, "A&A Faculty Agrees to Suspend Academics," *Yale Daily News*, May 8, 1969. © Yale Daily News Publishing Company, Inc. All rights reserved. Reprinted with permission.

War Protest Planned For Graduation Day

[see p. 23]

Between forty and fifty Yale College seniors met last Thursday night at Calhoun to plan an anti-war protest for Commencement Weekend. The meeting broke up after two hours of debate without reaching agreement on concerted action. But over the weekend several seniors met privately and agreed to work together on a common proposal.

The Thursday meeting was called by a group of Calhoun seniors to formulate a "unified class action" to express seniors' opposition to the war in Vietnam and the draft.

But by the meeting's end, several seniors had decided to individually sponsor four separate actions:

● Collection of signatures on a class petition asking that Commencement be dedicated to expressing opposition to the war and suggesting the Rev. William Sloan Coffin Jr. as special Commencement Day speaker.

● Establishment of Legal Defense Fund for seniors who refuse induction. Seniors would donate the $5 cap and gown returnable deposit to finance the fund.

● Circulation of "We Won't Go" statement for seniors who will refuse induction if drafted.

● Drafting of a moderate protest

Thompson said if 70-80 percent of the class sign the petition, then early this week the sponsors will ask the administration to approve some form of Commencement Day protest.

Thompson said the sponsors hope to get approval for several alternative forms of protest. He said he would suggest a prominent anti-war Senator be invited as Commencement speaker.

Those alternatives approved by the Administration would be voted upon by an open meeting of the Senior Class Council.

Publicity Wanted

The Thursday night meeting opened with general agreement that any protest should attempt to capture nation-wide attention. But conflict soon arose over which tactic would have the greatest impact.

One faction backed a moderate statement of opposition to the war that could attract support from the entire class.

A second group attacked this as "meaningless," claiming student unrest with the war and draft is already well known. This group felt a statement of refusal to accept induction and fight in Vietnam, even if signed by a minority of the class, would have a much greater impact on the nation and the government.

Michael Medved, William Thompson, and Gil Fuchs said they plan to circulate in the residential colleges a petition that seniors be allowed to express anti-war sentiments during Commencement. The petition did not suggest what form the protest would take. circulate a moderate anti-war statement. Paul Moore, 1969, agreed to collect signatures of seniors prepared to resist induction. Medved planned to circulate a class petition dedicating Commencement to anti-war protest and calling for Coffin to speak.

A & A Students Camp Out To Protest Financial Status

By Tom Warren

A dozen Art and Architecture students began camping out in the A & A building last night following a day of demonstrations in support of their demands for financial equity with the other graduate schools.

The decision for the "live-in" followed an unsuccessful attempt by a group of 40 students to enter the Yale Art Gallery.

The campus police kept the demonstrators locked out of the Gallery. They retired from the scene after about 15 minutes. But Gallery Director John Kirby decided not to risk reopening the gallery for the remainder of the day.

The Demonstrations at noon began when around 100 placard-bearing Art and Architecture students marched to Woodbridge Hall to receive President Kingman Brewster's answering letter to a number of their demands presented in a petition last week.

Brewster's letter acknowledged the financial plight of students in Music, Art and Architecture, and Drama, but it offered no hope that their demands for financial equity would be met for next year.

"The only honest answer," the letter said, "to the 'demands' for tuition abatement or greatly increased student aid for next year is that neither is possible."

After this reply was read to the demonstrators by architecture student Henry Stone, a smaller group of them marched to the Art Gallery, where they were refused entrance by a squad of campus police.

The protestors pounded on the locked doors of the main entrance for several minutes, shouting "Art is for the People and "More Money Now."

Before dispersing, they fastened the doors closed from the outside with bicycle locks and adorned the entrance with posters and palm prints of purple paint.

Kirby closed the Gallery on the advice of the campus police, who feared the demonstrators might return later in the afternoon.

The protesting students had meanwhile returned to the Art and Architecture Building, where they decided upon the tactic of a "live-in" to dramatize their situation.

"We don't exactly know how long we are going to stay," said architecture student Tom Carey. "Our attempt is merely to hold on to the momentum which has developed on this issue."

We want to emphasize that this is not an occupation," said Henry Stone. "We are simply trying to dramatize the seriousness of our situation."

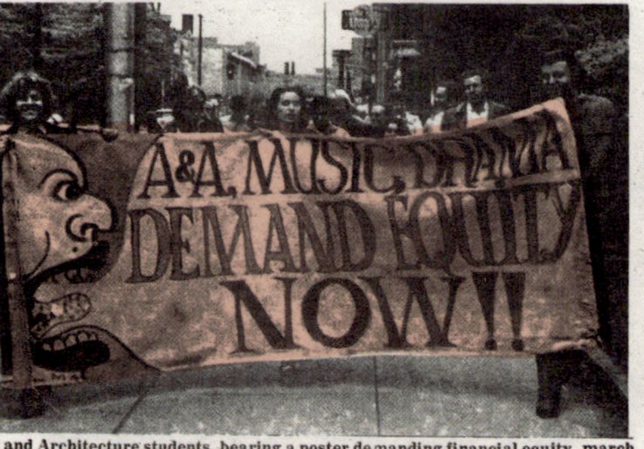

Art and Architecture students, bearing a poster demanding financial equity, march to demonstration in Beinecke Plaza.

As an example of the financial difficulty faced by many Art and Architecture students, Stone cited figures showing the 24 first-year students in the graduate school of painting were already in debt a total of $62,290.

The list showed individual debts averaged $2,400, and for several families the financial hardship had included going on welfare and having to feed their children with government food stamps.

"They're spending millions of dollars to build the Mellon Center, but they don't have enough to keep the art students from starving," Stone said, "The University seems more interested in storing paintings than in supporting artists."

Brewster's reply was delivered to the demonstrators outside Woodbridge Hall after several of their number were denied entrance to the building by campus policemen.

While rejecting outright the possibility that financial equity could be instituted for next year, it mentioned some avenues for future alleviation of the problem.

(continued on page 3)

* A&A Demonstration

(continued from page 1)

In particular, Brewster mentioned the efforts made this spring to interest foundations in putting up money for the arts. He added that if this showed promise, he would be willing to ask the provost advance funds against the prospect of foundation support.

He added that the relative financial disadvantage of the Art and Architecture, Drama, and Music Schools is "they are not as well supported by either government or by private restricted gifts and endowment."

He promised a more complete explanation of the University position in the near future.

Stone agreed most of the financial inequity between the graduate school of Arts and Sciences and the Art and Architecture School is a result of government and private funding over which the University has no control.

"That does not mean," he said, "they can simply sit back and let us try to get along on a pittance. We're asking them to confront the government for money if it is necessary."

In addition to the live-in, the protestors plan further demonstrations to keep the issue alive.

[see p. 23]

After Fire, Yale Smolders

By JOSEPH LELYVELD
Special to The New York Times

NEW HAVEN, June 25—A stately marble statue of the goddess Minerva presides over the charred rubble on the two floors of Yale's School of Art and Architecture that were swept by a fire just before dawn on June 14.

The statue, the only object of any consequence on the two floors that survived intact, is now doubly appropriate. Minerva was a goddess who both protected the arts and went to battle.

For more than a month before the blaze broke out, the School of Art and Architecture had been embattled by a complex of academic issues with strong political and racial overtones.

The sharpest of several simultaneous controversies concerned a decision taken jointly by the faculty and students of the department of city planning to reserve 10 places in an incoming class of 20 next fall for black and Spanish-speaking students.

The aroused university community still finds it hard to separate the fire from the unrest that preceded it, partly because of a provocative broadsheet that received wide circulation the week before the fire.

Arson Suspected

"Why has Yale not gone up in smoke?" it asked.

"See the A and A [Art and Architecture] building," the broadsheet advised. "See every building. See them soon."

Those words and the controversies that had swirled around the building were fresh in many minds the morning after the fire—including that of Fire Chief

C. A. Richardson

A statue of Minerva stands above the charred rubble of

[see p. 31]

Continued From Page 39

swiftly by relieving the chairman of the school's department of city planning, Christopher Tunnard, and its assistant dean, Louis S. DeLuca, of their administrative responsibilities.

He also wrote an unusual letter to the eight students first admitted to the department advising them not to come to Yale because the department might "not continue in its present form."

The administration never questioned the academic qualifications of the black candidates nor did it react directly to the proposal to divide the class on racial lines. However, virtually all the black students and some whites are convinced the racial question was a basic issue.

"Yale is an institution dedicated to perpetuating the status quo," says Donald Van Purnell, one of 10 students who have joined together in the Black Workshop, which has a storefront office near the School of Art and Architecture. Their aim is to weld their professional skills to their social commitment by working in black neighborhoods.

Sincerity Questioned

Recently, workshop members sent to the administration a memorandum that said: "Yale University is the university" are at stake,

"You sound as if you think Yale is immoral," a teacher in the department observed. "Relatively speaking, I think it should be," the Provost replied.

"Charlie," said the teacher, "you and I worship at different temples."

stood to have turned up no physical or other evidence of arson. He says he will have no comment until his investigation is finished, in about two weeks.

Five Yale students were responsible for the broadsheet. None was enrolled in the

ture; all are known to the authorities.

One member of the group declared that their intentions were the opposite of inciting violence.

He said they had meant merely to call attention to the deterioration of communications among students, faculty members and administrators on a campus that so far has escaped violent unrest. The fire, said the student—who insisted that his name be withheld—was "an extremely unfortunate coincidence."

The suspicion of arson still lingers like the stench of smoke in the building (itself a provocative and controversial structure, designed by the architect Paul Rudolph).

In the long run, the suspicion could do more damage to the school than the fire did to the building, unofficially estimated at more than $500,000.

Even before the blaze, fumes of suspicion filled the school.

The faculty and students of the city planning department, who were trying to run the department as an experiment in participatory democracy, denied they were

dividing the class on racial lines. Their decision, they said, reflected their sense of the urgent need for black professionals to work in slum neighborhoods.

Before the decision was taken, eight students—seven whites and one black—had already been admitted. The remaining 12, therefore, would have had to be nine blacks and three whites.

Administration Bridles

The administration bridled at the whole procedure on the ground that students could only advise the faculty on admissions, not share its responsibility for them. It maintained also that the department's limited budget would not allow it to underwrite the scholarships the 10 black students would need.

A clash came when the students and faculty members went ahead and sent out letters of admission to the 12 without the approval of Dean Howard S. Weaver or the signature of the faculty member who normally signed admissions letters.

Kingman Brewster Jr., Yale's president, responded

Continued on Page 74, Column 7

Yale's pioneering Afro-American Studies program and support given to the Black Workshop itself as evidence of their sincerity.

Next year, they note, the number of black students in the School of Art and Architecture will double from 11 to at least 22, if six of the nine black candidates to whom the "unauthorized" admission letters were sent accept the status of special students outside the degree program.

Charles H. Taylor, Jr., Yale's Provost, says the controversy over the city planning department involved "a challenge to the university's integrity."

Challenge Is Seen

The city planning faculty retorts that the administration's actions were a challenge to their department's academic integrity, a position that has been supported in a resolution by the faculty of the architecture department and in a petition circulated by Professor George A. Schrader, chairman of the philosophy department, which has been signed by 130 faculty members from all parts of the university.

The School of Art and Architecture has also been aroused over the low level of financial aid students there receive, compared with students in other graduate schools. A more general demand for "restructuring" of the school to make it more relevant to the social concerns of the students has given rise to a continuing series of discussions between students and faculty.

Mr. Taylor, who thinks "two different concepts of

YALE WILL DIVIDE DISPUTED SCHOOL

Art and Architecture to Be Separately Run Divisions

Special to The New York Times

NEW HAVEN, Sept. 20 — A major reorganization of Yale University's School of Art and Architecture, apparently in response to last spring's disorders, was announced this week by Yale's president, Kingman Brewster Jr.

The reorganization will split the school into two divisions—design and planning and the arts—each headed by a dean directly responsible to the university's provost and president.

Students See Victory

Howard S. Weaver, formerly dean of the entire school, will be dean of the arts faculties. Charles W. Moore, former chairman of the school's architecture department, has been named dean of the design and planning faculties.

Some students in the school, which was the scene of a prolonged internal administrative struggle, a month-long student strike and a fire that swept three floors of its building, see these changes as a reaction to the student activism and a measure to provide greater administration control in the future.

These students point to the portion of Mr. Brewster's announcement that said it was hoped the changes would assure "the lines of authority between those who preside over faculties in the arts and design professions and the central administration are more direct and less ambiguous."

Brewster Explains Action

A spokesman for Mr. Brewster denied the student contentions yesterday, but he conceded that the change was "a reaction in the sense that the administration is responding to the problems brought to our attention in the spring."

"It is our hope to put the school in a position where it can develop best," he said. "The division is designed for the benefit of all the disciplines."

Also involved in the reshuffling is Prof. Christopher Tunnard, who was dismissed as chairman of Yale's City Planning Department last spring because of his role in the sending of unauthorized letters of acceptance to 12 candidates for admission. Professor Tunnard will serve as director of studies in planning, centering on curriculum.

Mr. Brewster, in his statement, called the changes "interim arrangements" designed to provide "an opportunity for a balanced and objective, fundamental reappraisal of what Yale should be doing, and how it should do it, in the arts, design and planning."

The blaze that reduced three floors of the Art and Architecture Building to rubble in June was the climax of months of simmering discontent. The fire was called "of suspicious origin" by New Haven Fire Chief Francis Sweeney at the time. After a six-week investigation, however, it was ruled to be of "undetermined cause."

Among the issues that had festered throughout the spring were those of the school's relevance to the surrounding society and, after the dismissal of Professor Tunnard and his assistant, Louis S. DeLuca, the integrity of the university and its components.

Students struck the school in May, demanding a greater voice in curriculum planning and a higher level of financial aid.

[see p. 31]

Leary Praises Youth, Hits Old Moral Values

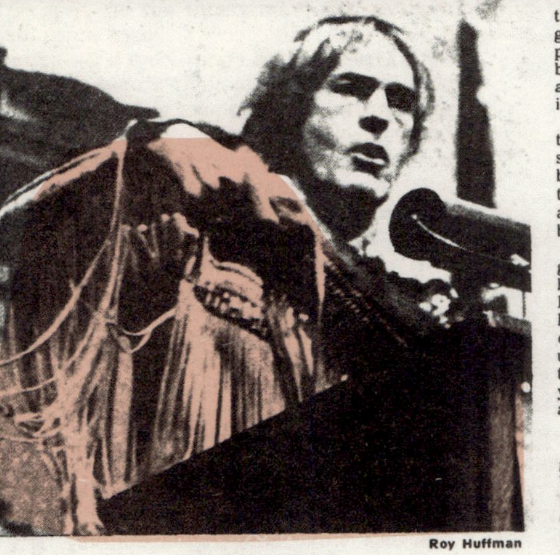

TIMOTHY LEARY

Praises Younger Generation

Dr. Timothy Leary spoke about the ramifications of the generation gap on religion, politics, dope, and sex last night before a packed Political Union audience in the Law School Auditorium.

"People who were born after the year of 1940 are a different species from those who were born before that," Leary stated. "I think you have to realize there are deep philosophic differences between the generations."

Leary said much of the younger generation has adopted the hedonistic hypothesis of "live and let live." He commented, "You have got to let people have their own style-no conformity, no uniformity…if you don't accept the 'live and let live' principle, you are going to have that law-and-order anthill."

Woodstock Dream

Leary said the peaceful gathering of 400,000 people at Woodstock was "a dream come true" and that young people all over the United States came together in several places during the summer. The ability of the younger generation to "share their hope and their dope" despite the Vietnamese War was praised by Leary.

Leary also lauded the communication between the people at Woodstock and their resourcefulness in solving problems despite the adverse weather conditions. Comparing the government's inability to deal with local problems, Leary commented, "The power of decision and the problems of day-to-day must be given back to the people."

Christian Faith

In contrast to the older generation's Christian philosophy that "life is a bad trip," Leary said, "The basic assumption of Woodstock was that we're all brothers and sisters and here to have a good time."

Leary referred to Judeo-Christianity as "a paranoia set-up that doesn't make sense any more." He said the political implications of the younger generation's desire to have a good time are "great" because "I believe deep down the Russians want to feel good too."

Leary said the older generation has their own dope in the forms of alcohol, barbituates and tranquilizers. The present

(continued on page 6)

Leary Sees Gap In Values Between Old, Young People

[see p. 23]

(continued from page 1)

leaders of the United States, Leary said, have been deeply influenced by prohibition which served to alcoholize a generation.

Leary said the older generation uses its dope to "take away some of the pain…from their dull, mechanical way of life."

Leary pointed out that millions in the United States are addicted to alcohol and barbituates and most of the auto accidents in the United States are caused by alcohol.

Leary said alcohol has a self-enhancing effect which has brought out the "my bar-right or wrong" attitude in the older generation, Leary added, "The alcohol mentality has really influenced the older generation."

Natural Life

Leary spends eight months each year living "close to nature" with his wife on a tall mountain in California where "I stay high and love God." Leary spends the other four months of the year lecturing at college campuses.

Leary, whose address was frequently interrupted by applause, began experimenting with hallucinatory drugs as a Harvard professor in 1961 and is currently appealing a 30-year jail sentence with a $40,000 fine for illegally transporting marijuana.

[see p. 75]

VOICE ARTS *Joyce Baronio on 42nd Street*

Tripping the Light Fantastic

By Edmund White

A sex performer named Cathy has just finished her stint on stage and come up to the photography studio for a break. She relaxes with her friend J.J., drinks half a beer, and lets J.J. fuss with her makeup. Then, in the infernally, bright summer afternoon light sweeping over the Hudson and through the open windows, she poses against the white wall. As they work they chat above the hoot and hiss of 42nd Street traffic. They talk about today's A.P. (audience participatioin), the moment at the end of a show when three or four male spectators come up on stage to be verbally humiliated, spanked, and forced to kiss Cathy's stiletto heels. Cathy's been in town just two years and she still retains traces of her Dallas accent. Something about her curly brown hair and innocent face leads J.J. to think Cathy might look nice as a bondage bride. Cathy loves the idea. She dons a wreath of white plastic flowers crowning a long veil that flows gauzily over her studded dog-collar, black bra, and garter belt. J.J. snaps a few pictures. At this moment fantasy, like pulled taffy, flows back and forth between the two women. The energy subsides and Cathy repeats a joke her male partner told her just before their last set. The women laugh—it's more like a pajama party than anything else.

"J.J." is the nickname Joyce Baronio attuned to the life of the imagination."

After studying anthropology and art history at the University of New Mexico, she got a job in Chicago casting models for a commercial photography studio. "Comparing people's real faces with their composites," she says, "helped me to gain an eye for how three dimensions translate into two." She also worked as a model herself, for which her looks are suited— heavy bolt of silken hair, snowstorm smile, Tartar eyes. But she married and became a faculty wife at Kenyon Colege. "While I was there I finished my degree and graduated Phi Beta, but I had a sense of how life could come to a . . . halt."

Her husband, Richard Baronio, designs exhibits. In 1974, when he went to Yale to help complete the interior of Louis Kahn's British art center, Joyce applied to the university's graduate program in photography. At that point she had been taking pictures for only six months. The two-year program, then headed by Walker Evans, accepted just four new students each fall. She was delighted to be chosen, still more so at spending every afternoon with Evans, looking over pictures, cataloguing negatives, sipping wine and chatting. From him she learned the art (perhaps the religion) of working only with natural light. Like Evans, Baronio can spend a whole day waiting for the exact nuance of sunlight. In her early work she also imitated the documentary approach that Evans had used in the pictures of Alabama tenant farmers and sharecroppers he made in the 1930s for the Farm Security Administration. And just as Evans had over the years photographed people's bedrooms, Baronio shot a bedroom in New England—except in her case Evans's literalism gave way to fantasy. She chose the bedroom of a dead woman, a shrine complete with dolls in the chair, a painting of the madonna above the pillow, and the wedding photo on the wall.

Continued on page 37

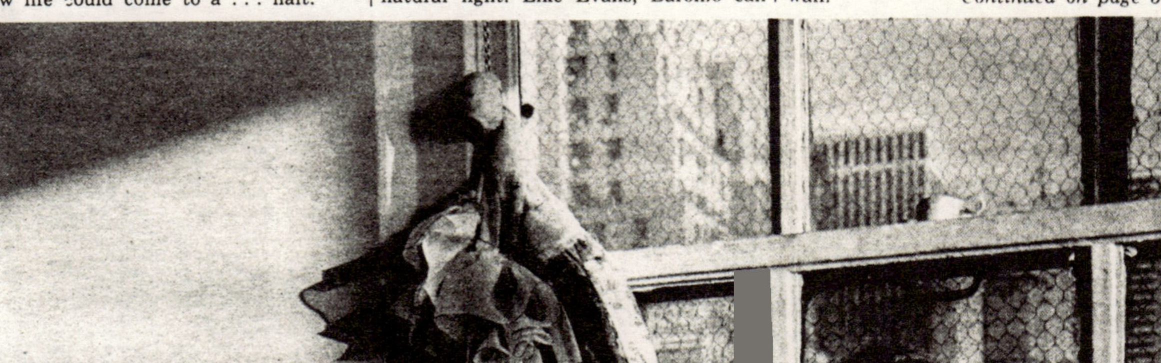

...years in a city studio, five feet by 12—or rather a reflector box, since its floor, ceiling, and walls are all painted white and the room is quite empty, designed to boost the already intense light. In this box she is slowly creating a series of images as mysterious and exalting as any we have.

Placing these photographs requires some exactness, for they come close to several familiar categories without falling into any of them. Though almost all of her recent pictures portray sex performers and strippers, none of them is pornographic. Though each model seems to be releasing a fantasy as if it were a pheromone, the work is in no sense surrealistic. And though the models might be considered exotic, the pictures resolutely avoid sensationalism. They are noble, often tender, and always admiring studies of healthy bodies and entranced faces.

Joyce Baronio is as unlikely at Show World as a pearl chaplet on punk green hair. She was brought up an only child across the street from the Presbyterian church in East Williston, a Wasp enclave on Long Island that pretends it's in Iowa. As a youngster she was given to dressing up as someone else, whether that someone was Princess Summer-Fall-Winter-Spring from *Howdy Doody* or the older sister of a girlfriend. By late adolescence she was inventing every detail about one imaginary person after another—and assuming each identity in turn. Baronio has a gift for what she calls "identity exchange." She once wrote, "From earliest memory I recall an almost overwhelming need to transcend my own existence. This took the outward form of dressing up and creating environments which would allow me, if only for an instant, to become one with another person. These other people were chosen purely intuitively; why one person and not dozens of others would inspire me to 'be' him or her is unclear." As she told me, "I can't take someone's picture unless I can identify with him or her—someone

Edmund White, "Tripping the Light Fantastic: Joyce Baronio on 42nd Street," *Village Voice*, August 6, 1979. Courtesy the *Village Voice* and Edmund White.

claimed. "I've seen them being hauled out in garbage cans."

True acceptance came when Show World flanked its entrance with blow-ups of two of Baronio's best photographs. They are not the familiar titillating fare. In one picture, a black woman in a maid's uniform with a white plume in her hair is pressing her cheek to the shoulder of a blond, bare-assed woman in the black cape and lingerie of a dominatrix. In the other, a pony-tailed woman in profile is gaily flipping up her skirt toward the city beyond the window.

The entertainers come to the studio still in costume, right after their shows, their glory still on them. Since sex shows are seldom directed, the performers must improvise dialogue and situations—and they are usually chosen because they already exude an air of drama. Baronio has to work fast, for a break lasts just half an hour. She is opposed, however, to snapping haphazardly. "I like the story about Brassai," she told me, "who was invited along with other younger photographers to shoot a celebrity during a very brief session. While the others clicked furiously away, Brassai had a glass of wine, chatted with the great man, fooled with the leg of his tripod, and snapped one perfect picture."

Technically, Baronio contradicts all precepts. When other photographers see her studio, they start to suggest ways of diffusing the light lest it bleach out half the face and cast the other half into illegible shadow. But Baronio waits for the brightest afternoon light and then, incredibly, *overexposes* the film at a shutter speed of a fourth of a second, the normal setting for twilight. In the developing process, she soaks the film longer than she develops it, both before and after. The soaking cuts down on the brightness. In the developing pan the blacks appear first; as soon as the whites come in she stops the process.

"The sunlight is wonderful," she says. "It stuns the performers the first time they

[see p. 75]

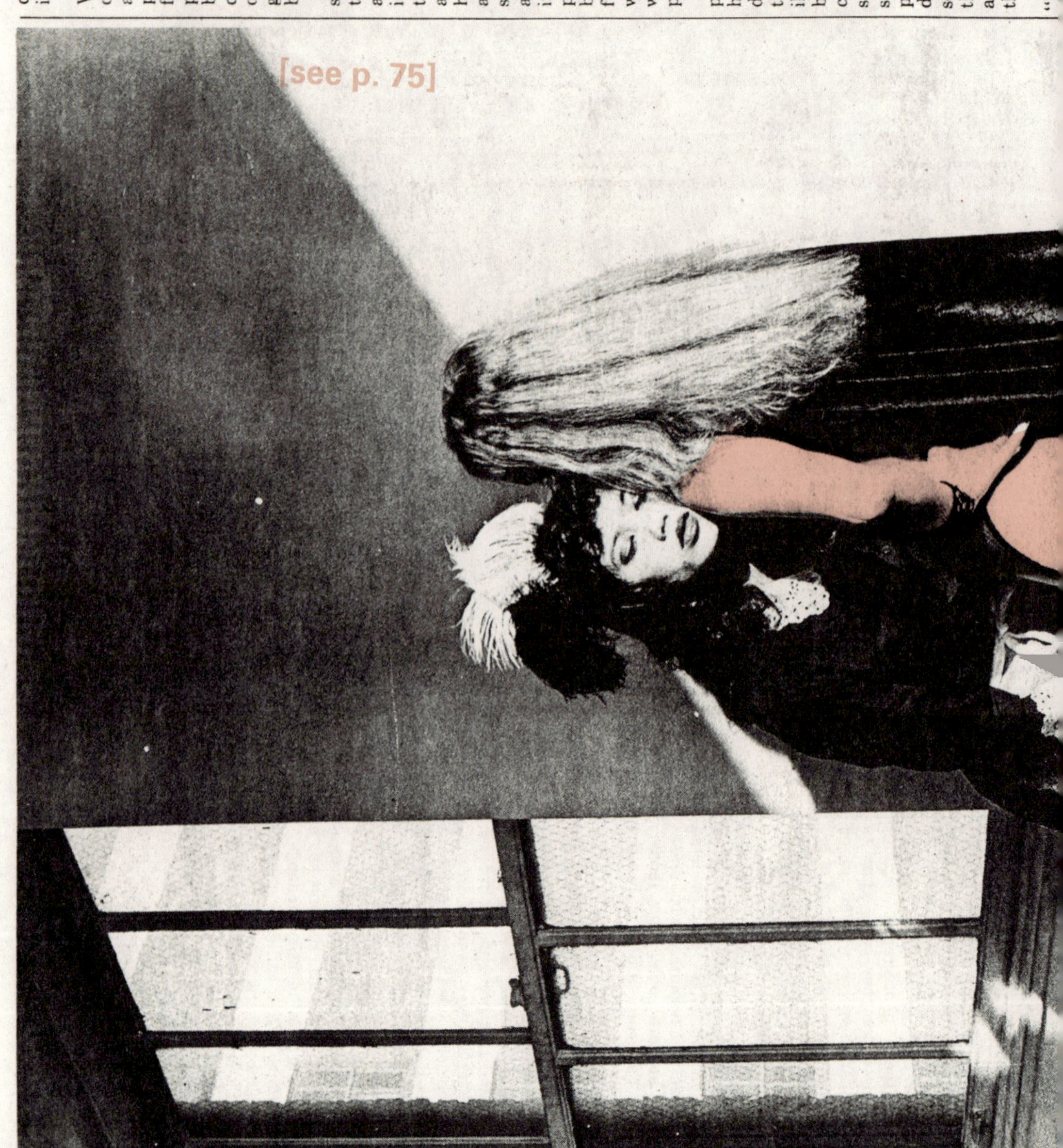

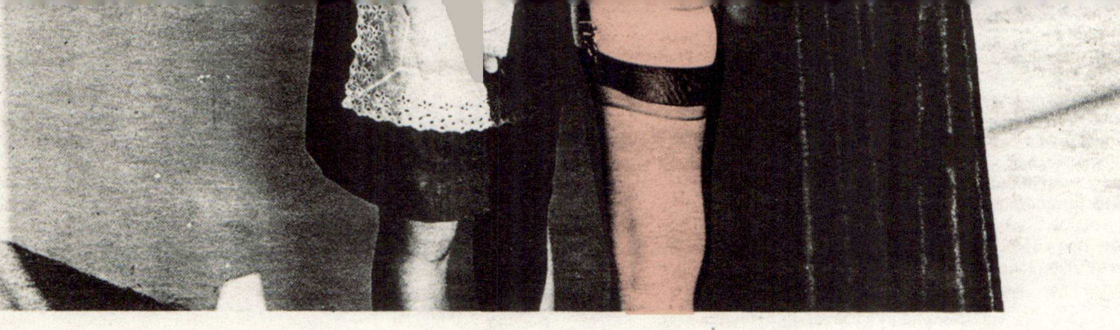

Continued from page 35

"I was spending all my time photographing people acting out fantasies at fashion shows or doll shows, square dances, parades, tractor pulls," Baronio says. "But in America fantasy occurs only on *weekends!* I was crazy about beauty contests, though I'd shoot only the preparations back stage, not the show itself. But I was always lugging around all this equipment and being forced to use the available light, usually artificial." Baronio speaks in the voice lady librarians adopt in telling stories to children, but she's less elocutionary, more likely to explode with a sudden word ("weekends!") or to trail off into mumbled ellipsis. Perhaps a listener is privy only to fragments of her constant inner reveries. Her thoughts often veer off from people to odd things. She will, for instance, begin to describe how her Chelsea loft was converted from a factory into living space, but she will become distracted by a description of the abandoned machines. Or she will be talking about how proper the men in the audiences at Show World appear to be until they step out of their J. Press trousers to be spanked on stage, but she will get lost in talking about the embossed initials on their attache cases. Or she will withdraw altogether into the delights of a catalogue from the Gordon Novelty Company—twirling pasties, animal hands, a poo-poo cushion, a rubber tongue ("Put this in your mouth and you can 'lick' the world").

Baronio's vision emerged when she began to photograph nude beauty contests, especially the 1976 Ms. All-Bare America contest in New York. An extraordinary picture of a young contestant standing in a dressing room foreshadows the later 42nd Street work. The woman, lips parted in fascinated pleasure, gazes through kohled Nefertiti eyes at her reflection in the mirror as she draws a scarf about her. The reflection is crisp, the real woman slightly out of focus. Many of the contestants in New York were performers in the sex entertainment industry.

These people were fantasists who lived their dreams all week long, and Baronio wanted to work with them—but in a different environment. As she has put it, "The faces and costumes of the contestants and my own experience with fantasy told me that they wanted—needed—if only for an instant to bypass the 'real' world for the world of the imagination. The photograph was my way to achieve this transformation, but it was impossible as long as the existing light fixed the contestants—and their fantasies—in the momentary specifics of their environment."

She rented her small studio in the crotch of the great L described by the sex industry, which runs across 42nd Street and up Eighth Avenue. By working as a staff photographer for *Pornocopia,* the trade paper of the sex entertainment business, she met strippers. Everyone was suspicious of her at first. She had no credentials they recognized. She looked and behaved like an ex-debutante. She did straight black-and-white portraits and didn't ask the models to spread their legs, bend over, or flip their nipples; in fact, she does not pose her models at all. Nor did she pay her subjects (and they don't pay her, though she gives them prints).

By just hanging out, Baronio has stilled fears and become a fixture on 42nd Street. She conducted me and a friend through Show World with the casualness of an old hand, waving at the skimpily clothed women in glass cubicles who talk dirty through a partition to men who keep pumping in quarters to hear the rest of the arousing rap. She chatted with the women at the ticket booth to the live sex show. She breezed through the corridors of shuffling men seeking congenial quarter movies. "All these *quarters,*" she explains—in the momentary specifics of their environ—angle and quality of the light shirts from month to month, the flow of time introduces another rhythm into the pictures.

Until recently Baronio worked just with individuals, most of them women. She speaks of these women with rapture. "She's a wonderful person," or "She's *so* beautiful," or "Her dress is real silk—*she's* real" are the comments she makes as she shows her prints. Not long ago Baronio began to photograph couples, who are themselves a fairly new feature at Show World. One picture is of a seated man and a kneeling woman on a leash, her head oscillating in a blur. When this picture was handed to a feminist on a radio talk show as a point of discussion (the subject of the show was pornography and romance), the woman stormed off the show in protest. I mentioned this response to Baronio, who seemed wounded. "They're wonderful people," she said, looking at her couple. "They're married in real life, they're musicians, but sex performing is a way of paying the bills." Perhaps that woman didn't like the mixing of power and sex. I understand that, though it's not exactly easy to uproot." Another glance at the photograph. "You should have seen this thing come up in the developer." Very solemn: "I'm in this picture."

Baronio has done nothing to push her work. Her integrity and patience remind me of some painters I know, Jasper Johns in particular. Like him, her output is small, her imagery restricted, her craftsmanship impeccable. Next year she will undoubtedly win an audience when she publishes her prints in a book to be called *Forty-Second Street Studio.* And she continues to win disciples at the New School, where she teaches.

I asked her what living for three years among sex entertainers has done to her head. "Sometimes I feel I'm on the edge. I'm so frightened or tired I want to stop, I'm numb—but that's when the work just begins to get good."

Deconstructionist revisits Yale

Derrida looks at nationalism and literature

By ROLAND SICARD

"American students are very open-minded and intellectually curious. More so than in France, they don't hesitate to participate, to express their opinion," said French philosopher Jacques Derrida, the father of the "Deconstruction" school of literary criticism. Derrida is in the middle of a four-week stay on campus, a visiting professor in Yale's Comparative Literature department.

"In reality, I'm not just invited by the Comp Lit department," Derrida said, pausing as he smoked his pipe. "At the beginning, it was a joint invitation from the French, the Philosophy, the English, and the Comp Lit departments. I found myself more deeply attached to Comp Lit because I felt especially close to Paul de Man [former chairman of the Comparative Literature department, who died in 1983] both on the personal and the academic levels."

For the last twenty years, Derrida has taught philosophy at the "Ecole normale superieure" and at present is at the "Ecole des hautes etudes en sciences sociales," both Parisian institutions of higher learning.

At Yale, Derrida has focused his teaching on the two-fold problem of the theory of translation and of comparative literature. Every year, he gives it a different twist.

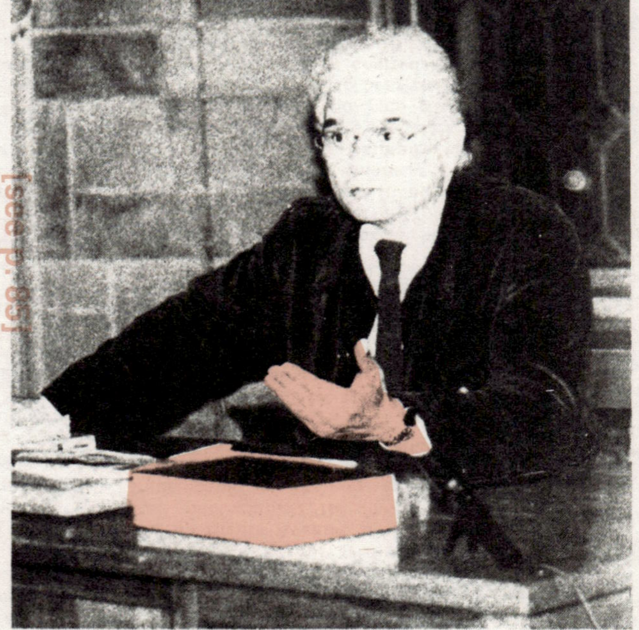

YDN-Tracy Burke

M. DECONSTRUCTION — Jacques Derrida, father of the deconstructionist school of literary criticism, is lecturing at Yale this month on the problem of nationalism in literature and philosophy.

This time, which is his 11th stay as a visiting professor to Yale, he is addressing the problem of nationalism in literature and philosophy. "The literary content is linked to an idiom," Derrida said. "I try to figure out when does a literary or philosophical work resist translation. Up to where is it translatable?"

This topic, which Derrida said he hopes will eventually lead to a publication, takes his work in a new direction. His previous works have dealt with linguistic and philosophical problems of reading. Among these works are *Writing and the Difference*, *Of Grammatology*, and *The Dissemination*, which have all been translated into English.

Although he can speak and discuss in English, "I must write in French," Derrida said. "This is the reason why my Monday lectures are in French. However, my students understand French well," he added.

Students "are interested in my work," Derrida said. "They make the effort to understand and to have a discussion."

Derrida said he does not find it hard to teach students who are not philosophy specialists. "I find the great interdisciplinarity here at Yale very appealing," he said. "The compartmentalization of subjects which I have come across at other places does not exist here," Derrida said, adding that "among others, Paul de Man's influences is to be credited for this situation."

The visiting professor system, which does not exist in France, is a good one because, "it adds a greater mobility to the academic institution," Derrida said.

"Considering what happens in France, I greatly appreciate the fact that one does not find here the petty Parisian quarrels which set the intellectuals apart," he said. "I am not saying that controversies don't exist here. Quite on the contrary, they exist and they can be very lively. But everything is out in the open. In Paris, it's mostly silence; intellectuals censor each other."

While in the United States, Derrida does not stay only at Yale. Currently he is an Andrew D. White Professor-At-Large at Cornell University, where he will be in September. This semester he will lecture on Heidegger at Johns Hopkins University and on Joyce at Brown University.

[see p. 85]

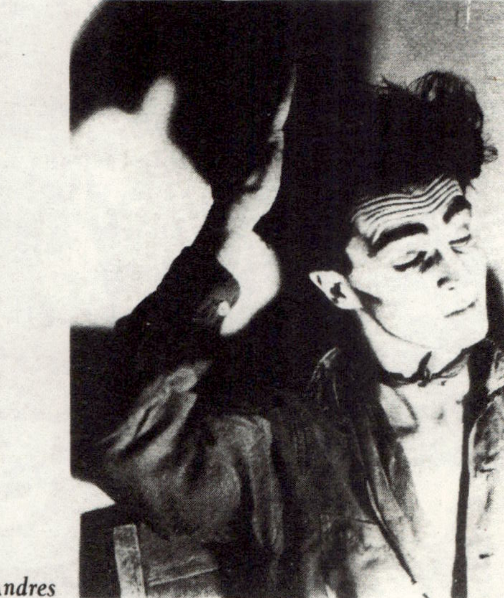

Jo Andres

[see p. 119]

John Kelly

Postmodernisms at Yale

by Richard Meyer

Art and illusion, illusion and art.
Are you really here or is it only art?
Am I really here or is it only art?
— Laurie Anderson

This weekend, for the first time in the Yale/New Haven area, perhaps for the first time anywhere, a postmodernism conference is convening. "Postmodernisms: Politics, Practices, Performance" will take place at the very postmodern Whitney Humanities Center today and tomorrow and the speakers will include artist Barbara Kruger, cultural critic Edward Said, performance artists Jo Andres and John Kelly, filmmaker Yvonne Rainer, and art critic Craig Owens.

According to Jennifer Wicke, Assistant Professor of Literature and the Coordinator of the Conference, the event is intended to address the problem of "defining the present moment." Wicke said that the speakers attending the conference represent "the most contemporary work in many fields."

Edward Said, for example, is a professor of comparative literature at Columbia known for his controversial Palestinian literary and political views. His book *Orientalism* has been termed post modern in that it attempts to break down the traditional notion of the East as other. Said will partake in a panel discussion entitled "Postmodern Politics" on Saturday morning.

Barbara Kruger attends the conference with a quite different post modern perspective. She is well known in the art world for her multi-media works, which appropriate images and then overlay words in the form of advertising print. Her past works have included a piece with an image of a statue of a woman in profile and the statement "Your Gaze Hits the Side of My Face" as well as an image of a woman with hair blown over her face and the overlay "We are your Favorite Embarrassments." Kruger will be part of a panel discussion on art practices this afternoon from 3-5 p.m.

The conference will also include two actual pieces of art, performances by Jo Andres and John Kelly. The performances, according to Wicke, break down the boundaries between dance, film, theatre, and art as well as between high and low culture. This traversing of tradition boundaries between disciplines is a central tenet of postmodernist art. The performances will take place tomorrow afternoon from 2-4 p.m.

Wicke said that the conference itself will be organized in post modern fashion. "It will not follow typical academic hierarchies by separating students and faculty or artists and nonartists." Wicke emphasized that the floor will be open to discussion at all times throughout the various events and that the conference is "as much a festival" as an intellectual undertaking.

Wicke said she hoped the conference would both "illuminate the condition of postmodern society and critique it." If, as the conference suggests, the contemporary moment is the postmodern age then what can possibly follow? Wicke responds by admitting that postmodernism is a paradoxical term in that it "cannibalizes itself. It is vacuous in a way, but it is also an inevitablity."

All Postmodern Conference events will be held at the Whitney Humanities Center, 53 Wall Street. For a complete listing of times and speakers, please consult the After Hours calendar, page 11.

Art under the specter of AIDS

Videos confront society's reaction to the disease

By RICHARD MEYER

Last Saturday, as part of the GAY/lesbian Arts Festival, an experimental film from 1981 called "Homosexual Desire in Minnesota" was screened. At one point during that film, a group of Minneapolis men protest the current raids on a gay bath-house. As the camera pans the group of men, it catches sight of a placard. For a moment, for just a freeze frame, the screen reads: "NO MORE AIDS," then the camera pans further to the left and the full message: "NO MORE RAIDS" becomes discernible. The bath-houses are all closed now, the days of police-raids on bars and baths one more

should be tattooed in the upper forearm, to protect common needle users, and on the buttocks to prevent the victimization of other homosexuals." The media perpetuates inaccuracies which threaten to prolong not only the viral raid

and hysteria, which hangs across the entire media industry of the Western world, and beyond." It is the linking of AIDS to a set of identities: gay promiscuous, evil, non-white, and simply "other" which must be contested at every turn. The interpretation of AIDS as a metaphor for moral misbehavior (Jerry Falwell stated that "AIDS is God's judgment of a society that does not live by His Rules") delays research, augments suffering, and insures the health and longevity of the HIV virus. Craig Owens, former Senior Editor of Art

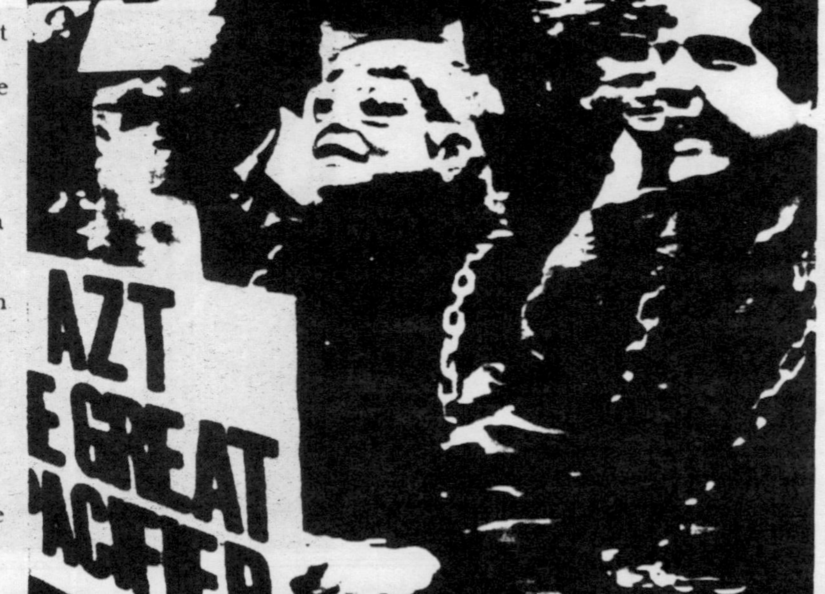

mer A gesture towards diespelling the media's AIDS hysteria, here visualized as a blinding mass of falesehood. 7:20-7:25 "The ADS Epidemic" by John Greyson Death in Venice (a parody) from the "Acquired Dread of Sex". 7:25-7:48 "Changing the Rules" by John Hoffman/AIDS films A clear-speaking call for understanding and prevention featuring Ron Reagan, Jr. 7:48 - 8:08 "Doctors, Liars, and Women: AIDS Activists Say No to Cosmo" by Maria Maggenti and Jean Carlemusto. Documents the recent protest by New York AIDS activists of Cosmoplitan magazine which has

After Hours

Editors

**Sharon Knauer
Andrew Reynlak
Richard Rothschild**

Photography Editor

Mark Harvie-Watt

Cover by Chris Kalb

nostalgia and present-day death, seems like sex heaven. Yet the raids on the lives of gay men, of lesbians, and of the straight community continue. Since it is through TV that we receive so many of our (mis)conceptions about AIDS, the medium of video is a particularly apt vessel for deconstructing AIDS misrepresentation. On Tuesday, March 1, "Visualizing AIDS," a series of six videos from the American Film Institute will be screened. The videos range in perspective from informational to parodic, from abstract and artistic to documentary and testimonial. With different narrative stategies and visual styles, each tape attempts to confront not only the epidemic of AIDS, but the dangerous lies and accusations which constitute a raid on all our lives. The police are wearing rubber gloves these days and they close down protests rather than pleasure domes. Cosmopolitan magazine murderously announces to its assumed white, straight-female readership that "there is almost no danger of contracting the virus through ordinary sexual intercourse" and William F. Buckley advises that "Everyone detected with AIDS

and emotional raids which AIDS-hysteria and misrepresentation foster. As Simon Watney has pointed out: "It is commonplace of medical history that every epidemic proceeds from an initially vulnerable community. The HIV virus [Human Immun-odeficieny virus has manifested itself in three constituencies which are already feared and marginalised in the West-blacks, intravenous drug users, and gay men. The presence of AIDS in these groups is generally perceived not as accidental but as a symbolic extension of some imagined innner essence of being, manifesting itself as disease. Further, in different ways for all three groups, AIDS has been used to articulate profound social fears and anxieties, in a dense web of racism, patriotism, and homophobia. It is this web, spun out in words sticky with blood lust, contempt, hatred

ber in the department of art history will introduce the series. Maria Maggenti and Gregg Bordowitz, creators of two of the videos will also speak and answer questions. Admission to "Visualizing AIDS" is free of charge and all members of the Yale and New

Haven communities are welcome. The tentative screening schedule is as follows:

7:00-7:15 Opening Remarks by Craig Owens 7:15-7:20 "Snow Job" by Barbara Ham-

Testing the Limits Collective This project has been described by Village Voice critic Gary Indiana as "an incitement to rage and to organized polit-cal action. 8:40-9:00 Discussion of video tapes by Maria Maggenti and Gregg Bordowitz, Question and Answer

9:00-9:10 Break

[see p. 118]

9:10-10:30 "Bright Eyes" by Stuart Marshall Produced for Britain's channel 4, an ambitious essay on how historical and social factors have colluded to misrepresent the true nature of AIDS.

Richard Meyer, an organizer of "Visualizing AIDS," is a senior in the history of art major. His senior essay is tentatively titled: "Rhetoric and Representations: Art about AIDS"

Yale Advocates Of Gay Rights Protest Arrests

President Forms Panel to Investigate Incident

By NICK RAVO

Special to The New York Times

NEW HAVEN, Nov. 1 — About 100 advocates for gay and lesbian rights, shouting slogans and waving pink- and lavender-lettered signs, rallied outside the office of Yale University's president today to protest the arrest of nine men last week in a confrontation with campus and city police officers over a sexually explicit poster.

The demonstration, the latest in a string of controversies involving homosexuals at Yale, underscored the growing role of gay students as the school's most militant minority group.

It also presented another highly publicized problem for Yale's president, Benno C. Schmidt Jr., a constitutional scholar and staunch advocate of freedom of expression, who has been criti-

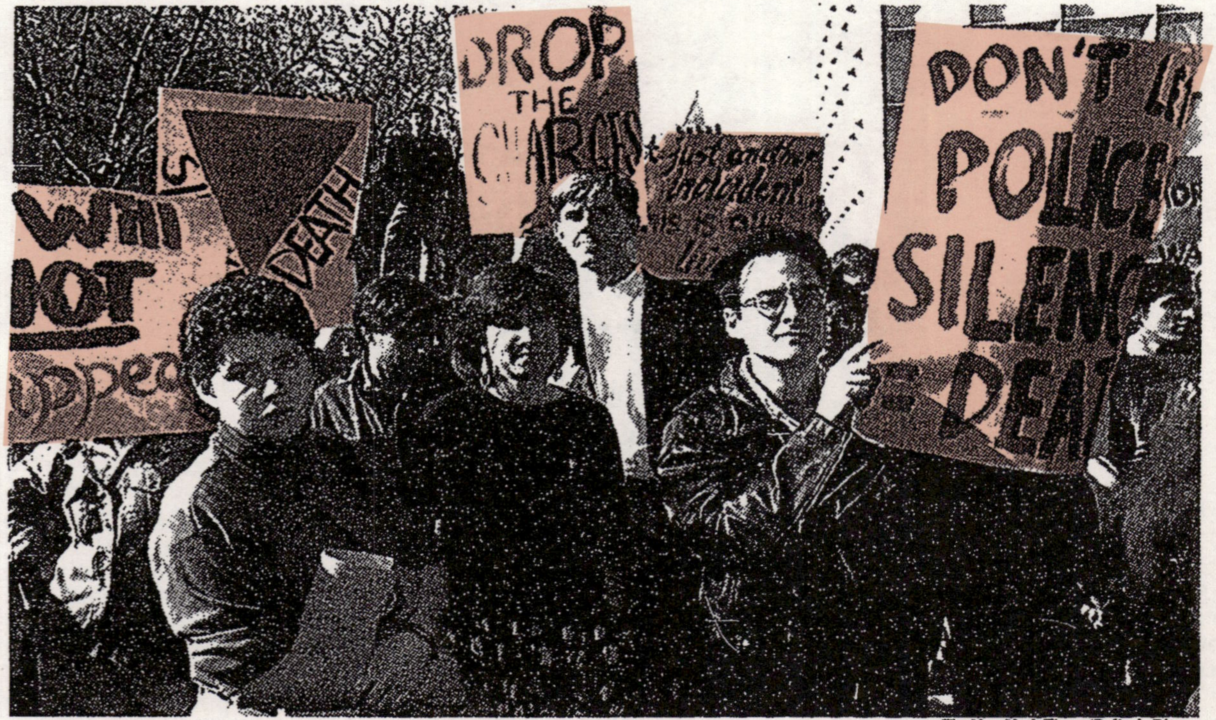

The New York Times/Rolin A. Riggs

Gay-rights advocates at Yale University yesterday protesting the arrest last week of nine men duri... a con-

several demands, including dropping the charges against the men, who were participating in a conference last weekend at the Lesbian and Gay Study Center at Yale.

'This Is a Nightmare'

They also demanded the dismissal of the officers involved in the arrests, and insisted that Mr. Schmidt make a public statement condemning "anti-gay, lesbian and bisexual violence and attitudes."

Sheila Wellington, Yale's secretary and the official who oversees the campus police force, said Mr. Schmidt had formed a committee to study the incident. She said dropping charges would be left to the state's attorney's office.

"This is a nightmare," she said.

Ms. Wellington said Mr. Schmidt met with faculty members and with gay leaders involved in the conference shortly after the arrests and made clear his "full commitment" to "free expression and the protection of diversity of opinion," as well as "his support of the presence of members of the gay and lesbian community at Yale."

Mr. Schmidt said in a telephone interview today: "I understand their concerns, and I share them. But we need to have a full investigation."

The confrontation began when a participant in the conference, William Dobbs, a New York lawyer, was arrested by Yale police officers about 9:30 P.M. Friday after he put up a sexually explicit poster in the law school, the police said.

The poster is one of a series made by a group of San Francisco artists known

... of the president, a new test of his sensitivity to gay rights.

as Boy with Arms Akimbo that show men posing in the nude. They also contain the phrase "Sex Is" or "Just Sex." The police became involved after a female law professor working in the building called them.

After the arrest of Mr. Dobbs, a shoving match erupted between conference participants and officers. That led to eight other arrests by the New Haven police, an impromptu protest march by about 300 people, and complaints of police harassment, false arrest, physical threats and slurs.

Eight of the nine men, most of them graduate students at Yale or other universities, are to appear in New Haven County Court Thursday. They have been charged with breach of peace and interfering with police, both misdemeanors.

Mr. Schmidt said the incident appeared to focus on two issues: whether the man hanging the poster was acting within the university's right of free expression and whether the police overreacted in making arrests. The New Haven police would not comment on the incident. And Mr. Schmidt said, "If New Haven police behaved in any way that was inappropriate, I'm going to say so."

was sparked more by the law professor's concern for her safety than a question of obscenity and free expression. "If I were working in my office," she said, "and it was late and a person I didn't know was putting up a poster. . . ."

Students at today's demonstration chanted "Hey, hey, ho, ho, this homophobia has got to go" and "Lez, lez, gay, gay — these words aren't so hard to say." They ended their protest by asking everyone to dance to a tape of Madonna, the rock star, singing "Express Yourself."

About 20 police officers, some wearing helmets, guarded the president's office in Woodbridge Hall.

The demonstrators also presented copies of a poster they characterized as a backlash against their protests. It said, "When gays act up, lock 'em up" and "The right to free speech does not include the right to put up sexually graphic photos wherever you damn well please."

Visible Gay Community

Homosexuals at Yale have been at the center of controversy several times in the last few years. In 1982, Newsweek magazine said Yale had an unusually visible gay community.

In 1986, a student was sentenced to two years' academic probation for satirizing a poster promoting Gay and Lesbian Awareness Day. Although the student was exonerated, the case prompted Mr. Schmidt to appoint a committee on freedom of expression last fall to address the conflict between free speech and harassment.

the nation's first lesbian and gay studies centers. And in 1988, The Wall Street Journal ran an article saying Yale Law School students were wearing pink triangles on their lapels during recruiting interviews and asking potential employers about their views and policies on homosexuals.

Perhaps the best-known incident occurred in 1987, when an essay in The Journal described Yale as a gay school. Mr. Schmidt, in a letter to about 2,000 potential fund-raisers, attacked the essay as "drivel." The letter's tone struck some members of the gay community as homophobic.

"Yale has a very vocal and strong gay and lesbian population," said Katherine Pradt, a junior English major from New Haven. "And because we have the Yale name, we get a lot more attention than gays and lesbians at other universities."

[see p. 118]

NO SUCH THING AS AN ABSTRACT WOMAN

Angela Y. Davis

Lecture delivered via Zoom during
"Diving Into the Wreck: Rethinking Critical Practices"
at the Yale School of Art, October 27, 2020

MARTA KUZMA   Welcome everyone. It is an honor and a privilege to have Professor Davis join us today, one week prior to the election, but also a day when a new Supreme Court judge has been confirmed, which will have an impact for years to come.

I will begin with a short introduction and then very much look forward to hearing Professor Davis' words.

Professor Davis was born in Birmingham, Alabama. She studied French literature at Brandeis University, followed by philosophy under Theodor Adorno at the University of Frankfurt, then part of West Germany. She returned to the United States and continued her studies under Herbert Marcuse at the University of California, San Diego. In her own words, she found Marcuse "committed to an immediate political activism." Professor Davis completed her doctoral thesis at Humboldt University in Berlin, with a dissertation that addressed Immanuel Kant's analysis of violence during the French Revolution. She went on to lead the Philosophy Department at UCLA in 1969, at the age of twenty-five, but was fired shortly thereafter by the Board of Regents of that university under pressure from then Governor of California, Ronald Reagan, for being a member of the Communist Party. Later, she was wrongfully imprisoned for more than a year, before her release in 1972, after which she continued to teach and speak internationally. She ran for vice president on the Communist Party ticket in 1980 and 1984. She was appointed the Presidential Chair of African American and Feminist Studies at the University of California, Santa Cruz, in 1994.

It's often overlooked that Professor Davis was hired onto the faculty of the San Francisco Art Institute, in 1976, where she taught aesthetics, but this is particularly relevant for us, and I am very happy to welcome Professor Davis to this course of Critical Practice, which is subtitled after Adrienne Rich's "Diving into the Wreck," a poem from the early 1970s.

Professor Davis' words and teachings include interpretation of Marcuse's *Eros and Liberation*—around instinctual repression, around the regime of an establishment—drawing from what has been understood as theory toward something called "practice" and "resistance."

As this course is not one lodged in any static armature of words and formulas, it has been our aim to continue an effort to understand ideas of radical injustice, racial injustice, and global capitalist exploitation, and to build—as a school and among our students—critical consciousness of what Marcuse would call "the extension of the executive arm into our souls." We attempt to build a vocabulary of resistance located in what Marcuse referred to as "a new sensibility that expresses the essence of life instincts," one which Professor Davis cites from Marcuse's own text as, "the need to address and dismantle political linguistics as the armor of the establishment."

In this most vulnerable and difficult of weeks, it is, again, an honor to have Professor Davis speak to us. Thank you.

ANGELA Y. DAVIS   Good morning, everyone. It's a little earlier for me than it is for you. I'm on the West Coast. You have to excuse me if I'm not as coherent as I normally am; I usually don't speak at this time of the morning, but I was just saying hello to Dean Kuzma, whom I haven't seen in person since she served as the Rector of the Royal Institute of Art in Stockholm. That seems like it was eons ago, doesn't it? Universes ago. Thank you for inviting me to participate in your class.

I was really intrigued by the title, "Diving into the Wreck: Rethinking Critical Practice." I know that there have been a number of phenomenal sessions—with Hortense Spillers, Fumi Okiji, and others—but I read the description of the course carefully, and I want to repeat one part of it, "taking 'Diving into the Wreck' as a point of departure, the course provides space for a cultivation of consciousness that extends self-knowledge outwards into a sense of community through the act of critical reflection."

Now, I'm not entirely sure where my comments will figure into your engagements with critical reflection as artists, but I can begin by saying that I so love the title of this course, which is taken from Adrienne Rich's phenomenal poem.

As I was thinking about the course, it gave me the opportunity
to revisit Adrienne Rich's words, and her contributions, her art,
her politics, her life. I met Adrienne Rich through the poet June
Jordan and got to know her because she and June were very
close friends. I'm not entirely sure why I'm telling you this—
I usually don't reveal this kind of information in my talks, but I want
to say that I was totally impressed by the way their friendship
survived, or was rather steeped, in political contradictions.
They were both extraordinary poets, and they were both deeply
committed to radical social transformation. They both used
their remarkable talents as artists to forge new knowledges and
new ways of critically engaging with our world.

I referred to their disagreements, so let me say very succinctly
that the disagreements were around Palestine, which was the
subject of a number of June Jordan's early poems, including the still
widely read poem, "Moving Toward Home," in which she writes:

> I was born a Black woman
> and now
> I am become a Palestinian
> against the relentless laughter of evil
> there is less and less living room
> and where are my loved ones?

> It is time to make our way home.

I know that eventually they resolved their differences and that,
like June Jordan, Adrienne Rich became an outspoken critic
of the occupation. I quote her here [from the Jewish Voice for
Peace, April 4, 2004]: "I've been asked to say a few words
about the importance of Jewish activism against the occupation.
Whether in the U.S., Israel, or elsewhere, I think every shred of
it matters. It's the embodiment of an ethical Judaism of, 'That
which is hateful to you, do not do to others. It is the rejection
of an idolatrous version of Israel and of the soil. It is a recognition
that history is not Jewish alone. It is a critical, educated response
to what has been claimed as Israel's right to exist at any cost
and on any terms, including a blindered self-destructiveness.'"

I am sharing this because Adrienne came a long way from her
initial conflict with June regarding Palestine and Israel in order
to make such an outspoken critique. Both of their deaths were

great losses. I'm thinking about Adrienne Rich, June Jordan, and Audre Lorde as artists who provided the most needed political direction without ever directly subordinating their artistic impulses to politics, especially at a time when we were searching for a way forward. All three of them showed us capacious versions of feminism and critical ways of apprehending the world that encouraged us to work with contradictions—to work with contradictions rather than striving to reconcile them or compelling us to choose one pole or the other.

All three of them, Adrienne, June, and Audre, powerfully demonstrated the leadership that creators of art, poetry, painting, films, sculpture, music, and dance can provide us as we move in the direction of radically transforming our worlds.

Now, as a person who has come to rely on written or spoken words of a more didactic sort as a way of contributing to the collective quest for human freedom, I've come increasingly to recognize that if we are really interested in creating change— *real* change—this change will never occur without the participation of—and I would probably go so far as to say without the explicit leadership of—artists.

I'm saying this to make the point that this session is very important to me—engaging with art students, with artists, with those who are in school, not only to develop their skills as painters, sculptors, photographers, printmakers, but also to imagine and reflect on the affairs of the world. So, why is art so important? Aside from the fact that it moves us and reminds us of the momentous power of beauty, or of that which is so strange as to convey a sense of possibility about which we might never have otherwise dreamed of … Why is art so important? Thinking about this period, this Black Lives Matter era, I remembered that when the [National Museum of African American History and Culture] in Washington opened, I was asked to write a short piece on one of the exhibits in the museum. The exhibit was a casket. It was a casket made of mirrors. I want to share this 2016 Mirror Casket project with you.

As art object, performance, and political statement, the Mirror Casket evokes a pivotal moment in the history of U.S. social justice struggles. Collaboratively produced by artists and activists involved in the protest that erupted in the aftermath of the August 2014 police killing of Michael Brown in Ferguson, Missouri, the coffin-shaped, mirror-clad casket reflects and performs the work that finally placed police violence in Black communities on mainstream U.S. political agendas. Conveyed on the shoulders of protestors, pallbearers, through the streets of Ferguson, the casket confronted police officers, activists, journalists, and others with their own reflected images—some whole, some fractured through glass, imparting the message that we are all implicated in different ways in the process of racist state violence and that we all bear the responsibility to end it.

In its inaugural exhibition during the protests that followed the news of the failure to indict Michael Brown's killer, police officer Darren Wilson, the Mirror Casket embodied the demonstration theme—funeral procession of justice—but while this sculpture quite literally conveyed the notion that justice is dead, it simultaneously exemplified and reflected the idea that people's robust demands for racial justice are very much alive. The mirror in fact serves as an apt metaphor for the role played by new technologies of communication in twenty-first-century movements against state violence. The rapidly accumulating archive of video images of police killings in Black communities is shifting popular consciousness. These images have helped to focus the world's gaze on mediated representations of the persistent brutality of racism.

Historical violence by armed bodies representing dominant political forces from slave catchers to post-slavery police forces, and lynching, as well as other extralegal forms of violence was always a characteristic feature of racism. Historically, this violence has been ideologically disguised either as necessary to keep a less than human population in check or as an exaggeration by those who putatively rely too much on victimhood as the determining factor of their social identity.

Since the 2014 protests erupted against the police killings of Michael Brown in Ferguson, Eric Garner in Staten Island, twelve-year-old Tamir Rice in Cleveland, and subsequent revelations of many more assaults on Black people, we have witnessed numerous video representations of police violence. Smartphones and body cameras have become the looking glass compelling the recognition that Black lives matter. Likewise, the Mirror Casket does not simply announce the death of justice but renews calls for more efficacious forms of justice today.

This short piece was written four years ago, and now it is possible to think of the art piece as a kind of harbinger of what we would experience in 2020. Perhaps during the conversation today we can talk a little bit more about the way art can help us imagine the future. I want to say a few more words, largely about the field of aesthetics, and then I want to open up a discussion with all of you.

As you heard, my training is in philosophy, in critical theory, and especially critical theory associated with the Frankfurt School. Many of the primary members of the Frankfurt School engaged extensively with art. Whether it was as artists or theorists, these philosophers strongly emphasized the value of aesthetics. Today, as I do intellectual and activist work, including with many artists and musicians, I am so thankful that the professors with whom I studied— especially Herbert Marcuse—gave me a vocabulary that allows me to engage with the transformative potential of art.

You heard that I taught for quite a few years at the San Francisco Art Institute. At the moment, I am working with SFJAZZ as a member of the board of trustees. I'm also on the advisory board of the Institute for Jazz and Gender Studies at Berklee College of Music in Boston. This institute is headed by the amazing drummer Terri Lyne Carrington, who, by the way, was the very first woman ever to receive a Grammy for instrumental jazz. Two issues ago in *DownBeat*, she won the *DownBeat* critics poll in three categories: Best Jazz Artist, Best Group, and Best Album. If you're interested in her, I urge you to listen to her most recent album, the one that won all these awards. It is called *Waiting Game*. Her group is called Social Science. It's so interesting that she released this album before this period that was initiated by the shelter-in-place order associated with the pandemic. In many ways, it was a harbinger of what has happened over the last several months. I've been especially interested in music and how it works against what you might call the individualizing consciousness of neoliberalism—how it gives us a sense of what it means to be a part of a collective process.

I should also tell you that I just participated in a program that comes out of UC Santa Cruz. A series of conversations—Zoom conversations—under the rubric Visualizing Abolition. The topic is visuality of abolition. If any of you are interested in listening to the conversations, they were recorded. Bryan Stevenson, who was head of the Equal Justice Institute in Montgomery, who has this amazing center [the National Memorial for Peace and Justice] that is a memorial to lynching—you've probably all

seen images of it—he's going to be in conversation with Gina
Dent this evening. There are many other interesting people in the
series, like Nicole Fleetwood, who recently published a book on
carceral art and aesthetics called *Marking Time: Art in the Age
of Mass Incarceration.* Visualizing Abolition is connected to an
exhibition, which is currently at the San Jose Museum of Art.
It is art by [incarcerated individuals] and about carceral issues,
by [the imprisoned] and about imprisonment. The title of the
exhibition at the San Jose Museum of Art is *Barring Freedom.*

Now, I know I'm kind of all over the place, but I thought I might
also share with you a conversation from the organizers of
Critical Resistance: Beyond the Prison Industrial Complex, which
jump-started the collective concern with abolition—prison abolition, police abolition—back in 1998. As we were organizing
this conference there was virtually no consciousness in the
broader communities about the expanding prison population,
and we wanted to use a visual image to convey to people what
the conference would be about. Of course, on the organizing
committee, so many people said, "Well, maybe something with
bars or maybe something with chains." I mean, how many
bars and chains have we seen? As a matter of fact, I know that
when I gave the opening statement of my trial, it was released in
a little pamphlet that had bars on it. Wherever we go, it's bars and
chains. Some of us said, "Well, if we use bars and chains, then
people who see this will think they already know what it's about."
We decided to ask a local artist, a wonderful artist by the name
of Rupert García, if he would come up with an idea for a poster.
I should have brought the poster up to show you—it's an image
of an eye, this kind of foreboding eye against a horizon. ... We
plastered the poster up everywhere, and it was so interesting,
because people couldn't figure out "What is this big eye? What
is this about?" Of course, in talking about it, we said, "Well,
this is the eye of surveillance, this is the eye of the state, but at
the same time, it's the eye that's looking toward the future. It's
the eye that gives us hope." I wanted to share that story with you,
because it taught us so much about representational practices
and about the way in which art can encourage us to discover
a very different kind of critical knowledge and engagement.

So, let me say a few more words, and then I want to open
it up. I promised you I would say something about the field
of philosophical aesthetics.

You've read some of Marcuse's work, "Essay on Liberation" and—

DEAN KUZMA   *Counterrevolution and Revolt* … then we've also read the preface to *Eros and Civilization.*

PROFESSOR DAVIS   I actually pulled my copy of *Eros and Civilization* off the shelf and looked at it. When I opened the paperback, it split in two, but I treasure this copy, which is more than fifty years old. But let me share a passage from *An Essay on Liberation.* It's about form. "In the aesthetic Form, the content (matter) is assembled, defined, and arranged to obtain a condition in which the immediate, unmastered forces of the matter, of the 'material,' are mastered, 'ordered.'" Of course, we would be critical of some of the vocabulary here, but let me continue, "Form is the negation, the mastery of disorder, violence, suffering, even when it presents disorder, violence, suffering. This triumph of art is achieved by subjecting the content to the aesthetic order, which is autonomous in its exigencies. The work of art sets its own limits and ends, it is *sinngebend* in relating the elements to each other according to its own law …"

Now, Marcuse was very much influenced by Immanuel Kant in his reflections on the work that the aesthetic does, and, in quite a number of his books, he emphasizes the subversive power of art and the aesthetic—not only in *An Essay on Liberation*, but also in *Counterrevolution and Revolt*, where chapter three is entitled "Art and Revolution," and Marcuse's last book was entitled *The Aesthetic Dimension.* Interestingly, this last book was published in the early 1970s, but "The Aesthetic Dimension" was also the title of chapter nine of *Eros and Civilization*, which was published in 1955. I make these points because, in the course, you're looking at the way art helps us to move toward critical engagements with the world. It's interesting that in the history of aesthetics, art or the aesthetic is initially introduced as an inferior form of knowledge. I'm referring to Alexander Baumgarten in his book *Aesthetica*, published in 1750. To simplify, because, of course, we don't have the time to delve deeply into this, Baumgarten defined aesthetics as knowledge through the senses rather than knowledge through reason and logic. And, so, Immanuel Kant took up this notion of aesthetics as an important field of philosophy, but he elevated aesthetics.

He said, "It's really not inferior knowledge." It is what he called a "judgment of taste." It's a judgment, rather than knowledge.

But precisely in the process of elevating the field, he deprived it of its potential to generate knowledge. This philosophical segregation of the field of aesthetics from the field of epistemology is, at one level, linked to the later insistence that art should not be polluted by political claims, that art should be for its own sake, and all of you are familiar with the whole notion of art for art's sake. Although, at the present moment, even the art world is changing under the impact of the social, economic, and political changes being demanded in this era of Black Lives Matter, which intersects with the #MeToo movement. And I was thinking that it's interesting that the most recent issue of *Artforum*, if you can see this, has Stanley Whitney's work, *No to Prison Life*, and also an interview with Nicole Fleetwood, [author of *Marking Time*]. But let's get back to the philosophy of aesthetics and back to Kant. What Kant did was to elevate aesthetics to the level of critique, even as he deprived the field of the possibility of generating knowledge or producing morality.

I'm going to try to give you a thirty-second introduction to Kant's critical work, which is, of course impossible. The three major works that Immanuel Kant produced were critiques. There was number one, the *Critique of Pure Reason,* which addressed the production of knowledge or epistemology—how is knowledge possible? Then the second was the *Critique of Practical Reason,* which engaged with morality—how is freedom possible? And freedom is defined as a moral phenomenon. And then the third is *The Critique of Judgment,* which includes *The Critique of Aesthetic Judgment* and *The Critique of Teleological Judgment.* And the questions there in relation to our conversation here are: How are beauty and art possible?

Let me just summarize the conundrum in which Kant found himself after writing the first two critiques. The first critique humanized the process of producing knowledge. Knowledge did not come from God, knowledge did not come from Hegel's absolute idea, it came from a lawful process emanating from the human mind. He argued that what we considered to be the laws governing the world, governing the world of appearances, as he put it—that these laws don't come from nature, but rather they come from the faculties of reason that produce these laws for the very purpose of understanding reality. This was what he called the realm of necessity. And the problem here is that freedom is nowhere to be found, even though the laws of governing reality emanate from the human mind. And I'm not being very precise here of course, but the problem is that there was no room for freedom, no room for freedom at all in the first critique.

Let me just say one other thing before I move on to the second critique. I found the really interesting issue was that we can never know the world except as it exists in the incarnation that is produced by our interaction, giving order and laws to the world. We can't know what Kant called the thing-in-itself (*das Ding an sich*), and, for me, that's one of the most interesting aspects of epistemology. It means that the object of our knowledge always exceeds our capacity to completely know it, and I will just say parenthetically that that creates a space for the epistemological work of art and the imagination.

The second critique is the *Critique of Practical Reason* whose mission is to rescue the very possibility of freedom. If freedom can't exist in the world where everything is governed by laws, even though these laws are subjective, so to speak—meaning that they come from the knower rather than from the known— the attempt to rescue the possibility of freedom happens like this: freedom is a moral phenomenon, and it can exist in my moral actions, but actually it resides not in the action itself but rather in the maxim or the law that governs that action. You can see that Kant was really concerned about laws, but here is an instance where we see autonomy. And what does autonomy mean? Autonomy means giving oneself the law. And, so, freedom is defined as the capacity to give oneself the law—to act as if the maxims of your action were to become through your will a universal law of nature. That's one of the instantiations of what Kant called the categorical imperative. What's interesting is that, in the second critique, *Critique of Practical Reason*, paragraph 59 is entitled, "Beauty As the Symbol of Morality."

We don't have time to go through this, but let me ask you to think about the notion of beauty as the symbol of morality and then point out again that the conundrum here is that there are two entirely separate realms: the realm of nature and the realm of morality. One is the realm of necessity; the other is the realm of freedom. So, the question arose—how is it possible to link the world of freedom and the world of necessity? How can one intervene in the realm of necessity? In the third critique, this happens through beauty and art, but it is through judgment, not knowledge.

Marcuse was very struck by this conscious decision to place aesthetics as a mediating force between knowledge and freedom. He was interested in the notion of art as revealing the work of the senses or sensibility—a kind of sensuous critical engagement. As a matter of fact, I think it's always important to recall that the etymological meaning of aesthetics is precisely the senses, and so you find Marcuse using aesthetics in the philosophical context we spoke about, but also aesthetics in relationship to a kind of critical engagement that emanates from the senses rather than only from reason. And we can return to that paragraph that I read from "An Essay on Liberation" on the role of form—I could go on because I'm still so interested in this material and in Kant's formulation of the *sensus communis*. There is something like a collective engagement that happens, an internalized sense of community or collectivity that gets generated by the process of engaging with art. Kant called it the *sensus communis*— common sense. The way Kant describes this notion is far too complicated and technical for me to explain here, but let me say that art unleashes our capacity not only to think, but our capacity to feel, and oftentimes we can feel what we do not yet know how to say. We can experience on that aesthetic level, the level of the senses, the level of the imagination, what we have not yet figured out how to express in didactic language. In this sense, I think that art really does show us the way to transform our world. In this contemporary era during which we are grappling with structural, systemic, institutional racism, it can help to chart our paths in an area where we've never dared to tread as a society or as a world. This means that we are redeveloping our sense of history, given that in many ways, what is happening now should have occurred in the aftermath of the abolition of slavery. This is why this period is so absolutely important, and why artists have such a critical role to play. And with that, I will conclude my presentation and invite you to ask questions.

RACHAEL ANDERSON   Thank you for speaking with us today. I was really excited when you mentioned how music, especially, can help us dismantle some of the oppressive things that neoliberalism has done to the culture, as far as making people kind of separated. I took from what you were saying that music brings people together in a special way. I'm wondering if you could speak more about that.

PROFESSOR DAVIS   What interests me so much about music—and we can talk about all the various genres of music—are the listening practices we develop, which also involve a sense of how others react to the same music. When we're moved by music, we are not only thinking about ourselves as individuals, but rather we imagine ourselves and our co-listeners as a larger collective audience. We have an implicit awareness of those who are listening with us. So, it's not an individualized experience. It's an experience that helps to create a sense of the extent to which we are all deeply steeped in communities and collectivities, and that we're not the individual subject that neoliberal ideology posits as the primary unit of society. Of course, we can examine the way popular music has had an impact on young people during this period and how it has been an integral part of the politicizing processes that led to the most massive demonstrations against racism in the entire history of this country … One could have never predicted that, in the midst of a horrendous pandemic, collectively witnessing the lynching of George Floyd—and I think that the videotaping also allowed us to experience being recruited to be a part of an audience that witnessed a lynching—that in that very difficult moment, more people poured out into the streets at their peril, even when there was a very clear possibility that they might be infected by the virus. They nevertheless went because, I think, there was a conjuncture that made us all recognize that we must address this issue that has been plaguing us since the foundation of this country: racism and racial capitalism. We must address it now or it will never be adequately confronted. And music, precisely, was and continues to be a part of this process of politicizing people at a different level, at the level of the senses, at the level of our interior constitution.

CHINAEDU NWADIBIA   Thank you so much for seeing us. I know how it is to be up so early on the West Coast. You look radiant. In the lecture today, you were talking about working with contradictions and embracing that, and I want to know if you could reflect on a time in your life where you navigated the contradictions of whatever you were immersed in and how that may or may not have been pivotal for you.

          ANGELA Y. DAVIS

      Well, I've had to recognize the value of embracing contradictions rather than trying to reconcile them or solve them, of course, and in my philosophical studies, I've read Hegel and Marx, both of whom insist on the productive power of contradiction. But that productive power emanates precisely from the reconciliation, from what Hegel called the *Aufhebung*, which allows one to reach a more advanced step. On the other hand, Audre Lorde informed us that we don't always have to engage in that frantic effort to reconcile contradictions. We can sometimes simply let them be, live with them, dwell within the contradictions. And, for me, this has become one of the most valuable lessons I've learned from feminism— from feminist approaches, radical feminist methodologies, anti-racist, anticapitalist feminist methodologies—and that, of course, in part is reflected in the notion of intersectionality that everybody's familiar with now, but it goes beyond that. It involves recognizing that sometimes we acquire important insights by eschewing frantic efforts to get rid of contradictions for the purpose of figuring out, for example, "Who am I?" To draw on my own personal history, when I was a younger activist trying to do work on gender issues, feminist issues, I was asked several times, "Well, you have to decide whether you are a woman or whether you are Black." So, okay, If I'm a woman, it means I can engage in feminist work, but if I'm Black, it means that I only get to do anti-racist work. And, I kid you not, this was a question that was posed to me on many occasions. Of course, now you see the flaws in the assumption that identity should determine political praxis, but this also points out the extent to which our analytical powers are often misrepresented as reflecting the actual world, the social reality. We use the category "woman," but there's no such thing as an abstract woman, and there's no such thing as an abstract Black person, right? Race is always gendered and classed, and class is always raced and gendered, et cetera, et cetera. So, I have come to embrace this idea that art can yield a kind of knowledge that is not categorical. We can learn from the way artists work and the way we engage with art. Contradictions don't bother us so much if they are a part of an autonomous creation. We can learn from these art practices. They can deepen our critical practices in relation to the world.

          Hello. Thank you so much for speaking with us. It's been really exciting, and to see your energy, that's also giving us energy, and that's great.

          And this is my early morning energy, wait until the afternoon!

          Okay, word, hopefully we'll get that chance, but I wanted to ask you a question about this Critical Practices class and how we've been really focusing on Black aesthetics and Black thought and thinking about Blackness in a broad scope, I think, because we've been having a lot of conversations, and we've been feeling as though, for me personally, out of this class, how can we continue a conversation about this and develop this as a way that, I don't know … I feel these are ways of perceiving and ways of aesthetics, and how can this conversation go past this class? How can it be an international conversation? How can Blackness be an international conversation? How can that be a way of fugitiveness, a way of … I'm still trying to understand these things, but I feel like a lot of people have been talking, and we've been saying that this is just a moment in time, and it'll pass, and I'm sort of worried about that. I'm worried that we're going to have this conversation, we're going to talk about all these things, and we'll pass through, and I'm curious what you think about that? Being international, and known, how do you manage this predicament?

          First of all, thank you so much for the question. There are so many ways in which I could engage with it, but I will begin by saying that the internationalization of our perspectives is so important. I should tell you that yesterday, I did a Zoom program in Barcelona at the Center for Contemporary Culture. I won't tell you what was required from my end because we had a planned electrical outage for fire prevention. In California, aside from everything else that is happening—the pandemic and our anti-racist work—we have to address climate change and the ways in which our worlds are going up in flames as a result of global capitalism. So I had to purchase a generator at the very last minute, in order to speak to a socially distanced audience in Barcelona about issues of anti-Black racism. I participated in a panel of Black people who live in Spain and who are addressing the ways in which the history of Spain reflects a particular engagement with structural racism and immigration. It was really fascinating. I think that in the U.S we lack a sense of belonging to a larger community, a planetary community, which means that we should not just focus on ourselves. In that context, I want to just say a few words about broadening our understanding of the meaning of this movement at this moment. I know that we will probably refer to this time as "the era of Black Lives Matter," but we should also recognize that racism emanates from other historical sources, not only the slave trade and the role that slavery played in producing capitalism, racial capitalism, but also the colonial period. Let's not forget that the original act of racism was the colonization of the land of Indigenous people, and that as a matter of fact, the resistance that Black people offered was precisely enabled by Indigenous people. The success of the very first slave uprising, which took place in 1526, was attributed to the assistance of Native people. So, let's try to be inclusive and more capacious and recognize that the history of anti-Black racism does not unfold in isolation from the history of racism directed at Indigenous people or Latinx communities, and I think that is so important, because if we are to imagine a possibility of a world where freedom and equality and justice prevail, we have to address a whole range of issues—racism, as it's directed against multiple communities—and we certainly have to deal with hetero-patriarchy. And we also have to address the climate change issues, issues of disability, etc. So, I guess I would answer your question by saying that intersectionality, which we often use as an analytical category that helps us to understand identity, is, I think, even more compelling when we think about the inter-sectionality of struggles. And that compels us to recognize that even though the entire world looks toward the U.S. and our current struggles to address structures of policing and structures of imprisonment and so forth, without recognizing that there are really interesting campaigns going on in Nigeria, for example— the campaigns for the abolition of SARS [Special Anti-Robbery Squad]. Brazil has the largest number of Black people outside of the continent of Africa, and in Brazil, Black people and Indigenous people have had to come together to address the militarization of the police, to address the burning of the Amazon. So, I guess the point I'm making is that we should not try to be neat, let's be messy. Artists help us in dealing with this. The world does not correspond to our beautifully formulated analytical categories. It always exceeds it, and art allows us to understand the extent to which the world and reality exceed our capacity to know it in traditional terms.

KENDRICK CORP   Thank you so much for speaking with us, it's been amazing. I was wondering if you could speak in context to abolition, to the emotives in past, present, and future; I think of abolition starting hundreds of years ago, but I feel like, when I talk about it with my friends, especially in the context of recent actions of federal officers going and using surveillance to disrupt—we were talking about the emotives of abolition and the difficulty there, because it's not necessarily plan-based, it's dealing with feelings, and you spoke about feelings earlier in the context of art, so I was wondering if you could just share some thoughts on the motives there in that context? Thank you.

PROFESSOR DAVIS   Abolition, of course, has different genealogies, and the genealogy that those of us who have been doing abolitionist work over the last twenty years—and then some of us have been doing it for the last fifty years or so—that genealogy is connected to the abolitionist movement against U.S. slavery. I think it's important to be specific because I'm working on a book right now with a number of collaborators, with three other co-authors, entitled *Abolition. Feminism. Now.*, and we are trying to point out that abolition actually is linked to feminism in many ways—including in relation to the antislavery abolitionist movement. But we also distance ourselves from feminist abolition, or abolitionist feminism, which addresses prostitution, because unfortunately sometimes, in Europe especially, when we speak about abolitionist feminism, people think that we're talking about abolishing prostitution. Not at all. We're very much in support of the rights of sex workers and their autonomy and their capacity to give leadership.

What could I say about abolition to answer your question in a short period of time, because this is a topic I've been thinking about for a very long time, since I first encountered the notion of prison abolition in 1971, when I was in jail myself. After George Jackson was assassinated at San Quentin, and prisoners in Attica prison in New York staged an uprising—the

Attica Prison rebellion—they raised the prospect of ultimately abolishing imprisonment as the primary mode of punishment. In the mid-seventies, in the aftermath of the Attica rebellion, the Quakers—the American Friends Service Committee—did an enormous amount of work promoting prison abolition. And what's interesting about that, of course, is that introducing the idea of prisons as punishment was originally considered a major reform, a more humane punishment—imprisonment rather than corporal punishment. So, Quakers were at the forefront of that original movement, but then they were also at the forefront of the movement to abolish prisons. There have always been critiques of policing, whose U.S. origins can be discovered in slavery.

To more specifically address your question, abolition requires imagination. It requires the kind of collective imagination that allows us to foresee a future in which these repressive structures are no longer necessary, and this is why art is so important. Who better to help us cultivate the capacity to imagine? Gayatri Spivak has a wonderful book called *An Aesthetic Education in the Era of Globalization*, where she makes a point that the imagination has to be educated, and, going back to Kant, imagination was the primary faculty engaged in the critique of judgment.

So, what's interesting about abolition in the ways in which it has been theorized up to this point, when it has begun to enter the mainstream, is that it's not simply about imagining the end of these structures and systems of policing and imprisonment. It's also about recognizing the extent to which we often internalize the impulses of the state—how, in our very emotional makeup, we often engage in punitive and retributive responses in our relations with one another. So, what is the connection between those impulses that appear to come from within the individual? What is ideological about that? What links the way we feel to the ideological work of the state? Abolition has also been concerned with this, recognizing that we not only have to imagine the actual concrete dismantling of these institutions, but we also have to work toward dismantling them as they render our own emotional responses ideological.

          Thank you for your presence and everything that you're sharing. I had some questions about the sort of beauty that you mentioned earlier in talking about art, and I think we've worked in this class to interrogate a sort of classical idea of beauty, but there's a sort of beauty that maybe I'm connecting with a vitality, or life force, or connectedness in what you were saying, and I'd like to hear more about that. Then, the second part of that interest in beauty is that I'm also thinking about the sort of vitality that you're embodying here with us today, and what it is to be able to maintain this level of deep connection to the world through all of the waves of transformation that you've been active in, and I am just so curious about how you are sustaining that and remaining tapped-in personally, but also for us, as well, knowing that this isn't ending anytime soon.

PROFESSOR DAVIS   What a beautiful question. I'm not sure that I can do justice to the way you formulated the question. I'm really intrigued by the way you formulated it. But what I will say is that I've been involved in movements against racism, for radical social change, to dismantle capitalism, all of my life. I think my first—well, I don't know whether this was actually my first venture into activism—but when I was eleven years old, I became involved in an interracial discussion group in Birmingham, Alabama, at my church. It was a Congregational church, so it was Black kids and white kids just talking. Just talking. And that was so threatening that the church was burned. Let's see ... I said eleven years old. I was born in 1944, so that must've been 1955, which was also the year of the Montgomery bus boycott. I guess I'm sharing this with you to make the point that a protracted engagement with the quest to help to produce a better world has also involved recognizing the role of pleasure and joy and beauty. Oftentimes people thank me for all my sacrifices, and my response is, "Well, I don't really feel like I've sacrificed anything. What else would I have done? How could I have had a better life?" But I've learned that engagement and activism and intellectual labor also have to be able to produce a pleasure, joy, and this is why I think art is so important, and that it should not be segregated from the work that we do, that it be part of that work. So, I can listen to amazing music and feel moved and feel connected to people, and also recognize at the same time that this music has transformative power—it's helping us to change the world.

And, as I said before, this is why I think that the sensibility of artists helps all of us to recognize that as we do this work, we're part of a very long continuum, and that basically what we're trying to do is enable new terrains of struggle for others, so I'm especially really excited at this moment, because, first of all, I never imagined I would experience anything like this. When we talked about abolition, it was like, "Well, I don't know, maybe fifty years from now, maybe one hundred years from now, maybe two hundred years from now …" We positioned ourselves as those, say, who were enslaved, who were struggling for freedom, who might not have exactly grasped what that freedom would mean. They were struggling for us, but, of course, they didn't have the capacity to picture us as we are—with our issues and institutions and so forth—but they did have the capacity to imagine the possibility that new generations would experience freedom in a very different way. I think that is what we're all doing now, and one hundred years from now, people will be thinking about this period, and many of them will probably be thankful to those who stood up and who insisted on trying to craft a different world, and we never know exactly what this work is going to bring us. There are never any guarantees. I really loved the way that Stuart Hall—amazing cultural theorist—if you haven't read Stuart Hall and his engagement with popular culture and art, read him—he always pointed out that there are no guarantees. We don't know exactly what our work is going to produce. But— I go back to Kant's categorical imperative—we have to act as if it were possible, and acting as if it were possible to change the world for the better allows us to become a part of this continuum that extends toward the past, but also far into the future. And this is my way of beginning a conversation in response to your wonderful question.

 One thing I was struck by and appreciated today, especially with Marta sharing with us the video of the May Day protests, and thinking about aesthetics and the historicizing of moments, watching in that video events taking place in New Haven, and knowing that we'd get to speak to you today, and reading your interview, "Angela Davis Still Believes the World Can Change"—I was really struck with this bringing-together of the time, as it related to the reminder of our role, while fighting against the historicizing of power and movements to be something from another time. I wanted to ask you on a very personal level, as it relates to the aesthetics of the movement, and one of the main things that creates that is this feeling of a conscious aesthetic amidst the 1970s Black Power movements. I wanted to know, as someone who has traveled through all of this, what your experience of the aesthetic was as it came, and your awareness as it shifted? Is that something that we can be aware of in the moment? How do we use it to unify the power of a collective movement, or fight against the historicizing of the elements that come in and push some things into the past as a way of separating our connection and role in that?

PROFESSOR DAVIS   That's a complicated question. So, I would first point towards the Black Art Movement, which is still having an impact on the way we think about the political power of art, and I'm thinking about poets like Sonia Sanchez and Amiri Baraka, and all of those who were involved in trying to produce an aesthetic deeply steeped in the political quest of Black liberation. There was a wonderful exhibition at the Hammer called *Now Dig This! Art and Black Los Angeles 1960–1980* with a Charles White image on the cover of the catalogue—you might be interested in looking at that work. I want to also mention the everyday aesthetic, which was quite powerful. I can tell you a personal story. There were these bumper stickers—some of you may know what bumper stickers are, but we don't use them as much anymore because we have social media. I had a couple of bumper stickers, orange bumper stickers, that said "Black is Beautiful." I remember putting one on my car—it was a 1959 Buick—but this was in the late 1960s. I was a teaching assistant and put another one on my office door. And you will not believe the negative reactions. People wrote all kinds of nasty—this was at a university—nasty stuff on the bumper sticker on my office door. Eventually, I had to take the bumper sticker off my car bumper, because I got run off the road on a freeway. So, I'm using this brief anecdote as an example of the power of the aesthetic. Simply to claim that "Black is Beautiful" was considered to be so subversive that it had to be eradicated. Of course, if we had enough time, we could talk about the politics of appearance, and the emergence of new hairstyles, and new fashion possibilities, and so forth, but all of that was very much a part of a quest for freedom and liberation. Thank you so much for the question.

ALVIN ASHIATEY   I wonder if you could speak to class reductionism and race reductionism insofar as Black Lives Matter has become the most visible struggle the left has become engaged in as of late?

          Yeah, reductionism never really works, whether it's class reductionism or race reductionism. In the context of a racist society, reductionism incorporates those racist impulses, so some people speak about the priority of class—and a lot of old-style Marxists do this—they think of the working class as white. The working class is an important driver of history, of course, but they imagine the working class as white—white workers, white male workers—when, as a matter of fact, if one looks at the history of the labor movement in this country, it was women who were responsible for the emergence of a radical proletariat with strikes in the Northeast at the end of the nineteenth century, the beginning of the twentieth century, and even before in the mid-nineteenth century with the rise of the Industrial Revolution. Of course, if one thinks of race reduc-tionism, gender usually gets excluded. So, in the past, Black men were considered the primary representatives of Black people, thus excluding women and non-binary people from that formu-lation. So, what is exciting now, I think, is that we're beginning to recognize the detrimental impact of these categories on our capacity to understand the world. And, I am so grateful to the trans movement, because new realms have been opened up in our capacity to imagine different modes of normalcy.

The very fact that we have been led through a process that has caused us to challenge the binary structure of gender helps us in other ways, because if we can challenge something we have so relied on and that has so anchored our sense of what constitutes normalcy, then we can also imagine a world that is not under the mastery of capitalism. We could also imagine a world in which ableism doesn't prevail in the way that it does. I'm thinking about those who used to be very reluctant to embrace the idea that Black lives matter, because they assumed that it was exclusive, that it meant that only Black lives matter. It's so interesting that this universalizing logic that so colors our popular epistemological practices prevents us from even recognizing that there are ways we can argue for universality that begin with the particular. And, again, this is an insight that comes from philosophical aesthetic theory. This was a point that Kant made—the importance of beginning with the particular and not involving oneself in a process that requires the subordination of the particular to the universal in this repressive way, but rather, understanding how the particular can move us toward a very different kind of universality. So, Black Lives Matter is not only Black lives matter. The meaning is that only if Black lives matter then we can imagine all lives mattering. So, there's a deep connection with the universal there. I think it's important for us to remember this as we talk about this as the era of Black Lives. This is not about Black lives only. It's about Indigenous lives. It's about Latinx lives. It's about Asian-American lives. It's about Muslim lives. It's about trans lives. We can go on, and on, and on. So, I think that is what is exciting about this period. It's perhaps moving us away from the kind of reductionism to which you refer.

AMARTYA DE   I was thinking about Schopenhauer and the differences between Schopenhauer and Kant. I was thinking of the idea of the tranquil experience when one is out in the world, and there's the information that we have, and also the experience of need and suffering—maybe not personal need and suffering but observed need and suffering. Oftentimes, when making work, I find that I have to think about both of these things and wonder where to go. Oftentimes, the tranquil is something that happens by chance, or need and suffering is something that's more conceptual and objective. I was thinking maybe you had some advice to give to artists for how to work with both, or just work with one and speak of the other?

PROFESSOR DAVIS   The most phenomenal aspect of art-making and art appreciation, one might say, is that there are no rules. I'll actually go back to the Marcusean formulation. It's precisely the capacity to create one's own rules at that moment that do not rely on the production of a formula or a general category or a category of knowledge. And so, I know, of course, if one looks at art history, we see all kinds of art, and we see artists who are deeply moved by suffering and pain, and we also see art that actually brings us to what you call the space of tranquility. Then on the other hand, the Schopenhauer— the assertion of the will! I think that it's about the imagination, and the imagination has no limits. But rather than you asking me the question, I should be asking you to reflect on your own experience in producing art. I like to think of art as something

that is not segregated into art schools and art worlds. And I like
to think about what is known as high art alongside popular art
and how both have the capacity to change all of us, whether it is
toward that tranquil space or whether it's the *Sturm und Drang*.
Thank you so much for the question.

ROSA POLIN   My question is phrased in a messy way,
and I'm not sure if I'm going to be able to express it any better.
I am also asking about imagination and the relationship between
Eros and Thanatos, and the dialectic process of actually achieving
or getting to that point where we can imagine a path, say, to
justice or freedom that's abolitionist, if that actually makes sense.
How do we get to this civilization that is based on love and life,
as opposed to death and violence, without violence? If it's the
carceral state on one side representing Thanatos and the death
drive, how do you combat that with love? Because now, in 2020,
we roll our eyes at this idea of "make love, not war," or that love
or peace is going to accomplish anything in the face of violence.
So, what is the role of imagination and contradiction and violence
in achieving this utopia?

PROFESSOR DAVIS   Well, of course, if you read "An Essay
on Liberation" by Herbert Marcuse, you will perhaps acquire
a different sense of the meaning of utopia, because he argues
there precisely that our tendency to think of utopia as no-place—
because that is the etymological meaning of the term—that
precisely as a result of the development of the kind of frantic
capitalist production and the world we inhabit now, that utopia has
not only become more meaningful, but it has become necessary,
and it is no longer the no-place, but it is an alternative. It becomes
that to which we have to resort in figuring out how to extricate
ourselves from all of the problems you referred to: Thanatos.
But at the same time, I don't know whether I would entirely
embrace that kind of binary positioning of Eros and Thanatos—
life as opposed to death. How can death itself be engaged
with in a more productive way, in a way that brings the living in
conversation with the dead? I'm thinking about in Latinx cultures
and in African cultures, the ways in which the dead are alive.
They are our ancestors. They enable us. They give us courage.
So, this is the beginning of a conversation that would be very
wide-ranging, but I don't forget the points that you made about

how to rid this world of violence, And, certainly, that is one of the major quests of our time.

I recently saw a film that you might be interested in seeing, a really remarkable documentary called *Belly of the Beast* (2020). It's about the work of an organization in the San Francisco Bay Area, Justice Now, that works with and for women in prison. The film follows a Black woman by the name of Kelli Dylan, who was sentenced to prison because she killed an abusive husband. But in prison, she was sterilized against her will and without her knowledge. As it turns out, in this prison, the Central California Women's Facility, quite a number of women, Black women especially, were sterilized—forcibly sterilized without their even knowing it. I'm mentioning this because I don't want to make light of what we have to do to rid our world of violence.

There are more guns in this country than anywhere else in the world, and more guns in civilian hands, but when we talk about disarming the population—I'm reminded of this, because almost every night in the neighborhood where I live in Oakland, I can hear gunshots—we should ask about the relationship between efforts to address the huge problem of intra-community violence, and the violence associated with police and other state apparatuses.

I would argue that we have to figure out how to articulate those issues and call for the disarming of the country. That would also have to include police. It's about imagining a different structure of safety. Why is it that we only think about safety and security in relation to police? I was talking about the ways in which the ideology of this state has taken residence in our hearts, so that we often assume that the only way we can address something negative that has been done to us is to engage in retributive behavior. So, again, this is the beginning of a very long conversation, and I totally appreciate your question.

I've thoroughly enjoyed this engagement with all of you of this morning.

DEAN KUZMA Professor Davis, thank you so much. I have to ask this question that was raised in the early morning session because we're one week away from the elections. A student, Grant Czuj, asked about the attempt by the establishment to dismantle your position as a thinker and a scholar for being a member of the Communist Party. Much of what has gone on in the political rhetoric of the last few years and certainly over the last few months has been about who is lodged as a socialist and who's not lodged as a socialist. There's this inability in America to think of a socialist imaginary, and to think of the left, not only within the categories of what we have known since neoliberalism, but within a socialist practice and habitation. So, on that point, I wondered if you could add something?

          I think the election is about all of this. We often separate electoral politics from our work as artists, our work as intellectuals, and in times of elections, we do our civic duty by going out to cast our vote. Of course, many of us confront the contradiction that there's no one to vote for, and so what is a meaningful participation in this process that does not force us into supporting candidates who we know are not going to provide viable alternatives to the other candidates who are running? I've often pointed out that my experience has been that electoral politics is not the best realm in which to engage in radical politics. I'm saying this as someone who once ran for vice president on the Communist Party ticket.

But I do think we have a responsibility to create better conditions for ourselves to do the work that can change the world, and that is what elections are all about. That is why it is so important to, at this particular moment … how should I put it? I think we're voting to clean out the White House, and it's like a negative process of cleaning it out so that we can actually begin to do work that is going to press us in more radical directions. Oftentimes, it is assumed that one goes to the polls and one votes, and we have the little "I Voted" sticker, and that's it. I think this was a real mistake during the previous election when Obama was president. People felt that just by electing a Black man to the presidency, the world was going to change, so we didn't come out into the streets, and we didn't protest, and we didn't pressure Obama. It was very important symbolically that he was elected, but there are so many things that could have happened during that period which did not. And because we didn't do the work of critique, because we didn't stand up and protest, we didn't demand that this person, Barack Obama, dismantle Guantanamo, for example, and take more progressive positions on immigration, and not—there were so many negative processes underway during the Obama administration that people didn't recognize because they were so excited that a Black man was in the presidency.

We did not do our work. That is how we ended up with this conundrum right now. So, it seems to me that imagining the part that electoral politics can play in our quest to transform the world is about recognizing that we're voting for candidates we think we can more effectively pressure and force to move in non-carceral directions, and to imagine the police as obsolete, to think about health and safety and security as not requiring armed human beings but creating other kinds of formations ensuring safety. When someone, for example, has a mental health crisis, the instinctive response should not be to call the police, but rather to call our imagined community mental health committee to reach someone who will compassionately address what is happening.

Schools, and jobs, and housing, and healthcare, and joy, and pleasure, and art—these are all the things that we need. Electoral politics is a small part of the process of attempting to move us in that direction, so, vote.

DEAN KUZMA   Professor Davis, thank you. Thank you for diving into the wreck with us today. It's phenomenal to hear your words, and it was great to see you again.

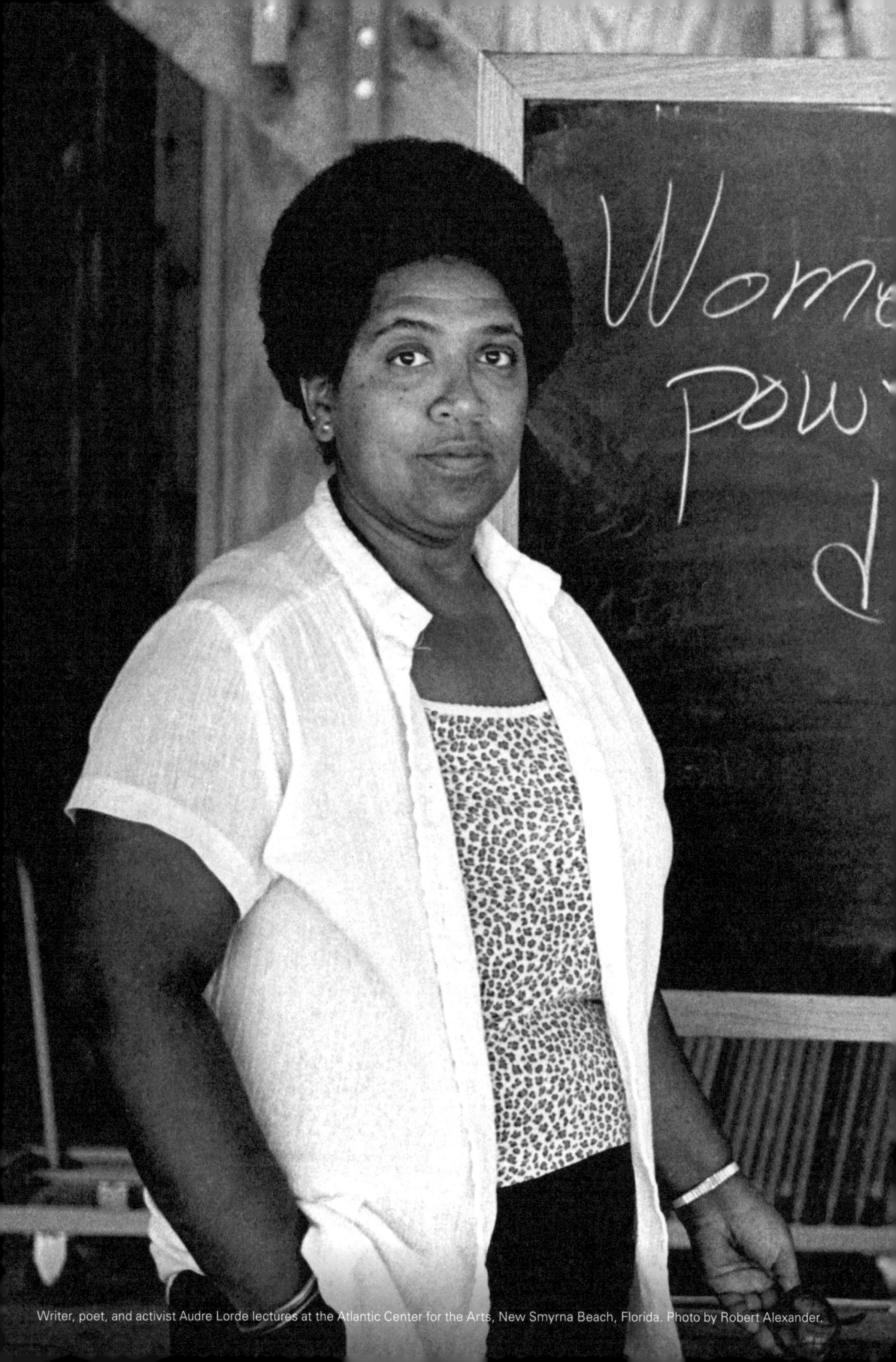

Writer, poet, and activist Audre Lorde lectures at the Atlantic Center for the Arts, New Smyrna Beach, Florida. Photo by Robert Alexander.

m are
rful and
ngerous i.

WHY HAVE THERE BEEN NO GREAT WOMEN ARTISTS?

Linda Nochlin

This essay originally appeared in the January 1971 issue of *ARTnews*

Reprinted courtesy of the Estate of Linda Nochlin,
with thanks to Daisy Pommer and Julia Trotta

1 Kate Millett's *Sexual Politics*, New York, 1970, and Mary Ellmann's *Thinking About Women*, New York, 1968 provide notable exceptions.

While the recent upsurge of feminist activity in this country has indeed been a liberating one, its force has been chiefly emotional—personal, psychological and subjective—centered, like the other radical movements to which it is related, on the present and its immediate needs, rather than on historical analysis of the basic intellectual issues which the feminist attack on the status quo automatically raises.[1] Like any revolution, however, the feminist one ultimately must come to grips with the intellectual and ideological basis of the various intellectual or scholarly disciplines—history, philosophy, sociology, psychology, etc.—in the same way that it questions the ideologies of present social institutions. If, as John Stuart Mill suggested, we tend to accept whatever is as natural, this is just as true in the realm of academic investigation as it is in our social arrangements. In the former, too, "natural" assumptions must be questioned and the mythic basis of much so-called fact brought to light. And it is here that the very position of woman as an acknowledged outsider, the maverick "she" instead of the presumably neutral "one"—in reality, the white-male-position-accepted-as-natural, or the hidden "he" as the subject of all scholarly predicates—is a decided advantage, rather than merely a hindrance of a subjective distortion.

In the field of art history, the white Western male viewpoint, unconsciously accepted as the viewpoint of the art historian, may—and does—prove to be inadequate not merely on moral and ethical grounds, or because it is elitist, but on purely intellectual ones. In revealing the failure of much academic art history, and a great deal of history in general, to take account of the unacknowledged value system, the very presence of an intruding subject in historical investigation, the feminist critique at the same time lays bare its conceptual smugness, its meta-historical naïveté. At a moment when all disciplines are becoming more self-conscious, more aware of the nature of their presuppositions as exhibited in the very languages and structures of the various fields of scholarship, such uncritical acceptance of "what is" as "natural" may be intellectually fatal. Just as Mill saw male domination as one of a long series of social injustices that had to be overcome if a truly just social order were to be created, so we may see the unstated domination of white male subjectivity as one in a series of intellectual distortions which must be corrected in order to achieve a more adequate and accurate view of historical situations.

It is the engaged feminist intellect (like John Stuart Mill's) that can pierce through the cultural-ideological limitations of the time and its specific "professionalism" to reveal biases and inadequacies not merely in the dealing with the question of women, but in the very way of formulating the crucial questions of the discipline as a whole. Thus, the so-called woman question, far from being a minor, peripheral and laughably provincial sub-issue grafted on to a serious, established discipline, can become a catalyst, an intellectual instrument, probing basic and "natural" assumptions, providing a paradigm for other kinds of internal questioning, and in turn providing links with paradigms established by radical approaches in other fields. Even a simple question like "Why have there been no great women artists?" can, if answered adequately, create a sort of chain reaction, expanding not merely to encompass the accepted assumptions of the single field, but outward to embrace history and the social sciences, or even psychology and literature, and thereby, from the outset, to challenge the assumption that the traditional divisions of intellectual inquiry are still adequate to deal with the meaningful questions of our time, rather than the merely convenient or self-generated ones.

Let us, for example, examine the implications of that perennial question (one can, of course, substitute almost any field of human endeavor, with appropriate changes in phrasing): "Well, if women really are equal to men, why have there never been any great women artists (or composers, or mathematicians, or philosophers, or so few of the same)?"

"Why have there been no great women artists?" The question tolls reproachfully in the background of most discussions of the so-called woman problem. But like so many other so-called questions involved in the feminist "controversy," it falsifies the nature of the issue at the same time that it insidiously supplies its own answer: "There are no great women artists because women are incapable of greatness."

The assumptions behind such a question are varied in range and sophistication, running anywhere from "scientifically proven" demonstrations of the inability of human beings with wombs rather than penises to create anything significant, to relatively open-minded wonderment that women, despite so many years of near-equality—and after all, a lot of men have had their disadvantages too—have still not achieved anything of exceptional significance in the visual arts.

The feminist's first reaction is to swallow the bait, hook, line and sinker, and to attempt to answer the question as it is put: i.e., to dig up examples of worthy or insufficiently appreciated women artists throughout history; to rehabilitate rather modest, if interesting and productive careers; to "re-discover" forgotten flower-painters or David-followers and make out a case for them; to demonstrate that Berthe Morisot was really less dependent upon Manet than one had been led to think—in other words, to engage in the normal activity of the specialist scholar who makes a case for the importance of his very own neglected or minor master. Such attempts, whether undertaken from a feminist point of view, like the ambitious article on women artists which appeared in the 1858 Westminster Review,[2] or more recent scholarly studies on such artists as Angelica Kauffmann and Artemisia Gentileschi,[3] are certainly worth the effort, both in adding to our knowledge of women's achievement and of art history generally. But they do nothing to question the assumptions lying behind the question "Why have there been no great women artists?" On the contrary, by attempting to answer it, they tacitly reinforce its negative implications.

Another attempt to answer the question involves shifting the ground slightly and asserting, as some contemporary feminists do, that there is a different kind of "greatness" for women's art than for men's, thereby postulating the existence of a distinctive and recognizable feminine style, different both in its formal and its expressive qualities and based on the special character of women's situation and experience.

This, on the surface of it, seems reasonable enough: in general, women's experience and situation in society, and hence as artists,

2 "Women Artists," Review of *Die Frauen in die Kunstgeschichte* by Ernst Guhl in *The Westminster Review* (American Edition), LXX, July, 1958, 91–104. I am grateful to Elaine Showalter for having brought this review to my attention.

3 See, for example, Peter S. Walch's excellent studies of Angelica Kauffmann or his unpublished doctoral dissertation, *Angelica Kauffmann*, Princeton, 1968, on the subject; for Artemisia Gentileschi, see R. Ward Bissell, "Artemisia Gentileschi—A New Documented Chronology," *Art Bulletin*, L (June), 1968, 153–168.

is different from men's, and certainly the art produced by a group
of consciously united and purposefully articulate women intent
on bodying forth a group consciousness of feminine experience
might indeed be stylistically identifiable as feminist, if not feminine, art. Unfortunately, though this remains within the realm of
possibility it has so far not occurred. While the members of the
Danube School, the followers of Caravaggio, the painters gathered
around Gauguin at Pont-Aven, the Blue Rider, or the Cubists may
be recognized by certain clearly defined stylistic or expressive
qualities, no such common qualities of "femininity" would seem
to link the styles of women artists generally, any more than such
qualities can be said to link women writers, a case brilliantly
argued, against the most devastating, and mutually contradictory,
masculine critical clichés, by Mary Ellmann in her Thinking about
Women.[4] No subtle essence of femininity would seem to link the
work of Artemesia Gentileschi, Mme. Vigée-Lebrun, Angelica
Kauffmann, Rosa Bonheur, Berthe Morisot, Suzanne Valadon,
Kaethe Kollwitz, Barbara Hepworth, Georgia O'Keeffe, Sophie
Taeuber-Arp, Helen Frankenthaler, Bridget Riley, Lee Bontecou or
Louise Nevelson, any more than that of Sappho, Marie de France,
Jane Austen, Emily Brontë, George Sand, George Eliot, Virginia
Woolf, Gertrude Stein, Anaïs Nin, Emily Dickinson, Sylvia Plath
and Susan Sontag. In every instance, women artists and writers
would seem to be closer to other artists and writers of their own
period and outlook than they are to each other.

Women artists are more inward-looking, more delicate and
nuanced in their treatment of their medium, it may be asserted.
But which of the women artists cited above is more inward-
turning than Redon, more subtle and nuanced in the handling
of pigment than Corot? Is Fragonard more or less feminine than
Mme. Vigée-Lebrun? Or is it not more a question of the whole
Rococo style of 18th-century France being "feminine," if judged
in terms of a two-valued scale of "masculinity" vs. "femininity"?
Certainly though, if daintiness, delicacy and preciousness are
to be counted as earmarks of a feminine style, there is nothing
fragile about Rosa Bonheur's Horse Fair, nor dainty and intro-
verted about Helen Frankenthaler's giant canvases. If women
have turned to scenes of domestic life, or of children, so did
Jan Steen, Chardin and the Impressionists—Renoir and Monet
as well as Morisot and Cassatt. In any case, the mere choice
of a certain realm of subject matter, or the restriction to certain

4   New York, 1968.

   LINDA NOCHLIN

subjects, is not to be equated with a style, much less with some
sort of quintessentially feminine style.

The problem lies not so much with the feminists' concept of
what femininity is, but rather with their misconception—shared
with the public at large—of what art is: with the naïve idea that
art is the direct, personal expression of individual emotional
experience, a translation of personal life into visual terms. Art is
almost never that, great art never is. The making of art involves
a self-consistent language of form, more or less dependent
upon, or free from, given temporally-defined conventions,
schemata or systems of notation, which have to be learned or
worked out, either through teaching, apprenticeship or a long
period of individual experimentation. The language of art is, more
materially, embodied in paint and line on canvas or paper, in
stone or clay or plastic or metal—it is neither a sob-story nor a
confidential whisper.

The fact of the matter is that there have been no supremely
great women artists, as far as we know, although there have been
many interesting and very good ones who remain insufficiently
investigated or appreciated; nor have there been any great
Lithuanian jazz pianists, nor Eskimo tennis players, no matter how
much we might wish there had been. That this should be the
case is regrettable, but no amount of manipulating the historical
or critical evidence will alter the situation; nor will accusations of
male-chauvinist distortion of history. The fact, dear sisters, is that
there are no women equivalents for Michelangelo or Rembrandt,
Delacroix or Cézanne, Picasso or Matisse, or even, in very recent
times, for de Kooning or Warhol, any more than there are Black
American equivalents for the same. If there actually were large
numbers of "hidden" great women artists, or if there really should
be different standards for women's art as opposed to men's—
and one can't have it both ways—then what are the feminists
fighting for? If women have in fact achieved the same status as
men in the arts, then the status quo is fine as it is.

But in actuality, as we all know, things as they are and as they
have been, in the arts as in a hundred other areas, are stulti-
fying, oppressive and discouraging to all those, women among
them, who did not have the good fortune to be born white,
preferably middle class and, above all, male. The fault, dear
brothers, lies not in our stars, our hormones, our menstrual
cycles or our empty internal spaces, but in our institutions and

our education—education understood to include everything
that happens to us from the moment we enter this world of
meaningful symbols, signs and signals. The miracle is, in fact,
that given the overwhelming odds against women, or blacks,
that so many of both have managed to achieve so much sheer
excellence, in those bailiwicks of white masculine prerogative
like science, politics or the arts.

It is when one really starts thinking about the implications of
"Why have there been no great women artists?" that one begins
to realize to what extent our consciousness of how things are
in the world has been conditioned—and often falsified—by the
way the most important questions are posed. We tend to take it
for granted that there really is an East Asian Problem, a Poverty
Problem, a Black Problem—and a Woman Problem. But first
we must ask ourselves who is formulating these "questions,"
and then, what purposes such formulations may serve. (We may,
of course, refresh our memories with the connotations of the
Nazi's "Jewish Problem.") Indeed, in our time of instant communication, "problems" are rapidly formulated to rationalize
the bad conscience of those with power: thus the problem
posed by Americans in Vietnam and Cambodia is referred to by
Americans as "the East Asian Problem," whereas East Asians
may view it, more realistically, as "the American Problem";
the so-called Poverty Problem might more directly be viewed
as the "Wealth Problem" by denizens of urban ghettos or rural
wastelands; the same irony twists the White Problem into its
opposite: a Black Problem; and the same inverse logic turns
up in the formulation of our own present state of affairs as the
"Woman Problem."

Now the "Woman Problem," like all human problems, so-called
(and the very idea of calling anything to do with human beings
a "problem" is, of course, a fairly recent one) is not amenable
to "solution" at all, since what human problems involve is re-
interpretation of the nature of the situation, or a radical alteration
of stance or program *on the part of the "problems" themselves*.
Thus women and their situation in the arts, as in other realms of
endeavor, are not a "problem" to be viewed through the eyes
of the dominant male power elite. Instead, *women* must conceive
of themselves as potentially, if not actually, equal subjects,
and must be willing to look the facts of their situation full in
the face, without self-pity, or cop-outs; at the same time they

must view their situation with that high degree of emotional and intellectual commitment necessary to create a world in which equal achievement will be not only made possible but actively encouraged by social institutions.

It is certainly not realistic to hope that a majority of men, in the arts, or in any other field, will soon see the light and find that it is in their own self-interest to grant complete equality to women, as some feminists optimistically assert, or to maintain that men themselves will soon realize that they are diminished by denying themselves access to traditionally "feminine" realms and emotional reactions. After all, there are few areas that are really "denied" to men, if the level of operations demanded be transcendent, responsible or rewarding enough: men who have a need for "feminine" involvement with babies or children gain status as pediatricians or child psychologists, with a nurse (female) to do the more routine work; those who feel the urge for kitchen creativity may gain fame as master chefs; and, of course, men who yearn to fulfill themselves through what are often termed "feminine" artistic interests can find themselves as painters or sculptors, rather than as volunteer museum aides or part time ceramists, as their female counterparts so often end up doing; as far as scholarship is concerned, how many men would be willing to change their jobs as teachers and researchers for those of unpaid, part-time research assistants and typists as well as full-time nannies and domestic workers?

Those who have privileges inevitably hold on to them, and hold tight, no matter how marginal the advantage involved, until compelled to bow to superior power of one sort or another.

Thus the question of women's equality—in art as in any other realm—devolves not upon the relative benevolence or ill-will of individual men, nor the self-confidence or abjectness of individual women, but rather on the very nature of our institutional structures themselves and the view of reality which they impose on the human beings who are part of them. As John Stuart Mill pointed out more than a century ago: "Everything which is usual appears natural. The subjection of women to men being a universal custom, any departure from it quite naturally appears unnatural."[5] Most men, despite lip-service to equality, are reluctant to give up this "natural" order of things in which their advantages are so great; for women, the case is further complicated by the fact that, as Mill astutely pointed out, unlike

5   John Stuart Mill, *The Subjection of Women* (1869) in *Three Essays by John Stuart Mill*, World's Classics Series, London, 1966, p. 441.

other oppressed groups or castes, men demand of her not only submission but unqualified affection as well; thus women are often weakened by the internalized demands of the male-dominated society itself, as well as by a plethora of material goods and comforts: the middle-class woman has a great deal more to lose than her chains.

The question "Why have there been no great women artists?" is simply the top tenth of an iceberg of misinterpretation and misconception; beneath lies a vast dark bulk of shaky *idées reçues* about the nature of art and its situational concomitants, about the nature of human abilities in general and of human excellence in particular, and the role that the social order plays in all of this. While the "woman problem" as such may be a pseudo-issue, the misconceptions involved in the question "Why have there been no great women artists?" points to major areas of intellectual obfuscation beyond the specific political and ideological issues involved in the subjection of women. Basic to the question are many naïve, distorted, uncritical assumptions about the making of art in general, as well as the making of great art. These assumptions, conscious or unconscious, link together such unlikely superstars as Michelangelo and van Gogh, Raphael and Jackson Pollock under the rubric of "Great"— an honorific attested to by the number of scholarly monographs devoted to the artist in question—and the Great Artist is, of course, conceived of as one who has "Genius"; Genius, in turn, is thought of as an atemporal and mysterious power somehow embedded in the person of the Great Artist.[6] Such ideas are related to unquestioned, often unconscious, meta-historical premises that make Hippolyte Taine's race-milieu-moment formulation of the dimensions of historical thought seem a model of sophistication. But these assumptions are intrinsic to a great deal of art-historical writing. It is no accident that the crucial question of the conditions *generally* productive of great art has so rarely been investigated, or that attempts to investigate such general problems have, until fairly recently, been dismissed as unscholarly, too broad, or the province of some other discipline, like sociology. To encourage a dispassionate, impersonal, sociological and institutionally-oriented approach would reveal the entire romantic, elitist, individual-glorifying and monograph-producing substructure upon which the profession of art history is based, and which has

6   For the relatively recent genesis of the emphasis on the artist as the nexus of esthetic experience, see M. H. Abrams, *The Mirror and the Lamp: Romantic Theory and the Critical Tradition*, New York, 1953, and Maurice Z. Shrader, *Icarus: The Image of the Artist in French Romanticism*, Cambridge, Massachusetts, 1961.

only recently been called in to question by a group of younger dissidents.

Underlying the question about woman as artist, then, we find the myth of the Great Artist—subject of a hundred monographs, unique, godlike—bearing within his person since birth a mysterious essence, rather like the golden nugget in Mrs. Grass' chicken soup, called Genius or Talent, which, like murder, must always out, no matter how unlikely or unpromising the circumstances.

The magical aura surrounding the representational arts and their creators has, of course, given birth to myths since the earliest times. Interestingly enough, the same magical abilities attributed by Pliny to the Greek sculptor Lysippos in antiquity—the mysterious inner call in early youth, the lack of any teacher but Nature herself—is repeated as late as the 19th century by Max Buchon in his biography of Courbet. The supernatural powers of the artist as imitator, his control of strong, possibly dangerous powers, have functioned historically to set him off from others as a godlike creator, one who creates Being out of nothing. The fairy tale of the Boy Wonder, discovered by an older artist or discerning patron, usually in the guise of a lowly shepherd boy, has been a stock-in-trade of artistic mythology ever since Vasari immortalized the young Giotto, discovered by the great Cimabue while the lad was guarding his flocks, drawing sheep on a stone; Cimabue, overcome with admiration by the realism of the drawing, immediately invited the humble youth to be his pupil.[7] Through some mysterious coincidence, later artists including Beccafumi, Andrea Sansovino, Andrea del Castagno, Mantegna, Zurbaran and Goya were all discovered in similar pastoral circumstances. Even when the young Great Artist was not fortunate enough to come equipped with a flock of sheep, his talent always seems to have manifested itself very early, and independent of any external encouragement: Filippo Lippi and Poussin, Courbet and Monet are all reported to have drawn caricatures in the margins of their schoolbooks instead of studying the required subjects—we never, of course, hear about the youths who neglected their studies and scribbled in the margins of their notebooks without ever becoming anything more elevated than department-store clerks or shoe salesmen. The great Michelangelo himself, according to his biographer and pupil, Vasari, did more drawing than studying as a child.

7   A comparison with the parallel myth for women, the Cinderella Story, is revealing: Cinderella gains higher status on the basis of a passive, "sex-object" attribute—small feet—whereas the Boy Wonder always proves himself through active accomplishment. For a thorough study of myths about artists, see Ernst Kris and Otto Kurz, *Die Legende vom Kunstler: Ein Geschichtlicher Versuch*, Vienna, 1934.

So pronounced was his talent, reports Vasari, that when his master, Ghirlandaio, absented himself momentarily from his work in Santa Maria Novella, and the young art student took the opportunity to draw "the scaffolding, trestles, pots of paint, brushes and the apprentices at their tasks" in this brief absence, he did it so skillfully that upon his return the master exclaimed: "This boy knows more than I do."

As is so often the case, such stories, which probably have some truth in them, tend both to reflect and perpetuate the attitudes they subsume. Despite any basis in fact of these myths about the early manifestations of Genius, the tenor of the tales is misleading. It is no doubt true, for example, that the young Picasso passed all the examinations for entrance to the Barcelona, and later to the Madrid, Academy of Art at the age of 15 in but a single day, a feat of such difficulty that most candidates required a month of preparation. But one would like to find out more about similar precocious qualifiers for art academies who then went on to achieve nothing but mediocrity or failure—in whom, of course, art historians are uninterested—or to study in greater detail the role played by Picasso's art-professor father in the pictorial precocity of his son. What if Picasso had been born a girl? Would Señor Ruiz have paid as much attention or stimulated as much ambition for achievement in a little Pablita?

What is stressed in all these stories is the apparently miraculous, non-determined and a-social nature of artistic achievement; this semi-religious conception of the artist's role is elevated to hagiography in the 19th century, when both art historians, critics and, not least, some of the artists themselves tended to elevate the making of art into a substitute religion, the last bulwark of Higher Values in a materialistic world. The artist, in the 19th-century Saints' Legend, struggles against the most determined parental and social opposition, suffering the slings and arrows of social opprobrium like any Christian martyr, and ultimately succeeds against all odds—generally, alas, after his death—because from deep within himself radiates that mysterious, holy effulgence: Genius. Here we have the mad van Gogh, spinning out sunflowers despite epileptic seizures and near-starvation; Cézanne, braving paternal rejection and public scorn in order to revolutionize painting; Gauguin throwing away respectability and financial security with a single existential gesture to pursue his Calling in the tropics, or Toulouse-Lautrec, dwarfed, crippled and alchoholic [*sic*], sacrificing his aristocratic birthright in favor of the squalid surroundings that provided him with inspiration, etc.

Now no serious contemporary art historian takes such obvious fairy tales at their face value. Yet it is this sort of mythology about artistic achievement and its concomitants which forms the unconscious or unquestioned assumptions of scholars, no matter how many crumbs are thrown to social influences, ideas of the times, economic crises and so on. Behind the most sophisticated investigations of great artists—more specifically, the art-historical monograph, which accepts the notion of the Great Artist as primary, and the social and institutional structures within which he lived and worked as mere secondary "influences" or "background"—lurks the golden-nugget theory of genius and the free-enterprise conception of individual achievement. On this basis, women's lack of major achievement in art may be formulated as a syllogism: If women had the golden nugget of artistic genius then it would reveal itself. But it has never revealed itself. Q.E.D. Women do not have the golden nugget of artistic genius. If Giotto, the obscure shepherd boy, and van Gogh with his fits could make it, why not women?

Yet as soon as one leaves behind the world of fairy-tale and self-fulfilling prophecy and, instead, casts a dispassionate eye on the actual situations in which important art production has existed, in the total range of its social and institutional structures throughout history, one finds that the very questions which are fruitful or relevant for the historian to ask shape up rather differently. One would like to ask, for instance, from what social classes artists were most likely to come at different periods of art history, from what castes and sub-group. What proportion of painters and sculptors, or more specifically, of major painters and sculptors, came from families in which their fathers or other close relatives were painters and sculptors or engaged in related professions? As Nikolaus Pevsner points out in his discussion of the French Academy in the 17th and 18th centuries, the transmission of the artistic profession from father to son was considered a matter of course (as it was with the Coypels, the Coustous, the Van Loos, etc); indeed, sons of academicians were exempted from the customary fees for lessons.[8] Despite the noteworthy and dramatically satisfying cases of the great father-rejecting *révoltés* of the 19th century, one might be forced to admit that a large

8   Nikolaus Pevsner, *Academies of Art, Past and Present*, Cambridge, 1940, p. 96f.

proportion of artists, great and not-so-great, in the days when
it was normal for sons to follow in their fathers' footsteps, had
artist fathers. In the rank of major artists, the names of Holbein
and Dürer, Raphael and Bernini, immediately spring to mind;
even in our own times, one can cite the names of Picasso,
Calder, Giacometti and Wyeth as members of artist-families.

As far as the relationship of artistic occupation and social
class is concerned, an interesting paradigm for the question
"Why have there been no great women artists?" might well be
provided by trying to answer the question: "Why have there been
no great artists from the aristocracy?" One can scarcely think,
before the anti-traditional 19th century at least, of any artist who
sprang from the ranks of any more elevated class than the upper
bourgeoisie; even in the 19th century, Degas came from the
lower nobility—more like the haute bourgeoisie, in fact—and only
Toulouse-Lautrec, metamorphosed into the ranks of the marginal
by accidental deformity, could be said to have come from the
loftier reaches of the upper classes. While the aristocracy has
always provided the lion's share of the patronage and the audience for art—as, indeed, the aristocracy of wealth does even
in our more democratic days—it has contributed little beyond
amateurish efforts to the creation of art itself, despite the fact
that aristocrats (like many women) have had more than their
share of educational advantages, plenty of leisure and, indeed,
like women, were often encouraged to dabble in the arts and
even develop into respectable amateurs, like Napoleon III's
cousin, the Princess Mathilde, who exhibited at the official
Salons, or Queen Victoria, who, with Prince Albert, studied art
with no less a figure than Landseer himself. Could it be that the
little golden nugget—Genius—is missing from the aristocratic
make-up in the same way that it is from the feminine psyche?
Or rather, is it not, that the kinds of demands and expectations
placed before both aristocrats and women—the amount of
time necessarily devoted to social functions, the very kinds of
activities demanded—simply made total devotion to professional
art production out of the question, indeed unthinkable, both for
upper-class males and for women generally, rather than its being
a question of genius and talent?

When the right questions are asked about the conditions for
producing art, of which the production of great art is a sub-
topic, there will no doubt have to be some discussion of the

situational concomitants of intelligence and talent generally, not merely of artistic genius. Piaget and others have stressed in their genetic epistemology that in the development of reason and in the unfolding of imagination in young children, intelligence—or, by implication, what we choose to call genius—is a dynamic activity rather than a static essence, and an activity of a subject *in a situation*. As further investigations in the field of child development imply, these abilities, or this intelligence, are built up minutely, step by step, from infancy onward, and the patterns of adaptation-accommodation may be established so early within the subject-in-an-environment that they may indeed *appear* to be innate to the unsophisticated observer. Such investigations imply that, even aside from meta-historical reasons, scholars will have to abandon the notion, consciously articulated or not, of individual genius as innate, and as primary to the creation of art.[9]

9 Contemporary directions—earthworks, conceptual art, art as information, etc.—certainly point away from emphasis on the individual genius and his salable products; in art history, Harrison C. and Cynthia A. White's *Canvases and Careers: Institutional Change in the French Painting World*, New York, 1965, opens up a fruitful new direction of investigation, as did Nikolaus Pevsner's pioneering *Academies of Art*. Ernst Gombrich and Pierre Francastel, in their very different ways, always have tended to view art and the artist as part of a total situation rather than in lofty isolation.

The question "Why have there been no great women artists?" has led us to the conclusion, so far, that art is not a free, autonomous activity of a super-endowed individual, "influenced" by previous artists, and, more vaguely and superficially, by "social forces," but rather, that the total situation of art making, both in terms of the development of the art maker and in the nature and quality of the work of art itself, occur in a social situation, are integral elements of this social structure, and are mediated and determined by specific and definable social institutions, be they art academies, systems of patronage, mythologies of the divine creator, artist as he-man or social outcast.

THE QUESTION OF THE NUDE

We can now approach our question from a more reasonable standpoint, since it seems probable that the answer to why there have been no great women artists lies not in the nature of individual genius or the lack of it, but in the nature of given social institutions and what they forbid or encourage in various classes or groups of individuals.

Let us first examine such a simple, but critical, issue as availability of the nude model to aspiring women artists, in the period extending from the Renaissance until near the end of

the 19th century, a period in which careful and prolonged study
of the nude model was essential to the training of every young
artist, to the production of any work with pretentions to grandeur,
and to the very essence of History Painting, generally accepted
as the highest category of art: indeed, it was argued by defenders
of traditional painting in the 19th century that there could be
no great painting *with* clothed figures, since costume inevitably
destroyed both the temporal universality and the classical
idealization required by great art. Needless to say, central to
the training programs of the academies since their inception late
in the 16th and early in the 17th centuries, was life drawing from
the nude, generally male, model. In addition, groups
of artists and their pupils often met privately for life
drawing sessions from the nude model in their studios.
In general, it might be added, while individual artists
and private academies employed the female model
extensively, the female nude was forbidden in almost
all public art schools as late as 1850 and after—
a state of affairs which Pevsner rightly designates as "hardly
believable."[10] Far more believable, unfortunately, was the
complete unavailability to the aspiring woman artist of any nude
models at all, male or female. As late as 1893, "lady" students
were not admitted to life drawing at the Royal Academy in
London, and even when they were, after that date, the model
had to be "partially draped."[11]

A brief survey of representations of life-drawing sessions
reveals: an all male clientele drawing from the female nude in
Rembrandt's studio; men working from male nudes in 18th-
century representations of academic instruction in The Hague
and Vienna; men working from the seated male nude in Bailly's
charming painting of the interior of Houdon's studio at the beginning of the 19th century; Mathieu Cochereau's scrupulously
veristic *Interior of David's Studio*, exhibited in the Salon of 1814,
reveals a group of young men diligently drawing or painting
from a male nude model, whose discarded shoes may be seen
before the models' stand.

The very plethora of surviving "Academies"—detailed, painstaking studies from the nude studio model—in the youthful
oeuvre of artists down through the time of Seurat and well
into the 20th century, attests to the central importance of
this branch of study in the pedagogy and development of the

10   Female models were
introduced in the life-class in
Berlin in 1875, in Stockholm
in 1839, in Naples in 1870,
at the Royal College of Art in
London, after 1875. Pevsner,
op. cit., p. 231. Female models
at the Pennsylvania Academy
of the Fine Arts wore masks
to hide their identity as late as
about 1866—as attested to in
a charcoal drawing by Thomas
Eakins—if not later.

11   Pevsner, op. cit., p. 231.

talented beginner. The formal academic program itself normally proceeded, as a matter of course, from copying from drawings and engravings, to drawing from casts of famous works of sculpture, to drawing from the living model. To be deprived of this ultimate stage of training meant, in effect, to be deprived of the possibility of creating major art works, unless one were a very ingenious lady indeed, or simply, as most of the women aspiring to be painters ultimately did, to restrict oneself to the "minor" fields of portraiture, genre, landscape or still-life. It is rather as though a medical student were denied the opportunity to dissect or even examine the naked human body.

There exist, to my knowledge, no representations of artists drawing from the nude model which include women in any role but that of the nude model itself, an interesting commentary on rules of propriety: i.e., it is all right for a ("low," of course) woman to reveal herself naked-as-an-object for a group of men, but forbidden to a woman to participate in the active study and recording of naked-man-as-an-object, or even of a fellow woman. An amusing example of this taboo on confronting a dressed lady with a naked man is embodied in a group portrait of the members of the Royal Academy in London in 1772, represented by Zoffany as gathered in the life room before two nude male models: all the distinguished members are present with but one noteworthy exception—the single female member, the renowned Angelica Kauffmann, who, for propriety's sake, is merely present in effigy, in the form of a portrait hanging on the wall. A slightly earlier drawing of *Ladies in the Studio* by the Polish artist Daniel Chodowiecki, shows the ladies portraying a modestly dressed member of their sex. In a lithograph dating from the relatively liberated epoch following the French Revolution, the lithographer Marlet has represented some women sketchers in a group of students working from the male model, but the model himself has been chastely provided with what appears to be a pair of bathing trunks, a garment hardly conducive to a sense of classical elevation: no doubt such license was considered daring in its day, and the young ladies in question suspected of doubtful morals, but even this liberated state of affairs seems to have lasted only a short while. In an English stereoscopic color view of the interior of a studio of about 1865, the standing, bearded male model is so heavily draped that not an iota of his anatomy escapes from the discreet toga, save for a single bare shoulder and arm: even so, he obviously had the grace to avert his eyes in the presence of the crinoline-clad young sketchers.

The women in the Women's Modeling Class at the Pennsylvania Academy were evidently not allowed even this modest privilege. A photograph by Thomas Eakins of about 1885 reveals these students modeling from a cow (bull? ox? the nether regions are obscure in the photograph), a naked cow to be sure, perhaps a daring liberty when one considers that even piano legs might be concealed beneath pantalettes during this era (the idea of introducing a bovine model into the artist's studio stems from Courbet, who brought a bull into his short-lived studio academy in the 1860s). Only at the very end of the 19th century, in the relatively liberated and open atmosphere of Repin's studio and circle in Russia, do we find representations of women art students working uninhibitedly from the nude—the female model, to be sure—in the company of men. Even in this case, it must be noted that certain photographs represent a private sketch group meeting in one of the women artists' homes; in the other, the model is draped; and the large group portrait, a co-operative effort by two men and two women students of Repin's, is an imaginary gathering together of all of the Russian realist's pupils, past and present, rather than a realistic studio view.

I have gone into the question of the availability of the nude model, a single aspect of the automatic, institutionally-maintained discrimination against women, in such detail simply to demonstrate both the universality of the discrimination against women and its consequences, as well as the institutional rather than individual nature of but one facet of the necessary preparation for achieving mere proficiency, much less greatness, in the realm of art during a long stretch of time. One could equally well examine other dimensions of the situation, such as the apprenticeship system, the academic educational pattern which, in France especially, was almost the only key to success and which had a regular progression and set competitions, crowned by the Prix de Rome which enabled the young winner to work in the French Academy in that city—unthinkable for women, of course—and for which women were unable to compete until the end of the 19th century, by which time, in fact, the whole academic system had lost its importance anyway. It seems clear, to take France in the 19th century as an example, a country which probably had a larger proportion of women artists than

12 H. C. and C. A. White, op. cit., p. 51.

13 Ibid., Table 5.

any other—that is to say, in terms of their percentage in the total number of artists exhibiting in the Salon—that "women were not accepted as professional painters."[12] In the middle of the century, there were only a third as many women as men artists, but even this mildly encouraging statistic is deceptive when we discover that out of this relatively meager number, none had attended that major stepping stone to artistic success, the Ecole des Beaux-Arts, only 7 percent had received any official commission or had held any official office—and these might include the most menial sort of work—only 7 percent had ever received any Salon medal, and *none* had ever received the Legion of Honor.[13] Deprived of encouragements, educational facilities and rewards, it is almost incredible that a certain percentage of women did persevere and seek a profession in the arts.

It also becomes apparent why women were able to compete on far more equal terms with men—and even become innovators—in literature. While art-making traditionally has demanded the learning of specific techniques and skills, in a certain sequence, in an institutional setting outside the home, as well as becoming familiar with a specific vocabulary of iconography and motifs, the same is by no means true for the poet or novelist. Anyone, even a women, has to learn the language, can learn to read and write, and can commit personal experiences to paper in the privacy of one's room. Naturally this oversimplifies the real difficulties and complexities involved in creating good or great literature, whether by man or woman, but it still gives a clue as to the possibility of the existence of Emily Brönte or an Emily Dickinson, and the lack of their counterparts, at least until quite recently, in the visual arts.

Of course we have not gone into the "fringe" requirements for major artists, which would have been, for the most part, both psychically and socially closed to women, even if hypothetically they could have achieved the requisite grandeur in the performance of their craft: in the Renaissance and after, the great artist, aside from participating in the affairs of an academy, might well be intimate with members of humanist circles with whom he could exchange ideas, establish suitable relationships with patrons, travel widely and freely, perhaps politic and intrigue; nor have we mentioned the sheer organizational acumen and ability involved in running a major studio-factory, like that of Rubens. An enormous amount of self-confidence and worldly

knowledgeability, as well as a natural sense of well-earned
dominance and power, was needed by the great *chef d'école*,
both in the running of the production end of painting, and in the
control and instruction of the numerous students and assistants.

In contrast to the single-mindedness and commitment demanded
of a *chef d'école*, we might set the image of the "lady painter"
established by 19th-century etiquette books and reinforced by
the literature of the times. It is precisely the insistence upon
a modest, proficient, self-demeaning level of amateurism as a
"suitable accomplishment" for the well-brought up young woman,
who naturally would want to direct her major attention to the
welfare of others—family and husband—that militated, and still
militates, against any real accomplishment on the part of women.
It is this emphasis which transforms serious commitment
to frivolous self-indulgence, busy work or occupational therapy,
and today, more than ever, in suburban bastions of the feminine
mystique, tends to distort the whole notion of what art is and
what kind of social role it plays. In Mrs. Ellis' widely read
The Family Monitor and Domestic Guide, published before the
middle of the 19th century, a book of advice popular both in
the United States and in England, women were warned against
the snare of trying too hard to excel in any one thing:

It must not be supposed that the writer is one who would
advocate, as essential to woman, any very extraordinary degree
of intellectual attainment, especially if confined to one particular
branch of study. "I should like to excel in something" is a frequent
and, to some extent, laudable expression; but in what does it
originate, and to what does it tend? To be able to do a great many
things tolerably well, is of infinitely more value to a woman, than to
be able to excel in any one. By the former, she may render herself
generally useful: by the latter, she may dazzle for an hour. By being
apt, and tolerably well skilled in everything, she may fall into any
situation in life with dignity and ease—by devoting her time to
excellence in one, she may remain incapable of every other.

So far as cleverness, learning, and knowledge are conducive
to woman's moral excellence, they are therefore desirable, and no
further. All that would occupy her mind to the exclusion of better
things, all that would involve her in the mazes of flattery and

admiration, all that would tend to draw away her thoughts from others and fix them on herself, ought to be avoided as an evil to her, however brilliant or attractive it may be in itself.[14]

Lest we are tempted to laugh, we may refresh ourselves with more recent samples of exactly the same message cited in Betty Friedan's *Feminine Mystique*, or in the pages of recent issues of popular women's magazines.

This advice has a familiar ring, of course: propped up by a bit of Freudianism and some tag-lines from the social sciences about the well-rounded personality, preparation for woman's chief career, marriage, and the unfemininity of deep involvement with work rather than sex, it is still the mainstay of the Feminine Mystique. Such an outlook helps guard man from unwanted competition in his "serious" professional activities and assures him of "well-rounded" assistance on the home front, so that he may have sex and family in addition to the fulfillment of his own specialized talent and excellence at the same time.

As far as painting specifically is concerned, Mrs. Ellis finds that it has one immediate advantage for the young lady over its rival branch of artistic activity, music—it is quiet and disturbs no one (this negative virtue, of course, would not be true of sculpture, but accomplishment with the hammer and chisel simply never occurs as a suitable accomplishment for the weaker sex); in addition, says Mrs. Ellis, "it [drawing] is an employment which beguiles the mind of many cares…Drawing is, of all other occupations, the one most calculated to keep the mind from brooding upon self, and to maintain that general cheerfulness which is a part of social and domestic duty…It can also," she adds, "be laid down and resumed, as circumstance or inclination may direct, and that without any serious loss."[15] Again, lest we feel that we have made a great deal of progress in this area in the past 100 years, I might bring up the remark of a bright young doctor who, when the conversation turned to his wife and her friends "dabbling" in the arts, snorted: "Well, at least it keeps them out of trouble!" Now as in the 19th century, amateurism and lack of real commitment as well as snobbery and emphasis on chic on the part of women in their artistic "hobbies," feeds the contempt of the successful, professionally committed man who is engaged in "real" work and can, with a certain justice, point to his wife's lack of seriousness in her artistic activities. For such men, the "real" work of women is only that which directly or indirectly

14   Mrs. Ellis, "The Daughters of England: Their Position in Society, Character, and Responsibilities" (1844) in *The Family Monitor*, New York, 1844, p. 35.

15   Ibid., 38–39.

serves the family; any other commitment falls under the rubric
of diversion, selfishness, egomania or, at the unspoken extreme,
castration. The circle is a vicious one, in which philistinism and
frivolity mutually re-enforce each other.

In literature, as in life, even if the woman's commitment to art
was a serious one, she was expected to drop her career and
give up this commitment at the behest of love and marriage: this
lesson is, today as in the 19th century, still inculcated in young
girls, directly or indirectly, from the moment they are born. Even
the determined and successful heroine of Mrs. Craik's mid-19th-
century novel about feminine artistic success, *Olive*, a young
woman who lives alone, strives for fame and independence
and actually supports herself through her art—such unfeminine
behavior is at least partly excused by the fact that she is a cripple
and automatically considers that marriage is denied to her—
even Olive ultimately succumbs to the blandishments of love
and marriage. To paraphrase the words of Patricia Thomson in
The Victorian Heroine, Mrs. Craik, having shot her bolt in the
course of her novel, is content, finally, to let her heroine, whose
ultimate greatness the reader has never been able to doubt,
sink gently into matrimony. "Of Olive, Mrs. Craik comments
imperturbably that her husband's influence is to deprive the
Scottish Academy of 'no one knew how many grand pictures.'"[16]
Then as now, despite men's greater "tolerance," the choice for
women seems always to be marriage or a career, i.e., solitude
as the price of success or sex and companionship at the price
of professional renunciation.

That achievement in the arts, as in any field of endeavor,
demands struggle and sacrifice, no one would deny; that this
has certainly been true after the middle of the 19th century,
when the traditional institutions of artistic support and patronage
no longer fulfilled their customary obligations, is undeniable:
one has only to think of Delacroix, Courbet, Degas, van Gogh
and Toulouse-Lautrec as examples of great artists who gave up
the distractions and obligations of family life, at least in part, so
that they could pursue their artistic careers more singlemindedly.
Yet none of them was automatically denied the pleasures of sex
or companionship on account of this choice. Nor did they ever
conceive that they had sacrificed their manhood or their sexual
role on account of their singleness and singlemindedness in order
to achieve professional fulfillment. But if the artist in question

16   Patricia Thomson, *The Victorian Heroine: A Changing Ideal*, London, 1956, p. 77.

happens to be a woman, 1,000 years of guilt, self-doubt and objecthood have been added to the undeniable difficulties of being an artist in the modern world.

The unconscious aura of titillation that arises from a visual representation of an aspiring woman artist in the mid-19th century, Emily Mary Osborne's heartfelt painting, *Nameless and Friendless*, 1857, a canvas representing a poor but lovely and respectable young girl at a London art dealer, nervously awaiting the verdict of the pompous proprietor about the worth of her canvases while two ogling "art lovers" look on, is really not too different in its underlying assumptions from an overtly salacious work like Bompard's *Debut of the Model*. The theme in both is innocence, delicious feminine innocence, exposed to the world. It is the charming *vulnerability* of the young woman artist, like that of the hesitating model, which is really the subject of Miss Osborne's painting, not the value of the young woman's work or her pride in it: the issue here is, as usual, sexual rather than serious. Always a model but never an artist might well have served as the motto of the seriously aspiring young woman in the arts of the 19th century.

SUCCESSES

But what of the small band of heroic women, who, throughout the ages, despite obstacles, have achieved pre-eminence, if not the pinnacles of grandeur of a Michelangelo, a Rembrandt or a Picasso? Are there any qualities that may be said to have characterized them as a group and as individuals? While we cannot go into such an investigation in depth in this article, we can point to a few striking characteristics of women artists generally: they all, almost without exception, were either the daughters of artist fathers, or, generally later, in the 19th and 20th centuries, had a close personal connection with a stronger or more dominant male artistic personality. Neither of these characteristics is, of course, unusual for men artists, either, as we have indicated above in the case of artist fathers and sons: it is simply true almost *without exception* for their feminine counterparts, at least until quite recently. From the legendary sculptor, Sabina von Steinbach, in the 13th century, who, according to local tradition, was responsible for South Portal groups on the Cathedral of Strasbourg, down to Rosa Bonheur, the most renowned animal painter of the 19th century, and including such eminent women artists as Marietta Robusti, daughter of Tintoretto, Lavinia Fontana, Artemisia Gentileschi, Elizabeth Chéron, Mme. Vigée-Lebrun and Angelica Kauffmann—all, without exception, were the daughters of artists; in the 19th century, Berthe Morisot was closely associated with Manet, later marrying his brother, and Mary Cassatt based a good deal of her work on the style of her close friend Degas. Precisely the same breaking of traditional bonds and discarding of time-honored practices that permitted men artists to strike out in directions quite different from those of their fathers in the second half of the 19th century enabled women, with additional difficulties, to be sure, to strike out on their own as well. Many of our more recent women artists, like Suzanne Valadon, Paula Modersohn-Becker, Kaethe Kollwitz or Louise Nevelson, have come from non-artistic backgrounds, although many contemporary and near-contemporary women artists have married fellow artists.

It would be interesting to investigate the role of benign, if not outright encouraging, fathers in the formation of women professionals: both Kaethe Kollwitz and Barbara Hepworth, for example, recall the influence of unusually sympathetic and supportive fathers on their artistic pursuits. In the absence of any thoroughgoing investigation, one can only gather impressionistic data about the presence or absence of rebellion against parental authority in women artists, and whether there may be more or less rebellion on the part of women artists than is true in the case of men or vice versa. One thing however is clear: for a woman to opt for a career at all, much less for a career in art, has required a certain amount of unconventionality, both in the past and at present; whether or not the woman artist rebels against or finds strength in the attitude of her family, she must in any case have a good strong streak of rebellion in her to make her way in the world of art at all, rather than submitting to the socially approved role of wife and mother, the only role to which every social institution consigns her automatically. It is only by adopting, however covertly, the "masculine" attributes of singlemindedness, concentration, tenaciousness and absorption in ideas and craftsmanship for their own sake, that women have succeeded, and continue to succeed, in the world of art.

It is instructive to examine in greater detail one of the most successful and accomplished women painters of all time, Rosa Bonheur (1822-1899), whose work, despite the ravages wrought upon its estimation by changes of taste and a certain admitted lack of variety, still stands as an impressive achievement to anyone interested in the art of the 19th century and in the history of taste generally. Rosa Bonheur is a woman artist in whom, partly because of the magnitude of her reputation, all the various conflicts, all the internal and external contradictions and struggles typical of her sex and profession, stand out in sharp relief.

The success of Rosa Bonheur firmly establishes the role of institutions, and institutional change, as a necessary, if not a sufficient cause of achievement in art. We might say that Bonheur picked a fortunate time to become an artist if she was, at the same time, to have the disadvantage of being a woman: she came into her own in the middle of the 19th century, a time in which the struggle between traditional History Painting as opposed to the less pretentious and more free-wheeling genre painting, landscape and still-life was won by the latter group hands down. A major change in the social and institutional support for art itself was well under way: with the rise of the bourgeoisie and the fall of the cultivated aristocracy, smaller paintings, generally of every-day subjects, rather than grandiose mythological or religious scenes were much in demand. To cite the Whites: "Three hundred provincial museums there might be, government commissions for public works there might be, but the only possible paid destinations for the rising flood of canvases were the homes of the bourgeoisie. History painting had not and never would rest comfortably in the middle-class parlor. 'Lesser' forms of image art—genre, landscape, still-life—did."[17] In mid-century France, as in 17th-century Holland, there was a tendency for artists to attempt to achieve some sort of security in a shaky market situation by specializing, by making a career out of a specific subject: animal painting was a very popular field, as the Whites point out, and Rosa Bonheur was no doubt its most accomplished and successful practitioner, followed in popularity only by the Barbizon painter Troyon (who at one time was so pressed for his paintings of cows that he hired another artist to brush in the backgrounds). Rosa Bonheur's rise to fame

17   H. C. and C. A. White, op. cit., p. 91.

accompanied that of the Barbizon landscapists, supported by
those canny dealers, the Durand-Ruels, who later moved on
to the Impressionists. The Durand-Ruels were among the first
dealers to tap the expanding market in movable decoration
for the middle classes, to use the Whites' terminology. Rosa
Bonheur's naturalism and ability to capture the individuality—
even the "soul"—of each of her animal subjects coincided
with bourgeois taste at the time. The same combination of
qualities, with a much stronger dose of sentimentality and
pathetic fallacy to be sure, likewise assured the success of
her *animalier* contemporary, Landseer, in England.

Daughter of an impoverished drawing master, Rosa Bonheur
quite naturally showed her interest in art early; at the same time,
she exhibited an independence of spirit and liberty of manner
which immediately earned her the label of tomboy. According
to her own later accounts, her "masculine protest" established
itself early; to what extent *any* show of persistence, stubbornness
and vigor would be counted as "masculine" in the first half of
the 19th century is conjectural. Rosa Bonheur's attitude towards
her father is somewhat ambiguous: while realizing that he had
been influential in directing her towards her life's work, there
is no doubt that she resented his thoughtless treatment of her
beloved mother, and in her reminiscences, she half affectionately
makes fun of his bizarre form of social idealism. Raimond Bonheur
had been an active member of the short-lived Saint-Simonian
community, established in the third decade of the 19th century
by "Le Père" Enfantin at Menilmontant. Although in her later
years Rosa Bonheur might have made fun of some of the more
far-fetched eccentricities of the members of the community,
and disapproved of the additional strain which her father's apos-
tolate placed on her overburdened mother, it is obvious that the
Saint-Simonian ideal of equality for women—they disapproved
of marriage, their trousered feminine costume was a token of
emancipation, and their spiritual leader, Le Père Enfantin, made
extraordinary efforts to find a Woman Messiah to share his
reign—made a strong impression on her as a child, and may
well have influenced her future course of behavior.

"Why shouldn't I be proud to be a woman?" she exclaimed to
an interviewer. "My father, that enthusiastic apostle of humanity,
many times reiterated to me that woman's mission was to elevate
the human race, that she was the Messiah of future centuries.

18 Anna Klumpke, *Rosa Bonheur: Sa Vie, son oeuvre*, Paris, 1908, p. 311.

It is to his doctrines that I owe the great, noble ambition I have conceived for the sex which I proudly affirm to be mine, and whose independence I will support to my dying day …"[18] When she was hardly more than a child, he instilled in her the ambition to surpass Mme. Vigée-Lebrun certainly the most eminent model she could be expected to follow, and he gave her early efforts every possible encouragement. At the same time, the spectacle of her uncomplaining mother's slow decline from sheer overwork and poverty might have been an even more realistic influence on her decision to control her own destiny and never to become the slave of a husband and children. What is particularly interesting from the modern feminist viewpoint is Rosa Bonheur's ability to combine the most vigorous and unapologetic masculine protest with unabashedly self-contradictory assertions of "basic" femininity.

In those refreshingly straightforward pre-Freudian days, Rosa Bonheur could explain to her biographer that she had never wanted to marry for fear of losing her independence—too many young girls let themselves be led to the altar like lambs to the sacrifice, she maintained. Yet at the same time that she rejected marriage for herself and implied an inevitable loss of selfhood for any woman who engaged in it, she, unlike the Saint-Simonians, considered marriage "a sacrament indispensable to the organization of society."

While remaining cool to offers of marriage, she joined in a seemingly cloudless, lifelong and apparently Platonic union with a fellow woman artist, Nathalie Micas, who evidently provided her with the companionship and emotional warmth which she needed. Obviously, the presence of this sympathetic friend did not seem to demand the same sacrifice of genuine commitment to her profession which marriage would have entailed: in any case, the advantages of such an arrangement for women who wished to avoid the distraction of children in the days before reliable contraception are obvious.

Yet at the same time that she frankly rejected the conventional feminine role of her times, Rosa Bonheur still was drawn into what Betty Friedan has called the "frilly blouse syndrome," that innocuous version of the feminine protest which even today compels successful women psychiatrists or professors to adopt some ultra-feminine item of clothing or insist on proving their prowess as pie-bakers.[19] Despite the fact that she had early

19 Betty Friedan, *The Feminine Mystique*, New York, 1963, p. 158.

cropped her hair and adopted men's clothes as her habitual attire, following the example of George Sand, whose rural Romanticism exerted a powerful influence over her imagination, to her biographer she insisted, and no doubt sincerely believed, that she did so only because of the specific demands of her profession. Indignantly denying rumors to the effect that she had run about the streets of Paris dressed as a boy in her youth, she proudly provided her biographer with a daguerreotype of herself at 16 years, dressed in perfectly conventional feminine fashion, except for her shorn head, which she excused as a practical measure taken after the death of her mother; "who would have taken care of my curls?" she demanded.[20]

As far as the question of masculine dress was concerned, she was quick to reject her interlocutor's suggestion that her trousers were a symbol of emancipation. "I strongly blame women who renounce their customary attire in the desire to make themselves pass for men," she affirmed. "If I had found that trousers suited my sex, I would have completely gotten rid of my skirts, but this is not the case, nor have I ever advised my sisters of the palette to wear men's clothes in the ordinary course of life. If, then, you see me dressed as I am, it is not at all with the aim of making myself interesting, as all too many women have tried, but simply in order to facilitate my work. Remember that at a certain period I spent whole days in the slaughterhouses. Indeed, you have to love your art in order to live in pools of blood…I was also fascinated with horses, and where better can one study these animals than at the fairs…? I had no alternative but to realize that the garments of my own sex were a total nuisance. That is why I decided to ask the Prefect of Police for the authorization to wear masculine clothing.[21] But the costume I am wearing is my working outfit, nothing else. The remarks of fools have never bothered me. Nathalie [her companion] makes fun of them as I do. It doesn't bother her at all to see me dressed as a man, but if you are even the slightest bit put off, I am completely prepared to put on a skirt, especially since all I have to do is to open a closet to find a whole assortment of feminine outfits."[22]

Yet at the same time Rosa Bonheur is forced to admit: "My trousers have been my great protectors…Many times I have congratulated myself for having dared to break with traditions which would have forced me to abstain from certain kinds

20 A. Klumpke, op. cit., p. 166.

21 Paris, like many cities even today, had laws against impersonation on its books.

22 A. Klumpke, op. cit., pp. 308–309.

of work, due to the obligation to drag my skirts everywhere..."
Yet the famous artist again feels obliged to qualify her honest
admission with an ill-assumed "femininity": "Despite my
metamorphoses of costume, there is not a daughter of Eve
who appreciates the niceties more than I do; my brusque and
even slightly unsociable nature has never prevented my heart
from remaining completely feminine."[23]

It is somewhat pathetic that this highly successful artist, unspar-
ing of herself in the painstaking study of animal anatomy, diligently
pursuing her bovine or equine subjects in the most unpleasant
surroundings, industriously producing popular canvases throughout
the course of a lengthy career, firm, assured and incontrovertably
masculine in her style, winner of a first medal in the Paris Salon,
Officer of the Legion of Honor, Commander of the Order of
Isabella the Catholic and the Order of Leopold of Belgium, friend
of Queen Victoria—that this world-renowned artist should feel
compelled late in life to justify and qualify her perfectly reasonable
assumption of masculine ways, for any reason whatsoever, and
to feel compelled to attack her less modest trouser-wearing
sisters at the same time, in order to satisfy the demands of her
own conscience. For her conscience, despite her supportive
father, her unconventional behavior and the accolade of worldly
success, still condemned her for not being a "feminine" woman.

The difficulties imposed by such demands on the woman
artist continue to add to her already difficult enterprise even
today. Compare, for example, the noted contemporary,
Louise Nevelson, with her combination of utter, "unfeminine"
dedication to her work and her conspicuously "feminine" false
eyelashes; her admission that she got married at 17 despite
her certainty that she couldn't live without creating because
"the world said you should get married."[24] Even in the case
of these two outstanding artists—and whether we like
The Horsefair or not, we still must admire Rosa Bonheur's
achievement—the voice of the feminine mystique with its
potpourri of ambivalent narcissism and guilt, internalized, subtly
dilutes and subverts that total inner confidence, that absolute
certitude and self-determination, moral and esthetic, demanded
by the highest and most innovative work in art.

23   Ibid., pp. 310–311.

24   Cited in Elizabeth Fisher, "The Woman as Artist, Louise Nevelson," *Aphra*, I (Spring), 1970, p. 32.

We have tried to deal with one of the perennial questions used to challenge women's demand for true, rather than token, equality, by examining the whole erroneous intellectual substructure upon which the question "Why have there been no great women artists?" is based; by questioning the validity of the formulation of so-called problems in general and the "problem" of women specifically; and then, by probing some of the limitations of the discipline of art history itself. Hopefully, by stressing the *institutional*—i.e., the public—rather than the *individual*, or private, pre-conditions for achievement or the lack of it in the arts, we have provided a paradigm for the investigation of other areas in the field. By examining in some detail a single instance of deprivation or disadvantage—the unavailability of nude models to women art students—we have suggested that it was indeed institutionally made impossible for women to achieve artistic excellence, or success, on the same footing as men, no matter what the potency of their so-called talent, or genius. The existence of a tiny band of successful, if not great, women artists throughout history does nothing to gainsay this fact, any more than does the existence of a few superstars or token achievers among the members of any minority groups. And while great achievement is rare and difficult at best, it is still rarer and more difficult if, while you work, you must at the same time wrestle with inner demons of self-doubt and guilt and outer monsters of ridicule or patronizing encouragement, neither of which have any specific connection with the quality of the artwork as such.

What is important is that women face up to the reality of their history and of their present situation, without making excuses or puffing mediocrity. Disadvantage may indeed be an excuse; it is not, however, an intellectual position. Rather, using as a vantage point their situation as underdogs in the realm of grandeur, and outsiders in that of ideology, women can reveal institutional and intellectual weaknesses in general, and, at the same time that they destroy false consciousness, take part in the creation of institutions in which clear thought—and true greatness—are challenges open to anyone, man or woman, courageous enough to take the necessary risk, the leap into the unknown.

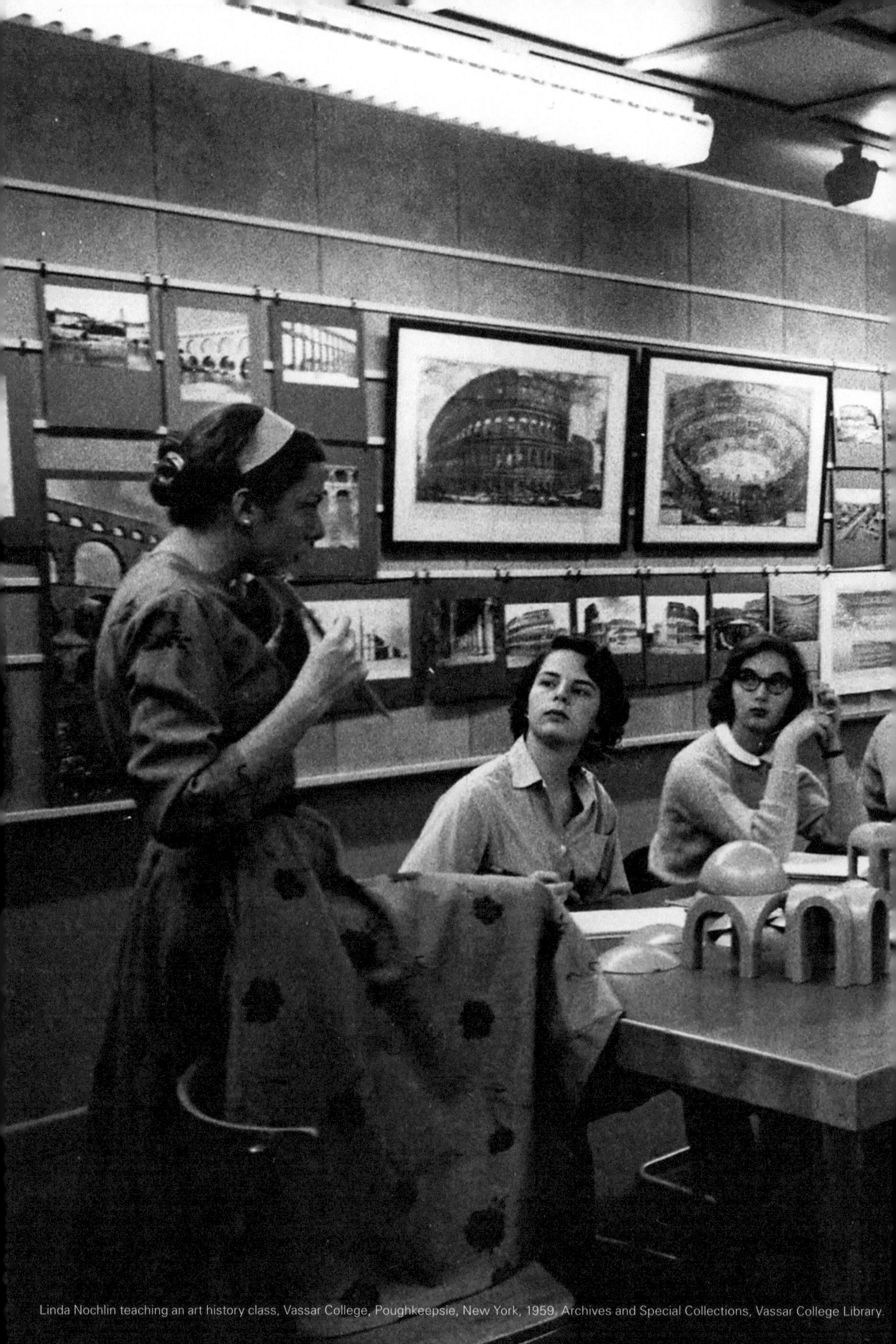

Linda Nochlin teaching an art history class, Vassar College, Poughkeepsie, New York, 1959. Archives and Special Collections, Vassar College Library.

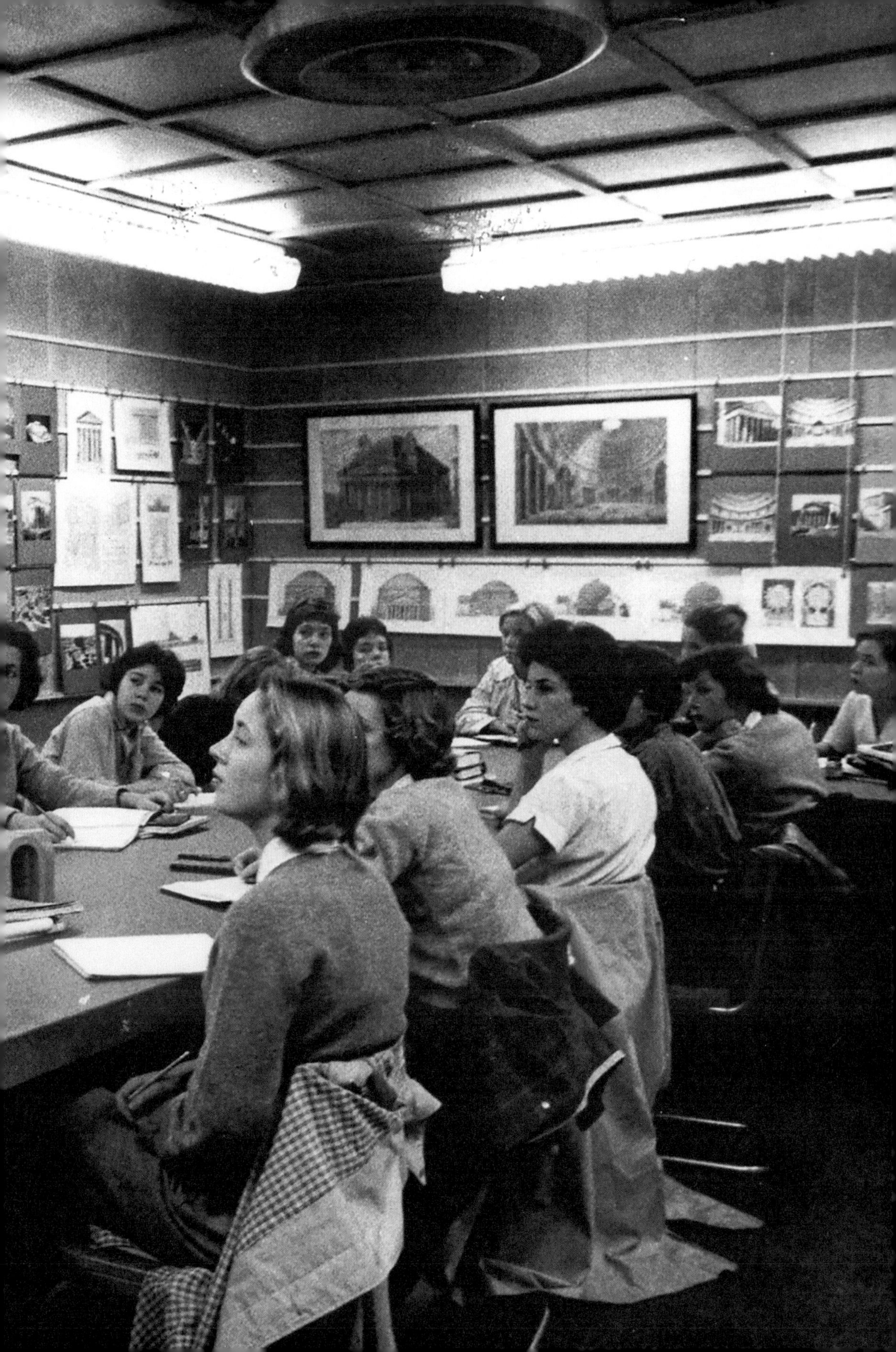

COLOPHON

History of an Art School
Marta Kuzma
with Angela Y. Davis and Linda Nochlin
edited by Angie Keefer

This book is published on the occasion of the 50th anniversary
of undergraduate coeducation at Yale College and the 150th
anniversary of the first women students at Yale University.

Reproduced texts
Angela Y. Davis' October 27, 2021, lecture in "Diving Into
the Wreck: Rethinking Critical Practices" at the Yale School
of Art has been reproduced courtesy of Angela Y. Davis.
Linda Nochlin's 1971 essay, "Why Have There Been No Great
Women Artists?" has been reproduced courtesy of the
Estate of Linda Nochlin.

Editor
    Angie Keefer

Associate editor
    Edi Dai

Copy editor
    Eugenia Bell

Photo editor
    Angela Chen

Publication coordinator
    Willis Kingery

Project manager
    Beth Lovell

Research assistants
    Angela Chen, Beth Lovell, Edi Dai, Willis Kingery

Design
    Irma Boom Office:
    Irma Boom, Anna Moschioni

Type
The fonts in use throughout this publication were drawn
by students of Letterform, an elective course within
the Department of Graphic Design at Yale School of Art.
    DW F-Grotesk by Dawoon Jeon
    New Normal by Emma Gregoline
    Nebula Regular by Hrefna Sigurðardóttir
    Almond and Apriori by Julia Schäfer
    Cambré and Selectic Pro by Kyla Arsadjaja
    Trilce by Lau Huaranga
    Ligne by Yuanbo Wang
The body typeface is Univers by Adrian Frutiger.

Lithography and Printing
    Zwaan Lenoir

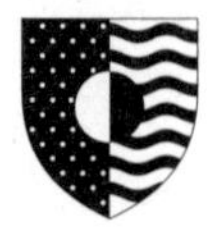